HAUNTED SKIES

Preserving the Social History of UFO Research

HAUNTED SKIES VOLUME 11 1989-1990

First paperback edition printed 2015 in the United Kingdom.

A catalogue record for this book is available from the British Library.

ISBN 978-0-957-4944-4-2

Published by

Haunted Skies Publishing

For more copies of this book, please email: johndawn1@sky.com

Telephone: 0121 445 0340

Designed and typeset by Bob Tibbitts ~ (iSET)

Printed in Great Britain

FOREWORD

RETIRED COLONEL USAF – CHARLES IRWIN HALT

My early years

A S a teenager growing up into adulthood I never had much interest in the UFO subject, but I can clearly remember reading a book which I came across during a church rummage sale, while assisting my mother, who was organizing the event entitled *The Flying Saucers Are Real*, by Donald Keyhoe. This book outlined numerous encounters between USAF fighters, personnel, and other aircraft and UFOs between 1947 and 1950.

Church rummage sales were the forerunner of today's American garage or yard sales – known as car boot, bric-a-brac, garage sales or church fayres, in the United Kingdom. Most household items could be found for sale – including clothing, kitchen accessories and books. I found Keyhoe's book fascinating but, after reading and putting it aside, forgot all about it.

Confronting the inexplicable!

Memories of it were resurrected in December 1980, when I found myself confronted with an experience I could not explain. The incidents that occurred over a three night period in Rendlesham Forest, Suffolk, left a lasting impression on me and tragically affected the lives of many concerned.

Lives changed for ever

Without reservation I can say that those involved in the incidents, which occurred on the first night, have never been the same – probably because of a combination of their experience in the forest and then being 'debriefed' afterwards by USAF and British 'spooks' officers, engaged in military intelligence.

We are not alone

Since then I have been privy to hearing of an unbelievable number of first-hand accounts of encounters by very reputable individuals, many occurring in Rendlesham, Suffolk area. I have become firmly convinced that we are not alone. Some type of intelligent life is in our midst, which has the ability to change shape, size, move at phenomenal speed and apparently, significantly affect people who have been witness to the appearance of these objects.

What lies behind the phenomenon is, of course, open to all manner of speculation. My own personal opinion is that whatever it is, it does not normally reside in our known universe unless it's from another dimension.

The 'Haunted Skies' Books

John Hanson and Dawn Holloway, assisted by Brenda Butler – a colleague of theirs (whom I have known for over 30 years) – have undertaken a mammoth task of now documenting British/American/Australian UFO sightings on a day-by-day basis, covering from the early 1940s, right up to the present date.

The current Volume 11 of *Haunted Skies* brings those UFO reports up to 1990, along with an update on other World UFO events from the period 1963 onwards.

All of the volumes of *Haunted Skies* have been produced at considerable personal expense and involve an unbelievable amount of personal time.

Not only have John and Dawn been able to sort out the facts but they have had to deal with many misleading and often possible cases of intentional misinformation, quite often self-serving. What happened at Bentwaters is a good example taking into consideration a popular book, published some years ago, which claims to present the facts but is wrong on so many issues.

Colonel Charles I. Halt displaying Volume 10 of 'Haunted Skies'

John and I have corresponded at great length and personally met. He and Dawn's work has not always seen the success it merits, despite it clearly laying out the facts requiring further official investigation.

Volume 8 (1980) covers the Rendlesham Forest Incident

Is it the case that nobody in a position of authority wants to face the truth, or could it be that the truth is known to a few? I leave that for the reader to decide. If you want to personally understand the scope of the issue, you need to read the entire *Haunted Skies* series. If you wish to know more about the events that took place in Rendlesham Forest, I suggest you purchase Volume 8, which covers many reports of unusual lights seen over the Forest, not only by the public but by various airmen, including my own assessment of what I and others saw during the end of December 1980.

Charles I. Halt, 2014

INTRODUCTION

The Triangular UFO

THE first part of this Volume of *Haunted Skies* covers the UFO events that took place in America, Australia and the UK, during 1989 and 1990.

Researchers of the UFO subject are aware of the interest displayed by the media during a surge in UFO activity which took place over Belgium in November 1989.

On November 29th, at least thirty separate witnesses, including police officers sighted a craft – described as being flat, triangular in shape, with lights underneath – silently and slowly moving across the landscape of Belgium in that grand and majestic manner now associated with the appearance of these objects, referred to as Triangular UFOs.

The Belgian UFO 'wave' peaked with the events taking place on the night of 30th/31st March 1990. On that night UFOs were tracked on radar, and chased by two Belgian Air Force F-16 Jet fighters and photographed. They were sighted by an estimated 13,500 people on the ground – 2,600 of whom filed written statements describing in detail what they had seen.

Following the incident, the Belgian Air Force released a report detailing the events of that night.

Fortunately, we are now able to see that in addition to the incidents which occurred over Belgium and other parts of Europe, there was an interesting development involving a previously unknown 'wave' of UFO activity over the Essex area obtained from archived material, collected by the late Ron West from Essex. This might, in other circumstances have been destroyed and lost from the public's eye.

The reader will learn of many sightings involving the appearance of three lights or globes hovering in the sky, set equidistantly from each other, sometimes over power and electrical installations.

They are reminiscent of the early 1950 reports of UFOs – often referred to as examples of the George Adamski craft, described as being a saucer or domed object, with a base in which three globes are set at equal distance from each other. Originally we both speculated on the authenticity of such craft. However, as time went on, we were to come across many such examples. These included reports from people like UFO researcher Margaret Fry – who, as a young housewife, witnessed a spectacular sighting of a near landed object in Kent, during October 1954.

The second part of this book continues our chronological examination of historical (USA, UK, Australia) UFO reports, which began in Volume 10 of *Haunted Skies*. This covers the period from 1963 to 1964.

We decided to reintroduce the UFO sightings from Volumes Two and Three of *Haunted Skies* into the framework of this book, so that the reader could now see for themselves that it was not just about a sighting in the UK on such and such a date, but what took place in Australia and the USA. This is important, as it allows us to see a worldwide perspective other than just British.

We are the first to accept that we could never fully cover the UFO events of the 20th Century, but will document as much as we can, as we have always maintained that we have never wanted to leave anything out – taking into consideration the valuable research carried out by many people who we have met over the years, some of whom are no longer with us.

Francis Ridge

We would also now like to thank people like Francis Ridge, of NICAP, and numerous other people from UFO research groups, such as MUFON whose work is now available on the internet. We should be proud of them, as they have laboured long over the years to ensure that this information is not lost from history.

Unlike UFOs and their probable occupants, we do not have the luxury of being able to live longer than the normal human expectation of life. It is clear that 'they' – whatever 'they' represent – are a very old phenomenon that exists alongside us rather than visitations of extraterrestrial species, although on occasion there appears to have been examples of the latter.

Without doubt, it is the greatest phenomena of all modern time, whether you are a sceptic or not, one day we will have the courage to go forward and face it, rather than telling ourselves it does not exist.

Finally we would like to dedicate this book to two old friends, who are shown here in Rendlesham Forest during a 'get together'. Brenda Butler and Dot Street were responsible for bringing the public's attention to what many consider to be the greatest UFO enigma of modern day times, and still subject of controversy over 34 years later – time marches on!

Dot Street (left) with Brenda Butler

Events of 1989

FOLLOWING extensive protests against the Berlin Wall, bringing about its collapse, the East German Government dismantle the barrier which led to the reunification of East and West Germany.

In China, pro-democracy protesters clash with Chinese security forces in Tiananmen Square, on 4th June; pictures of a man confronting a tank are shown on TV news throughout the world.

Russia pulls out of Afghanistan • Israel and The Palestinian Liberation Organization begin preliminary talks • Japan: the Tokyo stock market crash ends Japan's long period of high economic growth • Denmark: The Registered Partnership law is passed, which grants same sex couples many of the rights and responsibilities of marriage • South Africa: Violence in black townships worsens with over 2,500 killed. New Prime Minister in South Africa F.W. De Klerk starts to dismantle apartheid • Poland: Free elections in Poland bring solidarity to power • Czechoslovakia: 200,000 protesters in Prague call for the resignation of the country's communist government in the 'Velvet Revolution'. Following the protests, free elections are held in Czechoslovakia.

On 18th October 1989, NASA launched the Galileo spacecraft. Its mission was to probe Jupiter's atmosphere and study the largest planet and its moons for two years. The spacecraft was purposefully plunged into Jupiter's atmosphere in September. On its way to Jupiter, Galileo spent time studying Earth, Venus, the Moon, and two asteroids. It orbited Jupiter for two years and observed the surrounding satellites, collecting amazing photos of the planet and identifying evidence that there was possibly liquid water under the surface of Europa, a moon of Jupiter. The Galileo spacecraft was hugely successful in its missions and made several new and exciting discoveries.

Cost of Living, USA - 1989

Yearly inflation rate – 4.83% • Year end close, Dow Jones Industrial Average – 2753 • Interest rates year end, Federal Reserve – 10.50% • Average cost of new house - $120,000.00 • Average income per year – $27,450.00 • Average monthly rent – $420.00 • Average price for new car – $15,3500.00 • 1 gallon of gas - 97 cents • US postage stamp – 25 cents • BMW 325 - $21,400 • Ford Probe – $12,695 • Ham and cheese pizza – $2.59 • Rib-eye steak – Lb $3.79 • Ritz Crackers – $1.79 • Barbie's Dance-time Shop – $24.98 • Ghostbusters table-top pinball – $19.85

Cost of living, UK - 1989

FTSE 100 Average – 2200 • Average house price – £71,733 • Gallon of petrol – £1.68 • Yearly inflation rate – 7.8% • Interest rates year end, Bank of England – 14.88%

Technology

The 486 series of microprocessor is released by Intel, opening the way for the next generation of much more powerful PCs. Microsoft releases its Office Suite including Excel, Word and Powerpoint, spreadsheet, word processing and data and presentation software, which still dominates office software today.

Memorable and sometimes poignant events . . .

John Lennon assassination • Mount Saint Helen erupts killing 60 people • 'Who Shot JR'? • Abortion pill introduced in France • CNN is launched as the first all new Network • Saddam Hussein attacks Iran for close to a decade over oil rights and President Carter attempts a helicopter rescue of the hostages in Iran.

Favorite toys: He Man, My Little Pony and Care Bears! Favorite films: *Indiana Jones, The Last Crusade, Ghostbusters 2* and *Batman!*

Time differentials

The reader should take into consideration the time differentials involved with UFO sightings presented on the same date, understanding the different time zones around the world. This really only applies where more than one sighting relating to different time zones is given on or around the same day.

If this book was about chronicling British UFO activity we would have converted international sightings to GMT, in order to examine association between individual reports of UFO activity. Unfortunately, this would change the dates of some of the incidents and cause confusion.

No doubt the reader may wish to check for themselves whether there is any correlation between different UFO reports that have taken place many hundreds, if not thousands, of miles away.

Although we found little evidence of UFO activity intersecting time zones, we have on occasion found some similarities.

PART 1

JANUARY 1989

1st January 1989 (Australia) – Cigar-shaped UFO

IN the Western District of Victoria, at 7.15am, a large, dull silver, cigar-shaped object was seen hovering over a *farm shed where irrigation pumps were kept by a farmer's wife. The woman started her car up, intending to let her husband know what was going on, when approximately five minutes after the first sighting it disappeared from view. This happened in the same locality where a small circular object was seen to merge with a larger cigar-shaped UFO while irrigation was in progress. (**Source: *The Australian UFO Bulletin*, December 1989 Edition**) *This was the same farm where all the water in a small dam disappeared overnight.

1st January 1989 (Canada) – UFO seen over lake

At 9.15pm four people living near Lake Kashagawigamog, Ontario, Canada sighted an object in the sky for five minutes that had an appearance and performance beyond the capability of any known earthly aircraft. Identifying on occasion a possible affinity between the sightings of UFOs and localities, was a sighting over 20 years later by a group of people one of whom said:

"Just before dusk on October 2nd, 2010, my husband and I, from our cottage on the north shore of Lake, noticed a large bright shimmering yellow/amber light just above the south-west horizon of Lake Kashagawigamog, above a high promontory and across the lake from Puffer's Island. At first we thought it was a helicopter, because the light hovered motionless in the sky for about five minutes after we spotted it. The light shimmered like objects on the hot tarmac in the summertime and the colour shifted from yellow to golden to amber, and back again randomly. It was slightly overcast, but the horizon was clear of clouds. As we stood outside and watched there was no sound at all, which we found very unusual as sound carries quite well over the water. After at least three minutes, the 'light' slowly moved straight up and into the cloud bank. We watched for it to re-emerge from the cloud bank (which if it had been a plane or helicopter it would have) but there was no sign of it anywhere and absolute silence."

(**Source: *International UFO Reporter*, CUFOS/Brian Vike WWW.**)

2nd January 1989 (Canada) – UFO seen

At 9.40pm, Gloucester, Ontario another UFO was seen over this locality. (**Source:** *International UFO Reporter*, CUFOS)

3rd January 1989 (USA) – Four Diamond-shaped UFOs seen

On this day, at 6.20pm, four car-sized, silver-coloured objects, diamond in shape, were sighted about 300ft up in the air over the freeway at Corona, California by a young woman aged 23. (**Source: Paul Ferrughelli,** *Computer Catalogue of UFO Reports, 1988-94* –Author, Teaneck, 1992/Lary Hatch)

3rd January 1989 (UK) –Triangular light seen over Essex

A bright *'light'* was seen moving at phenomenal speed, backwards and forwards, between Southend and Basildon. Through binoculars a blue pulsing light, surrounded by a white glow, was observed. Other witnesses included David Lever (46) of Crays Hill, Billericay who, between 10pm and midnight, watched an object in the sky described as a . . .

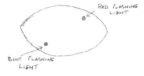

"triangular or shield-shaped light: which headed away at great speed across the sky, towards Southend; it then headed backwards to where it had first been seen and repeated this 'to' and 'fro' action many times. Through binoculars I saw a blue pulsating light on it.
At one point it seemed to separate into two parts with a gap down the middle, inside of which you could see different coloured lights."

(**Source: Brenda Butler & Ron West**)

Wickford Essex

At 7.30pm, Henry Shirmer (63) of Shotgate, Wickford, Essex, went outside to check on the animals. He noticed a line of *'bright lights'* in the sky to the East. After shutting away the rabbits, he glanced back into the sky and was surprised to see the *'lights'* heading towards his direction . . .

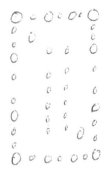

"As they came closer I saw that 'it' consisted of several rows of lights, forming an oblong shape. 'They', or 'it', passed overhead, allowing me to see a number of bright lights, with lesser lights between – ten lights on each (i.e. four bright, six dull ones) – gone in a couple of minutes. I saw the same object at 10.30pm for a minute. On the 8th January I saw it again, at 7.30pm, for about 30 seconds."

Marion Shirmer (59) – the wife of Henry – also corroborated the sighting, after having been called outside by her husband. (**Source: Ron West**)

4th January 1989 (UK) – Humming UFO

Mr Douglas Harrison (70) of Harvest Road, Canvey Island, contacted Ron West, after having sighted the following object at 7.30pm.

"I estimated it to be between 1,500ft and 5,000ft in the sky. I could hear a humming noise from it. It had a batch of lights on the front, with 'portholes' along its side. There was an elliptical 'feathery' blue light at the rear, and a white pulsating light at the end."

	YEAR	NUMBER	INVESTIGATOR	CASE SUMMARY	
GROUP			Ron West	DATE	
	1989	E/89/13	EVALUATOR	TIME	
INVEST REF: RWH189/2	REF.			LOCATION	
				EVAL'N	
RETURN FORM TO:–				UFO CLASS	CE1
				CLOSED	

EAST ANGLIAN U.F.O. & PARANORMAL RESEARCH ASSOCIATION

SIGHTING ACCOUNT FORM

SECTION A

Please write an account of your sighting, make a drawing of what you saw and then answer the questions in section B overleaf as fully as possible. Write in **BLOCK CAPITALS** using a ball point pen.

Sighting enter 7.50pm. very clear night facing north 1st floor Bedroom sighting over Led-on-sea three miles away at 2000ft The UFO housing one with twin light facing me one single light pulsating very fast & very bright. Notice white cloud like mist to left ran Binoculars + White cloud I see what appears to be the shape of a gold miners pan, extreamly large took at the twin UFO again they ran back to the white cloud & found it has changed it shape by rotating on a vertical axie Shape has now changed to a huge Spherical Black Ball looking to scale this out 1 mile across This Black sphere had a surface like the very & not scared No light on this object. All hovering in one spot for 10 minutes Wide absorbing two UFO in sight at same time.

Please continue on a separate sheet if necessary.

DRAWING*

1st Sighting

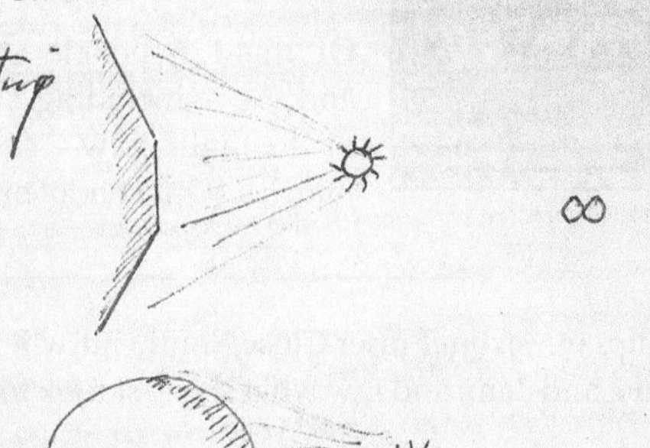

2nd Sighting BLACK

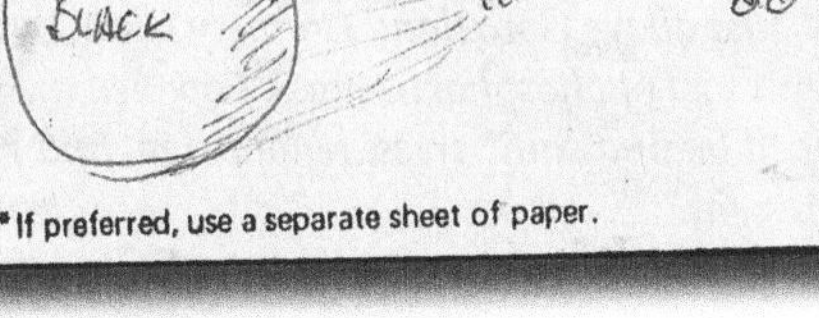

*If preferred, use a separate sheet of paper.

Your full name (Mr/~~Mrs~~/~~Miss~~/~~Ms~~)

D.W. HARRISON   Age 70

Address 58 HARVEST ROAD

CANVEY ISLAND ESSEX

Telephone No 692791 (STD 0268)

Occupation during last two years

RETIRED

Any professional, technical or academic qualifications or special interests

Senature artist, draftsman carpet saw, wood signs

Do you object to the publication of your name?
*~~Yes~~/No. *Delete as applicable.

Today's Date 8-2-1989

Signature D W Harrison

6th January 1989 (USA) – Orange *'ball'* seen

At Pensacola, Florida, two people driving over the Bay Bridge saw an orange *'ball'* in the sky, which then shot straight up and disappeared from view. (**Source:** MUFON/ **Paul Ferrughelli**, *Computer Catalog of UFO Reports, 1988-94/*Author, Teaneck, 1992/Larry Hatch)

Yorkshire – Bell-shaped UFO

At Askern, West Yorkshire, a family travelling in a car reported having sighted a *'bell-shaped'* object at close range. (**Source: Chris Gibson I.U.N.**)

7th January 1989 (UK) – Blue *'ball'* over the M1 Motorway

At 2am, Mr Andrews was heading towards Birmingham on the M1; his colleague was driving. Suddenly, to the men's amazement, a *'blue ball of light'*, estimated to be six inches in diameter (as seen with the naked eye) appeared in front of the car's windscreen, a few feet away from the car. Seconds later, it was gone from sight.

8th January 1989 (UK)– Kegworth air disaster

This was the day of the Kegworth air disaster, when British Midland Flight 92 – a Boeing 737-400 – crashed onto the embankment of the M1 motorway near Kegworth, Leicestershire. The aircraft was attempting to conduct an emergency landing at East Midlands Airport, during the evening.

Of the 126 people aboard, 47 died and 74 – including seven members of the flight crew – sustained serious injuries. (Our condolences are offered.)

Southend – UFO over Essex

This was also the same day, according to Mrs C. Philips (65) from Fraser Close, Southend, when she happened to be looking out of her bedroom window, between 2 and 3am, and saw what she first took to be a helicopter approaching from the North.

> *"It appeared to come down to a very low level, just above Courtland Country Club, Bournes Green. All I could see was a small light, surrounded by a sort of phosphorus mass. I opened the window and listened, but could not hear any noise. It dipped behind some trees, reappeared, and headed away fast, towards the North, before being lost from sight."*

(**Source:** Ron West)

UFO over Matlock

Flying object is seen in Matlock

AN Asker Lane resident of Matlock has reported an unidentified flying object allegedly seen over the town on Monday January 8.

He wishes to remain anonymous and claims the object was clearly visible after dark for a period of three minutes from 1816 hours to 1819 hours, and immediately made a full report on the incident.

'The evening was fine, clear and dry with good visibility and the resident claims the object was a very bright light of yellow and red colours roughly circular in shape.

The light appeared to pulsate or flicker and the upper part of the object occasionally changed colour on the outer edges from red to blue to green.

A number of flashes of the most beautiful blue colour came from underneath the object in well defined rays, and the lights bore no resemblance to conventional navigational lights

on normal aircraft.

The object approached the Matlock area from above Darley, NNW, flying in an approximate southerly direction, then swung in an easterly direction, eventually disappearing over Riber Hill.

There was no dark shape of an aircraft against a lighter sky and the light appeared to be the whole of the object.

The height was about 1500 feet at level flight and the resident estimated that the object covered

about 15 miles in the three minutes observed - giving an airspeed of about 300mph.'

He also stated the object was larger than any aircraft and appeared to be completely transparent and suspected the light produced inside was white but appeared yellow/red as the transparent material was tinted, and believed the blue light flashing downwards was probably ultra-violet light.

He has enclosed a rough sketch of his sighting and would like any other reader who may have seen a similar sighting to send their report to the Mercury (names and addresses will be held if required).

Send your details to: Flying Object, c/o Matlock Mercury, 24 Bakewell Road, Matlock DE4 3AY.

• NB. Don't accept any lift from little green men.

9th January 1989 (USA) – Luminous cloud of smoke seen

A luminous cloud of smoke, performing gyrations through the sky, was seen just before dawn over Key Largo, Florida. (**Source: Paul Ferrughelli,** *Computer Catalogue of UFO Reports, 1988-94*/**Author, Teaneck, 1992**)

Pennsylvania – Oval UFO

On the same day, this time over Indiana City, Pennsylvania, a large UFO – described as an oval object, showing red and white lights – was seen hovering in the sky over Indiana City, at 9pm.

Early January 1989 (Australia), Yunta

In early January 1989, Gary, an interstate truck driver was travelling from Newcastle to Adelaide when he decided to pull in around 4.30pm, at a Mobil petrol station in Yunta, South Australia, for refreshment and a nap. At approximately 9pm he set off for Adelaide. While driving along the road that had railway lines running parallel to it, he saw, between the road and the railway lines:

". . . a large, glowing orange 'ball', like a basketball, which was parallel to the height of my truck, and went straight past my direction, making a whooshing noise."

As he could still see the lights of Yunta in the distance in his rear vision mirror, he first thought it might have been a train on the lines, but as it turned out, it wasn't.

Gary:

"I just want to let you know I wasn't tired, I wasn't hallucinating. I was well rested, well fed and wide awake. It went so fast and then it vanished, in the blink of an eye. It was something I can't explain. I know there was no aircraft there and they weren't crop dusting either, as there's nothing there to dust. It is desert-like, no trees and a long lonely road. You don't see many cars, only a few trucks on the road. I can't explain what I saw."

10th January 1989 (UK) – *'Flying saucer'* over the A12

Mr John 'I', 43 (details on file) from Kelvedon, Essex, was driving home along the A12 from Chelmsford at midnight on the 10th January 1989 when he saw an object,

". . . the size of a rugby ball – silver-grey in colour – stationary in the sky over one of the road bridges that crosses the A12. It had red, blue, green and yellow, lights going through the centre of the object, which was rotating anticlockwise. It was oval, with a flat bottom and a dome on top. It was about 600ft above the bridge and about a mile away. After 20 minutes, it shot straight up into the sky and disappeared into a cloud bank."

Hockley, Essex

At 1.55am, Stanley William Smith (74) from The Spinneys, in Hockley, Essex, was returning home after having been to see friends with his wife – Mrs I. Smith (74) – when he noticed a *'light'*, stationary in the sky.

"It stayed there for about 15 seconds and then headed away in a North to South direction. Suddenly, it made a sharp left turn and moved away westwards, before disappearing behind clouds a couple of minutes later."

(Source: EAUFO & PRA, Ron West & Mr M. Bainbridge)

East Mayne – Group of *'lights'* seen

Although not sure of the exact date, music teacher Paul White (32) from Basildon, Essex, was driving southwards along East Mayne at 9pm when he saw a group of *'lights'* in the sky somewhere over the St. Nicholas Church area.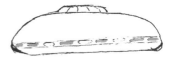

"I thought it was a helicopter, but the lights moved together so fast it couldn't have been the answer. They shot upwards into the sky, at tremendous speed – soon lost in the night sky and easily mistaken as a star."

(Source: Ron West)

Early January

In the same period of early January 1989 two UFOs were observed hovering over a field next to the A128, at Colchester – by two men driving along the Tilbury Road – accompanied by a scattering of orange *'lights'* in the sky – last seen heading towards the Horndon-on-the-Hill direction.

12th January 1989 (UK) – UFO display

Mrs Norma Bowshill (63) of Braintree, Essex, was at her home address at 12.30am when she saw:

> "... *a hexagonal object moving across the sky, at speed. Sometimes it turned erratically in flight in a zigzag manner, before disappearing into the sky.*"

(Source: Ron West)

Lancashire

On the same day, a man from Stacksteads Lancashire, was out walking his dog when he saw an unusual cloud on the skyline near a quarry top. Inside the *'cloud'* multi-coloured lights were seen for about five seconds before it moved to the right and vanished over a hill.

(Source: Rodney Howarth (I.U.N.)

12th January 1989 (USA) – *'Diamond'* UFO seen

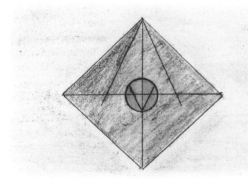

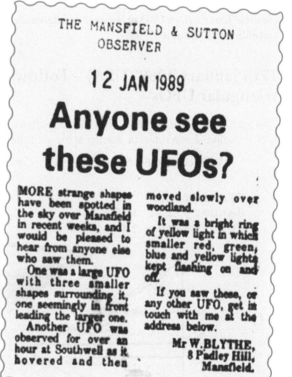

THE MANSFIELD & SUTTON OBSERVER

12 JAN 1989

Anyone see these UFOs?

MORE strange shapes have been spotted in the sky over Mansfield in recent weeks, and I would be pleased to hear from anyone else who saw them.

One was a large UFO with three smaller shapes surrounding it, one seemingly in front leading the larger one. Another UFO was observed for over an hour at Southwell as it hovered and then moved slowly over woodland.

It was a bright ring of yellow light in which smaller red, green, blue and yellow lights kept flashing on and off.

If you saw these, or any other UFO, get in touch with me at the address below.

Mr W. BLYTHE,
8 Padley Hill,
Mansfield.

At 8pm near Belleville, Illinois, two young men were out driving, when they noticed a bright light hovering in the distance. Curious, they stopped the car. An object, described as being multicoloured and diamond in shape, about 20ft across and around 300ft away, approached their position. As it did so, its exterior lights brightened. It then flew slowly overhead, before veering away and out of sight. (Source: MUFON)

16th January 1989 (UK) – Fish-shaped UFO sighted over Essex

At 7pm, Mrs E. Catlin (74) from East Woodbury Lane, Southend-on-Sea, Essex, was with her daughter – Sandra Ann Bush (41) – travelling on the 127 bus near Progress Road, approaching Kent Elm traffic

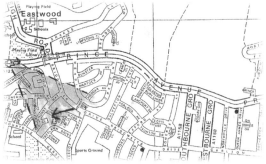

lights, heading towards Southend, when they saw an object in the sky, *"resembling a huge fish, with lights appearing on the 'tail', heading at a terrific speed, before disappearing into cloud."* The object, which had a large bright light to the front, a bluish light in the middle and a white light on the rear, appears to be similar in description to that of the 'Flying Triangle', which was said to haunt the European skies around this period of

> # UFO shaped just like a fish
>
> UFO investigators are interview-ing people who saw a large skate-shaped object in the sky which when it banked was about 30 feet deep. The mystery fish craft, about 100 feet long, was seen over Southend, inland and by people on the beach.
> If anyone else saw the craft they are asked to ring the UFO hotline on Basildon 286079.

time, although the terminology was not widely known to the public then as it is now.

(Source: *East Anglian UFO & Paranormal Research Association/* Geraldine and Deanne Dillon)

17th January 1989 (USA) – Followed by triangular UFOs

Two men driving a truck from Fort Wayne, Indiana, to Ohio, complained that they had been followed by two triangular-shaped objects, moving at low altitude through the sky for a period of 30 minutes, at 1.30am.

(Source: Paul Ferrughelli, *Computer Catalog of UFO Reports, 1988-94/* Author, Teaneck, 1992)

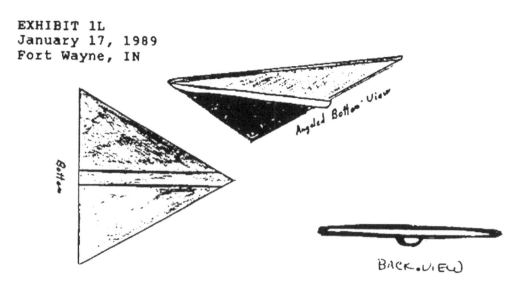

EXHIBIT 1L
January 17, 1989
Fort Wayne, IN

USA: Twelve UFOs seen

At 7am, twelve objects or more were seen moving across the sky over Fennimore, Wisconsin. The police who were contacted, confirmed that they had received several reports about this.

(Source: Paul Ferrughelli, *Computer Catalog of UFO Reports, 1988-94/* Author, Teaneck, 1992)

Canada: *Encounter with UFO*

At 11pm, this time over Kamloops, British Columbia, Canada, it is claimed a UFO was seen at close range.

(**Source: Rosales, Albert S.** *Humanoid Contact Database*/Garuda79@aol.com)

Canada: *Pilots sight UFO*

It is also claimed that the crew of an airliner flying over Rocky Mountain House, Alberta, Canada, saw a UFO for about five seconds, at 11.16pm, but there is little information about what promises to be an interesting incident, bearing in mind the professions of those involved. (**Source: CUFOS**)

17th January 1989 (UK) – Bright *'light'* seen

Southend was yet again the scene of further UFO activity – this time involving a bright *'light'* seen hovering over open land to the west of the town's airport, by Mary Lowe (18) and her mother from Eastwood before rising vertically upwards and heading slowly across the sky, towards Rayleigh.

(**Source: East Anglian UFO & Paranormal Research Association**/*Yellow Advertiser*, Colchester, 27.1.1989 – 'UFO spotted hovering near Airport – bigger than a star, and with no aircraft lights')

Bright light hovering in the sky over Essex

At 6.30pm Barbara Atkins (56) from Eastwood, Southend, was looking out of the window with her daughter when she saw a bright light hovering in the sky, between the Airport and Kent Elms, which slowly moved back and then rose vertically upwards at speed, and was gone from sight. (**Source: Ron West**)

17th January 1989 (USA) – Motorist paced by triangular UFO

At 1:30pm, a motorist was driving his truck towards Hicksville, Ohio, from Fort Wayne, Indiana, when he saw an object while exiting Woodbridge Apartments, travelling east on St. Joe Center Road. The object was then sighted again south of Route 37, apparently maintaining a parallel position approximately one mile south, at tree-top height.

Paced by the UFO

Several miles before Hicksville, Ohio, the object swooped across the road and positioned itself 50-75 yards in front of the witness's vehicle (still at treetop height) displaying three lights shining down for approximately half a mile. The driver pulled over to the right side of the road and stopped – so did the UFO. He got out of his truck and watched it for approximately 15-20 seconds (as it shined its three lights on him). The UFO then moved to the far side of his truck and then back over the field from where it came.

Two UFOs now seen

The man carried on to Hicksville and told his friend what had transpired. The two men then left at 2am to try and find the UFO. While driving westwards on Route 37, they sighted the object (still showing three lights) on their south side, and another UFO to their north. They followed these to the outskirts of Fort Wayne, where one crossed the road (from north to south) and headed back toward Hicksville. The men turned around on Route 37 and followed it back toward Hicksville. The UFO started to cross the road ahead of them, they accelerated to intercept it but it flew away westwards and was soon out of sight.

(**Source: MUFON, Indiana, Field Investigator Haddox**)

YELLOW ADVERTISER
-Colchester-

27 JAN 198?

UFO spotted hovering near airport

'Bigger than a star and with no aircraft lights'

MORE SIGHT-INGS of strange lights in the sky have been reported near Southend Airport.

A teenager and her mother from Eastwood watched a bright light hover for at least five minutes over open land to the west of the town's airport on Tuesday of last week.

The UFO was seen at around 6.30pm, hovering at just above rooftop height.

Eighteen-year-old Mary Lowe saw the light — "bigger than a star and without aircraft lights" — hover in the one position, then suddenly rise vertically to ten times its original height before moving off slowly in the direction of Rayleigh.

Southend police say there was no activity in the area on the night and the police helicopter was definitely not in use that evening.

When Mary's mother called Southend Airport to report the sighting, she was told nothing had shown on their radar screens at the time, nor were there any unusual aircraft operating.

Mrs Lowe's sighting is the third in the area this year. According to the Anglian UFO Research Group, previous sightings were reported on January 3 and 12.

The first involved three people who watched a bright light travel at phenomenal speed backwards and forwards between Southend and Basildon over a two-hour period. Through binoculars the three observed a blue light pulsating through a white glow.

Then on the evening of January 12, six people reported seeing two lights over Canvey. First one light revolved around the other, then it stopped and they appeared to switch roles.

Eventually the two lights separated, one flying towards Southend, the other in the direction of Basildon — where it disappeared, only to reappear suddenly over the sea not far from its original position, in close company with the first light once again.

Last year there was a whole spate of UFO sightings in southern Essex, some of the more spectacular phenomena being spotted by several dozen observers.

The Anglian UFO Research Group has asked anyone who thinks they have seen a UFO to call its emergency hotline on Basildon 286079.

18th January 1989 (UK) – Orange *'light'* seen

Erica 'C' of San Remo Road, Canvey Island, Essex, was driving home along Somes Avenue, after finishing work at 5.30pm.

> *"I saw a flashing orange 'light' in the sky – much bigger than any star – completely silent. It seemed to be hovering over the Hadleigh area. I watched it for five minutes until it just vanished from view."*

(Source: Ron West)

18th January 1989 (USA) – Domed UFO display, Somerville, Ohio

A family with an eleven-year-old child were living on a farm located 45 miles away from Wright-Patterson Air Force Base.

At 3.57am, on a clear morning, the barking of the dog awakened the family. When they went outside, they were astonished to see six or eight glowing elliptical objects in the sky, with flat sides.

For the next one-and-three-quarter hours (until having to leave for work and school) they watched the objects, described as being 4-10ft in diameter, hexagonal in appearance, with a dome on top, constantly changing colours from red, to yellow-orange and blue, as they hovered, landed, changed speed, disappeared and reappeared, while making a low humming noise, at a distance estimated to be between 100-500ft away from them.

Jet aircraft appears

At one point a jet aircraft flew over. As it did so, the objects – which were flying below treetop level over the family's (and their neighbour's) property – all disappeared. A ring of pulsing red, green and white, lights was sighted near the base of the objects. The evening after this sighting, a formation of jets passed slowly over their property, which the family considered an unusual occurrence. (**Source:** *MUFON UFO DATABASE*, **Portion of Reports from the Files at MUFON headquarters, July 1999, Sequin TX, CD-ROM, Case Log #890603, by Richard Seifried**)

Cylindrical UFO sighting, Massachusetts

At 7.30am, a deer hunter waiting in a tree stand on a clear morning, at Glen Allen, became aware that birds and squirrels in the locality became silent.

He looked up and saw a silent cylindrical object pass directly overhead, at an estimated altitude of 1,500ft. After it moved away out of sight, a minute later, the sounds of wildlife resumed. He estimated the size was the same as a Boeing 747 [230ft long] and with a speed of 300 mph. The man contacted an air traffic controller, at Greenville, and was told there was no aircraft listed in the area at the time of the sighting. (**Source:** *MUFON UFO DATABASE*, **Portion of Reports from the Files at MUFON Headquarters, July 1999, Sequin TX, CD-ROM, Case Log #900207, by James Scarborough**)

Over Florida

At 5.45pm, a woman, aged 64, of Gainsville, Florida, sighted a *'flying disc'*, about 80ft across, some 1,500ft away from her, showing what looked like smoke coming from it, followed by a solid-looking purple circle around a yellow-green centre, out of which a beam of light shone. (**Source: MUFON**)

21st January 1989 (UK) – Bright *'lights'* seen

Mr David Alan Giles (56) of Birchwood Drive, Leigh-on-Sea, was travelling with his wife along the B1012, one mile from Rettenden Turnpike, when they saw a bright *'light'* in the sky towards the south-east.

> *"It was stationary, quite large, and had a pointed appearance at the top. It was over Rayleigh. The weather was overcast and drizzling with rain. A few seconds later it vanished from sight."*

(Source: Ron West)

22nd January 1989 (USA) – UFO over Indiana

At 9.30pm, Green Fork couple – Mr and Mrs Gilmer – sighted a glowing bright *'light'*, low down in the sky. This was the third time in six days that the object had been seen by Mrs Gilmer. She had observed it previously on the 17th January, at 9pm, when it was accompanied by other smaller objects, and then on the 19th, around 6.30pm. On this occasion, the object was much closer and estimated to be at a distance of 1,000 yards, heading in a south to north-west direction. Mrs Gilmer shouted out to her husband, *"It's starting to move. It's coming this way!"* The object then flew silently over their home, at a height of about 500ft, before disappearing from view five minutes later. (**Source: MUFON Indiana, Field Investigator Mike Palmiter**)

```
EXHIBIT 2L
January 22, 1989
Greens Fork, IN
```

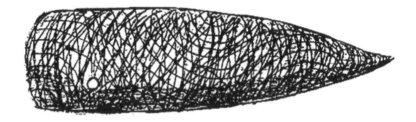

24th January 1989 (UK) (USA) (Australia) – Triangular *'lights'* seen

Essex

At 7.50pm, Rayleigh resident – Mr William Nicholls (66) – went outside to shut the gate, when he saw an unusual light in the sky – far bigger and brighter than any of the stars. He then alerted his wife, Maisey, who came outside. On fetching a pair of binoculars, he looked through and saw: *"...three stars, forming a triangular shape."* The lights then headed away, towards the direction of Romford, London, before being lost from view.

At 10.50pm, Southend resident – Robert Lister (43) – was outside his house in Oban Road, when he saw two star-like objects, motionless in the sky, south of Southend-on-Sea. He fetched a pair of binoculars, in order to observe them closer. A couple of minutes later one of the lights vanished, leaving the other – which was bluish in colour, with a faint red light around the outside before that too, faded away.

(Source: Brenda Butler & Martin Bainbridge)

USA: *Over Oklahoma*

At Valliant, Oklahoma, two large triangular objects accompanied by four to five smaller bright objects, were seen by dozens of people in the sky for over an hour. The large objects had red, white and blue lights. They hovered and moved slowly at treetop level. The smaller lights manoeuvred between them.

(Source: Richard F. Haines, *Project Delta: A Study of Multiple UFO*, p. 109; McCurtain (Oklahoma) Daily, 1st February 1989)

Over Tasmania

At 1am, two people (unable to sleep) went out for a walk to the nearby *Tamar River*, at Invermay, where they stopped on a jetty to talk.

High in the sky to the north-west, they noticed an object – like a star, falling towards the ground – and took it to be a shooting star. However, it came to a halt at an elevation of 20° to 40° and stopped for about 15 seconds, then moved horizontally across the sky towards the south-east. Twice more it stopped for some 10 seconds at a time, before it just disappeared into the far distance. Each time the *'light'* would move, it seemed to have a tail behind it. Two minutes later it was gone from view. (**Source: NLTA 1989-007**)

26th January 1989 (UK) – Triangular lights seen

Mr J.S. Hepworth (31) was driving westwards along the A127, at 8.45pm, approaching the Halfway House flyover, when he saw:

"...three round lights, motionless in the sky, in a triangular formation above the A127, west of the flyover. They were silent and appeared to be 250ft above the ground. I drove underneath the lights, which I estimated were 200ft between each other, and continued on my journey".

(Source: Steve Postoy)

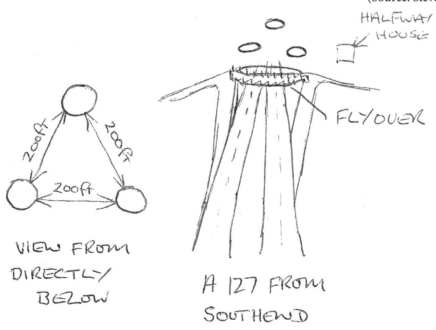

27th January 1989 (UK) – Mysterious blue flashes seen

Mrs Barbara Driscoll (58) of Victoria Avenue, Basildon, was getting the car ready at 8.30pm, to take the family away to meet her husband from Laindon Railway Station when the interior of the house was illuminated by a blue flash of light from the back and then from the front of the house, lasting between 5-8 seconds, agitating the dog. Barbara wondered if there was a storm approaching. She then got into the car and made her way to pick up her husband. Suddenly, she noticed what looked like searchlights sweeping across the sky.

28th January 1989 (UK) – Triangular UFO seen over Essex

A bright triangular, or shield-shaped, object was seen moving through the sky over Tiptree, during the evening. It was seen to dim in luminosity, before shooting across the sky towards Chelmsford, and was then lost from sight. (**Source: *Essex Chronicle*, Chelmsford, 17.2.1989 – 'Strange sightings in the skies'/Ron West**)

29th January 1989 (UK) – Triangular lights seen over Essex

Many of the readers will be familiar with the attention given to a massive 'wave' of UFO sightings that took place in 1989, over the Belgium area, and of the publicity given to those reports which involved the over-flight of three lights, set at equilateral distance from each other. On occasion, the Belgium Air Force gave chase, but was never able to intercept – although photographs were taken.

How many readers (up until now) were even aware that the Essex area was the target of UFO attention, during the early part of the year and that on the 29th January 1989, a number of people sighted a mysterious cluster of three lights moving across the sky?

7pm – UFO display, Basildon

Mrs Verity Ann Mathews (36) of The Gore, Basildon, was putting the dog out into the garden, when she happened to glance upwards and see three bright *'lights'* in the sky:

> *"…much brighter than any star, and forming the shape of a large triangle; the 'lights' appeared to be firing at each other. I then alerted my son, Nicholas, and daughter, Sarah, to come and have a look.*
>
> *After about half an hour, the 'triangle' moved slowly to the right, before returning to its original position. At this point I felt cold and went inside. I told my son, Nicholas – who, by then, had gone back into the house – to go and have a look to see if he could see them, 15 minutes later, but they had gone."*

(Source: Ron West/S. Postoy)

7.30pm – UFO display, Great Wakering, Essex

Enrolled nurse – Mrs Susan Sayer (31) of Beach Court, Great Wakering, reported having seen a number of lights in the sky, consisting of pairs or singular, prior to the three lights appearing at 8.15pm, forming a triangle in the sky. During this time aircraft were seen, but were completely separate from the UFO light display. Martin Bainbridge, from Ron West's UFO Group, who had been telephoned, arrived at the house and was in the fortunate position of being able to confirm the sighting himself, along with another witness – Mr Peter Sayer.

7.30pm – Three lights seen over Essex

Emir 'P' (43), of Stanford Road, Orsett, Essex – a qualified nurse by employment – was stood outside the Accident and Emergency Department, at Basildon Hospital, waiting to board an ambulance.

"I spotted two very large brilliant white lights in the sky. I didn't bring my colleagues attention to it, as I thought they might think I was being silly.

The ambulance turned up and off we went. While we were driving along One Tree Hill, the driver of the ambulance brought my attention to three strange lights he could see in the sky, towards Horndon-on-the-Hill. I told the crew I had seen two of these lights previously. At this point the traffic slowed down, enabling us to have a closer look at the three lights, situated in a triangular position in the sky. Suddenly, the lower light moved up between the other two and moved so close we thought there was going to be a collision, but it just circled the other one."

7.40pm – UFO display over Basildon

Mrs Hazel Caroline Wilkes (30) of Eric Road, Pitsea, Basildon, was in the back garden feeding her rabbits. She looked upwards into the clear night sky and saw what at first she took to be a large bright star. Any such notion was quickly vanquished when the *'star'* was joined by two others that moved over from different parts of the sky, then another forming a square of lights. She alerted her husband and two sons, who came outside.

"Two of the lights split away and headed across the sky, but returned to the original location. Two aircraft approached the lights, which moved away – as if wanting to avoid detection. The two that were left began an intricate display – like a laser show – across the sky; one stayed still, the other moved backwards and forwards at a terrific speed. A helicopter appeared and seemed to be watching them, but at quite a distance."

Hazel, whose legs were shaking with a mixture of fear and excitement, telephoned the 'UFO hotline' and was later interviewed by Martin Bainbridge, of the local UFO Group.

8pm – Bread and Cheese Hill

At the same time, Christopher Crawford (30) from Westcliff-on-sea, Essex – manager of a greengrocer shop – was waiting for the 9.15pm bus, with his wife, Julie, and father-in-law, at the bottom of Bread and Cheese Hill. They saw three fast moving objects above the horizon, which inexplicably halted in the sky.

"Two smaller discs appeared and headed away in the opposite direction, stopped, and then moved backwards to their original position – almost creating an impression they were going to collide. All of the time they were pulsating bright and dim, then they headed away and back again – it looked like they were breathing, that's the only way I can describe it. The bottom left object dropped quickly down onto the horizon, before rejoining the other three. The bottom right shot away and came back again. At this stage, a light aircraft appeared in the sky near the objects. As it did so the lights completely disappeared from view, but reappeared when the plane was out of sight. When the bus arrived at 8.15pm, the objects were still there."

8.10pm – Three lights sighted over Leigh-on-Sea
8.15pm – Rayleigh, three lights seen

Three lights were seen in the north-west direction of the sky, by Christopher Alan Cann, his wife – Jill (44) of Station Crescent, Rayleigh, and their two sons – Christopher and Stuart.

"They appeared to be stationary – then two of them very slowly crossed each other, as if changing places. They were still in the sky when we went inside."

At about the same time, Miss J. Barker (23) from Basildon, was in the process of locking the garage door when she, too, saw the three lights in the sky, moving overhead.

8.30pm – Basildon, three lights seen

Another witness was Stuart Conran (18) of Wickford, Essex. He saw them change from a triangular formation to a vertical line.

> *"The bottom right-hand side one faded away first, followed by the other two. The sighting lasted 15 minutes."*

9.15pm – Bury St. Edmunds, Suffolk, three white lights seen

Farmer's wife Anne Goddard (43) of Emswell, Suffolk, was checking the buildings with her husband when they sighted three white lights stationary in the sky over Bury St. Edmunds – 15 minutes later they had gone.

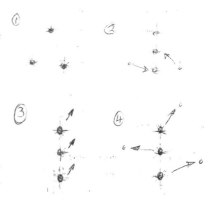

RED LIGHT SEEN HERE (APPROX

T ANGLIAN U.F.O. & PARANORMAL RESEARCH ASSOCIATIO

SECTION A   # SIGHTING ACCOUNT FORM

Please write an account of your sighting, make a drawing of what you saw and then answer the questions in section B overleaf as fully as possible. Write in **BLOCK CAPITALS** using a ball point pen.

On Monday 30th January 1989 the time was 7·15 p.m. I was standing in the front porch of my house, I was just about to go out for the evening, looking North over the river Thames, I saw a very bright ball of light, high in the sky, coming from the region of southend on sea. It was travelling from East to West. It seemed to come down at an angle, very fast, it then seemed to explode, with blue, green lights shooting all over the place, then it was gone. There was no noise, I watched for 2/3 seconds.

EAST ANGLIAN U.F.O. & PARANORMAL RESEARCH ASSOCIATION

SECTION A ## SIGHTING ACCOUNT FORM

Please write an account of your sighting, make a drawing of what you saw and then answer the questions in section B overleaf as fully as possible. Write in **BLOCK CAPITALS** using a ball point pen.

AT FIRST WE SAW TWO BRIGHT OBJECTS HOVERING THEN THEY STARTED TO CIRKLE EACH OTHER. AFTER A TIME A THIRD ONE APPERED AND THEY ALL FORMED A V FORMATION. THEN THAT THIRD FLEW AWAY AND THE OTHER TWO STARTED TO CIRCLE EACH OTHER AGAIN. THEN AFTER ABOUT 5 MINS OF CIRCLEING EACH OTHER THEY FLEW STRAIGHT UP VERY FAST, WE DID NOT SEE THEM AGAIN
   ALSO AT THE TIME AN AIRPLANE FLEW OVERHEAD AND THE THIRD ONE FLEW AWAY MUCH FASTER THAN THE AIRPLANE.

Please continue on a separate sheet if necessary.

DRAWING*

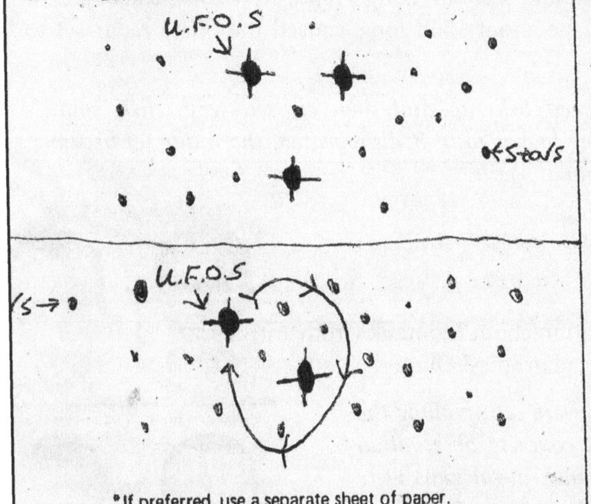

U.F.O.S

★ Stars

/S →

U.F.O.S

* If preferred, use a separate sheet of paper.

Your full name (Mr/Mrs/Miss/Ms)
JULIAN JAMES APPS Age 12

Address 29 FAIRFIELD GDNS
EASTWOOD LEIGH-ON-SEA

Telephone No. 526618 ....(STD.............)

Occupation during last two years. SCHOOLBOY

Any professional, technical or academic qualifications or special interests
AIRCRAFT OBSERVING

Do you object to the publication of your name?
Yes/No. *Delete as applicable.

Today's Date. 5·2·89

Signature J APPS

30th January 1989 (UK) (Canada) – Box-like UFO seen

Bright *'lights'* were sighted over Little Catins, Harlow, Essex, by local resident – Linda Pike – which turned red, just before she decided to go back into the house. The next morning, she was getting the children ready for school, when she saw:

". . . a big black thing – like a box – hovering and spinning, surrounded by haze, moving across the sky".

After discovering that her next door neighbour – Claire Prindiville (11) – had also seen strange things in the sky, she telephoned the police to report the matter. (**Source:** *Harlow & West Gazette*, **9.2.1989 – 'Mum calls Police after UFO sighting'/Personal interview**)

Benfleet, Essex

At 9.40pm, a witness reported seeing a large object *'the size of a double-decker bus'* moving slowly and silently across the sky, at about 800-1,000ft altitude. It had two sets of lights or windows along the centre, and the length was estimated at 250-300ft. (**Source: Ron West, East Anglian UFO & Paranormal Research Association**)

UFO sighted

At 10.05pm, an unidentified object was sighted over Nanaimo, British Columbia.

30th January 1989 (USA) – UFO over New York

Montauk Point Lighthouse

A triangular or diamond-shaped object was observed by Captain David Gaviola and two crew members of his fishing boat, just after leaving Montauk Harbour, Long Island, New York. The object, which appeared to be about 150ft long, caused the boat's radar set to fail. David:

"It turned belly-up and then cruised west, then south, climbing higher until it disappeared, the radar set became operational again."

(**Source: Star, East Hampton, NY, 9th February 1989**)

Operation 'Pastorius'

Interestingly, we discovered the following information about Montauk (from Wikipedia, 2014) which relates to a landing by German spies! Quote:

"During World War II, coastal fortifications were set up along the eastern tip of Long Island, at Montauk. A concrete observation tower was built next to the Lighthouse. 16 inch naval guns were placed in adjacent bunkers, at Camp Hero. The observation tower is still situated next to the lighthouse and the additional bunkers are visible at Camp Hero State Park, as well as Shadmoor State Park."

On 13th June 1942, as part of Operation Pastorius, four German agents, led by

George John Dasch

Ernest Peter Burger

Heinrich Harm Heinck

Richard Quirin

George John Dasch, were landed by U202, at what is now Atlantic Avenue Beach (sometimes called Coast Guard Beach) in Amagansett. Confronted by Coast Guardsman John C. Cullen, they said they were Southampton fishermen. When one of the four said something in a foreign tongue, they offered him $300 to keep quiet. The agents disappeared into the night, after he sought out his supervisor. When reinforcements arrived they discovered German cigarettes on the beach, along with four heavy, waterproof, oaken boxes, buried in the sand, filled with brick-sized blocks of high explosives, bombs disguised as lumps of coal, bomb-timing mechanisms of German make, and innocent-looking 'pen-and-pencil

sets' that were actually incendiary weapons. The agents rode the Long Island Railroad into New York City and were ultimately captured, along with four others who had come ashore at Jacksonville, Florida. Six of the agents were to be executed.

Montauk Project & the X-Files!

In 1992, Long Island residents – Preston B. Nichols and Peter Moon – published a science fiction book, *The Montauk Project: Experiments in Time*. They suggested that the radar was used by the government to conduct time travel experiments. Some readers believe their sci-fi account is true. The base has become of cult interest among conspiracy buffs. It was featured in a segment of *The X-Files*.

31st January 1989 (USA) – UFO ejects fireballs

At 6.40pm seven or eight blinking lights were reported in the sky over Versailles, Illinois – no doubt connected with the following report, fifteen minutes later – this time over Rushville, Illinois – a UFO was observed by a motorist, travelling along Route 67, which was seen to manoeuvre in the sky and then and eject what looked like several fireballs. Later, at 9.15pm, a bright light was seen stationary in the sky for a short time, over Leavenworth, Washington. Fifteen minutes later, at Valliant, Oklahoma, two objects were seen moving across the night sky, followed by four others.

FEBRUARY 1989

1st February 1989 (UK) – UFO over Wales

EDWARD and Irene Ward of Hoyland Drive, Haverfordwest, were driving to Tenby swimming pool, at 7.30am. As they turned off the main A77 road, at Sageston, passing ˙RAF Carew Airfield, they saw:

". . . a round silver coloured object, very high up, moving through the sky. It then stopped in front of us, but still high up, before darting across the sky over Kilgetty, then over the coast, followed by its appearance, once again, overhead, at fantastic speed – as if in a blink of the eye."

(Source: *Haverfordwest newspaper*, 7.2.1989 - 'Close Encounter for local couple')

2nd February 1989 (USA) – Cigar-shaped UFO seen

At 9.30am, a 3 year-old girl from Olympia Fields, Illinois, saw an unusual object in the sky outside and called her mother. The mother – who was presumably interviewed later – said it was as big as a 747 Jet airliner, which appeared to be crashing to the ground at a steep angle, before being lost from view.

(Source: MUFON, Illinois)

3rd February 1989 (UK) – Dome-shaped object, Lancashire

At 1.10am, Bryan Turner – manager of A1 Taxis, Waterfoot, Rossendale – was driving past Waterfoot Police Station, when he happened to look upwards into the sky and see a flashing light, which he took to be an aircraft, about 200ft off the ground.

"I thought it was too big for a helicopter. I stopped the car and got out to have a look, and saw this huge dome-shaped object, with stationary lights around the top, with red and amber flashing lights on the bottom. It seemed to be gliding soundlessly through the air, from east to west, and I thought it was going to crash into the top of the hillside, but it disappeared over quarries on Rooley Moor."

(Source: *Rossendale Free Press*, 11.2.1989 – 'RAF draws a veil over UFO riddle')

˙RAF Carew Cheriton was a Royal Air Force airfield of Coastal and Training Command near Carew, Pembrokeshire sited 4.7 miles North West of Tenby. It was built on the site of RNAS Pembroke (aka RNAS Milton) from the First World War, which had been decommissioned and sold off in the inter war years.

During the same month, Farnborough taxi driver – Gerry Hurn – had just picked up Danielle from her boyfriend's house in Keith Lucas Road, when they saw:

> *"...three bright blazing orange lights in the sky – like a helicopter formation – hovering. All of a sudden, they just veered away and vanished."*

3rd February 1989 (USA) – Paced by UFO

At 2.45am, two men driving near Ravenna, Michigan reported having sighted a UFO approach a car at treetop level, which then carried out what they referred to as *'games'* with the vehicle. (**Source: Not ascertained–Full details to be confirmed**)

4th February 1989 (USA) – UFO over Indiana

At 3am, over Lanesville, Indiana, a slowly moving object, showing lights, was sighted by two people, who estimated it was at a height of 300ft. (**Source: MUFON, Indiana, Field Investigator Janet Reising**)

5th February 1989 (UK) UFO – Display over South-East Buckinghamshire

At about 5pm, Luke Nichols (12) and his friend, Benny Haynes (13) were playing football in Westwood Park, Little Chalfont, with four other friends, when they sighted a number of objects in the sky, flashing with light. Luke:

> *"When we looked up again they were in a totally different place; they came really close to us and grew larger. There were lots of lights – red, blue, and white ones – all flashing together. When we first saw them, four of the boys ran away."*

The boys told their parents, who called the police. By the time they arrived there was nothing to be seen.

6th February 1989 (UK) – 'V'-shaped UFO seen

At 9pm, a 'V'-shaped object was seen spinning in different directions across the sky over Rochford, Essex, by a local man.

> *"At one stage it stopped still and a red light appeared. I also saw other lights that changed from blue to white, to red, and then orange-red."*

(**Source: Ron West/***Southend Evening Echo***, 9.2.1989 – 'UFO men probe 'V' shape spinner'**)

Was this an example of what was to become labelled as the 'Silent Vulcan,' but more commonly referred to as 'The Flying Triangle' which was to plague the skies of Europe?

It went thataway! Sumners UFO spotters point to the night skies. From left to right: Mrs Lin Pike, son Greg (nine), Mrs Barbara Prindiville and daughter Claire (11).

than black

UFO spotted

CASE E/89/123

REPORT; John Donaldson

...with brighter than bright strip lights along side

A BLACKER than black mystery flying machine and giant strip lights brighter than the moon has been spotted in skies over Harlow.

The bizarre UFO has been seen by several families in the Sumners area of the town.

Little Cattins mother-of-three Mrs Lin Pike wants to know exactly what's going on. For it's the third UFO sighting she's had in the past two months!

Twice she's seen gigantic hovering strip-lights blazing over the town centre. But this close encounter of the third kind, last Monday morning, left her stunned and desperately grasping for logical explanations.

Later she quickly sketched the black square lattice-shaped object, surrounded by a faint hazy circle, which she first spotted from her kitchen window.

Said Lin (32): "It was the most incredible thing ever — and it looked big...much bigger than a plane. I have never seen anything so black. It was the blackness that struck me.

"It looked like it was over Katherines and I thought was it a new kind of weather balloon, or has someone got a huge kite out? I would have given any money for a pair of binoculars.

"I first saw it edge on moving towards me. Then it began moving to the left and it started turning. That's when I saw the hole in the middle. I could see the grey sky through it," said Lin.

The mystery flying machine then rose quickly into the air until it became no more than a dot in the sky. Then it disappeared. The sighting lasted about 30 minutes.

The previous evening, around 6pm, Lin and several of her neighbours watched amazed as a huge bank of bright white lights hovered

An artist's impression of the mystery UFO, based on Lin's description.

original illustration

high above the Town Hall. Then the lights blinked out to be replaced by a row of faint red lights.

"It was so bright — brighter than the moon," said 40-year-old neighbour Barbara Prindiville. "We just couldn't think what it could be because it was so big.

"It really stood out," she added.

The sighting lasted about 10 minutes, during which no noise was heard. Then the faint red lights disappeared.

Harlow police Inspector Mike Walker said on Wednesday that Mrs Pike had reported the sighting to them and that a report would be sent to the Civil Aviation Authority.

On Thursday a spokesman at Stansted Airport radar control said there had been no unusual air traffic movements at the times of the sightings. And they had received no reports of UFOs.

7th February 1989 (UK) – Strange glow over Worcestershire

At 9am, Elsie Oakley (83) of Worcester Road, Kidderminster, contacted the *Kidderminster Times*, telling them of a strange experience which befell her, when she saw what looked like a powerful *'light'*, hovering above trees opposite her house, followed by a red glow – which rose higher, until it stopped well above the trees.

> *"A white cloud came over and it was shining through the cloud like the sun – then it began to beam down through the cloud. I went upstairs, but the 'light' was so bright, it hurt my eyes – then the 'glow' headed straight for the houses. I was so scared I didn't stop to see how far it went. I thought to myself – my God, if that thing falls on us, we could all be set alight."*

(Source: *Kidderminster Times*, 16.2.1989 – 'UFO fear has Elsie in a spin'/Personal interview)

7th February 1989 (USA) – Small UFO seen

At 10pm, a 17-year-old girl from New Haven, Connecticut, USA, observed a small sphere with red and blue lights, 60ft away, hovering three metres over her yard.

8th February 1989 (UK) – UFO sighted over Essex

This is what Alan Hollington and Christopher Bowman saw moving through the sky over Essex during the evening.

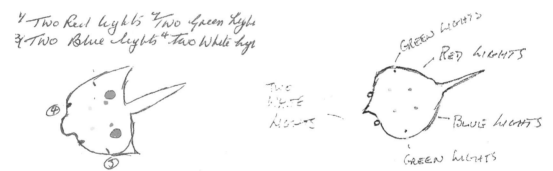

The object as seen by Alan Hollington   The object as seen by Christopher Bowman

9th February 1989 (UK) – Triangular UFO over Gloucestershire

At 9pm, several members of the public from Stroud, Gloucestershire – including motorists driving along the A46 near Stroud – sighted a triangular object in the sky and called the police. Police Sergeant Parr arrived and watched, with amazement: *"...a white triangular-shaped object – larger than a helicopter (definitely not an aircraft) – passing through the sky at 9pm one evening, over the A46 at Stroud"*. (**Source:** *Swindon Star*, Wiltshire, 16.2.1989)

9th February 1989 (USA) – Formation of *'lights'* seen

At 6.30pm, three adults and two children from DuQuoin, Illinois, sighted 15 large stationary *'red lights'* at treetop level, in a horizontal straight line formation, about 200ft from their house. After about two minutes, the silent *'lights'* broke formation, formed a cluster, and then moved about the local area before heading away out of sight, four minutes later. (**Source:** NUFORC)

10th February 1989 (UK) – UFO over Swindon

At 12.50am, Pinehurst couple – James and Doris Fisher – told of sighting a mass of lights, resembling a *'flying chandelier'* in the sky, over Poplar Avenue, Pinehurst, Swindon. At 1.10am, the lights disappeared from view. (**Sources:** *Swindon Star*, Wiltshire, 16.2.1989 – 'The night we saw a Flying Chandelier'/*Stroud News and Journal*, 16.2.1989 – UFO SITING) [-not sighting?!]/*Swindon Evening Advertiser*, 11.2.1989 – 'Couple claim UFO sighting over Town')

On the 24th of February *The Essex Chronicle* provided some but not all of the answers!

Essex Chronicle, Chelmsford

10 FEB 1989   723

UFOs are school's hot air

UFO SIGHTINGS over Chelmsford last week have turned out to be a lot of hot air.

And it is all down to the youngsters at the town's Melbourne Park Primary School. For the children caused the stir of UFO excitement when they launched model hot air balloons as part of a project on air movements.

Deputy headmaster, of the Melbourne Road school Mr Richard Sawyer said the connection between the sightings and hot air balloons was made by a friend, who, after hearing about the school project had read the UFO report in his Chronicle on Thurs.

Reports of UFOs over

town came last Monday, Tuesday and Wednesday. A former RAF man told police that he and his wife had seen an object in the sky Tuesday and Wednesday.

He described the object as "balloon shaped, grey at the top with a brown band at the bottom."

The balloons made from tissue paper, cane and wire were created by a class of 10 to 11 year-olds, then launched from the playground the same week as the UFO reports.

Mr Sawyer said, "We built four balloons altogether and

the best flight went about 2 to 3 miles to New Hall Convent.

The balloons which have a note attached asking to be returned have also landed at Chignal St James, Broomfield and Pump Lane, Chelmsford. Mr Sawyer added laughing that someone who had returned one balloon thought it was a parachute.

The class have two models left to launch, but are waiting for a calm day.

Mr Sawyer described the model making as "play-time with a purpose" and a similar project at a previous school he had taught at had failed to cause such interest.

Youngsters read about their hot air balloon UFO in last week's Essex Chronicle.

10 FEB 1989

SCHOOL REVEALS UFO MYSTERY

On the same day at Rawtenstall, Lancashire, a taxi-driver saw a *'domed disc'* flying low over the valley, in a North to South direction, at an estimated height of about 200ft –

"... as big as three jumbo-jets"

(**Source: Rodney Howarth and Andy Roberts**)

11th February 1989 (USA) – *'Flying Disc'* over Texas, and other UFOs

At 11.15pm, a woman resident of San Antonio, Texas, was at her home address, when she heard a humming noise coming from outside.

On going to investigate she saw an orange disc-shaped object, projecting a bright blue beam of light – strong enough to block out a nearby street light. (**Sources: Robert E. Morgan, MUFON field investigation case files, case #890402;** *MUFON UFO Journal*, **February 1990, p.15**)

11th/12th February 1989 (USA) – UFO Display over Alabama

Over two nights running, in the small town of Fyffe, Alabama, with a population of less than 2,000, over 50 people called the police department to report strange lights and shapes in the sky.

Police chased the UFO!

Police Chief 'junior' Garmany and Assistant Chief Fred Works (now a Fyffe councilman), were sent to investigate.

Artist's impression of what was seen at Fyffe, Alabama, US, during 11th and 12th February 1989. Some said the object was bigger than a Jumbo jet aircraft . . . others that it appeared banana-shaped with bright lights on the top and bottom. The event is still celebrated in Fyffe and hot air balloons are used in the publicity literature – epitomised in this art.

Garmany:

> *"It was completely silent; we got out of the car and turned off the engine and the radio. We followed the object in our car for about twelve miles, and then it suddenly reversed direction and silently flew over our heads at an estimated altitude of 1,000-1,500ft. We figured it was going about three or four hundred miles an hour."*

Officer Fred Works:

> *"It looked like an airplane, at first, but was moving fast."*

Garmany described the object as oval and being bigger than a Jumbo jet, while Works described it as triangular-shaped. The object appeared to be metallic in hue, and had no wings, windows or letterings, with flashing green, red, and white lights along the sides. White lights dotted the bottom, which appeared to be shining upward, illuminating the base of the strange aircraft.

Fired shotgun at UFO!

Other UFO sightings were reported from DeKalb City, Dawson, Dog Town, and Lick Skillet. The DeKalb County Sheriff's Office received over 50 telephone calls about the sightings. One terrified resident *"was about to have a heart attack and his wife was screaming"*, an official stated. He said:

> *"It came over at treetop level"* and that he *"had shot at it with a 12-gauge shotgun"*.

Spokesmen at various airports and Air Force and Air National Guard bases said none of their aircraft was in the DeKalb County area on the night in question. (**Sources: Elton Roberts, *Times Journal*, Fort Payne, Alabama, 14.2.1989; *News Journal*, Pensacola, Florida, 23.2.1989**)

Banana-shaped

Some witness reports stated that the object was banana-shaped and *"hovered at an angle from 1 o'clock to 7 o'clock, with bright lights at the top and bottom, and a real bright light at the centre. The curvature was outlined in green, with a real bright light in the centre"*.

Other witness reports stated it was triangular in shape and, even at close range, no sound emitted from it.

It should come of no surprise to see what appears to be an identical object to that seen on numerous occasions, over Essex.

Special Anniversary held in Fyffe

In 2005, the Mayor of Fyffe – Larry Lingerfelt – asked the City Council to consider implementing an annual two-day 'celebration' to commemorate the UFO sightings. Mayor Larry Lingerfelt said that although he didn't see anything himself, he is convinced there are those who did. He is also sure that people will once again be drawn to the town when about a dozen hot air balloons are seen hovering above it, during the event.

> *"I think we've got the connection – it's a unique one that will capture people's interest and imagination."*

Councilman Billy Carroll confirmed that the council unanimously supported the mayor's proposal. He said:

> *"We thought it's a good idea – anything to help the town"*

Carroll was formerly a member of the town's fire department, when the UFO sightings were reported in February 1989, and witnessed what he referred to as *"the weirdest thing I'd ever seen"*.

While several described the UFO as a banana-shaped bright light, Carroll said he saw:

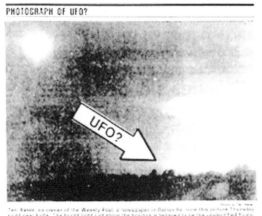

PHOTOGRAPH OF UFO?

Caption below photograph illegible.

UFO still stumping skeptics, believers

By ... ...

The above illustration is what two Fyffe officers said they saw in the sky on Feb. 12.

Crowds continue to flock to Fyffe

Nathan Jones prepares some T-shirts which were sold to sightseers Friday night in Fyffe.

"*...a white spot in the night sky that quickly disappeared. Alabama 75, through Fyffe, was like Panama City Beach, during spring break. Traffic was bumper to bumper all the way to Fort Payne, with motorists wanting to see a UFO*".

UFO (Unforgettable Family Outing)

Each year from 2005 onwards, a special anniversary is held to commemorate the UFO sightings of 1989 – which happened on the 25th/26th August.

This attracts between 4-5,000 visitors from all parts of the Country. The word UFO has now come to stand for 'Unforgettable Family Outing', which includes two days of hot air balloon and helicopter rides, food, and performances.

9th Annual

UFO DAYS

Saturday, August 24th

Gates Open at 9:00 a.m.
Entertainment Begins at 10:00 a.m.

LIVE MUSIC • ARTS & CRAFTS
ENTERTAINMENT & GAMES FOR THE KIDS
ANTIQUE TRACTORS & CARS

Entertainment Line-up:

Emcee: C.J. Jolley • National Anthem: Payton Sells

10:00 am - The Sharps
10:45 am - Michelle Norwood
11:30 am - Willing • The Phil Sexton Family
12:15 pm - Willie Underwood
1:00 pm - Danny Lee
1:45 pm - Stereo Revival
2:30 pm - Still Rockin' - Ronnie Osborn

3:15 pm - Jeff Martin & Caleb Chisenhall
4:00 pm - Payton Sells
4:45 pm - Picketts Charge - Fyffe FFA Stringband
5:30 pm - Thru the Roof - Hell Band
6:15 pm - Falt-er
7:00 pm - Smoking Gun
7:45 pm - The Bert David Newton Band

8:30 pm - The Big Band
(includes some members of the former Southern Flight Band)

Also Barney Fife will be there to mingle with the crowd & possibly sing a song or two

FREE ADMISSION

Mayor Larry Lingerfelt:

> *"Our UFO history started back in 1989, following UFOs spotted around Fyffe, as a result of which we received international exposure. We have people from all over the United States coming to this event, held annually. UFO days aren't just unforgettable for the family, it's also a record-setting weekend for the local economy. In the hotel business, in Rainsville, we completely fill up every room they have during UFO days. Jack's restaurant, downtown, breaks records every year during the UFO days' weekend".*

It seems ironic that while events involving the sightings of UFOs are used to fuel the economy of Fyffe (and who can blame them) no such interest has ever been displayed by their Essex counterparts.

12th February 1989 (Canada) – Four UFOs seen

At 10.30pm on the 12th February, over Ajax, Ontario, Canada, four objects were seen in the sky and observed by a couple for two hours.

12th February 1989 (UK) – UFO over Essex

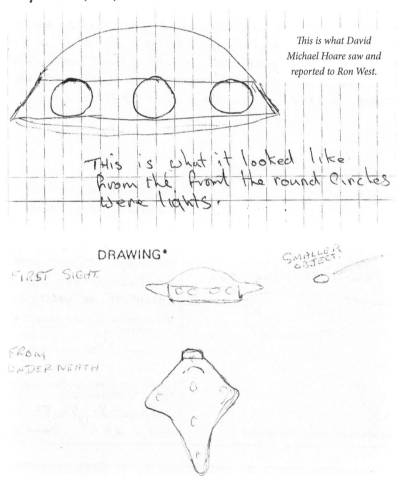

This is what David Michael Hoare saw and reported to Ron West.

EAST ANGLIAN U.F.O. & PARANORMAL RESEARCH ASSOCIATION

SECTION A   SIGHTING ACCOUNT FORM

Please write an account of your sighting, make a drawing of what you saw and then answer the questions in section B overleaf as fully as possible. Write in **BLOCK CAPITALS** using a ball point pen.

I WENT OUT OF MY BACK DOOR AT ABOUT 9.00 PM AND I SAW A BRIGHT LIGHT OVER THE HOUSES TOWARDS THE RIVER AND I WENT IN AND ASKED MY FRIENDS TO COME AND HAVE A LOOK. IT HAD THREE SPOT LIGHTS ON THE FRONT OF IT. AND WAS A FUNNY SHAPE LIKE A SUBMARINE. THEN I SAW A BRIGHT LIGHT COME FROM ABOVE THE OBJECT AT A VERRY FARST RATE AND STOPED OUTSIDE THE OBJECT. THEN THE SPOTLIGHTS WENT OUT LEAVING A HALE WHERE THE LIGHTS WHERE WERE. THEN IT STARTED MOVVING LEAVING A VAPOR IN THE SKY. IT THEN PARST OVER THE HOUSES. WANCE OVER THE HOUSE IT WENT VERRY FARST INDEED. IT LEFT THE VAPOR TRAIL IN THE SKY FOR SOME TIME

Please continue on a separate sheet if necessary.

DRAWING*

LOOKING FROM THE SIDE

* If preferred, use a separate sheet of paper.

Your full name (Mr/Mrs/Miss/Ms)
DAVID MICHAEL HOARE Age 43
Address 29 CHAPLE RD
ISLE OF GRAIN ROCHESTER
ME3 0BZ
Telephone No.................(STD ME 3 0BZ)
Occupation during last two years...... G A
ASSISTANT IN WORKS CANTEEN

Any professional, technical or academic qualifications or special interests
NIL

Do you object to the publication of your name?
*Yes/No. *Delete as applicable.
Today's Date 3 - 7 - 89
Signature D M Hoare

13th February 1989 (Canada) – UFO seen

The following day at 10.17pm, an unusual object was sighted in the sky, by two people, over Sydney Mines, Nova Scotia.

14th February 1989 (USA) – Flurry of UFOs seen

At 7.55pm, a circular object, displaying red, white and blue lights, was seen over Tehachapi, California; it appears that at least 10-12 other objects were also seen. At 10.44pm a UFO was sighted over Pemberton, British Columbia.

Night lights 'not from an aircraft'

18 FEB 1989

Swindon Evening Advertiser, Wiltshire

More mysterious lights have been seen in the sky above Wiltshire.

The couple who saw the latest aerial display, late in the evening at Barbury Castle, near Chiseldon, are convinced they were not from any aeroplane.

Eamonn Smyth, 18, watched the lights for more than half an hour with his girlfriend, Elizabeth Free.

"We first saw a triangle of orange lights moving slowly low to the ground. We thought at first they might be from a Druid party or Satanist sect," he said.

"They seemed to pass behind some trees and when a car came along they went out.

"Then they came back on and were joined by another group and moved off towards the horizon. There was a red glow in the sky with yellow and gold streaks.

"We also saw what looked like a spotlight going up into the sky."

Mr Smyth, who lives in Wood Street, Old Town, Swindon, previously had an open mind on UFOs.

"But what we saw on Thursday night was amazing – the flashing lights were definitely not from any aircraft," he said.

Mr Smyth plans to return to Barbury Castle – this time armed with a camera.

17th February 1989 (UK) – Triangle of orange lights over Wiltshire

Eamon Smythe (18) from Wood Street, Old Town, Swindon, and his girlfriend – Elizabeth Free – were near Barbury Castle, Chiseldon, when they saw a *'triangle of orange lights'* moving slowly through the sky, close to the ground.

"They seemed to pass behind some trees, and when a car came along they went out. Then they came back on and were joined by another group, before moving off towards the horizon. We saw a red glow in the sky, with yellow and golden streaks."

(Source: *Swindon Star*, 23.2.1989 – 'UFO reported by Barbury couple')

18th February 1989 (UK) – Car followed by UFOs

According to Ron West, of the Essex UFO Group, he was contacted by a man, who claimed to have seen flying disc-shaped objects following a car down East Mayne, Basildon. The man said the objects were *"about 12ins in diameter and 3ft above the road, and 25ft behind a car in front"*.

(Source: *Southend Evening Echo*, 23.2.1989 – 'UFO Probe into Discs') [Some accounts give the 20th February 1989]

The night we saw 'a flying chandelier'

AN UNIDENTIFIED flying object with pulsating lights has been reported over Swindon.

From their bedroom window on Poplar Avenue, Pinehurst, James and Doris Fisher watched the object for more than 20 minutes.

Said Mr Fisher: "it was in the early hours of Friday that we saw it — from ten minutes to one until ten past.

"It was like a chandelier hanging in the sky with red and green lights which changed brightness," said Mr Fisher, who is retired.

"It was a mass of lights and I called my wife who said it did look just like a chandelier.

"It was in a south westerly direction and high in the sky.

● An artist's impression of the UFO reported over the Cotswolds. Among the witnesses was a policeman.

"It was very hard to tell how large it was or how far away.

"I wanted to report it to the police but I thought they would think that I was a fool."

RAF Lyneham lies south west of Swindon but a spokesman there said he was not aware of any aircraft that could have resulted in such a sighting.

Meanwhile in the Cotswolds, several people, including a police constable, reported seeing a UFO.

A brightly lit object was spotted by motorists driving along the A46 near Stroud.

Again there were a number of lights. A spokesman for Gloucestershire police said the object had been described as larger than a helicopter, with more lights than a plane. "There were three green lights and the beams shone down in the form of a tripod," he said.

Sgt Parr said that people driving along the road had been so impressed by the sighting just after 9.00 pm on Thursday that they called into a police station and reported the matter.

He said that later a policeman, who had been about a mile from the road, had reported seeing the triangular shaped object

All witnesses said the mysterious object disappeared so suddenly that they were not able to say in which direction it had gone.

SWINDON STAR —Wilts— 16 FEB 1985

Essex Chronicle Chelmsford

-3 MAR 1989

More strange sky sightings

ANOTHER batch of UFO sightings over Chelmsford have been reported by flying object investigators East Anglian UFO.

They are the latest in a line of sightings by witnesses since the end of January.

The inverted triangle of lights seen in the area on January 28 and 29 were spotted again on February 17 at Springfield between 8.30 and 9pm.

And a large, glowing orange ball was witnessed over the county town at 11.30pm on February 15.

UFO investigator Ron West commented: "There must have been lots of people who saw that one."

But the strangest sighting was the 12" metallic disk followed by a Chelmsford man driving towards his home town on February 20.

The man was 75 yards behind the car in front of him when the disk appeared as he drove along the A12 from Brentwood.

It followed the car at a height of three foot before vanishing after ten minutes.

White glowing balls were seen heading towards Chelmsford at 8.45pm on Monday.

Anyone who witnessed these incidents can contact the UFO Hotline on Basildon 286079.

Swindon Evening Advertiser, Wiltshire

11 FEB 1989

Couple claim UFO sighting over town

An unidentified flying object with pulsating lights has been seen over Swindon this week.

James Fisher and his wife Doris watched it from the bedroom window of their home in Poplar Avenue, Pinehurst, for more than 20 minutes.

"It was like a chandelier hanging in the sky with red and green lights which changed brightness, a mass of lights in a south-westerly direction and high in the sky Mr Fisher said."

RAF Lyneham lies roughly in that direction from Swindon but a station spokesman did not know of any aircraft that could have resulted in such a sighting.

The couple's sighting follows reports of a UFO over the Cotswolds from members of the public and a policeman.

Exeter Express & Echo

21 FEB 1989

Driver spots 'flying jelly fish'

A DEVON lorry driver was still stunned today after seeing a giant jellyfish—like creature hovering above trees near Cullompton.

Adrian Redfern, of Tedburn St Mary, was driving along the M5 yesterday when he suddenly spotted the unidentified flying object.

Mr Redfern told the Express and Echo: "It was extraordinary. I have never seen anything like it."

The mystery creature was 30 ft wide. "It kept expanding and shrinking and then it suddenly disappeared," Mr Redfern said.

The lorry driver, who was delivering a load of concrete, says that he is normally extremely sceptical.

"People might think I am mad, but I am sure it was there," he added.

PC Gerry Leyman, at Cullompton Police Station, said that there had been no further reports of flying sea animals in the area.

"Normally this is the type of thing that is dealt with at headquarters," he added.

20th February 1989 (UK) – Jellyfish UFO seen over Devon & London

21st-22nd February 1989 (USA) – UFOs seen

At 2am, a *'craft'* was seen 50ft in the sky, above a resident's home at Philadelphia, Pennsylvania.

At 9.50am, a bright object was seen descending through the sky over Poway, California, at an estimated height of 1,000ft, which then made a 90° turn before being lost from view.

Wilson, Pennsylvania

At 10pm, an object displaying six to eight lights on its side was seen hovering in the sky over Wilson, Pennsylvania.

The following day, two people from Kansas saw a total of eleven objects moving across the sky – five of which were in formation, hovering over the town. Official explanation: 'Stars'.

Kansas

A group of lights was seen in the sky over Kansas. Other witnesses gave matching descriptions. The objects manoeuvred soundlessly. At one stage, five of the UFOs joined into a formation and hovered above the town. The objects reportedly moved swiftly, *'coming to a sudden dead stop and hovering'*.

In the hover position, the lights blinked in a specific pattern. (**Source: Irene Jepsen,** *Daily News*, Russell, Kansas, 24.2.1989)

23rd February 1989 (Canada) – UFO sighted

At 5am, a UFO was sighted in the sky over Vancouver, British Columbia, for 30 minutes.

23rd February 1989 (USA) – UFO Display over Kansas

An object was claimed to have landed east and slightly north of Russell, Kansas. An unnamed woman described it as *"huge, about the size of a football field . . . 'a city of lights'..."*. Frightened, she left the area.

Another report from Newport, Hampshire, tells of a large white *'light'* seen by the occupants of a car, while travelling along the road, at 11pm.

The two people concerned stopped to get out, fearing for their safety.

23 FEB 1989

UFO probe into discs

UFO researchers are investigating a motorist's claim that he saw metallic discs flying down East Mayne, Basildon.

The 12-inch diameter discs were moving at about three feet above the road and 25 feet behind the car in front.

The same day, Saturday, five white objects and red, green and blue lights were seen over Southend. At one stage a stream of light was beamed down on to the sea.

Anyone else who had sightings is asked to contact the UFO hotline on Basildon 286079.

SWINDON STAR
—Wilts—

23 FEB 1989

UFO reported by Barbury couple

MORE mysterious lights have been seen in the sky above Wiltshire.

The couple who saw the latest aerial display are convinced they were not from any aeroplane.

The latest sighting was at Barbury Castle, near Chiseldon, late on Friday evening. Eammon Smythe, 18, says he watched the lights for more than half an hour with his girlfriend Elizabeth Free.

"We first saw a triangle of orange lights moving slowly low to the ground.

"They seemed to pass behind some trees and when a car came along they went out.

"Then they came back on, were joined by another group and moved off towards the horizon. There was a red glow in the sky with yellow and gold streaks."

Mr Smyth, who lives in Wood Street, Old Town, Swindon, said other people must have seen the lights because they were so bright.

24th February 1989 (USA) – Triangular UFOs seen

This was a busy day of UFO activity for the United States. It appears, from the records available, that they unfortunately only contain scant details, which, to a great degree, can never possibly reflect the trauma and emotion involved with those luckless people – some of whose lives were changed forever. It began at Russell, Kansas (the scene of previous UFO reports) with a cluster of mysterious lights seen moving out of an alley, by a family, (**Source: Paul Ferrughelli**, *Computer Catalogue of UFO Reports*, 1988-94 Author, Teaneck, 1992)

At Lac St. Jean, Quebec, Canada, a *'flying disc'* was seen and photographed, just after midnight. (**Source:** *International UFO Reporter*, CUFOS/John Musgrave, *UFO Occupants and Critters*)

24 February 1989 – (Canada) 00:32

North Bay, Ontario – An unidentified object was sighted that had an unusual appearance or performance.

One object was observed by one witness for over 60 minutes. (**Source: CUFOS**)

Fyffe Albahama

A UFO, as big as house, was sighted hovering over a pond, lighting up the surroundings as bright as day before inexplicably vanishing. Another sighting involved a multicoloured triangular object seen in clear weather for five minutes by a women resident from the town. (**Source:** *MUFON investigation files*)

Timothy Good Lecture

At 2pm on 26th February 1989, the Yorkshire UFO Society held its meeting at Centenary House, North Street, in Leeds. Timothy Good was the speaker. Admission was free.

25th February 1989 (Australia) – Oblong UFO seen over Victoria

Mrs Nella Williams claimed to have observed a large oblong object, stationary in the sky for five minutes, at 7.30am.

> *"It was very bright and shiny, with a dome shape at the rear end, and it disappeared without any apparent movement. It was there one moment and gone the next."*

(Source: *Advocate*, Eden Hope, Victoria, 1.3.1989)

The UFO Hunter – Tony Dodd

DAILY STAR, Monday, February 27, 1989

EXCLUSIVE: The ex-cop

THE UFO HUNTER

☆ THERE are around 1,000 reported sightings of Unidentified Flying Objects every year in Britain. The true number could be far greater ... because many people who have had close encounters with other-world visitors keep quiet for fear of being ridiculed.

☆ Former policeman TONY DODD (left) used to be similarly silent. But now, after his own, fateful eerie experience, he is Director of Investigations for the Yorkshire UFO Society, and no longer scared to declare his beliefs.

☆ He claims at least 60 personal sightings of spacecraft keeping watch on Earth. And he is hunting more believers ... in a bid to force governments to admit they are hiding the truth about aliens.

☆ Tony, who cites instances of Britons being transported inside flying saucers for examination, stresses there IS Something Out There. Read his story. Then judge for yourself.

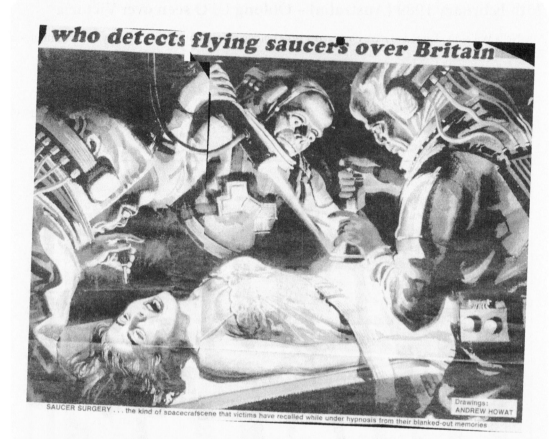

who detects flying saucers over Britain

Drawings: ANDREW HOWAT

SAUCER SURGERY . . . the kind of spacecraft scene that victims have recalled while under hypnosis from their blanked-out memories

BEAMED UP . . . how the saucers snatch their subjects

TONY DODD had been a tough, no-nonsense North Country copper for 25 years. But one black, moonless night he filed the strangest report of his career . . .

"Alien spacecraft hovering above the Skipton road. Eerie silence. Strange lights from portholes."

It was a night which changed Tony Dodd's life—the time when he realised that beings from another world are regular visitors to Earth.

"Call me crackers if you like," says Tony, with true Yorkshire bluntness, "but they are out there all right."

"There's no doubt about it."

During his quarter century of keeping watch over the good folk of North Yorkshire, Tony gained a reputation as a dedicated and sensible member of the community.

A plaque on the wall of his home in Grassington states: "His conduct was exemplary."

And before that fateful, frosty night in January, 1975, Tony gave as much credence to the existence of UFOs as he did to that of Santa Claus.

Glowing

But now he claims to have seen at least his flying saucers.

That first sighting came at 3.30 a.m. on five remote moors at Coniseley, near Skipton, as Tony was driving with his colleague, Pc Alan Dale.

He says: "Suddenly, there it was—a spectacular, shimmering flying saucer hovering 10ft over the road.

"It was staggering," says Tony.

"An actual spacecraft. A

By GORDON WILKINSON

magnificent saucer about 100ft across and glowing with an incandescent light.

"All around it were coloured lights, looking as if they were shining from portholes.

"But it made no noise. There was just an eerie silence, and then it sped away.

"We were flabbergasted. But it was a real spacecraft, all right.

"I was three years in the RAF before joining the police force—I know how to recognise conventional aircraft.

It was that close encounter that made Tony Dodd start to probe the UFO phenomenon.

Since his retirement from

the police last November, Tony has become Director of Investigations for the Yorkshire UFO Society.

"The part of the Yorkshire Dales where I live is a well-known spot for sightings," he says.

Patience

"The area around Carleton Moor has been visited by aliens many times.

"There are other hot spots around the country —such as Warminster, near Salisbury Plain.

"The UFOs are there to be seen if people take the time and patience to search for them.

"There are about a

thousand sighted in Britain every year.

"I've seen UFOs at least 60 times. One one occasion I actually flashed my car lights at a space craft and it signalled back to me.

"The aliens obviously have some reason for keeping to remote areas.

"Maybe they don't want to panic people—30 per cent of sightings are in rural areas.

"The aliens, obviously, are of a highly advanced intelligence and could make themselves known to us whenever they like."

As Director of Investigations for the UFO Society, Tony is compiling a computer record of all spacecraft sightings in the UK.

"The 300-member York-

shire Society has people all across the country.

"As soon as a UFO is spotted, Tony sends one of his regional investigators to the scene.

Observers use high powered telescopes, cameras and geiger counters.

Evidence

Suspected flying saucer landing sites can emit radiation, left by the craft power supplies.

Tony says: "We are the Yorkshire Society, but our members are all over the country.

"We are determined to compile so much evidence on UFOs that the Government will finally acknowledge the aliens are here.

"Governments around

Aliens are Tony's life

the world have known about the aliens for many years—but for their own reasons they refuse to let us know the truth.

"When I was on the force, I daren't speak out too much for fear of being branded a crank. But now I can come forward.

"What I want now is feedback from the public. Those who have had close encounters can contact me on the UFO hotline (0756 752216). All calls will be dealt with in confidence.

"Many policemen, and others who are out and about at night, have seen UFOs. But they are frightened of being ridiculed if they report them.

"There will be many more people in the air industry and scientific community with evidence.

"It's high time they came forward and the truth about the aliens was finally acknowledged.

"Newspapers and TV stations have plagued me for years for interviews.

"*But I know the Daily Star has always taken an interest in the UFO phenomenon and it is fitting that the paper should tell my story.*"

THE FORCE . . . ex-copper Tony

HYPNOTIC CLUE TO SPACE KIDNAPPERS

UFO watcher Tony Dodd claims spacemen kidnap Britons from their beds and beam them up to their flying saucers.

Once on board the spacecraft the humans are medically examined by the aliens.

Ex-cop Tony says the aliens blank out the memories of the people they have examined before setting them free.

But details of the encounters can still be unlocked under hypnosis.

People who experience the sensation of having lost part of their day may have been abducted by aliens, says Tony.

He claims a 41-year-old housewife from Colne, Lancs, was snatched from bed while her husband slept next to her.

Under hypnosis she recalled a three-hour ordeal at the hands of three silver-suited spacemen who examined her on an operating table in their craft.

Two friends from Keighley, Yorks, also experienced a 45-minute memory loss during a car journey together across local moors.

Ordeal

Under hypnosis they remembered being beamed up to an alien craft.

A 32-year-old Halifax woman is claimed to have been beamed up to a spacecraft in a ball of brilliant light. The terror of her ordeal was later unlocked by hypnosis.

On some occasions the examination of humans are carried out by robots under the aliens' command, say the UFO experts.

UFO alert as more sky-high mysteries sighted

By ALAN WHEELER

MORE unidentified flying objects have been spotted in the skies over South East Essex.

East Anglian UFO Research members are interviewing witnesses to the latest rash of sightings, probably due to the clearer skies.

One of the most interesting sightings was on Friday March 3 by an ex-RAF pilot in Grays.

The man, in his mid-40s, saw a brilliant white light in the sky surrounded by a glow. The former pilot estimated the object to be at 20,000 to 25,000 ft.

He watched the football-shaped object hover for three quarters of an hour and then it sped off at incredible speed in the direction of Kent.

Mr Ron West, senior investigator and founder of the group, said: "He said the RAF has nothing that can travel at that speed and he was convinced it was not a plane."

At 6.45pm on Sunday March 5 a woman and her son travelling on the A127 from London to Southend witnessed another UFO.

The Southend couple spotted a red ball of light through their windscreen at the Rayleigh Spur with the A130 to Chelmsford.

Wonder

Stunned at the unearthly sight they pulled into a layby and watched in wonder with their windows wound down for 15 minutes.

As they watched an aeroplane flew near the red light which suddenly went out only to reappear in the sky once the plane had flown past. Eventually the silent light just vanished.

The A127 again features in a case this month which Mr West's UFO team are investigating. It happened at 7.40pm on Wednesday March 8.

A mother and her two sons aged seven and nine were travelling towards Southend when they saw an object in the sky as they approached the Rayleigh Weir.

They described it as diamond-shaped with two glowing white lights at the front. As it passed overhead they noticed two more blinking white lights at the rear end.

The witnesses said it looked nothing like an aircraft and was travelling too fast to possibly be one.

Three independent reports from Southend, Leigh and Canvey on Saturday March 11 talk of a similar diamond-shaped craft being spotted in the skies between 8.30pm and 10pm, again with two lights at the front and two at the back.

Mr West is particularly excited about an incident which happened on Tuesday January 31 at the Southend home of nine-year-old Reginald Moran and his parents.

The little boy spotted an object from the living room window of his house and ran upstairs to get a closer look from a bedroom window, only to find the mysterious sight had vanished.

His parents, who say he is a very truthful boy, are convinced he did see something, and Mr West says he is very impressed with the detailed description given of the object.

He said: "The boy described it as rectangular in shape with a square-shaped box on top which was rotating. It had a bright hazy ring or a glow around it.

"The box part was described as the only visible moving part and it turned round slowly. We are sure this is an authentic and accurate description."

The team is ready to investigate UFO sightings day and night and have a hotline on 0268 286079 which anyone can call if they see anything mysterious in the skies.

MARCH 1989

1st March 1989 (USA) – Triangular UFO seen over Ohio

WHILE being driven home at 8.03pm, a 37-year-old mother and her 19-year-old daughter from Union City, spotted a triangular-shaped object stationary in the sky, about halfway between their car and their house, which was about a quarter of a mile away. The driver stopped the vehicle and the two women stared in disbelief at the object, which was *"gigantic"* in size, and five to six times larger than their house.

Suddenly the craft started to move slowly toward the two women. As it passed overhead, at a height of about 40ft, they were able to see the surface of the craft, which looked *"very metallic"*. During the 10minutes observation, a rumbling sound was heard coming from the UFO. Both women said they were terrified by the experience. (**Source: NUFORC**)

2nd March 1989 (USA) – Boomerang-shaped UFO seen

A man (60) living in Shrub Oak, Westchester County, New York, told of seeing a huge metallic boomerang-shaped UFO – showing many lights on its front, hovering over his head – just 50ft above the ground, at 9.35pm. Later, he complained that he was unable to account for about 20 minutes.

Could there have been any association with what was seen over Purton, UK, nearly 30 years ago?

(**Source: Paul Ferrughelli,** *Computer Catalog of UFO Reports*, **case 246, citing Robert Gribble, UFO Reporting Center**)

3rd March 1989 (UK) – UFO over Grays, Essex

An ex-RAF pilot from Grays, sighted a brilliant white *'light'* in the sky, at an estimated height of 25,000ft. He watched it for 45 minutes, before it moved rapidly away heading towards the Kent direction.

At 6.30pm taxi driver Basildon Kenneth Marsh (40) was driving towards Broadmayne traffic roundabout, Pitsea when he noticed a huge bright light in the sky moving slowly over the Southend-on-Sea area; he watched it for about five minutes until it was out of sight.

4th March 1989 (UK) – Pulsing UFO

Austin Rover workers from Swindon – Howard Carey, from Dores Road and Roy Townsend, of Alfred Street – sighted an irregular object showing a pulsing light at the front, heading northwards across the sky. *"It veered to the right and left, before heading off towards Cirencester."*

(Source: *Swindon Evening Advertiser*, 4.3.1989 – 'Another UFO mystery')

5th March 1989 (UK) – Red *'ball of light'*

A woman and her son, travelling along the A127 from London to Southend, sighted a red *'ball of light'* in the sky over Rayleigh, which was motionless for 15 minutes, before moving away. At about 7.45pm Vernon Wright (17) and his friend Keith Martin(17) were walking along Leighton Avenue, Southend , when they saw two lights stationary in the sky . Excited they ran down the road while keeping their eyes on the objects. Five minutes later they dropped downwards and headed away.

8th March 1989 (UK)

Another object was seen hovering in the sky over Rayleigh.

10th March 1989 (UK) – UFO sighted over Tamworth

11th March 1989 (UK) – UFO over nuclear power station

At 9.15pm, William Jones (57) of Whitaker Way, West Mersea, Colchester – a postman by occupation – was looking out of his lounge room window with his wife, when they saw an oval-shaped light, hovering approximately two miles away, over Bradwell Nuclear Power Station. At this point, Arnold Watson (62) – the next door neighbour – came round and told them he was also watching the object, which was about the size of a dustbin in the sky.

William:

> *"We watched for 20 minutes, and then it moved to the right, 30-40ft, stopped, and moved back to its original position. As*

SWINDON STAR
—Wilts—

9 MAR 1989

Two more say: We spotted a sky mystery

THE LATEST in a spate of UFO sightings was reported last week by two Austin Rover workers, Howard Carey and Roy Townsend.

They both saw a round brightly lit object travelling northwards over Swindon.

Mr Carey, who lives in Dores Road, Upper Stratton, said: "I have never before seen anything that could not have been explained.

"At first I thought it was a Hercules but there was no noise. It was bathed in a whitish glow and had a very irregular shape.

"There was an intense blue light at the front which pulsated.

"It veered to the right and to the left and then headed off towards Cirencester at a faster speed."

Fellow worker Roy Townsend, of Alfred Street, Swindon, said: "I just don't know what it was. It had a ring of lights and it was glowing."

10.3.89

(0827 285396)
Kean Jackson

6 Medina
Belgrave
Tamworth
Staffs

Dear Grayham,

Thankyou for your time on Monday after the meeting. I thought I'd write a compact summary of my sighting and after afects to see if any may conside with any of your own experiances or be of any use to your group. By the way the number for the group you did not inclose in it by any chance twelve? just a feeling!.

Friday 10th March 89 9.00 pm approx the first sighting was just a light in the sky I pay no attention to it but the second was right in front of me some one to two hundred feet above just hovering it had a white dome with a small Red/white light above. Around the dome were 6 Red and green lights flashing giving the appearance of rotating around the dome. Below this a red light cast down on the lower part of the object making it look like a cone with another red flashing light at the bottom of the cone. After watching it for about 30 seconds it slowly moved away from me. As I said on monday my outlook on life has change since and I have messages given to me I hope that you may let me come over and talk to you or some of your member I hope to hear from you soon

yours
sincerly

The Ambulance Station Staff at Hind Hill Street, Heywood, Lancs also spotted U.F.O. activity, in the vicinity of their station, in May 1989.
The lights went out in their station and phone lines went dead.
This article was printed in "The Heywood Advertiser" in May 1989.
I hope you can assist me, in any way, with research into these sightings in total confidence.

Yours faithfully,
P. Walker.
(PAUL WALKER)

it did so, it seemed to glow from dim to bright, before disappearing from view at 10.01pm. We then telephoned the police to report it."

The police confirmed that they had received several other reports of UFO activity that evening.

11.3.1989.

Dear Paul,
          Herewith a feature, on the East Anglian U.F.O & Paranormal Research Group.
     The East Anglian U.F.O & Paranormal Research Group, came into being on the 1st July 1988. Brenda Butler, who is very well know in the Suffolk area, for paranormal research, for the past twenty five years, also for being the main investigator on the " U.F.O. Mystery of Rendelsham Forest" RAF/USAF Bentwaters --- RAF/USAF Woodbridge, cases. Myself not as well known but also with over twenty years, investigating U.F.Os, Having been an A.I. investigator for the British U.F.O Research Association. Decided to set up our own research group, covering the Counties of Essex, Kent, Norfolk, Suffolk and Cambridgeshire, investigating all U.F.O and Paranormal sightings. We have at present over fourty members covering this area, but are still interested in hearing from anyone interested in becomeing either members or investigators, we hold meetings once a month, where we discuss all aspects relating to the U.F.O Phenomenon.
Through the newspapers we hope to attract the attention of people (general public) who have had an experience or seen something in the sky, that they cannot explain, and have no one to talk to about it, to contact us(in complete confidence) and discuss their experience/sighting. We are here to listen and where possible help, also to give information to other interested parties who have a desire to learn about the U.F.O Phenomenon.
Anyone contacting us, will be visited by one of our investigators, who will then ask if they would fill in one of our "sighting forms", this form will then be entered onto our computer, and cross-referenced with other reports on file. The case will be discussed, conclusions drawn, and if requested, the person who contacted us will be told of our findings. The whole idea is to collect as much information as possible. We are interested in hearing from people who have witnessed, lights in the sky, orange balls of light, lights doing things that normal aircraft could not possibly do. Have you seen a shape in the sky, that is not normal with conventional aircraft:- a black square shape, oblong, triangular or round shape. Had an paranormal experience. Then we would like to here from you, past or present experience's or sightings. Southend is a hotbed of U.F.O sightings, they must go somewhere so why not where you are. There is definitely something out there. We are trying to sort out what! The govenment do not want to know, the Air ministry say's that U.F.Os "are not a threat to our security" Well if they are not interested in U.F.Os, we are. So if you have seen something you cannot explain why not contact us.
Our number:- U.F.O.HOTLINE 0268 286079.

We also give talks, on U.F.Os to interested groups or clubs.

Ron West.

According to Ron West, hundreds of people witnessed the mysterious *'ball of light'* over the Estuary. They included Stanley Malvey (36) and his wife, Julia. They were driving their Ford Cortina car along the Esplanade, when they saw the *'orange ball'* and stopped to obtain a better view. Others were Jack Oakes (49) and his wife. Thomas got into his car and set off homewards. At 10.10pm he was astonished to see an orange coloured spinning object, showing red, green, and pink lights hovering in the sky, a short time later over Southend-on-Sea.

"It seemed to be stationary, but then it would go up and down again. I then lost sight of it behind the hospital building."

12th March 1989 (USA) – Fyffe, Alabama, USA

At 7.30pm, a local resident – Mr Gary Coker – observed an extremely large object, with red and green flashing lights on the side and two white lights on the base. The object suddenly vanished. Five miles away, another witness, at exactly the same time (7.30pm), said that an object – the size of a football field – hovered over his chicken house. It was described as being a metallic blue, with two white lights underneath, showing red and green lights on the sides. (**Source:** *Weekly Post, Rainsville*, **Alabama, 16th March 1989**)

13th March 1989 (UK) – Lights reported

Strange coloured lights were seen in the sky over Derby and were reported to the police and weathermen. Some of the callers believed the objects were UFOs, until it was established that they had, in fact, been the Northern Lights or Aurora Borealis, caused by electrons from the sun hitting the Earth's atmosphere.

Report of Space Shuttle Crew sight alien spacecraft

Space Shuttle Discovery (mission STS-20) was launched from The Kennedy Space Center at 9:57 a.m. on March 13th 1989. After achieving the required orbit the crew turned their attention to the primary mission right away, and the satellite and its booster were deployed without problem. This was fired off at 3:12 p.m., after only five hours in space. The primary objective was to orbit a tracking and data relay satellite, perform science experiments, and take over 3000 photographs of the earth's surface from space. Photographic equipment included a 70mm IMAX motion picture camera. The crew included Commander Michael L. Coats and Pilot John E. Blaha, and three mission specialists.

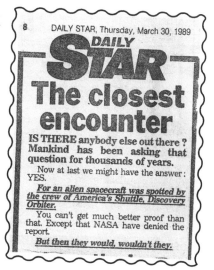

An American radio ham Donald Ratsch claimed to have intercepted radio transmission messages from Discovery to Mission Control that indicated the presence of a UFO. The exchange (recorded) spoke of a 'fire', which UFO researchers claim is NASA code for an unidentified object! Shortly after this followed the message *"we still have the alien spacecraft under observation"* – it

THURSDAY, MARCH 30, 1989

DAILY STAR

JUST WHAT YOU DIDN'T EXPECT!

20p (21p Cls)

NAVEL RATINGS EXTRA

SEE PAGES 3 & 7

SHUTTLE'S CREW SAW ALIENS

Discovery 'buzzed'

ALIENS buzzed the space shuttle Discovery high above Earth, it was revealed last night.

By FRANK CURRAN and ANTONELLA LAZZERI

Experts say a UFO tracked the American spaceship during its five-day flight earlier this month.

At one stage, the alien craft "locked" onto the shuttle's controls—causing a sudden loss of power.

The Discovery's five-man crew reported the close encounter with an "alien spacecraft" to NASA ground control.

And the conversation was picked up by astonished radio hams throughout America.

NASA chiefs in Houston, Texas, are refusing to release their recordings of their top-secret chats with Discovery pilot Colonel John Blaha.

But one man in Baltimore, Maryland, claims to have tuned into the NASA-Discovery and taped the talks.

Approached

The tape was played to the Daily Star yesterday—and Col. Blaha is clearly heard saying:

"Houston, this is Discovery. We still have the alien spacecraft under observation."

The radio exchange allegedly happened as Discovery orbited Earth for the 14th time exactly 20 hours, 45 minutes after being laun-

ched from Cape Canaveral on March 14.

Discovery also reported losing power at the time of the sighting—which experts claim means the alien craft was interfering with the supply.

Exception

Another radio ham in Ohio says he listened in just 6½ hours after the shuttle took off and heard the astronaut say:

"Houston, we have a problem. We have a fire"—believed to be a secret NASA codeword for a UFO.

And a third eavesdropper claims to have heard NASA order Col. Blaha to change to a classified radio frequency before continuing to discuss the UFO.

Discovery made a perfect landing in the Californian desert on March 19 after successfully "towing" a £60 million communications satellite

Turn to Page 2 Column 1

Col. Blaha . . . talks

Blast-off . . . Discovery's launch "led to brush with the unknown."

Pilot John E. Blaha

was then claimed for a few minutes Discovery was entirely drained of its power and rendered completely inoperative. Following Donald Ratsch's disclosure of the incident, the so-called 'Discovery Encounter' made headlines throughout the world. For their part, NASA vigorously denied the claims and was backed up by the crew of the Discovery who said it was an elaborate hoax!

Late March 1989 (UK) – *'Flying disc'* over Northamptonshire

A mysterious object was seen in the sky over the village of Moulton, in Northamptonshire, described as twice the size of a star, moving much slower than an aircraft, according to villagers – Sue and David Harrison – who said it resembled:

> "...a 'disc' – blue in the middle, with a white band around it; outside was a pulsating red band, making it look like a clock face going mad."

Beckenham & Penge news
The Advertiser, Friday, March 17, 1989

It came from outer space

By
BARBARA McSWEENEY

TALES of dwarfs running about in green overalls, taking specimens from stunned earthlings might bring a smile to anyone's lips.

Not, though, to those of Beckenham author, Timothy Good, whose book "Above Top Secret' has just appeared in paperback.

A man who relishes these tales of the unexpected, he frankly admits that some people are "compulsive liars", and that of others "you can't believe half of what they say".

Yet, he claims, many are credible witnesses.

'World's top people have secretly contacted ETs'

"After all, what have they got to gain except ridicule?"

Aged 47, his interest in UFOs dates back to his early teens, when a passion for aviation and space drew him to a book which detailed sightings by pilots, missile experts and air traffic controllers.

Working all over the world as a musician, he has gathered a huge amount of evidence for the book, which took two years to write but absorbed twenty years of research.

His first book, a Vanity Press publication, came out in 1983.

"George Adamski — The Untold Story" investigates the claims of an American to have filmed a 25 ft spaceship gently humming in a friend's front yard.

A semi-professional photographer himself, Mr Good rarely goes anywhere without his camera.

He was appalled to find he had forgotten it on 15 December 1980, when, walking home to his Beckenham flat, he suddenly saw a motionless, star-like object in the wrong position for a planet.

"I dashed the remaining distance home to observe it through my telescope and take photographs and movie film."

But, by the time he reached the window, it had vanished.

"Officials explained it away as a meteorite, but a meteorite doesn't split and regroup the way this did."

He would have been more disappointed, if he had not already had an exciting glimpse of the unknown 17 years earlier.

"We were listening to a record, when my mother called us into the garden.

"At first I thought it was a planet or a balloon, but through binoculars I could see it was a sharp-edged object, translucent like glass.

"All the neighbours came out onto the street, and we sat in deckchairs watching it, until it went behind a cloud and disappeared."

"The Air Ministry said it was probably a research balloon from the continent, but that does not explain how it stayed so still."

Mr Good is used to being ridiculed, particularly in the serious media.

"But anyone who spends more than an hour with me, talking about the subject, will take me seriously."

Recently he gave a talk in the USSR, and will be lecturing in the States three times this year.

At home he has talked to the Young Conservatives, the Rotary Club and the Round Table.

"People usually begin with scepticism, and end with astonishment at the wealth of evidence."

His aim in writing "Above Top Secret" was "to alert the media to the fact that something of unprecedented significance was happening."

This is not just the reality of extra-terrestrial visits, he says, but the reality that top level people all over the world believe in them, have been in contact with them, and are concealing what they know.

The US, he claims, is not only in possession of a crashed space ship, but of four humanoid bodies found in it.

Exactly who is concealing what is not entirely clear, since "UFOs ARE Classified even higher than the H-Bomb."

And he says, "It's doubtful if many people in government itself know what is going on."

This puts the spotlight on military and intelligence agencies.

"I think I have been able to prove the case."

But he has a frightening warning: "Not all extra-terrestrials may have our best interests at heart.

"They may be creating a hybrid: samples of blood, ova and sperm have all been taken from people.

"If we were told the truth, though, we'd learn to live with it - just like we've learnt to live with the threat of nuclear war."

"Above Top Secret" is published by Grafton Books at £5.99. Signed copies are available in the Beckenham Bookshop.

Timothy Good: "Beam me up, Scotty"

17th March 1989 (UK) – report of UFO sighted over Essex

MRS PULLEN.   17th March   11PM to 12½c

My son came home and asked if I would like to see a U.F.O. and took me into the garden at the back of the house overlooking fields. He showed me a brightly coloured changing light in the distance. There was also a similar light not as bright further over to the right. My husband and I set up a telescope in a stationary position to look closer the light changed colour gold, red, green and some blue. The other light was not as prominent. We knocked next door to our neighbour to witness what we were seeing, Mr Brooks & Mrs Brooks came out into their garden bring binoculars. We stayed watching for approximately 1hr. before the light eventually faded.

My son tells me he and some friends had been watching several lights grouped together for about 2hrs before he came home to tell us of the two left. The others disbursed apparently.

We are not sure what we were looking at but whatever it was stayed around for the hour that we were watching it moving up and down and sideways so slowly that we only noticed it was moving because it kept going out of telescope focus.

This is a true account of what I experienced

Mrs J Pullen   Date of birth
49-10-48

MR PULLEN   D.O.B - 21/3/1957.

On Saturday March 17th at around 10 pm my Stepson came in and said to my Wife and I that he had seen a UFO over to the back of our Garden.

We went into the Garden and noticed what appeared to be a bright ball of light that was changing colour.

We lined it up with a pylon in the foreground and watched it with the naked eye, binoculars and a telescope. Looking through the binoculars and the telescope just enlarged the object but did not bring out any details, just a bigger version that appeared to be vibrating thus making it impossible to focus.

The object moved very slowly to the right over a long period of time and eventually faded into the distance. At no time did it make any fast or sharp movements.

It was about 30° and in the direction of South West.

At the same time, another object the same was over to the West, but was nowhere near as spectacular and was completely stationary, looking very similar to a star, but changing colour as was the other one in the South West.

Although there is a flight path in the general direction of the sightings, several aircraft flew over at the time we were observing the lights and no way could what we saw have been a Civil Aircraft.

A.M. Pullen.

March 1989 – UFO 'buzzes' British Airliner

Some very peculiar 'lights' were seen by the pilot and 140 passengers aboard an British Island Airways aircraft en route from Malta to Gatwick. One of the passengers was *Suzy Walton – then a radio presenter for London Broadcasting Corporation. Another passenger was Brian Challis manager of Hogg Robinson Travel Agent, Newmarket. He told of seeing the distant sky light up. Moments later the aircraft plunged

MID-AIR PLUNGE PANIC AS UFO BUZZES PLANE

TODAY Thursday March 23 1989

by NICK CRAVEN

THE captain and passengers on a VIP flight watched in amazement as a UFO sped towards them.

They sat spellbound as a silvery glow with flashing lights appeared over the Mediterranean.

Seconds later, guests on the maiden flight were thrown forward as the shape disappeared and the plane plunged, spilling coffee and smoked salmon.

The chairman of British Island Airways, Peter Viller, was among executives and journalists who witnessed the drama on the inaugural flight of the firm's McDonnell Douglas 83.

At first captain Bob Taylor thought it was another plane and told passengers to look out of the window as they crossed Sardinia.

Susie Walton, a presenter with London's LBC Radio, said: "The sky lit up with shimmering lights. It was like a disco. It was very pretty, almost a romantic light.

"After the light disappeared, the captain came back on and said it wasn't an aircraft. He said it could have been a missile or a UFO. But if it was a missile he would have been warned about it in advance. There was no sound, it was silent.

"When the plane suddenly dropped a few minutes later, it was terrifying. I thought that was it. They later said the drop was due to 'wake disturbance' which you get if you fly into the vacuum created by a jumbo jet. But there were no other planes around."

Capt Taylor added: "I've never seen anything like it before. It looked like the remains of a condensation trail.

"It came towards us somewhat faster than normal, in fact it was obviously missing us and climbing tremendously high way above us.

"At first I thought it was an aircraft. It was the way it suddenly disappeared that made me change my mind. I can tell my grandchildren I might have seen a UFO."

No one has identified the object which did not show up on air control screens. But BIA chairman Peter Viller insisted: "The lights were anything from 500 to 3,000 miles away. I'm certain it was not a UFO."

Brian Challis

twice throwing the passengers forwards spilling after dinner coffee. An unnamed spokesman for British Island Airways later said, "*We saw some bright lights in the sky and then experienced some turbulence its been blow out of all proportion.*" [Apparently a number of National newspapers reported that the passengers were terrified]

Brian:

> "*I didn't see any sign of panicking; people were surprised, some were covered in coffee. The Captain told us to look out of the windows as we crossed Sardinia. As I was sat on the other side of the aircraft I didn't bother. But I did see the sky was brightly lit up in the distance, like a cloud swirl with white lights, very spectacular*"

The Captain then spoke to the passengers, he said that he had been listening to Air Traffic Control and said he had picked up a broadcast about it being a misfired missile, but assured the passengers the light was 250-300 miles away, there was no question of the plane being in danger.

(Source: *Newmarket Journal Suffolk* **6.4.1989**)

˙In 2014, according to the internet, Suzy is a chartered Director, chartered Scientist and deputy Chairman of the Royal Society for the encouragement of Arts, Manufacture and Commerce (RSA) and the University of Westminster. She recently finished a 6 year term as deputy Chairman of the Internet Watch Foundation, which regulates the internet against aspects of criminality.

She sits on a number of other boards, including the institute of Directors, Government committees, the State Honours Committee and writes, speaks and consults, on a range of topics.

For over a decade she was a senior Civil Servant in central Government and has been employed in the Prime Minister's Strategy Unit. She was also in the MOD and was awarded a PhD for her research into suicide in the military. Her early career included being editor and presenter for Sky News, BBC, and LBC radio. In addition she has been a West End actress, playing a leading role for three years, and has five children. We emailed her several times and also wrote to her, but never received any reply.

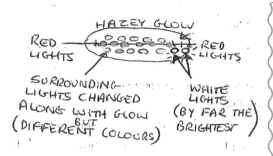

HAZEY GLOW
RED LIGHTS
RED LIGHTS
SURROUNDING LIGHTS CHANGED ALONG WITH GLOW (DIFFERENT BUT COLOURS)
WHITE LIGHTS (BY FAR THE BRIGHTEST)

21st March 1989 (USA) – Longmont, Colorado, UFO display

A member of the National Air Traffic Controllers Association disclosed that UFOs were tracked at the F.A.A's en route centre at Longmont, Colorado. Centre spokesman and safety chairman – Kevin Cain, had this to say:

> "Longmont air traffic controllers at several sectors were astonished to see numerous UFOs appearing on their radar displays. These unidentified targets looked like actual aircraft, with apparently normal speeds and altitudes; some controllers had a dozen or more of these targets over a half-hour period."

However, Mitch Barker – an FAA spokesman at the regional office in Seattle – rejected the report, saying:

> "They were having a problem with the transponders that automatically send information from the aircraft to the centre."

(Source: *Coloradoan*, Fort Collins, Colorado, 26.3.1989)

23rd March 1989 (UK) – Diamond-shaped UFO seen over Essex

At 7.30pm, Peter Bolton (29) from Harold Hill, Essex, was parked alongside the A127 dual carriageway in his Vauxhall Cavalier 1600cc, facing

---

2 0 MAR 1989

UFO alert as more sky-high mysteries sighted

MORE unidentified flying objects have been spotted in the skies over South East Essex.

East Anglian UFO Research members are interviewing witnesses to the latest rash of sightings, probably due to the clearer skies.

One of the most interesting sightings was on Friday March 3 by an ex-RAF pilot in Grays.

The man, in his mid-40s, saw a brilliant white light in the sky surrounded by a glow. The former pilot estimated the object to be at 20,000 to 25,000 ft.

He watched the football-shaped object hover for three quarters of an hour and then it sped off at incredible speed in the direction of Kent.

Mr Ron West, senior investigator and founder of the group, said: "He said the RAF has nothing that can travel at that speed and he was convinced it was not a plane."

At 6.45pm on Sunday March 5 a woman and her son travelling on the A127 from London to Southend witnessed another UFO.

The Southend couple spotted a red ball of light through their windscreen at the Rayleigh Spur with the A130 to Chelmsford.

Wonder

Stunned at the unearthly sight they pulled into a layby and watched in wonder with their windows wound down for 15 minutes.

As they watched an aeroplane flew near the red light which suddenly went out only to reappear in the sky once the plane had flown past. Eventually the silent light just vanished.

The A127 again features in a case this month which Mr West's UFO team are investigating. It happened at 7.10pm on Wednesday

By ALAN WHEELER

A mother and her two sons aged seven and nine were travelling towards Southend when they saw an object in the sky as they approached the Rayleigh Weir.

They described it as diamond-shaped with two glowing white lights at the front. As it passed overhead they noticed two more blinking white lights at the rear end.

The witnesses said it looked nothing like an aircraft and was travelling too fast to possibly be one.

Three independent reports from Southend, Leigh and Canvey on Saturday March 11 talk of a similar diamond-shaped craft being spotted in the skies between 8.30pm and 10pm, again with two lights at the front and two at the back.

Mr West is particularly excited about an incident which happened on Tuesday January 31 at the Southend home of nine-year-old Reginald Moran and his parents.

The little boy spotted an object from the living room window of his house and ran upstairs to get a closer look from a bedroom window, only to find the mysterious sight had vanished.

His parents, who say he is a very truthful boy, are convinced he did see something, and Mr West says he is very impressed with the detailed description given of the object.

He said: "The boy described it as rectangular in shape with a square-shaped box on top which was rotating. It had a bright hazy ring or a glow around it.

"The box part was described as the only visible moving part and it turned round slowly. We are sure this is an authentic and accurate description."

The team is ready to investigate UFO sightings day and night and have a hotline on 0268 . 286079 which anyone can call if they see anything mysterious in the skies.

the Canvey Island direction, accompanied by members of the Penson family, when they saw a diamond-shaped object in the sky, showing red, white, and blue lights. Peter:

> *"There was a main object and three smaller lights around. It disappeared behind the cloud but then reappeared; it looked like it was over the sea."*

This was an interesting report, as it contained not only what appeared to be the arrival of what should, by now, be an all too familiar appearance of the three UFOs (as seen, on numerous occasions, over the Essex area) but also an object, which we had come across many times before .

It appears that the objects were very similar to what Essex man Christopher Penson saw during March April 1989.

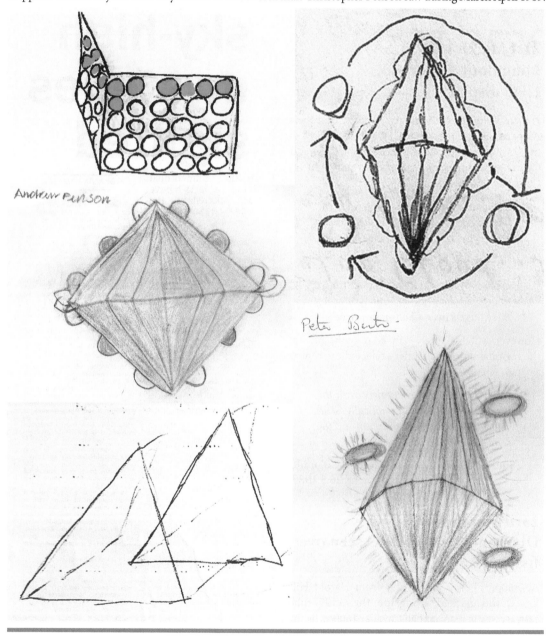

Andrew Penson

Peter Berto

RAF Church Lawford

In particular, it reminded us of the UFO seen over Southend, in 1995, involving a number of police officers. (More details about that in a later Volume of *Haunted Skies*). Not forgetting the sighting in July 1951, involving Mr Leonard Burrell from Kessingland, Suffolk who was completing his National Service at RAF Church Lawford, just outside Rugby, Northamptonshire.

> "Something caught my eye – a bright light, brighter than the sun behind it. It seemed to flash on and off at one second intervals, clearly visible against a blue sky, with a few high feathery clouds far away on the horizon. I looked at my wristwatch (12.35pm) and continued to observe the object. Approximately ten minutes later, the object had descended low enough for me to make out precisely what it looked like. I estimated it to be between five and ten feet long and three to six feet wide in the middle. It was silver metallic in appearance, with a very high gloss to its outer surface, and seemed to have been constructed from glass-like material, with a mirror finish.
>
> It reminded me of a very large diamond, with finely cut edges. The object was now at its lowest point – about 500ft off the ground and 2-300 yards away – appearing to rest for a while, for several seconds, over a group of trees near the school buildings. Suddenly, a number of birds that had been roosting in the trees flew up into the air and headed towards the UFO, as though attracted by it. None of them actually went near it but, within a split second, they all turned and headed away from the object, screeching as they went. The whole area around the school went completely quiet. You could not hear one bird until the object disappeared, when they started to sing again. As the birds flew off, the UFO began to move slowly upwards, still turning at the same speed and flashing regularly, with bright sunlight reflecting off each facet of its surface. Within 20 minutes it had gone."

Len contacted the nearest RAF weather station and explained what he had seen. They confirmed that no weather balloons were in the area that day, and could not offer any logical explanation for the sighting.

(**Source: Ron West/Roy Lake**)

Taxi driver adds to growing 'We saw it' list, but . .

RAF draws a veil over UFO riddle

ROYAL Air Force chiefs refuse to comment on sightings of Unidentified Flying Object seen over Rossendale.

The Ministry of Defence Press officer in London would not comment on the UFO sightings and insisted it was a matter for the Air Force.

The Air Force Press spokesman in London stressed: "We never take part in any discussions about interplanetary flying objects.

"We defend the airspace of the UK. If a responsible authority such as air traffic controllers or police say to us, 'There is an unauthorised aircraft in the sky we are anxious about it; will

By JEAN GILLATT

you establish what it is?' we would investigate that there is nothing in the sky that has not the authority to be there.

"We do take steps to prevent unauthorised aircraft, that is our job. But we would never talk about space flights or UFOs."

At about 1.10 am last Friday Mr Bryan Turner (55), manager of A1 Taxis, Waterfoot, saw what he believes was a UFO similar to the one recently seen landing in a Stacksteads quarry.

He described what happened as he was returning from his last taxi job of that night!

"I was driving past Waterfoot Police Station from the direction of Stacksteads and stopped to let a wagon turn. I just happened to look upwards and saw a flashing light, which appeared to be an aircraft flying really low. It was maybe 200ft above.

"I thought that was funny. It was too big for any helicopter. I jumped out to take a better look. I saw this huge dome-shaped object with stationary lights around the top, and red and amber flashing lights around the bottom, which seemed to be revolving. It wasn't like any aircraft I have ever seen!"

Mr Turner of Bury Road, Raw-

tenstall, added: "I could not hear any sound. It seemed to be gliding from East to West. I thought it would crash into the hillside but it skimmed the top and disappeared towards the quarries over Rooley Moor.

"I do not believe in spaceships or UFOs or anything like that, but I do know I saw an unidentifiable aircraft."

Two people living at Cloughfold have phoned the Free Press since we reported on 21 January that Mr Harry Aspinall of Cutler Lane, Stacksteads, saw a UFO in Lee Quarries while walking his dog. They claimed to have seen a similar sight, a low-flying brightly lit aircraft, behind the Smith and Nephew factory at Cloughfold.

26th March 1989 (UK) – As seen by Bobby Craven over Essex, that evening

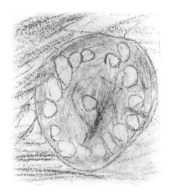

28th March 1989 – Rusian Phobos 2 probe lost

The Phobos program was an unmanned space mission consisting of two probes launched by the Soviet Union to study Mars and its moons, Phobos and Deimos. Phobos 2 became a Mars orbiter and returned 38 images with a resolution of up to 40 meters. Both probes suffered from critical failures. Phobos 1 and 2 were of a new spacecraft design, succeeding the type used in the Venera planetary missions of 1975-1985, last used during the Vega 1 and Vega 2 missions to comet Halley. Phobos 1 was launched on July 7, 1988 and Phobos 2 on July 12, 1988, each aboard a Proton-K rocket. They each had a mass of 2600 kg (6220 kg with orbital insertion hardware attached).

The program featured co-operation from 14 other nations including Sweden, Switzerland, Austria, France, West Germany, and the United States (who contributed the use of its Deep Space Network for tracking the twin spacecraft). Phobos 2 arrived in January 1989 and entered an orbit around Mars as the first phase towards its real destination, a small Martian moon called Phobos. The mission was flawless until the craft aligned itself with the moon. On March 28, 1989 an elliptical object was detected moving towards the satellite seconds before it failed. All indications were that the elliptical object had attacked the satellite which was now dead and left spinning out of control.

On March 28, 1989 *Tass*, the official Soviet news agency stated:

> *"Phobos 2 failed to communicate with Earth as scheduled after completing an operation yesterday around the Martian moon Phobos. Scientists at mission control have been unable to establish stable radio contact."*

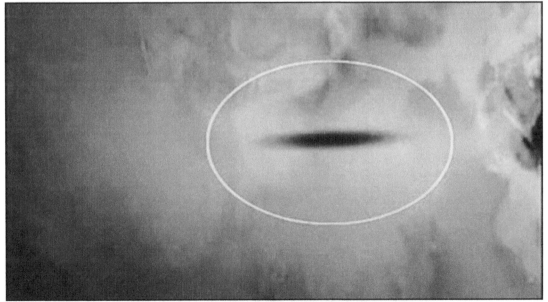

Russian Mars probe Phobos 2 – Unidentified shadow on Martian surface. This appeared on the final three frames before contact was mysteriously lost.

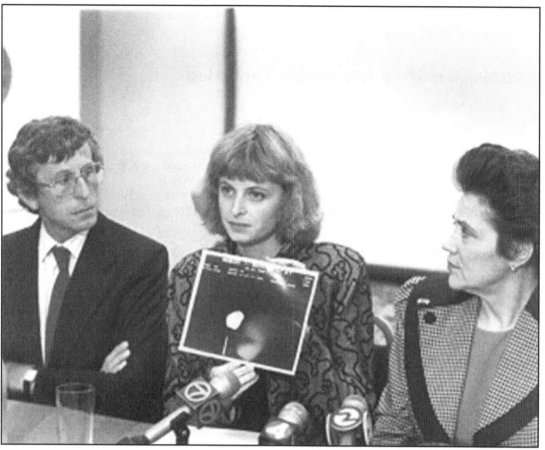

Marina Popovitch, a Russian Cosmonaut at a Press conference held at the San Francisco Russian Consulate. She is shown with a photograph of a cylindrical-shaped UFO taken by the Russian Probe Phobos 2 shortly before it ceased operating.
(Colin Andrews is on the left, Marina Popovitch on the right. Centre is Marina's interpreter, holding the photograph.)

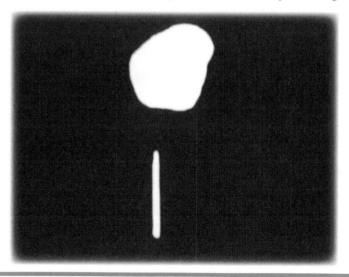

APRIL 1989

PRESENTED below: An overview of March 1989 UFO activity, as published in the *Thurrock Gazette* on the 7th April 1989.

More UFO sightings reported

A RECORD number of UFO sightings were reported in Grays last month as more people related their experiences to a team of experts.

Mr Ron West, founder member of the East Anglian UFO and Paranormal Research Group, said that details of six Grays sightings in March had been reported to the Group.

by Clair Orton
Thurrock Gazette 7.4.1989

Various sorts of UFO have been seen, including a craft shaped like a doughnut with red, green and blue lights around the edge.

Mr West said: "This seems to be a very popular craft and has been spotted all over South East Essex and reported to us on numerous occasions."

This UFO was reported by two different people who gave similar descriptions, adding that it had been seen in the area of Lenthall Avenue.

Another two of the sightings also occurred in this particular area, although the type of UFO described was different.

Mr West is delighted that the response from people in Grays is now picking up and that sightings are being reported.

He said: "It is not surprising that UFOs should be seen in the Grays area because we think these objects come up the Thames estuary heading towards or coming back from London.

"Obviously, people in Grays are now starting to look at such objects and think about what they could be.

"Now we have investigators working in the Grays area, people are beginning to report these things and now we are getting as many sightings in Grays as we are in other parts of South East Essex."

If anyone has seen a craft which they would like to report, they can contact the special UFO Hotline on Basildon 286079.

1st April 1989 – Obituary, Raymond Drake

Raymond Drake held a season ticket for Sunderland United Football Club for many years. He died at a match at Roker, not far from his home, on 1st April 1989, aged 76. Born 2nd January 1913, Drake followed a career as a civil servant; he eventually became head of HM Customs and Excise in Sunderland. Raymond was known for his "Gods and Spacemen" books, the first of which – *Gods or Spacemen?* – was published by Ray Palmer, in Amherst, Wisconsin, in 1964. In the *BUFORA Journal* (March 1980) Raymond said:

> *"We descend not from ape-men, but from glorious celestials from the stars. Today we use only a fraction of our potential brain-power. My friends, we are more than men, we are the Sons of Gods!"*

Raymond's writing included plays, science fiction novels and poetry – much of which went unpublished, or was only privately circulated.

A twenty verse whimsical SF poem, *The Stolen Bride*, appeared in *Space-link* magazine, Volume 5, Nos. 2 and 3.

> *"Raymond and I were amongst contributors to a glossy book,* Beyond This Horizon – *an anthology of science fiction and science fact, published in conjunction with the BTH Festival in 1973, where we appeared on the platform together at the Sunderland Arts Centre."*

Gods or Spacemen? (1964) ISBN: 0-451-07192-1 – *Gods and Spacemen in the Ancient East* (1968) – *Mystery of the Gods – Are they coming back to Earth?* (1972) – *The Ancient Secrets of Mysterious America – Is Our Destiny upon Us?* (1973) – *Gods and Spacemen in the Ancient West* (1974) ISBN: 0-451-06055-5 – *Gods and Spacemen in the Ancient Past* (1975) ISBN: 0-451-06140-3 – *Gods and Spacemen Throughout History* (1975) ISBN: 0-85435-332-1 – *Gods and Spacemen in Greece and Rome* (1976) ISBN: 0-451-07620-6 – *Gods and Spacemen in Ancient Israel* (1976) ISBN: 0-7221-3034-1 – *Messengers from the Stars* (1977) – *Cosmic Continents* (1986) (**Source: Wikipedia, 2014**)

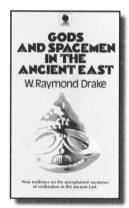 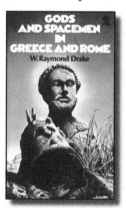  

3rd April 1989 (UK) – UFO over Essex

At 8.45pm, Vanessa Duff (22) – then living at Wellington Road, Tilbury – contacted the 'UFO Hotline', after sighting a *'bright light'* zig-zagging and occasionally stopping, in flight across the sky.

4th April 1989 (UK) – Spinning top UFO over Derbyshire

At 9.15pm, two 18-year-old students were sat in a car, parked on the top of Stanage Edge, above the village of Hathersage – on what was a cold, clear night, with 2ft of snow on the ground – when they saw a strange 'light' in the sky, in a southerly direction. The 'light', now low in the sky, disappeared from view but then reappeared. It was described as:

> "...*shaped like a spinning top, with white and red lights*".

As the students drove towards Sheffield, the object appeared to land on the hillside, lighting up the ground, apparently following the car at low altitude. Upon reaching the outskirts of the city, the silent object seemed to split into two lights – which vanished into fields. It was claimed that when the students returned to the scene, the next day, they discovered an area of snow was melted under where the object appeared to land. This matter was reported to the Derbyshire Police, MOD, and RAF Finningley.

(**Source:** David Kelly, David Clarke, IUN)

5th April 1989 (USA) – Saucer-shaped UFO seen

At 3am, two farm owners – one female, the other male – living close to each other in Plainfield, Indiana, reported having sighted a hovering '*disc*', showing lights on its external structure. The woman told of being awakened by a light and, on going to see the cause, saw a '*flying disc*' hovering silently in the sky, about 200ft away, at an altitude of 100-200ft. She then went back to sleep. The man, in his 60s – a retired labourer – was awoken by his dog and saw the object as described above. Both described:

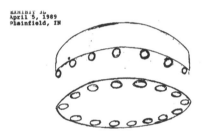

> "...*a bright 'disc', with estimated diameter of 15ft. The body of the 'disc' was blue-white, and bright as a security light but much larger, with steady amber, blue, and white lights, on the bottom*".

Five to six lights were seen on the base of the UFO.

The woman reported power and telephone outages for the next three days. Both witnesses reported elation and memory lapse during the sighting. (The woman did not remember the sighting until the next night).

(**Source:** *MUFON UFO DATABASE*, **Portion of reports from the files at MUFON Headquarters, July 1999, Sequin TX, CD-ROM, Case Log #890708, by Norma J. Croda**)

6th April 1989 (UK) – 'Flying saucer' lecture

Emphasising the growth in interest of the UFO subject then, as opposed to now, was shown during a lecture on 'flying saucers', at Leigh Library, Lancashire. The organisers had to turn away 160 people. At 7.30pm on this day, veteran UFO researcher – Arthur Tomlinson, B.Sc., spoke about UFO crashes at the Derby Room, Leigh Library, following the release of information under the Freedom of Information Act. Admission was £1.

7th April 1989 (UK) – UFO over Kent

At 11am, a silver-blue saucer-shaped object, with a white 'halo' around it, was seen in the western sky over Kings Close, Kingsdown, near Deal, Kent, by Mr Clarence Gilbert Searle (72) and his wife, Dorothy Alice (68).

> *"It was moving in a series of fast, horizontal, and vertical movements."*

At 8.30pm, the couple were astonished to sight what appeared to be the same object, traversing in a series of horizontal and vertical movements through the south-eastern part of the sky. Clarence ran in and picked up a pair of binoculars. By the time he arrived back outside, it had gone. Clarence:

> *"This was the second time. Last year I saw what looked like a sharply defined, low crowned, bowler hat in shape, object – silver in colour – flying across the sky."*

(Source: John Robson Lydd/*Adscene*, Canterbury, Kent, 19.5.89 – 'Have you seen these UFOs?')

8th April 1989 (UK) – Corby, Northamptonshire

At 10pm, a retired technician sighted a bright *'light'* in the sky from his back garden which appeared stationary for around 30 seconds, before moving away in a northerly direction, at an elevation of 40°. It was a clear sky, with moon and stars visible. (**Source: Ernest Still, BUFORA**)

On the same day, Police Sergeant Tony Dodd's interest in the UFO subject was featured in the *Bradford Telegraph & Argus* newspaper.

UFO hunt chief's close encounter

Bradford Telegraph & Argus West Yorkshire 8.4.1989

MORE THAN a decade has passed since former police sergeant Tony Dodd saw the phenomenon which turned him into one of Britain's leading UFO experts.

He and a colleague from the North Yorkshire force had been called out to an incident in the South Craven village of Cononley, when they spotted a pool of bright light on the road ahead.

Emerging from the police car, they looked up to the darkened skies and saw a glowing disc-shaped craft, with rotating coloured lights around its base, hovering about 100ft above them.

It was his first encounter with what he believed was an alien overflight and one which was to

EVIDENCE: One of Tony's UFO picture collection

to help solve the mystery of UFO's.

Since then, Mr Dodd, 54, has seen more than 60 similar objects, mostly in the Cononley and Carleton Moor areas.

Now, following his retirement from the police after 25 years service at Skipton and in his home community of Grassington, he has just been appointed to a top post in

As Director of Research and Investigation with the country's biggest sky-watching organisation, Quest International, which has links throughout the world, he has an overview of exactly what is happening and where.

Mr Dodd has charge of a team of 90 investigators, who look into reports of unusual occurrences, aided if necessary by high-quality photographic equipment as well as geiger-counters and site sampling kits if there are indications a craft has landed.

"The reason I haven't been able to give up sky watching is that I know UFO's are operating in our air space and I want to help prove it," said Mr Dodd.

"The Government denies the existence of UFOs, but I feel the sheer volume of reports coming in is bound to take the cover off in the not too distant future."

Quest International's Hotline

ON THE LOOKOUT ... Tony Dodd searches the sky

9th April 1989 (UK)

At 11pm, Mr Norman Garry Gubb (32), from Canvey Island, was awoken by a bright flashing *'light'*. He looked out of the window and saw a multicoloured object heading through the sky before being lost from view. (**Source: Ron West/Ron Smith**)

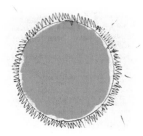

10th April 1989 (UK)

At 10pm, Ronald (35) and Kim Goodge (31) of Earls Avenue, Southend-on-Sea, sighted a round red-orange flame coloured object, stationary in the sky.

"It then began to move away in a north-west direction; 25 minutes later it was out of view."

11th April 1989 (UK)

At 7.45pm, this object was sighted in the sky by Mr S. Dennett (64) of Canvey Island. The matter was brought to the attention of Ron West, who asked Jeff Smith – an investigator for the group – to go and interview him.

At 9.30pm, schoolgirl Addy Carter (11) of Blenheim Chase, Leigh-on-Sea, happened to see an object passing through the sky.

"It was green and blue coloured, with white flashing lights on it. It was small – then it got bigger and just stopped all of a sudden. It hovered in one spot for a while, and then disappeared."

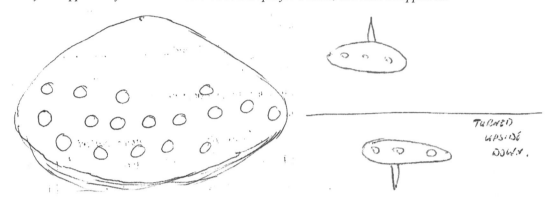

11th April 1989 (USA) – UFO over Lebanon

At 10.30pm, after watching the news, a farmer drove out in his pick-up to check on an Angus heifer, which was past due on delivery of her calf. When he arrived at the location, he heard the cows making far more noise than usual. He found the entire herd gathered in the south-east corner and the Angus standing beside her newborn bull calf. He turned off the engine and lights, because the battery wasn't very good, and noticed a red glow through the trees to the North and thought it was a campfire somebody had left. When he got out of the truck he heard a crackling sound coming from that direction. Since the fire appeared to be most certainly on his property and much closer, he went back to the pick-up and grabbed a flashlight. When he turned around, he said:

"I got the biggest shock of my life. Hovering above the trees was a huge red 'ball', about 20-35ft in diameter, less than 50 yards away from me, showing yellow speckles on its surface, accompanied by a crackling sound. After bobbing slightly up and down in the air the object started to move off a few minutes later, and then rapidly climbed at a steep angle to the north-west, slowly at first – then a distant dim red star in 10-12 seconds. A moment later it was gone."

(Source: www.Interent NICAP *The 1989 UFO Chronology*)

Also seen on the 11th April, this time over the UK, for the third time running…

12th April 1989 (UK) – UFO seen near Wickford

At 3am, a man living in Grays, Essex, sighted an object flashing with lights, hovering over the river for half an hour before loosing it in clouds.

Within hours, people living in Canvey and Rettendon also saw what appears to have been the same, if not similar, object.

One of those witnesses was Mr Derek Norman Perry and his wife, from Rettendedon Common.

At 4.15am, the family dog began to whine – as if in distress. Mr Perry opened the window and checked the animal was alright and now back in its kennel.

UFO lights over Thames

ALIEN lights have been reported over Canvey.

UFO researchers will be interviewing two witnesses who contacted the UFO Hotline after watching a disc-shaped object travelling up the Thames Estuary at a height of about 500 feet.

UFO investigator Ron West said the pair watched it for a few minutes before it disappeared behind some houses.

They said it seemed to be spinning and had red, green, blue and yellow lights.

More strange sightings were seen over Southend when people reported seeing a large round orange-red ball in the sky. They watched it for 20 minutes before it disappeared.

The East Anglian UFO and Paranormal Research group is looking for more members to be researchers or investigators.

At the moment there are 65 members and anyone interested in delving into the unknown should contact the UFO Hotline on 0268 286079.

"I noticed some bright lights, resembling a chandelier, about 500ft off the ground, in the direction of the local school, in a north-east position. The UFO then stopped and sat there, completely silent in the sky. It started to move again but this time losing height, before disappearing behind the church. I ran to the front bedroom of the house and waited. In a short time, it reappeared – still moving slowly. Suddenly, with a great roar, it shot away at a 45° angle and was lost from view as it entered a cloud. It was colossal in size and its speed was terrific."

A MASS OF LIGHTS (BRIGHT.)

EVENING ECHO   Tuesday, April 18, 1989   Page 13

Rugby ball UFO hovers above Thames

By JONATHAN GUY

A MYSTERY object spotted by families throughout South East Essex has been classified as a UFO by the East Anglian UFO Society.

The rugby ball-shaped object was spotted in Canvey, Grays and Rettendon, and Ron West of the UFO society feels it could have been spotted by others yet to come forward.

The object was first sighted off Canvey at around midnight on April 11 when a man saw what he described as a "rugby ball with a tail" hovering out in the estuary.

The man, who went into his garden to watch the object for more than 30 minutes, said it was covered in flashing lights and disappeared behind the clouds.

Three hours later a man in Grays spotted the object, which he too described to the UFO society as rugby ball-shaped, bedecked with flashing lights hovering over the estuary.

He watched the object for half an hour before losing it in the clouds.

The final sighting was over Rettendon Common where Mrs Janet Perry and her husband were woken by the sound of their dog barking.

Frightened

She said: "My husband looked out of the window to check on the dog, but saw this balloon-type object covered in lights.

"He called me and we watched the object hover and then it went round to the other side of the house. My husband rushed to the other window and saw it speed off.

"We did not tell anyone until a couple of days later when we heard a boy who lives nearby had been frightened by the object."

The pair went to see a neighbour who had a mass of electronic equipment in his house.

Mrs Perry said: "He said that one of his monitors had been shut down mysteriously that evening and that the only thing which would have caused the monitor to shut down was a power cut, although his other equipment was still fine."

Hotline

At 6.15pm, Mr Kevin John Brooks (34) – a cost accounting analyst of Folkestone, Kent – was stood waiting on Platform 4, Charring Cross Railway Station, London, when he saw:

"…a grey metallic object in the sky. I wondered if it was a balloon. It was high in the sky and in an eastwards direction, revolving about two revolutions per second. I watched it for some 15mins, during which time I asked others to look at it; nobody had an idea what it was. At this point our train arrived and I sat in the carriage, continuing to keep it under observation. Four smaller objects appeared in the sky and moved closer to the larger object, in a random manner. I saw a Jumbo Jet flying underneath it, which showed how massive the object was. The train set off and the object was still visible past London Bridge."

At 9pm, an elderly woman, living in Grays, Essex, was putting out the milk bottles when she saw an object in the sky for about 10 minutes – *"similar to a bonfire night sparkler"* – before it headed towards the direction of the river.

Peter Oliver – spokesman for the East Anglian UFO & Paranormal Research Association – disclosed that in the last few months the group had investigated 18 sightings in the area.

Another witness was Mrs Thompson (73) of Nutbury Avenue, Grays, Essex, who was outside her house, looking towards the direction of the A13, when she noticed:

> *"...a green flashing light in the sky. It then changed to orange in colour. Its outer edges were sparkling green, yellow, and white. My daughter and granddaughter came out to see it and, after ten minutes, it disappeared over nearby houses."*

At 9.30pm a bright object, showing flashing lights, was seen stationary in the sky over Leigh-on-sea, by a man living on Cliff Parade. He watched it until 9.50pm, when it vanished from sight.

(Source: Peter Oliver/Ron West)

14th April 1989 (UK)

At 8.45am, a flashing light was seen slowly crossing the sky over Southend, by school 'lollipop' lady – Jean Stephenson (45) and her son.

> *"It appeared to have a shadow at the back – like a tail, which was moving from side to side as it passed overhead, taking 30 minutes to do so."*

(Source: Ron West)

15th April 1989 (UK)

During the evening Moulton, Derbyshire couple, Sue and David Harrison, reported having sighted a UFO over their village once again in the company of at least three other villagers, who watched it through a telescope.

(Source: *Northampton Chronicle and Echo*, 20.4.1989 – 'UFO spotted flying high over village')

18th April 1989 (UK) – Three *'lights'* seen over Lancashire

Kenneth and Lillian Bond – owners of a newsagents shop at Nelson, Lancashire – sighted three coloured *'lights'*, shining in the sky above the village.

Ken:

> *"We saw the perfectly still white, green and blue, lights in the sky and wondered if it could have been the police helicopter – then felt this wasn't the explanation. It's the first time my wife and I have seen anything like this before."*

UFO spotted flying high over village

A MYSTERIOUS object has been spotted high over a Northamptonshire village three times in the last two weeks.

The UFO first appeared in the night sky over the Easter Bank holiday above the village of Moulton.

Villagers Sue and Dave Harrison who spotted the object from their bedroom window, said it was about twice the size of the brightest star in the sky and moved much more slowly than a plane.

"I'd love to know what it is. It looks like a disc, blue in the middle with a white band round it.

Pulsating

"Then outside that there is a pulsating red band, which looks like a clock face going mad," said 27-year-old Sue.

"The first time we saw it, it was in the sky outside our window for about half-an-hour.

"If it turned out to be Martians, I'd put the kettle on and make them a cup of tea and make them

by Richard Thomas

feel welcome . . . if there is anyone up there of course," joked Sue.

In case you think Sue and Dave, 38, are seeing things, the object appeared again on Saturday . . . and three other villagers saw it when they came round and looked through Sue's grandfather's telescope.

And now work colleagues at Hestair Maclaren in Northampton want Sue to tell them the moment she sees it again so they can come round and view it though the telescope as well.

"I really don't know what it is, but it surely can't be a spaceship," added Sue, who now checks the skies every night for the object which last appeared on Tuesday.

Northampton Chronicle & Echo
20 APR 1989

19th April 1989 (USA) – Angels seen!

During the evening, a 10-year-old girl from Fayette, County, Pennsylvania reported having seen two short white glowing figures, which she called angels, near a large glowing UFO. An adult witness saw the UFO shoot straight up into the sky when it departed. (**Source:** *Humanoid Contact Database 1989*, case 925, citing Stan Gordon, PASU Data Exchange, August 1989)

19th April 1989 (UK) – Also on the same date was a sighting by Wickford boy – Kerry Byrne (9)

EAST ANGLIAN U.F.O. & PARANORMAL RESEARCH ASSOCIATION

SECTION A   **SIGHTING ACCOUNT FORM**

Please write an account of your sighting, make a drawing of what you saw and then answer the questions in section B overleaf as fully as possible. Write in **BLOCK CAPITALS** using a ball point pen.

I saw a great big sun like object. And it had lots of lovely pretty lights on. The lights had colours like looking through a crystal. The sky was pure white everywhere. I saw a close up veiw of it it took off from a hovering position like a luminous Green laser beam.

DRAWING*

Greeny whity colour glow →

Glow →
Yellow

Red —
Lights

Light beams ↑

*If preferred, use a separate sheet of paper.

Your full name (Mr/~~Mrs/Miss/Ms~~) MASTER
KERRY BYRNE   Age ...9..
Address... 16. Meadow Rd

c/o Wickford
Telephone No. 733.189 ....(STD 0268 ...)
Occupation during last two years... Schoolboy

Any professional, technical or academic qualifications or special interests

Do you object to the publication of your name?
*~~Yes~~/No. *Delete as applicable.
Today's Date. 19/4/89
Signature... Kerry Byrne

(a) Number of objects 1. Large .... (b) Colour walt light bulb close up.. (c) Sound. coming ....
(d) Shape... like a radish clows upside .... was this sharply defined or hazy?...... both ....
(e) Brightness..... Sun .... (compared to star, venus, moon, sun etc.)

20th April 1989 (UK) – Three UFOs seen over Suffolk

Michael 'B' (28) – a trainee accountant of Crown Street, Bury St. Edmunds – was on his way home along Angel Hill, at 11pm, when he noticed three lights in the sky.

"They formed a triangle in shape and were moving very slowly towards the direction of the east of Ipswich. They suddenly stopped in mid-air. Another set of three lights then appeared over the top of me. They were about the size of footballs and were completely silent. These drew level with the first set of three and both sets moved slowly away, heading eastwards. Forty minutes later, I lost sight of them."

His sighting was corroborated by Peter Fox (52) of Eastgate Street, Bury St. Edmunds. Peter and his wife, Joyce, were out walking the dog at 11pm, when they saw:

> "...three white lights, stationary in the sky over the Industrial Estate. We were surprised to see another set of three lights arrive, at which point the six lights began to move along the A45 road, towards Ipswich. Ten minutes later, they were gone from view."

21st April 1989 (USA) – Close encounter; weapon discharged at UFO

At 9.15pm, a man living in a wooded area of Crestview, Florida, heard his dog barking and went outside to investigate, when he saw an object hovering over the driveway. He described it as being:

> "...circular, possibly 90ft in diameter, with windows around the circumference, and appeared to have a rotating beacon in the centre, which shone through the windows, giving a flashing-in-sequence effect. The object's base was brilliantly illuminated."

He fired at the object with his .22 calibre semi-automatic rifle, just as a bright beam struck him on his face coming from the centre bottom of the UFO, but the gun misfired and, before he could reload, the object sped away, making a sound like the wind as it departed. He reported feeling anxiety and fear when he saw the object, estimated to be at least 100ft away. The bullet that misfired was later analysed by Remington Arms Co., Inc., who said the powder in the cartridge was contaminated, possibly during manufacture.

(Source: *MUFON UFO DATABASE*, Portion of reports from the files at MUFON Headquarters, July 1999, Sequin TX, CD-ROM, Case Log #890614, By Allen Reynolds)

21st April 1989 (UK) – UFO over power lines

At 9.15pm, Alan Blackburn (38) of Risbygate Street, Bury St. Edmunds, was outside when he noticed a strange *'ball of light'* travelling across the sky, heading in an east to west direction.

> "It suddenly slowed down and then descended to about 500ft in a sort of jerky movement, and stopped dead still. I started to walk towards the location, which was about half a mile away. As I got closer, I was able to see it was oval-shaped and about 20-30ft in length, hovering over the power lines. Suddenly, it shot straight up into the sky, completely silently, and was gone."

(Source: Ron West)

ESSEX CHRONICLE : 21.4.89

'Rugby ball' UFO seen over river

RESEARCHERS have been investigating a surge of UFO activity in the skies over Thurrock in the last ten weeks.

Strange lights and mysterious objects have been spotted with increasing frequency, says the East Anglian UFO and Paranormal Association.

by Staff Reporter

"In the last two to three months we have had 18 reports of UFOs in this area," said investigator Peter Oliver. "That is a big increase on the number of reports we had been receiving previously."

The association has now set up a hotline so that members of the public who spot UFOs can contact them without delay.

Among the latest sightings have been a bright object described as a "rugby ball with a tail," and a brilliant green light hovering over the A13. Both are being investigated by the society which has ruled out the possibility of them being normal aircraft.

The "rugby ball" was seen by a man in Grays, at about 3am on April 12. It was covered in flashing lights and he watched it hovering over the river for half an hour

before losing it in the clouds.

The object was seen by people in Canvey and Rettendon within hours of the Grays' sighting.

Later the same day, the brilliant green light was spotted by an elderly Grays woman at about 9pm as she was putting out her milk bottles.

She said she watched it for about ten minutes and during that time it changed from green to yellow and then to white.

The edges of the object gave off light similar to a Bonfire Night sparkler, she said. Eventually it moved off in the direction of the river.

Mr. Oliver said he had interviewed the woman and it was certainly not a helicopter or any other form of aircraft that she had

seen.

"We would like to hear from anyone else who saw these objects in the sky," he said.

"We would also like to hear of any other UFO sightings or supernatural experiences.

"Many people are reluctant to talk about these kind of things because they fear ridicule by neighbours, workmates or even family and close friends.

"But we have carried out many interviews and take these things very seriously. The data we gather is processed and used to try to find out what these things are and where they come from."

Anyone with information should contact the society's hot line on Basildon (0268) 286079.

22nd April 1989 (UK) – Mysterious light through the window

At around midnight, Susan Whitley (29) of Park Lane, Southend-on-Sea was at her home address, when she heard the sound of an engine. She looked out but could not see any car. A strong burst of different coloured light shot through the window, startling her and frightening the dog – which ran under the bed.

Susan later contacted Ron West to tell him what had taken place.

22nd April 1989 (USA) – Orange domed *'ball of light'* seen

At 9.22pm, two people living in St. Louis were on their balcony when they saw an orange *'ball of light'* in the sky, towards the East. The object then appeared in front of the witnesses, between nearby buildings. It was described as disc-shaped, without tapered edges, with an orange dome on top, orange stripe around mid-section, and a black base with many blue lights underneath. The witnesses ran into the street and watched the object for about 25secs, until it was lost from view in the westward direction.

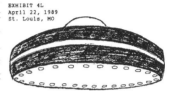

EXHIBIT 4L
April 22, 1989
St. Louis, MO

Also on this date – a lecture on the UFO subject by David Barclay

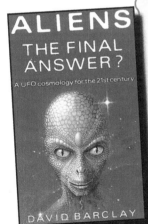

UFO enthusiasts meet at library

2374

UFO enthusiasts from all over Britain will be hoping to prove that 'we are not alone' at a seminar at Central Library on Saturday.

Members of the Independent UFO Network (IUN) and the British UFO Research Association will be the joint hosts of a discussion on extra-terrestrial abductions which have allegedly occurred throughout the country.

David Barclay, of Stubbing Way, Shipley, editor of the magazine The UFO Debate, says the meeting will be of particular importance.

He says: "Hopefully, it will draw attention away from occurrences in the South of England, to the experiences of people in this part of the country.

David, who has believed in the existence of beings other than ourselves for the past 40 years or so, admits

that UFO enthusiasts have had some 'bad Press' recently, but says they are not all cranks.

David hopes the seminar will do much to dispel people's fears by providing a forum for debate on the subject.

Two speakers will be making a presentation at the seminar, both of which will be fully illustrated by photographs.

Andy Roberts, from Brighouse, will give a short introduction to abductions before concentrating on abductions in the north of England.

John Spencer, internationally renowned UFO researcher and author, will then concentrate on abductions world-wide.

David Barclay says "Everyone is welcome to the seminars – aliens and all!"

The meeting will begin at 2pm at Room 1 of the library. A UFO-line information service is also available on 0898 654 637.

24th April 1989 (USA) – Golden object seen

At 2.30pm, a woman aged 76, from Seville, Ohio, was looking out of her window, when she saw:

> "...a bright gold octagon-shaped object, 3-4ft in diameter, on the ground in a neighbour's field".

After watching for about two minutes, the silent object ascended slightly and moved to within 300ft of the woman's house and landed. A short time later, it was seen to move back to its original landing site. After further observation, lasting several minutes, it ascended and moved out of sight. (**Source: NUFORC**)

28th April 1989 (UK) – Three orange lights seen

At 9pm, Dr. Alan Whitcomb (48) of Long Road, Canvey Island, was driving along Hawkesbury Road, when he noticed a bright light in the south-west direction over the River Thames.

> "I watched it for about 10 minutes, before it vanished from view. Two small orange lights then appeared travelling in the same direction, south to east."

29th April 1989 (UK) – Bright *'ball'* of blue light seen

At about 1.15am, Mr Reginald Apthorpe (63) – a resident of Hockley Mobile Homes, Lower Road, Hockley – had just parked his car. He looked out over the River Thames and sighted a bright *'ball'* of blue light moving across the sky at tremendous speed, a few hundred feet off the ground. It then made a sharp right-hand turn, before moving away and out of sight.

29th April 1989 (UK) – Flashes of light seen

At 10pm, John T. Robson – an investigator for Ron West's group – was out 'sky watching' with Geoffrey Boon, at 'Brenzett', Romney Marsh.

> "We had parked the car off the main road, which carries on to Rye – a small town in Sussex. It was a bright, starry, night but no Moon.
>
> Suddenly, Geoff saw a brilliant blue flash, which occurred twice, at the base of the Plough constellation, due east"

Mysterious white beam seen

At 11.45pm, Mrs Margaret Rose Harvey (49) of Broad Green Steeple, Bumpstead, Haverhill, Suffolk, was on her way home with her husband, in Fell Lane, Birdbrook.

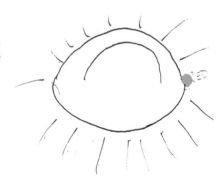

> "I saw this object in the sky, showing a white beam shining in all directions. There was a red light to one side. I had it in view for ten minutes, before it disappeared. It had been completely silent and I found the experience frightening, leaving me shaking."

In an interview conducted by Peter Fleming and Julie Rondeau, Mr Fleming expressed concern that their sighting would be treated with mockery.

Anybody reading the weight of evidence offered by us in just this Volume of *Haunted Skies* alone, should now no longer treat such reports with any flippancy.

Also on this date was a report from Jane Seale and her husband, Richard. Jane wrote to the local newspaper, explaining what they had seen – so did Mr R Harvey.

Strange Light in the sky

CONCERNING the strange light in the sky reported in a recent Echo my friend Richard Crooks and I were standing in my garden talking at around that time (10.30pm), when we both were aware of what seemed like lightning.

But there was no noise, rather like a floodlight effect for a second or two. I looked up into the sky and saw something like a firework rocket way above shooting across the sky. Several seconds later we heard directly above us, very faintly 'boom, boom'. Thunder?

Richard thought perhaps it was ball lightning, and I thought it could have been a shooting star.
MISS JANE SEALE,
2 Poplar View,
Little Bradley,

A frightening experience

ON reading the letter from Mr Kettridge, in the Echo of June 8, I saw a stange glow in the sky on April 29 at approx 11.45pm on my way home from Birdbrook. The glow was larger than anything I have ever seen, it sent out a beam the full width of the glow in all directions over the ground, just like a search-light it is as frightening now just thinking about it, as it was then, watching.

I watched it all the way home, it didn't seem to be moving, then it just disappeared, one minute it was there the next it had gone, my husband saw this as well as myself and even he says it was too big to be a plane or helicopter. I to am surprised that no official reports were made on this.

I didn't write before in case every one laughed at me, but knowing I'm not the only one to see strange lights is comforting.
M. R. HARVEY
4 Broad Green,
Steeple Bumpstead.

30th April 1989 (UK) – Rugby ball-shaped UFO seen

Between 9.30pm and 11.30pm, a UFO was seen flying above the River Thames, heading towards London. Residents from Shoebury, Canvey, and Kent, telephoned the 'UFO Hotline', set-up by Ron West, telling of having sighted:

> "...a rugby ball-shaped object, showing yellow, white, blue and green, lights along its side, flying across the sky"

(Source: Ron West Archives/*Colchester Yellow Advertiser*, 12.5.1989 – 'Busy May day for UFO spotters')

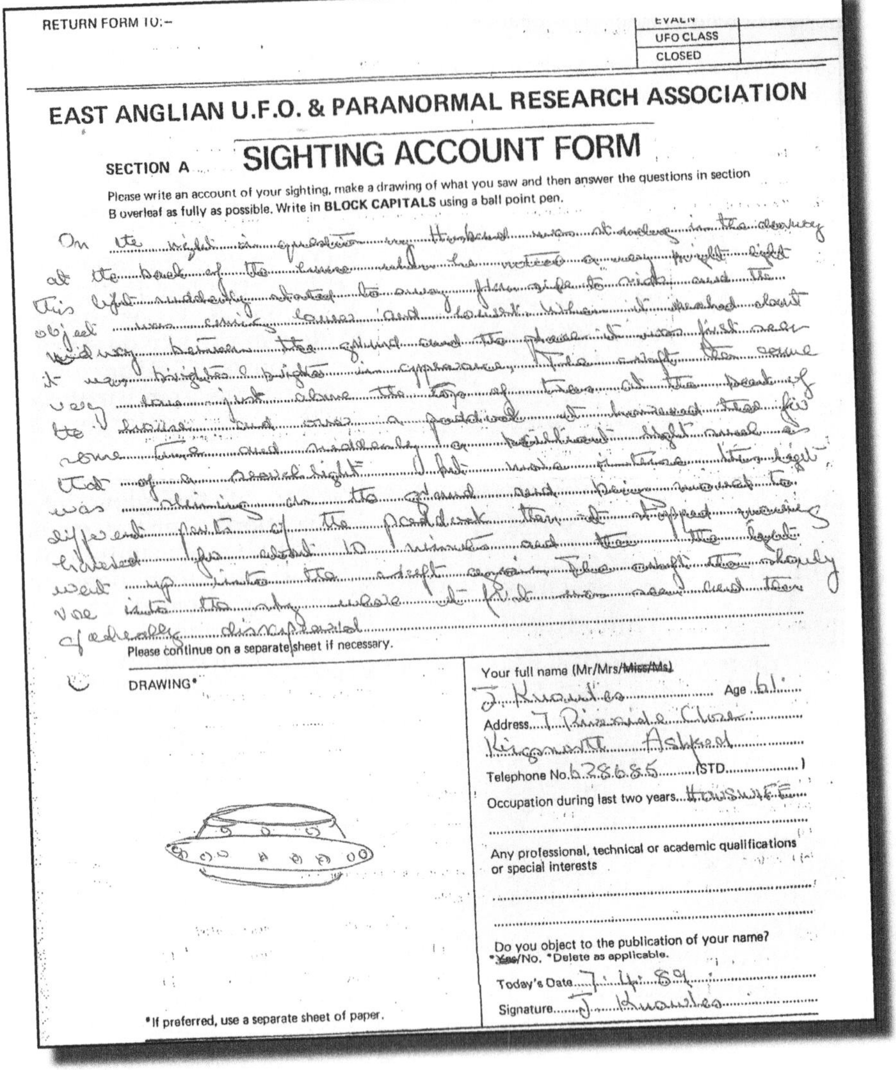

RETURN FORM TO:–

EVALN	
UFO CLASS	
CLOSED	

EAST ANGLIAN U.F.O. & PARANORMAL RESEARCH ASSOCIATION

SECTION A **SIGHTING ACCOUNT FORM**

Please write an account of your sighting, make a drawing of what you saw and then answer the questions in section B overleaf as fully as possible. Write in **BLOCK CAPITALS** using a ball point pen.

On the night in question my husband was standing in the doorway at the back of the house when he noticed a very bright light. This light suddenly started to sway from side to side and the object was coming lower and lower. When it reached about midway between the ground and the place it was first seen it was brighter & brighter in appearance. The craft then came very low just above the tops of trees at the back of the houses and over a paddock. It hovered there for some time and suddenly a brilliant light much as that of a searchlight [illegible] intense. This light was shining on the ground and being moved to different parts of the paddock then it stopped moving, hovered for about 10 minutes and then the light went up into the craft again. The craft then slowly rose into the sky where it first was seen and then gradually disappeared.

Please continue on a separate sheet if necessary.

DRAWING*

*If preferred, use a separate sheet of paper.

Your full name (Mr/Mrs/~~Miss/Ms~~) J. Knowles Age 61

Address 7 Riverside Close, Kingsnorth Ashford

Telephone No. 628685 (STD)

Occupation during last two years Housewife

Any professional, technical or academic qualifications or special interests

Do you object to the publication of your name? ~~Yes~~/No. *Delete as applicable.

Today's Date 7. 4. 89.

Signature J. Knowles

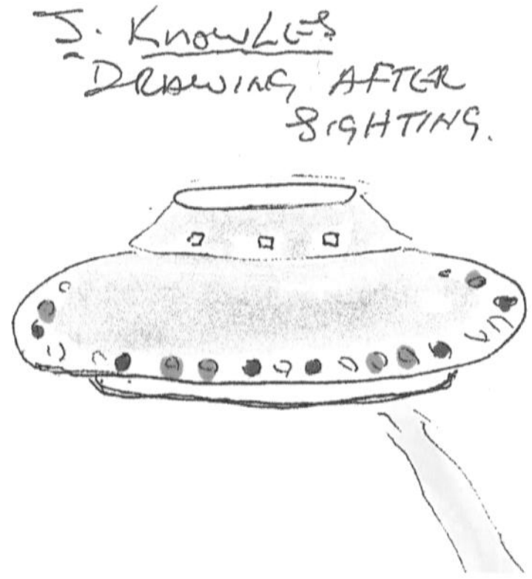

MAY 1989

1st May 1989 (UK) – Cylindrical object over Wales

AT 5.30pm, Llandudno residents – Douglas Haig Hughes, a retired RAF Gunner, and his wife, Catherine – were walking along Ffordd Maelgwyn, when they noticed a cylindrical-shaped object, heading towards them from the direction of Glan Conwy area, about 600ft up in the air, moving at approximately 50mph.

"It then slowed down and flashed a bright red light – like infrared – onto us from out of one of the 'windows', before heading away towards Llandudno."

A spokesman for RAF Valley confirmed that they had not been flying any aircraft over the last few days.

(Source: Personal interview)

1st May 1989 (USA) – Aliens under attack!

In Metcalf, Illinois, a female resident claimed that following a visit to the bathroom at 2.30am, she noticed the electricity was off. At this point she saw a pair of large eyes looking through the window and screamed. This elicited the assistance of another person [presumably, her partner or husband?] who fired four shots at the *'being'* through the window. It is then claimed that four other tall humanoids, with dangling arms, were seen stood near a power pole. Undoubtedly there had to be far more to this matter than just a reference on the Internet (2014), bearing in mind the impeccable source – Francis Ridge.

Hollywood woman claims abduction

A report of alien abduction was claimed to have happened in Hollywood, California, involving [albeit scant details] a woman, who said that while on her way to work, at 5am, she experienced a long period of missing time. Later, she recalled having been taken onboard an object and greeted by a man in a blue coverall. She was then taken to a room with a large screen and was told they were going to visit a planet called 'Erra', where, on arrival, numerous forests and trails – very rich in oxygen – were found.

(Source: Jim Brandt, Far out summer, 1993)

2nd May 1989 (USA) – Unusual light

At Louisville, Kentucky, an unusual light was seen under cloud cover that was claimed to have followed a vehicle the witness was in.

Louisville, Kentucky

At 5.15am, a big bright *'light'* was sighted stationary in the sky over Louisville, by a 31-year-old man who was delivering newspapers. The *'light'* then began to move in a circular pattern, before heading towards his position at speed. By the time he had started the engine of the vehicle and put the headlights on, *'it'* was only 125ft away from him. Within seconds the object moved from right to left in front of him, before moving away out of sight. (**Source:** NUFORC)

2nd May 1989 (UK) – Triangular UFO seen

A black triangular object, described as being completely silent, showing no lights, 100ft across, was seen moving slowly through the sky over Essex, heading in a north-west direction. Ron West contacted a spokeswoman at Southend Airport, who confirmed there had been an airship flying above The Thames Estuary at the time of the sighting, although Ron was sceptical of this as being the explanation. One of the witnesses was Tony Ford.

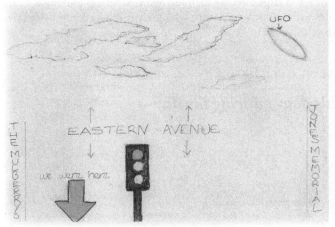

BOTTOM OF OBJECT

3rd May 1989 (UK) – UFO seen

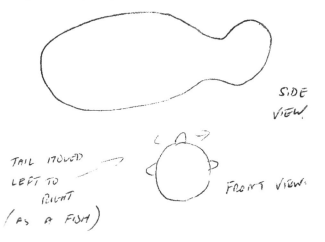

3rd May 1989 (Australia) – Pulsating UFO & 'V'-shaped object seen

At 9.20pm, Barry from Waterford, Brisbane, Queensland, was playing with his dog in the backyard of the house, when he saw a pulsating aqua coloured object, with red edges, in the south-west part of the sky. Owing to his vision being partly obscured by trees, Barry went upstairs to the balcony and looked out, when he saw another identical object. Barry watched it for an hour, until 10.20pm, at which point the objects started to move west and north-west respectively.

Another resident, from Holland Park, Brisbane, appears to have seen the same UFO. The man concerned was was on his way back into his house, between 9.30pm and 10pm, when, out of the corner of his eye,

Southend Evening Echo, Essex.

4 MAY 1989

Did you sight this UFO?

By FRED HAMMERTON

A MYSTERY object with yellow, white, green and blue lights and shaped like a rugby ball has been seen by 26 people in Canvey, Shoebury and Southend.

The latest sightings were over the Bank Holiday weekend.

The object, looking like two saucers joined by a single blue light, was watched by a Canvey man for three-quarters of an hour on Sunday night.

It was first seen about 9.30pm from Canvey and about 10pm spotted from Leigh and Westcliff.

Four people also saw the object between Canvey and Leigh.

Early Monday morning, about 3.20am, a Southend milkman saw it on his way to work and another worker on his way home saw the "rugby ball" along the Estuary.

At 10.15pm on Monday it was also seen from Kent. People there said it was spinning and watched it for about half an hour.

There was another sighting from Great Wakering.

All were reported to the East Anglian UFO Research Association.

Anyone with information can contact it on the hotline. 0268 286079.

his attention was drawn to what he thought was a large bird. He then realised that he was looking at a large boomerang or 'V'-shaped object, with a faint white glow, moving through the clear sky. It silently glided away to the south and was out of view in nin seconds.

5th May 1989 (UK) – UFO seen over Essex

Doreen Anderson saw this object during the day

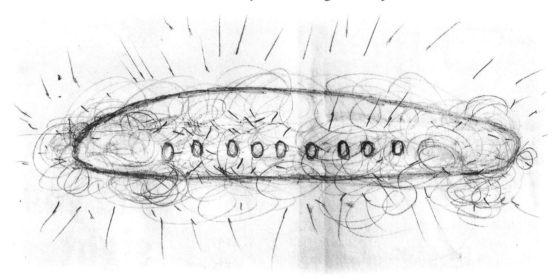

6th May 1989 (UK) – UFO seen to land in Thetford Forest, Suffolk

At 11.55pm, Lewis 'M' (21) – a member of the Armed Forces – was on leave and parked up with his girlfriend, Brenda Monks, in the picnic area in Thetford Forest, Suffolk.

> *"We saw a large white 'ball of light', which seemed to descend into the forest. After about 30 minutes, it shot straight up into the sky – no noise and about the size of a dustbin lid."*

Another couple also saw the UFO. Unfortunately, they also wished their identities be kept secret.

Leonard 'F':

> *"I was parked in Thetford Forest on the Spring Bank Holiday, with my girlfriend, listening to the car radio. We noticed a very large 'ball of light' come down and seem to land in the forest, completely silently. Thinking it was aircraft descending we got out of the car, but could only see a faint light. As we never heard any explosion, we decided to get back into the car and, after waiting five minutes, left. When we reached the main road, the radio suddenly came back on again. I checked the car clock; it had stopped at 11.52pm. I looked at my wristwatch; it read 12.10pm."*

Mr Digby also reported having sighted this object on the same day.

(Source: Ron West)

Newcastle Journal

5 MAY 1989

UFO hotline

THINGS that go bump in the night and glow in the dark might not be all they seem.

Investigators have launched a 24-hour international UFO hotline to improve research into the phenomenon. Any sightings or conversations with little green men should be reported by telephoning 0756 752216. Na-noo. na-noo.

EAST ANGLIAN U.F.O. & PARANORMAL RESEARCH ASSOCIATION

SECTION A ## SIGHTING ACCOUNT FORM

Please write an account of your sighting, make a drawing of what you saw and then answer the questions in section
B overleaf as fully as possible. Write in **BLOCK CAPITALS** using a ball point pen.

Standing in my bedroom I normally spend a period of time
looking at the sky + area's around, prior to settling down.
I spotted this exceptionally colourful, large, object
falling through the sky, similar to a dart falling.
I reported to the Hotline but for various reasons the
investigator never managed to arrive. Three persons came
to see me on 11·7·89.

TIME.
1·07

E/89/2210b. Ject
seen.

...igby   Age 68
...n Road, Basildon
...S14 3R.
8   (STD: SS11 3R)
...o years... Retired

...l or academic qualifications

Do you object to the publication of your name?
*Yes/No. *Delete as applicable.

Today's Date 11·7·89
Signature X ... A.O Digby

* If preferred, use a separate sheet of paper.

6th May 1989 (USA) – UFOs over Washington

At 10pm over Ferndale, in Washington, five people sighted an apparent stationary light in the sky. As they watched, a second huge one (also silent), joined the first, then moved away at high speed, descended towards the ground and moved toward the group, passing overhead at rooftop level, where it appeared to land in a nearby field and vanish from view 15 minutes after the initial sighting.

6/7th May 1989 (New Zealand) – *'Monkey-like'* beings seen on golf course

On the weekend, Mr John Harris – a resident of Taupo – was out with two other friends, playing golf at the Wairakei Golf Course. As he was about to 'tee' off, he looked down the fairway and saw, with great astonishment, coming out of the mist:

> *"...three bright green 'creatures'. I couldn't believe it. I shouted to the others, who were standing next to the tee. They looked and were freaked out.*
>
> *We jumped into the buggy and took off down the fairway, to try and see if these 'things' were for real. When we got to about 50 metres from them, they took off. We tried to find them, but it was hopeless. Only then did we realise how shaken we were – it was terrifying. They were about 2 meters in height, slim, coloured bright green, with a luxuriant growth of hair."*

According to enquiries made locally, by presumably John and his colleagues, this was the third time the *'creatures'* had been seen on this golf course – the first having taken place in 1984. The second incident took place earlier in 1989, and involved two Americans who declined to be named. They told of having seen what they first took to be:

> *"...big green hounds. When we moved closer, they made a high-pitched squeaking sound and darted into the trees. We didn't report it at the time. Would you have done?"*

(Source: *Sunday News*, New Zealand, 14.5.1989 – 'Stunned New Zealand golfers see green monkey-like beings on the fairway')

Lake Taupo (New Zealand) – Green UFO seen, 1960s

Bearing in mind the close proximity to Lake Taupo, we made a search on the internet and found, on the following website – *UFOInfo.com* – a letter from an unsigned person, which may have nothing to do with what the golfers saw, but should be taken into consideration.

> *"I was in my mid-twenties and out fishing at the mouth of the* Waitetoko *stream, about half a kilometer north of Te Rangiita, on the shores of* Lake Taupo. *It was a Monday night (I remembered this as I had a small transistor in the pocket of my waders, listening to the YA stations radio play) and it was just before 11pm (when fishing closed for the night).*
>
> *In the northern sky a light bulb-shaped object appeared at about 30° over Kinloch. I measured it with my arm at full stretch and my fingers spread. The width was a little wider than my spread fingers. It was half as long again lengthwise. The colour was the shape of a light bulb and electric green and sharp edged – not fuzzy or ill-defined. It just was there and it lit up the whole lake, taking about 15 seconds to float down below the horizon. When it first appeared I looked to see if there were any house lights on, but there were none. (TV used to stop at about 10.30pm.) In the Taupo newspaper it was mentioned that others had seen it, along with the official line (just space debris re-entering the atmosphere), which didn't make sense to me. There was no tail, just very faint red sparks popping out from the narrower top end, where the light socket would have been. I have never mentioned it too much, as people tend to look at me as to question my sanity."*

8th May 1989 – further sightings

8th May 1989 (USA) – Whale-shaped object seen over New York

At 9.45pm, at an undisclosed address, two people were looking out of the window when they noticed a *'whale-shaped'* object, black in colour about 50ft long, approaching below treetop level. The unidentified aerial object made a noise loud enough to shake the house – then it flew away and out of sight.

10th May 1989 (USA) – Motorist chased by UFO

At midnight on this date, a 38-year-old man, accompanied by a 16-year-old girl, were driving near Farmington, Michigan, when they realised they were being pursued by a silvery disc-shaped object, with a greenish tinge. It is believed that the presence of the UFO caused interference to the electrical system of the car [never mind what it probably did to the people!] Unfortunately, like so many other cases we were to come across from NICAP, and other US UFO websites, we have only limited knowledge as to what exactly took place and who was involved. This is not a criticism of the organisations concerned – far from it. Without this valuable information, we would be worse off. No doubt the reader may wish to conduct their own research into matters such as these – that defy explanation.

Bautista Canyon (USA) – Entities seen

On the same date at Bautista Canyon, Anza, California, an elderly woman was driving from the Bautista Canyon area, when she noticed a mushroom-shaped luminous craft, measuring an estimated 30ft in diameter that descended and hovered slightly above power lines. She stopped her vehicle and observed about 6-8 *'beings'* emerge from the craft and begin working on the outside. After approximately 10 minutes, they re-entered the object, which departed with a loud humming sound and a burst of blue flame. There were reports of TV and electrical interference at the time. (**Source: Debbie Steinberg,** *Anza Valley Outlook*, **Anza, California, 2.6.1989/Paul Ferrughelli,** *Computer Catalogue of UFO Reports*, **1988-1994, citing Robert Gribble, National UFO Reporting Center, Seattle**)

15th May 1989 (USA) – Allegation of abduction and implant found

At 2am, a 4-year-old girl from Tyler, Texas, was sleeping alone in her father's camper at a truck stop. She suddenly woke up, realising that she was no longer in the truck. Everything around her was white and she found herself unable to see the rest of her body, and felt very cold. Her right foot began to hurt on the left side. She saw *'figures'* around her that were *'darker than light'*, with indiscernible features, and then found herself back in the truck.

The young girl climbed out of the camper and ran to the parking lot. She looked up and saw three pink-red *'lights'* zigzag around, hovering in a triangular shape. The *'lights'* suddenly disappeared.

This was yet again one of those instances where one would have to treat the allegation made with some suspicion (especially with regard to the tender age of the witness) not that this implies fabrication – far from it – just that we cannot form any conclusions without having access to the original source material, or the names of the personnel involved in the investigation. It is of interest to hear of a possible implant recovered ten years later, but where is the medical evidence, never mind the testimonials of those concerned? We appreciate the importance of cataloguing such reports for posterity. However, nothing can be proved, despite it being a very odd story but not that rare! (**Source:** NUFORC)

17th May 1989 (UK) – Car-sized object falls to the ground

We have to admit that this was the first time we had heard of this incident, which took place at Hartlepool, from the *Think about it* website, involving 23-year-old student – Jenny Cook – who was a trainee teacher at Sunderland University. She was sat in her car on Osborne Road, waiting for a friend, when she looked up to see:

> *"...a metallic silver-like, drop-shaped object, about two metres long, was falling from the sky. It looked like a piece of glass, about the size of a small car."*

Jenny first thought it was a model airplane, but then realised that this was not the case. It fell to the left of her at very high speed, showing white hot at the front end, before vanishing behind houses four to five seconds later. We do not know if she was the only witness, or who contacted the police, but we are told that very soon after the encounter the military arrived at the place of the possible impact. The area was cordoned off and soldiers searched the terrain. An hour later, military lorries arrived at the location where the *'strange piece of metal'* had fallen. The Royal Air Force allegedly reported that the object had just been a meteor and had been sent to a laboratory for study. (**Source:** *Anomalous News*, **St Petersburg, Russia**)

Once again there is little information on the internet, or in our files, to corroborate what exactly happened here. There is, however, an Osborne Road in Hartlepool.

We have looked through our extensive records but cannot find any other information which would clarify exactly what took place here. Neither can we find any report of space debris or meteorites landing at this location, or further information in the newspaper/magazine *Anomalous News*.

30th May 1989 (USA) – Humanoid seen

A resident of Baker City, Oregon, was out walking, at 9pm, when he noticed a *'bright light'* approaching from the south. At first he thought it was a star, but then realised this was not the case, as it had the appearance of Jupiter, was gold in colour and glowing steadily. The object approached closer to the witness location, at which point he noticed two dark shapes, in what appeared to be a window of the completely silent object.

> *"They were human-looking in size and were only visible from the waist up. Since the gold light was so strong behind them, I could not see any features – just the shape of heads and shoulders, side by side, not quite touching."*

The man was unable to later recollect details of the exact time he saw the object, or how long it lasted. He could only remember watching the approach of the craft. When the craft was almost out of sight, heading towards the north, he ran to a nearby gas station to see if anyone else had witnessed the object, but was unable to find anybody in. (**Source:** NUFORC)

18th May 1989 (UK) – UFO over Heywood, Lancashire

On 20th May 1989, the *Daily Mail* published an article relating to an incident that had occurred at Heywood Ambulance Station, two days previously, involving two ambulance men, who claimed to have had a close encounter with *'Aliens from Outer Space'* ('Flashing Lights Shock, 999 Men'), during which it was disclosed that an attempt had been made to communicate with the UFOs by means of Morse code, and the police had chased the object in a patrol car.

We felt unprepared to accept the explanation offered that what the men had seen was either Venus, or unusual atmospheric effects, and spoke to Mr Stuart Golding – one of the ambulance men involved, who told us:

> *"I stand by what happened. You read about it in the paper, but I can't see the point of discussing it any further because of all the 'stick' that I was given after reporting the incident, which had nothing to do with any atmospheric conditions."*

Paul Walker

As a result of an appeal in the local newspaper, we were contacted by Paul Walker from Blackley, near Manchester:

> *"In March 1989, 1 was walking past Heywood Community School, with my cousin, when we saw an object, shaped like a rugby-ball, with bright lights around its centre, hovering a few feet above the building. It then shot up vertically into the sky and disappeared from view. We telephoned Air Traffic Control, at Manchester Airport, and explained what happened. They told us they had no reports of foreign aircraft."*

Dear Sir/Madam, I am writing in reply to your letter "AND BY THE WAY" MANCHESTER METRO NEWS (4-5-2000). Me and my nephew spotted U.F.O. activity over the Darnhill/Heywood area (March-April 1989).

The U.F.O. was hovering above Heywood Community School for about 5 minutes. WED/THURS in March, from about 11.30pm. My nephew took a photo of this but it didn't develop! We also telephoned "Air TRAFFIC CONTROL" at Manchester Airport but they said "They had no sightings of foreign aircraft."

I would like to know if other readers experienced any of these "incidents"? The U.F.O. was about 7 to 8ft in height, was shaped like a rugby ball and had bright lights around the Centre. after it had stayed hovering for about 5 minutes, it then shot up vertically in the sky in a split second and disappeared like a MICRO DOT in the sky.

Michael Thomas

We were contacted by Mr Michael Thomas – a resident of the area and ex-UFO Investigator for BUFORA – who spoke of having seen a UFO crossing the path of a light aircraft travelling towards Barton Aerodrome, at a height of 2,000-3,000ft. During further conversation with Mr Thomas, we learnt of his particular interest into the events that had taken place concerning the two ambulance men, following a conversation held with Mr Golding, on the 21st May 1989.

Michael:

"On the 21st May 1989, 1 was obliged to call out an ambulance to take my wife, who was expecting a baby, to hospital. While on the way there, I spoke at some length to the driver, Mr Golding, about

One of the ambulancemen was quite shaken up the one that banged on the police station door when they could not dial 999, The police station (sub) is on the same street Hind Hill Street, all I was interested in was "did the phones go dead" adamant "yes" from them, Topmost in my mind was Todmorden and the dead Radio. He told me that the U.F.O sent out coloured lights in all directions at this point I still thought it might be Venus. He did not mention (to my knowledge) having flashed his/Their head lights at the UFO. But if that is in the "Manchester Evening News" then its possibly true.

Just picture the scene, these two men having slept most of the day sleeping having finished their night shift. Only to be confront by an article on the front page of the Evening News. a poster on the door, it was mayhem a lot of people talking all at once trying to make some sense out of it all. Me prattling on about Venus. One thing I did tell one of them was yes they can do that, knock the phone(s) out — We had no time to exchange names they knew mine from my B.U.F.O.R.A. membership card. By the way the dialing code for the ambulance station was 0161 whereas the code for Heywood is 0706. I done a check around the town to see if any other phones went taxis 2ct — none,

When Gordon Creighton asked me to check up something in the ambulance station I rang the old number and got through to a Restaurant. It was later I found out they had gone ex-directory. Granted this will keep the cranks away as they

Michael Thomas

Heywood, Lancashire

the UFO incident, which happened a few days previously, on the 18th May 1989. You might think it rather odd that I would engage in UFO conversations when my wife was in labour, but my family were well used to me. In fact, my baby daughter, Ruth, was born on that day. Mr Golding told me he had received a lot of 'stick' from his colleagues for reporting the incident, which included posters depicting 'Little Green Men – This Way' stuck onto the wall at the station. I knew that it couldn't have been Venus, because it was too low on the horizon when the incident happened. I suspected there was a connection with the appearance of the UFO and sub-electricity power station, sighted next door to the ambulance station in Hind Hill Street. He told me the telephones had been rendered inoperative during the time that the UFO had hovered over the depot, stopping them from telephoning the police."

It was obviously of paramount importance to contact the other ambulance man concerned – Mr Walter Gorse – so we wrote a number of letters to the National Health Trust, at Whitefield, in Manchester, asking them for any information relating to the incident. To our surprise, they denied any knowledge of the incident but promised to forward a letter on to Mr Gorse.

UFO 'buzz' still riddle

WAS it a UFO? Observers of the 'thing' spotted in the sky by Heywood ambulancemen and Leigh factory workers in the early hours of Friday morning, are today still no wiser as to what they saw.

On Friday two Heywood ambulanceman reported seeing an unidentified flying object. Police contacted Manchester Airport who cited "climatic conditions" as the cause of the sighting.

But night shift workers at Leigh's BICC factory were as puzzled as the ambulancemen Unhappily, the factory worker who would most like to have seen the mysterious 'flashing

By ALWYN GRAHAM

lights' was not on duty duty when they appeared.

He is Steve Balon, North-west investigator for the Direct Investigation Group on Aerial Phenomena, the second oldest UFO society in England.

Flashing

Steve told colleagues they should have woken him at 2am when the objects appeared in the night sky. But no-one did, and he had to content himself with second-hand accounts from workmates.

Steve said he had investigated and been told the two ambulancemen had seen coloured flashing lights in the sky — but when they switched their headlights towards the 'object', the telephone lines at their ambulance station went dead and, unable to dial 999, they went to a police station and a policeman followed the

'lights' for more than a mile in his car before the quarry "suddenly shot off at speed".

He said he had spoken to air traffic control, and aurora borealis had been suggested as the cause of the sighting. But the evidence he had heard did not indicate the northern lights.

Star

One man who did see the phenomena was 50-years-old Jack Hollis, a night shift machinist at the BICC factory.

He told the BEN: "Something kept flashing red, white, and then green. I have never seen anything like it before. One man thought it was a star, but it was too big for a star.

"You couldn't make the shape out, but it kept changing colour. It wasn't an aircraft because it was in the same place for two hours."

Jack said there was a similar object, about the same height, but further away.

Bolton Evening News 22nd May 1989

Greater Manchester Police

We also wrote to the Greater Manchester Police, asking if they could put us in touch with the police officers who had been involved in the incident. We received a letter from Chief Inspector Ian Lomax, saying:

"I refer to your letter of 11th April, 2001, concerning the incident on 18th May 1989, outside Heywood Ambulance Station. I can confirm that Sergeant Morris and a Constable Bennett did respond to a call from the Ambulance Service about lights seen in the sky. As I understand it, the officers saw the lights. Both officers did make statements to the Manchester Research Association, the following day, which was, at that time, chaired by Mr Peter Hough. Unfortunately, our correspondence records of that time have since been destroyed. Both officers have retired from the service. I have taken the liberty of copying your letter to the Directorate of Air Staff Secretariat Ministry of Defence, for their information."

Police chase a UFO

Manchester Evening News
19 MAY 1989

Phones cut as objects hover over station

Mercy crew in UFO alert

Riddle as objects light up night sky

By Matt Finnegan

AN AMBULANCE crew today claimed to have had a close encounter with a UFO which hovered over their station for more than an hour.

Stuart Goulding and Walter Gorse watched in disbelief as three objects appeared in the night sky directly over Heywood ambulance station in Hind Hill Street.

They say one of the objects, flanked by two white lights, sent out red, white and blue flashes.

And when they turned on the headlights of their ambulance they say the UFO went "haywire." Phone lines at the station went dead and they were unable even to dial 999.

One of the men ran to the nearby police station to summon help. A policeman then followed the lights for more than a mile, but they suddenly darted away.

Air traffic controllers say they didn't see any UFOs and police are investigating one theory that the sighting may have been a star which reacted to atmospheric conditions.

Sightings

Over the years there have been several sightings of UFOs in the area and just a few miles away the area around the Rossendale Valley has earned the nick name of UFO Valley for having the highest number of sightings in Britain.

Unexplained objects have also been reported over nearby moorland. A team of UFO experts was today due to investigate the latest sighting.

Both ambulancemen were off duty and unavailable for comment today. But a colleague said "They were scared stiff by what happened. They just couldn't believe what they had seen. When the police confirmed the sighting they knew they weren't hallucinating.

Bolton Evening News
19 MAY 1989

MERCY MEN 'SPOT UFO'

2 ambulancemen reported seeing UFO in sky above Heywood, near Bury.

Police contacted Manchester Airport where spokesman said object was lights caused by "climatic conditions".

One of the objects was spinning round with lights all around the outer rim. They were multi-coloured and two other white objects were on either side

"When they tried to phone up to report it the phones went dead and they couldn't get through. Both of them are convinced that what they saw was real."

A police spokesman said flashing lights were seen over Heywood by several other people including police officers.

"But it has been suggested that it may have been a star and at the moment we are satisfied with that explanation. We certainly don't think we were being invaded."

Mr Gorse

We received a letter from Mr Gorse:

"Just after 1.15am, on the 18th May 1989, we were delivering a patient to Darnhill, Greater Manchester, when I noticed, from the driving seat position, a number of people stood outside a nearby block of flats who seemed to be pointing to the nearside of the ambulance, but I chose to ignore it thinking they were just 'messing about'. After dropping off the patient, and in the process of updating Ambulance Control of our movements, I noticed four luminous 'globes of light', the same distance between each other, moving across the sky in a horizontal formation.

When I looked upwards again, I saw that there were now only three of these 'globes of light' and brought it to the attention of my partner, who confirmed he could also see them. As we continued on our journey back to the Ambulance Station, my partner shouted to me that we were being followed by one of these 'globes'. I immediately stopped the ambulance, but I couldn't see anything. By the time we had reached the depot, I was beginning to become a little irritated by the jocularity of the conversation taking place, so I switched on the blue emergency lights and was shocked to see the appearance of one of these 'globes' hovering a few hundred yards away in the sky. I could see this object quite clearly. It had a band, like a bracelet – red, white and blue in colour – rotating clockwise around its centre.

I reversed the ambulance into the bay, at the same time flashing the blue lights again, noticing the 'band' – previously rotating in a 'ten-to-two' position – was now rotating horizontally and that there were now two other 'globes of light' behind the first one, forming a triangle. I radioed Ambulance Control and asked them if they could see the UFOs from the Whitefield Building. They told me 'Radio Piccadilly' wanted to speak to us 'live on air' about what we were seeing. I had no objection to this and a conversation ensued between us and the Radio Station. Ambulance Control then asked us to call the police. When we went over to the telephone, it was found to be out-of-order, although I can confirm that it was working perfectly after the UFOs had left. A short time later, a Police Sergeant arrived driving a Land-Rover and, after watching the UFO, told me he was going to drive over towards Ashworth Valley to obtain a closer look. When he tried to use the police radio, he couldn't get through for about ten minutes.

At 3.10am, as dawn began to break, the 'globe of light' forming the base of the triangle began to turn, presenting a different visual image, before accelerating upwards into the sky in a curious corkscrew manner. That was the last I saw of it."

Retired Police Constable Brennan

"All I can remember is a bright light high in the (northern?) sky over the moors. It was quite large, larger than a star – probably about the size of the moon, but not the moon. I have the impression (now) that it was pulsing very slightly and emitting not just a white light but possibly bluish and yellow in different areas. I first saw it while driving through Heywood, whilst on the way back to the Police Station. Later, when arriving at the Ambulance Station, I saw Sergeant Morris and the ambulance men were also looking at it. I believe I then travelled with Sergeant Morris in the police Land-Rover to a part of the sub-division, up on the moors, but nothing came of it. I know that Divisional Radio Control checked with Manchester Airport, who claims to know nothing about it. That's all I can really tell you without having access to my original statement made to Mr Hough."

According to the *Manchester Evening News*, Jenny Randles – Director of Investigations for BUFORA – suggested it had been the Northern Lights!

18 June 2001

Dear Mr Hanson,

I received this morning a letter from you which had been forwarded to me by Chief Inspector Lomax of Greater Manchester Police, Rochdale Division. You are asking about the incident in May 1989 in which I saw, together with Sgt Morris and some ambulancemen, some lights in the sky which were later described by others (not by me) as a UFO. To be honest, I can barely remember the incident, so probably the most accurate record of what I saw will be with the person who interviewed me the day after. You say he is called Peter Hough. By all means, do contact him for his records of what I said at the time. I wouldn't set much store by what I remember today.

All I can remember is that there was a bright light high in the (northern?) sky over the moors. It was quite large - larger than a star, certainly, probably about moon-size (but not the moon). I have the impression (now) that it was pulsing very slightly and emitted not just a white light but possibly bluish and yellow in different areas. I saw it over a period of time, that is, over about an hour. I first saw it on my own while I was driving in an area of Heywood which is quite high. After some time I returned to the station and on my way saw that Sgt Morris and the ambulancemen were also looking at it. I think I then travelled with Sgt Morris in the police land rover to a part of the subdivision which is up on the moors in the direction of the strange light, but nothing came of it. I know that divisional radio control checked with Manchester Airport, but they claimed to know nothing about it. I didn't see the strange light disappear (as I hadn't seen it 'come') and thought no more about it.

This is all I can remember. As I said, what I said to Peter Hough (if he is the man who interviewed me the next evening) is bound to be far more accurate and useful than what I remember today.

I would prefer to leave matters at this point, but I hope you are successful in your research.

With best wishes,

Yours sincerely,

Abrennan (former PCW, GMP)

Triangular UFO seen by ambulance crew

Several weeks later, Walter Gorse was to become involved in another UFO sighting, whilst driving the same ambulance (Registration Number C25 BNE):

> *"I was accompanied by Debbie Hanson and responding to an emergency in Heywood, driving back from Rochdale, late one evening, when we both saw a small black triangular object nearly collide with power lines at the side of the road. As it headed towards us, I instructed Debbie to switch-off the blue emergency beacon. As soon as this was done, the 'craft' swerved and moved away from us. When we arrived at the scene of the incident, there were a number of police officers present. I casually showed one of the officers a sketch of what I had just drawn and asked him if Air India 99 (police helicopter) was up. He looked at me and said, 'Don't start up with UFOs tonight'.*

> *After loading the patient into the rear of the ambulance, we made our way to Bury General Hospital where, after delivering him, we were astonished to see the same 'craft' again – this time at a height of about 100ft – apparently following the M66 down to Heap Bridge. We discovered that another ambulance crew from Bury had also seen something strange in the sky over Holcombe Brook, which they took to be an aircraft light, until it split into separate parts and moved off across the sky. They urged me not to disclose their names, for fear of ridicule. I was amazed to find out, while listening to the local radio station, the next day, that an airline pilot, on his way into Manchester Airport, had complained of being 'buzzed' by a UFO."*

ADSCENE
Canterbury, Kent

19 MAY 1989

Have you seen these UFOs?

ABOUT four weeks ago you very kindly printed a letter for us, and we say thank you - the response was great.

We are now looking for witnesses to these events in the following areas:

Christmas 1988 around the coastguard station at Deal - a large disc with a number of lights underneath slowly coasting over the houses lighting up the surrounding area.

Saltwood area - a bright blue/white light around Castle Road area, at about 1am, emitting a sound like a large electrical spark was seen in November last year.

Kingsnorth/Ashford area late October 1988 - a UFO in the Riverside Close area and Ashford. A large disc was extremely low over these areas between 500 and 30ft off the ground, with a silver body and lights underneath - circular in shape and about 10ft in diameter.

Charing Cross/London - we would like more witnesses to come forward about a UFO at or over the railway station, at 6.15pm, on 8 April. A number of people travel this line into Folkestone.

Maidstone/Charing in February, 1989 -

a very large object exploded in the sky at Charing or nearby, at about 6pm. There was a lot of traffic on the road at the time.

Maidstone/Birnam Square, on 20 February, 1989 - an oval object whitish/yellow and red in colour, with no sound but controlled movement up high then very low, at about 6.40pm.

The UFO stayed in the area for about 10 minutes, and was about the size of a large dinner plate.

Kingsdown/Deal, on 7 April, 1989 - the shape of a low-crowned bowler hat, silver in colour with no sound. This lasted for about four minutes ,at 11am.

These are just a few of the reports that I have received in the south of Kent and in the northern part, reports are still coming in by phone and letter.

We would like more people to come forward who saw these events to contact me on 0679 20599.

John Robson
Sunset Cottage
New Street
Lydd.

We should like to thank Michael Thomas for his investigation into the incident, and for putting us in touch with some of the parties concerned. Sadly, Michael died from a heart attack some months afterwards.

(Source: *Daily Mail*, 20.5.1989 – 'Flashing lights shock 999 Men'/Greater Manchester Ambulance Service, NHS /Michael Thomas, UFO researcher/ Peter Hough /*Evening News*, 19.5.1989 – 'Manchester Police Chase UFO'/ Unknown newspaper, 20.5.1989 – 'Hello, hello, that looks like a UFO')

Editor comments

On 1st June 1989, Alan Fitzsimmons, Editor of the Heywood Advertiser, commented on this matter. He dismissed the official explanation that a star was the answer and pointed out that the ambulance men had seen three objects. In addition to this, a star would not have knocked out the telephone lines at the Ambulance Station. He then reminded the readers of his own experience, many years ago, in 1957, when as a young reporter with the same newspaper, following a *UFO sighting brought to the attention of the newspaper, the MOD had called in to the office and read out the Official Secrets Act to him , warning them to discontinue reporting!

ROCHDALE,
LANCS.

27th MARCH 2001

Dear Mr. Hanson,

thank you for your letter, and may I apologise for my ex-colleagues for trying to safeguard my privacy, I think you will appreciate that we were some what harassed by every "crank" under the sun.

May I assure you that what was witnessed was not a fleeting glance, but went on from 01.15 hrs to 03.15 hrs of that particular incident. At the first encounter of the objects we were mobile in the Dam Hill area of Heywood, I noticed that persons in the high rise flats were or appeared to be engrossed at their windows looking towards my nearside.

We dropped a patient off on Dam Hill and was pulling into the kerb to receive instructions from our control. At this moment I espied four luminated globes 0 0 0 0 all at an equal height and distance apart, I pulled the vehicle into the kerb and encountered a grid, this caused light distortion down the windscreen, I then noticed that there now was only 0 00 three. I mentioned this to Stuart who had not noticed them at this time, control gave us R.T.B.

As we proceeded towards the depot Stuart who was in the passenger seat said " they are following us. We stopped and started a couple of times and because I had an obscured view could not see them. By the time we reached the station yard I was getting a little fed-up with Stuart so as a bit of devilment switched on the blue lights and verbally mimicked an "alien craft", I looked out of my side window to see this globe on my right. Across the globe was a band like a bracelet, red, white and blue rotating anti-clockwise.

I reversed into the bay and again flashed my blue lights

SINGING STATION / STOREY / yard / MARKET ? distance. Globe.

②

and the response from the globe was that the barrel which had been running like at "ten to" to 20 past was now rotating quarters to to quarters past. We now observed that the other two globes

had gone into a "V" formation [GLOBE A]

B DISTANT

Some distance apart, and to a higher position. I contacted control to see if they could see anything from Whitefield, and then went out to make up a red light in response to the lights on the barrel, yet they did not copy the indicator lights. The PAX line went a few minutes later and control notified us that "Radio Piccadilly" was about to ring us on the other line.

Stuart spoke to Piccadilly for some time "live on the air", and when he had finished the PAX went again, control "Have you notified the police", our reply "we thought that they had already done this". In response we attempted to use the "OUTSIDE LINE" and found that it was dead "possibly a fault at Radio Piccadilly or a phenomenon, ironically only clearing after they left.

The police arrived, observed what was going on, the sergeant deciding on getting the land rover out and going towards ASHWORTH VALLEY to get a closer look. There was a bit of a scare when contact was lost with the sergeant for approximately 10 minutes, but he could find nothing and yet the Objects were still there.

At approximately 03 10 hrs and dawn breaking I was outside on my own still signalling with the lamps the globe suddenly turned to like say goodbye, and presented to following to us. This was in view for about 3 minutes, it then turned with the white convex towards me (less the coloured band) and moved off at a great acceleration leaving a cork screw shaped hole through the cloud.

Red convex glow

WHITE CONVEX WHICH HAD BEEN FACING US.

SIMILAR COLOUR TO SKY BACKGROUND or transparent.

Cloud.

Cork screw hole.

Cont 3.

③

We then had statement to make to the police, but have never had to sign a typed one, or official statement. We were also visited by MUFOSA (Manchester U.F.O. Society) with their official documents.

I would also like to disclose that several weeks later and using the same ambulance C251 BNE and working with another colleague (female). We were on a blue light job responding back from Rochdale to Heywood and was buzzed by a small craft, in its haste it nearly collided with the power lines and I instinctively instructed my colleague to douse the blue lights, the craft veered away in an unbelievable 360° turn away from the pylon. We arrived at the incident which had a number of Police Officers present, copied the craft similar in size to a small helicopter but with a triangular luminated panel underneath, On asking a police officer if "India 99" (Police Helicopter) was about and pointing to the said craft, I was told "do not start up with UFO's tonight")

TRIANGULAR LUMINATION

We transported the patient to BURY General Hospital and was returning to Heywood when we spotted the craft again, this time it was at a height of about 100 ft. following the M66 down to HEAP BRIDGE, the Bury/Heywood boundary and although it was doing about 50 mph it perfectly followed the natural hollows etc. managing to keep the same uniform height. (REPORTED ON NEWS BY AIRLINE PILOT WHO WAS BUZZED ON APPROACHING RINGWAY AIRPORT.

A few weeks after this encounter I was working with another colleague and noticed two other small craft, (same ambulance), I did not say anything to my colleague, but several minutes later he said out of the 'blue' "Your mates are out again tonight", my reply "I am saying nothing", and left it at that.

GREYISH   RED GLOWING CONVEX.

To make things even sound more sinister, at about this time and for a few years had trouble with E.S.P. The most sinister was at about 03:00hrs having a dream of looking through some one elses eyes. I saw petrol pumps in a Large, the voices of someone saying "he has a gun" then some minutes later Police, then the sound of a motor cycle being driven at speed EAST Bound. On the M62. This was the shooting of a POLICE INSPECTOR and a POLICE SERGEANT. at BIRCH SERVICES M62 near Heywood, if I had been on nights and not earlier I would have been on the call.

Trusting that you don't find this too incredible.
Yours respectfully
Walter Byrne.

Superintendent G. Varley
Sub-Divisional Commander

Mr J Hanson
P O Box 6371
BIRMINGHAM
B48 7RW

GREATER MANCHESTER POLICE

Our ref: IML.YT
Your ref:

When calling or telephoning
please ask for Middleton Police Station,
Oldham Road, Middleton M24 1AY
24 April 2001

Dear Mr Hanson

I refer to your letter of 11th April 2001 concerning the incident on 18th May 1989 outside Heywood Ambulance Station.

I can confirm that Sergeant Morris and a Constable Bennett did respond to a call from the Ambulance Service about lights seen in the sky.   As I understand it the officers saw the lights.

Both officers did make statements to the Manchester UFO Research Association the following day which was, at that time, chaired by Mr Peter Hough.

Unfortunately our corresponding records of that time have since been destroyed.   Both officers have retired from the service.

I have taken the liberty of copying your letter to the Directorate of Air Staff Secretariat, Ministry of Defence, for their information.

I am sorry I cannot assist further.

Yours sincerely

Ian M Lomax
Chief Inspector

20th-23rd May 1989 (UK) – UFOs over Essex

At 10pm on the 20th May 1989, two teenage girls from South Woodham Ferrers were out walking along Hullbridge Road, when they were confronted by a *'red ball'* of glowing light. The girls ran away but after plucking up their courage returned to the scene, whereupon the lights appeared and chased them along the street. On the same evening, a large orange *'light'* was seen in the sky over the Pitsea area.

On the 21st May 1989 a UFO, described as an oval object with white lights around the centre, was seem motionless in the sky. A short time later it shot away.

Alan and Dawn Cook of Grosvenor Gardens, Biggleswade, sighted a white object, flashing across the sky at 10.20pm on the 22nd May 1989.

At 5pm on the 23rd May, two silver glowing *'lights'* were seen hovering in the sky for 10 minutes, by holiday-makers on the beach at Southend.

(**Source: Ron West/***Biggleswade Chronicle***, Bedfordshire, 26.5.1989 – 'Close Encounter')**

27th May 1989 (USA) – Humanoid seen

At Odenton, Maryland, during the evening, it is claimed that two young boys encountered a 3-4ft tall brown/black, hairy humanoid, with one white stripe running down the back of one of its legs. The being ran through a clearing behind the house, and then disappeared into some woods. (**Source:** *Strange Magazine #5*)

28th May 1989 (Canada) – UFO over Edmonton, Alberta

Shortly after 1.30am, a Mr Gilmore claimed to have had a close encounter with a UFO.

> *"I could see depth and everything into it; the bottom was shaped like the bow of a boat . . . It looked large to me, but there was nothing to judge it against.*
>
> *I held up my index finger to get a comparison of size, but it's hard to judge. I guess it was about 1,500 to 2,000ft away and about 800ft wide . . . It was shimmering and what looked like heat waves radiated from it, but there was no heat."*

(**Source: Randy LaBoucane,** *Examiner*, **Edmonton, Alberta, 11.6.1989)**

30th May 1989 (UK) – Police called out

At 8.15pm, a large white *'light'* with red, yellow, and blue lights flashing inside it, was seen in the night sky over Highfields, Stafford, by a number of residents, who called the police, following which PC Terrence Gibbs and Kevin Muller arrived at 9pm. After watching it for an hour, they left – unable to offer any explanation. Other reports for the same evening tell of a cone-shaped object, with lights flashing underneath it, seen over Weston Downs, and a strange red light, seen heading across the night sky at 11.15pm, before merging with another bright light. (**Source: UFOSIS)**

HAVERHILL ECHO, *Thursday, June 22, 1989* **5**

Couple see the light after UFO sighting

STRANGE objects and lights in the sky are of special interest to a Haverhill couple who have become investigators after seeing a cigar-shaped UFO over Ladygate Woods.

Peter Fleming (20) and girlfriend Julie Rondeau (18) are currently looking into Haverhill's latest phenomenon – a blue glow which shone around Haverhill on the night of May 22 reported by several people who contacted the Echo.

The couple, who live at Argyll Court, joined EAUFOPRA – the East Anglian UFO Paranormal Research Association – after an incident just about a year ago while they were walking at night with their dog in the vicinity of Puddlebrook.

Peter, a forklift truck driver with Davis Engineering, said they were convinced what they saw was extra-terrestrial because of its behaviour.

'It came up as a distant

Peter and Julie ... no longer sceptical about UFO sightings.

glow and settled over Ladygate Woods,' he said. 'It gave off a strong beam of light that shone up the area. Then it zig-zagged around and moved up and down.

'After several minutes the light moved round in an arc and we could see it was a cigar-shaped object, very large, with portholes, showing green, yellow and

red lights. There was no noise. When it moved away towards the south east we heard a sonic boom.'

Peter said for most of the time they were mesmerised, a little scared. Their labrador-cross dog, Smudle, was also unsettled by it.

Their sighting was reported to EAUFOPRA,

who checked everything out and found there was nothing from local air bases or airports that particular night that could account for their story.

The experience prompted them to join the UFO group and they have been issued with ID cards to investigate strange sky sightings in the Haverhill area.

Julie, a secretary at the Welding Institute at Abington, is just as enthusiastic as Peter after what they saw.

Peter said up to that night they were sceptical about UFO stories. Now they really do believe UFOs exist. Where they came from was anybody's guess but it was only by monitoring and investigating the phenomenon that they were ever likely to find out.

The couple can be contacted through the UFO hotline at Clacton , telephone 0255 431391.

31st May 1989 (Australia) – Two golden bands

A woman resident of Townsville, Queensland, was looking into the sky shortly after sunset, at 5.45pm, when she noticed a pink/orange *'cloud'* in the north-west. She fetched her binoculars and through them saw what appeared to be *"two solid looking golden bands, standing side by side"*.

The object was moving slowly, so she went to the front gate to steady the binoculars and continued to keep it under observation for 15 minutes, until it was finally lost from sight over Paluma Range. (**Source: UFORA**)

JUNE 1989

4th June 1989 (USA) – Three UFOs seen

AT 7.45pm, a security guard and an air traffic controller at Air Force Facility 42, in Palmdale, California, sighted a silver flying object and three orb-shaped UFOs during testing of the B1 bomber.

(Source: MUFON UFO Journal, November 1990)

Rectangular UFO seen

At 11.30pm, while driving along the Express Connector roadway at Frankfort, Kentucky, a 36-year-old woman observed two large bright white lights, moving in her direction. She stopped her car for a better look and as the lights got closer, she saw that they were attached to *"a rectangular-shaped object, massive in size"*.

The woman stopped and got out of the car, in time to see the craft halt directly overhead and remain there for about two minutes.

> *"I could see what appeared to be numerous pipes laying flat against the underside of the UFO, which was illuminated by several lights."*

(Source: NUFORC – 'The witness experienced an episode of missing time'/Paul Ferrughilli, *Computer Catalogue of UFO Reports, 1988-1994*, case #265/some accounts give the 13th June 1989)

5th June 1989 (Australia) – UFO tracked on radar

At Dorrigo, New South Wales, two pilots tracked an object at 4,000km on the aircraft's weather radar. The jet cargo aircraft's crew noted a big return on the radar. Over a period of four minutes, it was seen to travel from 60 nautical miles ahead, and off their screen in a straight line track. **(Source: Bill Chalker)**

6th June 1989 (UK) – UFO display over Suffolk

Mr Norman Trent (79) was at his home address in Denham, Suffolk, when he saw something unusual in the sky – as a result of which he later contacted Ron West, who asked him to complete a sighting report.

EAST ANGLIAN U.F.O. & PARANORMAL RESEARCH ASSOCIATION

SECTION A **SIGHTING ACCOUNT FORM**

Please write an account of your sighting, make a drawing of what you saw and then answer the questions in section B overleaf as fully as possible. Write in **BLOCK CAPITALS** using a ball point pen.

6/6/89

Late in the evening, there was a clearance in the dull showery weather. The sun was shining through very thin whispy cloud in the West and appeared to be some 10 to 15 degrees above the horizon as seen from our rear garden.

From a position on the horizon just under the sun dark circular shapes arose in a continuous stream. Some were single, others we in groups of 2 or 3, one group consisted of seven discs. Each shape was slightly smaller than that of the sun. As each disc rose high in the sky it became transparent, then disappeared from sight.

About one hour later, I went out with a hand bearing compass to obtain a bearing of the incident, when just over the position of the first sighting I saw a bright yellow/white burst of light similar to that of an explosion

Please continue on a separate sheet if necessary. Twice size of Sun

DRAWING*

overlapping

Edge White

Burst of light

Centre Yellow

* If preferred, use a separate sheet of paper.

Your full name (Mr/Mrs/Miss/Ms)
Mr. Norman E. Trent   Age 79
Address The Bungalow, Hoxne Rd
Denham, EYE, Suffolk
Telephone No. 0379 75 270 (STD   )

Occupation during last two years
Retired

Any professional, technical or academic qualifications or special interests

Do you object to the publication of your name?
*Yes/No. *Delete as applicable.

Today's Date 25-6-89
Signature N. E. Trent

10th June 1989 (UK) – UFO display over Woodford Green, Essex

At 10.10pm, two objects – described as red and orange in colour – were seen moving in and out of cloud and weaving across the sky, for over 20 minutes, by Mr Rogers and Miss P. Reeves.

Triangular UFO over Essex

Patricia Irene Page (69) of Witham, Essex, had this to say:

> "I was driving along the B1053 near Sampford Peverell, during the evening, at about 9.40pm, in my Ford Fiesta 950cc, when I saw two black triangular 'craft' appear over the roofs of some cottages. I was fascinated, as I had never seen anything like that before. They were moving slowly across the road in front of me. I stopped the car and observed them for about two minutes, before they went out of sight. The objects, which were about 300ft high in the air, seemed to be examining the ground beneath them as they flew over fields."

The sighting took place near Wethersfield USAF Base. Was there a connection? (**Source: Ron West**)

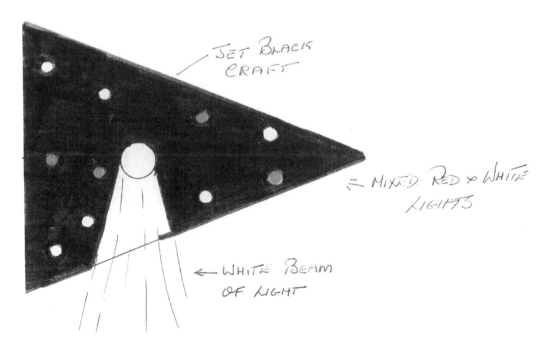

10th June 1989 (Tasmania) – Strange lights seen

At 8pm, a father and his son were en-route to a local shop at George Town when they noticed some flashing lights in the sky to the north-west, but did not take much notice. On walking home they saw the lights again, which appeared to move towards them and then change into a white ball shape. The two men became upset and ran the last block home. The son looked out and saw some lights moving away westwards.

Enquiries made with Civil Aviation revealed no aircraft listed in that area. (**Source:** TUFOIC)

11th June 1989 (Canada) – UFO display

At 7am, a Canadian Airlines International plane was flying near St. John's, Newfoundland, when the crew noticed a dark grey or black ovoid object, estimated to be about two meters in length, making complex manoeuvres in the sky for three minutes. (**Source:** Chris Rutkowski, *International UFO Reporter*, July 1990, p.10)

16th June 1989 (Australia) – Formation of UFOs seen

Two brothers from Yowah Opal Field, Western Queensland, were opal mining at around 3.15am, on a bright moonlit night, when the older brother's attention was drawn to a large shadow passing over him and the surrounding area. He looked up to see an immense object, four to five times the size of a football field, recede quickly towards the moon and come to rest near it. By blocking the moon out with a nearby overhang he could observe the object clearly, which he described as being, *"about one and a half times the apparent size of the moon, with a shiny gun-metal appearance."* and then alerted his brother. In addition to the larger object, the two men then saw six smaller ones moving through the sky.

The brothers then decided to wake up their friends, but by the time they had done this the objects had disappeared. The first brother just caught a glimpse of a silvery object, streaking past the perimeter of the moon between the ten and eleven o'clock positions. (**Source:** Australian UFO Research Network)

17th June 1989 – Diamond-shaped UFO over Essex

A UFO was seen by four people over Hadleigh, Colchester, described as being: *". . . 100ft long, by 30ft high, and flying at a height of 150ft."*

Diamond in the sky

A DIAMOND shaped UFO was spotted by 4 people last Saturday June 17. The witnesses reported the sighting to the East Anglian UFO Research Society. They watched it for half an hour in the Hadleigh area and described it as one hundred feet long and 30 feet high and at an altitude of about 150 feet.

UFO investigators plan to interview the witnesses this week.

15 JUN 1989

COASTAL EXPRESS
-Colchester-

Club lists 892 UFO sightings

THE Essex skies are alive with mysterious objects, according to a UFO spotters group in the county.

In the last nine months a staggering 892 flying objects or strange lights in the sky were reported to the Boxted-based East Anglian UFO and Paranormal Research Association.

And several witnesses claim to have actually made contact with creatures not of this Earth.

Spokeswoman Sheridan Lane said between July 31 and December 31 last year, 532 sightings were reported in Essex.

After the group investigated them, 189 turned out to be aircraft or other every day explicable objects.

But the remaining 343 were impossible to explain, and have been classified as UFOs.

A further 360 objects were spotted and reported between January 1 and April 30 this year.

Investigations are still going on into 160 of them, while 150 have been classified at UFOs.

But all the incidents are not mere sightings of distant indistinct objects, claims Miss Lane.

Of the recent 360 cases, 270 were from people who spotted bright lights in the sky.

But ten were actual cases of contact with alien lifeforms, with one Clacton woman claiming she was abducted by a spacecraft before having the event erased from her mind.

She later relived her close encounter under hypnosis with the UFO research team.

If you're still sceptical, the team has organised a UFO talk by author Timothy Good, at Cecil Jones School, Southchurch, Southend, at 7.30pm, on June 24.

15.6.89

During the same period, a silver *'disc'*, showing many lights, was seen in the sky over Southend, by dozens of people, which was just one of a number of reports received by Ron West and his group. The other sightings told of *"a black-grey object, with orange lights"*, seen over the Thames Estuary, and *"a silver spinning UFO, with approximately 20 orange lights around it"*, seen by people attending a barbecue at Southend.

(Source: *Yellow Advertiser*, Colchester, 23.6.1989 – 'Diamond in the Sky'/*Southend Evening Echo*, Essex, 4.7.1989)

19th June 1989 – UFO over North Warwickshire

Mr Alan Cooke of Weddington, Nuneaton, was just about to go to bed when he noticed a motionless blinding light, low in the sky over the village of Caldicott, and wondered what it could be.

> *"It was far too bright to be any aircraft, or police helicopter. I looked through a pair of binoculars but was unable to make out any other details. I looked away for a split second and it was gone."*

(Source *Nuneaton Evening Times*, 23.6.1989 – 'UFO sighting to be probed')

20th June 1989 (UK) – Four UFOs sighted

At 11pm, three men were travelling in a car along the A1067 towards Fakenham, driving past scattered bungalows between Drayton and Taverham, Norwich, when they saw a *'light'* in the sky ahead of them and to their left.

At first they took the *'light'* to be an aircraft, en route to Norwich Airport, but thought otherwise after seeing how close the *'light'* appeared to be.

The driver slowed down the car and then stopped, allowing them to see behind the *'beam of light'*, four more lights – red in colour, arranged in an oblong pattern, about 8ft high and 16ft long – forming the four corners of an oblong shape, darker than the sky. The object was estimated to be about 75yds away from them and at a height of about 60ft. As the car drew level, the *'beam'* or *'cone of light'* was seen pointing towards their left. It then began to slowly move in the direction of Norwich and soon became hidden from sight. According to the men concerned, they believed that their arrival in the car had, in some way, disturbed it from hovering over one of the bungalows.

> **Southend Evening Echo, Essex.**
>
> ## 19 JUN 1989
>
> ### School UFO talk
>
> EAST Anglian UFO Research Association will have author Timothy Good talking to it at Cecil Jones School, Southend, on June 24 starting at 2pm. Mr Good who wrote Top Secret, about alleged UFO cover-ups, will answer questions.
>
> Admittance is £1.50 to pay for the hire of the hall.

(Source: Letter to Gordon Creighton, *FSR*)

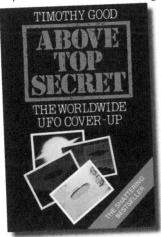

24th June 1989 – Timothy Good lectures on UFOs

Author and veteran UFO researcher Timothy Good appeared at Cecil Jones School, Southend, this evening, to talk about UFOs. Admission was £1.50 pence.

> **Southend Evening Echo, Essex.**
>
> ## 22 JUN 1989
>
> ### UFO author lecture
>
> AUTHOR Timothy Good who wrote about UFOs in his book Above Top Secret is lecturing on Saturday afternoon at 2pm at Cecil Jones High School, Eastern Avenue, Southend.
>
> Entry is £1.50 which is to pay for the hire of the hall.

Writer sighted at UFO talk

Timothy Good with his book Above Top Secret which exposes a UFO scandal

Southend Standard

2 3 JUN 1989

Probe into UFO sightings

A STRANGE object spotted in the sky by a Hockley couple is being investigated by a team of UFO specialists.

And they are already being kept busy looking into a number of other recent sightings of unidentified flying objects in South East Essex.

The Hockley couple saw a ball of intense white light one afternoon about 2.30pm and watched it for about 25 minutes before it disappeared.

About the same time a Thorpe Bay couple spotted a cigar-shaped object which was shining brightly.

And at 2.15pm the same day a couple from Canvey told East Anglian UFO investigators they saw an object which they at first thought was a balloon. They realised it was not and watched the noiseless craft for 40 minutes before it disappeared in the Shoebury area.

25th June 1989 (UK) – Bright UFO over Worcester

At 11pm, Mrs Shirley Baddeley of Ripon Road, Ronkswood, Worcester, was returning home after having walked the dog, when she noticed:

> "...a light in the sky, about five or six times the size of a star. At first it didn't seem to be moving – then it moved across the sky. As it did so, a bright orange light began to flash on one side. It was a good imitation of an aircraft but it didn't make any noise."

The object was last seen heading towards the direction of Tibberton.

(Source: *Worcester Evening News*, 26.6.1989 – 'UFO seen over City')

26th June 1989 (UK) – Strange light over Essex

At 10.15pm, Mrs Pauline Woodley (50) – shop owner – of Snakes Lane, Southend, was driving near Leigh Elms petrol station and crossing over the London road, with her daughter Kate (11) and husband.

Pauline:

> "We had been visiting my mother, who lives near Southend General Hospital, when we saw a strange 'light' in the sky, which appeared to be following us. After filling up with petrol we continued on our journey, but stopped in Blenheim Crescent in order to obtain a closer look, where we saw a beam of light rotating around itself in the sky."

(Source: Ron West/Geraldine Dillon)

Would you please try to draw what you saw.

27th June 1989 (UK) – *'Ball of light'*

At 11pm, John Stone (28) from South Crockerford, Basildon, Essex, was in his back garden, when he saw:

> *"...what looked like a round 'ball of light', showing an orange 'tail', making a rushing noise, in an eastern direction."*

30th June 1989 (UK) – UFO display over police station

At 10.30pm, two police officers observed a total of twelve large lights directly above Hornsey Police Station, repeatedly making circular patterns in the sky above them, for approximately 15 minutes.

(Source: FOI Documentation)

ARE UFOs PIE IN THE SKY? NOT TO GRASSINGTON'S SOBER EX-POLICEMAN

TONY DODD: Looking for answers

DetectiveDodd's lights fantastic

RETIRED policeman Tony Dodd handed me the scoop of the century.

Long-lived aliens from outer space who feed on the bodily fluids of humans and cattle are holed up in a New Mexican underground bunker and have wiped out soldiers sent to dislodge them.

The alien life form, known as ALF, are described as hairless, three to five feet high, with large tear-shaped eyes, thin lips and four-fingered, claw-like hands and toes, grey reptile-like skin and arms which reach their knees. They are particularly partial to strawberry ice-cream. Science fiction? Utter fantasy? Not according to 54-year-old Tony.

His bizarre claim, he said, comes from a bemedalled American air force and naval intelligence officer Milton William Cooper, who had access to secret documents, and claims to have seen a huge UFO rising form the sea next to his submarine.

Cooper has challenged the White House by charging the Government with treason against the American people.

His story is that the aliens have temporarily abducted and medically probed thousands of people. The American top military have known about about them for years and have given them them several remote underground bases in exchange of the kind of technology which enabled them to build the Stealth bomber.

But since then the aliens have shown their true, malevolent colours.

"It is the biggest cover up of all time," said Mr Dodd. "And my information is that something dramatic on UFOs is going to happen in 1992."

Tony, director of research and investigations for the Yorkshire UFO Society, is co-director of

their magazine, the smartly-produced Quest International, which goes out to 300 members worldwide.

What comes as a jolt is that Mr Dodd, who lives at Hardy Meadows, a backwater in the tourist town of Grassington, is eminently sane.

He will admit to being somewhat obsessed by UFOs. "But I want to find out what it is all about. I am searching for the truth, just as I

OBJECT LESSON: Tony's drawing of a UFO seen at Cononley

ALIENS are here, living in America and with a taste for strawberry ice-cream, says former policeman Tony Dodd. And he means it! JOHN HEWITT wasn't sure what to believe.

MYSTERY SIGHTS: A UFO (or cloud?) over a California lake (top) and Tony Dodd's photo of unexplained lights above Carleton Moors (above)

was when I was on the force," he said.

He does not mean the Stars Wars variety. He is talking about the North Yorkshire Police, where he served for 25 years, based at Skipton.

He was out with a colleague on night patrol in a country lane at Cononley in January 1978 when a 100ft UFO floated across the road in front of their car.

"It had three great spheres underneath and there were coloured lights flashing and rotating. The whole thing was giving out an incandescent glow."

Since then he had been out with binoculars and geiger counter on the Carleton Moors, near Skipton, which he claims is prime UFO-spotting territory. He reckons he has seen about 60 UFOs.

"It was as though it was signalling, and it was so close I could see the dimpled glass windows," he said.

The authorities ridicule UFOs, but they are interested in them, Mr Dodd asserts.

JULY 1989

2nd July 1989 (UK) – *'Flying disc'* over Essex

BETWEEN 2.30am and 3am, Emma Huff (18) and Gary Attwood were parked up in a car behind Gloucester Park Swimming Pool, Basildon, when they saw a silvery disc-shaped object, flashing with red and white light, moving towards the pool and then back again – an action repeated twice.

After watching it for about two hours, it inexplicably vanished from view. Oddly, during an interview later made with Mr P. Oliver and J. Smith, from the Essex UFO Group, Gary denied seeing anything at all.

Later that evening, between 10pm and 11pm, Mrs Jane Barry (42) and her husband, from Sherwood Way, Southend-on-Sea, were in the bedroom, looking out of the window, when they saw a long tadpole-shaped, red-orange coloured object, about an inch wide, moving through the air *"followed by a ping and then a thud, as if it had hit a brick wall."*

3rd July 1989 (UK) – Orange lights seen

At 10.30pm, Lesley Metcalfe (28) of Lee Hall Road, Leigh-on-Sea, Essex, was sat in the lounge of her home. She went to draw the curtains and looked out to see:

> *"...a perfect circle of orange lights in the sky, moving eastwards over Southend-on-Sea – gone in seconds".*

4th July 1989 (UK) – Orange *'light'* seen

At 10pm, Dorothy Jones (79) of Sherbourne Gardens, Prittlewell, Southend-on-Sea, was sat in her sun lounge with an elderly neighbour, when they saw a strange bright orange *'light'* in the sky, heading towards the Shoebury direction.

Her neighbour – Mrs J. Cordess (75) – also corroborated the sighting. She described the flight of the object as jumping through the sky, rather than flying in a straight course, and that the object was in view for 15 minutes before being lost from sight.

They were not the only witnesses. At the same time, Daren Porter (13) of Perry Street, Chelmsford, was lying in bed looking out at the sky, when he saw:

> "...*a bright 'light' hovering in the sky over the Mayflower School. I got out of bed and watched, as it passed over our house.*"

8th July 1989 (UK) – Two *'lights'*

At 11.30pm, Mr Andrew William Saul (31) was driving along the A12 at Newbury Park, Ilford, near Ley Street, with his fiancée – Helen Marie Smalley – when he noticed two *'lights'* in a diagonal formation, moving from west to south-east across the sky.

> "*I first thought they were balloons but then realised this was not the case, as there was no movement between the two of them. The traffic lights changed to green and I continued on my journey – soon to lose sight of them.*"

9th July 1989 (UK) – Silver UFO

Mr Frank Mackie saw a silver UFO flying through the sky over Essex. It appears he was not the only one. The *Southend Evening Echo* reported that others had also sighted the 'silver UFO'.

OBJECT REAL CLOSE

9th July 1989 (Australia) – *'Light'* seen inside the house

At 5.40am at Clare, Southern Australia, a one metre diameter yellow-white *'ball'* was seen hovering over a sofa in the lounge, by people in bed. Simultaneously, they noted that their feet were *'glowing'* like an X-ray. The light and glow disappeared and they fell back to sleep. (**Source: Keith Basterfield**)

Southend Evening Echo, Essex

11 JUL 89

Have you spotted a flying saucer?

A LARGE unidentified flying object described by some witnesses as large as a two-storey block of flats and only a few hundred feet from the ground seen over Southend and parts of Essex and Suffolk is still puzzling UFO investigators.

It is believed the the UFO was in trouble and landed on the North Essex and Suffolk border for a couple of hours before it disappeared. That was in 1980, but the British Unidentified Flying Object Research Association is still trying to find more witnesses to the sightings.

They would like to hear from a Georger Emslie, then of Cossington Road, Westcliff, who was a witness to that saucer-shaped object in the December of that year.

Witnesses can contact Essex BUFORA representative Ron West on 0255 431391. He will also be pleased to hear from anyone who believes they have seen a UFO.

Southend Evening Echo – Essex.

10 JUL 1989

Silver UFO still around

THE silver disc with accompanying orange lights is still floating around the Southend area.

UFO researchers have had four more reported sightings.

The noiseless object in one sighting had the orange lights flashing in a circle round it.

There have now been more than a dozen separate reports.

If anyone else saw the disc they are asked to contact the UFO hotline on Basildon 286079.

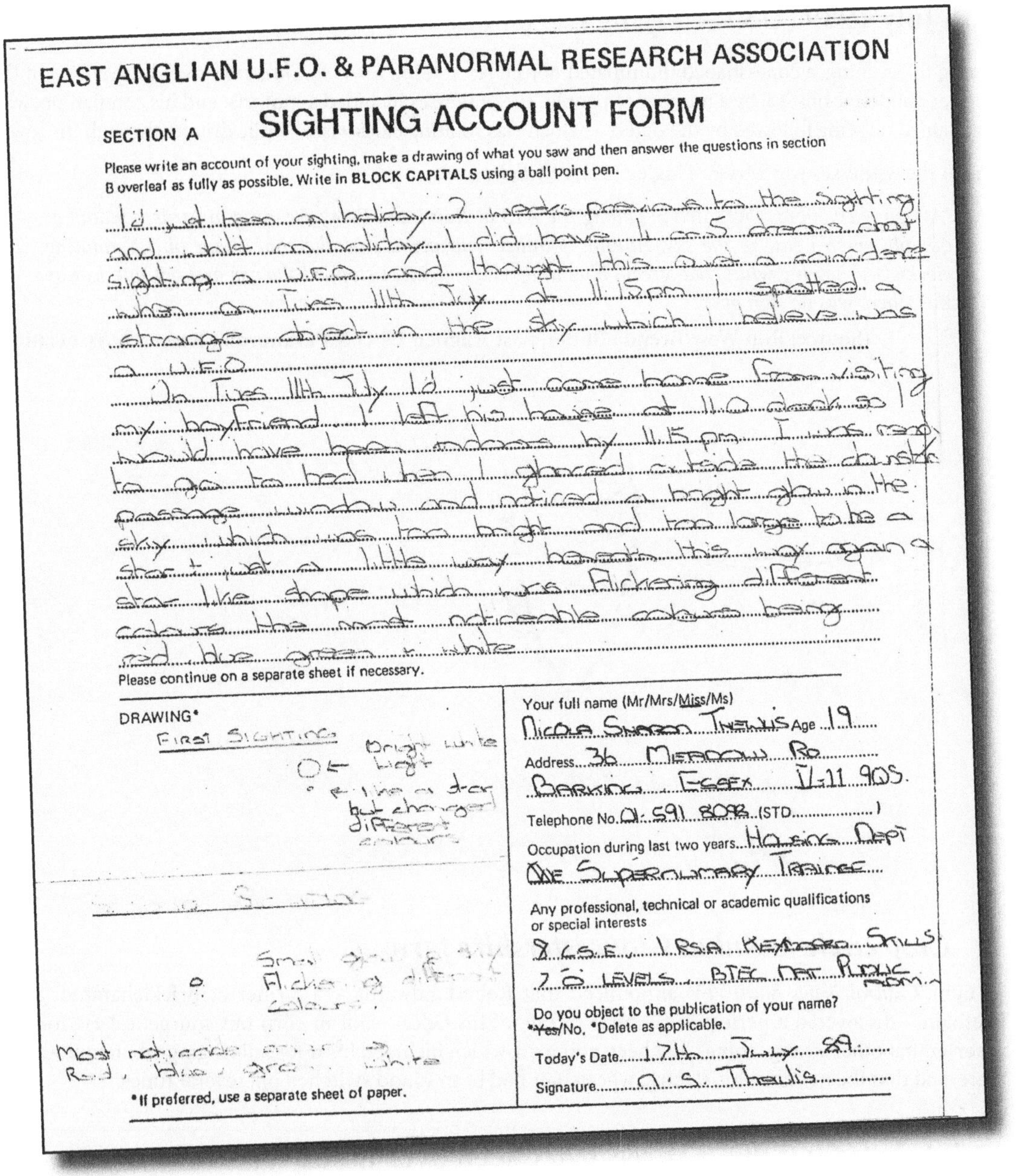
EAST ANGLIAN U.F.O. & PARANORMAL RESEARCH ASSOCIATION

SECTION A **SIGHTING ACCOUNT FORM**

Please write an account of your sighting, make a drawing of what you saw and then answer the questions in section B overleaf as fully as possible. Write in **BLOCK CAPITALS** using a ball point pen.

I'd just been on holiday 2 weeks previous to the sighting and whilst on holiday I did have 4 or 5 dreams about sighting a U.F.O. and thought this was a coincidence when on Tues 11th July at 11.15pm I spotted a strange object in the sky which I believe was a U.F.O.

On Tues 11th July I'd just come home from visiting my boyfriend. I left his house at 11.0 clock so I would have been indoors by 11.15pm. I was ready to go to bed when I glanced outside the double passage window and noticed a bright glow in the sky which was too bright and too large to be a star, just a little way beneath this was again a star like shape which was flickering different colours the most noticeable colours being red blue green & white

Please continue on a separate sheet if necessary.

DRAWING*

FIRST SIGHTING

Bright white light

like a star but changed different colours

SECOND SIGHTING

Small star like flickering different colours.

Most noticeable colours Red, blue, green, white

*If preferred, use a separate sheet of paper.

Your full name (Mr/Mrs/Miss/Ms) Nicola Sharon Thewlis Age 19

Address 36 Meadow Rd Barking Essex IG11 9QS.

Telephone No. 01 591 8098 (STD)

Occupation during last two years Housing Dept One Supernumerary Trainee

Any professional, technical or academic qualifications or special interests

8 G.C.S.E. 1 RSA Keyboard Skills

2 'O' Levels BTEC Cert Public Adm.

Do you object to the publication of your name?

*Yes/No. *Delete as applicable.

Today's Date 17th July 89.

Signature N.S. Thewlis

11th July 1989 (UK) – Flickering lights

At 11.15pm, Nicola Sharon Trent (19) of Meadow Road, Barking, Essex, was about to enter her house, when she glanced into the sky and saw:

> *"...a bright glow flickering with red, blue, green and white, lights. I was so excited I rushed upstairs to wake up my brother, Jason, and then looked out of the landing window. The bright glow had gone, but the flickering lights were still present. I watched it for about 45 minutes, before I lost sight of it."*

(Source: Roy Lake)

12th July 1989 (UK) – *'Flying Christmas tree'*

During the evening, a cone-shaped illuminated object, resembling a *'flying Christmas tree'*, was sighted in the sky over Southend-on-Sea, by a number of people. The witnesses included a motorist and his companion, who complained of being followed by the object – which was rotating clockwise – while driving through the town.

One of the witnesses was Mrs B. Tingley (52), of Chelmsford.

> *"At about 10.30pm, I was driving along the A13 at Rainham, Essex, heading towards London, at 60mph, when I saw in the sky, running parallel with me, a metallic cone shape object, rotating clockwise, showing white, red, green, blue and yellow, lights. I stopped the car and got out, but by then there was no sign of it."*

(Source: Ron West/Brenda Butler, East Anglian UFO & Paranormal Research Association)

Crop circle found at Gloucestershire farm

At 6pm, *Central News South TV* announced that Robert Edwards – a farmer at Bricklehampton, near Evesham – discovered a perfect huge circle in one of his fields – not in corn but courgettes! He told the reporter that other strange things had been going on, which included his doorbell ringing when nobody was there, and that the lights on his electric wheelchair had been found switched on, several times.

15th July 1989 (UK) – Three *'stars'* seen over Essex

At 4.40pm, Gillian Goring (32) – wife of Dan Goring (Essex UFO researcher) – was sat at her home address in Enfield, London, when she saw:

> *"...what looked like three twinkling 'stars' moving across the sky, forming a triangle, seen between scattered clouds. They then rose upwards and disappeared from sight. About 15 minutes later, another group of 'lights' appeared; this time there were about fifteen sets of three lights, in the middle of which was a red object. An aircraft moved near to them. As it did so, the 'lights' veered away, at speed, and were gone from view in seconds. The whole incident was over in 30 minutes."*

15·7·89   1989-7-1

FOR OFFICIAL USE ONLY

		YEAR	NUMBER	INVESTIGATOR	CASE SUMMARY
GROUP	BUFORA REF.				DATE
/INVEST REF:				EVALUATOR	TIME
					LOCATION
RETURN FORM TO:-					EVAL'N
					UFO CLASS
					CLOSED

UFO SIGHTING ACCOUNT FORM

SECTION A

Please write an account of your sighting, make a drawing of what you saw and then answer the questions in section B overleaf as fully as possible. Write in **BLOCK CAPITALS** using a ball point pen.

I WAS SITTING IN MY GARDEN, LOOKING UP AT THE SKY. WHEN I NOTICED WHAT LOOKED LIKE THREE TWINKLING STARS MOVING ACROSS THE SKY BETWEEN SCATTERED CLOUD. IN THE FORM OF A TRIANGLE: ONE IN FRONT Y TWO BEHIND. AS I WATCHED, ANOTHER ONE SEEMED TO JOIN THEM AT THE BACK. GOING IN THE SAME DIRECTION. THEY SEEMED TO BE FLYING IN FORMATION. THEY ROSE HIGHER INTO THE SKY & THEN DISAPPEARED. I CONTINUED WATCHING THE SAME AREA. & SOME FIFTEEN MINUTES LATER ANOTHER GROUP OF THE SAME OBJECTS APPEARED FROM THE AREA THAT I FIRST SAW THEM. THIS TIME THERE WAS EVEN MORE (AT FIRST 8 THEN 15 OBJECTS) THAT MASSED TOGETHER IN A SORT OF FORMATION. WITH A CENTRAL OBJECT THAT WAS RED. WHEN A PASSING AIRLINER WHENT NEAR. THEY ALL SEEMED TO VEER AWAY FROM IT AT SPEED AND CONTINUED ACROSS THE SKY TO A HIGH POINT AND DISSAPEARED FROM VIEW IN A MINUTE. LIKE FADING AWAY. HIGHER AND HIGHER UP INTO THE ATMOSPHERE.

Please continue on a separate sheet if necessary.

DRAWING*

①   ②

③

Your full name (Mr/Mrs/Miss/Ms)
GILLIAN GORING .... Age 32

Address........
GREAT CAMBRIDGE RD · EDMONTON · N.18

Telephone No. 807 ....(STD ....)

Occupation during last two years CASHIER

Any professional, technical or academic qualifications or special interests
PSYCHIC MATTERS

Do you object to the publication of your name?
*Yes/No. *Delete as applicable.

Today's Date 16.7.89

Signature........ G. Goring

*If preferred, use a separate sheet of paper.

Published by the British UFO Research Association (BUFORA LTD.) for the use of investigators throughout Great Britain. Further copies may be obtained from BUFORA Research Headquarters., Newchapel Observatory,

15th July 1989 (USA) – Cylindrical UFO seen

At 8.20pm a man, his wife (who was driving), their 15-year-old daughter and her friend, were travelling north on Interstate 29, approximately 30 miles south of Sioux Falls, South Dakota. The husband, who was looking out onto the horizon for buildings that would indicate they were approaching the outskirts of the city, noticed a dark, cylindrical-shaped object (apparently flat on both ends) hovering in the sky to the north and west of their location on the highway, at an elevation of about 20° to 25° above the western horizon.

Although he was unable to determine its actual size or distance, it appeared to be about as large as a typical farm grain storage silo would be when viewed from about a quarter of a mile away on the ground. He pointed out the object to the others in the car and joked about it being an *'oddball UFO'*. At first they all laughed, because of the odd shape and position of the object. The girls said it looked like a *'flying garbage can';* the wife said it looked like a *'soup can'* and he said it looked like a *'flying silo'*. He was able to view the object through a pair of small binoculars (8x21) and managed to keep it in sight for several seconds at a time, on a number of occasions. During the whole of the sighting, the object remained in a vertical position at the same angular elevation above the horizon, and appeared to remain totally stationary in the sky as they moved north on the Interstate. No markings, protrusions, lights, signs of ropes, cables, or other objects (including balloons, airplanes, helicopters) either above or below the object, could be seen. It appeared to be located above a large, open field. The sky conditions were clear to partly cloudy, with little or no wind, and the sun was setting in the west. (**Source: MUFON, Indiana**)

16th July 1989 (USA) – Was this space debris?

At 10.15pm over New Harmony, Indiana, an object was reportedly seen hovering silently at treetop level, before being seen to float toward the end of the street, heading eastwards, and then disappearing from view. One witness said it was so big that it looked like:

> *"...one of those satellite TV dishes. It was right over the top of me. It was so huge! It was white as day (outside) – no sound at all. It hovered, kind of hesitated. It didn't fly – it just floated, and it was huge".*

According to the researchers involved in conducting an investigation into this matter, there was only one problem – it may have been just a coincidence, but there had been a spectacular Russian satellite re-entry at the time of the sighting.

(**Source: MUFON, Indiana, Field Investigator Fran Ridge**)

UFO over South Carolina

At 1.30am, a security supervisor from Hilton Head Island, South Carolina, reported having sighted:

> *"...an illuminated oblong-shaped object, the length of a football field – with a large window on one side and a greyish metallic back end – moving across the sky, at about 20mph."*

The witness was able to observe the object for nearly five minutes – during which time he alerted his wife, before it picked up speed and disappeared in a streak of light.

(**Source: Greg Barrett, *Hilton Head News*, Hilton Head Island, South Carolina, 20.7.1989**)

16th July 1989 (UK) – A visit to a crop circle

Ron West received a telephone call from Melvin Grant – head of the Mansfield, Nottingham, UFO Group – with regard to the discovery of an 18ft x 17ft circle found in the crop, and visited the scene for himself.

```
REPORT ON CORNFIELD CIRCLE NEAR MANSFIELD, NOTTS
------------------------------------------------
             by Duncan Walters

Investigator,E.A.U.F.O.P.R.A; Chairman, Mansfield UFO Group.
```

The circle was first brought to the attention of Mansfield UFO Group after a married couple spotted it whilst out walking on the afternoon of Sunday July 16th. As far as we can determine, it is the first occurrance of a cornfield circle in this part of Nottinghamshire.

During the week which followed, several trips were made to the site of the circle, investigators from the National UFO Investigation Society were invited along with members of Mansfield UFO Group to take photographs, samples and measurements. Ron West of E.A.U.F.O.P.R.A. also paid the circle a visit whilst he was in the area.

Shortly afterwards, I was contacted by Ralph Noyes, after Ron told him about the circle. I sent Ralph a number of photographs as well as details of the circle.

The 'technical' information obtained from the site of the circle is as follows:

The 'circle' is in fact slightly oval, being 18 feet across at the widest diameter, and 17 feet at the narrowest.

The circle is in a field of oats, which are swirled around in a clockwise direction.

It lies 50 feet from one of two openings in the high hedgerow which borders the field.

The field in which the circle lies is only a short distance from the site of a prehistoric Barrow, called Hamilton Hill, which lies between Mansfield and Sutton-in-Ashfield.

After a report and a photograph of the circle appeareed in the Mansfield CHAD newspaper, I was contacted by a producer from BBC Radio Nottingham who came with me to the site of the circle to record an interview with me. The interview was broadcast during the morning of Tuesday August 8th.

We are at present awaiting results of soil and corn analysis.

The accompanying drawings show details of the area where the circle is.

17th July 1989 (UK) – Orange *'ball of light'* seen

At 10.30pm, Mrs M. May of Arnold Road, Dagenham, Essex, was in the process of closing the back door, when she saw an orange *'ball of light'* shoot across the sky, at terrific speed.

> *"It terrified me. I had never seen anything like that before – gone in a couple of seconds. I did tell some people about it; they looked at me as if I was 'crackers', but I know what I saw."*

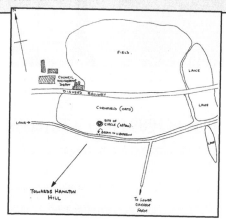

Ralph Noyes, who retired as the under-Secretary of State, in 1977, was another British government official, whose letters petitioning that the UFO matter be taken seriously, can be found in the *UK UFO* files. In 1969 he was head of Defence Secretariat 8 (DS8), and one of his responsibilities was to answer public questions about UFOs. He says he was not able to share his true opinions on the subject. In the files he states:

> *"It is only since I left the MOD (in 1977) that I have seriously tried to consider what may possibly lie behind the 'UFO phenomenon'. It was impossible to discuss it seriously within the Department; I would merely have 'rubbished' my working relationship with the RAF and scientific colleagues if I had disclosed the interest I felt in the better reports which reached us. What I retain from my MOD experience – greatly reinforced by much that I have since read – is that the 'phenomenon' is of importance."*

(From right to left, back) Ralph Noyes, Timothy Good, Gordon Creighton, with wife Joan. (Far left) Brenda Butler. (Front row) Japanese film director with (right), Dot Street

19th July 1989 (UK) – Three *'lights'* over Bradford

At 11.40pm, Engineer Keith Duggan (55) of Fraser Road, Calverley, was looking out of his bedroom window, when he saw:

> *"...a circular white 'light' – bright on its underside – drifting across the sky. This was joined by two others".*

(Source: *Bradford Telegraph & Argus*, West Yorkshire, 24.7.1989 – 'Strange lights spotted')

22nd July 1989 (USA) – Metallic *'disc'* over Trenton, Maine

At 3.30pm, 'Randy' Rhodes – a police dispatcher for the City of Ellsworth – and Bill Reiff – an attorney – took off in a Beechcraft Bonanza from the Hancock County Bar Harbour-Trenton Airport. At around 3.45pm, they spotted a huge metallic *'disc'*, shining like polished aluminium, at the 9 o'clock position, apparently at the same altitude as their plane – approximately 5,100-5,200ft. The object then suddenly moved dead ahead to the 12 o'clock position and took on a reddish or rose colour, before heading in the direction of the Maine Yankee Nuclear Power Plant in Wiscasset.

Feeling reluctant about continuing with the object in front of them, they turned back towards the Airport.

The Aerial Direction Finder was working at the time, but the DME (Distance Measuring Equipment) was not receiving. It had never before given them a problem. Three or four minutes after the object disappeared, the DME came back on.

When the two men landed, they discovered there had been power surges and outages on the ground. A spokesman for the Bangor Hydroelectric Company later reported that three limbs, falling over a transmission line when a resident cut down a tree, caused the outage.

(Source: *UFOE Vol. II*, Section III; Leland Bechtel, *MUFON UFO Journal*, November 1989, p19/ Polly Saltonstall, *Times*, Bar Harbor, Maine, 3.8.1989)

28th July 1989 (UK) – Crop circle found

Farmer John Webb (51) of Maddox Farm, Littley Green, Chelmsford, Essex, contacted the *Essex Chronicle* after being told (by one of his tractor drivers) of an area of flattened wheat in the field he was harvesting. The article was then seen by Sheridan Lane and Ron West, who spoke to Mr Webb and arranged to see him on the 19th August 1989.

At 11.30pm, Barry Kerry (47), from Colchester, was with his wife and two sons, when they saw four blue and red lights, forming a square, stationary in the sky, about two miles away. After five minutes of observation, the lights just vanished from view.

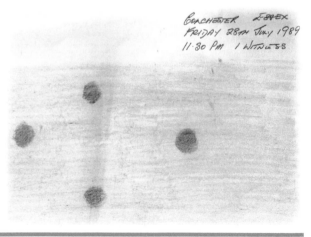

29th July 1989 (UK) – UFO over Horsham, Surrey

At 10.10pm, Jim Chambers – then head gamekeeper of the Ghyll House Farm Estate, Copsale – was sat watching a film, when his

West Sussex County Times, Horsham

4 AUG 1989

RIDDLE OF LIGHTS IN HORSHAM'S NIGHT SKY

Was this a UFO?

234

They are all sure it was

ALL of these people witnessed the strange lights in the Horsham sky on Saturday night. They are all convinced that something strange was going on. The Copsale UFO spotters are, from left: Julie Chambers, Kevin Phillips-Hill, Jamie Chambers, Ann Chambers, Jessica Chambers, Jayne Phillips-Hill, Nicholas Phillips-Hill, Alistair Phillips-Hill and Jim Chambers with Karen Phillips-Hill in front.

THE SKIES over Horsham were lit up on Saturday night by what the Chambers family of Copsale and their neighbours are convinced were UFOs.

"I've never in my life seen anything like it," said Jim Chambers, head gamekeeper on the Ghyll House Farm Estate, Copsale, describing the Unidentified Flying Objects.

"We first saw the thing about ten past ten. The film had just started on the satellite channel and our daughters came into the living room and said there was a light outside shining into their faces.

"I told them I'd come out. I looked out to the front of the house and there, across the lake and above the trees, about 300 yards away, was this great round, white light about 25 or 30 feet across with a series of lights around the edge."

His wife Ann continued: "It sat there hovering over the trees for two or three minutes and then went across to what we call The Wilderness. It went in a big circle, maybe a mile across, but all in a split second. It looked as though maybe it was mapping the area because it moved over towards Southwater and moved around in a circle again."

The Chambers telephoned their neighbours, Jayne and Kevin Phillips-Hill, who came out of their house to see the bizarre sight.

"I've never seen anything like that before in my entire life," said Mrs Phillips-Hill. "The speed of the thing was absolutely incredible."

Mr Chambers said that they had also seen an airplane in the sky at the same time. "The difference between the two was remarkable. The lights were moving so quickly that the normal aircraft looked as though it was standing still. After it moved over towards Southwater another one appeared just above and to the left of the first one. They were each going around in circles at the same rate."

The object made no noise and Mr Chambers says they have seen no signs of any kind that it may have left behind.

by Jan Hatwell

"No burning or trampled grass or anything like that. And it was perfectly quiet. The children didn't hear any noise at first either. Jessica, our four-year-old, thought it was her mum shining a torch in through her bedroom window for a joke."

Both families, a total of ten people, sat and watched the phenomenon for about 45 minutes after which it disappeared in the direction of Broadbridge Heath. "We called the airport and Gatwick said they didn't have anything on their radar. The police gave us two numbers to call if we thought we'd seen a UFO, one in Dorking and one in Redhill, but they were both unobtainable."

Derek Head of Cape Copse, Rudgwick, said he was travelling from Five Oaks towards Rudgwick on Saturday night about midnight. He stopped his car and got out to watch the sky.

"There were four white hazy lights and they appeared to be elliptical shapes radiating from a central point which wasn't moving at all." He said that there should have been a logical explanation but he couldn't see any lights from the ground projecting upwards on to a cloud.

Reports of a laser show on Saturday night in the Godalming area were confirmed by Surrey Police. A spokesman said that there had been a large party in Thursley, near Hindhead, a distance of about 20 miles as the crow flies from Horsham.

"We were inundated with phone calls. Godalming police station in particular. We despatched a unit to an address in Thursley where we found a noisy but orderly party, with the guests enjoying a laser light show.

"It consisted of a set of rotating lights and there was so much low cloud that the lower half of the beam wasn't visible. So it wasn't apparent that the lights were coming from ground level. The party continued and we had sightings of the lights reported from as far away as Haslemere and North Guildford."

But Kevin Phillips-Hill was adamant. "Nothing anyone can say will convince me that it wasn't a UFO. We're on the flight path here and we know the difference between a plane or a helicopter and what we saw."

daughters told him about a *'light'* seen outside, shining into their faces. Jim and his wife, Ann, went outside and saw, approximately 300yds away, across the lake and above the trees, a white *'light'*, 25-30ft across, with a series of lights around its edges.

> *"It sat there, hovering over the trees, for two to three minutes, and then went across to what we call the wilderness; it went in a big circle – maybe a mile across – but all in a split second. It looked as though it was mapping the area, because it moved towards Southwater in a circle again."*

The Chambers telephoned their neighbours – Jayne and Kevin Philips-Hill – who came out of their house to look for themselves. *"I've never seen anything like it before in my life; the speed of the thing was absolutely incredible",* said Mrs Philips-Hill.

A total of 10 people watched the object for 45 minutes, until it disappeared in the direction of Broadbridge Heath.

Ghyll House Farm

The family strongly rejected an explanation put forward, later, that they had seen laser lights being operated from the Godalming area, on the same evening.

(Source: *West Sussex County Times*, Horsham, 4.8.1989 – 'Was this a UFO?')

Deptford & Peckham Mercury

10 AUG 1989

THEY'VE SEEN THE LIGHT!

2374

Were they UFOs?

UFO SPOTTERS have been flooding the Mercury with calls since a couple spotted strange lights two weeks ago.

In last week's Mercury we reported that Catford couple Don and Lynette Simpson had seen the bright, white lights sweeping across the sky.

Suggestions as to the cause of the unexplained sighting have ranged from fireworks displays to the 21st birthday celebrations of London Weekend Television, but these lines of inquiry have drawn blanks.

Civil servant John Costin told the Mercury he'd seen the same sort of thing before and wasn't particularly bothered when he saw the four bright lights as

he walked along Peckham's Southampton Way at midnight on Saturday, July 29.

"The lights were going into the centre and then fanning out again, and I remembered I'd seen the same sort of thing before over the area," John said.

Polytechnic lecturer Nick Dunleavy, of Alanthus Close, Lee, spotted the lights as he was leaving the Royal Festival Hall.

"They seemed to be coming from the Fleet Street area, but they definitely weren't fireworks. They were more like spotlights," he said.

Landscape gardener David Champion saw the lights when he was taking his dog for a walk along Scarlet Road, on the Downham Estate.

Camden Town-based company Theatre Projects Services laid claim this week to the mysterious UFOs.

The company said the strange sights in SE London were in fact the result of their lights being used at a bash for barristers in the city.

The lights were also used at celebrations marking this week's premiere of Batman.

30th July 1989 (UK) – UFO over Essex

In the evening, Cherie Grant, from Colchester, heard a *'whooshing'* sound, followed by the sighting of an illuminated circular object, estimated to be 10-15ft across, showing half a dozen or more green lights underneath it, slowly drifting across the sky, travelling from the direction of Leinster Road, towards Arterial Road, 20-30ft off the ground.

The incident was reported to the MOD. A representative of that department dismissed the sighting, saying:

> *"I don't believe in UFOs. The Air Traffic Control Radar, at West Drayton, is more interested in keeping a lookout over the North Sea for possible hostile aircraft."*

(Source: *Yellow Advertiser*, 4.8.1989 – 'Flying Saucer' whoos Cherie with soft green lights')

'Flying Saucer' whoos Cherie with soft, green lights

A WHOOING sound was the first indication Cherie Grant had of possibly other worldly mysteries gliding past her Laindon home.

And hearing the sound shortly after midnight on Sunday morning she looked from her bedroom window to see a round, illuminated object drifting slowly past overhead.

"It was about 10 to 15 feet across and had half-a-dozen or more green lights beneath it," said 23-year-old Cherie.

The object seemed in no hurry, and was drifting some several feet higher than a telegraph pole, recalled Cherie.

"It seemed to come from the direction of Leinster Road and travel towards the Arterial Road," added Cherie.

A spokesman at West Drayton air traffic control was unable to confirm if any unusual radar contact had been made over the area.

But a spokesman at the Ministry of Defence admitted the MoD "did not believe in UFOs."

He said: "The air traffic control radar at West Drayton is more interested in keeping a look out over the north sea regions for possible hostile aircraft."

Mail on Sunday, London

30 JUL 1989

Night sky poser

STRANGE lights in the sky over southern England left scores of people baffled last night.

Some thought that the mystery objects were UFOs and alerted police.

Scotland Yard received dozens of calls from as far apart as Hackney in London's East End and Haslemere, Surrey, from people who saw bright white lights darting across the night sky.

Police mechanic Peter Ridley, who lives in Limehouse, said: 'The lights looked really strange. I've never seen anything like them. They went round in circles, and moved at enormous speed.'

London Weekend Television's 21st birthday celebrations were blamed for the phenomenon, but a LWT spokesman said celebrations do not start until today.

31st July 1989 (UK) – Hamburger-shaped UFO

Katherine Briscoe from Streatham, London, was driving home from a holiday to Worcester, and had just passed Bristol on the M5 Motorway, when she was forced to brake, as vehicles in front began to slow down. Looking out of the window, she saw a huge hamburger-shaped object – dark metallic in colour, with a band of windows around the centre – hovering over the right-hand side of the southbound carriageway, about 90ft in the air, with rings of coloured light underneath it.

> *"It seemed to be watching or waiting for something. As we drew level, it suddenly moved a mile away to the east, leaving a faint trail behind it. The next day or soon after, I read about a UFO being seen in the newspapers."*

UFO? No, it's just some light entertainment

by Peter Gruner

LONDON'S strangest UFO mystery was explained today with the likelihood that the lights spotted over London were two or more laser shows.

People who saw the searchbeam-style lights for up to 20 minutes said they moved in circles at enormous speed, came together and then separated, finally shooting off across the sky.

Rock star Roger Taylor, of Queen, held a laser light show and party at his home near Godalming. A Surrey police spokesman said: "That would explain many of the reports we received that night." But he was baffled about how people 40 miles away in North London could have seen the same lights.

That was explained by advertising executive Sarah Tellerman, 26, who tracked the mystery lights in her car to the Grays Inn Ball in a square off Grays Inn Road.

She said: "I saw the lights over Covent Garden and then followed them to the source, a private party being held by solicitors.

"The police arrived and so did other light spotters. The party was a very big affair and that's where the lights appeared to come from."

One of the party guests later revealed that four large blue searchlights were used, and may have been seen over a wide area.

A Scotland Yard spokesman said: "We received dozens of reports from very normal and quite sober citizens. At first we thought someone in North London was holding a laser show, but could find no report of one."

One witness, Malcolm Cox, said: "We were walking to a party in Islington when we saw the lights and watched them for about 15 minutes. There were about 10 of them moving in circles and eclipsing each other. I've never seen anything like it."

Another theory—quickly discounted—was that it was London Weekend Television holding a 21st anniversary light show over the Thames. That wasn't until last night.

The lights were explained by weatherman Philip Eden, who said they had been reflected in cloud.

"Cloud formations were very low over the weekend, about 1500 ft above the ground," he said. "It is quite common for headlights or laser lights to be reflected off clouds and it would explain the lights."

ROGER TAYLOR: Laser party

LONDON EVENING STANDARD 31 JULY 1989

Barking & Dagenham Post. Essex
−2 AUG 1989

15 more saw orange UFOs

EVERYONE'S seeing UFOs!

Since the Post reported last week that three people had reported strange orange objects in the night sky over Barking and Ilford, another 15 witnesses have come forward.

Roy Lake of the East Anglian UFO and Paranormal Society said most of the people who contacted the society did so after reading the report about mystery objects in the north-eastern sky.

Isle of Wight County Press, Newport, I.O.W.
4 AUG 1989

Woman sees mystery object in night sky

A WOOTTON woman looked out of her bedroom window on Sunday night and saw what she believes to be a UFO.

Mrs. Dorrie Smith, of St. Edmund's Walk, said, "It was 11.55 pm and when I looked out of the window I saw a brilliant white object in the sky.

"It was completely round and a mass of lights. It went right over the house.

"At first I thought it was a star but it definitely was not, and it was not an aircraft," said Mrs. Smith.

Island police said they had received no reports from other people in the area of strange objects in the sky.

AUGUST 1989

1st August 1989 – The meteorite season

THURROCK RECORDER

6 AUG 1990

MORE SECRET THAN A-BOMBS!

Sky watching for UFOs

AUGUST signals the start of the meteorite season and hundreds of people throughout Britain will begin watching the sky at night.

Peter Oliver, from Lucas Avenue, Grays, and Roy Lake, from Barking, will be looking for more than just meteorites.

For Peter, 42, and Roy, 51, are chairman and president respectively of the East Anglian Unidentified Flying Object and Paranormal Research Association which numbers churchmen, spiritualists and former army personnel among its members.

Peter said: "Before anyone starts ridiculing us, let me say I do not believe in little green men jumping out of saucer-shaped spaceships and terrorising the public."

REPORTS: SUE FENWICK

"But I do believe there are UFOs in our skies and some very strange events have happened over the years which defy explanation."

Roy said: "A lot of the time, what seem like UFOs or paranormal events can be explained after rigorous research which we carry out.

Peter added: "For every 100 UFO sightings, only two will remain unidentified, the rest will turn out to be aircraft, searchlights, hoaxes or other phenomena."

Peter went on: "The famous Project Blue Book, the American Air Force's UFO research programme for investigating UFOs ran from 1947 to 1969, then stopped suddenly.

"UFO sightings have increased dramatically since then but no government will admit publicly their existence - UFOs are more secret than nuclear arms!

"With people's help, we want to build up a dossier of factual evidence on UFO sightings so the government can no longer deny their existence.

"Something is going on up there and not many people know what it is."

'Evidence'

He added with a wry smile: "We have an inkling but we can't say without further evidence from the public!"

So get your telescopes out and get sky-watching.

There's an organised skywatch at Thames-view, Chadwell St Mary, on Saturday August 11 between 7.30-8pm.

And if you see anything out of the ordinary, telephone their 24-hour hotline on Grays Thurrock 373065.

If you are over 18 and fancy becoming a UFO/paranormal investigator, telephone the hotline or Grays Thurrock 377280 or 081-594-4797.

Something odd is going on in our skies and these two men are determined to find out what. Roy Lake (left), president, and Peter Oliver, chairman of the East Anglian UFO and Paranormal Research Association, spend their evenings sky-watching with the help of powerful telescopes, maps and compasses.

'Dossier of evidence'

QUEST PUBLICATIONS
12 MILES HILL STREET,
LEEDS LS7 2EQ
ENGLAND.

29/≡90

22 AUG 1990

2374

Pete has his eyes on the skies

A GRAYS man is waging his own personal war against Government defence chiefs as he watches the Thurrock skies for strange, nocturnal lights.

Peter Oliver, of Lucas Road, is determined to lift the lid off the UFO mystery and at the same time dispel the 'little green man' myth, so often associated with the subject.

The 42-year-old is head of the East Anglian Unidentified Flying Object and Paranormal Research Association and, with the help of his members, hopes to unearth the truth about the flying saucers - seen by thousands of reliable witnesses the world over.

The father-of-two said: "I must stress that I do not believe in little green men from Mars jetting around in their spacecraft and then jumping out on unsuspecting victims.

"I believe the occupants of the crafts frequently spotted in our skies would be very much like us.

"I have had letters and reports from 'so many genuine people who have seen strange things, they just can't be ignored."

Peter, an electrician's mate at Tilbury Power Station, keeps huge files of witness reports and is in constant contact with

Pete with his telescope and dog Casey

some of the most prominent authorities connected with the subject.

But he is disillusioned by the Government's denial of the extra-terrestrials' existence and plans to gather enough hard-core evidence to prove once and for all the Ministry of Defence are covering something up.

He said: "Earth cannot be the only inhabited planet in the entire universe. There must be other life-forms out there somewhere.

"What we need is for the governments of the world - who have undeniable proof of alien existence - to publicly admit it."

2nd August 1989 (UK) – Four small lights seen

At 1.45am, two police officers observed four small white lights, moving in an erratic manner, constantly fading and brightening across an almost clear sky above Kings Lynn. (**Source: FOI Documentation**)

Dome-shaped object seen

At 10.15pm the same day (2.8.1989) Julie Chant of Greenhill Road, Norton Radstock, Avon, was settling her son – Michael – down for the night, when she heard a distinct humming sound. Looking out of the window she saw a dome-shaped object with a flashing red light on top and four bright lights in front of it, emitting an amber glow. She shouted for her husband – Richard – who came to have a look. After the UFO had gone, they telephoned the police and reported the matter to Police Sergeant Martin Purchase, who said they had made a note of the incident and were interested in further reports. (**Source:** *Norton & Radstock Star*, **2.8.1989** – 'UFO sighting by Mum')

2nd August 1989 (Tasmania) – UFO over Jericho, Tasmania

At 10.22pm, a taxi driver was taking two train drivers to the railway station on the north-south line. They saw an object hovering in the clear north-eastern part of the sky over Jericho, Tasmania, described as disc shape, showing four dark square areas along its base, and giving off a very powerful white glare. Seconds later it was gone. No other reports were received and the local police know of no 'local' explanation. (**Source: TUFOIC**)

10th August 1989 (UK) – UFO over Essex & Kent

At midnight, two people saw a very large round object, apparently made of a dark metallic material, about 200ft in diameter, with blue, green, and red lights, spinning silently in an anticlockwise direction, hovering at a height of about 150ft. Suddenly, it shot out to sea, at tremendous speed.

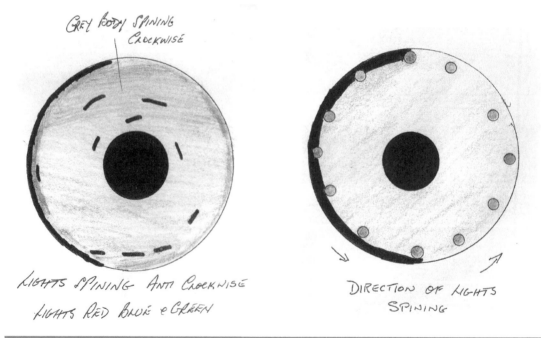

EAST ANGLIAN U.F.O. & PARANORMAL RESEARCH ASSOCIATION

SECTION A   SIGHTING ACCOUNT FORM

Please write an account of your sighting, make a drawing of what you saw and then answer the questions in section B overleaf as fully as possible. Write in BLOCK CAPITALS using a ball point pen.

On Wednesday Night / Thursday morning 9th / 10th August 1989 I was driving along the Sea front, along Belton Gardens — New Road the time being 12.05 pm. Suddenly this huge object shot straight across my field of vision, it was about 150-200 foot up, in the sky. It was a roundish metallic object with Red, Blue Green and Yellow lights spinning in an anti clockwise direction the object of a dark grey colour seemed to be moving in a clockwise direction, It was at least 200/250 foot across, domed shaped, It had a dark circle in the underneath, I only saw it for a few seconds it was moving so fast. It crossed the estuary going into Kent where I lost sight of it There was no noise, and that was strange for an object that size...

Please continue on a separate sheet if necessary.

DRAWING*

LIGHTS MOVING ANTI CLOCKWISE

→ KENT

DARK CIRCLE

Your full name (Mr/Mrs/~~Miss/Ms~~)
..... ANGELA ..... Age 47
Address..... BROOMFIELD AVE
LEIGH ON SEA ESSEX
Telephone No. ..... (STD 0702)
Occupation during last two years.....
Housewife

Any professional, technical or academic qualifications or special interests
.....

Do you object to the publication of your name?
Yes/No. *Delete as applicable.

Today's Date. 26-8-1989
Signature..... (MRS)

* If preferred, use a separate sheet of paper.

A woman in Leigh-on-Sea, driving home at midnight, was astonished when:

"...*a huge round object shot right across my view. It was approximately 200-250 ft across and the same distance up, and had blue, green and red lights, spinning anticlockwise. The object then crossed the Thames Estuary and headed towards the direction of Kent*".

Three other witnesses reported a similar object in Leigh-on-Sea at the same time

(Source: Ron West, East Anglian UFO & Paranormal Research Association)

EAST ANGLIAN U.F.O. & PARANORMAL RESEARCH ASSOCIATION

SECTION A

SIGHTING ACCOUNT FORM

Please write an account of your sighting, make a drawing of what you saw and then answer the questions in section B overleaf as fully as possible. Write in **BLOCK CAPITALS** using a ball point pen.

I RECALL LYING IN MY FRIENDS BACK GARDEN WATCHING THE METEOR SHOWER WHEN DURING A SPACE OF TIME DURING WHICH WE SAW NOTHING WE ALL SUDDENLY NOTICED AN OBJECT IN THE SKY WHICH AS I RECALL WAS A DULL ORANGE GLOW & DIAMOND IN SHAPE. IT SEEMED TO APPEAR FROM OUT OF THIN AIR & SEEMED TO BE MOVING NOT ONLY DOWNWARDS BUT SIDEWAYS AS WELL AT SOME A CONSIDERABLE SPEED. THIS MAY SOUND CONTRADICTORY WHEN I SAY THAT THE TOTAL TIME SPAN INVOLVED IN MY SIGHTING WAS NO MORE THAN TWO SECONDS BUT THAT IS WHAT MY MEMORY TELLS ME.

THE OBJECT WAS LIKE NOTHING I HAD SEEN BEFORE & THIS EFFECT WAS OBVIOUSLY HEIGHTENED BY IT BEING IN THE SKY & VISABLE IN DARKNESS.

Please continue on a separate sheet if necessary.

DRAWING*

A VERY APPROXIMATE & VERY BASIC SKETCH.

*If preferred, use a separate sheet of paper.

Your full name (Mr/~~Mrs/Miss/Ms~~)
CHRISTOPHER P. MADDOX. Age 25
Address 6, POOLE ROAD, HORN-
CHURCH, ESSEX, RM11 3AS
Telephone No. 50482 (STD. 04024)
Occupation during last two years LIFE ASSURANCE TECHNICAL ADVISOR

Any professional, technical or academic qualifications or special interests
A'LEVEL, O'LEVELS, GENERAL INTERESTS

Do you object to the publication of your name?
*~~Yes~~/No. *Delete as applicable. NO
Today's Date 7/9/89
Signature [signature]

EAST ANGLIAN U.F.O. & PARANORMAL RESEARCH ASSOCIATION

SECTION A **SIGHTING ACCOUNT FORM**

Please write an account of your sighting, make a drawing of what you saw and then answer the questions in section B overleaf as fully as possible. Write in **BLOCK CAPITALS** using a ball point pen.

TWO OBJECTS WERE OBSERVED FROM THE GARDEN AT 21.09 THEY WERE CIRCULAR IN SHAPE AND MOVING ABOUT SOMETIMES SLOWLY AND FAIRLY FAST AT TIMES SIMILAR TO A SEARCH LIGHT BEING OPERATED BUT THERE WAS NO BEAM FROM THE GROUND WHERE THE OBJECTS WERE OBSERVED WAS A FAIR AMOUNT OF CLOUD AND TO THE SOUTH OF THE OBJECTS WAS A LARGE AREA OF CLOUDNESS SKY AND THE OBJECTS AT NO TIME ENTERED THE CLOUDNESS SKY

Please continue on a separate sheet if necessary.

DRAWING*

CLEAR SKIES   CLOUD   2 OBJECTS

MOON

*If preferred, use a separate sheet of paper.

Your full name (Mr/Mrs/Miss/Mst) J T CAMPBELL Age 73

Address 39 LUCAS ROAD GRAYS

Telephone No. 72031 (STD)

Occupation during last two years RETIRED

Any professional, technical or academic qualifications or special interests

Do you object to the publication of your name? *Yes/No. *Delete as applicable.

Today's Date 2-10-89

Signature J J Campbell

13th August 1989 (USA) – UFO leaves ground traces

A resident (84) of Mansura, Las Vegas, was in the backyard of his house when he saw a small yellow oval or disc-shaped object a short distance away, at ground level. He called out to a female neighbour, who also saw it from the back door of her house. The 3ft wide object hovered silently and moved about at ground level, for approximately five minutes, some 30ft away, and then circled a tree, before flying away vertically and soon out of sight. A search of the area revealed some ground traces on the lawn.

(**Sources:** Hal Price, *MUFON Field Investigations Database,* case 890806; Dan Wright, *MUFON UFO Journal,* December 1992)

At 11pm on a clear night, a 31-year-old woman from Cantonment, Florida, was watching TV when she heard what sounded like drag racers outside.

She looked out of a window and saw an object *"like two paper plates, one inverted on top of the other, hovering above the house across the street from me"*.

She went to get a camera. When she returned, the object was gone. She estimated the object as about 12ft high and 40ft wide. It was silver in colour and had two rows of ten lights, each about 3ft in diameter, along the centre-line. The top row of lights were red, and the bottom row white. The object was moving about 5mph west to east, and appeared to rotate. The witness reported seeing a similar object in Germany, in 1976.

(Source: *MUFON UFO DATABASE*, Portion of Reports from the Files at MUFON Headquarters, July 1999, Sequin TX, CD-ROM, Case Log #891006a, by Carol Salisberry and Rex Salisberry)

14th August 1989 (UK) – UFO seen over Mildenhall

16th August 1989 (UK) – West Yorkshire UFOs

RAF MILDENHALL

---

16 AUG 1989 Bradford Telegraph & Argus
West Yorkshire

Mystery of the flying 'traffic lights'

FLYING 'traffic lights' are the latest in a string of UFO sightings.

"It is unusual because the object or its effects were seen by three people independently," said Dave Barclay of the West Yorkshire UFO-watchers organisation Independent UFO Network.

The first report came from a Horsforth man who has a responsible position at Leeds-Bradford Airport,

said Mr Barclay. "At 2.45am he saw a bright object as large as the full moon cross the sky in about five seconds. He thought at first it was a plane about to crash and was about to alert the emergency services. But it kept on flying until it was out of view."

The second report at 2.44am came from an amateur astronomer who lives near Bingley.

"He saw the same thing but as he watched it went through a colour change from bright greenish white to a very bright red and then it became

a dark object before it went out of view.

"It was visible for seven seconds." He put it down to a meteorite burning up, but a group of 50 Todmorden astronomers who were out on the same night saw nothing at all."

The third report came from a Baildon woman who woke up at 2.48am to find her bedroom bathed in an incredible green light. "It changed from green to brilliant red and made her lace curtains look as though they had been dipped in phosphorescent

blood. But when she looked out of the window the source of the light had disappeared," said Mr Barclay.

"We have had many UFO reports in the Bradford area. The Pennines are undoubtedly a 'hot spot' and many UFO spotters from the south come up her to investigate reports

● The Independent UFO Network is inviting top American UFO researcher, nuclear physicist Dr Stanton Friedman to speak at a seminar in the Library Theatre, Sheffield in October 23.

Mansfield UFO Group

Members of this organisation canvassed shoppers in the town centre, handing out leaflets and asking people to report any UFO sightings they might have come across.

17th August 1989 (UK) – A visit to a crop circle

18th August (USA) – Triangular UFO over Carolina

At 3pm on the above date (some accounts give the 8th) security guard Paul Moore at the McGuire Nuclear Plant, Lake Norman, North Carolina, sighted a reddish-brown triangular shaped UFO, at an altitude of about 300ft, moving at a 45° angle, heading directly for the Nuclear Plant's sub-station.

"It was completely silent. The pointed end was forward. It was about the size of a Stealth bomber. Within seconds, it vanished from sight."

(Source: *Lincoln Times-News*, 6.9.1989/George D. Fawcett, MUFON State Director, North Carolina)

19th August 1989 (UK) – A visit to a crop circle, Littley Green, Essex

After learning of a crop circle found in a farmer's field, Ron West and Sheridan Lane went to have a look. These are their written notes:

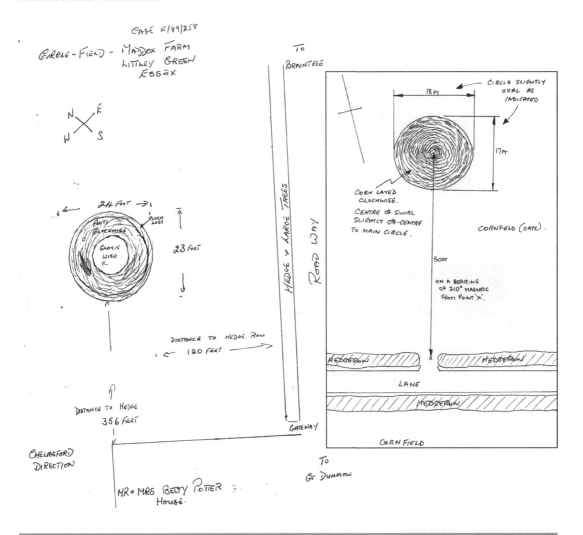

Report by Sheridan Lane on the 'Wheat Field' Circle at Littley Green, Near
Chelmsford, Essex.
Date of visit: Saturday 19th August 1989.
Date of this report: Sunday 10th September 1989.

I walked slowly towards the circle, and when I reached a distance of 12ft
from it I began to feel a mild energy coming up out of the ground. I stood
still for a few minutes, experiencing this. Three feet nearer, this same
energy became stronger, while similtaneously I felt energy penetrating me
from the actual circle. This came towards me in a horizontal line. From
this point onwards these same two energies continued, but 3ft from the
circle the power once more strengthened, while at the same time a third
power source made itself felt. I could sense tiny circles of energy
entering my finger tips and hands. Through one hand they moved clockwise,
and through the other one - anti-clockwise. Unfortunately, due to being
very busy, and then going on holiday, I have been unable to type this
report sooner, and consequently have forgotten which hand experienced
clockwise circular motion, and vis versa. Ron West kindly took notes
for me on my feelings at the time, but this detail has not been entered
by him. I couldn't have written my own notes because such actions would
have formed a distraction to the actual 'sensing'.

From the distance of 3 ft I began to pace the circle, moving towards the
South, and on around it to reach East. Between South and East the sensations
began to diminish. This continued around to the North orientation. Between
North and West, and on between West and South the strength of the field
of force returned. My initial approach to the circle had been from this
direction, in a straight line of walking.

Inside the actual circle the energy was different. It seemed to flow in
tiny circles, clockwise, and anti- clockwise; similar to air movements.
I stood within different parts of the circle, and moved round it several
times to establish this.

Three days later, Ron West and I returned to the scene with Mark Parnham
and my eight year old son. (I could find no-one to look after him).
My son had been told nothing of my original 'sensing'. He only knew we
were coming to look at a strange circle of Wheat. When he was standing
3ft from it, he said: "Mummy, my skin feels all funny, it's tingling".
Inside the circle he found several 'hot spots' where he told us he felt
heat coming up out of the ground under his feet. I felt it where he stood.

Three days earlier the weather had been sunny and hot. On this day - Teusday
22nd August - it was cooler and much more cloudy, with only occasional bursts
of sunshine. My son felt these 'hot spots' under a cloudy sky. The presence
of hot sunshine disguised it.

CASE E/89/258

 **East Anglian UFO & Paranormal Research**

Ron West
95 Chilburn Road
Great Clacton
Essex
CO15 4PE

TEL:
(0255) 431391

REPORT OF A CIRCLE IN A WHEAT FIELD INVESTIGATED BY;-
RON WEST. CHAIRMAN E.A.U.F.O.P.R.A.
SHERIDAN LANE. INVESTIGATOR & RESEARCHER E.A.U.F.O.P.R.A.

On the 17th August 1989, Sheridan and myself were sent a newspaper cutting
from the Essex Chronical dated 11th August 1989. It was headed " Have
Littley Green Men Landed," and showed a picture of a Mr John Webb, Farm
Bailiff, standing just outside the circle. I made contact with Mr Webb,
and arrainged to visit him on Saturday 19th August 1989, with Sheridan Lane.
Sheridan Lane's report on a seperate sheet.
On entering the field at Littley Green, we found that it had been harvested
but a circle of wheat had been left around the circle of flattened wheat.
On looking at the circle of flattened wheat, the first thing that I noted,
was that the wheat within the circle had been flattened in two ways i.e;
From the outer circumferance, approx six foot of the wheat was flattened in
a anti-clockwise direction, but the inner section of wheat was flattened in
clockwise direction. All the wheat was ' matted and entwined '.
The circle was sharply defined at the edges. On taking the measurement of
the circle, I found it to be slightly oval, i.e 24 feet by 23 feet.
The soil within the circle had not been disturbed in anyway. (lose soil, or
holes.) The wheat within the circle, looked to be, old, darkened an weathered.
Yet the wheat still standing seemed to be fresh looking and thriving.
Samples of wheat from within and from outside the circle, have been taken,
also samples of the soil from with and outside, for testing.
The circle lies 120 feet from a hedge of bushes and trees boardering a road
way, and 356 feet from the garden hedge of a Mr & Mrs Potter, of Coombe Hill,
Littley Green.
My own view on this circle is that it is genuine. I have seen too many circles
in corn and wheat fields. So I can say that this circle is not a hoax.

Ron West.
Chairman, Investigator.
E.A.U.F.O.P.R.A.

A SIGHTING ACCOUNT FORM (East Anglian U.F.O. & Paranormal Research Association), REF. 1989, E/89/258, RW/GL 28789.

Account: "One of my tractor drivers informed me that we had a circle of flattened wheat in the field, he was harvesting. I went with him and inspected the circle. I then reported it to the farm owner also the owner of farm workers."

DRAWING: WHEAT FIELD. (24' × 23')

Your full name: JOHN WEBB, Age 51
Address: MADDOCK FARM, LITLEY GREEN, ESSEX
Telephone No. 361473 (STD 0245)
Occupation during last two years: FARM BAILIFF
Do you object to the publication of your name? Yes/No
Today's Date: 19-8-89
Signature: J. Webb

Mid-August 1989 (UK) – Did a UFO land in Kent?

At 1.30am, Wilfred Gomez and Simon Millington were driving along Nash Road, Margate, when they saw:

> "...what looked like an upturned satellite TV dish, covered in flashing lights, making a peculiar noise, descending through the sky about a quarter of a mile away. We went to investigate further and found a 60ft circle in the field, with a smaller one nearby".

The next morning, after contacting the Canterbury-based *Adscene Newspaper*, the couple returned to the location, along with photographer – Malcolm Ganderton – who took a photo, which was published in an edition of the newspaper, dated 18th August 1989. A police spokesman was quoted as saying: "*We have no record of this sighting. However, American A-10 Aircraft, based at Manston, often fly at night and, from a distance, can look strange.*" (**Source: *Adscene Newspaper*, Canterbury, Kent, 18.8.1989 – 'Saucer Mystery'/ Quest Publications, Yorkshire**) [Authors: It has been claimed this report was a hoax, but we have found no evidence to corroborate whether it was or wasn't]

26th August 1989 (UK) – Triangular UFO refuels!

In August 1989, ˙Chris Gibson – a Scottish oil-exploration engineer and, at the time, a member of the British Royal Observer Corps (ROC) – was working on the oil rig *'Galveston Key'* in the North Sea when he noticed an aircraft in the shape of a pure isosceles triangle, refuelling from a KC-135 Stratotanker alongside two F-111s.

The sighting was to lead to much speculation as to its identity, bearing in mind the circumstances one supposes that it may have been the mysterious Aurora hypersonic spy plane. Another possible explanation is Northrop's A-17 Stealth attack plane.

Triangular craft seen

"I was working in the indefatigable field on the jack-up rig 'Galveston Key', *in August 1989. My colleague, Graeme Winton, went out on deck but returned immediately. He told me to 'have a look at this'. We went outside and Graeme pointed skywards. I had been at university with Graeme and he knew of my interest in aircraft. As far as Graeme was concerned it was a formation of aircraft and he reckoned I'd be interested. I looked up, saw the tanker and the F-111s, but was amazed to see the triangle. I am trained in instant recognition, but this triangle stopped me dead in my tracks. My first thought was that it was another F-111, but there were no 'gaps'; it was too long and it didn't look like one. My next thought was that it was an F-117, as the highly swept platform of the F-117 had just been made public. Again the triangle was too long and had no gaps. After considering and rejecting a Mirage IV, I was totally out of ideas. Here was an aircraft, flying overhead, not too high and not particularly fast. A recognition gift and I was clueless. This was a new experience. Graeme asked me what was going on. I watched as the formation flew overhead and told him that the big one was a KC-135 Stratotanker, the two on the left were F-111s and that I didn't know what the fourth aircraft was. Graeme said, 'I thought you were an expert?' I said 'I am', to which Graeme replied, 'Some expert!'*

It was obvious to me that this aircraft was something 'dodgy'. I watched the formation for a minute or two and went back inside with Graeme.

At the time I was writing the aircraft recognition manual and had a Danish Luftmelderkorpset Flykendingsbog in my briefcase. This is probably the best aircraft recognition book ever produced. I looked through it, but nothing matched.

Restrictions of the Official Secrets Act

I then sketched what I had seen and sent this to Peter Edwards, who was a Group Officer in the ROC and was also on the recognition team. We discussed what to do about it but decided that if it was reported through official channels, it would be at best rubbished, at worst lead to trouble. Having signed the Official Secrets Act I didn't want to jeopardize my position in the recognition team, so I kept my mouth shut. I told other members of the recognition team in the hope that they could shed some light on the subject. On returning home I had a look through my book collection. The only aircraft which came close to matching what I had seen was a Handley Page HP115. It was not one of them. Whether this aircraft was an Aurora is debatable – my background precludes jumping to conclusions based on a single piece of evidence."

(Source: *Chris Gibson's Aurora Sighting* by Simon Gray)

˙Chris Gibson was working as a drilling technologist for a major oilfield service company. He holds an Honour degree in geology, with some knowledge of engineering, geophysics and chemistry. He has also completed a postgraduate course in systems analysis, and was a member of the Royal Observers Corps for 13 years and member of the ROC's aircraft recognition team for 12 of those years. He is considered to be an expert and produced an aircraft recognition manual for the ROC.

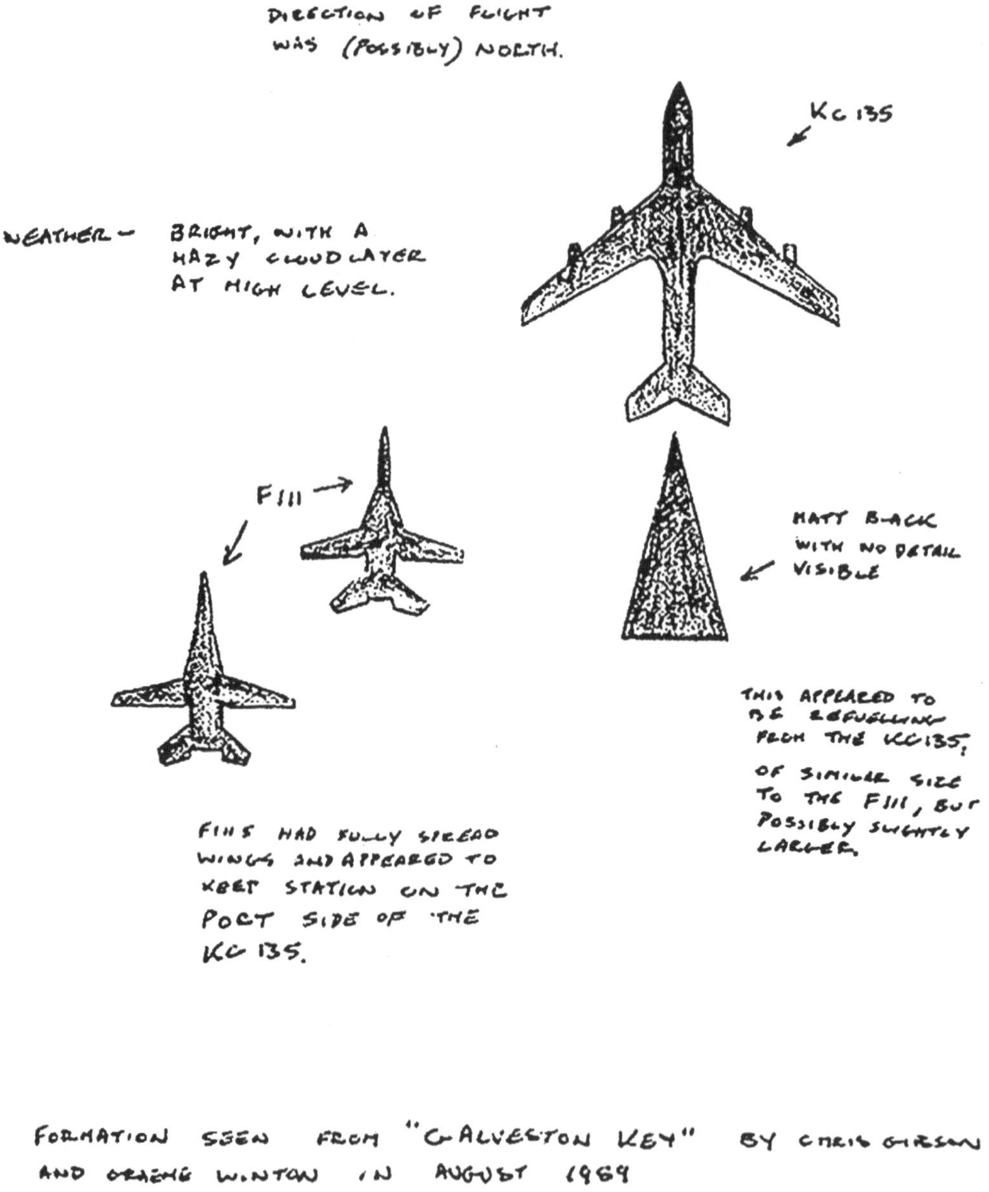

DIRECTION OF FLIGHT
WAS (POSSIBLY) NORTH.

KC 135

WEATHER — BRIGHT, WITH A
HAZY CLOUD LAYER
AT HIGH LEVEL.

F111

MATT BLACK
WITH NO DETAIL
VISIBLE

THIS APPEARED TO
BE REFUELLING
FROM THE KC135,
OF SIMILAR SIZE
TO THE F111, BUT
POSSIBLY SLIGHTLY
LARGER.

F111 HAD FULLY SPREAD
WINGS AND APPEARED TO
KEEP STATION ON THE
PORT SIDE OF THE
KC 135.

FORMATION SEEN FROM "GALVESTON KEY" BY CHRIS GIBSON
AND GRAEME WINTON IN AUGUST 1969

SKETCH by CHRIS GIBSON

28th August 1989 (UK) – Triangular UFO over Essex

DUP			YEAR	NUMBER	INVESTIGATOR		CASE SUMMARY		DATE	
		REF.	1989	E/89/	*Ron West*				TIME	
INVEST REF:	28989				EVALUATOR				LOCATION	
RETURN FORM TO:-									EVAL'N	
									UFO CLASS	
									CLOSED	

EAST ANGLIAN U.F.O. & PARANORMAL RESEARCH ASSOCIATION

SECTION A   **SIGHTING ACCOUNT FORM**

Please write an account of your sighting, make a drawing of what you saw and then answer the questions in section B overleaf as fully as possible. Write in **BLOCK CAPITALS** using a ball point pen.

At 4.20 pm on the 28th August 1989 Monday morning it was. I let my dog out he had been scratching at the door to go out I walked out a little way with him. I looked up into the sky, I saw a diamond shaped object, the size of the bungalow roof it had a brilliant round white light in its centre which had a glow but no beam. I walked further down the garden path to investigate further. The object then moved overhead, there was no sound as it went overhead and I did not feel frightened, Yes there was a noise It was like a flight of ducks or geese. It was then that I felt very cold, I had come out without any shoes on, and the cold was coming up through my feet So I went in not thinking anymore about the object

Please continue on a separate sheet if necessary.

DRAWING*

Your full name (Mr/Mrs/~~Miss~~/~~Ms~~)
BRENDA EAST   Age 82
Address 32 RUTLAND ROAD
CHELMSFORD ESSEX
Telephone No. 283348 (STD. 0245)
Occupation during last two years
Housewife
Any professional, technical or academic qualifications or special interests

Do you object to the publication of your name?
*Yes/No. *Delete as applicable.
Today's Date 15th September 89
Signature Brenda East

* If preferred, use a separate sheet of paper.

30th August 1989 (UK) – Police search Clacton Airstrip for UFO

31st August 1989 (USA) – Triangular UFO seen

At Trumbull, Connecticut, two witnesses saw small white lights in what appeared to be a triangular shape, moving very slowly through the sky and making a low humming sound. At one point it was motionless for about a minute, before disappearing in an easterly direction.

(Source: Ellen Beveridge, *Times*, Trumbull, Connecticut, 7.9.1989)

SOUTH BUCKS STAR.
-High Wycombe-

16 AUG 1989

And visitors from space come here...

SEEN a flying saucer or Unidentified Flying Object? Then Contact International UK want to hear from you!

They are an organisation devoted to the investigation of such outer space phenomena and so far have 85,000 cases on file. Their cases are from all over the world but they are able to carry out in-depth probes on cases in the South Bucks Star area. They are based in Oxford.

Chairman Michael Soper said: "It is very important to interview the witnesses and see the spot where they saw the object."

Michael explained that evidence they have shows governments in America and Britain are taking a very serious interest in the subject, despite the glib statements of 'govenment spokesmen' that they are simply misidentified lights.

Contact International UK have set up a hotline that anyone can phone day or night with reports of sightings. The number is Oxford (0865) 726908.

Have you seen a UFO or had a close encounter of the mysterious kind? Write to The Star, Gomm Road, High Wycombe, Bucks HP13 7DW and share your experience.

Above: As seen by Mr Britton at 6pm over the Colchester, Essex area on the 31st of August 1989 (**Source: Ron West**)

East Anglian Times, Ipswich

31 AUG 1989

Report of UFO but no trace found

POLICE searched Clacton airstrip for signs of an unidentified flying object early yesterday.

The UFO, said to be 30 metres wide, was seen by two men at 3.30 am. They said that it was hovering 40 to 50 metres above the ground and making a humming noise.

The men claimed the UFO was round, with red, blue, green and yellow flashing lights. They saw it above the airstrip while they were driving in West Road.

Police told Stansted air traffic control and the Ministry of Defence.

Air traffic controllers found no trace of the UFO on their radar screens and there was no record of any flights from Clacton airstrip then.

The men said the UFO flew low over the Three Jays in Jaywick Lane, turned right and moved towards St. John's Road.

UFOs

Do they exist, or are they all of our own making?

PETROL

4 STAR ★★★★

'Fill her up please mate...'

THERE you are driving down the road at night, minding your own business, when suddenly you catch sight of something in the sky.

It's not like any aircraft you've ever seen; it's flashing colourful lights and moving erratically at enormous speed. As it passes overhead your radio goes dead. Then it disappears.

Scoff not ... this kind of thing seems to happen to several hundred apparently sane and respectable Britons every year.

Most of them shake their heads in disbelief and swear never to drink again; others are so frightened that they dare not tell a soul; and a small percentage enjoy a brief moment of glory in the spotlight of the local press.

Such a story invariably prompts similar, often embellished revelations and 'experts' dust off the old theories about little green men from Mars. But is the invasion of Planet Earth really imminent? Or is there a simple explanation?

There have been mysterious sightings in the sky for as long as written records have been kept — for example, The Bible appears to contain several references in the chapters of Ezekiel.

Modern sightings appear to date from 1947 when an American businessman reported seeing nine silvery objects flying very swiftly near Washington.

His description prompted the tag 'flying saucers' and similar sightings have been made by supposedly serious, well-trained professional people like police, servicemen and even ex-President Reagan at frequent intervals ever.

Take the incident in London last year when no less than eight policemen swore they had seen a 'saucer' through the telescope of a teenager. It later turned out to have been the planet Jupiter, and in fact nine out of ten sightings can be explained away fairly easily.

Saucer shapes are frequently formed naturally in the atmosphere by pollution, pulverised dust and water particles, and lights can be caused by many things.

Ball lightning is a favourite among the natural phenomena and it is now

by JULIE COCKCROFT

known that moving lights often occur in the months before an earthquake, emitted by rocks under pressure.

Otherwise a 'spaceship' could really be an aircraft, weather balloon, meteorite or burned-out debris from satellites and other space junk falling to Earth.

EVIDENCE

Scares have even been started in America by what turned out to be loads of illegal marijuana, blasted over the Mexican border by a rocket launcher to beat the border patrolmen.

And it is possible that some supposed UFOs are really top secret military or scientific experiments that have been

Colchester Evening Gazette.

16 AUG 1989

seen accidentally but cannot be officially explained away.

NASA has even claimed that the Russians use apparent UFO sightings to cover up tests of strategic weapons which violate international treaties.

Sadly, there is not a scrap of real evidence to indicate that we are being watched or visited by super-intelligent beings from another planet.

Stories that various governments have actually made contact or possess the bodies of aliens who died on Earth, have to be taken with the proverbial pinch of salt. Credibility is decidedly challenged by those people who say they have been kidnapped and examined by strange creatures.

Yet a survey in America as long ago as 1966 indicated that five million Americans claimed to have seen a UFO or to have met aliens. Six out of ten say they believe in the phenomenon as do 20 per cent of Britons.

In Britain as many as 400 sightings are reported each year although UFO societies believe that ten times as

many more go unreported because people are afraid of being ridiculed.

Some are not afraid to speak out. Twenty years ago, Peter Hough was a schoolboy doing a morning paper round when he spotted something unusual.

"I saw an object that looked very crudely like an aircraft. It resembled two pieces of wood nailed together like a cross. I thought it was something caught in a tree until I realised it was quite some distance away.

"It was blunt at either end and the wings were at right angles to the fuselage. There were two rows of white lights winking on and off like Christmas tree lights. It did a very strange right-angled turn that I've never seen an aircraft do before or since."

Today he is chairman of the Manchester UFO Research Association. "Most of the sightings we have reported to us are easily explained away as satellites, aircraft or weather phenomena. We're not in the business of promoting myths. We

are seriously investigating the phenomenon."

Jenny Randles, director of investigations with the British UFO Research Association, co-ordinates the team of investigators who look into reported sightings.

She said: "You must realise that 90 to 95 per cent of UFO sightings turn out to be identifiable."

SIGHTINGS

BUFORA works closely with the police, the Ministry of Defence and Jodrell Bank to whom most UFO sightings are usually reported.

She said there are about 160 different phenomena which have been misinterpreted as UFOs in one way or another.

Writer David Barclay, from West Yorkshire, thinks there is a psychological explanation for the phenomenon — that we are compensating for the lack of romance and mystery in our modern lives.

SEPTEMBER 1989

5th September 1989 (UK) – Three lights over Essex

JUST after midnight what looked like *"three light bulbs"* were seen in the sky over Canley, by a local woman.

At 12.15am Robert Haskins, from Billericay, sighted *"a long rectangular object, showing white lights, moving across the sky, heading towards the Basildon direction, before coming to a halt."*

At around the same time, a woman from

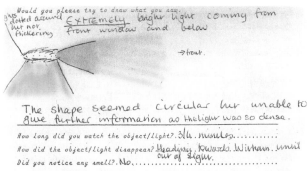

Southend watched a large circle of lights in the sky. Minutes later Mr Barton, from Southend, saw:

"…an object, hovering over the airport. It was huge, showing red, white, and green lights. A short time later, it moved towards the Basildon area."

At 2.45am Mrs Kay also from Southend sighted something unusual in the sky from her back garden.

At 3am, the Jones family, from Basildon, was awoken by a humming noise. When they went outside they saw a long object, showing a bright light, hovering in the sky. They watched it for 10 minutes, until it shot away towards Southend. Another witness was Southend man Mr Lowe.

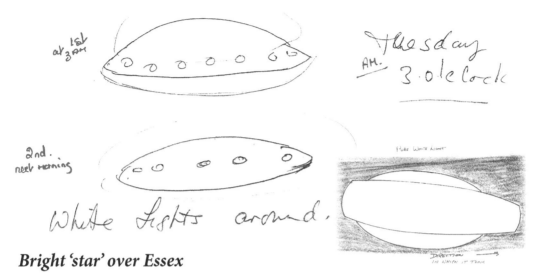

Bright 'star' over Essex

At 12.15pm, Mr Tony Jenkins – a novelist by occupation, of Queen's Park, Billericay, in Essex – happened to be looking out of his bedroom window, saying goodbye to his son – Anthony John Jenkins – when they saw what looked like a huge bright star in the sky. To their surprise, the *star* moved slowly away, before accelerating across the sky – where it halted in-mid air, once again. His son confirmed what had happened, although he remembers seeing a vapour trail, which dissipated a few seconds later.

> "Upon further inspection of the night sky, I noticed that other bright objects were dashing across the sky in all different directions – one every 30 seconds. I did my utmost to capture the strange events on videotape and was pleasantly surprised at the results, the next morning."

The matter was investigated by Roy Hale and Ron West, of the East Anglian UFO and Paranormal Research Association. Unfortunately, the current whereabouts of the video taken by Mr Jenkins is unknown, although it was examined initially and apparently pronounced genuine.

(Source: Ron West)

Roy Hale

6th September 1989 (UK) – *'Flying cigar'* over York

At 8.30pm, a large, bright, cigar-shaped object was seen hovering over York City racecourse, by local residents – Eric Fairburn and his wife, Kathleen.

In an interview conducted with the *Yorkshire Evening Post*, he had this to say, quote:

> "My wife saw this funny light in the sky and, at first, I thought it was the gas jet from a hot air balloon, because we see a lot of them go over.
>
> After studying it, I saw the light flashing on and off – similar to a beacon of a police car. When I looked through my race glasses, it was so bright it seemed to be giving off little stars. It hovered for about two minutes. The flashing lights became faster and then it whizzed off, at incredible speed, across the sky."

> **(Source: *Yorkshire Evening Post*, 7.9.1989 – 'Riddle of UFO stumps couple'/Personal interview)**

UFO over Colchester

Southend Evening Echo 21.9.1989

Good grief! UFO hovers near as expert Tim talks

A UFO hovered over Basildon while flying saucer expert Timothy Good gave a lecture.

The author of Above Top Secret — The World Wide UFO Cover-up was talking at The Bullseye pub around the time four people claimed they saw a large round ball-shaped object hovering over the town centre.

It was white with a ring of multi-coloured lights and made no sound.

The witnesses watched it for two minutes while they were stuck in a traffic jam.

Also on Friday night five people on Canvey spotted seven lights in the sky coloured red, green and yellow hovering at 3,000 ft for 10 minutes.

The East Anglia UFO and Paranormal Research Association also received a call from a couple who saw six coloured lights making geometric patterns in the sky in Stanford-le-Hope on Sunday at 8.30pm.

Anyone who saw these unexplained objects and lights should contact the East Anglia UFO hotline on 0268 286079.

On the same day, a round, white, ball-shaped object, showing multicoloured lights, was seen hovering in the sky over the *Bull's-eye* public house, Colchester, at 9.05pm. Incredibly, a talk was being given on the UFO subject. Was this just coincidence? A similar object was seen, 10 minutes later, over Canvey Island. (**Source: East Anglian UFO & Paranormal Research Association/** *Yellow Advertiser,* Colchester, 29.9.1989 – 'UFO gazers in puzzle')

8th September 1989 (UK) – *'Sky watch'* on the Moors

Andy Walmsey of the Independent UFO Network (IUN) was told about a number of strange lights seen on various occasions over the 'Withens Moor area of West Yorkshire – a high moorland expanse in the vicinity of a large stone monument, known as Stoodley Pike – a locality associated with reports of *'dancing lights'*, ghosts, and paranormal happenings. Our now good friend and well-established veteran researcher, Philip Mantle, first heard of this unidentified light phenomena following contact with a witness, and passed the details onto Andy. Andy spoke to the man concerned – a hospital porter – who told him that the *'lights'* had been seen at the same time, three nights running, and decided to set up a *'sky watch'* with the witness, who offered to show him the exact location. (Grid reference 037315, 0S Sheet 104)

A visit to the location – UFO display

On the evening of 8th September 1989, Andy made his way to the location, accompanied by his girlfriend and witness, and began their vigil at 8pm.

A short time later, the witness let out a shout. Andy turned around and saw eight or nine *'lights'* in the sky, at approximately 30° elevation off the horizon. Andy:

> *"I began to take photographs, and periodically look at them through binoculars. They moved erratically through the sky and changed intensity as they did so. Five of them demonstrated an uncanny ability to align themselves along geometrically perfect horizontal and vertical planes. At times, these 'lights' appeared to be accompanied by red, green, and white lights. This amazing light show went on for about an hour, before one detached itself from the rest and began to move towards us, illuminating the hill around it as it did so. I took two more photographs before it climbed vertically, at tremendous speed – then lost from view in cloud, only to appear behind us!*

'The site is inaccessible to vehicles, including off-road vehicles and quad bikes, (the Pike stands on Langfield Common, so is the responsibility of Calderdale Council) and overlooks Todmorden. Langfield Common is a true moor. Stoodley Pike Monument contains a spiral staircase of 39 steps, accessed from its north side. During repairs, in 1889, a grill was added to the top step, allowing more light in, so that only 6 or 7 steps are in darkness. There are no windows. The entrance to the balcony – the highest point that can be reached, and some 40ft above ground level – is on the west face. It serves primarily as a destination for hikers, fell-runners and cyclists, being close to Mankinholes Youth Hostel and the *Top Brink* public house. Just below it, on the roughly 200 metres contour shelf, is the Harvelin Park housing estate. From here, walkers can enjoy an easy 30 minutes walk to the Pike.

The witness then had the idea of flashing the car lights at them. To our amazement, three of the 'lights' in the sky flashed back at us, so we flashed again and got a response. Bad weather started, so we were forced to leave before our trail became waterlogged."

When Andy arrived home, he contacted other members of the group – Philip Mantle, Andy Roberts and Rodney Howarth – to tell them what had transpired. The next night, the four men staked out the location but saw nothing. Unfortunately, the photographs taken by Andy inexplicably failed to come out at all – which was very odd.

In April 2013 we spoke to Philip, wondering if he could remember what had happened to the missing witness and the photographs taken. Unfortunately, he could not assist but spoke emotively of the freezing cold and arduous journey undertaken on the *'sky watch'* that night, which yielded no result.

UFO over London

At 9pm on the same date, Mrs T. Yakici of Walthamstow, London, went upstairs to prepare the baby for bed. She happened to glance out of the back window, when she saw . . .

". . . a large triangular 'light' in the sky, about the size of a front door, hovering over the roof of a nearby house. A few minutes later it moved slowly and silently across to my right, behind trees, and then was lost from view".

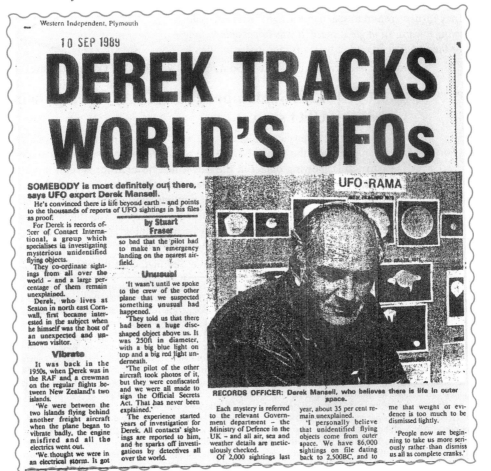

Western Independent, Plymouth

10 SEP 1989

DEREK TRACKS WORLD'S UFOs

UFO-RAMA

SOMEBODY is most definitely out there, says UFO expert Derek Mansell.

He's convinced there is life beyond earth – and points to the thousands of reports of UFO sightings in his files as proof.

For Derek is records officer of Contact International, a group which specialises in investigating mysterious unidentified flying objects.

They co-ordinate sightings from all over the world – and a large percentage of them remain unexplained.

Derek, who lives at Seaton in north east Cornwall, first became interested in the subject when he himself was the host of an unexpected and unknown visitor.

by Stuart Fraser

Vibrate

It was back in the 1950s, when Derek was in the RAF and a crewman on the regular flights between New Zealand's two islands.

'We were between the two islands flying behind another freight aircraft when the plane began to vibrate badly, the engine misfired and all the electrics went out.

'We thought we were in an electrical storm. It got so bad that the pilot had to make an emergency landing on the nearest airfield.

Unusual

'It wasn't until we spoke to the crew of the other plane that we suspected something unusual had happened.

'They told us that there had been a huge disc-shaped object above us. It was 250ft in diameter, with a big blue light on top and a big red light underneath.

'The pilot of the other aircraft took photos of it, but they were confiscated and we were all made to sign the Official Secrets Act. That has never been explained.'

The experience started years of investigation for Derek. All contacts' sightings are reported to him, and he sparks off investigations by detectives all over the world.

Each mystery is referred to the relevant Government department – the Ministry of Defence in the UK – and all air, sea and weather details are meticulously checked.

Of 2,000 sightings last

RECORDS OFFICER: Derek Mansell, who believes there is life in outer space.

year, about 35 per cent remain unexplained.

'I personally believe that unidentified flying objects come from outer space. We have 86,000 sightings on file dating back to 2,500BC, and to

me that weight of evidence is too much to be dismissed lightly.

'People now are beginning to take us more seriously rather than dismiss us all as complete cranks.'

10th September 1989 (UK) - Green object flies over Bristol

At 8.19pm, Colin Pulsford from Filton, Bristol, and his wife, Linda, were out walking when they saw a bright green object, with a 'tail', about one eighth diameter of the moon, shooting across the sky - which he first took to be a rocket. It was also seen some miles away, over Yate.

(Source: *Bristol Evening Post*, 12.9.1989 – 'Mystery of the flying object')

12 SEP 1989

Mystery of the flying object

SOMETHING mysterious hurtled through the night sky over the Bristol area — but what was it?

Colin Pulsford of Branksome Way Drive, Filton, thought at first it was a rocket sent up by somebody with very early access to Guy Fawkes fireworks.

But it travelled horizontally rather than vertically and made no noise.

It was bright green and from ground level appeared to be one-eighth of the diameter of the moon. It had a tail. As suddenly as it had appeared it disappeared.

Mr Pulsford was baffled, but put the incident out of his mind — until next morning when a colleague at work spoke of a similar sighting miles away at Yate.

"It wasn't a meteor," said Mr Pulsford. He was out taking a walk with his wife Lilian over playing fields on Sunday evening when he saw the mysterious object. The time: 8.19 pm..

Bristol University physics lecturer Dr Rodney Hillier, could offer no explanation

11th September 1989 (UK) - UFO over Somerset

At 7.45pm, Mike and Wendy Wood from South Petherton, Somerset, were walking their dog over fields at Coombe Bottom, near Compton Durville, when they became aware of a *'bright light'* behind them. Their first thoughts were that it was a firework. They turned around to see *"a green 'light', with red-yellow edging, heading towards us at great speed. It was impossible to judge how high, or the size of it. Seconds later, it disappeared from view".*

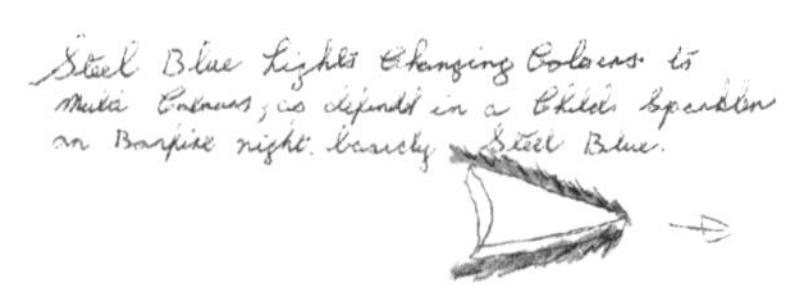
Steel Blue Lights Changing Colours to Multi Colours, as defined in a Child's Sparkler on Bonfire night. basicly Steel Blue.

(Source: *Western Gazette*, Yeovil, Somerset, 14.9.1989 – 'UFO scare terrifies villagers')

Ed Walters with wife, Frances

12th September 1989 (USA) - Red glowing UFO seen

At Pensacola, Florida, a total of 35 people, including twelve investigators for the Mutual UFO Network (MUFON) sighted an elliptical, red glowing object in the sky, which hovered for several minutes, before ascending towards the east. The object then entered cloud cover but could still be seen. Seven minutes later, a white object was observed at 10°, moving swiftly towards the west before disappearing. *Ed Walters, the well-known witness who had photographed many UFOs in nearby Gulf Breeze, took two photographs with his *Instamatic 110* camera.

(Source: *Sentinel*, Gulf Breeze, Florida, 21.9.1989)

*Wikipedia 2014 – The Gulf Breeze UFO incident is a famous series of UFO sightings that occurred beginning on November 11, 1987. Gulf Breeze was a small city in Florida of approximately 6,000 at the time of a wave of UFO sightings that began in late 1987. News of high-quality UFO photos spread rapidly and worldwide and became the subject of newspaper and magazine articles, television talk shows and feature programs. The "Gulf Breeze UFO Incident" most definitive evidence is a series of photographs and contact claims made by Ed Walters that began, for him, on November 11, 1987. Walters reported and documented a series of UFO sightings over a period of three weeks. The photographs of the craft were unusually clear and initially Walters' claims generated great excitement. Research by Jerry Black in the early 1990s revealed a trail of suspicious money leading to Walters, giving the initial indications that the case was a hoax. The later discovery of a model in a house once owned by Walters, similar to the UFOs shown in his photographs, shifted majority opinion to believe that Walters' UFO photos were faked. The model was found by Robert Menzer, who was quoted stating, "*The model was nine inches long across the top and five inches deep. Made of "two nine-inch foam plates attached to two six-inch foam plates; a six inch square blue-color gel (plastic film) and on six inch round orange paper ring, a 3.5 inch long tube, and a two inch wide paper ring between the two nine-inch plates. There were windows drawn on the model which was covered with drafting paper.*" Although Ed Walters was the nexus of the Gulf Breeze sightings, he was not the only person to claim a sighting. According to ufocasebook.com, an estimated 200+ others came forward with sightings, videos and/or photographs during a three-year period. On December 2, 2010, the Syfy series *Fact or Faked* investigated another UFO video shot in 2009 where the object in the video is similar to the one(s) Ed Walters caught on camera.

model found

Photographer: Critics out to discredit him

13th September 1989 (UK) – UFO display

Miss M. Page of Seabroooke Rise, Grays, Essex (a block of flats adjacent to the *River Thames*) was at home, at 7pm, when her friend – Bobette – called to tell her about some strange objects in the sky.

> *"We stood watching two lights 'dancing' in the sky. After about 25 minutes we went round to see John, from 310, who was also watching them.*

I noticed that one of them was much brighter than the rest, and may have been over the direction of Thurrock Power Station, and continued watching them. At some stage, I heard a car horn and went onto the back balcony, but was surprised to see the sky was clear.

I returned to the front of the flat and saw they were still there. After 15mins, they just stopped in front of what looked like layered clouds."

In an interview later conducted by Peter Oliver with the witnesses, it was remarked on the strangeness of the clouds themselves, which were seen initially as normal dark grey, before changing into blue-mauve streaks in horizontal layers that began to move away, followed by the discontinuance of the phenomena. Another witness was Jonathan Sansom (14) – then living in the same block of flats. (**Source: Ron West**)

15th September 1989 (UK) – UFO over Colchester

Linda Cooke (24) – a housewife from Lampets Lane, Corringham, Essex – was at home when her husband called her outside. She went out and saw:

"...lots of different 'lights', darting all over the sky – red, green, and white ones – flashing. I counted thirty sets of them. I watched for half an hour and went back inside at 8.30pm."

Michelle Knight was another witness to strange phenomena this evening.

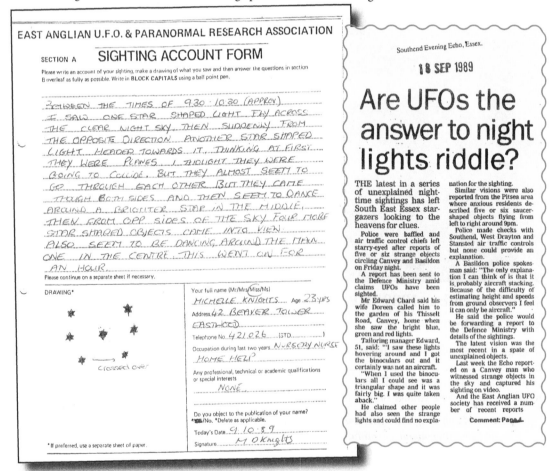

EAST ANGLIAN U.F.O. & PARANORMAL RESEARCH ASSOCIATION

SECTION A   **SIGHTING ACCOUNT FORM**

Please write an account of your sighting, make a drawing of what you saw and then answer the questions in section B overleaf as fully as possible. Write in **BLOCK CAPITALS** using a ball point pen.

BETWEEN THE TIMES OF 9.30 : 10.30 (APPROX) I SAW ONE STAR SHAPED LIGHT FLY ACROSS THE CLEAR NIGHT SKY, THEN SUDDENLY FROM THE OPPOSITE DIRECTION ANOTHER STAR SHAPED LIGHT HEADED TOWARDS IT. THINKING AT FIRST THEY WERE PLANES, I THOUGHT THEY WERE GOING TO COLLIDE, BUT THEY ALMOST SEEM TO GO THROUGH EACH OTHER. BUT THEY CAME THRGH BOTH SIDES AND THEN SEEM TO DANCE AROUND A BRIGHTER STAR IN THE MIDDLE. THEN FROM OPP SIDES OF THE SKY FOUR MORE STAR SHAPED OBJECTS CAME INTO VIEW ALSO SEEM TO BE DANCING AROUND THE MAIN ONE IN THE CENTRE THIS WENT ON FOR AN HOUR.

Please continue on a separate sheet if necessary.

DRAWING*

Crossed over

Your full name (Mr/Mrs/Miss/Ms)
MICHELE KNIGHTS .... Age 23yrs
Address 42 BEAVER TOWER EASTWOOD
Telephone No. 421026 .... (STD.......)
Occupation during last two years NURSERY NURSE / HOME HELP

Any professional, technical or academic qualifications or special interests
NONE

Do you object to the publication of your name?
*Yes/No. *Delete as applicable.
Today's Date 9.10.89
Signature M O Knights

*If preferred, use a separate sheet of paper.

Southend Evening Echo, Essex.

18 SEP 1989

Are UFOs the answer to night lights riddle?

THE latest in a series of unexplained night-time sightings has left South East Essex stargazers looking to the heavens for clues.

Police were baffled and air traffic control chiefs left starry-eyed after reports of five or six strange objects circling Canvey and Basildon on Friday night.

A report has been sent to the Defence Ministry amid claims UFOs have been sighted.

Mr Edward Chard said his wife Doreen called him to the garden of his Thissell Road, Canvey, home when she saw the bright blue, green and red lights.

Tailoring manager Edward, 51, said: "I saw these lights hovering around and I got the binoculars out and it certainly was not an aircraft.

"When I used the binoculars all I could see was a triangular shape and it was fairly big. I was quite taken aback."

He claimed other people had also seen the strange lights and could find no expla-

nation for the sighting.

Similar visions were also reported from the Pitsea area where anxious residents described five or six saucer-shaped objects flying from left to right around 9pm.

Police made checks with Southend, West Drayton and Stansted air traffic controls but none could provide an explanation.

A Basildon police spokesman said: "The only explanation I can think of is that it is, probably aircraft stacking. Because of the difficulty of estimating height and speeds from ground observers I feel it can only be aircraft."

He said the police would be forwarding a report to the Defence Ministry with details of the sightings.

The latest vision was the most recent in a spate of unexplained objects.

Last week the Echo reported on a Canvey man who witnessed strange objects in the sky and captured his sighting on video.

And the East Anglian UFO society has received a number of recent reports

Comment: Page 4

Timothy Good lecture, UFO seen overhead!

UFOs were also the subject of much discussion at Ossett Town Hall, during the same evening, when members of the Yorkshire UFO Society assembled to enthral a crowd of around 250 people with stories of downed *'flying saucers'*, crop circles, Government plots and conspiracies.

Graham Birdsall – President of YUFOS – apologised to the audience, after the meeting, which should have finished at 5.40pm, because two of the speakers still had not given their talks! Other speakers were Timothy Good, George Wingfield, Dr. Henry Azadehdel and Ralph Noyes, who spoke about the Rendlesham Forest incident.

Mark and brother, Graham Birdsall, seen here with Philip Mantle (right).

16th September 1989 – (UK)

At 12.15am, Mr Warren from Old School Lane, Elmstead Market, Colchester, had just parked his car in fields behind his house, after having been to a wedding.

> *"I saw some orange lights in the sky and stopped to watch. A separate light appeared in the distance and to my astonishment came to within 500yds, where it halted in mid-air. I shouted my wife, Maureen (53) to come and see it (she had already gone inside). She came out and we watched it for 45 minutes, until it flew away. The next morning I examined the ground under which it had been, but there was nothing of any note."*

Mr Warren's drawing shows a triangular or heart-shaped object, with what appears to be sparks falling away from it. Maureen's drawing shows a defined triangle, with sparks falling away.

Lights set off UFO panic

Report for SR by SANDRA HEMBERY

FAMILIES went UFO potty as strange lights hovered over the Basildon district.

UFO researchers were flooded with calls after the latest in a series of unexplained sightings baffled stargazers.

The calls came on Friday night as the SR's special report on unidentified flying objects hit thousands of homes.

East Anglian UFO Society chairman Ray West said everything went potty as sky-watchers reported a series of red, white and green objects circling the night sky.

Calls came in from Laindon, Basildon and surrounding areas after the strange objects were seen at around 8pm.

Eye witnesses reported stopping their cars and gazing for more than half an hour at the diamond-shaped objects.

Darting

Mr West said: "There is no way they could have been aircraft. People have explained these sightings away by saying they were aircraft stacking.

"This couldn't have been the case as they were darting about the sky."

One Basildon eyewitness took a video recording of the objects and will be handing over the evidence to the UFO society.

Another Laindon family reported one of the objects flying low. It was described as a diamond-shaped object with flashing lights on its underside.

Mr West added: "We get odds and ends now and again. But all of a sudden we get an abundance of them. That is the case here."

Just over a week ago calls came in to Basildon police of similar sightings in South East Essex. The previous week a man caught a saucer-shaped object on video after seeing flashing lights in the sky.

Now Mr West has urged anyone who saw strange objects on Friday night to contact the UFO hotline on Basildon 286079.

17th September 1989 (UK) – UFO display

At 8.30pm, Mr and Mrs Debra Jane Allen (23) of Stanford-Le-Hope were in their garden.

"We saw six blue, white, silver, green, and red lights, circling around in the sky, as if doing a formation dance. We watched them for 15 minutes and then went inside."

Mr Allen:

"I agree fully with what my wife has said, but I saw what appeared to be a humming top-shaped object, with lights rotating around it, shortly before my wife saw it. They departed in different directions."
(Source: Peter Oliver)

19th September 1989 (UK) – UFO over Essex

Mr Eric Milner, from Laindon, was taking his dog out for a walk, just after midnight, when he saw:

"...a round, stationary object, 25-30metres in length, showing flashes of red, white,

---

SR FEATURES

Unidentified Flying Objects, or Utterly Foolish Observations?

Whatever our attitude to UFOs — baloney or new beginning — the fact remains that they are back in the news.

A spate of recent sightings suggests that if the Force is with anybody at the moment, it's the people of South-East Essex.

When the first UFO lands, is it likely to be in Essex?

UFO sightings seem to be concentrated in particular places at particular times. Recent areas to be favoured include the north of Italy and South Island, New Zealand.

But the Thames Estuary does appear to be very much in favour of the year in alien circles, if only because the river may not as a guideline to London and tea with the Queen.

By March 1989 there had been over 70 sightings, putting south-east Essex at the top of the national league, although the concentrated population may mean that there are simply more eyes to look, particularly during the repeat season on television.

What do the UFOs look like?
IF EVEN a fraction of the accounts are to be believed, UFO builders offer more range and variety of models than the Ford Motor Company over its entire history.

Descriptions of the craft include the following: a rugby ball, fish, cigar glowing at the smoker's end, half a water melon, a (whole) pear, transformer robot, and loaf of cottage bread. Oh, and saucer.

Have any UFO incidents been satisfactorily explained away?
YES — and occasionally the explanation has proved almost as bizarre as anything that could be laid on by little green men.

In June 1979 anglers sitting around Hanningfield Reservoir were startled by a large object that plummeted into the middle of the reservoir. Fishing was reported to be particularly poor for the rest of the day.

The object was variously described as like "a flaming comet" and "an

Do UFOs appear to those who really want to see them?

Bright blue, green and red lights over Canvey... saucer shapes hovering over Pitsea... A Saturn shaped comet's tail tail caught on video by a Billericay novelist... Something is going on up there.

The Standard Recorder has examined the whole phenomenon of

express cannonball". But witnesses generally agreed that it had been moving too fast too see at all. It had made an almighty splash.

Essex police frogmen made a thorough search but could find nothing. Science fiction afficionados will, however, recall the Steven Spielberg produced film Cocoon, in which alien spacemen are suspended in deep sleep at the bottom of the sea until their colleagues can return to rescue them.

The Hanningfield UFO was no alien. Almost two years later, water bailiffs succeeded where the frogmen had failed. Out of the water they fished — a weather balloon.

Who owned the balloon and why it had come down remained a mystery. Someone, somewhere, must have restored a very damp weather forecast.

Another closely identified UFO was the "green glowing thing" described by alarmed housewife Mrs Pat Busby of Pitsea and Mr William Jones in June 1981.

Pat Miles of the British Astronomical Association also saw it.

"It was a brilliant fireball, a piece of rock," he explained. "They come from minor planets between Mars and Jupiter." So minor, indeed, that unlike Southend they don't have their names all through the rock.

Who gets the prize for the most ingenious investigation of UFOs?
UNDOUBTEDLY a special team that asked members of Basildon police force traffic control and other flight experts from Southend airport. One night in early October 1987 a spate of UFO reports arrived on their desk and they set to work.

The team were initially puzzled by the reports of large, bright lights hover-

UFOs in this part of the country in a bid to discover just how seriously we should take them.

Some sightings are just plain fanciful. Others can be explained away. But there remains a small core that can only be described as inexplicable.

One fact remains clear. Flying saucers have never yet harmed anybody. Nobody has even fallen off a bike while spotting them.

And whether or not the things themselves are real, one thing remains for sure about flying saucers — their entertainment value.

The latest sightings

MR EDWARD Chard, of Thissell Road, Canvey, was called into the garden of his home by his wife Doreen.

It was the night of Friday, September 16, and Mrs Chard was astonished by flashing blue, green and red lights.

Tailoring manager Edward, 31, said: "I saw these lights hovering around and I got the binoculars out and it certainly was no aircraft.

When I used the binoculars all I could see was a triangular shape and it was fairly big. It was quite taken aback."

He claimed other people had also seen the strange lights and could find no explanation for the sighting.

Similar visions were also reported from the Pitsea area where anxious residents described five or six saucer shaped objects fly-

ving from left to right around 9pm.

Police made checks with Southend, West Drayton and Stansted air traffic controls but none of them could provide any explanation.

A Basildon police spokesman said: "The only explanation I can think of is that it is probably aircraft stacking. Because of the difficulty of estimating height and speed by ground observers, I feel it can only be aircraft.

The police will be forwarding a report to the Defence Ministry with details of the sightings.

Five days before that, romantic novelist Anthony Jenkins of Billericay was startled by a particularly striking UFO which appeared in the night sky above his head.

Anthony said: "Before this hap-

pened I did not really believe in UFO sightings.

"It was one o'clock in the morning and I was saying goodbye to a relative of mine.

"There were things flying across the sky with lights shooting all over the place.

"I first saw something with a tail. It was bright and shot across the sky.

"You could be forgiven for thinking it was a comet."

Anthony described the aircraft as domed on top and underneath with a disk running around the edge — like Saturn.

Wife Teresa, 31, had earlier seen the strange objects but had been too embarrassed to say.

He stood poised, video camera in hand, for more than three-quarters of an hour, watching the objects "dance" around each other.

---

and green lights, circling around its base. It was completely silent and about 3,000ft up in the sky. I watched it for about five minsute; suddenly, it shot upwards and was gone."

A similar object was seen by a couple, living in Basildon, at around the same time.

At 6pm the same day, a black cigar-shaped object was seen in the sky over Boxted, Colchester, by Mr R. Stowe, who was driving along the Brentwood by-pass, heading towards Chelmsford. (Source: *Yellow Advertiser,* Colchester, 12.9.1989 – 'Is anybody up there?'/ *Standard Recorder,* 29.9.1989 – 'Lights set off UFO panic')

Stow-on-the-Wold, Gloucestershire

At 9.30pm, two police officers saw a multicoloured object moving through the sky, at an estimated altitude of 1,000-1,500ft.

It then went on to perform a series of bizarre manoeuvres for 15 minutes, which included silent hovering, before transforming into a single orange light, at which point it disappeared at speed.

(Source: Declassified documents)

20th September 1989 (UK) – Mysterious beam of light seen

At 7.30pm, Mr Gary Singleton (33) from Wickford, Essex, was driving down the A414 – a semi rural road near Danbury, Essex – when:

> *"I became aware of a very bright light on my left-hand side. It was pulsating between a vivid blue and green and moving in a straight line across the sky – much faster than any aircraft. It then went behind trees and I lost sight of it."*

At about 8.15pm, Margaret Stanton (40) of Little Oaks High Road, Laindon, Essex, was walking down Knock Hill, when she saw a *'ring of lights'* projecting a sharp beam of light downwards onto an open field nearby.

> *"I thought it might have been a searchlight, but then realised that if this was the case then the beam would be narrow at the bottom and wide going upwards, but this beam was in reverse. Also the ground was not illuminated below the beam."*

(Source: Ron West)

22nd September 1989 (UK) – UFOs over Essex

At 7pm, Ian Trevor Sales (23) – an actor by profession – was walking up Underhill Road, Benfleet, when he saw a triangle of three lights, motionless in the sky. Intrigued, he stopped to watch. About 15mins later, they moved away towards Basildon. (**Source: Karl Kauter, Essex UFO Group**)

At 7.55pm, Mrs Edna Peck (65) and her husband, of Popes Avenue, Pitsea, Basildon, Essex, were walking up the road when they noticed a group of about seven white lights, moving around in an anticlockwise direction across the sky. Her husband fetched a pair of binoculars and looked through them. All he was able to make out was that they were over the Basildon area; 20 minutes later, they were out of view.

Also at 7.55pm, Driving Instructor Martin Reeves (29) was driving along the A13, towards Laindon, with a friend, when they saw lights in the distant sky, moving in an erratic manner.

> *"There were about seven or 10 of them, flying towards each other and stopping. People stopped their cars to look. When we reached our destination, which was my Aunt Carol and Uncle Tom's house, the lights were still showing. At this point a diamond-shaped object passed overhead, making this humming noise."*

Westcliff-on-Sea

At 8.16pm, Mrs Janet Gray (34) of Cavendish Gardens, Westcliff-on-Sea, was summoned outside by her daughter, Laura, who told her mother and son, Peter, about a strange object she could see in the sky. The family then observed a pair of oval silver objects, stationary in the sky. A short time later the objects headed off, at speed, over the *River Thames* direction. Basildon

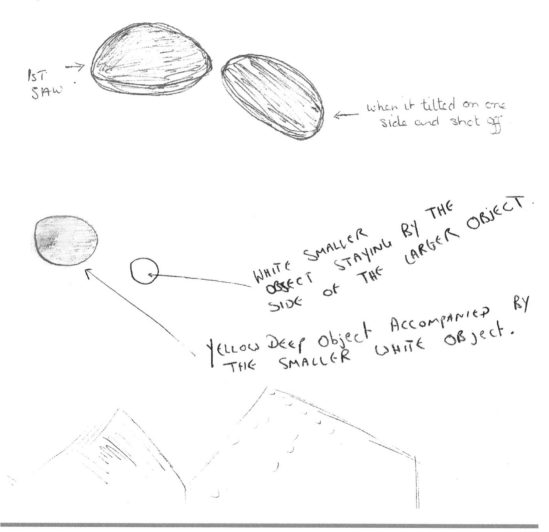

Basildon

At 8.05pm, Thomas Wright (46) was stood outside his house at Langdon Hills, Basildon, in Essex, talking to his nephew, when they saw an object in the sky, showing red, green, and white lights.

> *"Above that were three or four other objects higher up. One of them dropped down over the larger one, while the others began to more erratically. Suddenly the larger object started to move slowly away, then shot off."*

Other witnesses were Carole Wright (45):

> *"My nephew told me they were watching something in the sky. I said to him, 'Are they bats?' He said, 'No'. I looked and saw something resembling the front of a straight back winged plane, heading over the garage opposite. When it was directly overhead I saw it was a diamond-shaped object, showing red, green, and white lights, making a humming noise as it flew away, after hovering above us for a few seconds before being lost from view."*

Southend Evening Echo, Essex.

25 SEP 1989

'Diamond' UFOs alert

UFO researchers were flooded with calls after the latest in a series of unexplained sightings baffled South East Essex stargazers.

East Anglian UFO Society chairman Ray West said everything went potty on Friday night as sky-watchers reported a series of red, white and green objects circling the night sky.

Calls came in from Laindon, Basildon and surrounding areas after the strange objects were seen.

People stopping their cars, gazing for more than half an hour at the diamond-shaped objects.

One Basildon eye witness took a video of the objects and will hand over the tape to the UFO society.

Another Laindon family reported one of the objects flying low. It was diamond-shaped with flashing lights.

Mr West urges anyone who saw strange objects on Friday night to contact Basildon 286079.

Pitsea

At 9pm Lesley Spiteri (30) from Sandon Road, Pitsea, was at her home, when she happened to look out of the window and see:

> *"...a green and red flashing bright light, moving through the sky over the rooftop of a nearby house. This was followed by another eight or nine more, which went in different directions".*

23rd September 1989 (UK) – UFO display

At 12.06am, Adrian Charles Court (30) and his wife were holidaying at the Colchester Caravanning Park with other members of the family, when they received a visit from Adrian's brother, telling him about something unusual in the sky.

> *"I looked and saw, about five miles away, four lights, which appeared circular in shape, moving in a circular and elliptical pattern. There were three lights in the middle and one light constantly moving around the other three."* **(Source: Peter Oliver)**

At 12.15am, Jackie Pennington from Finborough, Stowmarket – a beauty therapist by occupation – was stood outside, talking to her husband, Lance, and other members of the family, when they saw four *'white circles'* in the sky,

> *"...which began to move into the centre of the sky and then went back again, showing an overall rotational effect; there were no clouds until after the circles had disappeared – then the clouds*

seemed to form a petal effect where the lights had been. We didn't see any beams or light, although the light given off by whatever the things were seemed to reflect downwards onto our house."

The family watched the strange effects for approximately 45 minutes, before it came to an end. Could these have been laser lights?

Other witnesses to what appears to be the same phenomena were John Robbins (28) of Woodford Close, Great Clacton, Essex. He was talking to Shaun Bullman (17) – a friend at the end of the road – when they noticed four lights, circling in the sky over an adjacent field. At this stage Dee Elsley (26) (a member of Ron West's group) and her friend turned up.

John:

"We went to the far end of the field and saw two 'lights' making these circular movements, high above us – possibly over the Heathrow tracker Beacon Thorpe. We stayed in the field for about one and a half hours, watching them, until they disappeared at about 2am."

(Source: East Anglian UFO & Paranormal Research Association)

24th September 1989 (UK) – Five UFOs seen

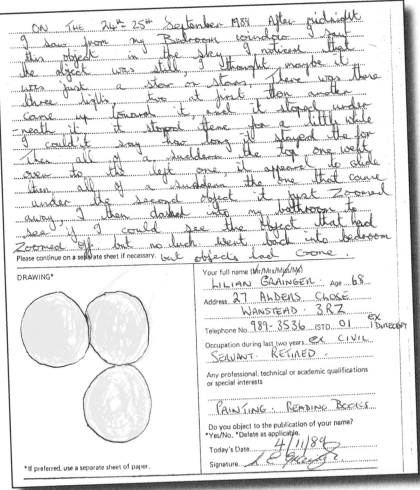

The report submitted by Lillian was not the only one that evening. Mr Polyket (62) of Nether Priors, Basildon, and his wife and son, saw five red, green, and a large white flashing light, moving around the sky in a row of three, with two alongside.

> *"One of them (white) was stationary above the Telephone Exchange – the others then circled around it; 30 minutes later, they all moved away."*

26th September 1989 (UK) – UFO over Quantock Hills

At 10.15pm, Greta Thrush – a former chairperson for Dunster Parish Council – was driving home along the A358, from Taunton, with her husband, David and daughter-in-law, Ruth. As they passed the Crowcombe and Halsey Manor area, they saw:

> *"...a bright yellow object, hovering above trees at the foot of the hills, banana in shape, with something pink pulsating in the middle. It was very low and gave the impression it was going to land on the Quantock Hills, above the village of Crowcombe. We watched it for five minutes, before losing sight of it. Even now, nearly 20 years later, what we saw still enthrals me."*

Greta, intrigued by what she and her family had seen, wrote a letter to the *West Somerset Press*, appealing for any other witnesses, and was rewarded with a reply from a woman at Porlock, Devon, who sighted something unusual through binoculars, for 10-15 minutes over the *Bristol Channel,* before it headed over the Quantock Hills. (**Source:** *West Somerset Press*, **28.9.1989** – 'Police Probe UFO sighting'/Personal interview)

29th September 1989 (UK) – UFO display

At 8.15pm, Mr Peter Hamilton (21) was looking out of the window of his house at Mellow Close, Laindon, Basildon, in Essex, to ensure his car was secure, when he saw:

> *"...eight or 10 objects in the sky. I shouted jokingly to my girlfriend... 'UFOs', as I first thought they were aircraft but then realised that they weren't.*
>
> *A couple of them flew over the flat. They were made up of blue, white, and red lights. The white was still with the others, flashing. We counted eight objects; six of them seemed to be stacking in the sky, leaving the other one on its own for a short time – then a couple more came. There were 10 now, showing three or four lights on each. Soon they were all gone."*

(**Source: Peter Oliver**)

‌LLOW ADVERTISER
-Colchester-
27 OCT 1989

Bases already on earth

Twelve-feet tall aliens 'on their way here'

WAR OF the worlds may not be far away, as reports of a UFO landing in the Russian town of Voronezh filter through from the Kremlin.

Ron West, chairman of the UFO research organisation in Britain feels that the story released by the Russian news agency Tass is true.

The agency claims that three aliens, 12 feet tall, strolled around a park in the remote town 300 miles south-east of Moscow.

Tass did not say when the landing occurred, but that it took place shortly after a bright shining ball was seen in the sky. A depression 20 yards in diameter was left in the ground when the spaceship lifted off.

Russian investigators discovered two rocks on the ground where the spacecraft had landed. They were analysed and found to be inconsistent with rocks normally found on earth.

Mr West said: "The landing has been authenticated by Genrikh Silanov, a respected Russian scientist.

"In any case, this isn't the first time aliens have met with humans.

"Six cases of aliens being seen by humans have been reported to our organisation this year — and that is just in the Southend and Benfleet areas."

Purpose

Mr West feels there must have been a purpose for the visit, and is sure the Russians have not released all the details.

He said: "You don' know if the aliens hav abducted anybody."

Last month Mr Wes was given an amateu video of a spaceship cir cling the area. It has beer sent to a specialist labora tory in Nottinghamshir to be analysed.

"I believe it to be au thentic, or a remarkabl clever hoax," he said. "We shall find out in couple of weeks."

Mr West believes it i likely that the aliens wil soon be visiting Britair "I have documents th aliens already have base on earth," he said.

If you have seen any thing strange in the sky telephone the UFO ho line, 0268 286079.

UFO over telephone exchange

A COUPLE from Basildon have reported seeing a UF hovering over the town telephone exchange.

They watched the circle of red, green and white ligh for about 30 minutes before it moved off.

Twelve other witnesses reported a similar sighting.

OCTOBER 1989

2nd October 1989 (UK) – Triangular UFO over Staffordshire

GRAHAM Allen was to witness something strange, on this date at 7.30pm. Graham – then head of Staffordshire UFO Group – was out walking with his children on Etching Hill, a mile outside the small town of Rugeley.

"We saw a bright light in the sky, which divided into two separate lights, and then what looked like a spark came away and headed off in the direction of Stafford. The two lights approached us; they reminded me of car headlights. As they moved closer I saw that they formed part of a massive triangular object, covered in lights – like something out of 'Star Wars'. I crouched down, covering the children with my arms. As the object silently passed overhead, I looked up and saw a rectangular orange section to the rear. If there had been anyone waving at us, we would have seen them – that's how close we were.

We watched as it drifted over towards Rugeley Power Station. When I arrived home, I asked the children to draw the object – which they did."

Graham Allen

Graham freely admits he does not comprehend what these things are, or where they come from, but knows they certainly exist. The experiences sustained by him have altered his perception of life and brought about a new found desire to help others come to terms following their own close encounters.

On the same day, a family walking their dog along Underhill Road, South Benfleet, watched a large triangular craft, displaying red, green, blue and white, lights in the sky for 20 minutes, until it disappeared from view.

4th October 1989 (UK) – Fish UFO seen!

At 9.30pm, a huge saucer-shaped object, resembling a 'skate' fish, was seen in the sky over Canvey Island.

(**Source: Sheridan Lane, East Anglian UFO and Paranormal Research Association**)

5th October 1989 (UK) – UFO display

Stephen Kenneth Jeffrey (37) of Fulham Road, London SW6 – employed as a ticket collector for the London Underground – was on duty at 7.45pm, when he noticed strange lights in the sky over Kensington Underground Station.

"They were very faint and hazy, darting about all over the place in various directions, and flashing onto the cloud. I considered whether they could have been the Northern Lights, or even perhaps laser being used at a rock concert."

Other witnesses included Ralph Yorke and Christina, from Harrow, who told Stephen they had seen the lights while travelling to the Underground Station.

5th October 1989 (UK) – Three white lights seen over RAF Lakenheath

At 10.45pm, housewife Karen Smith (31) was looking out of her bedroom window in the High Street, Lakenheath, in Suffolk (which overlooks RAF Lakenheath) when she noticed three large white lights, stationary in the sky over the airbase.

"They formed a triangular shape, with a faint orange halo around them, and were about 2000ft up – the size of tennis balls from the ground. Suddenly, all the lights on the airbase went out and I could see a lot of vehicles moving about. I saw two aircraft take off; as they did so, the lights faded away. The only noise was the aircraft taking off."

On the 9th October, Ron West contacted the Duty Officer at RAF Lakenheath. He explained the reason for the call and was told:

"No comment. I wasn't on duty on that date."

On the 12th, Ron contacted the base again and was told:

"Nothing unusual happened on the night of the 5th October 1989."

OSSETT OBSERVER -6 OCT 1989

Extra-terrestrial finds a home in the town hall

AN extra-terrestrial showpiece is to become a fixture at Ossett Town Hall following the soaraway success of the recent UFO conference.

The delighted organisers from the Yorkshire UFO Society have announced their intention to make the conference an annual attraction after this year's event drew in people from across the country.

Visitors from as far afield as Reading, Berkshire and Liverpool attended the event which organisers promised would blow the lid off the UFO debate once and for all.

In all, more than 350 people arrived to hear revelations about the shooting down and capture of an alien spaceship in South Africa earlier this year.

And they squirmed in their seats as Timothy Good, author of the bestselling UFO book "Above Top Secret," showed slides of alleged alien experimentation and surgery on animals.

"The response of the public has been tremendous and there would have been even more people but for traffic delays on the M1. I think the event has been a resounding success and Ossett is the ideal place for it."

9th October 1989 (UK)

A silver sphere with a black base, was seen apparently following the course of the Oxford to Didcot railway line, by Mr Fred Bradley of Kennington, Oxford. (**Source: Personal interview**)

9th October 1989 (USA) – Pilot sights sphere

At 5.45am, a crop-duster pilot was flying to an assignment near Tunica, Mississippi, when he spotted an aluminium coloured sphere, moving rapidly through the sky, estimated to be 300ft or more in diameter, which passed diagonally and below his plane at about 800-900mph, half-a-mile away.

(**Source: James Scarborough,** *MUFON UFO Journal,* **No. 264, 1990**)

9th October 1989 (Australia) – Effects of massive radiation

At 9.15pm, two people were driving through Melbourne when they sighted an orange-red object, about 20ft in diameter, hovering at ground level near some power lines. The object was then seen to climb into the sky, fly over the car, and disappear from view over a nearby hill.

John Auchetti, of the Victorian UFO Research Society, discovered unusual markings on the ground near where the UFO had been seen.

Laboratory analysis of grass samples showed the cells to the upper exposed side of the grass stems were dead, while those on the bottom side were still alive. Tests conducted at Monash University showed that yellowing of the grass and the surrounding organic material was caused by intense or massive amounts of ultraviolet radiation.

(**Source: John Auchetti,** *The Churchill Park UFO Encounter/Ground Ring Summary/The Australian UFO Bulletin,* **Victorian UFO Research Society, March 1990**)

John Auchetti with Bill Chalker (right).

10th October 1989 (USA) – UFO over Tennessee

Pilot Bill Kimmel reported, while flying between Clarksdale and Memphis, he had observed a round, metallic UFO, which kept changing colours and was moving at 800-900mph, 3,000ft off his left wing. He said:

> *"There was no way it was a weather balloon, because no balloon can travel that fast."*

(**Source***: Commercial Appeal,* **Memphis, Tennessee, 12.10.1989**)

The Aetherius Society

The Standard London 10 OCT 1989

UFO story isn't alien to us, say scientists

ON THE far side of the scientific community, the news of 12 ft aliens taking a walk in a Russian park comes as final proof that a belief in UFOs is not a definition of lunacy.

At the Aetherius Society, spokeswoman Chrissie Aubry noted with satisfaction that the description of a "shining ball or disc" seen landing in a park in the southern town of Voronezh matched their own reports almost exactly.

It gave her the opportunity once again to call for the Defence Ministry to release its own secret files on UFO sightings, adding: "Tass never jokes and if they take it seriously, so should the authorities in Britain."

According to the society, the description of craft seen by the people of Voronezh bears a striking resemblance to what they know as a scout craft—a disc-shaped craft with four domes underneath which are apparently the landing gear.

She went on: "We have been saying for years that alien spacecraft have been visiting this planet. They have been coming for thou-

JOHNSTON

"Take me to West Berlin!"

by John Passmore

sands of years and helping mankind."

It was at this point that the society's explanation began to stretch credulity as Chrissie said: "We believe that some of the great teachers like Buddha and Jesus were interplanetary. Our own president George King has been contacted and received some 600 transmissions from the inter-planetary parliament."

But such credentials carry little weight at the Defence Ministry, where one person deals with all UFO reports—and that is only one part of his job.

A spokesman explained: "We only look at them if they have some military connection.

"For instance, if a space-ship hovered over Aldershot and little green men got out, we would be interested. We simply don't have the man-power to look at all these things. This Russian thing is no big deal and has absolutely nothing to do with us."

With official reaction like that, it is hardly surprising that Colin Andrews, the engineer who has been studying mysterious circles found

in cornfields all over south-west England is treating the Russian report very carefully.

He said: "We're certainly following up this sighting. It's very interesting that they found a 20-metre circular depression in the park which is very similar to our circles. But we are far from saying the circles are made by alien craft. We have to be very careful about this."

Chrissie Aubry with a model of one of the space vehicles her society believes have visited Earth

Picture: ALISON McDOUGALL

11th October 1989 (UK) – Cigar-shaped UFO seen

Local writer – Glynis O'Shea, and her husband, Michael – from Wicken, near Milton Keynes, described seeing:

> "...a 'light', stationary in the sky ahead. It then got bigger and apparently got closer, until almost at the end of the dual carriageway stretch, we could see its shape. It was like a fat cigar, with lights flashing at either end, and in the middle were two headlights. As we passed underneath, I turned around to look behind – it had disappeared."

The couple were adamant that the object, which had been flying at only a few thousand feet, and similar to a *'blimp'*, was not the *Fuji Airship*, based at Bedford, as they had seen this many times previously, and declared it was totally unlike anything they had ever seen before.

(**Source:** *Newport Pagnel Citizen*, 12.10.1989 – 'Weird sighting of mystery aircraft')

NEWPORT PAGNELL CITIZEN

12 OCT 1989

WEIRD SIGHTING OF MYSTERY AIRCRAFT

By STEVE LARNER

WRITER GLYNIS O'Shea is used to telling stories — but she claims her encounter with a UFO is no work of fiction.

She and husband Michael were "buzzed" by a mystery craft as they drove south along the A5 through Milton Keynes.

The incident occurred just weeks after a man claimed his car was forced off the road by a spaceship. Now Glynis, of Wicken, wants other people who have experienced strange happenings along that stretch to come forward.

"When we first saw it it was just a light, stationary in the sky ahead. Then it got bigger, apparently as we got closer, until almost at the end of the dual carriageway stretch we could see its shape.

"It was shaped like a fat cigar, with lights flashing at either end and in the middle two headlights. As we passed beneath I turned round to look behind — and it had disappeared," she said.

Glynis said the object was flying at only a few thousand feet and although similar to a blimp was not the familiar Fuji airship based at Bedford.

"I have seen that many times but this was unlike anything I have seen before."

And she says demon drink can be ruled out: "We were on our way to a dinner party — and I only touch Perrier water. I have got to know if anyone else saw something."

● Is Milton Keynes the close encounters capital of the country? Have you seen something strange in the sky locally? Then tell us at the Citizen by phoning the newsdesk on MK 664777.

● Fact, not fiction — writer Glynis O'Shea is convinced she saw a spaceship.

11th October 1989 (UK) – UFO over Kent

In October 1989, Mrs Solange Hando was driving towards the family home at Herne Bay, in Kent, accompanied by her son – Giles, and friend – Richard, when they saw

> ". . . a small red light in the sky just under cloud cover, projecting two powerful beams of white light. To our astonishment, the beams of light moved towards our position but fell short over nearby rooftops."

Frightened, Mrs Hando decided to make her way home but still felt sufficiently curious to look back. When she did so, she saw that the beams of light had been replaced by an amber glow on either side of the red light, with a green single light higher up. The following morning, she contacted the police and Air Traffic Control; they were as mystified as she was by the sighting. She then contacted the local newspaper, who published their story, as a result of which another member of the public came forward to tell of a similar sighting, a couple of miles away, on the same evening. Mrs Hando still remains mystified to the present day as to what it was that she and her companions saw, and is now a firm believer in the existence of UFOs.

(Source: David Haith/Colin Andrews/*Woman,* London, 23.7.1990 – 'I saw a Flying Saucer!')

13th October 1989 (UK) – UFO crash-lands?

At 7.15pm, Mrs Cecile Woodford of Carmen Court, Willingdon, Eastbourne – an author of books by profession – was at her home address when she noticed a bank of cloud in the distance, followed by the appearance of a pear-shaped object that descended from the sky.

Eastbourne Gazette

18 OC, 1989

2374

Pear-shaped UFO stuns author

A PEAR-SHAPED UFO has been sighted near the Downs.

The dark ominus shape came plummeting towards the earth and burst into flames at dusk on Friday, according to a startled eyewitness.

After it crashed to the ground in the Wannock and Folkington area a huge cloud of smoke rose above it.

When most of the smoke had cleared odd lights were spotted flitting around it which suddenly disappeared.

Local author Cecile Woodford stood stunned at her top flat window in Carmen Court, Willingdon, too frightened to investigate any wreckage.

She said, 'It was about 7.15pm and was beginning to get dark. There was a bank of cloud in the far distance when this pear-shaped thing started to come down lower and lower.

'It came in front of the cloud and burst into flames, not just a flare it really burst and then it went down.

'Up came a huge cloud of smoke then odd dots of light were around it.

'It was as if something was following it.'

The larger than life UFO was too big to be an air balloon, she said.

And nearby museum owner, Paul Foulkes-Halbard of Filching Manor, said he heard a loud explosion coming from the same area at about the same time.

'I was sitting in my study and heard this noise. It sounded like a metallic explosion and reminded me of a bad crash where a car had tumbled over and over.'

No wreckage could be found.

The Ministry of Defence could offer no explanation as to what the strange object was.

School stages UFO event (UK) – 15 years later!

Ironically, on the 22nd July 2004, year six pupils at Willingdon Primary School staged a play about aliens landing on Earth, which had a strong anti-bullying message. Inevitably of course, a matter such as this gained much media attention.

13th October 1989 (Canada) – UFO hovers over barn

At 10.20am Rose Neumeier, who was living on a farm near Langenburg, Saskatchewan, was surprised by a *'flash of light'* which occurred.

Looking out of the window she saw:

"...an oblong, silver object, hovering soundlessly above the garage. It had a bright silver band around the middle, which was the light I had initially seen. It then moved off to the north, paused, and then returned to hover over the barn. After a few seconds, it took off and disappeared in almost an instant".

A number of other sightings were reported in the area in mid-October.

(Source: George Bentley, *Leader-Post,* Regina, Saskatchewan 4.11.1989)

Saskatchewan residents abuzz at UFO sightings

REGINA (CP) — Residents of Langenburg, Sask., are craning their necks skyward these days after reports of a strange flying object hovering silently in the air around town.

"Everybody is talking about it," said RCMP Sgt. Herman Fogen, who is investigating the sightings. "Everybody is looking for some positive proof this really is a UFO."

A group of high school students and two teachers first reported seeing a brightly lit object near the town of 1,400 on the night of Oct. 11.

Two days later — on Friday the 13th — a similar object reportedly paid a morning visit to a farm 10 kilometres south of the community, in southeastern Saskatchewan near the Manitoba boundary.

"I am convinced there is something strange happening in the area," said teacher Bob Markham, who said he watched the strange object for 10 to 15 minutes after students alerted him and another teacher.

Fogen said he has no reason to think the reports are a hoax or disbelieve the witnesses. He said he is compiling statements and will forward the results of the investigation to the National Research Council.

"According to the paper we read the Russian people are talking to aliens so there's no reason we shouldn't be able to see them at least," said Fogen.

Rose Neumeier, 39, said she was sitting at her kitchen table talking on the phone shortly after 10 a.m. Oct. 13 when she saw a huge, silvery object silently float over her farmyard for two to five minutes.

"There was sort of a flash of light and at first I kind of chalked it off to a passing car on the road," she said. "But the light was sort of stationary. It was there and I looked up and saw it. I was scared at first and curious. You're transfixed."

The object, about nine metres long and three metres thick, hovered about 30 metres in the air no more than 15 metres from the house, said Neumeier. She said it looked like two pie plates face-to-face and had a flat top and a bottom like corrugated steel.

"It made no noise at all," she said. "The cattle weren't disturbed, the dog wasn't disturbed. If I hadn't caught the flash of light I probably wouldn't even have noticed it.

Neumeier said she didn't report the sighting to police — Fogen asked her about it after hearing a secondhand report — because she didn't think anyone would believe her.

Could there have been a connection with a UFO sighted over the country some years previously?

13th October 1989 (UK) – Three objects seen in the sky

On the same date, but this time in the UK, Essex mechanic Anthony Walden (40) was driving home in his Ford Escort MK2 with his daughter and wife, at 8.30pm, after having been shopping. As they approached a roundabout at Waltham Cross, Essex, they noticed a group of boys looking upwards into the sky and pointing. Curious, Antony stopped the car and got out to have a look, when:

> *"I saw three objects in the sky, moving slowly in a line, about a quarter of a mile away. It was about the size of a ten pence piece from where we stood, to start with, but when it moved closer it was as big as a saucer in size.*
>
> *One of them seemed to go to the left, the other straight ahead, the other to the right. I told my daughter to get my binoculars. As the objects(s) came closer, the light changed colour along the side. It then tipped to one side, showing a circular base, before gliding away silently into the distance."*

Strange dreams

Although it might have been sheer coincidence and nothing to do with the encounter with the UFO, Anthony developed an increased awareness and precognitive feeling that something was going to happen. Interestingly he had a dream, involving meeting a beautiful girl with cat-like eyes. His illustration of the *'eyes'* reminds us of other incidents involving close encounters, where people have reported seeing unusual black eyes – whether on an animal, or human being. Some will regard this as a trait of behaviour associated with an abduction experience – but there is no proof, intriguing as the concept may appear.

14th October 1989 (USA) – USAF fighter jets chase UFOs

As dusk fell at San Marcos, near San Diego, California, Jerry and Janet Clark noticed some *'red lights'* in the sky, forming an oval pattern.

Shortly afterwards, with six other witnesses, the Clarks watched as a dark object passed silently over their heads, its perimeter lights turned off.

Janet: *"It looked like a boomerang, and it was massively huge – about the size of a football field."*

Twenty minutes later, a second triangular-shaped object passed over the Clark group, being pursued by six fighter jets. Other sightings were reported in the immediate vicinity that night.

(Source: *Brae Canlen*/San Diego, *Reader,* California, 8.2.1990)

15th October 1989 (UK) – UFO over Kent; discovery of rash on body

At 8.35pm, Miss Dionne Beresford (21) – a VDU Operator from Windsor Avenue, Chadwell-St-Mary, Grays, in Essex – was watching TV in her bedroom, when she saw a bright white *'light'* appear outside the bedroom window. On going to investigate, the *'light'* dropped down out of view but reappeared – this time flashing red and green lights on either side.

> *"All of a sudden, eight 'lights' appeared; three of them formed into triangular shapes, one flew over the top of the house, flashing red and green, the other flashed white, then green and red lights, each side of the house. I could hear a dull humming noise. They stayed in the sky for about an hour, before moving away. It reminded me of a 'flying plaice' in shape."*

Mr P. Oliver, who was responsible for interviewing Dionne and her parents with regard to this matter, concluded this to be a genuine account and remarked on the admission made by her of the *"discovery of a rash on her legs, the following morning"*, which was brought to the attention of her doctor, who suggested it was an allergy rash. (**Source: Mr P. Oliver, East Anglian UFO and Paranormal Research Association**)

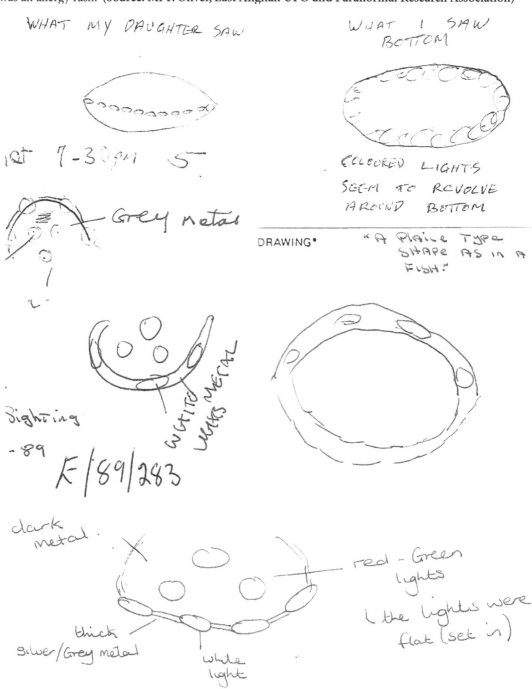

At 9pm, an employee at Tilbury Power Station sighted a diamond-shaped craft hovering in the sky. He was later interviewed by Peter Oliver and was most reluctant to be named, or supply any further information, fearing ridicule.

17th October 1989 (UK) – UFOs over Staffordshire

Mr D. Walters – Secretary of the Mansfield UFO Group – and Mr L. Truman, were travelling by car to Ilkeston from Mansfield, Nottinghamshire, to investigate a report of a UFO seen at that location; little did they know that they, themselves, were to witness something unusual in the sky.

```
REPORT OF UNIDENTIFIED FLYING OBJECT.
-------------------------------------------
WITNESSES: MR.D.WALTERS AND MR.L.TRUEMAN.    F/89/282        DATE: 17-10-89
TIME:1925 to 1930 HOURS BST (APPROX)

ACCOUNT OF SIGHTING:
--------------------

Mr.Trueman and I were travelling by car to Ilkeston from Mansfield on the
night of Tuesday 17th October last.  The reason for our trip was to
investigate a reported UFO sighting by a witness at Ilkeston.
Our route took us along Derby Road, Kirkby-in-Ashfield and through Annesley
where we took a right hand turn on to the road leading towards the
roundabout at M1 Motorway Junction 27.

We were leaving the roundabout on the road towards Underwood and Eastwood.
We had travelled only a few tens of yards from the roundabout when
Mr.Trueman brought my attention to a glowing object in the sky to the front
of us and slightly over to our left hand side.  It appeared to be travelling
very slowly indeed across our field of view.

Mr.Trueman commented that it looked rather strange for an aircraft, so I
wound down the car window (passenger side) and using Mr.Trueman's
binoculars, focussed on the object.

What I saw through the binoculars amazed me.  I am used to a variety of
different aircraft light arrangements, but this was nothing like anything I
had encountered so far.  It appeared like two Vee formations of light, one
above the other a short distance apart, and was composed of numerous small
lights. The Vees pointed downwards, with white lights forming the left hand
parts of the Vee, whilst the right hand sides were made up from red lights.

As we watched, a faint sound of engines was heard above the sound of
traffic which was passing us for most of the time on the road.

We stood watching the object,which was about 45 degrees high in the sky,
slowly travel from right to left, from approximately over the Derby
direction towards the direction of Mansfield.  As it turned away from us,
the Vee configuration changed until it appeared as two clusters of light
separated horizontally by a space. By this time it was further away and the
clusters of light appeared to be mixed red and white.  A small red flashing
light appeared to be on the top of each cluster of light.
We watched it until it went out of sight over the tree tops.
I looked at my watch which said 7.30.
```

D.Walters 20-10-89.

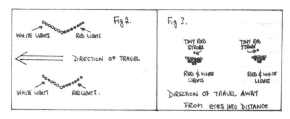

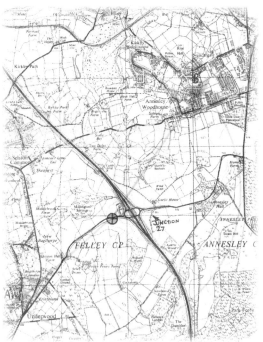

SIZE OF OBJECT: SIZE OF PEA HELD AT ARMS LENGTH (NAKED EYE).

NOT SURE WHETHER ALL LIGHTS BELONG TO ONE OBJECT OR TO TWO OBJECTS CLOSE TOGETHER.

FIG 2 SHOWS HOW OBJECT(S) APPEARED WHEN SEEN AT FIRST IN DIRECTION OF ARROW 'A' ON MAP.

FIG 3 SHOWS HOW OBJECT(S) APPEARED WHEN SEEN TO BE GOING AWAY INTO DISTANCE IN DIRECTION OF ARROW 'B' ON MAP.

MAP INDICATES THE LOCATION WHERE OBJECT WAS OBSERVED FROM AND THE RANGE OVER WHICH IT WAS SEEN TO MOVE AROUND THE SKY.

AT NO TIME DID THE OBJECT PASS OVERHEAD, IT REMAINED APPROX. 45° HIGH.

20-10-89.

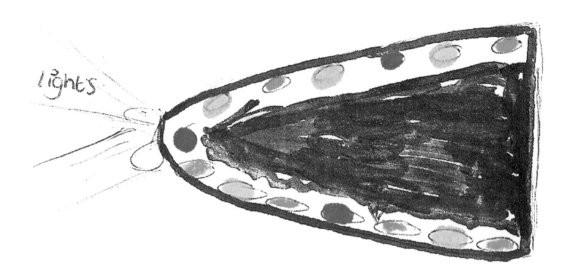

Mrs Dawn Aiken's illustration of what she witnessed

18th October 1989 (UK)

Essex woman – Mrs Susan Charmley contacted Ron West, after sighting a UFO. This is what she wrote:

Another witness was Dawn Aiken.

EAST ANGLIAN U.F.O. & PARANORMAL RESEARCH ASSOCIATION

SIGHTING ACCOUNT FORM

SECTION A

Please write an account of your sighting, make a drawing of what you saw and then answer the questions in section B overleaf as fully as possible. Write in **BLOCK CAPITALS** using a ball point pen.

THE THING I SAW WAS HOVERING ABOUT 25FT ABOVE A BUNGALOW, NEAR TO SEVERAL TREES. IT WAS STATIONARY FOR ALMOST FOUR MINUTES. THERE WERE BRIGHT LIGHTS UNDERNEATH, WITH LIGHTBEAMS OF WHITE LIGHT SIMILAR TO CAR HEADLIGHTS. THERE WAS NO SOUND THAT I RECALL. THE LIGHTBEAMS WENT OFF, THEN THIS THING SHOT OFF IN A SOUTH-EASTERN DIRECTION. THERE WERE NO SOUNDS, AND NO MOVEMENTS IN THE TREES, SO I ASSUMED IT WASN'T A HELICOPTER. I WAS ONLY STANDING ABOUT 15FT-20FT FROM THE BUNGALOW SO I COULD SEE THIS OBJECT QUITE CLEARLY. THE LIGHTS UNDERNEATH WERE RED, BLUE + GREEN, THEY WERE CIRCULAR IN SHAPE, I CAN'T REMEMBER HOW MANY.

Please continue on a separate sheet if necessary.

DRAWING*

120FT X 10FT

Light beams.

Your full name (Mr/Mrs/Miss/Ms)
SUSAN CHARMLEY ... Age 23

Address... THE BADGERS
LANGDON HILLS ESSEX

Telephone No.................(STD. 0268.)
Occupation during last two years... NANNY

Any professional, technical or academic qualifications or special interests

Do you object to the publication of your name?
*Yes/No. *Delete as applicable.
Today's Date... 22ND JANUARY 1990
Signature... S.E. Charmley

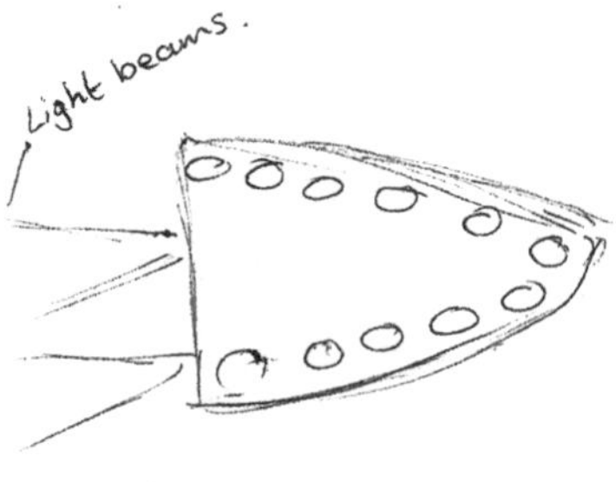

* If preferred, use a separate sheet of paper.

20th October 1989 (UK) – Seen by the police

At 8.15pm, Mr Michael 'T' (27) of Langdon Hills, Basildon, Essex, was picking up his wife from work. They saw five objects moving through the sky, while driving along the road.

Between 10.48pm and 11.30pm, at Hapton, near Accrington, numerous members of the public and four uniformed police officers sighted a circular-shaped UFO, displaying nine lights around its circumference, with a single orange light in the centre, surrounded by a mist, moving slowly and erratically across the sky.

(Source: Gary Heseltine, PRUFOS)

23rd October 1989 (UK) – Oblong UFO over Poole

At 8.39pm, a mysterious light formation was seen hovering over the motorway, between Glossop and Manchester, almost bringing traffic to a standstill. A few minutes later on the same evening, Mrs Anita Larby of Waterloo Estate, Broadstone, Dorset, was at her home address, when her two young children – Danny (11) and Rosie (10) – told her about seeing something in the sky. Mrs Larby presumed they had seen fireworks, until she went to see for herself and realised that this was not the case.

> *"It was over the Poole town centre, and had come from the direction of Broadstone, and was heading towards Creekmoor. It was oblong-shaped, with flashing lights. It wasn't a plane, because as soon as a plane came over it disappeared. I tried to take a photo, but it was too far away by the time I fetched a camera. I then reported it to the police."*

(Source: *Metro News,* 10.11.1989 – 'UFO sheds light on motorway madness'/*Bournemouth Evening Echo,* 25.10.1989 – 'Mystery UFO spotted again'/Jenny Randles, Reports Coordinator for the Manchester UFO Research Association/ 24.10.1989 – *Bournemouth Evening Echo* – 'Couple report sighting of UFO over Dorchester 'Sighing of the unexplained' – Glowing UFO seen over the Giant at Cerne Abbas Dorchester)

Bournemouth Evening Echo
25 OCT 1989

Mystery UFO spotted again

THE mysterious UFO which is travelling through Dorset skies at night has been spotted by a Broadstone family.

Mrs Anita Larby (37) of Allenby Road, Waterloo Estate, saw an oblong-shaped flying craft with flashing blue, red and yellow lights on Monday night and reported the event to the police on Tuesday morning.

That was just hours before the Echo printed a report in yesterday's newspaper detailing how a Yeovil couple spied a glowing UFO over the giant at Cerne Abbas.

Mrs Larby, a divorced mother of two, couldn't believe it when she saw the UFO and then read the Echo report. She said: "I was amazed that someone else had seen it. I didn't know about the Echo story at the time."

Police confirmed the call at 10.30am yesterday and that the UFO had been seen between 8.30pm and 8.45pm the previous night.

Mrs Larby said her two children, Danny (11) and Rosie (10), saw the strange object from a bedroom window. Mrs Larby thought they were talking about fireworks until she also cast eyes on the slow-moving thing.

She said: "It was over Poole town centre. It had come from Broadstone and was heading towards Creekmoor. It was hovering and very slow. We watched it for a full 15 minutes.

"It was oblong-shaped and rotating with flashing lights. It wasn't a plane because as soon as it disappeared a plane came over and it wasn't anything like that."

Mrs Larby said she tried to take a photo but it was too far away by the time she got hold of a camera.

She said: "I was not surprised to see it. I believe in UFOs and life on other planets. I am not afraid of the unknown."

She said the unusual sighting would probably be reported to the MOD.

UFO spotters Anita Larby, Rosie and Danny

UFO sheds light on motorway madness

UFOlogist of the year Jenny Randles

REPORTS of a "rotating disc" in the sky, which could have caused an accident on Manchester's M67 are being investigated by the country's only professional UFOlogist.

Manchester's Ms Jenny Randles, who has just received the prestigious UFOlogist of the Year Award in America, is appealing for people to come forward after reports of the mysterious "light formation" which hovered above the motorway between Glossop and Manchester.

"The sighting occurred around 8.39 pm on October 23 and almost brought traffic to a stand-still" said Ms Randles.

And this was not the only sighting on that night. A North West policeman and his wife were driving through Delamere Forest, Cheshire when a large triangular object appeared and hovered above their car.

"This is a common sighting," said Ms Randles, author and lecturer on the subject of UFOs, "We call it a Silent Vulcan because it is a similar shape to the Vulcan Bomber."

Many of the incidents are related to military testing of aircraft, but so far no satisfactory explanation has come to light of the two sightings.

"We work closely with the Ministry of Defence who monitor all the recorded sightings. We also work with Manchester Airport, Jodrell Bank, local weather stations and have contacts with astronomers," said Ms Randles who is reports co-ordinator of Manchester UFO Research Association (MUFORA).

Although she has never spotted a UFO herself, Ms Randles has helped compile a record of over 2,500 sightings in the North of England — all of which are stored in a regional archive at Manchester University.

And the university takes an active

By a Staff Reporter

interest in the findings of MUFORA. Dr Raymond Leonard, head of the total Technology Department of UMIST has been involved with the group for two years.

"MUFORA have few research facilities but, here at UMIST we have experts in all fields and if we can help with scientific experiments then we do," he said.

There are about 100 Manchester sightings reported each year all of which are investigated.

Members of MUFORA are holding a joint public meeting with the British UFO Research Association on Saturday, November 18, 1 15 pm at Manchester's Central Library.

METRO NEWS 10.11.89

Triangular object over Delamere Forest, Cheshire

At 7.15pm, an off-duty police officer and his family were driving past the forest, near the village of Alvanley, when they encountered a triangular object, covered with white, red, and blue lights, which hovered silently for 2mins before accelerating away. (**Source: Peter Hough,** *Northern UFO News,* **No. 142**)

24th October 1989 (USA) – Pilots sight boomerang-shaped UFO

At 6.15am a commercial airline crew, in flight over Northern Indiana, sighted a boomerang-shaped UFO passing through the sky overhead.

A vertical *'beam of light'* was seen shining downward from the underside of the object, which passed from view in 30 seconds. (**Source: Franklin Reams,** *MUFON UFO Journal,* **No. 264, April 1990**)

'Ball of light' seen

At 5am, on the same date in the UK, Glywn Edwards of Pontypool went downstairs to fetch a drink of water, when he noticed *"a 'ball of light', moving silently North to South"* along the valley. His wife, Toni, confirmed the sighting, but added she had seen very bright lights – like searchlights – being trained onto trees, before the object became lost from view. (**Source:** *South Wales Weekly Argus,* **Newport, 16.11.1989 – 'Couple's close encounter with a suspected UFO'**)

Orange domed UFO seen

On the same evening, Alan and Lee Thackeray were motorcycling between High Dunmow and Roding, when they saw an orange *'light'* in the sky, followed by the appearance of an orange dome, which the boys claimed had landed in a nearby field. A sceptical MOD spokesperson told the *Dunmow Broadcast & Receiver* Newspaper (1.11.1989) that *'unless a UFO actually landed in military territory',* they weren't interested.

(**Sources:** Edward Harris/*Dunmow Broadcast & Recorder,* 1.11.1989 – 'Family baffled by strange UFO')

The *Bournemouth Evening Echo,* in their edition of the 24th October 1989, told of a sighting over Cerne Abbas, near Dorchester.

Couple report sighting of UFO over Dorchester

Sighting of the unexplained

by Andy Nicholls

A GLOWING UFO has been spotted zooming above the giant at Cerne Abbas near Dorchester.

The oblong craft, fluorescent green with a red circular glow towards its rear, was travelling at great speed over the famous 180 foot long figure carved from chalk.

It then just disappeared from view to the amazement of the couple who saw it.

Incredibly, unknown to this couple, a similar sighting was reported the following night at South Petherton in Somerset.

The couple from Yeovil, who do not wish to be named, said they saw the unidentified flying object while travelling on the A352 road to Sherborne.

The woman said: "I thought it was a shooting star first of all. But it was too big and the wrong colour. It was only there for a few seconds and then it zipped off.

"It was travelling extremely fast, much faster than a plane. I have never seen anything like it before. I had always been sceptical about talk of flying saucers before, but not now."

She said her husband, who works with aircraft, said it was a flying saucer straight away. She said: "He knew it wasn't a plane. He said it must be a UFO."

She said they did not wish to be identified because of possible public reaction to their story. She said: "People don't believe you half the time. They would

probably think we were making it up or imagining it." She added this was why they had not reported.

Talk of UFOS has seemingly become respectable after the Russians reported that

aliens had landed in their country.

There have been a number of reported ufo sightings in Dorset but the last mystery in the Poole area was six years ago.

UNEXPLAINED GREEN AND ORANGE LIGHTS IN THE SKY

Family baffled by 'strange UFO'

DUNMOW BROADCAST & RECORDER, NOVEMBER 1, 1989

DID anyone else see unusual flashing lights in the sky over Dunmow last week? That's what Mrs Sandra Thackray would like to know.

For although her family were not all in the same place at the time, they all saw a strange green light "flashing all over the place" last Tuesday evening, October 24.

"It seemed to be moving much too fast for an aeroplane," said Mrs Thackray, a house manager at Croft House. She was driving from her home in Dunmow towards Little Easton at the time, with her elder son, Alan, 21.

"It was still in the sky when we got home and must have been there a good half-hour. We were intrigued by it."

But, she said, the following evening, Alan and his younger brother, Lee, 18, had an even stranger experience when they were out on their motor bikes with a friend.

"They were returning home from a karate class in Aythorpe Roding," their mother explained, "when they saw an orange light in the sky and a terrific orange dome hovered over a field and then landed."

By BROADCAST STAFF

She said one of the boys told her afterwards that he had seen someone running around inside the light.

She said the incident happened on an isolated stretch of road between High Roding and Dunmow.

A spokesman for Stansted said that the airport did not keep a log of unusual sightings but individuals passed on their own reports to the Civil Aviation Authority.

The Civil Aviation Authority said such reports were taken by the RAF "for reasons of national security", but at the Ministry of Defence, a sceptical spokesman said that unless a UFO actually landed in military territory, they were not really interested.

The Thackray family would love an explanation for their sightings. So if you saw something similar or can shed some light on the mystery, do let us know.

UFO sighted by USS Memphis?

What can we make of an intriguing claim from an unnamed sailor, about a UFO sighting, while in the Navy?

"I was assigned to USS Memphis (SSN-698), Homeport – Titusville, FL. (Cape Canaveral). Our mission was Special Assignments, which meant we protected the Space Program. We would go to sea and patrol while the shuttle was on the pad."

Electronic problems – Nuclear reactor shut down

"On October 24th and 25th, 1989, our ship was on patrol about 150 miles off the Florida coast, cruising at about 500ft, when the submarine started experiencing electronics problems. Our tanks were blowing out of control; we were losing navigation ability and the communications area was totally lost. We went to all stop and tried to access what was happening. The controls in the reactor area started to malfunction. This presented a serious danger to our safety, so the captain ordered us to shut down the reactor, surface, and go to diesel motors."

Submarine surfaced – 'V'-shaped UFO seen

When the ship surfaced, the seaman (whose rank is also not known – presumably an officer) went to his watch station. He tells that the ship was still experiencing electronic difficulties but mechanical devices such as diesel engines, cook stoves and turbines, were not affected.

> *"It was raining and the entire sky was red – like a red neon sign. I saw a large inverted 'V'-shaped UFO off the port side. The executive officer told me to stand fast and he would speak to the captain. In a minute, the captain appeared on the tower and asked me for a distance to the craft.*

> *Use of the laser rangefinder determined the closest point was 200 meters; the farthest point was 1000 meters off the port. The UFO was not perpendicular to our ship but at about a 45° angle. This huge vessel was over a half mile across. The UFO made a half circle around our ship – then passed across the stern, causing our electronics systems to go crazy.*

> *We had permanent damage in communications and the sonar room. As the craft flew over the stern, I could see the rain stop under its red glow. The water seemed to rise almost a foot as the UFO passed over silently. When the UFO finished its swing across the stern, it paused – the sky got brighter red and it simply moved off at tremendous speed inside 15 seconds – following which our boat returned to normal, with the exception of the radio and sonar."*

Reactor power then engaged

> *"The captain ordered us to return to reactor power and get underway. The captain took two petty officers – the executive officer, and me – into the wardroom. He told us to not spread any rumours until we had a chance to talk to Commander Submarine Fleet – Atlantic."*

Taken into protective custody

"We reached port in about seven hours, where I was taken into 'protective custody'. Two enlisted men, and I, agreed we had witnessed a real UFO. I was the one who shot it with a laser rangefinder, so I was the only one that had its exact sizes. I shot that vessel as it hovered and I got solid readings – not spotty like I would on debris."

Exploding weather satellite!

"We were in holding for about three hours, when an officer from the Air Force arrived and gave us a 'line of bull' about an exploding weather satellite. The Navy then transferred virtually everyone on the crew to new assignments. This included the captain, the executive officer and the entire crew. They were split up, which almost never happens unless one of them gets a promotion or a new command – neither of which happened.

The military just split up a four-year team. I was watching a program tonight that gave me the courage to share it."

Serious discrepancies

Unless the witness to this event has made a mistake with regard to the serial number of the submarine, (highly unlikely, one would have thought) then there is already a glaring discrepancy, as SSN-698 was *USS Bremerton* – a *Los Angeles*-class submarine, and the second ship of the United States Navy to be named for Bremerton, Washington. The contract to build her was awarded to the Electric Boat Division of General Dynamics Corporation in Groton, Connecticut, on 24th January 1972, and her keel was laid down on 8th May 1976. She was launched on 22nd July 1978, sponsored by Mrs Henry M. Jackson, and commissioned on 28th March 1981 with Captain Thomas H. Anderson in command. In addition to this, the shutting down or restarting a nuclear reactor is not like turning a light off and on: the normal periodic refurbishment/refuelling of a nuclear sub takes a couple of years!

David Bryant – Adviser to 'Haunted Skies'

"In an emergency, the reactor is designed to shut down automatically: US nuclear submarines have control rods that don't just drop into the reactor core, but are actually forced in by springs. The control rods are driven into the reactor if the control mechanism fails, even if the submarine is upside-down. The US Navy reactors shut down even if all the rods are not driven into the core. To restart the reactor, the cooling system has to be restarted first: this requires either an electrical supply provided by a diesel generator or a diesel pump. In any event, it would take a day at least to restart the power plant, even if nothing was damaged: no captain would order a reboot until every part of the system was checked. Logic dictates that this report <u>should not be taken seriously</u> at this stage."

(Source: www.ufocasebook.com/2011/1989ussubmarine, 2014)

Wikipedia: *USS Memphis* (**SSN-691**), – a Los Angeles-class submarine, was the sixth ship to be named for Memphis, Tennessee. The contract to build her was awarded to Newport News Shipbuilding and Dr. Dock Company, Virginia, on 4th February 1971, and her keel was laid down on 23rd June 1973. She was launched on 3rd April 1976, sponsored by Mrs Cathy Beard, and commissioned on 17th December 1977, with Commander G. Dennis Hicks in command. In March 1981, *Memphis* completed an around-the-world cruise, via the Panama Canal, including operations with both the 6th and 7th fleets. *Memphis* was re-designated an experimental submarine, during 1989, to test composite hull structures, unmanned underwater vehicles, advanced sonar's, hull friction reduction, and other advanced technologies for the *Los Angeles* and *Seawolf* classes, but remained combat-capable.

Rockbank, Victoria, Melbourne (Australia)

At 7.30pm, a triangular-shaped fluorescent green craft, estimated to be 10^2 metres in size, was seen by two people, who were 30 to 40 metres away at the time of sighting.

> *"It rotated clockwise, as a fifty cent coin would if you rolled it on the ground and rotated slowly. I observed it for three to four minutes, before it accelerated to create a blur in my vision. It then disappeared into infinity – not vertical but horizontally – towards Bass Strait Sea. I could see that it seemed to glow – like liquid inside a glow stick."*

(Source: UFOINFO Online Sighting Report)

25th October 1989 (UK) – UFO over Colchester Barracks

An army officer (name on file) at the 42nd Ordnance Company was carrying out a security check of the building and grounds at 10.30pm. While near the eastern edge of the building, he noticed:

> *"...a rotating light in the sky towards Berechurch Road, over the playing field. At first I thought it was the beacon of a police car, but it was too high up and no light or beam was being projected. I kept it under observation for 30 minutes and was still unable to determine its source, as it was in a section of low cloud which wasn't moving – unlike the clouds above it that were. It then vanished from sight. Shortly afterwards, the small cloud itself dissipated. It reminded me of a lighthouse beacon."*

We decided not to include the name of the officer, as his report may have breached the Official Secrets Act, as it happened while he was at work and on MOD property. (**Source: Ron West**)

'Flying saucer' over Sussex

During the same month, children and teachers outside St. Joseph's Catholic School, Haywards Heath, Sussex, were amazed to see a grey-peach coloured object hovering above the school, with what looked like *'legs'* dangling from it.

We traced some of the children, including Melissa Morrison – (aged 10 at the time of the sighting) – who still remembers the incident vividly.

> *"It was saucer-shaped, and had windows all around it, with these 'dangly things' hanging out of the bottom."*

26th October 1989 (UK) – Triangular UFO

At 12.45am, Simon Carter was walking along a main road at Mangotsfield, when he suddenly became aware of two bright lights approaching – as bright as floodlights used at a football ground. As they passed silently within 150ft, Mr Carter was able to make out

> *"... a triangular-shaped object – as large as five articulated lorries – which was almost transparent. It had two lights on the underside, pointing downwards. It then moved away at less than 50mph.*
>
> *As it did so the lights suddenly increased in intensity, until the whole structure became engulfed in the glow, before suddenly disappearing."*

(Source: Tony Dodd, *Quest International*, Vol. 9, No. 3, 1990/*Yellow Advertiser*, Colchester, 27.10.1989 – 'Twelve feet tall aliens on their way here'/*Peterborough Evening Telegraph*, Northants., 27.11.1989 – 'The night a UFO chased off women')

30th October 1989 (UK) – Lecture at the *Golden Lion Hotel,* Leeds

Stanton T. Friedman – an American nuclear physicist – gave a talk, which was organised by the Yorkshire UFO Society, during the evening.

(Source: *Yorkshire Evening Post,* 31.10.1989 – 'Spaced-out over great cosmic plot')

Thursday, Oct. 26, 1989   Star Phoen.

'They've returned,' Langenburg man says of UFOs

By Dave Yanko
of the Star-Phoenix

For Edwin Fuhr, the Langenburg UFO flap means "they've" returned.

Fuhr was swathing in his rape field 15 autumns ago when he came upon what looked like a goose blind near a small slough.

As he got closer to the "pothole," he realized it was no goose blind.

"There were five of them. They scared the hell out me."

The swather stopped. He couldn't get it started.

So he just looked on in fear as two saucers five metres in diameter, and three slightly smaller ones, hovered half a metre off the ground in front of him.

They had the classical shape popularized in the 1950s movies: "They looked like upside-down saucers, with lips, and domes on the top.

"There was nothing holding them up. They were just revolving."

Fuhr says it was about 9:30 a.m. that Sept. 1 morning, when he first encountered the crafts.

He watched them for an hour and a half, and his descriptions are vivid.

But somewhere, he lost two and a half hours.

Fuhr has no memory of events between 11 a.m. and 1:30 p.m., when he recalls seeing the saucers leave "in step formation, one at a time."

He recalls a feeling that his body had received an electrical jolt.

Reporters, Mounties, the FBI and UFO researchers from across North America flocked to Langenburg to interview him and study the pothole, says Fuhr.

An American government researcher told him he'd receive a copy of the report he compiled on the sighting, but Fuhr says he got nothing.

"Afterwards, they said it was mushrooms I saw," he said.

"I've never seen mushrooms that fly, and I've never seen them leave a pool radioactive."

Fuhr says he saw the colored lights in the sky two weeks ago. At the time, he thought they belonged to a distant airplane.

He's no longer the only man in Langenburg with a story about UFOs.

31st October 1989 (UK) – Girls sight UFO

At 5.30pm on this date, Miss Joanna Lumley (14) of Greenland Grove, St. Osyth, was out exercising horses on the local marsh, with her friend – Lisa Allen – when they saw a bright egg-shaped object hovering in the sky, about half a mile away. They stopped to watch, and after 10 minutes it changed colour from bright red to yellow. Half an hour later,

". . . it shot off into bushes. We rode towards it and it moved again, frightening the horses, then it moved away eastwards and was lost from view".

Indicating the possibility that the two girls had come into close proximity to the object was the revelation made – a couple

CHANGED SHAPE / LIKE TURNED
When it CHANGED COLOUR. GLITTERY.

of days later – that they both suffered unusual out-of-character, severe, nosebleeds. Whilst we cannot say categorically that they were attributed to the appearance of the UFO, we would be surprised if there was not a connection. One senses that there is far more to this incident than we shall ever know.

(Source: Peter Oliver/Ron West/Ros Reynolds)

Northumberland

At 6.30pm, two objects – approximately 40ft apart and bright white in colour – were seen against a clear sky, over Ashington, Northumberland, by a member of the public and a police constable.

(Source: *FOI Documentation*/**Gary Heseltine, PRUFOS)**

At 7.30pm, Miss Dionne Beresford (21) – a VDU Operator from Windsor Avenue, Chadwell-St-Mary, Grays, in Essex, was to experience another UFO sighting from her home address.

> *"A bright light flickered and shone directly into the bedroom window, illuminating the room with red and green light – then disappeared. I looked out and saw four objects, moving around in a circular fashion. One large object approached the window of the house, showing four white lights, and passed overhead – then they all moved away and out of sight."*

NOVEMBER 1989

2nd November 1989 (UK) – *'Flying saucer'* over Gwent

AT 5.30pm, three schoolboys – Lee Holt, Carl Jones, and Sidney McLoughlin – were out playing near Cwmtillery Lake, by an old farmhouse, when they saw a *'bright light'* coming down the hillside. The object – now seen as silver and saucer-shaped – came down even lower, clipping the tops of trees, before circling several times over the boys, and then flew rapidly away. This was followed by a huge fireball, which came down through the sky and fell to earth near the farm. After reporting it to their parents – who initially thought they had seen fireworks, or were making it up (until one look at their terrified state showed otherwise) – contacted the police, at Abertillery, who spoke to the boys and were quite satisfied that they had apparently seen something very strange. Inspector Brian Heal, of the Abertillery Police, was quoted as saying:

> *"We have to take any incident like this seriously, and whatever it was the boys saw they were very scared by it".*

(Source: *South Wales Argus,* Newport, 7.11.1989 – 'The UFO Paradox')

Boys tell of UFO terror

THREE north Gwent youngsters are convinced they have seen a UFO following a close encounter at Cwmtillery.

Lee Holt, Carl Jones and Sidney McLoughlin, all of Cwmtillery, thought their days on earth were numbered when a "flying saucer" homed in on them at 5.30pm last Thursday evening.

And even now they cannot think of a logical explanation for what they saw.

"We were playing up at Cwmtillery Lake near an old farmhouse when we saw a bright light coming down the hillside," said Lee, who has drawn a picture of what he saw.

"It was really low in the sky, clipping the tops of the trees. It circled above our heads several times, then flew off really quickly.

"It was silver, disc-shaped, with a domed top and luminous lights, about the size of a car, and it made no noise.

"We were really scared. I thought whatever it was was going to take us away.

"A few minutes after it vanished their was a huge fireball which came down near the farm."

The youngsters rushed home to tell their parents and at first Lee's mum Melinda was sceptical.

"I thought they had made it up, or that what they had seen was fireworks, but then I realised they were absolutely terrified," said Mrs Holt, of White Horse Court, Cwmtillery.

Abertillery police, who have investigated the boys' story, have been unable to offer any down-to-earth explanation.

"We have to take any incident like this seriously and whatever it was the boys saw they were very scared by it," said Inspector Brian Heal.

3rd November 1989 (UK) – 'Wriggling lights' over Staffordshire

At 10pm, Gillian Sergeant was sat in the front passenger seat of a car being driven by her father travelling along the A34 Cannock Road, Staffordshire, when they noticed a bright flashing light through a clump of nearby trees, and first thought it was a reflection or fireworks.

"I wound down the window and was shocked to see a number of curious 'globes of light' rotating clockwise around a much larger object, which contained a number of smaller wriggling objects – amoeba in appearance. We stopped the car and got out to watch the swirling object, which dwarfed in brightness

the street lights of Telford in the distance, for about 20 minutes. We continued on our journey towards Stafford, occasionally catching sight of the object in the sky when it wasn't obstructed by buildings. As we passed the crematorium at Stafford, on our left, the object – now fainter in luminosity – was moving over Within Lane, near RAF Stafford, but soon it was lost from view."

Gillian was to become plagued by mysterious swirls of light that appeared on photographs taken of her over the years.

My father & I were travelling from Cannock via Stafford to Stoke-on-Trent on November 3 1989, along the A34. Glancing through the passenger side window, (time about 10 o'clock) I noticed flashing white lights through a copse of trees. I wound down the window to see if a reflection of some sort was causing the effect, even though there was really nothing to reflect, only oncoming car headlights, so this was soon ruled out. (Street lights have only recently been installed here) Fireworks came to mind considering the date but I have never seen any that resemble balls of spiral swirling lights with 'wriggling' phenomena in the centre Energy circles in the sky. Stopping at the next lay-by we studied the lights more closely, the ordinary lights of Telford yonder paling into insignificance compared to those we witnessed now. They circled in a clockwise direction, similar to amoeba. This was no 'nuts and bolts' U.F.O., but my first real sighting of a 'U.F.O phenomenon', so I got out of the car and stared intently, which may have been a mistake. Some time later upon reaching

CIRCLING LIGHTS

he Crematorium (Stafford) lo and behold to my left appeared the same lights circling and swirling only a bit fainter, this certainly ruled out laser lights. Travelling along Within Lane past RAF Stafford we spotted another sighting at the end of the Lane, the lights swirling and spiralling faster and brighter, so much so that I could see them through the rear window (going on our way along Hilderstone Road) there in the distance.

Soon after my eyes became sore and red and I suffered from a long and nasty virus which was difficult to eradicate, losing my taste, smell and my whole metabolism was affected; several courses of anti-biotics and other medications were required.

At this point in time, although I admit to being somewhat psychic in nature but not drastically so, I started to seek — and find. Book after book I read in fact I was fortunate in having a relative who worked in the library.!

Trevor James Constable's book 'The Cosmic Pulse of Life'

hed a lot of light on the subject and Dion Fortune's The 'Mystical Qabala' answered a lot of questions for me, also 'The Tree of Life' by Z'ev Ben Shimon. I started reading 'Psychic News' and enjoyed watching paranormal programmes on T.V. even when the ubiquitous sceptics shot everything psychic down in flames.

Attending a Spiritualist Church is now part of my life, even on holiday I seek one out, and often receive messages. Seeing Stephen O'Brien three times at theatres has also been a highlight in my pursuit of knowledge. Phenomena has appeared on photos too. The 'Cannock lights' have much to answer for.

Understandably I am rather reticent about these things and prefer to keep quiet, but, if any of the information or photos helps to endorse the existence of knowledge of a spiritual calibre, then please feel free to use it at your discretion. Thank you.

Yours faithfully
G. F. Sargeant.
(Miss)

Creative Stationary

Gillian pictured here on the right (taken 1995 at Stratford upon Avon)

Cigar-shaped UFO

On the same day a luminous, golden-coloured, cigar-shaped object – described as resembling *"a test-tube with a domed nose but a flatter, less defined end, with what appeared to be a flickering and moving 'fluid' inside it"* – was seen over Whitefield, Manchester, by two people.

(Source: Personal interview/Michael Cookson, *Northern UFO News*, No. 141, February 1990)

4th November 1989 (Canada) – Did a UFO crash-land or was it a hoax?

This incident has received considerable publicity in the media, over the years, in various TV documentaries such as *Unsolved Mysteries*, *Sightings,* and *Encounters,* all over North America. Internationally, magazines, newspapers and newsletters, have devoted hundreds of pages to it and UFO conferences around the planet have intrigued many thousands of attendees with its seemingly startling details.

A letter is received from the 'Guardian'

It all began when Tom Theofanous – a UFO investigator with The Canadian UFO Research Network (CUFORN) – received a package from someone calling themselves 'Guardian'. It had no return address.

Tom:

> *"The package contained a story about a UFO crash that supposedly happened close to Carlton Place, which is about a half-hour drive from Ottawa. There was also a photo-copied picture of an alien. For the most part, we thought it was a joke."*

Decision to investigate

CUFORN director Harry Tokarz decided to call Arthur Bray – a retired Navy Pilot and well-respected UFO author and researcher, who lives in Ottawa – and ask him if he had someone in the Carlton area that could check out the story. As luck would have it, Arthur knew a fellow who was fascinated by the field of UFO research – Graham Lightfoot.

Arthur Bray

'Bright light' passes overhead – helicopters later seen

Graham began his investigation and located a number of witnesses – one of whom was Diane Labanek. She told of having seen an intense *'bright light'* pass overhead, going towards a swamp at the far end of the field behind and south of her home. Diane also saw several helicopters earlier that evening, using bright lights to scan the area. Another West Carlton resident recalled that it was the same weekend

when some cattle escaped from a nearby pasture, and that it took until late Sunday to round them up. A couple told Graham about the wife being scared by a very *'bright light'*, shone through their south-facing bathroom window. *"It reached right down our hallway!"*

The wife also mentioned that she vaguely remembered hearing the sound of helicopters at the time. Others talked of *"dogs and cattle being disturbed"*.

However, there were many others who did not see anything unusual during the course of the weekend, including a couple who had a telescope set-up. Graham reported those findings to CUFORN, along with results of his examination of the field and swamp behind Labanek's home – which revealed no signs on the ground, indicating the use of heavy equipment required to recover a *'crashed object'*. His report closed with: *"...although I could find nothing conclusive to support or disprove any of the witnesses' claims. I shall check back around the area later this summer."*

The former Provincial Director of MUFON, Ontario – Clive Nadin – and the current Quebec Director – Christian Page – also visited the area on separate occasions, and spoke to the 'witnesses'. They concurred with what Graham had to say and effectively wrote off the matter as being a hoax at that time.

The 'Guardian' makes contact again, in 1991

In the middle of October 1991, CUFORN began receiving more 'Guardian information', via the mail, and all postmarked 'Ottawa'. An envelope with some documents that mention a 'conspiracy' between the Chinese and 'grey aliens that are planning to take over the world' arrived first – then came a Polaroid photograph of a 'UFO' flying across an unidentified road; a while later came a black and white picture of a grey-type 'alien'.

The fourth delivery in the series was a package. It contained the now infamous VHS videotape, with a green label on the cassette, with a thumb print and the word GUARDIAN printed on the label. There were also three playing cards in the package – all with hand-written notes on them – an Ace, King and Joker. A photo-copied map showed the *'grey's landing area'*, along with notes explaining that the flares in the video were used to help the UFO, which can out-manoeuvre anything on the planet, and fly under the radar and know where to land! There were also 'Canadian Department of National Defense documents' enclosed – which, upon later investigation, proved to be forgeries.

There is, of course, much more to this matter than space permits. One thing appears clear – while there is no reason to mistrust the version of events as given by Diane, it appears that someone (whose name is freely available on the internet) – decided, like others we had come across during the years, to carry out a campaign of disinformation, making available documents and video clips pertaining to convince others of a landing of an alien craft, when, in fact, reading further into the comprehensive investigation, nothing of the sort happened. We should perhaps leave the matter there, other than to point out that wild assertions like this will always attract the attention of the Media, and will continue to do so.

(Source: *UFO Casebook, The Carp Case* – MUFON, Ontario) (Credits: **March, May & July 1994 issues of** *The MUFON, Ontario Newsletter*)

Arthur Bray was interviewed by David Haisell the editor of *Journal UFO* in 1979).

Extract from interview:

David:

"Do you have any personal opinion as to what is behind the UFO phenomenon?"

Arthur:

"You're looking for theories now, are you? Well, I think there are several possible explanations. A couple come to mind immediately. Certainly, the extraterrestrial hypothesis is one possibility which may explain some UFOs. I also have come to the conclusion after many years of looking into this that some UFOs may very well originate in a parallel universe. I think the evidence is growing all the time to support that particular theory, and I deal with this aspect in my new book. I think that those are the two most likely explanations in my personal opinion. I realise that there are many other explanations as well put forth by various people, but those happen to be the two that I think are likely to account for most UFOs."

David:

"What is it about the extraterrestrial hypothesis that leads you to believe that it may not necessarily explain UFOs?"

Arthur:

> "Well, I don't think it explains all UFOs. I think some UFOs can be accounted for as probably physical craft from elsewhere, but certainly there are many sightings which cannot be explained in that way due to the various circumstances surrounding many cases such as disappearance, materialization and dematerialization. I think these are more likely to be explained by a departure into a parallel universe. I think this is what has happened in some cases, and I think the evidence is very strong for this. Certainly there have been many cases going back for as long as I have been studying the subject, which involved materialization and dematerialization of UFOs, and I think we have to look somewhere other than the nuts and bolts theory to account for this, and certainly there are many aspects of parapsychology which would indicate that there is a parallel universe."

5th November 1989 (UK) – *'Flying saucer'* sighted

On the 5th November 1989, Brierfield woman Andrea Varley contacted the *Colne Times,* after she was convinced that she had seen a *'flying saucer'* over the town. She was not the only one. Dorothy Baker of Highgate, Nelson, saw something very long and flying low through the sky, showing portholes, on the same evening. Another witness was Ronald Jackson of Barkerhouse Road, Nelson. He was taking the dog out for a walk when he saw a bright stationary light in the sky, surrounded by lights which formed a banana shape.

Jennifer Rhodes (43) of Eastwood Boulevard, Westcliff-on-Sea – a hairdresser by occupation – was driving along the road near the A127 roundabout, heading towards Canvey Island, at 6pm, near Benfleet, when:

> "I saw, from my left-hand back seat, a bright orange-red light, shaped like a ball, with what looked like steam coming out of the top and bottom, moving slowly through the sky, before it disappeared. I arrived at my mum's house at 6.20pm, and happened to look outside the kitchen window, when I saw it again – now much larger. I ran into the garden and observed it shoot off towards the direction of Basildon, and then move behind cloud."

In conversation with Jennifer by members of Ron West's group Jennifer complained that it was so bright that it hurt to look at the object for very long.

Her mother also confirmed having seen the object.

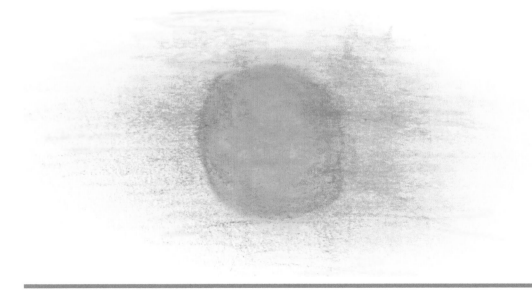

9th November 1989 (UK)

Mr Glen Kamiya (32) of Brent Avenue, Southwoodham Ferries, Essex – a shopkeeper by trade – had just locked up the family shop and was fetching some goods from the warehouse, when he noticed an unusual orange glow in the sky. He fetched the rest of the family and they came out to see:

> *"...an oval-shaped object with a black band around the middle, stationary in the sky, about three miles away. We watched it for 30 minutes, until it then 'blinked' out."*

Glen was to have a further sighting of what appears to have been a similar object on the 12th January 1990.

11th/12th November 1989 (UK) – UFOs sighted

At 11.45pm on 11th November 1989, Harry Willet – a former public schoolboy from Canterbury – sighted unusual *'bright lights'* outside his bedroom window, so he picked up a pair of binoculars and went outside, where he saw something that sent a shiver down his spine.

> *"...four green 'lights' clumped together, with flashing red lights on top, forming a 'V' shape. At first I thought it was an aircraft, but knew this couldn't be, as it was completely silent. I picked up the binoculars and looked through, seeing a revolving saucer-shaped object, with some sort of cabin on top, beaming down a white light. After about an hour, it vanished from sight."*

Harry contacted the police, who asked him to fill in a questionnaire – a copy of which was sent to RAF Manston. Incredibly, the Meteorological Officer at Manston suggested that he had seen the navigation lights of a ship, refracted in the sky! (**Source:** *Adscene,* **17.11.1989** – 'Mystery in the sky')

On the evening of the 12th November 1989, Janet Nicholson was driving down Cherwell Avenue, Darnhill, Heywood, Lancashire, with her husband, when she noticed a large white *'light'*, motionless in the sky over Darkhill Way – far too large and bright to be a star. By the time the couple arrived home, the *'light'* was still prominent. After 30 minutes, it began to move towards them.

> *"As it approached closer and moved overhead, we saw that it was triangular in shape and showing two white lights and a red one. It was an incredible experience and I am sure other people in Heywood must have seen it as well."*

(**Source: Heywood UFO Research Group**)

15th November 1989 (UK) – UFO display

Musician Helga Douglas (57) who, we presume, was the mother of Rosalind Reynolds – then living in Plough Corner, Little Clacton, Essex [all will be clear in the next paragraph] had this to say:

> *"Precisely at 9pm, when the BBC News came on, I decided to get on with the wallpapering. As I did so, I heard what I thought was a squadron of aircraft moving overhead, causing the windows and doors to rattle. My dogs cowered in fright and then barked uncontrollably. I went outside but saw nothing, because of clouds. I was puzzled, as they appeared to be so low. At about 1.45am, unable to sleep, I made myself a hot drink, when I heard what I took to be the sound of an aircraft, which lasted about one-and-a-half minutes."*

Boxted, Colchester

At 11.30pm, Mr J. Lane (21) of Boxted, Colchester, was awoken by his wife, who asked him to go outside where a friend of the family, Rachel, stood. He dressed and went out.

> *"I looked up and saw a dozen or so lights, all moving slowly in the same direction across the sky, eastwards. We watched them for about five minutes, then I went back to bed."*

It appears that they were not the only ones to see the lights. Sheridan Lane (44) Publicity Officer for EAUFOPRA – then living in Boxted – was to witness the phenomena at 11.15pm. Her written letter, in its most unusual style of handwriting, describes what took place. Shortly before the sighting, she and her friend, ˙Rosalind Reynolds, were writing-up some reports for the UFO group.

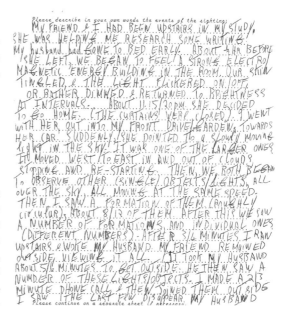

Ros:

> *"I was just leaving, when I noticed the moon was full in the sky and directly behind the house. I then saw a star, as bright as Venus, pass in front of it. I pointed it out to Sheridan, who then saw another one with two behind it. As the clouds were thickly spread and moving quite fast, I initially believed this was creating the effect that the stars were moving – then several groups of up to 12 apparently randomly formed objects appeared moving across the sky, at the speed of a jet aircraft. They were joined by more and more objects, all heading in the same direction. I went and fetched my camera and took some photographs, while Sheridan awoke her husband. A short time later they were lost from view, after clouds built up restricting visibility."*

Enquiries made with the RAF

Enquiries made with the local RAF Station revealed that eight aircraft were on an exercise from RAF Mildenhall that night, which is unlikely to be the explanation in this case, judging from the eyewitness accounts. Further enquiries were made with the following:

Southend Airport – Nothing picked up on Radar; Stansted Airport – Nothing picked up on Radar; RAF Watton/Lakenheath/Woodbridge/Bentwaters – No Comment.

BEWARE! THEY'RE

Aliens raped me on their then they stole my body

HOUSEWIFE Ros Reynolds-Parnham is still plagued by aliens – more than 13 years after she was abducted and raped on a spaceship.

"They won't leave me alone," says Ros, her voice trembling with emotion. "I live in fear of them whisking me up into the sky and using my body to study human life.

"Anyone who doesn't believe me should spend a night in my shoes."

Softly-spoken Ros, 34, first told The People last year how she had experienced an extra-terrestrial encounter that she says left her

EXCLUSIVE by LOUISE OSWALD

unable to have children and terrified she could be kidnapped by aliens again.

Now for the first time she is revealing the full effect of the aliens' crude sex experiments, as she was stripped naked and was used as a human guinea pig during a four-hour examination.

And she is also saying how she is still pestered by UFOs.

"Only last month I was woken by a strange trembling over the house," says Ros, of Clacton, Essex. "It sounded like an enormous helicopter. A bolt of blinding light shot through my

bedroom window. It focused on my husband Mark and all I thought was, 'Oh no, they're not going to take him too'.

"I leapt up to the curtains and shouted, 'Just leave us alone'. Then they vanished.

"I was like any ordinary young woman before this all happened. I was nine stone, attractive and enjoyed a great social life.

"Now I'm a size 18, I've lost all my friends and only have Mark and my mum for support.

"I stare at the sky whenever I go outside. In the last year alone I've seen at least four UFOs. I

get angry with them now. They've had their way with me. What more could they possibly want?

"I still can't believe that I went through this ordeal but, believe me, every word is true.

"I will never ever forget the night the aliens ruined my life. Those creatures told me their race was in danger of extinction and they had to look to other life forms to sustain themselves.

"They told me they were dying and that they needed 'juice'. I had no idea what they meant. It could have been blood, teardrops – anything.

ALIEN: Ros's chilling sketch of one kidnapper

1982 – UFO over Sudbury, Suffolk

In late September 1982, Ros Reynolds-Parnham, from Little Clacton, Essex, and her boyfriend, at the time – Philip, decided to visit her relatives, in Corby, Northamptonshire, and were travelling along the A1902, at Sudbury, in Suffolk, near the village of Stoke by Clare.

"At 8pm, a horseshoe-shaped group of lights flew very low over the car, as we passed under some power cables. I remember the lights, the silence, and the blue tendrils bouncing off the cables. My first thought was it may have been a 'helicopter', but everything was wrong – its movement, speed, silence, etc. As we drove out through the town, through Long Melford, and headed along the Clare to Haverhill Road, it came back and zipped over the car, two or three times, scaring the pair of us. The 'thing' matched our speed and ran parallel with us, for some time, along the road.

Egg-shaped light

From the side it was a big, bright, egg-shaped light, with a faint set of smaller coloured lights rotating around inside. I guess it was between 50 and 100ft away and the whole thing was at least the size of the length of our car, as it negotiated the hedges and telegraph wires. Philip was so scared that he just looked straight ahead. The car suddenly acted as if it had run out of petrol and died, along with the lights. We both had an argument as to who would look under the bonnet, and then got out together – me to keep my eyes on this thing, as it hovered silently over the field. The next thing I knew was that we were both back in the car – the engine now running, and lights on, with the 'thing' still hovering. We basically felt very quiet and subdued, for want of a better explanation, and just drove off as fast as possible. We never spoke the rest of the way, or I do not think we did. We arrived at Corby – not at 10pm, as expected, but 1.30-1.45am!"

Burn mark found on her chest

Ros and Philip made their excuses, without even mentioning what had taken place and returned home. Philip (for some reason only known to him) decided to hand paint the Ford Cortina a different colour, on the same

OUT THERE...

spaceship ... juices and skin

day. The following day, Ros (completely out of character) suffered a severe nosebleed (she never had one before, or since) a very bad burn mark on her chest, which has scarred, and a 'V'-shaped incision on her back. Her lifestyle, eating habits and personality, was to completely change dramatically, including an avid interest in drawings, writing, and typing, although generally feeling quite ill but fine before the UFO encounter.

CLOSE ENCOUNTER: *Ros has turned to Mark for comfort following her space ordeal*

Ros:

"I gave up drinking and smoking and developed a craving for sweets. Even stranger, I began to write complex notes on how the Universe was formed, and wrote up the engine plans of the 'spacecraft'. This was so unlike me. Eventually, we split up. For three years I was afraid to go outside. I split with Philip on very violent terms; he was never a violent person before. I sought medical help over some of the problems, but never mentioned my fears of it being possibly UFO, partly as I didn't admit it to myself, and partly as I was embarrassed and felt I would be laughed at as a fool."

Hypnotised

As a result of contacting a UFO organisation, who came to see her, it was suggested she be hypnotised, to extract further information regarding her encounter.

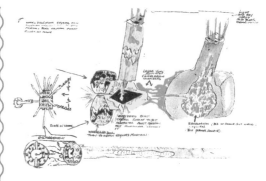

"I was stretched out on a perspex pedestal. They kept repeating the word 'juice' and I could feel them poking and prodding my body. I was screeching at them, "Leave me alone. Why me?"

"But it was no good. I was completely helpless. Those beasts wanted my body and there was nothing I could do. They raped me.

"If I went to the police or a doctor and said I was raped by a man everyone would be sympathetic, but no-one wants to believe a story like mine despite my mental trauma."

Ros's ordeal began on a warm evening in September 1982 as she drove with Philip, her boyfriend at the time, to visit relatives in Corby, Northants.

"Suddenly I noticed a horse-shoe of bright lights in the sky. Then the car's engine began to splutter and we jerked to a halt.

"The lights formed a spaceship which hovered noiselessly in the sky.

"Philip was shaking and we argued about who should check the engine. We both climbed out of the car and I watched the lights while Philip tinkered under the bonnet.

"Then we were suddenly back in our seats and the car was running. I don't remember getting back in. I felt strangely docile as if I had been doped with something.

"By the time we arrived at our friends' we'd lost four hours and I had no idea where I'd been for that time."

Gradually, signs emerged that Ros had been the victim of a bizarre kidnap.

She says: "Within three weeks I began to draw aliens and maps of engine rooms on spaceships in my sleep. These were all things I knew nothing about. I couldn't work out what was going on.

"Then my periods stopped. I found two two-inch scars on my chest and lower abdomen. I suffered horrendous headaches all the time."

'They had blue-green heads and their mouths were slits'

Ros contacted a local UFO research group and agreed to be hypnotised to piece together her experiences. That's when she met psychic Mark Reynolds-Parnham, who she married in 1991.

She says: "During a hypnosis session with Mark my dark secret came tumbling out. I remembered being guided on to the spaceship by three aliens who were about 3ft 6in to 4ft tall.

"They had blue-green heads and weedy bodies with almond-shaped eyes. Their mouths were just slits and none of them had hair or eyebrows. Each

had four fingers that they used to prod me..

"They had no voices but communicated to me through my mind. I was taken to a room that stank of rotten eggs. The atmosphere was very thick and suffocating and I felt paralysed.

"I then described how a larger alien, about 7ft tall, took skin and fluid samples from me. I could feel them poking in my private parts."

Since her encounter, Ros has been diagnosed as clinically depressed and prescribed strong tranquillisers.

She says: "I kept going

According to Ros:

"As the hypnotist started to put me under, a 'beam of light' appeared in the room. The video and audio equipment malfunctioned and spun around. The sceptic, who came to observe, was pinned to the chair with such force as to leave claw marks on his arms and all the clocks in the house stopped. I never got hypnotised, but they did bring in a psychic investigator."

Some of her memory has returned.

"I was in a room with a large Perspex type pedestal table in the centre. I remember being led to it. I didn't struggle (don't know why not) and was laid down on the thing. I remember sensing the whole procedure was clinical – like the tagging, weighing and measuring, of a wild animal. The 'Greys' never spoke out aloud, just telepathically, and there was a taller, blond haired person – that's all I remember. I get very emotional if I try and remember more."

We have to say that we were astonished at the depth of detail shown in the 'engine plans' of the 'craft', powered by a Rhubinium crystal – a power source unknown to our science, although curiously, Rubidium, discovered in 1861 (being a soft silvery-white element of the alkali group, which ignites spontaneously in the air) was considered for use in ion engines for space flight. (**Source: Personal interview**)

16th November 1989 (UK) –Triangular object

At 8pm, Mrs Doreen Woods (51) of Rantree Fold, Basildon, had just got out of her car when she saw what she took to be aircraft.

"I said to my husband, 'there are a lot of planes about tonight'. I looked up again and saw eight objects in the sky, which were very close together – far too close to have been airplanes. They were circling in the sky over the houses in an anticlockwise fashion. The closest object appeared triangular. I could see red and green flashing lights. Five minutes later they were out of sight."

Just after midnight, Elizabeth Riley (46) of Dunster Avenue, Westcliff-on-Sea was saying goodnight to a friend at the top of the drive, which overlooks the south-east direction over *The Thames*.

> *"It was a lovely clear night; suddenly we both noticed a flashing light in the south-eastern sky, at an angle of 45° off the horizon. I went inside and picked up the telescope but was unable to locate the light, which was covered in red, green, blue and white lights, shining brilliantly, giving an impression that the light or object was continually moving up and down – so left it until 1.15am, when I looked through again and found that it had moved SSE to SSW, now right in front of the house. I checked my Ephemeris to ascertain the movement of the planets in a 24 hour cycle, and found nothing that matched what I had just seen. I went to bed at 2.15am; it was still there."*

Later the same day, at 9.30pm, Susan Haines (20) was driving near Woodfield Road, South Benfleet, when she saw:

> *"...five large white lights forming a square, with a fifth light in the middle, heading across the sky. Five seconds later they just disappeared from view."*

17th November 1989 (UK) – Triangular lights seen over water tower

At 8pm, Mrs Wendy Cordell (34) of Broomfield Crescent, Wivenhoe, Essex, was walking the dog.

> *"I happened to look up into the sky and see, to the left of the water tower, three yellow-greenish lights spinning around in the sky in a triangular shape. My dog became agitated and kept pulling back."*

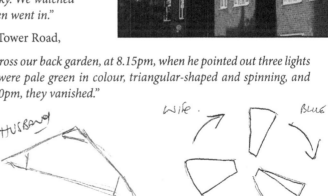

Her illustration is identical to the one supplied by another resident Mr Peter Wiseman, whose account follows.

Postman Michael Grover (39) of Heath Road, was stood on the doorway talking to the 'Avon' lady, along with his wife and two sons, at 8.15pm, when they saw:

> *"...three pale green rotating lights forming a triangular shape, hovering in the sky. We watched them for about 15 minutes and then went in."*

Another witness was Steven Darvill of Tower Road,

> *"I was talking to Peter Wiseman across our back garden, at 8.15pm, when he pointed out three lights hovering silently in the sky. They were pale green in colour, triangular-shaped and spinning, and formed a triangle in the air. At 8.30pm, they vanished."*

In all, there were eight people that saw these objects in the sky. Peter Wiseman (76) and his wife Jane (72) confirmed the sighting. Here is their account.

(Source: Ron West)

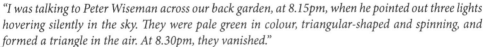

;T ANGLIAN U.F.O. & PARANORMAL RESEARCH ASSOCIATIOI

SECTION A **SIGHTING ACCOUNT FORM**

Please write an account of your sighting, make a drawing of what you saw and then answer the questions in section B overleaf as fully as possible. Write in BLOCK CAPITALS using a ball point pen.

I was in the back garden with my wife, when we noticed these three white to pale green lights hovering in the sky. They seemed to be spinning or rotating on them selves. I watched for a good 15 minutes but they did not move at all. Then, just as suddenly, they just went out, gone I heard no noise at all.

DRAWING*

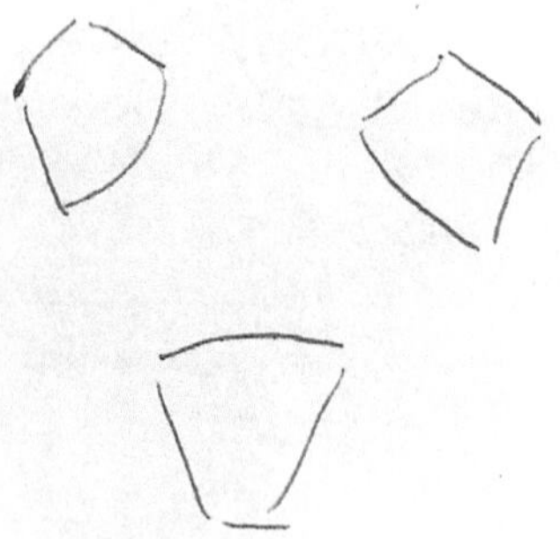

Your full name (Mr/Mrs/Miss/Ms)
Peter Wiseman Age 76
Address 10 Rosebank Rd
Wivenhoe Colchester Essex

Telephone No. (STD)

Occupation during last two years
Retired

Any professional, technical or academic qualifications or special interests

Do you object to the publication of your name?
*Yes/No. *Delete as applicable.

Today's Date 19-2-90

Signature

* If preferred, use a separate sheet of paper.

18th November 1989 (UK) – UFO over Devon

A cylindrical-shaped, fluorescent object, possibly 100ft in length, was seen hovering about 200ft above the sea, at Torquay, in Devon.

20th November 1989 (UK) – Were aliens seen at Norwich?

According to declassified MOD reports (2009) we learn of an incident involving a Norwich citizen, who was out walking her dog, when she claimed she met a man from another planet, who told her that aliens were behind crop circles. The anonymous woman telephoned RAF Wattisham, in Suffolk, in a state of distress, to describe her 'out-of-this-world' encounter, the previous night. A covering letter in the MOD files notes, dryly, that it is *"one of our more unusual UFO reports"*. The woman told the operator at the Base that the incident happened as she was walking her dog on a sports field, close to her home near Norwich, at about 10.30pm, when she was approached by a man with a 'Scandinavian-type' accent, dressed in a light-brown garment – like a flying suit.

> *"He asked me if I was aware of stories about large, circular, flattened areas, appearing in fields of wheat. He then went on to explain that he was from another planet similar to Earth, and that the circles had been caused by others like him, who had travelled to Earth."*

The woman said she was *"completely terrified"* and, as she ran home, she heard a loud buzzing noise behind her and turned to see a large, glowing, orange-white spherical object rise vertically from behind trees. The RAF operator, who took the statement from the woman, said the conversation lasted about an hour and described it as a 'genuine call'. Unfortunately, without knowing the woman's identity and having the opportunity of interviewing her ourselves, we cannot conclude anything but remain intrigued by the version of events given.

22nd November 1989 (USA)

At Cooper City, Florida, a couple observed a very large, dark triangle (arrowhead-shaped) flying low and silently from east to west. They counted seven circular white lights on the underside of the *'craft'*, which was moving at a high rate of speed, surrounded by a white haze.

CHAD, Mansfield

7 DEC 1989

Objects in the sky

On behalf of Mansfield UFO group and its investigation team A-U-RIS-A I would like to ask the public if anyone saw any strange lights or objects in the sky during the first week of November around the Langwith area, and on 22nd November in the Mansfield area at 5 pm approximately. Anyone with information, contact Mansfield 751889.

L. TRUEMAN

6 West Hill Drive,
Mansfield.

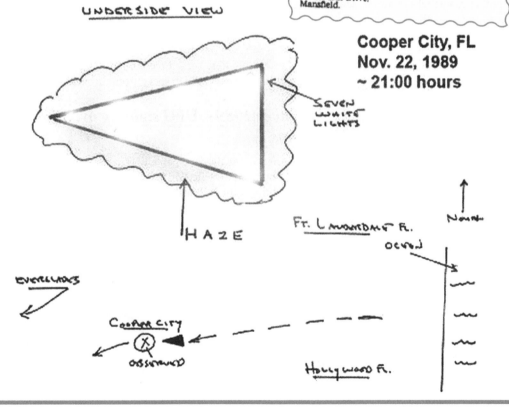

25th November 1989 (UK) – 'Flying cross' over Hampshire

At 10.30am, Mrs P. Parker (57) and her husband were driving home from shopping in Basildon Town Centre, when they saw a plane travelling overhead. Her husband remarked:

"That's no plane – there are another two of them."

Mrs Parker:

"There were three of them – oval in shape, a white green colour – just floating across the sky in a triangular formation, towards the south- west direction – no noise, no smoke – out of sight two minutes later."

At 10.44pm, Malcolm Handley from Southsea, Hampshire, and founder member of the Southampton-based UFO Group – WATSUP (The Wessex Association for the Study of Unexplained Phenomena) – was looking through his telescope, when he saw:

"...a number of objects, passing south-west to north-east. They formed a twisted cross and moved apart, and back again, at least three times during my observation. My impression was that they were outside the Earth's atmosphere. Rather oddly, I suffered from sore eyes over the next few days."

November 1989 – UFO seen over Lancashire

Another report tells of an incident that occurred during the same month, at 6.05am, near Wigan, when a man driving on the A1 motorway, towards his place of work was passing along an area of open land, when he was startled to see a huge object hovering about 60ft above a field. The object was metallic and segmented – like a hand grenade. It had a huge transparent window on one side, and on the opposite side there was something resembling a radar dish. Inside the window were seen three human-looking men – apparently sitting at a table, talking. The man, now frightened, drove off at high speed from the area.

November 1989 – UFO sighting over the Brecon Beacons

Dave Hodrien, of the Birmingham UFO Group, learned of the following UFO sighting from his wife, which happened when she was 11 years of age. At the time of the sighting, she and her brother Tim (5) were on their way back home from having been to see their Great Aunt Janice, at Leamington Spa, who was driving them to Neath, in South West Wales.

Driving over the Brecon Beacons

During the early evening, they crossed over the Brecon Beacons. It was quite dark in the sky, but the moorland was still partially visible.

The weather was clear and there was very little cloud. The road was deserted and there were no other cars on it. The girl was sitting on the back seat, next to her brother and staring out of the back window of the car, when she noticed an object with a row of coloured lights along it.

Dave Hodrien

The object was quite far away and high up, moving slowly across the sky, with far too many lights along it to be a normal aircraft.

A UFO is seen

These were flashing and changing colours, mostly white and red, but some other colours too. The girl brought her great aunt's attention to this, who glanced back at the object – which seemed to keep changing position in the sky one minute, then gone the next, reappearing in different places in relation to the moving car. Janice was trying to lighten the mood by telling them that the object *"was going to come and get them"*.

Suddenly the object appeared much closer to the car and much lower in the sky, estimated to be less than 100ft up. Both children could now clearly see that the lights formed a curved line, as if along the edge of a large disc-shaped object – presumably hiding the main body of the 'craft', which appeared to be about twice the size of a house.

Janice:

> *"It then went behind and to the right of the car, hovering in the sky. At this point I decided to stop to get a photograph of the object, as I was very interested in what it could be. I pulled up at the side of the road and got out, and went around to the back of the car and opened the boot to get my camera. The object appeared to now be stationary and it was completely silent."*

The girl started to panic and was screaming at Janice to get back in the car. Janice, now a little unnerved by the object but mostly fascinated by it, picked up the camera – but after being unable to determine how to use the night setting on it, and the fact that the girl was now very frightened, decided to get back into the car and drive away.

Shortly after continuing on their journey, suddenly, a huge glow of bluish-white light lit up the hills in front of the car. The 'glow' lasted for about 10 seconds, before dying away. Janice felt it was linked to the object which they had seen, but did not tell her about it.

June 2008 – Mysterious 'lights' seen over the Brecon Beacons

'Dr. Simon Griffey saw mysterious lights over the Brecon Beacons. His reported sighting has numerous similarities with what the family had witnessed. According to the *Sun* newspaper, this is what they had to say, quote:

> *"A baffled university don, who spotted a UFO over the Brecon Beacons, last night, said 'There is no logical explanation'.*

Dr. Simon Griffey saw lights loom over a mountain village – before they disappeared. His close encounter is the third reported in the space of just five days, following sightings by the army and police. Simon, a Doctor of Psychology at Cardiff University, said: 'I've had loads of theories proposed by friends and neighbours, but none of them add up.' Dr. Griffey, 50, and his son Jack, 23, were driving near Llangynidr Mountain in the Brecon Beacons, Powys, when they spotted lights over Talybont-on-Usk.

He said, 'There was no noise whatsoever, it was a bit eerie. I've driven over this mountain for 17 years and have never seen anything like it. There were seven lights and having read the description from the soldiers in Shropshire, there are some similarities. They were the same sort of colour and the same spherical shape that they reported. I know I wasn't seeing things, because Jack saw exactly the same as I did – and two other cars pulled over to look'."

Sceptics have suggested the sightings could be huge man-made lanterns, floating into the sky. However, the boffin of Llangynidr, said: 'It was too big. It was way above the horizon and stayed there for 15 minutes. It was a bit smaller than a full moon – quite big and high up."

Jack recorded the phenomenon on his mobile phone – but when they examined the pictures, later, they found only three of the seven lights.

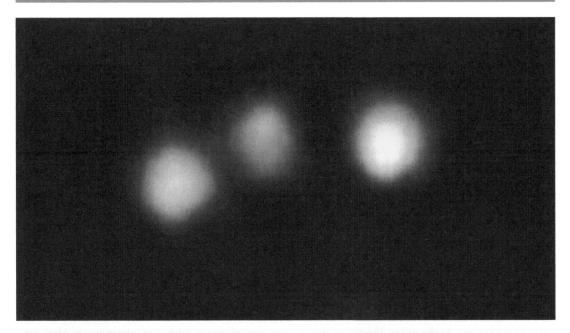

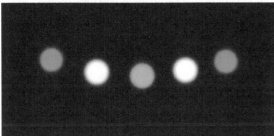

The lights as they appeared at a distance.

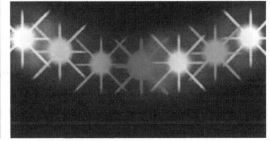

The lights as they appeared closer to the witnesses.

To this day, the parties are convinced the object they saw was definitely not a conventional aircraft or helicopter of any kind. The arrangement and number of lights on the object, and the way that they were changing colours, seem to suggest something very unusual. Both children mentioned independently that the object was very large and disc-shaped, even though the main body of it could not be made out. Also the object was completely silent, even when it approached, and it seemed to be able to move or hover in the air at will.

The area of the Brecon Beacons is used for military training and often jets are flown over it. Could the object have been a secret advanced aircraft of some kind? This is a possibility but, if this were the case, then why did it appear to be following the witness's car as if interested in it? Surely the pilots would have wanted to keep such a 'craft' away from the eyes of the public? (**Source:** *The Sun,* **27th June 2008/***The Green, Green Men of Home,* **by John Coles/Dave Hodrien, Birmingham UFO Group)**

*Dr. Simon Griffey started work in the School of Psychology at Cardiff University, in 2004, during which time he was seconded from Newport City Council to work as a professional tutor on the MSc. in Educational Psychology. Simon joined Cardiff University as an employee in 2006, and as a tutor as well as director of research, he was part of the team responsible for developing the Education Psychology doctoral programme in the School, which was the first of its kind in Wales. Simon was also influential in developing and maintaining the post-qualification doctoral programme that runs alongside the main programme. Dr. Simon Griffey, who was the Research Director as well as a tutor on the Doctorate in Educational Psychology programme died unexpectedly on June 3rd leaving his wife, Helen, and three children. We offer our condolences to the family for his loss.

28th November 1989 (Belgium) – UFO over the Cemetery

We would like to feel that the evidence presented in our Volumes of *Haunted Skies* is overwhelming in its entirety, despite the clamours made by those who would want us to believe that such objects do not exist. Those few who speak out are often ridiculed, sometimes vilified . . . such is the price that many pay for having the courage to simply tell what they saw. We realise that it would be impossible to include Belguim UFO reports, as space is at a premium, but we felt the following incident worthy of mention as it was so interesting, irrespective of the fact that it was explained away later as a hallucination!

A mother and her schoolgirl daughter, Evelyn, from Weywertz, went to pay their respects to the grave of the older sister, at around 7pm, on what was a clear evening, with no wind. As they reached the cemetery, they heard a strange noise. Evelyn joked with her mother, suggesting it was the nearby chickens. As they continued on their journey towards the gravestone, they noticed the noise was coming from a huge light shining about 30 metres down, above a row of fir trees. Whatever it was kept changing shape in front of their eyes, from triangular to quadrangular, accompanied by the continual movement of lights, and a humming or groaning noise. Evelyn tried to dissuade her mother from looking at the object. However, her mother was fascinated and wanted to get even closer, but her daughter thought this was unwise. At some point, her mother began to walk backwards. As she did so, the object shone some rays of orange-white light downwards. After about 10mins, the object moved away.

The next day, Evelyn suffered from a bad headache and had to leave school. A few days later, there was an article in the local newspaper – the *Grenz Echo* – about a similar object having been seen in the nearby town of *Eupen. (**Source:** *The UFO Report, 1991,* Timothy Good)

30th November 1989 (UK) – UFO sighted

Ken De'Ath (31) of Laindon, Essex, was driving near Hadleigh, at 4.50pm, near to the seafront, when he saw what he first took to be an aircraft, but then changed his mind after seeing it move slowly through the sky, showing a white light at each end, with six flashing red lights in between. It moved from his right to left, and headed towards the direction of Hadleigh Castle, before he lost sight of it.

30th November 1989 (USA) – Abduction of Linda (Cortile) Napolitano

On 30th November 1989, Linda (41) from Manhattan, New York, living in an apartment building on the lower east side of the city, near the bridge, telephoned Budd Hopkins and reported that she had been abducted during the early morning hours. She reported having gone to bed, but awoke at 3am to feel a paralyzing numbness starting at her feet, then moving up her body. She attempted to awake her husband, who was asleep, but failed.

---

*Eupen Communal Cemetery contains a separate German plot with 122 war graves from the First World War and 37 from the Second World War. After the Second World War, the graves should have been brought to a larger war cemetery, but the Eupen community did not allow that because they did not want to disturb the peace of the dead. Now Eupen takes care of the maintenance.

Hypnosis

According to Linda, following hypnosis, she claimed that three or four *'beings'* appeared in the room. She was then floated through her closed 12th story apartment window, and into a craft hovering overhead, in a blue beam of light.

"I'm standing up on nothing, and they take me out all the way up, way above the building. Ooh, I hope I don't fall. The UFO opens up almost like a clam and then I'm inside, I see benches similar to regular benches. And they're bringing me down a hallway. Doors open – like sliding doors. Inside are all these lights and buttons and a big long table. I don't want to get up on that table. They get me on the table anyway. They start saying things to me and I'm yelling. I can still yell. One of them says something that sounds like {Nobbyegg}. I think they were trying to tell me to be quiet, because he put his hand over my mouth."

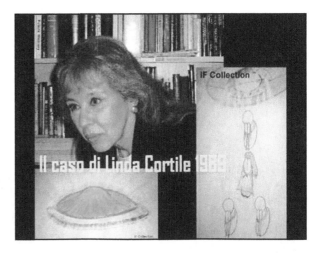

After a medical exam, she was literally dropped back into her bed, which still did not wake her sleeping husband.

Other witnesses

Unusually, in contrast to other similar complaints from people who allege alien abduction, it was claimed that there were three witnesses two blocks away, who saw Linda and the perceived 'aliens' floating out of the window and ascend into a craft.

Janet Kimball

In addition it is claimed by Budd, that a retired lady, Janet Kimball, was driving across the Brooklyn Bridge towards Manhattan on her way home to upstate New York after a late party, when she witnessed the event.

In letters, on the phone, and in person, she told him her car had stopped, along with other drivers. The scene she describes was quite chaotic, with people honking horns and shouting in dismay. She watched what she first thought was a movie being filmed, though she quickly realised that this could not be.

Budd Hopkins

We had the pleasure of meeting Budd, some years ago, at the UK Truro UFO Conference and discussing, albeit briefly, his involvement in this matter. On the surface it is a spectacular allegation, matched only by the enormous media interest which followed, after details were released to the Press.

Author, researcher and artist – Budd Hopkins – sharing a moment with Dawn Holloway at the UK Truro UFO Conference.

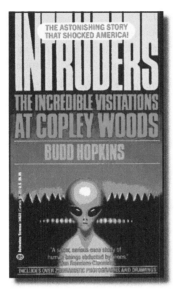

Budd Hopkins – signing a copy of his book, 'Sight Unseen', at the UK Truro UFO Conference.

Budd Hopkins wrote two popular books (*Missing Time*, 1981, and *Intruders*, 1987). He established the Intruders Foundation and has made innumerable appearances at conferences and in the media. Because of such strong endorsements and impressive affiliations, and because of his untiring work on behalf of abductees, Hopkins became an influential figure in the UFO abduction field. We remember him complaining to us at that:

> *"I couldn't enjoy my lunch, as people wouldn't leave me alone; they kept pestering me for photographs."*

This is the price of fame. Perhaps we are better off without it! No disrespect to Budd, a likeable man, who was accompanied by Carole Rainey, but he was a worldwide celebrity and people treated him as such. Of course he is not the only one. We have met many others, over the years, whose knowledge does not match their fans' expectations! However, this does not stop them demanding to be treated like royalty!

Nosebleeds and nasal implant

The reported incident generated worldwide interest. It has been discussed in the Wall Street Journal (Jefferson, 1992) *Omni* (Baskin, 1992) *Paris Match* (De Brosses, 1992) the *New York Times* (Sontag, 1992) and Hopkins and Napolitano have appeared on the television show *Inside Edition*. The *MUFON UFO Journal* labelled it "The Abduction Case of the Century" (Stacy, 1992, p9). Even the technical magazine *ADVANCE for Radiologic Science Professionals* carried a discussion of Linda's nasal implant (Hatfield, 1992).

Police witnesses Dan and Richard

In February 1991, Budd Hopkins received a letter signed from a 'Richard and Dan', who claimed they were police officers under cover in a car beneath the elevated FDR Drive, between 3am and 3.30am, in late November 1989. They told of having observed a large, bright reddish-orange object, with green lights around its side, and then saw a woman and several strange *'figures'* float out of a window and up into the object.

Richard and Dan told of being extremely concerned about the woman's well-being, and wanted to locate the woman, talk to her, and be assured that she was alive and safe. The two also mentioned that they could identify the building and window from which she emerged. After receiving the letter, Hopkins telephoned Linda and told her to expect a possible visit from the two officers.

The 'police officers' visit Linda

A few days later, Linda telephoned Hopkins to tell him that she had received a visit by Richard and Dan, who had introduced themselves as police officers. She initially thought they were enquiring about a crime related incident, rather than her allegation, believing – despite the call made to her by Budd – that they would not come to see her.

Oddly, after what Linda says was an emotional greeting – they expressed relief that she was alive – both men appeared to have been disinclined to meet with or talk to Budd Hopkins, despite the fact they had written to him earlier and Linda's entreaties to do so. Richard asked Linda if it was acceptable for them to write out an account of their experience and then read it into a tape recorder. She agreed, and a couple of weeks later Hopkins received a tape-recording from Richard, describing their experience. Some time afterwards, Budd Hopkins received a letter from Dan containing further information. The letter reported that Richard had taken a leave of absence, because the close encounter had been so emotionally traumatic. Dan also mentioned that Richard secretly watched Linda. (This information is from Budd Hopkins oral presentation at the 1992 MUFON symposium, in Albuquerque.) At the Portsmouth, New Hampshire conference, Hopkins said that he had received a letter from Richard, saying that Dan was forced to take leave of absence.

Not police officers but special protection for a VIP!

Subsequently Budd Hopkins received a further letter from Dan, in which he said that he and Richard were not really police officers but actually security officers, who had been driving a very important person (VIP) to a helicopter pad in lower Manhattan when the sighting occurred. The letter claimed that their car stalled, and Richard had pushed it, parking it beneath the Franklin D Roosevelt Drive. According to Dan, the VIP had also witnessed the abduction event and had become hysterical.

Snatched from the street

Linda claimed, in April 1991, of having encountered Richard on the street near her apartment. She was asked to get into a car that Dan was driving, but she refused. Richard picked her up and, with some struggle, forced her into the vehicle. Linda reported that she was driven around for three and a half hours, interrogated about the aliens, and asked whether she worked for the government. She also said that she was forced to remove her shoes, so they could examine her feet to determine whether she was an ET alien (they later claimed that aliens lack toes).

United Nations Secretary General Javier Perez de Cuellar

Linda did remember another car being involved with the kidnapping, and under hypnotic regression she recalled the license plate number of that car, as well as part of the number of the car in which she rode. It is claimed the vehicle was licensed to United Nations Secretary General Javier Perez de Cuellar.

General Javier Perez de Cuellar has denied he was involved on many occasions – once, in a fax to the PBS science shows *Nova* (which was preparing its 1996 abduction episode), he said:

> *"I cannot but strongly deny the claim that I have had an abduction experience at any time. On several occasions, when questioned about the matter, I reiterated that these allegations were completely false and I hope that this statement will definitely put an end to these unfounded rumours."*

1992 – MUFON Symposium, most important case

At the 1992 MUFON convention in Albuquerque, New Mexico, in July, both Hopkins and Linda appeared on the podium and presented the case.

In a short article previewing his 1992 MUFON symposium presentation, Budd Hopkins wrote:

> *"I will be presenting what I believe to be the most important case for establishing the objective reality of UFO abductions that I have yet encountered."* (Hopkins, 1992, p. 20)

During his lecture at the symposium, he stated:

> *"This is probably the most important case I've ever run into in my life."*

In his abstract for the Massachusetts Institute of Technology Abduction Study Conference, held in June 1992, he wrote:

"The importance of this case is virtually immeasurable, as it powerfully supports both the objective reality of UFO abductions and the accuracy of regressive hypnosis as employed with abductees."

Incidents involving claims of alien abduction (for want of better interpretation) following a close encounter with a UFO are an emotive issue. Over the years we have spoken to people who have made similar claims. The penalty for having the courage to report such matters is normally ridicule and scepticism, not forgetting the mental and physical traumas incurred.

Yancy Spence – The Brooklyn Bridge abductions

We were intrigued to come across details of another witness who claimed knowledge of the incident. This was Yancy Spence, employed by the Manhattan Offices of the *New York Post* for over 28 years, which may corroborate the account given by Janet Kimball – others may suggest differently.

"About a dozen people remember the procession of stretch limos that was parked on South Street (where the New York Post *is located). These obviously belonged to some very important people. I, myself, remember the ugly coloured Rolls Royce parked at the end of the little pedestrian island that faces the loading bays for the delivery trucks. The Rolls was parked the wrong way on South Street, and the chauffeur was standing just outside the driver's side door. He had his driving hat off and placed on the Rolls' long hood. His arms were crossed like Superman, daring some crazy New York cabbies to run him down. The Rolls has been linked to the then Secretary-General of the United Nations. The four men I tracked down all remembered the Rolls and line of more than a dozen dark limos.*

At 2.30am, I was upstairs in the South Street Diner, on the corner of South Street and Catherine Slip. I was told to report in early for my route, which didn't go out until 4am."

Lights and engine fail

"One of my bosses asked me to give his cousin a ride to Shore Parkway, the 'Riviera of Brooklyn', or so he told me before I dropped him off. To get back to the plant, I took the Manhattan Bridge. At that time, both lanes under the pedestrian's walkway were carrying Manhattan-bound traffic.

At exactly 3.15am, I was a third of the way over the crest, with no traffic ahead of me, when my truck's lights and engine shut down, and the truck coasted to a stop. I tried the emergency lights, but they didn't work either. I looked into my side-view mirror to see if anybody was going to pile into me, and then saw all of the headlights of the vehicles behind me go out and slowly coast to a stop. It felt like everything was going into slow motion. The bridge's lights went out and everything went dark. In retrospect, I believe that a power grid in Lower Manhattan shut down. It was an eerie sight, to say the least."

Beam of red light

"Outside my window, I caught sight of a beam of red light, playing across the nearby buildings. The light changed to a greenish-white colour and became pencil thin as it travelled across the building facades; whoever was outside at the time had to see it because the beam of light was the only power source in the blackout. One of my thoughts was that this must be some kind of laser test that the Brooklyn Navy Yard was conducting, but the source of the light stopped before the East River.*"*

Oblong oval to perfect circle

"The shape of the light kept changing from an oblong oval to a perfect circle. It focused in on one of the top floors of a nearby building. At first, I couldn't make out what building it was, but as

if to answer my thoughts, the beam of light shot down to street level and ran the length of the block, exposing the two sets of very distinctive 15ft-high inverted metal fishhook gates. These were riot gates, used to protect the only two entrance ways into the courtyards of the Knickerbocker apartment complex, on Cherry Street. I've seen that building thousands of times. How could I not know it was the Knickerbocker? The light beam then shot back up to the top floor of the centre building, the one with the exposed water tank, and focused on the bottom half of a double-pane window. There was a window to the right of it that was half the size – probably a bathroom window. This greenish-white light beam started to grow brighter and more intense."

Sky became lit up – vehicles stalled

"Then, for some reason, I looked at my side view mirror, and at that instant the sky lit up. I saw maybe two-dozen people who were now outside of their stalled vehicles; the flash illuminated them through the bridge's superstructure. Some of them were screaming and looked like crazed birds, locked in a cage, as others pointed back towards Knickerbocker. It was surreal, and it scared the hell out of me."

'Four balls' ascending in arrowhead formation

"When I looked back toward Knickerbocker, there was a totally different light. It was bluish-white with a cloudy mist and shaped like a stage spotlight coming down from above. Within this light appeared what looked like 'four balls', ascending in an arrowhead formation. They were tumbling,

and as they got closer to the source of the light, the balls opened up like blooming flowers. I could see that there were three gray aliens in dark jumpsuits in a triangular formation, surrounding an angelic-looking, dark-haired woman in a white gown. Her long hair flowed out in all directions, as if in a pool of water. They all looked like they were being pulled up by their mid-sections. I thought, at the time, that each body was being lifted on cables and that they were making a movie."

Might there be some similarities with a UFO sighted in the UK by Jennifer Cooke in 1977?

More details surfaced

"That's all I remembered of the experience, at first. Over the course of the next four weeks, however, more details resurfaced and that's when I 'remembered' the spacecraft. It was saucer-shaped and the bottom half was outer space black with angled sections, like a Stealth fighter. The 'saucer's' top half was mushroom-shaped – very 'organic' and smooth, with a gray metallic colour. The construction looked as if it was laminated. At the crown was an open donut-shaped hole, and inside was what looked molten metal or some kind of fluid. Whatever that substance was, it was percolating like a volcanic mud bed. The rim was a bright red and the centre was an even brighter yellow. In a fraction of a second, that molten mass dissipated to the inside of the dome, turning to liquid fire and spinning around counter-clockwise, like a giant cotton candy machine. The outside of the dome turned a bright red, and then the 'saucer' and its occupants just disappeared. Afterwards, I remember everyone casually getting back into her or his vehicle, starting them up, and then continuing their drive off the bridge. They were all probably thinking the same thing I was, that whatever it was we had just seen would be on the news or in the papers – but, by the time I went 10ft, the entire incident was forgotten.

Subsequent events were pieced together over time, as more memories of that morning returned.

"I arrived back at the 'Post' in just a few minutes, since it was only six blocks from the bridge. I parked on the opposite side of the island from the ugly Rolls (I noticed it right away), still parked across from the diner. All of the limos were parked on both sides of South Street. They were blocking the corner and were told to move so the newspaper delivery drivers could back the trucks in for the 4am edition – but, of course, they didn't move! I commented to someone that the Rolls was a beautiful car, but what an ugly colour, and that it would look great in white; some of the chauffeurs were outside of their Limos, milling around. One of them walked over to see what the straw boss wanted from the chauffeur who was double-parked and blocking the trucks from turning the corner, so they could back into the loading docks. This one chauffeur looked like 'Odd Job'. He was oriental and his suit was two sizes too small. Evidently, the chauffeurs were wondering why they were hanging out and waiting. To this day they're probably still wondering why. They sat there for close to 45 minutes."

Reporter Steve Dunleavy

"One of the people who remembered some of what happened that morning was reporter – Steve Dunleavy – whom I gave a lift home to Shore Parkway. I clearly recall what was discussed. I called Mr Dunleavy recently and asked if he remembered the conversation we had about most Americans did not know what the Vietnam War was all about! I then asked him if he remembered the driver who had to hail a cab for him. He chuckled and said, 'Yeah, I remember that too'."

Parked limos

"I then asked him if he remembered all the limos outside that morning. He replied, 'Yeah, I remember them'. I asked, 'Did you ever find out what that was all about?' To this he replied, 'We looked into it, but I can't remember what we found out.' I then said, 'there was a UFO about 150 ft over your head

that morning.' He then asked if I could call him in a couple of weeks, as he was preoccupied by the World Trade Centre tragedy and the war in Afghanistan."

Budd Hopkins visits Yancy

"About 14 months ago Mr Budd Hopkins visited me to document my information. On the July 4th weekend of 2002, I attended the MUFON conference in Rochester, to see if Mr Hopkins was going to discuss the case. The only time I had spoken publicly about this experience was at an Intruders Foundation meeting on September 8th, 2001. At the symposium, Mr Hopkins did mention that two delivery workers at the New York Post had come forward to describe the Rolls Royce that they had seen on South Street on the morning of November 30th – very important evidence in this abduction case.

The other driver he was speaking of is a friend of mine. When I began looking for people to corroborate the facts that I knew, I was very careful to be vague in discussing the particulars. You can't just spring the subjects of UFOs and abductions on people, especially if they've been personally involved – so I tried to figure out who was there that morning, over a dozen years ago. The first person I thought of was Bobby. He lives close by, and we get together now and then. During a conversation, I asked him, 'What was the brightest light you have ever seen?' His answer was, 'At the 'Post', one night.' He also said, 'It scared the hell out of me!' He explained that he thought some guys in the neighbourhood were 'messing around or something'. That one question was all that was needed to jog his memory. Over the next couple of months he started to remember more and more – so I suggested that he speak to Mr Hopkins. It took 10 months, but he finally did. I could tell he had been traumatized by the events of that night, just like I had been, and everyone else who witnessed the event, had to have been. Finally, to the former Secretary-General of the United Nations: It's been reported in the media that, through a spokesperson you claim that you were home sleeping. Well, maybe you were? But your chauffeur and Rolls were on South Street with the limos of the Security Council, who were home sleeping too, I suppose? The position you were elected to demands for you to find the courage – the machismo – to tell the people of the world what happened that morning. I know you are caught between the rock and hard place, but I believe you to be a God-fearing man. And, I also know that the truth is the truth."

Authors' comments

We felt the involvement of the so-called two men, Dan and Richard, was dubious. Could their actions have been deliberately orchestrated to bring ridicule to the incident? Or was it part of some staged performance to highlight the incident itself, and promote interest in the media – if so it was certainly successful. One suspects that this wasn't their real first names; we don't even know their real names. Even more suspicious.

We have the disadvantage of not having spoken to any of the parties involved (apart from a brief conversation with Budd) and can only rely on investigations carried out by others who are unable to categorically prove that this incident took place, especially bearing in mind Linda was on her own – unlike the Telford, Shropshire, case with the three ladies that we researched into some years ago, and other similar incidents.

We would have liked to have seen some of the original letters and documents pertaining to this case, and ascertain the authenticity of the *New York Post* employee – Yancy Spence – who provides an interesting, apparently authentic account, available on the internet, in which he describes (as does Janet Kimball) the car coming to a stop – which infers some sort of electrical interference, caused by the presence of the UFO. If this was the case it would be a first for us, as most of the vehicle interferences we have come across (and there have been many) normally occur at a reasonably short distance away from the vehicle, rather than 12 storeys up. If some inexplicable phenomena had immobilised vehicles driving over the Brooklyn Bridge at the time in question, then one would presume this in itself would have drawn newspaper publicity the following day.

Ironically, in a way it is not that we do not believe the account given by Linda – far from it. We have come across some very inexplicable, almost unbelievable, accounts from people we have been talking to for now a number of years.

In all probability, it appears something very strange happened to Linda during that early morning. Unfortunately, the evidence given by other witnesses has convoluted rather than clarified completely the events which, if happened, would have been the most spectacular UFO case of all time. If so, this should worry us all as it would not have been the only time! (**Source: Richard Dolan/WWW Internet 2014**)

Wikipedia 2014 – Budd Hopkins

In 1994, Hopkins met writer, filmmaker Carol Rainey, who became his third wife in 1996. They shared a mutual fascination with alien abduction stories and, according to Rainey, possibility that people on Earth may have been *"seeded here by highly advanced beings or a Big Being from 'out there."* The two co-authored a book *Sight Unseen, Science, UFO Invisibility and Transgenic Beings*, which was published in 2003. They were married for 10 years.

Also in 1996, Hopkins' book *Witnessed: The True Story of the Brooklyn Bridge UFO Abductions* was published. The book portrayed an abduction case that was alleged to have occurred in late 1989 near the Brooklyn Bridge in New York City.

In January 2011 Carol Rainey released an article titled *The Priests of High Strangeness: co-creation of the "alien abduction" phenomenon.*

In that article she, among other things, made a series of unsubstantiated and derogatory claims about her ex-husband Budd Hopkins, his colleague Dr. David M. Jacobs and the primary witness Linda Cortile. Rainey publicly impugned the quality of both Hopkins' and Jacobs' work, as well as the nature of their personal ethics and levels of credulity. She impugned Linda Cortile's way of life as a mother and housewife and went on to insinuate, without proof, that Cortile was a hoaxer. Contrary to Rainey's prior support of the alien abduction phenomenon she now characterized it as *"...an entire genre of performance art..."*

Budd Hopkins, in ill health and just months before his death, managed to construct and publish two rebuttals to Carol Rainey's allegations against him and his work. The first rebuttal, released in February 2011, was titled *"Deconstructing the Debunkers: A Response".* The second rebuttal, released in March 2011, was titled *"Comparison of Handwriting and Drawing Samples by Two Different Witnesses in the Linda Case".*

Carol Rainey's inaccurate claims against Hopkins, Jacobs and Cortile, disseminated in her article and in a collection of 'You Tube' videos, were refuted in detail over a series of fully referenced rebuttals, written by independent UFO abduction researcher Sean F. Meers.

Evidence of Rainey's apparent personal bias against Budd Hopkins and Linda Cortile became apparent when she sent an unsolicited abusive email to Linda Cortile and Sean F. Meers. Further evidence of her animosity and irrationality came to light in subsequent communications she publicly posted online, as well as in further unsolicited emails she sent to Cortile and Meers.

Hopkins died on August 21, 2011 from complications of cancer. Fans and supporters of Hopkins from around the world paid tribute. At the time of his death, he was in a relationship with journalist Leslie Kean.

DECEMBER 1989

7th December 1989 (USA) – Strange *'being'* seen

A T 4.30am, Tony Arias – a night watchman at the Colonial Palms Shopping Center, Miami, Florida – claimed to have encountered a strange *'being'*, in the parking lot, described as *"seven feet five inches tall, bald, with a big head and cat eyes"*. He then called the police and Officer Juan Santana responded and later said:

> *"This was one of the weirdest reports I've ever attended. On my arrival an extensive search was conducted for the 'thing', with negative results".*

Reporters believe he saw two other *'things'* with the first one.

Police Sgt. Joe Wyche:

> *"My first thought was that it was someone in some kind of scary costume, but I just don't know. Whatever he saw shook him up enough to call us."*

(Source: Jon O'Neill, *Miami Herald,* 10.12.1989)

8th December 1989 (USA) – UFO (three light) display over California

Two hospital secretaries saw unusual lights in the sky as they were driving southbound, on Interstate 5, at San Diego. Curious as to what they could be, they pulled into a parking lot and watched the lights manoeuvring over San Diego for half an hour.

Suddenly the lights approached the witnesses, and a silvery-blue object passed silently over their pick-up truck. *"It was so close, if I'd had a gun, I could have shot at it"*, said Martha – one of the women involved. She described the object as an *"...octagon, with a V-shaped appendage on the back. Under the 'V' were three bright pulsating lights"*.

Source: *Brae Canlen, Reader,* San Diego, California, 8.2.1990)

Evening Sentinel – Stoke-on-Trent

7 DEC 1989

UFO sighting baffles police

By Gill Abbott

POLICE are baffled by an Unidentified Flying Object which hovered over a North Staffordshire beauty spot for two hours.

Officers from Kidsgrove saw a large bright light above Mow Cop in the early hours of the morning.

They went to investigate the bizarre object after air traffic controllers at Manchester Airport spotted a static blob on their radar which they were unable to explain.

During the police investigation, their portable car radios went dead.

In the end, the town's police chief super-intendent, Peter Grocott, decided to take a look at the UFO himself.

He said: "We didn't get to the bottom of it – We just don't know if it was atmospherics or somebody from Mars.

Disappeared

"The traffic controllers called us because they thought it could have been the county's helicopter but it was not flying that night."

He added: "We checked the Air Force too and they

said it was nothing to do with them."

The police station log shows that as well as the air traffic controllers, several people called in to report the phenomenon at 5am.

Supt Grocott and his men kept an eye on it until 7am, until it disappeared into the morning sky.

Mr Chris Mason, of Civil Aviation Authority, blamed the radar blip on unusual weather conditions. But a spokesman for the Ministry of Defence said a UFO report has been received from police and an inquiry would be carried out.

The Visitor, Morecambe & Heysham & Lancaster

13 DEC 1989

Mystery lights over Bay

TWO Morecambe residents have had a close encounter in the past month with some unusual aircraft, which they think are types of UFO.

Mr Keith Tassart, of Kings Crescent, Morecambe, said he saw some lights in the sky over the Bay when walking home one evening. When he took a closer look, it was triangular-shaped with a brightly-lit dome at the front. "I had my binoculars with me, so I could see it very clearly.

"There were lights down each wing too. When it took off it had a red light underneath. I would say it was no higher than 2,000 feet."

Mr Tassart said knew it wasn't any ordinary aircraft because it hovered for several minutes before taking off, and did not make a sound.

A similar incident was recorded by Clair Allen (16), of Ruskin Avenue, Bare, who spotted what she is sure was a UFO in the sky over the Bay about three weeks ago.

"All I could see was a lot of lights. They were flashing, as if they were hitting off something.

"It was very low, and was there for about half-an-hour. I was terrified."

14th December 1989 (UK) – Three lights seen

Mrs A. Tinsley (33) from Basildon was driving home through Broadmayne, when she saw:

> *"...three lights, forming a triangle in the sky. I continued to keep my eyes on it, until it suddenly flew away"*.

20th December 1989 (UK) – Mysterious lights over Lancashire

UFO lands, alien occupants are seen

At about 6.30pm, Mr T. Murphy (53) – a taxi driver by occupation – was in his back garden, when he was surprised to see what looked like half of a dome, or circle, low down in the sky, with its bottom half lit up. Wondering what it could be, he fetched a pair of binoculars and looked through.

"I saw a small green and red light underneath it. I watched it on and off for about an hour, until it headed off seawards and was gone."

Mr Murphy estimated the object to have been at a height of 800ft and about a mile and a half away.

Herne Bay, Kent – Disc-like object seen

Mervyn Newell (49) of The Grove, Greenhill, Herne Bay, Kent – a builder by trade, married with three children – was awake in the front bedroom of his house, during the early hours of the morning. He happened to look through the window, when he saw a disc-shaped object in the sky, on its side, over a bungalow, some 3-4000ft away.

Aliens seen

"I then became aware of three alien 'figures' on the other side of a 4ft fence, which divided my fence from the neighbours.

Their waists were above the height of the fence. Their arms were longer than human ones. They had four fingers on each hand;

Circling shapes in sky

By GRAHAM LAWTHER

CHRISTMAS brought a surprise with a difference for a Netherthong man—a possible UFO sighting!

Keith Robson was taking an evening stroll near his home when he spotted discs of light in the sky as he approached the Moor Lane / Bradshaw Road junction.

Mr Robson said the four lights seemed to be at the corners of a shape maybe 200ft in diameter. In complete silence, they revolved for up to 45 minutes at a height of around 3,000ft until they faded away, each revolution taking just a few seconds.

"They were continuous lights circling around, in one position all the time, not going on and off," he said. The cloud base had been around 3,000ft, he added, but visibility was good. "You couldn't really miss them!"

He had first put the sighting down to car headlights. But he had always had an open mind on UFOs—and as he walked Bradshaw Lane, it became obvious the lights could not be from a vehicle but were hovering a few thousand feet above him.

Insp Terry Jepson, of Holmfirth Police, said the station had received no reports at that time—around 7.30pm, Wednesday, December 20—but suggested aircraft landing lights as a possible explanation. Planes left Manchester, flew low parallel to the A635, and then switched off their landing lights, causing previous spates of UFO sightings.

Oldham Police said their station had received many UFO reports recently—the sightings beginning when Oldham's Christmas lights were switched on! But those reports had come from the Ashton / Stalybridge area, where the town centre laser light show appeared as discs of light in the sky.

HOLME VALLEY
EXPRESS
-Yorks-

29 DEC 1989

two of the fingers were longer than the other two. Their heads were longer than their bodies with a skin tone being greyish-white.

They had teardrop-shaped eyes, with no reflection – no noses, but just two slits (for nostrils?) Their mouths did not move, and they had no ears.

I could see this quite clearly, because of the nearby street lamp which gave off a sodium yellow light. One 'figure' had a box like device on its waist, showing three lights – red, white, and green."

Telepathic message received

"I received a telepathic message 'Come with us'. I replied 'no' and walked towards the bed, at which point I felt a beam hit me, followed by a trilling noise. I felt paralysed and couldn't move. I asked 'them' to stop and it appears they did so, as I could now move again. I got into bed and awoke at 7.30am. Straight away, I remembered vividly what had taken place and believed it was no dream."

Chest pains experienced

On the 21st December, while shopping in Herne Bay, Mervyn had a panic attack in *Woolworths* and thought he was having a heart attack. He went to see his doctor, who suggested he had flu! Following further 'attacks' he was rushed into the Kent and Canterbury Hospital, where he was examined but found not to have suffered any heart problems – which was a relief. On the 26th December he suffered another attack, followed by several more – roughly two a week. After each attack he heard a ringing noise in his ears and was later examined for tinnitus, but was deemed clear of this.

"I was asked if I had been subjected to any high frequency noise. I said 'no'. The doctor then said a very strange thing to me – 'Your brain will sort out the problem. You must stop making yourself a prisoner and get back to normal life'."

The next thing that happened was that Mervyn's stomach swelled up for no apparent reason. Once again, tests carried out revealed nothing untoward.

Since the incident and at the time when these notes were taken, in March 1992, Mervyn has put on two stones in weight, although his normal intake of food had not altered. He wonders if there has been a change in his metabolism. Six months after the event he did, in fact, speak to Susan Stebbing, of Herne Bay, about the incident, as a result of which he was interviewed by Valerie Martin, of Herne Bay – a member of the Essex UFO Research Group.

As we have said before, if this was the only incident involving allegations of this nature, following a UFO sighting, one may be inclined to treat the matter with some scepticism, but it is not.

21st December 1989 (USA) – Motorist reports UFO sighting

At 1.30am, a woman and her husband, Daniel, were driving to Indianapolis from Bloomington, along *Highway 37*, when they saw an object, with lights, hovering over a field.

"It was hard to tell the actual shape of the craft, but the lights appeared circular. There were orange-yellow lights on the bottom, but I couldn't see all the way around it."

As they approached closer some 200 yards away, they were able to see clearly the object was hovering above the ground, about as high as a helicopter.

"We turned around, and made our way back at the scene where we saw the 'craft' now on the other side of the car take off, heading west – over a ridge of hills – the lights went out as it did so."

[Unsurprisingly, enquiries made later revealed an Indianapolis Power and Light generating plant was located just over the ridge, near to where the object disappeared.]

Another 'craft' appears

The couple had driven about seven miles along their journey and discussed what had taken place. The woman passenger was searching the sky when, on her side of the road, in the direction of the east, appeared:

> "...a craft that was huge and it was right there! It hung in the air. It was a large craft – like an aircraft carrier, or barge. It was angled or tilted toward me. It had a dome on the back and a long flat area on the front, with two huge searchlights. It made me nervous. It just hung there!
>
> We stopped the car and I rolled down the window. I could not hear any noise except my heart beating very fast. Daniel was trying to lean around me to see it, but he could not see the whole thing but could see the lights and felt the presence of it (a strange feeling in the joints, energy rushing through his body). That physical feeling stayed with us for quite a while afterward. So we sat and watched it, then it began to move toward me. I did not want the lights to shine on my car and I told Daniel to go. It stopped turning and as we drove away I continued to watch it, until I could not see it anymore."

The second craft was described as being:

> "...very industrial looking – too heavy to be hanging in the sky – industrial metallic with intricate squares on the outer sides, metal working that might have been indentations. If this had been a boat, the indentations would be for stairs – wasn't smooth. Dome was smooth looking, iridescent, illuminated from inside. It was not a high dome. The two lights on front of the craft were like searchlights."

(Source: MUFON, Indiana, Field Investigator Norma Croda)

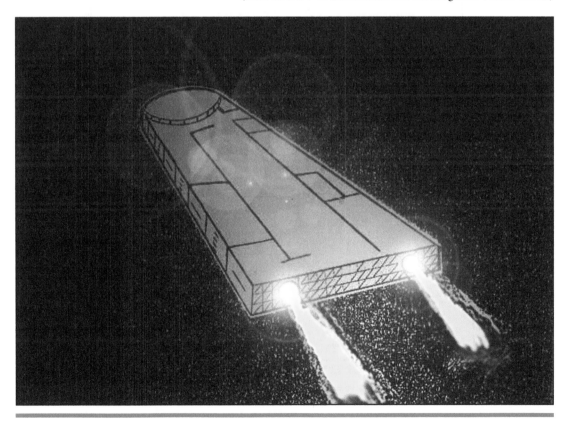

22nd December 1989 (UK) – UFO seen

At 11.42am, at High Wycombe, in Buckinghamshire, UK Aviation expert Peter Halliday, and his wife, sighted a disc-shaped aircraft speeding across the sky. He said,

> "I know what I saw was no aircraft, or weather balloon, or a satellite . . . it was definitely a UFO".

(Source: *Bucks Free Press,* High Wycombe, 29.12.1989)

UFO over Portsmouth

At 11.30pm, in late December 1989, Lawrence Bailey was attending a barbecue at *HMS Dryad*, in Portsmouth, when he noticed a *'bright light'* in the sky, heading towards his direction.

> "It stopped and hovered over a building. I could make out it was star-shaped, with a bright light at each corner or tip, and had what I took to be a hatch in the middle, although the brightness of the object prevented me from making out all details. Everything seemed to go quiet. I could no longer hear the sounds of the barbecue; I felt cold. About 15 minutes later, it moved away and out of sight. Everything then went back to normal."

(Source: Personal interview)

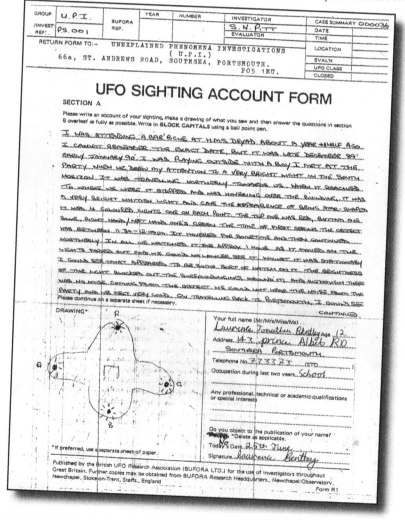

UFO over BBC transmitter

Also in the same month was a report from two security guard dog handlers, who were on duty at the Crystal Palace Sports Centre. Unfortunately, the date of the actual sighting was not given. Gordon Dare (61) from Surrey – then employed as a dog handler – was one of those concerned. He saw:

> *"...a long, grey, elliptical object, about 200 yards away, circling the top of the Crystal Palace BBC Tower, at 11pm; it was completely silent".*

Gordon then contacted his partner – John Freeman (28) – and asked him to take a look, which he did. His drawing was identical to Gordon's.

This was of course not the only occasion we were to hear of reports of UFOs seen near to transmission masts. During Spring/Summer 1950 Dennis Maycroft from Nottinghamshire was carrying out electrical installation work to the BBC transmitter at Holme Moss, Yorkshire a few miles from Holmfirth.

He was working on a mast platform approximately 600ft off the ground with Mr Frederick Binchell, a senior engineer from the BBC, and four steel erectors from the Birmingham area. At 2.30pm they noticed something in the sky roughly two miles away over the Huddersfield area.

> *"It was shaped like an upturned saucer, silver in colour, and approximately a hundred feet in length. We watched it move slowly up and down in the sky, noting when it was in the 'up' position, the underside appeared dark. When it was 'down', you could see a bluish 'energy' around the top of it."*

Details of the sighting were passed by telephone to Mr Binchell, who was now on the ground.

> *"After some two hours had elapsed the saucer-shaped object climbed upwards at tremendous speed before being lost from view. When Dennis returned to the ground he discovered over twenty people*

had seen the unidentified flying object, including the senior engineer who had already left on his way to London to report the incident. "A few weeks later, when somebody enquired about the sighting, he was told it had been a weather balloon. If this had been the case, how could it have hovered in the same position for two hours and moved at such fantastic speed?"

Although we were unable to trace any other witnesses to this incident or obtain any information from the BBC, we discovered a mysterious object displaying green and red lights was seen travelling across the sky over Yorkshire at a speed estimated to be in excess of more than a thousand miles per hour during the early part of 1950. Among the numerous witnesses were coastguards. A subsequent investigation launched by the RAF and scientists from Durham University, (who discounted the theory that it was a meteorite), failed to come up with any satisfactory explanation. (**Source: Personal interview**)

28th December 1989 (USA) – UFO interference

At 8.10pm, at Mount Vernon, Indiana, a family were watching television. Their nine-year-old son was playing with his Christmas gift, a remote- controlled car, which he was having trouble controlling it. A minute or two later, the 'touch-light' in the family room went out, and then came on, followed by the front door being burst open and the 13 year-old daughter and her two friends came screaming in shouting:

"Dad, come out here quick!"

There in the east of the sky, just two or three blocks away, was the most brilliant reddish-orange navigation light he had ever seen

According to the unnamed witness:

"Through binoculars a white strobe could be seen in the front of the object – now very low in the sky, approximately 10° off the horizon. It then made a turn toward the south-east. There was no green wing light or white navigation light showing on the craft, which was completely silent, rather the opposite if it had been a jet, prop engine, or helicopter.

Neither was it an ultra light aircraft and, based on its departure path, must have passed almost directly over the house, at low level, going west to east, before turning south-east. I am of the opinion it must have been in close proximity about the time of the electrical interference, unless this was all a coincidence. The object faded low in the distance, heading south-east."

The next day, the next door neighbour became frustrated with his new garage door opener, which appeared to be faulty and kept going up and down the night before. He removed it, and installed another one!

(**Source: MUFON Indiana, Field Investigator Fran Ridge**)

Events of 1990

Important events of 1990 include:

The Reunification of Germany and Yemeni unification, the separation of Namibia from South Africa.

Desert Shield, and the launch of the Hubble Space Telescope.

The Baltic declared independence from the Soviet Union amidst Perestroika.

Nelson Mandela was released from prison.

Margaret Thatcher resigned as Prime Minister of the United Kingdom after over 11 years.

1990 was an important year in the Internet's early history.

In autumn 1990, Tim Berners-Lee created the first web server and the foundation for the World Wide Web; it would be released to the public in 1991.

Gulf War begins....

Encyclopedia Britannica, which ceased printing in 2012, saw its highest all time sales in 1990; 120,000 volumes were sold that year. The number of librarians in the United States also peaked around 1990.
(Source: Wikipedia)

JANUARY 1990

1st January 1990 (UK) – Four red lights seen in the sky

AT 11pm, Sarah Mordon (19) of Peldon, near Colchester, Essex, was looking out of her bedroom window, when she saw:

> "...*four red lights, stationary in the sky over the Colchester area, and under cloud for about 10 seconds. I then went back to bed.*"

The newspaper cutting, which is shown (next page), identifies twelve separate UFO sightings. The reality is, of course, quite shockingly different!

1st January 1990 (Australia) – UFO seen by family

At approximately 8.50pm, Mrs 'D' entered the main bedroom at the back of the house near Malanda, Queensland, where her husband was sleeping, and told him about a light source that was entering through the window. The light was white – then went brilliant reddish. Looking out of the window, her husband saw the source of the light was coming through trees from the north-west direction. His wife then alerted the grandsons (15) (20) and (23) who were watching TV, and asked them to come and have a look. [No interference was noted on the set.]

The family of five walked up a slope at the rear of the house and saw the light source approaching from behind trees, until it was at an approximate 60° elevation, where it stopped in mid-air.

Mr 'D' estimated the height of the UFO was approximately at an altitude of 1,500ft and about 200yds away. He also estimated that it was approximately 200 to 250mm at arm's length in size. The object glowed, while extremely bright, and could be looked at without any discomfort.

> "*About 150ft above this object was a smaller white, clear light, similar to a spotlight, approximately the size of a car. This light seemed dimmed down by the intense red surrounding the main object. Both moved as one unit. After some thirty seconds the UFO moved away from us at a roughly 45°*

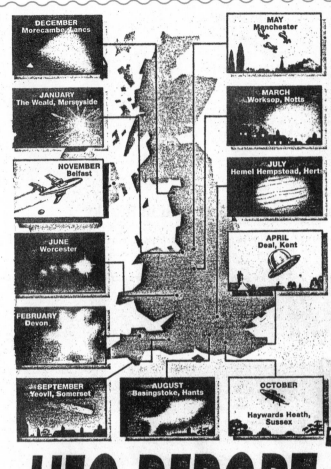

DECEMBER
Morecambe, Lancs

JANUARY
The Weald, Merseyside

NOVEMBER
Belfast

JUNE
Worcester

FEBRUARY
Devon

SEPTEMBER
Yeovil, Somerset

AUGUST
Basingstoke, Hants

OCTOBER
Haywards Heath,
Sussex

MAY
Manchester

MARCH
Worksop, Notts

JULY
Hemel Hempstead, Herts

APRIL
Deal, Kent

UFO REPORT 1990

TOP SECRET

The Fishers: no one can explain'

SIGHTED

A 'CHANDELIER' IN THE SKY

Jim Fisher, of Swindon in Wiltshire, glanced out of the window one night and saw a UFO. 'It looked like a chandelier hanging in the sky, something full of red and green lights. I fetched my binoculars and studied it further. I wondered if I was dreaming.'

Mr Fisher, 67 and retired, called his wife Doris. Without telling her what he'd seen, he handed her the binoculars. 'I see it — yes, it's like a chandelier,' she said. The couple watched for about half an hour.

'It couldn't have been an aircraft because it was motionless,' says Mr Fisher. 'If it had been a balloon it would have drifted away. I just don't know what it was.

'I got calls from other witnesses saying they'd seen the same thing. But no one — not even the police — can explain what it was.'

Illustration: Bill Le Feuve

SIGHTED

A ROUND SAUCER WITH WINDOWS

Morning break at St Joseph's Roman Catholic School, Haywards Heath, Sussex, in October 1989. The children are playing outside. Suddenly they stop and all eyes turn skywards. Hovering above them is a greyish-peach coloured craft with legs dangling below it. The pupils cluster around their teachers.

Of all recent UFO sightings, this is probably the most corroborated. Teachers Sue Weller, Jo Ferris and Mary Wells all saw it. Their testimony is backed up by dozens of pupils who have beens asked by the teachers to draw the object they saw. Most drawings are very similar.

'It was a round saucer with windows all around and dangly things hanging out of the bottom,' said Melissa Morrison, 10.

Enquiries made at nearby Gatwick Airport to see if anything unusual has registered on radar screens reveal nothing.

The mystery remains. . .

St Joseph's pupils' UFO drawings

angle, heading north-north-west. The object moved fast and went beyond the visible horizon (three kilometres) in five to seven seconds, where it then disappeared downwards; a red glow emanated, which illuminated the cloud base for 15 seconds. A white glow was also seen to the left of this, initially."

Approximately 30 seconds after the UFO departure, the lights of an aircraft were seen in the same general direction, though more distant, perhaps heading towards Atherton. The whole episode was over in two minutes. The sighting was confirmed by two other people who lived nearby.

(Source: Robert Frola and Diane Harrison)

2nd January 1990 (UK) – Two cigar-shaped objects seen over Suffolk

At 1.20am on 2nd January 1990, Peter John Maddocks (21) of Woodbridge, Suffolk – a RAF serviceman – was walking home near Woodbridge, when:

"I noticed two cigar-shaped objects in the sky, heading in a north-south direction towards Essex. They were below cloud bank and completely silent.

A cigarette, at arm's length, would have covered them. Ten seconds later, they were gone form sight."

At 1.30am, Anthony Weldon (49) was driving home with his wife, daughter, and her boyfriend, along the A12 between Chelmsford and Ingatestone, after having celebrated New Year's Eve, when they saw two objects, side by side, heading across the sky towards the direction of Brentwood, some 1,500ft up in the air. Five seconds later, they were lost from view.

Others that saw something highly unusual on this date were George T. Brown (26) of Sir Francois Way, Brentwood, Essex. He was standing outside his girlfriend's house in Park Road with his girlfriend Susan Watson (20) at 1.30am, when they noticed:

"...two very large silver-grey in colour oval-shaped objects, moving at speed across the sky. They were at a height of about 2,000ft, moving at 2,000mph. The ends of the objects were pointed and the fronts rounded. I last saw them heading towards the coast. Susan was so petrified, she ran indoors."

At 11pm this evening a fireball was seen crossing the sky over Scotland.

3rd January 1990 – Ralph Noyes writes to Ron West

9, Oakley Street,
London SW3 5NN
071-351 6659

3rd January, 1990

Ron West, Esq.

Dear Ron,

Happy new year ! Sorry not to have had time to return your recent 'phone call - desperately busy at the moment.

A delicate point... Thanks for your membership-renewal form... Trouble is that I already subscribe to 15 or 16 orgs./mags. at national level (I've lost count) and simply can't afford to subscribe to the dozen or so local groups with which I'm also in touch and to whom I give occasional talks. Perhaps you'd consider noting me as a temporary, unpaid consultatnt or some such ?!

I'm keen that somebody from CCCS should give your group a further talk before too long, and I would enjoy doing it myself. But heavy demands are now falling on rather a few of us: I've got seven lecture dates myself in the first few months of 1991 (not to mention an endless round of other work for CCCS); and I know that the few other stalwarts (eg. George Wingfield and Busty Taylor) are similarly hard-pressed. The problem is also going to increase as local CCCS branches are set up around the country, each with its own local programme of events. Moreover, I don't think we can any longer expect the few experts to travel countrywide without at least being given their travelling expenses.

I'm sure you see the problems. But we hope that before too long CCCS will manage to set up a Lectures & Training Secretary who can draw up a panel of speakers and to whom CCCS Branches and non-CCCS groups can apply for the name (and terms) of a good lecturer. We'll let you know the arrangements asap.

Yours ever,

(Ralph Noyes)

Lights in the night sky!

RICHARD KNIGHT and Anthony Yeo have had a close encounter with a bright, flashing UFO which definitely WASN'T the star of David!

They were at Richard's house in Mortehoe when, glancing out of the window, they saw an extra terrestial vision in the sky which they say would have stumped even Patrick Moore.

The question is: Was the green, blue, red and white flashing object, in the sky for nearly an hour, E.T's revenge?

NORTH DEVON JOURNAL HERALD 04.01.90

4th January 1990 (UK) – Mysterious *'light'* over Thetford Forest

At 7.30pm, Mrs B. Bellamy (65) of Thetford, Norfolk, was driving home after picking up the children from their grandparents, at Wootton, near Thetford Forest.

"I noticed that part of it was lit up with a brilliant white 'light', at ground level, emanating from inside the forest. There was no beam – just an intense white glow that extending to an area of about 100 yards. I slowed down, but then became frightened and drove as fast as I could past the 'light' and arrived home at 7.45pm."

Daily Record – Glasgow.

-4 JAN 1990

Night caller from outer space

THE mystery of the heavenly body in the sky was solved yesterday.

It wasn't a spaceship from another world ...

It was a METEOR. And probably the biggest seen for years over Scotland.

The fireball, 80 miles up with a 100 mile trail, was spotted around 11pm on Tuesday.

It sparked off calls to air traffic controllers at Edinburgh Airport.

But a researcher at the Royal Observatory in Edinburgh killed off any thoughts of a UFO.

Richard Dixon said there is no doubt it was a meteor. "And from the size, it was one of the rarer sightings."

It was seen as far apart as Fife and Ross-shire – where it split.

Dr Colin Steele of the British Astronomical Association asked people to send details of sightings to him at St Andrews University.

According to Ron West, who interviewed Mrs Bellamy, she was still very frightened about what she had witnessed, when seen a couple of months later.

At midnight, a couple living in Drysdale Avenue, Chingford, London, watched a very bright stationary orange *'light'* in the sky for about five minutes, until it suddenly shot straight upwards and out of sight.

Triangular UFO seen over Wales

At 8.45pm, Consultant Chiropodist Mr Heddwyn Jones (46), of Bala, was travelling back from Aberystwyth to Dolgellau when:

"I saw a triangular-shaped object, showing green and white lights, parked in a field near Rhydymain. I first thought that someone might have put coloured lights on a tree, but the lights were very straight. I stopped the car between the Drwys Nant traffic lights and the Old Creamery; the lights were still there and not moving. It was about 35ft high. I turned the car engine off and it flew away very fast – now just showing the white lights on its front, heading towards Dolgellau and the mountains."

(Source: Margaret Fry)

UFO seen over East London

A UFO has been reported over **Waltham Forest** and more may follow, says an organisation dedicated to studying the strange phenomena.

The East Anglian UFO and Paranormal Research Association says it has been contacted by two sets of people who have seen UFOs - Unidentified Flying Objects.

Spokeswoman Sheridan Lane said: "These are the first examples we have had in the London area. Others often follow. They seem to come in groups."

The first sighting was by a couple in Drysdale Avenue, Chingford, at midnight on Thursday January 4.

A woman is reported to have said: "I noticed this very bright stationary orange light. I watched it for between five and 10 minutes.

"I called my husband. We both watched it for about

Could there be more? say sky watchers

five minutes, when suddenly it shot vertically upwards very fast." A second sighting came on the night of Sunday January 14 in Hackney by a man who said he saw a 'bright light' in the sky.

He said he saw the light travel silently through the sky, then shoot suddenly to the left and disappear from view.

Sheridan Lane said: "We investigate all sightings very carefully, by checking all possible explanations, including aircraft movements and weather.

"Since the organisation was founded in 1988 we have received over 2000 UFO reports and only one quarter can be accounted for by normal means." The association has a UFO hotline. If you think you have seen a UFO ring 594 4797.

5th January 1990 (UK) – Triangular UFO seen over Norfolk

At 9.30pm, Peter Hulmes (64) was talking to Roy Jackson (45) – landlord of the *Queen's Head* Public House, Stowmarket – prior to going home, when they saw:

> "...three white lights in the sky, forming a triangle. We watched them for 10 minutes and I then walked home."

6th January 1990 (UK) – Contact International UK UFO meeting, Oxford

This was held at the Town Hall, Oxford, by Contact International UK, run by Michael Soper and Geoff Ambler – both of whom we know.

Michael:

"We have 80,000 cases on file, from all over the world, but only one in ten is inexplicable because we take a scientific approach."

MARSTON IS HQ OF NATIONAL UFO SOCIETY

Monitoring alien activity: Michael Soper at his home, HQ of Contact International

Keeping tabs on the visitors from space

By CHRISTOPHER KOENIG

THERE may be more in heaven and earth than in most of our philosophies — but in a semi-detached house in Ousley Close, Marston, the existence of UFOs on this planet is an unquestioned fact.

The house is the UK headquarters of Contact International, an organisation that monitors the comings and goings of spaceships, flying saucers and the like.

It is home to Michael Soper, a freelance maths tutor and chairman of the 250-strong organisation.

"I don't see it as my job to convince others of the existence of UFOs anymore," he says. "I now consider there is easily enough proof.

"Since American military papers have become declassified under a new open information law, too many well documented and professionally researched accounts of sightings have come to light to allow for doubt," he goes on.

"For us its not a matter of believing but of investigating."

Mr Soper says that Oxfordshire is a good place for spotting UFOs - the group is currently investigating a report from a Kidlington woman who saw a bright blue light shining down on her, and an Otmoor girl who, while out with her boyfriend, came across a flying saucer hovering over a haystack.

Then there is the Cumnor couple who saw something that looked like Concorde standing on its tail and gleaming with magnesium lights.

Mr Soper became interested in the study of unexplained flying objects during 1959 when he saw something oscillating above a Valiant bomber before zooming off to the north-east.

Since then he has looked at hundreds of reported cases. About nine out of ten reports turn out to be false, he says.

Cover-up

For example there was the man who saw lights that turned out to be caused by a switching operation at Didcot power station.

Since the international organisation was set up in 1967 it has recorded over 80,000 reports. More than 3,500 were of alleged landings.

"My own view is that there are intelligent beings surveying us.

"They seem to be particularly interested in our plants and hedgerows and they seem to be able to alter the usual space-time continuum.

"I think these beings are able to communicate with people and then make them forget the experience.

"I also think that the Government is covering up a lot of evidence of UFOs because they want to keep secret any research they are doing into the extraordinary powers of locomotion these machines have."

Anyone wanting to join Contact UK should ring Oxford 726908.

Serious

Mr Soper is puzzled about the scepticism of the British.

He points out that a recent poll shows that two out of every three people in USA believe that craft piloted by intelligent aliens exist.

"We don't get a good press, but we're really very serious." he said.

"We receive and analyse about 80 reports of sightings every month from all over the world.

"We also try and awaken public interest in the subject, and of course we speculate as to what UFOs are."

At a symposium held recently by Contact International at Oxford Town Hall, some 120 people were shown slides of "genuine" flying saucers.

They were also told of a mysterious "proven" UFO incident in New Mexico which, the group claims, was formerly hushed up but has now come to light through the release of official papers.

Closer to home — and

1648

OXFORD STAR

18 JAN 1990

Minster man reports lights in the sky

WITNEY GAZETTE
25 JAN 1991
1990

Oxford-based UFO investigators have been investigating reports of circling lights in the sky over Buckinghamshire seen by a Minster Lovell man.

Contact International, based in New Marston, received a number of reports at the weekend about objects with white and red lights circling and hovering over Stoke Mandeville.

Mr Mervin Neal of Wychwood View, Minster Lovell, was in the area visiting friends, and spotted seven mysterious lights flying silently in the sky.

Mr Neal said the lights were seen by many people in the area.

He told the Witney Gazette: "I am as sceptical as anyone about the existence of UFOs, but there certainly didn't seem to be any explanation for these lights."

Mr Michael Soper of Contact International said: "Somebody living in Hampden Road, Stoke Mandeville, reckoned there were about 20 objects, some hovering, some circling and going to the horizon and back again very quickly."

He said there were 12 witnesses there, and people watched the lights for around 30 minutes before they moved off in the Wendover direction.

Mr Soper said: "We can't be certain what they were. We are checking if they were microlight aircraft. The lights, white at the extremities and a central red light, fits the theory of a microlight and the circling also fits. We are trying to find out if it was a local air training school practising night flying."

UFO experts shed light on phenomena

STARRY-eyed UFO fans gathered at Oxford's Town Hall on Saturday for an out of this world experience.

Passers-by and hard-core enthusiasts listened to mysterious tales of a spaceship over Otmoor and lights seen around Kidlington at the Contact International UK meeting.

And the New Marston-based UFO group revealed scientific documentary proof of sightings, as well as light-hearted cartoon.

Despite the fact that UFO sightings are often treated with suspicion, the group still get 50 reports a month.

By STAFF REPORTER

UK chairman, Michael Soper said: "We have over 80,000 cases from all over the world on file, but only one in 10 is really inexplicable because we do take a very scientific approach.

"The recent release of American official documents has lent us credibility because they show such definite proof. We no longer have to strive to prove the phenomena."

Mr Soper said Oxford is a good place for UFO sightings. He added: "We used to get a lot of hoax calls from the Abingdon area, and when Venus is bright people get confused.

"But last year some Oxfordshire girls saw a light in a nearby field and later discovered there were melted rocks there which had been unusually carbonised. It's difficult to explain away."

Vice-president Geoff Ambler added: "We don't have little green men in our association. But we want to make friends if they are coming here."

All sightings which include reports of visitors have been in country areas, leading the experts to believe that they come to collect and study plant and animal life.

Silent flight of circling light

OXFORD JOURNAL

11 JAN 1990

Oxford-based Unidentified Flying Object investigators have been investigating reports of circling lights in the sky over Buckinghamshire.

Contact International, based in New Marston.

"Somebody living in Hampden Road, Stoke Mandeville, reckoned there were about 20 objects, some hovering and some circling and going to the horizon and back again very quickly."

He said there were 12

UFOs attracted to Oxon

A spaceship hovering above Otmoor and strange stationary lights over Kidlington were among numerous sightings of unidentified flying objects (UFOs) in Oxfordshire last year.

Contact International UK, a UFO group based in New Marston, says that the Oxfordshire sightings are just two examples of the many similar reports they receive from all over the world each year.

At a UFO symposium at Oxford Town Hall on Saturday, more than 100 fans were shown slides of presumed alien objects.

Chairman Mr Michael Soper said a recent Gallop Poll in America found that one person in four claimed to have seen a UFO. But in this country people would appear to be less perceptive as the figure is much lower.

Contact International receives about 50 reports a sightings a month from America and about 10 from Europe, but it believes that there are a great number of sightings which never get reported.

According to Mr Soper, Oxfordshire is a good area for spotting a UFO.

He believes that UFO spotters have have an unjustified stigma attached to them. People are not aware, he says, of the work and skill which goes into examining photographs and the physical evidence of sightings.

Contact International publishes a magazine with world-wide circulation as well as an annual UFO register. There is also a 24-hour telephone hot line (Oxford 726908).

NO 10/1/90 THE OXFORD TIMES

6th January 1990 (USA) – Orange light seen Indiana

At 2.30am, two people living in Crawfordsville sighted a large orange light, low in the sky and visible for one to three minutes; it was seen to circle the area and hover over a house about a half a mile away. The matter was later reported to the National UFO Reporting Center in Seattle, Washington, who then contacted MUFON at Indiana. (**Source: MUFON, Indiana, Field Investigator I. Roger Lamberson**)

8th January 1990 (UK) – Flashing UFO seen over Matlock

The Matlock Mercury newspaper, in their edition of the 26th January 1990 – 'Flying object is seen in Matlock' – told of being contacted by an Asker Lane resident, who reported seeing a bright yellow and red object, circular in appearance, apparently pulsating or flickering as it moved across the sky, on the 8th of the month. The witness, Nick Frank, said:

> "A number of flashes of the most beautiful blue came from underneath the object in well-defined rays. They bore no resemblance to conventional navigation lights and it covered 15 miles in three minutes. It was completely transparent and seen between 6.16pm and 6.19pm on that date."

The newspaper ended the article by saying: "NB: Don't accept a lift from little green men".

Another witness was Nick Frank of Wensley, near Matlock. He reported having sighted a strange object in the sky over Masson Hill.

> "It was two overlapping circular white lights. The next day, at work, one of my colleagues told me she was driving her car towards Matlock, when she noticed an identical object in the sky to what I had seen, although she saw red and blue colours emanating from the object."

(Source: *Matlock Mercury*, Derbyshire, 9.2.1990 – 'UFO sighting is noted in Matlock')

By the light of the silvery moon: Richard Tarr, ready to explore strange phenomena in Wiltshire

Watcher of the skies goes to ground

Bristol Evening Post – 8 JAN 1990

IF you see something strange in the neighbourhood, there's someone you should call, and it's not Ghostbusters.

Richard Tarr has been interested in Unexplained Flying Objects for as long as he can remember.

By day he works for a training company, but at night he scans the skies for strange phenomena.

Now he intends to lead a team of 11 people to delve into the mysterious and unknown.

He and his team will investigate the origin of the controversial circles which have appeared in Wiltshire cornfields.

Mr Tarr, aged 24, of Gloucester Road, Horfield Common, said: "We will be working with the Circles Phenomenon Research Group.

A special 24-hour hotline number has been set up to take details of sightings of unexplained phenomena.

Genuine examples of the weird and wonderful should be phoned through to 0756 752216 or you can contact Richard himself on 0272 514089.

Oxford Mail

8 JAN 1990

Aliens 'take an interest in Oxon'

A SPACESHIP hovered over Otmoor and strange stationary lights were seen above Kidlington according to sightings reported to UFO organisation, Contact International UK, based in New Marston.

The organisation says that they were just two of many received from all over the world each year.

At a symposium in Oxford Town Hall, more than 100 people, many UFO enthusiasts but others with a more casual interest, proved the phenomena of Unidentified Flying Objects continues to fascinate.

Revelations

They were shown slides of what they have determined to be genuine UFOs. And there were revelations about a flying saucer incident in New Mexico in 1947, which has come to light through the recent release of official papers.

Contact International members carried out a street poll in Summertown, asking passers—by whether they believed in UFOs.

Chairman Mr Michael Soper said a recent Gallop Poll in America found one person in four claimed to have seen a UFO.

According to Mr Soper, Oxfordshire is a good area for spotting a UFO.

8th January 1990 (USA) – Gulf Breeze, Florida

Gulf Breeze resident – Brenda Pollak, and eight others, observed a black disc, hovering in the sky for about 15 minutes.

(Source: *Sentinel*, Gulf Breeze, Florida, 18.1.1990)

9th January 1990 (UK) – Triangular UFO seen over Yorkshire

At 6.30pm, Skipton resident – John Sharp – was walking his dog on the outskirts of the town, when he noticed a pale yellow pulsating light in the southern sky, approaching his position. As it came closer, he was astonished to see:

> *"…a black triangular object, showing a yellow pulsating light on the underside, with a single tail fin at the rear, about 25ft across at the widest point. It passed overhead, banked and turned, heading away at approximately 50mph, making a swishing sound, before being lost from view."*

(Source: Tony Dodd, *Quest International*, Vol. 9, No. 3, 1990)

Other witnesses to strange things seen this evening was Suffolk housewife – Betty, her daughter, and Harold Williams. After contacting the Essex UFO Group, they filled out a sighting report.

Please write an account of your sighting, make a drawing of what you saw and then answer the questions in section B overleaf as fully as possible. Write in **BLOCK CAPITALS** using a ball point pen.

My daughter and I went into our back garden to collect our washing, this was Monday the 9th January 90, the time was 8.35pm. I know this because I suddenly looked at our clock and said "My washing is still outside" We were collecting it I looked up into the sky and there was this orange to red glowing object, I thought it was the moon at first, but I could also see the moon. It was stationary in the sky, then it moved and then stopped, my daughter was frightened at this stage so we came in, leaving the rest of my washing outside. We heard no noise, I again saw it through my kitchen window it had moved again, then in a flash it was gone

Please continue on a separate sheet if necessary.

Harold's illustration

DRAWING*
ORANGE GLOWING

Your full name (Mr/Mrs/~~Miss~~/~~Ms~~)
Betty .... Age *32*

Address ....:
WALSHAM LE WILLOWS SUFFOLK

Telephone No.......................(STD.................)

Occupation during last two years.......................
Housewife

Any professional, technical or academic qualifications or special interests

11th January 1990 (UK) – Golden object seen over Westcliff

At 10pm, a resident of Addiscombe Grove, Croydon, was stood on his front porch, taking in the night air, when he heard:

> "...a whirring sound coming in bursts of noise. I looked up and saw a grey, metallic, ellipse-shaped object, more like a soup bowl than saucer, hovering about 250ft above the rooftops. A minute later, it vanished."

(Source: *Croydon News & Property News*, 18.1 1990 – 'Was it a bird...? Was it a plane? Was it a UFO?')

At 10.50pm, a couple was feeding their dog at their house in Southbourne Grove, when they sighted an object that shone like burnished gold in the night sky. Ten minutes later, it shot off upwards at great speed and was gone.

At 11pm, another couple from Rectory Close, Hadleigh, reported having sighted four of five large square or oblong windows, set into a larger object, pass silently in front of them, several hundred yards in the air. (Source: Sheridan Lane/*Yellow Advertiser,* Colchester, 19.1.1990 – 'UFO shone like gold'/*Southend Evening Echo*, 17.1.1990 – 'More UFO sighting claims in Southend')

12th January 1990 (UK) – Two *'lights'* seen over Colchester

At 8.30pm, Ellena Sherlock (58) from Collingwood Road, Colchester, was in her back garden when she saw two rotating *'lights'*, moving anticlockwise across the sky – one red, the other green.

Two hours later, at 10.30pm, Glen Kemiya (32) of Brent Avenue, South Woodham Ferries, was returning home from a night out with his wife and parents, and were parking the car, when his wife shouted out, "What's that up there?"

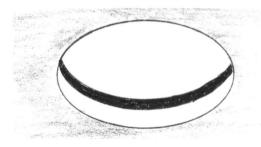

Glen:

> "I looked towards the Shoeburyness area and saw this saucer-shaped white 'light', stationary in the sky. It had a black band around its middle. We stood there watching it for about 15 minutes, by which time some of my neighbours had come out to look. Suddenly, it shot off across the sky at speed."

Another witness was Robert Kent.

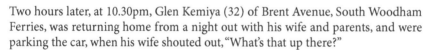

Direction of travel

S.L.
(Searchlight)

12th Jan 1990 (USA) – Indianapolis, Indiana

At 8.30pm, a man (33) and his three daughters (ages 15, 11, and 9) were driving north on Five-Points Road, when the 11-year-old brought their attention to a circle of lights in the sky to their left. The driver slowed down the car, in order for the occupants of the vehicle to obtain a closer look. As it appeared so strange, they then pulled onto a driveway leading to an old barn.

The family sat there for a few minutes and watched the object with an unobstructed view and had this to say:

> *"You could tell the object was circular by the pattern of red, white, green, and blue lights, which apparently went all the way around in a perfect circle. The object was definitely round. You've got the front view of the lights, but as the lights were rotating, you could see the back side of the lights. When the object moved, there was some tilting involved (as much as 60°), and the first time it tilted, a spotlight came on; another time it tilted and a little dark thing, somewhat dome-shaped, was seen."*

The first time the object tilted, the circle of coloured lights went out and a large white light came on underneath, in the form of a beam, which went down to the ground.

The witnesses who had the car windows down never heard any sounds associated with the presence of the object. When asked about the altitude, the main witness stated that the object was probably higher that 400-500ft. Later estimates of the object's distance were 0.8 of a mile south of Interstate 465. (**Source: MUFON, Indiana, Field Investigator Norma Croda/CUFOS**)

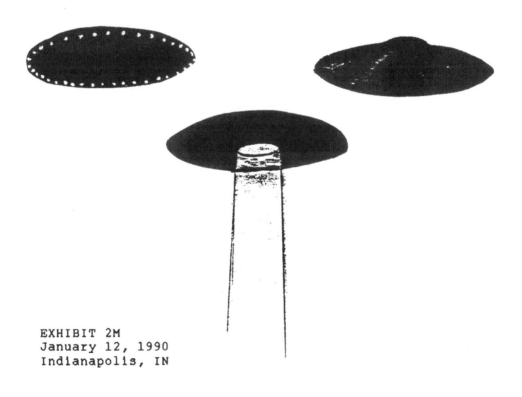

EXHIBIT 2M
January 12, 1990
Indianapolis, IN

14th January 1990 (UK) – Triangular UFO seen!

At 9.15pm, Sylvia 'V' (54) of Stowmarket, Suffolk (who asked that her details be kept confidential, as her husband was a local doctor) was at her home in Lime Tree Place, looking out of the bedroom window, when she saw:

> *"…three white lights, in the shape of a triangle, stationary in the sky. I watched them for 20 minutes and then decided to go downstairs."*

Also on the same evening was a report of a strange light seen in the sky over Hackney, London. It then made a sharp turn to the left, before moving away and out of view.

16th January 1990 (UK) – Triangular UFO seen over Thetford Forest, Suffolk

'Silver balls' seen in the sky over Essex

UFOs in the night sky!

WHEN weird silver balls appeared in the night sky over Highams Park, residents stood and stared in awe — where they UFOs?

The objects, slightly larger than footballs, were revolving and travelling across the sky in an anti-clockwise direction. Sometimes they travelled in threes and fours, but there was no apparent pattern to their movements.

After 10 minutes or so, the lights stopped but began again about five minutes later, and went on for hours.

Christine Wright of Harman Close, was the first person to see them. Mrs Wright said: "I was in the garden when I saw the lights. At first I thought it was my eyes, then I thought I was going mad."

Mrs Wright called to her neighbour who stood and watched the mysterious lights with her.

She said: "The lights were revolving, it was almost as though they were on the underside of a huge flying saucer. I must admit it was a bit scary."

But any chance they might have been space invaders in UFOs was discounted by the experts.

A spokesman for the Meterological Office said: "It was a clear night with just a little low cloud and there was no unusual weather which would have caused this phenomenon. They could possibly have

REPORT: Doreen Friend

be dicso lights reflecting over an area.

"When you first see them you wonder what's hit you," she added.

And Howard Miles of the British Astronomical Association backed up this theory: "We have had this type of query before. They appear to be some sort of laser beam shining on low clouds."

But a different theory is put forward by Inspector Paul Clulow of Chingford Police. Mr Clulow saw similar lights and investigated. He found out they were anti-collision lights used by planes when trying to fly under clouds at night. The light reflects off the cloud in the shape of a silver ball.

Chingford and Walthamstow areas since the weekend. We take all reports seriously and will check into this particular sighting."

So for the residents of Harman Close, it was goodbye to any hopes of meeting little green men — or was it?

DID YOU

● In March 1978 after the great January blizzard, Alec MacLennan uncovered a live sheep near the River Skinsdale, Sutherland, which had been buried in the snow for 50 days.

KNOW?

All party round up

● Leyton Labour MP Harry Cohen has bowled over school cricket players. He has donated two House of Commons pens to the London Community Cricket Association raffle. The Association aims to raise funds to revive cricket in London schools.

● And Walthamstow Tory MP Hugo Summerson is about to become an expert on inner city problems. Mr Summerson has been elected Secretary of the Urban and Inner Cities Committee.

● Social and Liberal Democrats from North Chingford say the Water Park being built in Larkshall Road has "risen like some overgrown wigwam" to mar the landscape.

UFO sighted

Brenda 'B' (44) of Thetford, Norfolk, was driving home through Thetford Forest, at 9.50pm.

"My husband pointed out a silver grey object, stationary in the sky, and slowed down the car. We looked and saw something like two saucers, one on top of each other. Seconds later, it began to fade away and then disappeared from sight." **(Source: Ron West)**

Travelling in our car home on Tuesday 16th January 90 the time was 9.50pm. My husband pointed out to me this object, stationary in the sky. We were passing through Thetford forest at the time. My husband slowed the car down to a crawl, and we looked at this object. It was saucer shaped, (two saucers, one on top of the other) as big as a dustbin lid. No lights were showing. We could hear no noise. We kept watching it, not knowing what it was or what to expect, then it suddenly started to fad out until it had completly disappeared. We saw no markings or indentations on it. It was a silver grey colour.

Please continue on a separate sheet if necessary.

DRAWING*

Your full name (Mr/Mrs/~~Miss~~/Ms)
BRENDA   Age 44
Address: QUEENSWAY
         THETFORD, NORFOLK
Telephone No. ...
Occupation during last two years
         Housewife

At 10.40pm, Thetford woman Betty Rhodes (31) was putting the milk bottles out when she saw:

> *"...a rugby ball-shaped object, moving silently and quickly across the sky. Five seconds later, it was gone from view".*

17th January 1990 (UK) – UFOs sighted over Canvey Island, Essex

At 9.30pm, two orange objects were seen hovering silently above Canvey Golf Course, for about 15 minutes, before disappearing from view – according to three people, who individually saw them. (**Source: Ron West/ *Yellow Advertiser*, Colchester, 26.1.1990 – 'Orange UFOs'**)

18th January 1990 (UK) – Triangular UFOs sighted, Clacton-on-Sea

At 3.30am, William Anderson (87) of Trafalgar Road, Clacton-on-Sea, was on the seafront when he saw:

> *"...three lights moving overhead, followed by one light. The three lights then appeared in a triangular formation, followed by three more lights – this time in a row."*

Please describe in your own words the events of the sighting;

Being my age, you do not sleep very well or much. I was sat looking out of my bedroom window, out over the Sea, when I noticed these strange lights, there was one on its own, two sets of three lights in a straight line, and one set of three lights in a triangular shape. I watched these lights for over an hour, only the single white light moved, it moved across towards the triangular shape, it didnot join them but stayed a fair distance from them, none of the other white to orange lights moved at all. I was watching the triangular lights through my binoculars, when I noticed a slight flash, over towards the East, I looked over there and the 3 lights in a straight line had gone, then appone looking back I noticed that all the lights had gone except for the triangular set. I watched them for a further twenty minutes when they just dimmed then went out. I had my windows closed so I do not know if there was any noise.

Aylesbury, Buckinghamshire

At 8.30am, Parish Councillor – Michael Whitney – was taking his two children to school at Haddenham, Aylesbury, Buckinghamshire, when he saw a translucent object moving through the sky, in the direction of Stone, 150-200ft high.

> *"It was over Church Way, Haddenham. It was unnerving, because it was so quiet. It appeared to have a 'figure' inside. The thing looked like a teardrop, about the size of a small helicopter, but it definitely wasn't a helicopter."*

(Source: *Bucks Advertiser*, 19.1.1990 – 'Councillor spots UFO')

Councillor spots U.F.O.

STUNNED parish councillor Michael Whitney saw a U.F.O while taking his children to school this week.

The amazed Haddenham councillor spotted the translucent object moving at about 60mph in the direction of Stone on Thursday morning.

Mr Whitney was with his five-year-old son Nicholas and eight-year-old daughter Victoria when the mysterious object was seen near Church Way, Haddenham.

He said: "It was unnerving because it was so quiet. It appeared to have a figure inside. It was like a teardrop, about the size of a small helicopter but it definitely wasn't a helicopter. I've never seen anything like it.

"It was doing quite a speed as if it was motorised but there was no sound and it wasn't being carried along on the wind. It was about 150-200ft up."

The dad-of-three from Rosemary Lane, Haddenham wonders if anyone else saw it.

"Perhaps they could tell me what it was. I couldn't believe my eyes."

18th January 1990 (UK) – Triangular UFO seen over Stansted Airport

During the late afternoon, Elizabeth Merry (11) of Chapel Road, Stanway, Colchester, who had been outside playing with her friend, Emma Worsley, and others, on the nearby playing field – was walking home when:

"I heard one of them shout, 'It's a UFO'. I looked up and saw this whitish-grey triangular object in the sky, about half a mile away from us. It had rounded corners and was showing red and green lights. It then began to move slowly, at first, and then increased speed, heading in a north-west direction."

The girls ran home and told their parents what they had seen. They later contacted the *Yellow Advertiser* and then Ron West to report the incident, who asked UFO investigator – Les Stacey – to interview the girls. In conversation with Emma and her mother, on the 24th March 1990, Les was told that the day after the UFO sighting, Emma became aware of a rash on the back of her neck, which disappeared the next day. Whether this may be attributed to the UFO sighting, we cannot say. Emma also made mentioned of waking up early from sleep on a number of occasions, following the sighting, and finding herself crying, but was unable to understand why. She was asked if she had experienced any strange dreams and answered in the negative.

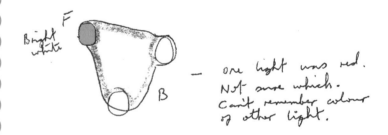

Great Oakley

At 6.30pm, Great Oakley housewife – Mrs Nice – was on her way to evening classes.

"As I went through the village, I saw an object hovering in the sky. It looked like a pyramidal line of lights – triangular in shape and tilted at an angle. There was a red flashing light on top. I got into my car and drove to Little Oakley, keeping an eye on it. It moved slowly from left to right and then stopped. When it did this, the red light flickered – then it moved back along the same route, before moving backwards again and vanishing from sight at about 6.34pm."

Talk on UFOs!

Ironically, the spate of UFO activity recorded for this date took place on the same evening as the East Anglian UFO & Paranormal Research Association, held a talk in Room 5, the Council Offices, Hockley Road, Rayleigh. At 7.30pm, Stan Conway gave the talk on UFOs.

Colchester

At 7.45pm, Mrs Pamela Brown (39) was collecting her son Neil (10) from cubs, by St. John's School playing field, Clay Lane, Colchester.

> *"I saw a shape in the sky made up of three golden balls of light, which began to merge together. I was struck by the size and its brightness. It reminded me of a 'fire' in the sky – far too big to have been an aircraft. It glowed for about 30 seconds and then appeared to turn and disappeared from view."*

Pamela was accompanied by her daughter – Anna Brown (10) and friend, James Batchelor (8).

The matter was later reported to Ron West, who interviewed her about the incident.

Cambridgeshire

At 9.10pm, Mary Street (69) of Merlin Drive, Ely, was out with her husband, walking the family dogs.

> *"We saw three white to orange coloured lights in the sky, forming a triangle, completely stationary and about the size of tennis balls. We kept watch on them while we carried on walking for 30 minutes, until they extinguished at 9.50pm."*

At 9.30pm, her neighbour – Ann Moorcroft (56) of Merlin Drive, Ely, Cambridgeshire – was out collecting the washing when she saw three white *'lights'*, with a hint of orange around them, hovering in the sky. By the time she had fetched her husband to come and have a look, they had gone.

Five minutes later, shop owner – Joseph Collett (59) also of Ely, was on his way home when he, too, saw exactly the same phenomena as described by Mary Street. He confirms that the lights disappeared from view at 9.50pm.

Norfolk

At 9.45pm, Betty Knowles (32) and her husband were entering their house in Silfield Road, Wymondham, Norfolk, when they happened to glance upwards and see:

> *"...three round white lights, forming a triangular shape, just hanging in the sky. They had an orange glint around them and, from the ground, looked to be about the size of peas. At 10.10pm they just went out."*

Janette Stokes (60) from Breckland, Mundford, Norfolk, was in her living room when, just as the 10pm *BBC News* had started, she saw

> *". . . a large orange light shoot silently straight across the sky, heading in a north to south direction. I ran outside; seconds later it had gone."*

18 JAN 1990   Edgware, Mill Hill & Kingsbury Times.

Zooming in on mystery lights over Hendon

The music of the spheres?

EIGHT-YEAR-OLD Ricardo Sidoli thought Hendon was being invaded by aliens on Thursday night.

And he was not the only one.

An amazing array of spinning lights in the night sky brought the residents of Barford Close out on to the streets in amazement.

Ricardo's father Richard, 40, compared the freak light dance to the fantastic scenes in the film Close Encounters of the Third Kind — and he should know because he works in the film industry.

But Mr Sidoli and his family weren't the first to spot the unexplained lights chasing the clouds.

"My neighbour Bert Leggett saw it first at about 6.30pm. He came and got me because I've got some binoculars," he explained.

But no matter how they scoured the horizon there appeared to be no explanation.

Mr Leggett's son David, eight, was also bemused but dubious about how his adventures would be received by classmates at Sunnyfields School.

"I think I'll keep it a secret. I don't think they'd believe me," he said

Was it really UFO's lighting up the night sky last week? District Editor ELIZABETH HAMMOND was determined to find out what it was that was causing wide-eyed wonder over North London

The display continued and harassed mothers appeared with warm coats for their children who refused to go indoors.

Meanwhile, I phoned the London Air Traffic Control Centre to ask for what I was sure would be a rational explanation.

My inquiries were met by a rather timid, and distressed, employee.

"I'm going to have to call the press officer, there have been so many inquiries," he said apologetically.

Hours later, and still on terra firma, I was told by the official spokesman that no pilots had reported anything strange on their flightpaths across London.

"It could have been a plane circling while waiting to land at Heathrow but other than that I'm afraid I can only say that I can't shed any light on it, if you'll excuse the pun," he said sheepishly.

At the Ministry of Defence, officers suggested the strange pattern of lights was the result of a laser show.

The next day Wembley Stadium confirmed that the display which had caused such a stir were actually stage lights from the Paul McCartney concert bouncing off the clouds.

But I, like the residents of Barford Close, remain unconvinced.

The trail of light appeared to be coming from the far side of the clouds.

"In my business I've seen plenty of arc lights and you would be able to see the beam from a lamp on the ground — like the old wartime searchlights," said Mr Sidoli.

The effect was like enormous fire flies in the sky.

"Perhaps that's really what it is," suggested David.

But I think we'd all prefer to think we'd witnessed a visiting spaceship.

You could say we'd seen the light.

Back over Colchester!

At 10.15pm, shop manager Barry Davies (52) of Mumford Road, West Bergholt, Colchester, was waiting for a bus in High Street, Colchester.

He noticed:

> "Three white lights in the sky, forming a triangular shape. I watched them for about 15 minutes, as they moved slowly and silently across the sky, before being lost from view as they went behind the Town Hall."

Norfolk

At 11pm, Teresa Moss (23) of Rose Street, Norwich, Norfolk, was walking home with her sister, when she saw three white lights in the sky over Norwich Cathedral.

My sister and I were walking home from work, we are both nurses, at Norwich hospital, we had just finished our shift, this was on Thursday Evening at 11pm, (18-1-90). We were walking down Ipswich Road, when we noticed these three white lights, stationary in the sky. We stopped and looked, they did not move, I would say the size of tennis balls, They were in a triangular shape as my drawing. We watched for about two minutes when they just went out, just like turning the light out, There was no noise. We did not see them again, We gave no more thought to them, until we saw your article in the newspaper.

UFO light display over Hendon, London

Somewhat as a footnote to this activity were reports from the Hendon area of London, of a light display seen by residents living in Barford Close.

Ricardo Sidoli (8) and his father, Richard, were first alerted by their neighbour, Bert Leggett, and his son, David (8), who told of seeing *'spinning lights'* chasing each other across the sky on the Thursday evening, described as resembling enormous fire flies. Enquiries made with London Air Traffic Control revealed they had received many reports of this phenomenon, which was initially explained away as an aircraft waiting to land at Heathrow. They were laser lights!

19th January 1990 (UK) – UFO over Essex

Miss Kyriaki Manoli (23) of King Cole Road, Stanway, Colchester, Essex, was waiting for a bus in Crouch Street, after college.

> *"I looked towards Balkerne Hill and saw an object in the sky, about 400ft away. It was moving slowly and was divided into three colours – navy blue, silver and cinnamon. I thought it might have been an aeroplane, although it didn't look like one. I felt a strange tingling feeling in my spine. At this point the bus came and I got on it. When I arrived home my friend greeted me excitedly with a newspaper in her hand, and she said people had been reporting seeing UFOs."*

Following the matter being brought to the attention of Essex UFO group investigator Les Stacey, he arranged for an interview to take place with 'Kiki', who has only a limited amount of English, which took place on the 22nd March 1990, along with a Mrs Lansley – a Greek lady, married to a British born person, who acted as an interpreter.

Les:

> *"The interview had just begun, when we were interrupted by the arrival of a Greek orthodox priest. He sat in and commented that 'UFOs and such phenomena are the manifestations of the devil'. He was friendly enough and, at the conclusion of the interview, I was thanked for conducting the interview in a professional and skilful manner."*

Chingford, Essex

Mrs Cadwallader (35) – a telephonist by occupation from Normanshire Drive, Chingford, Essex, located near Waltham Forest – was driving home after having picked up her daughter, Natalie, from the hairdressers, at 7.10pm, when she saw something resembling a red and white dinner plate – vaguely triangular – moving across the sky, which she believes was not an aeroplane. By 7.25pm, whatever it was could no longer be seen.

Colchester

At 11pm, Civil Service worker – Colin Collings (59) of Corwinders Close, East Bergholt, Colchester – was in his back garden, investigating a strange noise heard (which he thought might have been his fence falling down, following strong winds being experienced in the locality).

> *"I saw this very dark grey/black saucer-shaped object, gliding across the sky. It was just like two saucers, one placed on top of the other and heading eastwards at very fast speed. As it disappeared, two minutes later, a blue flash lit up the sky."*

(Sources: Ron West/*Yellow Advertiser*, 19.1.1990 – 'Strange lights over Colchester bring UFO claim')

20th January 1990 (USA) – Cone-shaped UFO, Boyle, Mississippi

A man was driving home when he sighted a slow-moving silvery object, at tree-top height. A crease in the surface near the rounded top was the only variation in an otherwise cone-shaped exterior. Two rows of numerous lights, each in a blue-green pattern, shone steadily. One row was situated near the base, the other along the perimeter of the flat bottom. The object picked up speed and paced just above and in front of the car for two to three miles, repeatedly moving left and right to avoid larger trees along the roadside. Abruptly the car's engine, lights, and instruments, died. The witness pulled to a halt and watched as the object continued down the road, then executed a smooth turn and climbed out of sight. He was then able to restart the engine. (Source: James Scarborough, *MUFON UFO Journal*, No. 264, April 1990)

BRISTOL OBSERVER

19 JAN 1990

Inside the '90s

HI-TECH UFO TEAM ARE WATCHING SKIES

Report by Christine Lewis

A TEAM of UFO spotters in Bristol are raring to go in the search for mystery sightings.

Shop assistant Richard Tarr, 24, is regional co-ordinator in the South West for Quest International, an organisation dedicated to UFO investigation.

He claims an 11-strong team of experienced observers ready to answer calls from anyone who sees unexplained phenomena.

Winston Keech, also 24, who has a degree in computing and in-strumentation, and unemployed Steven Fielding, 26, of Bangrove Walk, Lawrence Weston, are ready to cross rough terrain on motor bikes in pursuit of the truth.

They go armed with hi-tech computer equipment and cameras.

Says Winston, of Gloucester Road, Horfield: "A lot of people see strange things and don't know who to ask. We can tell them — even if it was only the latest air flight.

"A lot of things are unusual, like circles around the moon. That is the defraction effect caused by ice particles in the upper atmosphere.

"We are a scientific research team. We are not a bunch of cranks."

Winston is convinced sightings are genuine.

"There have been too many reports for it to be said that it was people hallucinating."

He believes the United States government has been investigating for years — but scientists do not like to reveal their interest for fear of being labelled cranks.

Richard, also of Gloucester Road, says the emphasis this year is on strange circles which have appeared in cornfields in Wiltshire and Hampshire.

"The corn is being manipulated by some form of energy," said Richard. Much more research is needed to find an explanation.

One call the Quest team investigated was in early December.

"We got people phoning up thinking the aliens had landed. But it was just laser tests for the 125th anniversary celebrations for the Clifton Suspension Bridge," said Richard.

They also researched odd illuminations, hovering over Leigh Woods for more than an hour, and were assured by the authorities it was not caused by military or civilian aircraft.

But their masters at Quest International said it was probably a helicopter — so the sighting remains a mystery.

You can contact Quest on 0756 752216 and Richard Tarr on 514089.

Mysterious circles in cornfields are high on the group's list of assignments.

Scanning the skies...Unidentified Flying Object hunters Richard Tarr, foreground holding a Geiger Counter, and fellow 'UFOlogists' Winston Keech and Steven Fielding, all from Horfield, keep a regular watch for extra-terrestrial visitors.

20th January 1990 (UK) – UFO over Norfolk

Baker, Colin Bourd (46) of Howdale Road, Downham Market, arose at 3am to prepare for work. He looked through the bedroom window and was surprised to see two large round *'lights'* in the sky, apparently hovering over the nearby river, about three-quarters of a mile away.

> *"They were the size of footballs – then one vanished, the other dimmed and faded away. I checked the time; it was 3.12am."*

Ely, Cambridgeshire

Mrs Brenda Monks (54) from Downham Road, Ely, Cambridgeshire, had just left the house to go shopping, when she saw:

> *"...a silver, disc-shaped object, heading silently in a west to east direction, at tremendous speed. If it hadn't been for the sun reflecting off it, I may not have witnessed anything."*

Thetford, Norfolk

At 10.30m, a white *'light'* was seen moving across the sky over Station Road, Thetford, by Mr E. Curtiss. The object stopped in mid-flight, for about two minutes, before heading away on its journey.

Norfolk

At 11.50pm the same day, Jon Flowers (46) was driving along the A11, towards Wymondham, Norfolk, when he saw a large orange *'ball of light'*, with an inner ring, stationary in the sky.

> *"As I drove closer, it appeared to increase in size. After turning off the A11, I lost sight of it. The object was not the moon and it was below cloud cover."*

22nd January 1990 (UK) – Triangular UFO seen over London, Essex, and Suffolk

At 4.40pm, Mr Ian James was walking home from work, when he saw something very odd in the sky. As a result of this, he later contacted Dan Goring, who interviewed him, following which a sighting form was filled out.

UFO SIGHTING ACCOUNT FORM

SECTION A

Please write an account of your sighting, make a drawing of what you saw and then answer the questions in section B overleaf as fully as possible. Write in **BLOCK CAPITALS** using a ball point pen.

IAN WAS WALKING HOME FROM WORK & AS HE WAS GOING ALONG DERBY ROAD HE SAW A SINGLE "DENSE BLACK CLOUD" IN AN AREA OF THE SKY THAT WAS STILL BLUE IN A DEEPENING TWILIGHT. HOWEVER, OTHER DARK CLOUDS WERE IN OTHER PARTS OF THE SKY & OVERHEAD, BUT THIS ONE SEEMED ISOLATED. WHAT CAUGHT HIS ATTENTION THOUGH WAS THE SHAPE THIS CLOUD HAD ADOPTED FOR IT LOOKED LIKE CONCORDE! IAN CONTINUED WALKING ALONG THE ROAD & UPON LOOKING UP AT THIS CLOUD AGAIN SAW THAT IT NOW GREATLY RESEMBLED A PTERODACTYL DINOSAUR & WAS VERY PRONOUNCED. SOON AFTERWARD HE LOOKED UP AGAIN & THE CLOUD NOW LOOKED LIKE A CHICKEN, BUT THE CLOUD WAS BEGINNING TO BREAK UP & DISSIPATE WITH HOLES APPEARING IN IT. IAN REACHED THE END OF DERBY ROAD & TURNED INTO THE HERTFORD ROAD & NEVER LOOKED UP AT THE CLOUDS AGAIN; HOUSES WERE IN THE WAY ANYWAY. HE ADDED THAT HE IMMEDIATELY RECOGNISED THE SHAPES THAT THE CLOUD'S OUTLINES DELINEATED. OTHERS HE TOLD AT HIS PLACE OF WORK MADE LIGHT OF THE STORY (DJG IS A

Please continue on a separate sheet if necessary. [WITNESS TO THIS]. D.J. Goring

DRAWING*

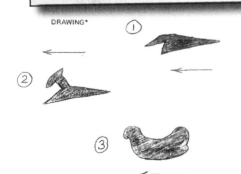

At 8.40pm, Mrs J. Robinson (37) of Cranston Gardens, Chingford, London, was walking her dog, when she saw what she took to be a shooting star in the western sky.

> *"I stopped and saw that this was not a shooting star but a group of spherical shapes, giving off a soft white glow, and moving in what looked to be some sort of pattern. There were five 'shapes' in all. Three moved together in a circular orbit around the sky, heading in an east to west*

direction. Seconds later, two of the 'shapes' appeared from the right-hand side close together, moving in an oval orbit. They then disappeared from view but reappeared a few seconds later. This motion went on until 11pm, by which time they were slowly fading away."

Clacton

At 9pm, Mr R.J. Hogkins (51) – a carpenter by trade from Anchor Road, Clacton – was out exercising the dogs near Tyler Road, when he saw:

"...three downward pointing bright lights. They then moved a few hundred yards to the west and began to hover again, before silently flying away towards Manningtree."

Woodbridge, Suffolk

At 9pm on 22nd January 1990, Woodbridge, Suffolk, resident – John Peterson (61) – was out with his wife (59) walking the dogs along Haugh Lane. The couple were astonished to see three large white *'lights'*, completely motionless in the sky, forming a triangle. The *'lights'* were still there at 10pm – by the time they returned home.

Norwich

At 9.20pm, two sets of three white lights, forming a triangle in the sky, were seen by Mr D. Walters and his wife, Jennifer, of Daivey Place, Norwich. The couple were returning home, at the time, and noticed the lights hovering above the Castle Museum, at a height they estimated to be 3,000ft and about three-quarters of a mile away.

"One set began to move away at a few miles per hour, before disappearing from view over the Royal Hotel. *The second set continued to hover over the Museum. Suddenly they just vanished from view. There were about thirty people watching these phenomena."*

Essex

At 9.35pm, David Fairclough (39) – a builder by trade – was leaving the *White Hart* Public House in Clacton-on-Sea, when he saw:

"...three lights, forming a triangle. I wondered what on earth they were and watched them for a few minute, before they dropped down behind some woods."

Cambridgeshire

At 10.50pm, Jack Simpkin (38) from St Augustine's Road, Wisbech, Cambridgeshire, sighted three lights in the sky forming a triangle. He watched them for a minute, until he lost his view of them. Ten minutes later, heating engineer – Mr Brian Wayland (53) also of Wisbech, Cambridgeshire – was exercising the family dog outside when he saw,

"I noticed three white round lights, stationary in the sky. They had a sort of an orange tint or halo around them. I watched them for about five minutes and they began to move towards each other, until joined together forming one light. Five minutes later they just vanished, leaving a halo which faded away a few seconds later."

Bury St. Edmunds

At 11pm, David Hillman (14) of Northgate Avenue, Bury St. Edmunds, was looking out of the bedroom window, when he saw three white lights hovering in the sky over the British Sugar Corporation factory, off the A45 (now A14).

"After 25 minutes, they began to move towards the direction of Ipswich, apparently following the road, before suddenly disappearing from sight."

Forty minutes later, at 11.40pm, another Bury St. Edmunds resident – Mrs Betty Brown – was looking out of her kitchen window, when she noticed:

"...three white lights, the size of saucers forming a triangular shape, apparently over the British Sugar Corporation works. I watched them for about 20 minutes, before they moved away."

At 11.45pm, Mr .Peter Jackson (36) and his wife (35) from Avenue approach, Bury St. Edmunds, were looking out of the bedroom window, when they saw:

"...three white round lights, hovering in the sky over the A45, near the British Sugar Corporation Plant."

The couple watched them for 15 minutes, until they flew away eastwards, and out of sight.

23rd January 1990 (UK) – Green light seen over The Wirral

A mysterious green *'light'* was seen flying across the sky, at about midnight on this date, by Ellesmere Port man – Neil Dunn, and his three friends, who were travelling along the M53.

Neil:

"As we arrived at the Eastham turn-off, we all saw a bright green 'light', with a tail, shooting towards Liverpool. We watched it for 15 seconds, until it disappeared."

(**Source:** *Liverpool Echo*, **25.1.1990** – 'Green light UFO leaves 'em baffled')

24th January 1990 (UK) – UFO display

At 8pm, Peter Allbright (50) of Station Road, Thetford – an engineer by profession – was in his back bedroom, looking out of the window with his wife, when he saw:

"...three round white lights, motionless in the sky. They were hovering over a nearby industrial estate and were about the size of tennis balls.

I watched them until 9.15pm, when they suddenly shot straight up into the sky, keeping in a triangular formation as they did so."

Jeanne Dorothy Holmes (48) was another witness to this phenomenon. She was at her home in Hale End Road, Waltham Forest, at 9pm, when her two sons came into the house and told her they had seen a UFO. She said:

"We ran into the back garden but our view was obstructed by the houses, so we went into Cobham Road. Suddenly, a circle of lights, five or six of them, appeared just in front of us, heading to our left and disappeared into clouds. A few seconds later, this was repeated. I asked my son to try and capture it on video. By the time he fetched his video camera, the lights had gone. It appeared to me that the lights were on the bottom of a large craft, circling as it moved through the sky. The formation was very similar to the markings left in the cornfields of Hampshire each year."

Mark David Holmes (18) – employed as helicopter ground crew – corroborates what was observed and tells of sighting:

> *"...three 'balls of light' in a cluster, moving about in the sky, followed by single lights moving in and out of cloud."*

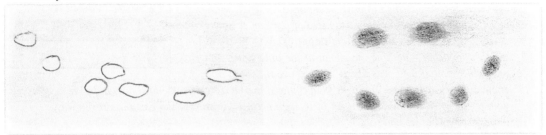

Liz 'D' (46) – a social worker from Millfield Avenue, London – was returning from the local shop, at 9.30pm, when her friend drew her attention to what she took to be fast moving clouds, heading across the sky. In an interview, later conducted with Roy Hale of the London UFO Studies Group, she said:

> *"They were rotating in a circle as they moved along. We watched them for about 10 minutes, until we arrived home. We then went into the back garden and continued observing until 11pm, during which time they carried on rotating in the sky."*

It appears that the *'lights'* were seen over a reservoir and factory area nearby. (**Source: Ron West**)

King George Reservoir

Mr Dereham was at home in Chingford, London, when his son, Lee (13) and his friend, Craig Watson (14) told him about having sighted a UFO they had seen circling over the King George Reservoir. Mr Dereham did not believe them, but sent his wife to go and have a look. As a result of her call, he then went outside himself and saw:

> *"...two sets of lights, three in each set, circling clockwise in the sky over the reservoir, at an angle of 180°. They were moving very fast. I watched them for at least 15 minutes, between 9.15pm and 9.30pm; they were not aircraft."*

At 10pm, Jamie Richards (12) of Drysdale Avenue, Chingford, London, sighted something very odd in the sky over the direction of the reservoir. He then called his mother and father.

Jamie:

> *"They looked like hazy blob-like forms of lights, speeding in an arc across the sky behind one cloud to another – sometimes bright; other times dim. They were very high. We looked through binoculars but couldn't make out any further detail."*

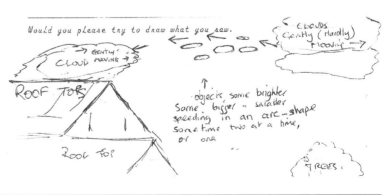

UFO seen over Thetford Forest

At 10.50pm, Julia Viking (18) and her boyfriend, Bernard Jones, were parked up in the car park in Thetford Forest, Norfolk.

"We were listening to the radio when, all of a sudden, a white 'light' appeared in the sky about the size of our car. It slowly descended. As it did so, the car radio stopped playing. Bernard tried the switches – nothing, no signal at all, only static. The now white 'ball of light' was about 250ft above the forest and about 600ft away from us. The 'light' then changed to a glare, which extended outwards. We jumped with fright when the radio came on of its own accord. We started the car and drove away, very unnerved by what we had seen."

[This was now one of other reports involving the sighting of UFOs over Thetford Forest. Please see 1st May 1989 and 3rd August 1989.]

Keighley News. Yorks.

2 FEB 1990

UFO sighting.

An amazed Laycock pensioner watched a glowing object shoot across the night sky.

The capsule-shaped UFO hurtled low across the village before disappearing.

Last Thursday night's incident is the latest in a string of reported UFO sightings around Laycock and Oakworth.

The 67-year-old woman, who does not want to be named, says: "It was definitely not a plane. It came quite low but there was little noise. I have never seen anything like it before in my life."

● The first-ever college course on UFOs is being staged at the Adult Education Centre, Storrs Hill Road, Ossett, on February 24 and March 3.

Case material from around the world, including photographic and video-taped evidence, will be presented.

Enrolment is on the opening day and costs £8.

25th January 1990 (UK) – UFO display, Hertfordshire

At 10.45pm, Heather Bartholomew, from Barnet, was taking her dog for a walk when she saw droplet-shaped *'lights'* in the sky.

"The sky was very cloudy and it looked as if the 'lights' were shining from above and radiating through the cloud. They seemed to follow me – that was the oddest thing about it. They followed me down Bells Hill and hovered around my flat for half an hour. It really was a unique thing; it is extraordinary. I definitely thought it was a UFO."

Another witness was Corrine Bedford of Berkley Crescent, East Barnet, who also rejected the explanation, provided later by the police, that she had seen laser lights in use at Paul McCartney's Wembley concert.

"I was with my two friends, when we saw what appeared to be three clouds over Barnet, which began to chase each other in a circle across the sky, soon to be joined by a total of sixteen little pools of light that made weird patterns in the sky. It looked like little fuzzy balls, dancing around. Every five seconds they met in the middle and then flew off and did their own thing. At 11.20pm, they disappeared completely."

The concert in question finished at 10.30pm! (**Source:** *Barnet Borough Times*, 1.2.1990 – 'Woman claims she saw UFO in Barnet sky')

BARNET BOROUGH TIMES
1 FEB 1990

'It looked like fuzzy balls dancing around'

Woman claims she saw UFOs in Barnet sky

A WOMAN out walking her dog believed she saw UFOs circling the sky above New Barnet and Totteridge last week.

Corrina Bedford, 23, from Berkeley Crescent, East Barnet, will not accept the police view that what she saw was lights from Paul McCartney's Wembley concert.

She was out at about 10.25pm on Wednesday when she saw what appeared to be three clouds over New Barnet.

"Then I thought — clouds don't chase each other in a circle," she said.

She went inside to get boyfriend Dan Reynolds and friend David Copestake. Although David had had a few drinks, Corrina was sober, she said.

All of a sudden, instead of only three, they saw about 16 little pools of light below the clouds.

There were no beams coming from the ground, so

Report by JANE O'BRIEN

they quickly ruled out the possibility of floodlights.

And they were sure it was not an aeroplane or helicopter.

The lights went off towards Totteridge and Whetstone so they walked after them to try to find out more.

Standing on a green near Oakleigh Park train station they watched the weird patterns in the sky. Another person out walking a dog stood and watched them too, said Corrina.

"It just looked like little fuzzy balls dancing around. Every five seconds they met in the middle and then flew off and did their own thing and then came back again," said Corrina.

"At about 11.20pm they disappeared completely," she said.

A few other people out walking seemed to see the lights but did not acknowledge them.

"I came back feeling like I was just a pinpoint on the earth. I felt very privileged to see it," she said.

A spokesman from Barnet Police Station said there were no other sightings reported last week, but the previous week there was a similar call when the caller accepted the lights must have come from Wembley.

He said they would not take any action on the strength of one call.

"We believe them to be laser beams," he said.

A spokesman from Wembley arena box office said search lights coming from the arena could be seen in the sky for long distances if there was low cloud.

He said he could see them from his home in Pinner where they were even frightening some of the local cats.

But he added the Paul McCartney concert was scheduled to end at 10.30pm.

26th January 1990 – further reports of UFO activity

Time 5.20 AM. Ba 10n Friday 26TH Jan
1990
Morning after the high winds

I was very restless after going to bed
the night before, usually I get up
for work as a self employed
Caterer at 6 AM.
 I always sleep facing my bedroom
window with my blind up, suddenly
I saw something in the sky
traveling accross my window a
plane I thought from Southend
Airport on looking out my window
to my amazement saw a round
object moving to the right, it
was a combination of pink and
blue colours, I watched fascinated,
then it seemed to get larger as
it got further away and I saw
then as it grew it was surrounded
in lights all around it just
like my domestic light bulls
in my house Could it be a
U.F.O?

Jm Daly.

SPINING. ANTI CLOCKWISE

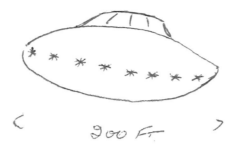

< 200 FT >

27th January 1990 – UFO over Essex

		YEAR	NUMBER	INVESTIGATOR		CASE SUMMARY	
RL27190				R LAKE		DATE	
RL/A25	REF.	1990	E/90/70	EVALUATOR		TIME	
						LOCATION	
IRN FORM TO:-						EVAL'N	
						UFO CLASS	
						CLOSED	

ST ANGLIAN U.F.O. & PARANORMAL RESEARCH ASSOCIATION

SIGHTING ACCOUNT FORM

SECTION A

Please write an account of your sighting, make a drawing of what you saw and then answer the questions in section B overleaf as fully as possible. Write in **BLOCK CAPITALS** using a ball point pen.

SATURDAY EVENING (JAN 27TH 90) MYSELF AND MY WIFE AND DAUGHTER WERE WATCHING THE TELEVISION. MY WIFE WAS FACING THE WINDOW OVERLOOKING THE SCHOOL PLAYGROUND, ALL OF A SUDDEN MY WIFE SAID "WHATS THAT? AND POINTED TO THE WINDOW. WE ALL LOOKED OUT OF THE WINDOW THEN RAN TO IT. WE SAW OUT OF THE WINDOW WHICH SEEMED ABOUT 100 YARDS AWAY A LARGE BALL SHAPE, THE OUTLINE OF THE BALL WAS VERY PROMINENT AND THE COLOUR WAS A BRIGHT CERISE PINK. WE STUDIED IT CAREFULLY. TRYING TO MAKE OUT WHAT IT WAS. IT HAD BEAMS OF THE SAME CERISE COLOUR COMING OFF IT. IT WAS GOING ACROSS FROM RIGHT TO LEFT AND MOVING QUIET SLOWLY. UNFORTUNATLY IT MOVED BEHIND THE SCHOOL AND OUT OF SIGHT FROM US. MY DAUGHTER AND I PUT ON OUR COATS AND RUN INTO THE PLAY- GROUND TO SEE IF WE COULD SEE IT, BUT IT SEEMED TO HAVE DISAPPEARED. WE NOTED THE TIME AND TALKED ABOUT WHAT WE HAD SEEN FOR A WHILE THEN SAW YOUR REPORT IN THE YELLOW ADVERT-

Please continue on a separate sheet if necessary. ISER AND DECIDED TO CALL YOU ABOUT OUR SIGHTING

DRAWING*

Your full name (Mr/Mrs/Miss/Ms)
JAMES RONALD SUDDELL Age 60
Address 41 TUNMARSH LANE
PLAISTOW LONDON E13 9NE
Telephone No. 471-9658 (STD 01)
Occupation during last two years
RETIRED

Any professional, technical or academic qualifications or special interests
—

Do you object to the publication of your name?
Yes/No. *Delete as applicable.

Today's Date 1 FEBRUARY 1990
Signature

CERISE PINK

* If preferred, use a separate sheet of paper.

Sherri Suddell's illustration of the object

28th January 1990 (UK) – UFO display over London

Karen Lentz (24) of Cathall Road, Leytonstone, and her sister were witness to something spectacular which took place, at 7.30pm, involving the sighting of:

"...three flashing lights in the sky, followed by ten or twelve more that appeared as if from nowhere. I called my sister and we watched on the balcony, for about 90 minutes. We also saw triangular-shaped objects in the sky. One of the objects approached the flat made up of nine flashing lights forming a triangle. Three helicopters then arrived and flew over the area. One of them attempted to pursue one of the UFOs but, to my amazement, the UFO turned around and chased the helicopter. The UFOs left by heading vertically upwards at 8.32pm."

28th January 1990 (USA) – UFO filmed over Gulf Breeze

During the afternoon a MUFON UFO investigator and three others videotaped a round, orange UFO that emitted white flashes of light from the top and bottom of the object. (**Sources: Paul Ferrughelli,** *Computer Catalogue of UFO Reports*, **1988-1994;** *MUFON UFO Journal*, **May 1990**)

31st January 1990 (USA) – *'Manta Ray'* UFO seen, showing three lights

A huge manta ray-shaped object, described as bigger than a 747, without the fuselage, showing flashing lights, was seen at 6.30pm, by many witnesses in Piketown, Dauphin County, estimated to be flying at 10,000ft altitude. On the same day at Halifax, Pennsylvania, Donna and Tom Rode were driving to Harrisburg, at 6.30pm, when they encountered a strange object, shaped like a *"stingray, with three lights – one blinking"*.

The object had no fuselage and Donna, who was familiar with aircraft specifications, estimated it was much larger than a Boeing 747 and flying at about 10-15,000ft, heading in a northerly direction – out of sight in 10 minutes.

(**Source: Lori Schoffstall,** *Sentinel*, **Dauphin, Pennsylvania, 20.2.1990/Timothy Good,** *The UFO Report*, **1991, p.238**)

31st January 1990 (UK) – *'Lights'* seen over Charing Cross, London

Strange *'lights'* were seen in the sky over Finchley, in the London Borough of Barnet, 11 miles north-west of Charing Cross, attracting newspaper attention. The witnesses included Anthony Perry and his wife, Margaret, who rejected the explanation, offered to them that they had seen laser lights.

FEBRUARY 1990

6th February 1990 (UK) – Three *'lights'* seen

AT 10pm, Peter Tweddle (33) was just about to enter his flat at Berefield Way, Colchester, when he saw *"a translucent cube-shaped object in the sky, about as bright as four large houses. I watched it for five to ten seconds and then went inside."*

At 11pm, Ray Briggs (34) of Forest Road, Colchester, was out fishing at Frinton Wall. He had just cast out and placed the fishing rod against the wall.

YELLOW ADVERTISER
-Colchester-
15 FEB 1990

UFOs sighted over Newham

ALIENS have taken a shine to East London with a record number of UFO sightings over the area last month!

And the East Anglian UFO and Paranormal Research Association are over the moon with the news.

The group which studies "observable phenomena" is asking locals to contact them if they see anything odd over the East London sky.

There were 24 UFO sightings over East London during January, all of which were reported by the group to the Ministry of Defence.

But the MoD reported back that only a quarter of the sightings were identifiable.

Over Newham there were five UFO sightings in January. These were:—

30 Jan 6, 10-11pm — several people in Stratford saw a saucer shaped object with red, green and blue lights spinning high over the East London sky. It was larger than a football, noiseless and was observed for an hour.

31 Jan 17, 4.40-4.50am, Plaistow — a married couple in Plaistow saw three lights in a triangular shape hovering over them. They estimated its size to be that of a golf ball, and was white in colour. Suddenly another similar 'craft' appeared and then both objects disappeared.

32 Jan 20, 11.45pm, East Ham — one witness saw a blue light, round in shape and noiseless, travel very fast across the sky.

33 Jan 23, 11pm over the A13 — a married couple driving along the A13 saw a blue light disappear into the distance. It was the size of a football.

34 Jan 27, 9.15-9.25pm, Plaistow — an orange ball of light, with an estimated 20-foot circumference, was seen revolving above a roof top by three friends.

Sheridan Lane, publicity officer for the group, said: "These are all extremely interesting sightings and made even more so by the fact that they cannot be accounted for by the MoD.

"There seems to be an increase in observable phenomena over the East London area which nobody can explain.

"We welcome news of UFO sightings and anyone who has seen anything odd in the sky should contact us on our hotline 594-4797."

Flying saucery or pie in the sky?

Report by Gavin Hinks

IN January this year the skies over Essex were alive with UFOs.

Of the 51 reports of UFO sightings in the skies over Essex, 26 sightings were in Colchester and involved a total of 84 people. Can 84 people really be imagining things?

Sheridan Lane, an investigator with the East Anglian and Paranormal Research Association, is working overtime investigating these reports and says that the figures for January are the highest in such a short space of time for years.

But though she is surprised by the number of reports coming in, they follow last year's trend when more than 2,000 reports of UFO sightings in the region were made.

She said: "We are moving towards a time when it becomes unavoidable but to accept the idea of extra-terrestrials, and this will have many implications."

Mrs Lane, of Straight Road, Boxted, has been a UFO investigator for just over a year. Before that she was a political journalist and was writing a book about the conflict between Israel and Palestine, when she got involved with the association.

"My personal belief is that people, through the mass media are becoming more comfortable with the concept.

"Television programmes, books and films all have a role to play, even if they are fictitious.

"Most of what is imagined is possible and we don't use our imaginations enough."

The East Anglian association is a breakaway group from the national British UFO Research Organisation and was founded in July 1988 by just two members. It now has over 100 members and more people are joining all the time.

But they do not just see their role as documenting UFO reports, they also play an active part in investigation, rigorously questioning any report.

As soon as a report comes in the association arranges to meet the witness and asks him or her to make another statement about the sighting so it can be cross-checked with the original report.

The witness is then asked to fill out a questionnaire in which they might be asked if they have developed any unexplained rashes, or if there was any feeling of nausea at the time of the incident.

"After this," said Mrs Lane, "we check out other details. We phone the civil and military aviation authorities to check if planes were in the area at the time of the incident. Then we call meteorological authorities to check the weather conditions.

"Last year we threw out a quarter of the reports after investigation, but this does in no way mean that the rest of the sightings were flying saucers or extra-terrestrial spacemen. It just means we have been unable to explain the sightings."

Sightings in this area include people in Harwich, Colchester, Frinton and Clacton who simultaneously saw a cigar shaped object hovering in the sky, and people in

OVERTIME...Sheridan Lane

West Mersea and Clacton who saw a column of three lights hovering in the sky and then flying away vertically at great speed.

However, Mrs Lane is convinced that in some way or another beings from another planet are visiting and may even be communicating with us.

And just like star gazing she says people can take practical steps to spot their own UFO.

"I would encourage people who are interested to get a good pair of binoculars, they're often better than telescopes, and just be patient."

Good hunting.

Barnsley Chronicle, Yorks.
2 FEB 1990

Glimpses of Venus or was it a UFO?

A LIGHT in the sky seen over Goldthorpe on Tuesday has baffled observers but not the RAF. People who saw the light at about 7.05am say it was high up, did not move, seemed to change its shape and beams of light came off it.

Mrs. Pat Dale, a supervisor at S.R. Gent's, saw the light as she was on her way to catch a bus to work from her home in Windsor Crescent, Middlecliffe. "The light was bright and a ray would occasionally come off it. I stayed and watched it for about eight minutes and its shape seemed to change," she said.

Retired miner Wilfred Addy, aged 60, said: "This had me puzzled. I watched it for about 10 minutes to check if it was a plane but it never moved. The light was very bright and in the east towards Goldthorpe. It would give off flashes of light," he said.

Yorkshire Traction secretary Sandra Potter said: "Beams of light came off it and it seemed to keep changing shape. It is a bit of a mystery although, at the time, all I could do was laugh about it being a flying saucer."

A spokesman at Royal Air Force Finningley, near Doncaster, said no reports about unidentified flying objects had been received and that there was no record of planes flying in the area at the time.

"What people could have seen is the planet Venus which is visible on early mornings and evenings at this time of the year.

"I bent down to tighten the line when I saw three objects, heading fast across the sky, following the coastline. I stood up. As I did so, they stopped for a few seconds. One of them to the left moved away in one direction; the others went off in other directions and that was the last I saw of them."

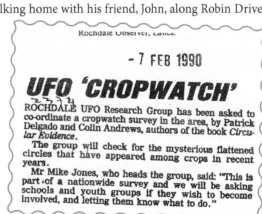

8th February 1990 (UK) – Three UFOs seen over Suffolk and Essex

Dorothy White's illustration

Between 8.30pm and 9pm, a number of people living in the Colchester, Braintree, Clacton, Romford, Chelmsford and Ipswich areas, reported having sighted three *'globes of light'*, forming a triangle in the sky. They included Dorothy White (52) of Mapleford Sweep, Basildon, who saw a number of strange lights in the sky, forming a circle, at 6.45pm.

Seen over Suffolk 1990 (UK) – Two sets of three lights

Doreen Jones (29) of Allenby Road, Ipswich, and her husband, were just leaving the house to go for a drink at the local pub …

"when we noticed these lights in the sky. They were round and appeared to be in a triangular formation, i.e., two set of three lights, moving slowly from the East. We watched them for five minutes, trying to gauge their height. Soon they had dropped down behind the flats, opposite, and that was the last we saw of them."

(Source: Ron West/*Southend Echo*, 20.2.1990 – 'Golf ball lights seen in the sky')

Observed over Kent (UK) 1990 – Pulsating UFO seen

At 8pm Shirley Gibbons (54) of Beckenham, Kent, and her husband, told of seeing a flashing or pulsating orange oval *'light'*, motionless in the sky, over the Croydon area. After watching the *'light'* for 30 minutes, they went inside. She later contacted the Croydon Property News to tell them about it.

Ipswich (UK) 1990 – Two sets of three lights seen

At 8.30pm, Peter Rowland (16), from Ispwich, was walking home with his friend, John, along Robin Drive, when they saw two sets of three silent lights in the sky, forming a triangle, moving slowly through the air.

"One of the set stopped for about a minute and then carried on following the first one, before both were lost from view in the distance."

Hockley, Essex (UK) 1990 – Three large yellow lights seen

Also at 8.30pm, Mrs Phyllis Binns (70) of Broadlands Avenue, Hockley, Essex, was letting the cats out into the back garden, when she saw:

Rochdale Observer, Lancs.

– 7 FEB 1990

UFO 'CROPWATCH'

ROCHDALE UFO Research Group has been asked to co-ordinate a cropwatch survey in the area, by Patrick Delgado and Colin Andrews, authors of the book *Circular Evidence*.

The group will check for the mysterious flattened circles that have appeared among crops in recent years.

Mr Mike Jones, who heads the group, said: "This is part of a nationwide survey and we will be asking schools and youth groups if they wish to become involved, and letting them know what to do."

"...an unusual thing in the sky, shaped like a triangle, showing three large yellow lights, with a small one almost unnoticeable at the bottom of the 'triangle'. I called my husband to come and have a look, thinking he would scoff at me. We watched it for about 15 minutes, until it was out of sight towards the north direction."

Ipswich 1990 (UK) – Two sets of three lights seen

John Costa (59) of Hadleigh Road, Ipswich, had this to say:

"I was looking out of the lounge window when I noticed two sets of three round white lights, forming two triangles in the sky, heading in an east to north direction. I estimated they were about 5,000ft high and silent. I watched them for four minutes, until they were out of view at 8.34pm."

Downham Market 1990 (UK) – Two UFOs seen hovering over power lines

At 9.30pm George Davies was driving home, going towards Downham Market, having just left Wisbech where he had a business.

"I was outside Downham Market, near to Downham Building Supplies, when I noticed two saucer-shaped objects hovering 300ft above the ground, about three-quarters of a mile away. I stopped the car, opened the window and looked out, when I realised they were hovering silently over power line cables. Sparks were shooting out from them at different angles. Suddenly, a pencil light shot straight upwards into the sky. I looked at my watch; it was 9.12pm. I then continued home."

9th February 1990 (UK) – Two UFOs seen over cathedral

At 8.45pm, an accountant – William Hambro (58) of Fore Hill, Ely, Cambridgeshire – and his wife, were out walking the dog through the town centre, heading towards the Cathedral, when they noticed:

"...two silver-grey, large, oval-shaped objects, hovering about 1,500ft above the spires. They had red, green and yellow, lights spinning around the centre in an anticlockwise direction. Our dog refused to go any further. He kept dragging himself backwards and lying down, but recovered when we walked away from the area. At arm's length, it looked to be about two and a half feet across."

At 10.45pm, typist Margareta Downs (18) was on her way home with her boyfriend, Bill Williamson, and in Downham Road, Ely, when they also saw:

> "...three lights, forming a triangle – one up, two down. They stopped for a minute and then continued moving. They halted again and repeated this behaviour twice more. On the third occasion, the 'lights' hovered over the RAF Hospital in Downham Road, where they stopped. After about 20 minutes, we decided to carry on our journey home."

10th February 1990 (UK) – UFOs over East Ham

London UFO Investigator – Roy Lake – told of having received a dozen UFO reports in and around the East Ham locality, during February 1990.

One of the witnesses was Mabel Flitton of Central Park, East Ham – a retired bank typist – who was preparing for bed, at 12.30am, when she saw

> "a bluish-white triangular light, with rounded edges and lights along its sides, moving very slowly eastwards across the sky, towards the Barking area."

Roy Lake with Brenda Butler

The MOD, who was consulted, said:

> "The unit dealing with UFOs had been disbanded years ago."
>
> (Sources: *Docklands Recorder*, 15.3.90 – 'Spacecraft Surprise')

12th February 1990 (UK) – Triangular UFOs over Suffolk

At 8.30pm, Mrs Julia Simpson (36) of Dickens Road, Ipswich, was stood in her kitchen, washing up. She said:

> "I glanced out of the window and saw six sets of white lights, moving across the sky; they were gone in seconds."

Norfolk 1990 (UK) – UFO observed out to sea

At 9.45pm a number of people in the Norfolk area saw a black, oval-shaped object (not unlike a grey-silver airship in shape) heading across the sky. They included Mr A. Smith, of Great Yarmouth. He was walking the dogs along the seafront when:

> "...an object caught my eye; it was shaped like an airship, just drifting about – no lights and no noise. It was about 5-600ft up in the air and about a mile away out to sea. Suddenly, it picked up speed and was gone in seconds – so fast that it must have been moving at 3,000mph! I last saw it heading towards Lowestoft."

14th February 1990 (UK) – *'Mushroom'* UFO seen

At 8pm, Joyce Brushett (61) of Surrey Avenue, Leigh-On-Sea, Essex, was stood at her front door waiting for an ice-cream van, when:

> "I noticed a mushroom-shaped light in the sky; it got bigger and was soon the size of a saucer, held

at arm's length. I called my next door neighbour, Tim, to come and have a look at the object, which was hovering over the Benfleet area for a few minutes, before shooting away at speed. After the ice-cream van turned up, I purchased some ice-cream; at which point I saw it returning back along the same path. It stopped in the sky, once again, and then shot away and out of sight."

15th February 1990 (UK) – Bell-shaped UFO seen

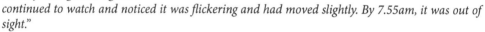

At 6.15am, Mrs Edith Cave (67) of Heathway, Dagenham, Essex, was getting dressed, when she happened to look out of the window and observe:

"...what I thought was an aircraft in the sky. I couldn't see any navigation lights. I continued to watch and noticed it was flickering and had moved slightly. By 7.55am, it was out of sight."

In addition to this, she told of having seen an unusual object in the sky, about two years previously, in 1988.

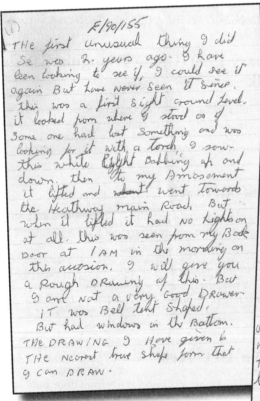

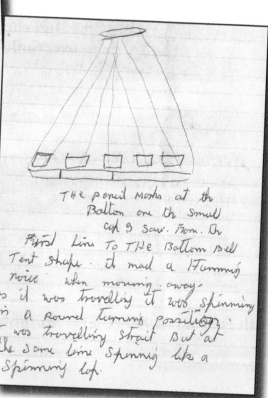

Three UFOs seen over Cambridgeshire (UK)

At 9pm, Audrey Adams (41) of Broad Street, Cambridgeshire, was looking out of her window, when she saw *"three balls of light"* in the night sky. She immediately called her husband. The couple watched the *'lights'*, set at equal distance from each other, as they hovered in the sky for about 10 minutes – until they then shot upwards and out of sight.

'Ring of lights' over Essex (UK)

At 11.50pm, Paul Walker (20) from Meadow Road, Stifford Clays, Essex, was collecting the washing from the line, when he noticed a huge *'ring of lights'* in the sky and immediately called his mother and father outside to come and have a look. They watched the strange object, until it became lost from view after moving behind cloud cover. **(Source: Peter Oliver)**

15th February 1990 (USA) – Three UFO's seen over Massachusetts

A motorist and his passenger were driving north along Route 3, between Brockton and Plymouth, at about 8.15pm, when a very large *'craft'* passed overhead, travelling in a south-east to north-west direction, at about 200mph, followed shortly by another, and then a third, which stopped directly overhead.

> *"We pulled off the highway, along with about 40 other vehicles, and we got out having a better look. The 'craft' was unlike any other I had ever seen and I have seen plenty. I have worked in aviation for about 15 years, including a tour in the US Air Force. The massive black or dark grey 'craft' stopped and hovered over us for about six minutes. It had very few lights, but there was enough residual light from the highway street lights to allow us to see the size and shape of the craft and some of its massive dimensions. I would have some difficulty giving an exact lateral measurement, except to say that it could have easily contained a nuclear aircraft carrier. It was nearly as tall as it was long, if you were to include the vertical projections. It was hexagonal in shape and had three vertical projections above the upper surface, ending in a tail formation located equidistant at the 120, 240 and 360 degree locations, if you were to look at the 'craft' as a disc. There was one white light in the center of the bottom surface of the 'craft' and a red and blue light on each side of the horizontal element of the vertical projections. The 'craft' was completely silent; after about eight minutes, the 'craft' moved suddenly and rapidly away towards the north-west in the same direction taken by the other two. A short time later, five F-16 Fighters, from what I believe was Otis Air National Guard Base near the towns of Sandwich and Falmouth, appeared in the sky. When I arrived home I was shocked to find that the television news had reported that there had been sightings reported to be UFOs up and down the east coast, from Virginia to Newfoundland in Canada."*

(Source: NUFORC 2014.WWW)

TODMORDEN NEWS & ADVERTISER

2 3 FEB 1990

UFOs on the horizon

TODMORDEN is no stranger to supposed extra terrestrial activity and interest will be high once again with a visit by Mr Arthur Tomlinson.

Manchester-based Mr Tomlinson is a UFO researcher who has spent 36 years studying the phenomenon. On Monday March 5 he will give a presentation at Todmorden Town Hall.

He promises videos, more than 100 slides, and Top Secret documents released under the Freedom of Information Act in the United States.

The lecture lasts nearly three hours and doubtlessly the most exciting attraction will be photographs of aliens which he promises to display.

16th February 1990 (UK) – UFOs over Essex and Norfolk

At 8.30pm, Norwich woman – Iris Eagling (48) – was walking home from the Norwich and Norfolk Hospital, after having been to see her husband.

As she turned out of the entrance she noticed a large *'ball'* of orange glowing light, motionless in the sky, towards Norwich Airport. She continued on her journey when, a few minutes later, it vanished from sight.

Essex (UK) – Gold light in the sky

Another witness was Mrs Janet Carvell (41) and her daughter – Emmanuel (8). They were driving back from Clacton to Colchester, at 7.45pm, near the Wheeley roundabout, when they noticed a large, gold coloured *'light'* in the sky, apparently hovering over adjacent fields. They stopped the car and got out to obtain a closer look.

> *"A small white light appeared in the sky and headed towards the larger light, which promptly went out – then four flashing lights appeared and moved overhead, making a droning noise, until out of sight."*

Leigh-on-Sea (UK) – Eight lights seen

At 10.15pm, Timothy Paul Southland (30) – a traffic clerk of Surrey Avenue, Leigh-on-Sea – was called outside by his wife, who told him she could see a strange *'ring of lights'* in the sky.

> *"I went outside and saw eight lights in total, forming a perfect circle. We carried on watching it and then all of the lights extinguished, leaving dark sky. Three white lights came on – a large oval one*

at the front and two smaller ones at the sides. A red pulsating one appeared and the object – which was completely noiseless – began to move away, allowing us to see a cigar shape at the front and a large circle at the rear. It was then lost from sight, a short time later."

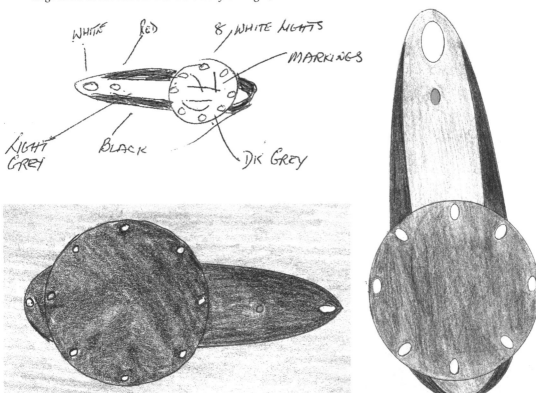

17th February 1990 (Australia) – Spherical UFO seen

At 6.30am, an elderly lady was out walking in Sherwood Park, Brisbane, Queensland, when she saw an orange-red object moving slowly northwards. Several others also witnessed the event. All agreed as to its appearance. It was first seen at an elevation of 30° to the East and disappeared behind trees, after about five to six minutes. The object was described as being:

> *"...spherical, with a cylindrical column below; this column was about half the diameter of the upper part. It appeared to be larger than the rising sun."*

Sherwood Arboretum, Brisbane, Queensland, Australia

17th February 1990 (UK) – Triangular UFOs over Essex

During the evening two *'Flying Saucers'* with multicoloured spinning lights were seen hovering in the sky, over Basildon. A short time later, they moved away. Other sightings of what appears to have been the same UFOs were reported from Colchester and Southend. They included a report from Mr L. Kittredge of Stratford, London, who was outside looking up into the sky, when he noticed a strange *'ball of blue light'* which was completely stationary. He watched as aircraft moved past it and then, seconds later, it disappeared from view.

London Docklands sighting (UK) – Three UFOs seen

Was this connected with what Sarah Garcher (14) and her mother witnessed?

> *"On the 17th February 1990, I went with my mother, June, on a day out to London We left Liverpool Street Railway Station and arrived at Custom House, at 6pm. We were walking down Victoria Dock Road, East 16, when I happened to glance up into the sky and saw what I thought were three light bulbs, attached to some sort of wire. I looked down, then up again, and realised they weren't attached at all and appeared to be moving toward us."*

Sarah's mother wondered if it could have been the control tower or an aeroplane, at the nearby Docklands Airport, but then discounted this as an explanation, as no lights were being displayed and no noise was heard. At this stage the object(s) came very low in the sky (which was now dark) and to the couple's amazement glided down behind a nearby fence, about 25ft away from where they were stood, and disappeared from view.

19th February 1990 (UK) – Elsie Oakensen mentioned

Daily Star - London

19 FEB 1990

Victims warn of a mind-blowing threat to Earth...

CLOSE ENCOUNTER: What Elsie Oakensen saw the night an alien spacecraft swooped on her car   Drawing: KEN TAYLOR

HUNTED BY A UFO

Teacher Elsie fails 'examination' by an alien spaceship

By STEVE PURCELL

TEACHER Elsie Oakensen and her friend Rita Gould are two ordinary women ... but they're all set to shock Britain's UFO-watchers.

For their true-life close encounters have convinced them that aliens are not only watching us — but HUNTING us.

The women's amazing stories are to be scrutinised by flying saucer experts at a special seminar later this week, and the evidence will be hard to dismiss.

Stalked

Elsie, 61, the wife of a police inspector, believes she was stalked, mind-probed ... and then rejected by alien forces.

She was a few miles from home when she spotted two bright lights hovering over the A5 near Daventry, Northants.

"At first I thought it was a low flying aircraft," she says. "But as I drove underneath I could see it was a 30ft-wide, dumbbell-shaped object about 100ft up.

Moments later, as she drove down a lane near her home in Church Stowe, the car lost power.

"I had my foot right down on the accelerator but the car just stopped.

"There was complete blackness and I couldn't see the car or the road.

"Then brilliant white circles of light, about a yard in diameter, appeared from nowhere flashing on and off around the car.

"When the last circle disappeared I was 100 yards down the road, driving normally. I hadn't

HUGE LIGHT SWOOPED ON RITA

WRITER Rita Gould was driving down an old Roman road when a UFO swooped on her.

"I'd seen a white light ahead and slowed as the light moved on to the road," she says.

Just as with Elsie Oakensen, the car seemed to stop by itself.

Disbelief

Passenger Clive Potter stared in disbelief as the light approached. Suddenly, the UFO shot off.

"A man later reported seeing a white oval shape that night in the sky over the Fosse road near Brinklow, Warwicks, where our encounter happened," says 51-year-old Rita.

"Two other people reported seeing something strange in the sky, and a huge corn ring appeared overnight in the field near the road."

TESTED: Elsie was rejected   Picture: BOB BARCLAY

started the car or put it into gear. It seemed to happen by remote control."

Elsie checked her watch. She'd LOST 15 minutes.

Once home, she saw two parallel white lines shoot into the sky above the spot where she had almost fallen prey.

Then she suffered an acute pain "like a band being tightened around my head."

Three investigators from nationally-known UFO organisations checked out Elsie's story. They discovered remarkable similarities between her experience and those

of other close encounter victims.

These included a sighting, at nearby Preston Capes, by four women just two hours after Elsie's experience.

Devoted

Elsie, now devoted to UFO research, is convinced she was tested by the aliens on that dark night in 1978, and that she failed that test.

● ELSIE and Rita will both speak of the BUFORA (Independent UFO Network) two-weekend course at the Adult Education Centre, Ossett, West Yorks, on February 24 and March

21st February 1990 (UK) – UFOs over Essex

Terry Carvell (44) of Mile End Rise, Colchester, was driving towards Mill End Road, when he noticed a *'bright light'* in the sky, which was surrounded by cloud, to the right of the Sun.

> *"I could see what looked like a dark shape within the 'light' and put my Polaroid glasses on. I was shocked to see a dark saucer-shaped object, with a dome on top, from which a number of rays of light projected. Five minutes later it was gone."*

At 10.15pm, a couple in Laindon, Essex, sighted a large orange coloured object, hovering over Langdon (Laindon) Hill. They watched it for about 15 minutes and noticed that it was surrounded by what appeared to be a halo.

(Source: Ron West/*Colchester Yellow Advertiser*, 2.3.1990 – 'Have we been visited by creatures from space?'

23rd March 2014 – Similar UFO seen in same locality

A check on the Internet in 2014 reveals another sighting over the same location, involving Steven – whose account was found on the *UK UFO* sighting website. This one happened on the 23rd March 2014. Unfortunately, we cannot verify the authenticity of it as we haven't traced the witness, although it appears to be genuine.

> *"I awoke very early, due to a pain in my foot giving me a restless night. My home is situated at the top of Langdon Hills Nature Reserve, and my bed looks out across the night sky, facing north-west. I regularly see planes en-route from/to Stansted. At around 4am, I looked out of the window into the clear night sky, when a very bright circular ball shape suddenly came into view from the right of my window. It remained completely motionless, very clear and above the tree line, for approximately one minute. Its scale was hard to determine, but appeared approximately the size of a golf ball, so no real idea of dimensions or distance away. It did seem, however, to be a significant distance behind/above the tree line and seemed on a par with the altitude of the planes I regularly see. After wondering what on earth this was, suddenly at a very high speed, it dropped straight down to earth, disappearing vertically behind the tree line, and out of view. I was very excited by what I had seen, as this was the first sighting I have ever had. It was definitely not a plane or helicopter, and moved unlike anything I know. Extremely bright, and white/yellow in colour, I rather hoped someone else may have seen it."*

22nd February 1990 (USA) – UFO over Indiana

At 5.30pm, a 17-year-old girl was at her home address. There was a clear sky, with a few clouds, when she heard what she took to be the wind blowing. She looked out of the window and saw a *'bright light'* in the sky. She went outside and stood on the porch and saw a bright silver *'disc'* – about the size of a car, with white lights around the centre – hovering over trees, about 100ft off the ground in the south direction.

> *"It then moved over a nearby trailer and went straight up into the sky, very fast, accompanied by a gush of wind that caused the trees to sway. There was no sound or smell present at any time."*

According to the investigators that interviewed the girl, no electromagnetic disturbance was noted and no other citizens in the nearby trailers noticed anything. The girl told them that the family dog (a mixed breed) was barking and howling during the sighting, which was over in a couple of minutes.

(Source: MUFON Indiana)

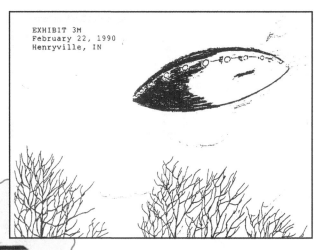

EXHIBIT 3M
February 22, 1990
Henryville, IN

February 24th 1990 – UFO Lecture

BATLEY NEWS

~ 8 FEB 1990

Learn about UFOs

CLOSE encounters of the third kind are just one of the topics up for discussion in a special weekend college course on Unidentified Flying Objects.

Organised by Batley ufologist, Philip Mantel, and Andy Roberts of the Independent UFO Network, the two-day course will run at the Adult Education Centre, Ossett School, Storrs Hill Road, on February 24 and March 3.

This course is the first of its kind on UFO's and will concentrate on two eye witness accounts of UFO sightings in Leicestershire and Northampton and people on the course will have the opportunity to discuss their own experiences.

The two tutors will present case material from around the world including photographic and video taped evidence and will be on hand to answer any questions.

Anyone interested should arrive at the Ossett Centre before 10am on Saturday February 24 and pay the £8 enrollment fee.

25th February 1990 (USA) – Triangular UFO seen

A man was visiting his parents just west of Wimberley, Texas, near the Blanco Bend River, over the weekend of February 24th and 25th, 1990.

At about 10.15pm, he was walking home from a nearby fast food restaurant. It was a quiet, dark, and very cool evening, with clear skies (a moonless night) and bright stars.

Triangular object seen – curious geometric shapes

He happened to look up into the sky and saw an object . . .

> *"triangular in shape, but it was as if the points of the triangle had been cut off. The cut was perpendicular to the bisection of the angle for the leading apex, and the other two points were either cut the same as the leading apex or cut perpendicular to the trailing edge of the UFO. I could only see the underside surface of the object, which was glowing faintly orange over its entirety, like very hot metal. There were no lights and no visible protuberances, but it had what appeared to be geometric shapes on the surface, formed with straight lines."*

These *'shapes'* appeared to form part of the object's structure, rather than being painted onto its exterior. He estimated the object must have been over 1,000ft away, although he accepted he was not too precise about scales or distances. It was moving very slowly and in a straight line from south to north (from his right to his

left) perpendicular to his walking direction. There was no sound of any kind from the vehicle or otherwise. After the object disappeared from view, the witness continued to stand and look for several minutes, totally awestruck by the experience.

Police received other calls

After returning home, he telephoned Hays County Sheriff's Department and reported the sighting. The dispatcher told him that *"there had been other calls received, regarding A UFO seen during the same evening".* Later, early Monday morning, he called a local Austin FM Radio Station and told a DJ friend of his sighting.

(**Source:** NUFORC)

Other sightings of interest

1962 – UFO sighted over the Norwegian coast

Ex-soldier William Jefferson, living in Hull, contacted us in 2007, with regard to an unusual event, involving his late father, Bill a Chief Engineer aboard the trawler St Chad's from Hull. On a calm and tranquil day some time in 1962, while fishing off the Norwegian coast. Bill had just 'turned in', after the skipper had instructed the trawling nets to be winched back aboard, as no fish were being caught. As he was settling down in his bunk after four hours on call, the officer on the bridge ordered him to get back up on deck quickly. Wondering what was going on Bill rushed up to the bridge, where he was stunned to see a huge dark grey 'disc', larger than the trawler, hovering a few feet above the funnel, making a slight humming noise.

> "It was so close you could see the panels joined by small squares and strange writing. Different coloured lights could be seen, but they weren't illuminated. The skipper ordered the radio operator to contact the authorities and report what was happening. About thirty minutes later, three low-flying Norwegian jet fighters arrived. As they entered the airspace, the 'thing' shot away and disappeared out of sight. The Captain advised us we were not to say anything about the matter, as nobody would believe us."

We also include an illustration from Ian Glasby of what he saw in 1974.

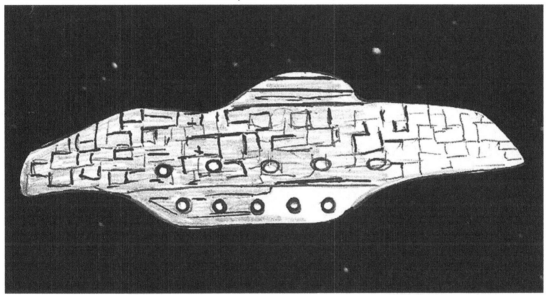

17th July 1976 – UFO seen over Kent

During the afternoon Mr Hedge – a resident of Bexleyheath, Kent, and a neighbour of Margaret Fry – were outside, gardening, when they saw what they took to be an aircraft, moving over the suburb. Suddenly, it 'exploded' in mid-air. Margaret ran into the house to alert her husband, Ron, and telephone the authorities, fearing the worst. When she came back outside, she was astonished to see:

> "...one of the strangest things I have ever seen in my life – a long, curved arm, salmon pink in colour, motionless in the sky, one side of which was the same width along its outer edge, attached to a regular box-like grid. The other side of the 'arm' ended in another box-like section It then began to rotate slowly, allowing us to take note of the 'revolutions' every 15 minutes, until it finally moved away some hours later."

1977 – Rectangular UFO seen

During the spring/summer, "*a rectangular object, hundreds of feet long*", showing bright lights, set behind some form of grid structure, was seen hovering over the Shell Refinery, at Carrington, (which lies between

Flixton, Partington, Daveyhulme and Sale) by a number of shoppers. A short time later, Police Sergeant Butts was travelling along Washway Road, Sale, when he and his colleague saw what appeared to be the same UFO.

June 1978 – UFO over Weybridge, Surrey

Ex-West Mercia Police Officer – Matt Sanders – spoke of what he saw, while a schoolboy, at Heathside County Secondary School, Weybridge, in Surrey.

"It was in June 1978. I was on the school playing field, when I noticed a silver/grey shallow 'flying disc', with a centre rectangular section comprising large square box shapes that looked like darkened unlit windows, hovering silently, about thirty to forty feet above the ground in front of trees over an area of woodland, separating Heathside School from Brooklands College. It looked a bit like an old pocket watch on its side – its profile split between the rectangular, middle section. I estimated it was about one hundred-and-fifty feet away from where I was stood. I didn't feel threatened, or frightened, by the sight of what looked like a classic 'flying saucer'. When I turned my attention away from it for a brief second, and looked back, it had gone. Over the years, I thought long and hard about what I saw. Could there have been a connection with the nearby electricity sub-station, the railway line, situated close to the school, or the British Aerospace factory site, about a mile away from the scene of the incident? I was amazed to find out that I was apparently the only person to see this UFO because there were about sixty other people in the area, some of whom were involved in a games lesson."

(Source: Personal interview)

Triangular object seen by Roy Hale on July 20th 1996

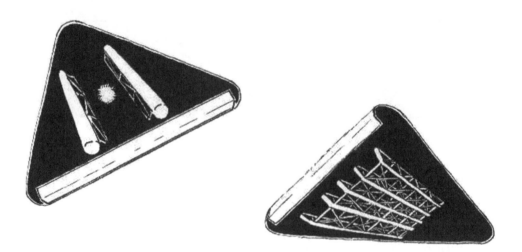

31st March 1999 – Similar sighting in the UK

Colin Saunders – a design draughtsman, employed on Aircraft Design for Airbus Industries was travelling home with his family, towards the Fosse Way, Leicestershire.

As they turned onto the Fosse Way, they noticed a cluster of deep red lights, with a hint of white, hovering in the sky about half-a-mile away.

Colin:

"We all commented on the lights. My wife said it was too low for a plane and too many lights for a helicopter.

We drove down the road parallel to the lights that I estimated to be only 80ft away. I noticed the lights were in a row but not level with the ground, tilted at approximately 25° to the horizon. I stared into the light on the far left. This light was the highest side of the tilt, with the far right light being the anchor point for the 25° angle. I then noticed a fifth, smaller, spurious light off to the left-hand side. (This turned out to be the one underneath the front of the 'triangle'.) In the middle of the end light I could see a criss-cross of lines – a bit like a traffic light lens. Somehow hypnotic, it seemed to pulse very rapidly in a digital fashion. I began to see a shape start to appear around these lights. The edges looked like the sky was rippling, due to what I believed was their transparency at the time. I could see the shape of a diamond around the lights. You needed a sharp eye to make out the shape. At some point, I thought I saw a mist – like cotton wool, around the wing tips. The whole thing then tilted upwards in a most peculiar fashion to reveal a large 'triangle'. The tilting action was not from the centre of the 'craft' but from the rear, i.e., the rear end stayed where it was and the 'nose' rose in the air. The surface of the 'triangle' looked to be alive. It was like a lake of dark grey liquid, similar to mercury, with waves running up and down the surface – like ripples on a lake in a breeze. On top of this 'lake' were silver lines that looked like box sections raised off the surface, interlocking like an old-fashioned maze. I thought to myself, 'My God, aliens do exist and abductions must be true. This explains why we have ancient mysteries'.

The next thing I recall is shouting to my wife, who was driving, to stop the car, as my view of the object was being restricted by a large hedge.

When we got out of the car, it was gone. We could see a large 'craft' in the distance, with strange red lights at the rear. It seemed enormous to me, with a huge wingspan. At the end of each wing was a white light, shining up along the top surface.

We couldn't decide if it was conventional, or not. There were no smells of any burnt fuel in the air at all."

Colin's daughter, Victoria, like other members of the family, confirmed that the sighting took place and that her father telephoned Coventry Airport, the following morning, but they told him there had been no other UFO sightings reported to them.

We were disturbed to learn that she sustained a sensation like sunburn to both of her ears, noticeable as dark and light patches. Although this medical condition soon cleared-up, being put down to an allergy, such as hairspray, it seems rather coincidental that this condition occurred shortly after the family's encounter with the UFO. The UFO incident was to become just part of a catalogue of unexplained phenomenon, spasmodically interrupting Colin's life, over the years, following the UFO incident – matters to which Colin still seeks the answers.

Illustration © 2009 www.davidsankey.com

26th February 1990 (UK) – Strange *'beam of light'*

At 8.20pm, Leonard Butterfield (44) of Roman Road, Colchester, Essex – an employee of British Telecom – was walking over to the window when his attention was caught by a very bright shining object above the houses, opposite.

> *"I thought it was a star – then realised it could not be this, as it was so unusually bright. It then began to move slowly from the east towards the south-east direction, at a height I estimated to be 1,000ft up (looking the size of a tennis ball) changing from one light to three lights, forming a triangular shape. As it did so, the two white lights at the top changed to a bright silver-gold colour, while the one at the bottom changed to blue. I watched as it moved away when, to my surprise, it changed to one bright light again before being lost from view."*

At 10.20pm, Andrew Smithdale (79) and his wife, Hilda, were watching TV at the family home in Victoria Street, Ely, Cambridgeshire, when they noticed a bright *'beam of light'* shining down from the sky. Thinking it might have been a helicopter they went into the garden and saw it was illuminating an area of about 50ft in diameter. Fifteen minutes later the light extinguished, leaving the couple perplexed as to what it could have been.

27th February 1990 (UK) – UFOs over Suffolk

At 7pm, Miss Josephine 'S' (name on file) (20) of St. Andrew's Street, Mildenhall, Suffolk – a typist by employment, at a military establishment – was on her way home in her Vauxhall Cavalier. As she drove past

RAF Mildenhall, she noticed three white lights, forming a triangle, stationary in the sky above the Base.

> *"I stopped the car, thinking they might have been aircraft about to land. After having done so, I noticed an orange glow around the lights. I continued to watch them until 7.10pm, when they faded away leaving a slight halo in the sky."*

The matter was reported to Ron West, who telephoned the duty officer at the airbase. He told him that nothing was recorded for the 27th February and declined to comment further.

At 7.30pm, Patrick Lumley (49) of Point Clear, St. Osyth, Essex, was on his way home, when he saw:

> *"...a long thin white pencil light streak across the sky and was gone in seconds."*

Was this a laser light, space debris, or could there have been a connection with what was seen half an hour previously?

MARCH 1990

1st March 1990 (USA) – Allegation of abduction, Minnesota

DURING the night, it was reported that following a foot of snow, a woman resident of Otter Tail County ran outside into the front yard and saw a disc-shaped craft, hovering in the sky, which then ascended into a larger object above it.

She then suffered a blackout and believes she may have been abducted, after vaguely recalling having been taken onboard by *"tall, blond, Nordic type beings, who predicted that catastrophe would befall Earth between the years 2000 and 2011".*

She also claims an implant was inserted into her head through one of her nostrils.

(Source: Albert S. Rosales, *Humanoid Contact Database 1990*, case #2330 citing Don Worley, UFOs: Alien Encounters, 1995)

1st March 1990 (UK)

At 5.05am, Mrs Hilda Aldridge (62) of Sandpiper Close, Shoeburyness, Essex, woke up to fetch a drink. She casually looked out into the night sky and saw what she first took to be a star and then rejected that idea. After monitoring its movement, she wrote a letter and diagram to Ron West. (See next page).

2nd March 1990 (USA) – UFO over Charlestown, Indiana

At 5.15pm Glenn (18) was driving home near Charlestown and looking out of the window into a large open field, when he saw:

> "...an oval-shaped, grey coloured object (like tree bark) hovering 40ft above the trees. I was amazed and nervous at what I was seeing. After about five seconds, the object shot upwards and disappeared from view at high speed."

According to investigations carried out, later, it was established that there had been no interference with his car engine or radio. Glenn said he was unable to confirm the presence of any sound made by the UFO, because his radio was playing at a very high volume. The distance to the tree line where the object had been seen was 300 yards. (**Source: MUFON, Indiana, Jim Delehanty and Mike Baker**)

DATE 1st MARCH 1990 (B)

To whom it may concern.

At 5:05am today, I woke to get a drink. Whenever I do, I look out of my lounge window. I looked up to the sky. There was a very bright star. Then it occured to me, it was a cloudy sky and there were no others. This "star" puzzled me. I found the binoculars and was amazed to see it wasn't what I thought. Living near the M.O.D Proof: Experimental area, we are used to bangs and sometimes funny things happening. So I thought there must be a connection there. But it fascinated me so much that I made a coffee and sat until 6·35am when it had almost dis-appeared. It seemed to hover for an hour then very very slowly moved away. It either went higher and higher or moved out to sea. Judging by the distance between "it" and the rooftops I would say it went up. I am not a crank, but a perfectly sane 62year old housewife.

2

I've always been "inclined" to believe the stories I've read about U.F.Os, but felt I would have to see one for myself to be convinced. My husband, who dismisses stories as nonsense and rubbish also saw this object, because I woke him and got him out of bed to see it.

Now, I'm no judge of distances so I will try to draw what I saw. This thing changed shape quite often and on two occassions I saw a Red light and I believe a yellow one. At times there appeared an aura of light which I will try to explain.

I would love to hear from you, in the hope that you can explain. Have I at last seen a U.F.O or something the R.A.F sent up. It could not possibly have been a helicopter. I do hope my drawings will be understood.

H.G.Aldridge. (Mrs)

(B) SHOEBURYNESS, 5·05 AM
1-3-90 2 WITNESSES

The thing itself was too far away for me to determine a size. Blurrs may have been caused by my glasses but I don't believe so.

My first sight, was rather like this

Changes of shape took place often and at regular intervals.

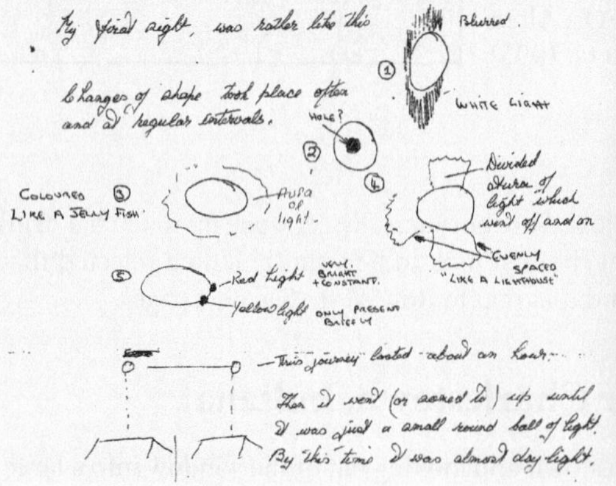
Blurred.
1
WHITE LIGHT
HOLE?
2
3
4
COLOURED LIKE A JELLY FISH
AURA OF light.
Divided Aura of light which went off and on
EVENLY SPACED "LIKE A LIGHTHOUSE"
5
Red light VERY BRIGHT + CONSTANT.
Yellow light ONLY PRESENT BRIEFLY
This journey lasted about an hour.

Then it went (or seemed to) up until it was just a small round ball of light. By this time it was almost day light.

I hope this drawing makes some sense. It is hard to describe. I've indicated it was over the houses but of course that is only as I saw it. On reflection I think it must have been well out to sea.

H.G.Aldridge

(2)(3)(4) WENT IN A CYCLE AT REGULAR INTERVALS 3 TIMES THEN (5) AS IT DISAPPEARED.

UFO chases car, Beavercreek, Colorado

At 11pm on the same day, a motorist and his companion, from Beavercreek, saw a bright pulsating oval *'light,'* which they chased for five minutes, before it then overtook their vehicle. The *'light and structured object'* was completely silent, and moved 30ft over the truck and bathed it in a 20-30ft circle of white light. The *'light'*, estimated to move at a speed from a hovering position to 70mph, followed them for a few minutes. The whole incident was over in 20 minutes. (**Source:** ***UFOE II*, Sections IX, X**)

2nd March 1990 (UK) – Huge fireball seen

At 10pm, a huge red fireball was seen over the Kegworth area by at least four people. (**Source:** ***Nottingham Evening Post*, 2.3.1990 – 'So Red'**)

Two UFO sightings puzzling to military

A FAMILY of four and an elderly man from neighbouring Suffolk villages claim to have seen UFOs that looked like "lemons falling out of the sky."

"Seeing is believing," said pensioner Victor Byford of Bury Road, Stanningfield.

"On Monday morning I got up at 8.30 and looked out the window across the woods towards Long Melford and thought an orange or lemon had fallen out of the sky.

"Then, about 5.25 in the evening, I was having my tea when I saw another lemon falling out of the sky in the wood.

"Then I heard on the radio about this family who had seen the same thing down the road in Cockfield, so I looked them up in the phone book and spoke to the lady, who said it was the same.'

Linda Shotbolt of Bury Road, Cockfield, said, "On Friday night I was busy getting the dinner ready. My son was standing at the kitchen window when he zoomed outside and came rushing back in to get us. John, my husband, went to have a look and called me so I went as well. We had to hold my youngest son up so he could see it.

"We stood there for about half an hour and watched it. There were three yellow lights. One was larger and the other two were hovering above ground level. It was a bit like a triangle. The left one took off to the left and then the right one went off to the left. The third started hovering and then took off.

"It was either a big light a long way away or a little light close by. We were looking towards Cockfield Green, in the same direction as Mr Byford had seen it, which is about a mile away, and it seemed about as far away as that—maybe a bit closer.

"The way Mr Byford described it was exactly the same," she said.

Her older son, Benjamin, 14, had a normal interest in UFOs "like any boy his age" and the family had no particular interest until they saw a programme about unexplained circles in American corn fields before Christmas, she said.

Flt. Lieut. Rusty Russell, a spokesman from RAF Honington, said, "We have a 24-hour air traffic watch, which includes radar, and a 24-hour meteorological watch. If it was in visual or radar range then we would have seen it.

IPSWICH MERCURY
-Suffolk-

-8 MAR 1990

Three yellow 'lights' over Suffolk

Linda Shotbolt of Bury Road, Cockfield, Bury St Edmunds was preparing the family tea, when she was fetched outside by her husband, John, who told her about something strange in the sky.

> *"We stood and watched these three yellow 'lights', hovering over Cockfield Green. One was bigger than the rest; it looked like a triangle. The left one moved to the left, so did the right-hand one. The third one then took off across the sky, at speed."*

(Source: Personal interview)

3rd March 1990 (UK) – UFO reappears over Essex

At 5am, Mrs Hilda Aldridge found herself in the fortunate position of seeing something else strange over the family home. Once again, she tells of sighting an oval-shaped object, with two lights at the side, which continually changed shape as it silently hovered in the sky.

Circle of oval lights seen

At 10pm, Southchurch, Southend man – Vernon Thurlow (42) – was out in his garden.

> *"I saw a circle of oval lights, stationary the sky; they were spinning anticlockwise. They had blue and yellow lights and seemed to be above my house. I called my wife and we watched them until 10.15pm, when they left at tremendous speed."*

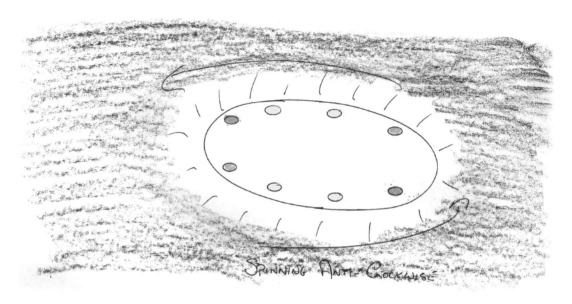

SOUTHCHURCH, SOUTHEND ON SEA, ESSEX
WEDNESDAY THE 3rd MARCH 1990
10 PM - 10.15 PM 2 WITNESSES

SPINNING ANTI-CLOCKWISE

4th March 1990 (USA) – Strange sphere seen, Massachusetts

At Wood End, Provincetown, a *'sphere',* with windows, was seen from a boat near the lighthouse. Several objects were observed to take-off at high speed, accompanied by loud booms. The object then stopped, hovered, and flashed bright white lights. (**Source:** *UFOE II,* Section VI)

'Flying Wing' or wedge-shaped UFO, seen over Louisville

At 10.10pm the same day two men were driving their car through Floyd Knobs – a hilly rural area of Louisville. It was cold, with a clear sky. As they drove past an intersection, they noticed a strange orange coloured *'light'* in the distance. The *'light'* then rose from behind a group of trees and moved towards them. After driving a short distance, curiosity overcame them. They stopped the car, turned off the ignition and watched the *'light',* wondering what it could be.

As it passed directly over them, gliding at an estimated altitude of 1,000-1,500ft, at an estimated speed of 100-150mph, heading north to south-west, both men clearly saw an outline of an unusual shape, like a wedge or *'Flying Wing',* stealth design. It was very large, about the size of a 747, wider than long, with three coloured lights visible (amber/yellow on left side, blue on right, and a pink-orange colour at the front). It disappeared from view, minutes later. One of the men said:

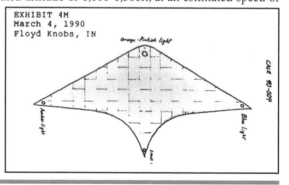

EXHIBIT 4M
March 4, 1990
Floyd Knobs, IN

Orange-Pinkish light

Amber light

Blue light

> *"It sounded like a blank tape, running through a stereo system".*

The illustration provided shows once again, what will become an all too familiar pattern across the surface of the object. (**Source:** MUFON, Indiana, Field Investigators Mike Baker and Jim Delehanty)

4th March 1990 (UK) – Triangular lights, Cambridgeshire

At 10pm, Mr William Dunn (23) and his wife were out walking near Breckland Farm, Wisbech, Cambridgeshire, when they sighted three round white lights, forming a triangle in the sky, hovering over the farm – which was estimated to be half a mile away from them. They watched the object for about five minutes, before it disappeared behind farm buildings, and then the couple continued their journey home.

5th March1990 (UK) – Orange objects seen descending

Victor Byford of Bury Road, Stanningfield, Bury St. Edmunds, happened to look out of his window, at 8.30am, and see what looked like *"an orange or lemon, falling through the sky over the woods, towards Long Melford."*

East Anglian Times. Ipswich

7 MAR 1990

RAF unable to explain separate UFO sightings

A PENSIONER and a family-of-four from neighbouring Suffolk villages claim to have seen UFOs which looked like "lemons falling out of the sky".

"Seeing is believing," said pensioner Mr. Victor Byford, of Bury Road, Stanningfield. "On Monday I got up at 8.30 and looked out the window across the woods towards Long Melford and thought an orange or lemon had fallen out of the sky.

"Then, about 5.25 in the evening I was having my tea when I saw another lemon falling out of the sky in the wood. My wife didn't see it either time because it vanished in a few seconds. I suppose it looked about the size of a pint mug but I couldn't tell how far away it was.

"Then I heard on the radio about this family who had seen the same thing down the road in Cockfield so I looked them up in the phone book and spoke to the lady who said it was the same."

Mrs. Linda Shotbolt, of Bury Road, Cockfield, said, "On Friday night I was busy getting the dinner ready. My son was standing at the kitchen window when he zoomed outside and came rushing back in to get us. John, my husband, went to have a look and called me so I went as well. We had to hold my youngest son up so he could see it.

"We stood there for about half an hour and watched it. There were three yellow lights. One was larger and the other two were hovering above ground level. It was a bit like a triangle. The left one took off to the left and then the right one went off to the left. The third started hovering and then took off."

Flt. Lieut. Rusty Russell, an RAF Honington spokesman, said nothing had been detected. "We have a 24-hour air traffic watch, which includes radar, and a 24-hour meteorological watch. If it was in visual or radar range then we would have seen it."

The lemon drops from outer space

PENSIONER Victor Byford thought he'd gone bananas when he saw a lemon fall from the sky.

"But I saw another lemon-shaped light later when I was having my tea," he said.

Victor, of Stanningfield, Suffolk, wasn't the only one to keep his eyes peeled — the Shotbolt family of nearby Cockfield saw three yellow lights near their home.

But the sightings baffled radar experts at RAF Honington, a few miles away.

Flt Lt Rusty Russel said: "It wasn't anything to do with us and we didn't pick up anything on our 24-hour radar watch. It's a mystery."

At 5.25pm the same evening, he was having a cup of tea when he saw another *'lemon or orange-shaped object'* falling out of the sky over the woods. It was only when he heard about what Linda had seen, while listening to the local radio, that he then contacted her.

Flt Lt. 'Rusty' Russell – a spokesman from RAF Honnington – said:

> *"We have a 24-hour air traffic watch, which includes radar, and a 24-hour meteorological watch. If it was in visual or radar range, we would have seen it."*

(Source: *Ipswich Mercury*, Suffolk, 8.3.1990 – 'Two UFO sightings puzzling to military'/Personal interview)

- 2 MAR 1990

UFO excitement

UNIDENTIFIED flying objects have been spotted by dozens of witnesses all over Essex and East London in recent weeks.

The East Anglian UFO and Paranormal Research Association says it is excited by reports from Colchester, Romford, Braintree, Clacton, Chelmsford and Ipswich of three white lights forming a triangle in the sky.

Anyone who saw it or any other paranormal phenomena should ring the association hotline on either 0268 286079 or 01 5944797.

7th March 1990 (USA) – Triangular UFO over Argos, Indiana

At 9.45pm, Gary Flagg – a security guard from Argos – was driving to work, when he saw [reading from his log]:

> *"...a white, triangular-shaped object, as large as a football field. I stopped on 17th Road (in Marshall County), got out of the car and watched. It was about 500ft over the top of the car. It moved extremely slowly. I don't even know how it stayed in the air."*

Gary didn't report the sighting to police, but told his wife.

A lady, who worked at (Mr Flagg's) place of employment, saw the same object that evening whilst driving to work.

(Source: MUFON, Indiana, Field Investigator Jim Delehanty and Mike Baker)

7th March 1990 (UK) – UFO over Essex

At 8.20pm, Mrs J. Camp (60) of Frinton Lodge, Frinton-on-Sea, Essex, was looking out of the window, when she saw three amber lights, forming a triangle, in the sky. Five minutes later, they were gone from view.

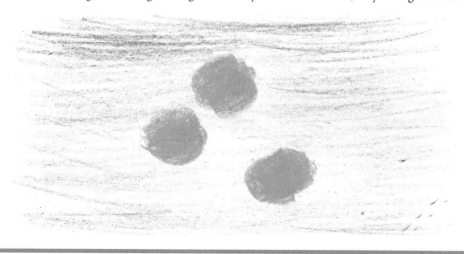

8th March 1990 (UK) – Red *'ball of light'* seen

At 7.25pm, a red *'ball of light'* was seen moving at speed across the sky, heading northwards, towards the direction of Kings Lynn, by Mrs D. Canning from Wisbech, Cambridgeshire. Within a few seconds it was out of sight.

9th March 1990 (UK)

At 7pm, Alex Stone (9) was outside Boxted Youth Club, at Boxted, Essex, when he saw a bright, square-shaped, silvery light, heading across the sky, which took 30 seconds to fade from view. He then contacted Sheridan Lane, who came to interview him about the incident.

10th March 1990 (UK)

At 10am, Mrs J. Holloway (59) was walking her two dogs in Burlington Gardens, Hadleigh, in Essex.

> *"I saw what looked like a bright star in the sky, towards the East. By the time I had got to the end of Burlington Gardens, it was moving southwards.*
>
> *It passed silently overhead, showing white and red lights. I don't know what it was, but I am adamant it wasn't an aircraft."*

11th March 1990 (UK) – *'Ball of light'* over the River Thames

Mrs Carole Bailey (31) of Maplin Way, Shoeburyness, Southend-on-Sea, was looking out of her daughter's window, when she saw a round, yellow- orange coloured *'ball of light'* in the sky, over the River Thames. She watched it for five minutes, before it vanished from view.

UFO seen over power station

At 9.30pm, Brenda Williams (38) of Nayland Road, Colchester, was on her way home, driving along West Parade, West Mersea, when :

> *"I noticed a huge white and yellow 'ball', perfect circle of light in the sky, hovering about 20ft over Bradwell Power Station. I stopped the car and got out. About five minutes later it moved to the right and then stopped again, before moving back to where it had originally been. Ten minutes later, it just disappeared from view."*

AIRE VALLEY TARGET
-Bingley-

- 6 MAR 1990

Mystery of UFOs tackled in 'mag'

SHIPLEY author and Ufologist David Barclay has brought out a new magazine which explores the mystery of the 'saucers' in the sky which no-one seems able to solve.

Mr Barclay, 53, of Stubbing Way, Shipley, is editor of the UFO Debate which he intends to bring out regularly. And the first publication is filled with stories about sightings in the Bradford area as well as the rest of the world.

He said he intended the magazine to be an open forum for Ufological speculation.

"I hope people will submit articles. It is a very interesting subject and there is a question to be answered," he said.

Mr Barclay, who has been studying Ufology for 40 years, is working with his daughter, Therese, to produce the magazine.

Over Rayleigh

Mr John Cooper (50) of Richmond Drive, Rayleigh, was in the kitchen when his wife called him outside to come and have a look at something in the sky.

> *"I looked and saw a yellow-orange coloured object in the eastern sky, at about 15° elevation. About five minutes later, it headed away towards the south-west direction."*

Over Rochford

At 10.10pm, Rochford resident – Mr R. Howard (48) – was walking his dog by the airport, along Alton Gardens and into Oaken Grange Drive, when he noticed a bright stationary light in the eastern sky.

> *"I couldn't take my eyes off it. It changed from white to orange and also changed in shape to that resembling an onion. I almost had the impression it was trying to attract my attention. Blue, green, and pink coloured lights appeared two thirds of the way down. The object then flipped over from horizontal to vertical. The lights were moving round from right to left while vertical. Half a minute later, it shot off eastwards and disappeared from sight."*

Southend Police and Airport were contacted. They denied any knowledge of other reports made concerning this sighting, and gave him a London telephone number (presumably the MOD) – which he did not ring. Instead he contacted Ron West, who sent Geraldine Dillon to interview him.

13th March 1990 (USA) – UFOs seen, Pensacola Beach

At 3pm, two women were out driving when they saw what looked like two white milk bottle-shaped objects, estimated to be about 20-30ft in length, reflecting the sunlight, making an angular descent over Pensacola Bay. When about 150ft above the water, at an estimated distance of two miles, the objects suddenly vanished seconds later. (**Source: MUFON Field Investigations database, case 900422C, citing Field Investigators Carol and Rex Salisberry**)

14th March 1990 (UK)

At 10pm, five *'lights'* were seen moving through the sky, about a mile high over Rayleigh, Essex, by Mr Clive Martin Horsemen (31).

15th March 1990 (UK) – Two bright *'stars'* seen

At 5.05am, Mr Pilgrim (39) of Blenheim Chase, Leigh-on-Sea, told of seeing what looked like two bright *'stars'*, one behind the other, moving through the sky over where he lived. At 7.20pm the same day, Terry Chambers (70) of Wakefield Street, East Ham, sighted a group of blue and red flashing lights in the sky over the Docklands Airport direction.

17th March 1990 (UK) – UFO over Essex

At 10pm, Tony Pullen (33) of Kelvenden Close, Rayleigh, Essex, received a visit from his stepson, telling him about a UFO in the sky. The next door neighbour, Mr K. Brooks (28) – a carpenter by trade – also went out to have a look and told of seeing . . .

> *"it shaking up and down, and changing colours from red, green, gold, and pale blue, lights. About three-quarters of an hour later, it moved away."*

The reports attracted the attention of the media, as can be seen from the comments made by people like Roy Lake and Ron West.

Southend Evening Echo – Essex.
15 MAR 1990

Calls flood in after UFO is sighted

UFO experts have been flooded with calls after the sighting of a white rotating light in the skies over Southend.

The large white ball, which was ringed by blue, red and green lights, was spotted on two nights at the weekend by witnesses from Rochford, Shoebury and Hadleigh.

UFO boffin Ron West said 18 witnesses had called the East Anglian UFO Watch to report the sightings of what he claims can only be an unidentified flying object.

Mr West said: "What makes these sightings all the more exciting is that the accounts from the witnesses are virtually the same.

"They all claim to have seen a large white ball which was rotating but making no noise whatsoever.

"Three witnesses in Rochford saw this ball, which they described as white or yellowish in colour, which hovered for 20 minutes before it shot out to sea on Saturday.

"On Sunday, 15 separate witnesses from Southend, Shoebury, Leigh, Thorpe Bay, and Rochford all reported seeing the ball.

"All the calls said they saw the ball between 9.50pm and 10.10pm.

"It hovered over in the east of the town for eight or 10 minutes before moving quickly towards Westcliff where it hovered again before flying off towards Kent at a very low altitude.

"All the witnesses say the ball was ringed with revolving lights, and it was making no noise whatsoever.

"To my knowledge there is nothing in the RAF or the US Air Force which could do this sort of thing, and until there is proof otherwise it has to be a UFO."

One of the witnesses phoned Southend Airport at the time to ask if they had any explanation, but they said there was nothing showing up on their radar screens.

Witness Marion Morgan, of Common Hall Lane, Hadleigh, said: "I could not believe my eyes. I woke the children up and called my husband. It was just hovering in the sky.

"My husband said it must be a bright star. Then it just seemed to take off.

"The only thing I could compare its movements with would be a Harrier jet or a very fast helicopter, but I am certain it is not one of those."

26th March 1990 (UK) – UFO reported over Lancashire

During the early hours of this morning, following a report of a fireball seen moving across the skies over the Chorley/Blackburn borders of Lancashire, the police helicopter was scrambled. In addition to this, what appeared to be an aircraft in trouble was reported over the Belmont and Rivington area. The RAF was contacted and searches were conducted, but nothing was found.

(Source: *Lancashire Evening Post*, 27.3.1990 – 'Mystery of UFO sightings')

Oddly, the police were also to receive reports from frightened motorists on the A1, who claimed having seen *'flying saucers'*. The answer was laser lights, used to celebrate the opening of the Megatron Spaceship Restaurant, at Alconbury, by children's TV presenter – Andy Crane.

(Source: *Peterborough Evening Telegraph*, 27.3.1990 – 'A1 show sparks UFO fear')

28th March 1990 (UK) – UFOs over London

During the early hours of 28th March 1990, former RAF Pilot David Lee and his wife were driving along Felixstowe seafront, when they saw:

"...a huge oblong-shaped object with red, green and white lights moving across the sky, heading inland".

The couple watched with astonishment as it skimmed over the tops of nearby buildings, before being lost from view.

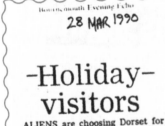

Bournemouth Evening Echo

28 MAR 1990

-Holiday- visitors

ALIENS are choosing Dorset for their summer holidays, according to a new survey.

In a list of British UFO sightings for last year, compiled in a book The UFO Report 1990, Dorset has emerged as one of the most visited counties in the UK.

And the unidentified flying objects are particularly prevalent over our skies from June to October.

In June an oval craft with lights was spotted in Bournemouth and in October a glowing oblong craft was seen hovering over the chalk giant at Cerne Abbas.

The latter sighting prompted even more suspicious sightings in the Poole area. But there was not one UFO spotted in Dorset from January to June and there has not been one recorded since October.

29th March 1990 (UK) – UFOs reported over Hertford

At 8.45pm a resident of Mile End Road, Colchester, sighted a large, pulsating, red circular light in the sky, hovering over a nearby hospital.

A few minutes later, it moved away and was soon out of sight. On the same evening, Hertford resident Sandra Frostick, and her son, sighted:

"...two extremely bright greenish lights, with a red light on top"

...hovering silently in the sky over Standon.

At 10pm, the *"frightening spectacle"* disappeared.

The MOD said they had received a number of reports of laser lights, reflecting off the clouds and creating a peculiar effect.

(Source: *Hertfordshire Mercury*, 30.3.1990 – 'Mystery sky lights baffle and bemuse villagers'/Hertfordshire Star, 28.3.1990 – 'UFO seen')

30th/31st March 1990 – Triangular UFOs tracked on radar over Belgium

This period is now generally associated with heavy UFO activity reported over Belgium. It involved UFOs being tracked on radar, and then pursued by Belgian Air Force F-16 jet fighters, who were ordered to intercept the intruders. The objects were photographed by the pilots and were also sighted by an estimated 13,500 people on the ground – 2,600 of whom filed written statements, describing in detail what they had seen.

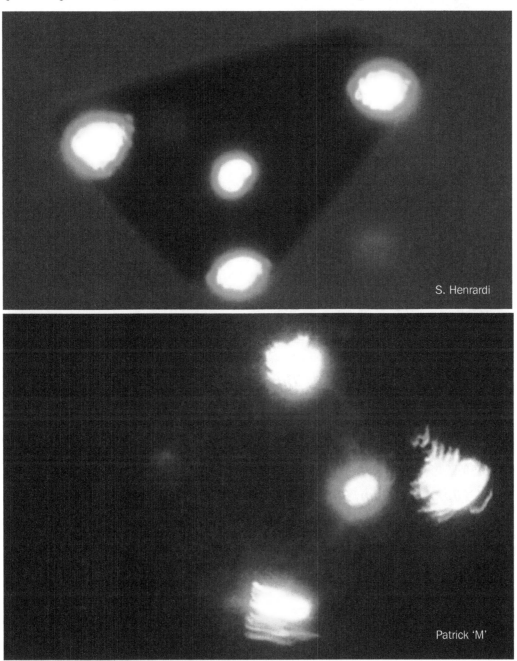

S. Henrardi

Patrick 'M'

It is, to us, a familiar story, but how many people realise that the Essex area was also subjected to heavy UFO activity during this period? If it wasn't for Essex UFO researcher Ron West, history would not be able to record just how prolific this was. One question begs to be asked – why did the RAF not, at any stage (as far as we know), scramble jets to intercept, as did their Belgium counterparts?

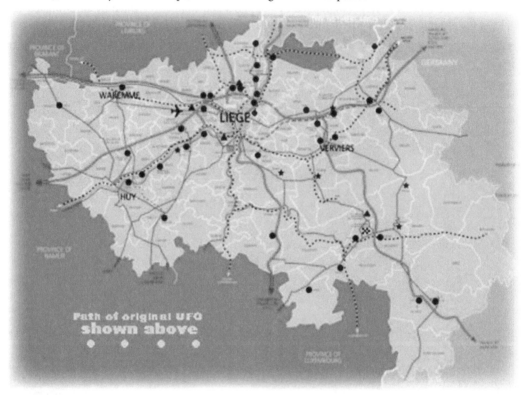

11pm, 30th March 1990 – Three unusual lights seen

At around 11pm on 30th March, the supervisor at the Control Reporting Centre (CRC) at Glons, received reports of three unusual lights seen moving towards Thorembais-Gembloux, which lies to the south-east of Brussels. The lights were reported to be brighter than stars, changing colour between red, green, and yellow, and appeared to be fixed, forming an equilateral triangle. At this point, Glons CRC requested the Wavre gendarmerie to send a patrol to confirm the sighting.

11.10pm-11.30pm, 30th March 1990 – Second set of lights seen

Approximately 10 minutes later, a second set of lights was sighted moving towards the first triangle. By around 11.30pm, the Wavre gendarmerie had confirmed the initial sightings and Glons CRC had been able to observe the phenomenon on radar. During this time the second set of lights, after some erratic manoeuvres, had also formed themselves into a smaller triangle.

Jet fighters scrambled

After tracking the targets and receiving a second radar confirmation from the Traffic Centre Control at Semmerzake, Glons CRC gave the order to scramble two F-16 Fighters from Beauvechain Airbase, shortly before midnight. Throughout this time the phenomenon was still clearly visible from the ground, with witnesses describing the whole formation as maintaining their relative positions while moving slowly across the sky. Witnesses also sighted two dimmer lights towards the municipality of Eghezee, displaying similar erratic movements to the second set of lights.

Nine separate interceptions attempted

Over the next hour, the two scrambled F-16s attempted nine separate interceptions of the targets. On three occasions they managed to obtain a radar lock for a few seconds, but each time the targets changed position and speed so rapidly that the lock was broken. During the first radar lock, the target accelerated from 240km/h to over 1,770km/h, while changing altitude from 2,700m to 1,500m, then up to 3,350m, before descending to almost ground level – the first descent of more than 900m taking less than two seconds. Similar manoeuvres were observed during both subsequent radar locks. On no occasion were the F-16 pilots able to make visual contact with the targets and at no point, despite the speeds involved, was there any indication of a sonic boom.

Smaller triangle disappears from sight

During this time, ground witnesses broadly corroborated the information obtained by radar. They described seeing the smaller triangle completely disappear from sight at one point, while the larger triangle moved upwards very rapidly as the F-16s flew past.

After 00:30hrs, radar contact became much more sporadic and the final confirmed lock took place at 00:40hrs. This final lock was once again broken by an acceleration from around 160km/h to 1,120km/h, after which the radar of the F-16s and those at Glons and Semmerzake all lost contact.

Fighters returned to base

Following several further unconfirmed contacts, the F-16s eventually returned to base shortly after 1am. The final sighting was provided by members of the Wavre gendarmerie. They described seeing four lights arranged in a square formation, making short jerky movements, before gradually losing their luminosity and disappearing in four separate directions, at around 01:30hrs.

2010 – Declassified letter

In a letter declassified by the MOD, in February 2010, sent to the MOD by the Public Relations Officer at the Belgium Air Force, we learn, quote:

> *"Relating to your questions, I can confirm that two F-16s had been scrambled on March 30th, 1990, as a reaction to both visual and radar observations. The scramble was co–coordinated with and authorised by the Sector Commander of the NATO Air Defence System."*

(Source: DEFE 24 1966)

Major P. Lambrechts report released to SOBEPS

A preliminary report, prepared by Major P. Lambrechts of the Belgian Air Force General Staff, was released to ˙SOBEPS. It includes a detailed chronology of events during the night of 30th-31st March 1990, and dismisses several hypotheses such as optical illusions, balloons, meteorological inversions, military aircraft, holographic projections, etc.

Major Lambrechts:

> *"The aircraft had brief radar contacts on several occasions, [but the pilots]... at no time established visual contact with the UFOs... each time the pilots were able to secure a lock-on one of the targets*

Explanation – Terrestrial objects, or street light?

DEPARTMENT OF THE AIR FORCE
WASHINGTON, D.C. 20330

OFFICE OF THE SECRETARY

19 December, 1990

Dear Mr. ▓▓▓▓▓▓

LtCol. Cox requested that I write you, as you know the situation in the Gulf has been occupying us round the clock. LtCol. Cox sends his regrets, but as the situation stabilizes, he will be in touch.

First, there are still some concerns over the October issue of Av-Week. We could not understand why they would run the Edwards story without review. This is still under review. What are your ideas?

The Belgium situation has been corrected to all our satisfaction. I understand that another show will air on the tabloid program that will show that the sightings could be a mis-identification of terrestrial objects, say a street light. This should air in January.

The Nevada situation has been brought under control by the inclusion of the "porno" queen along with the Nellis allegations. That was a brilliant coup. This entire issue is under constant monitoring. Anything else you may hear will be of great interest.

The last area to be addressed concerns our "friend" Mr. Cooper. As you can see by the attachment included, the reason for Mr. Cooper leaving Naval service. I believe back in the old days, the phrase would be keel hauling. Cooper has worked out beyond our expectations. With his paranoid personality, and alcohol abuse not to mention the crowds he draws, we feel that the field has been covered. Cooper, as expected, will self-destruct at some point, and with that, a large part and parcel of this field will go with him. We were concerned last year when he drew police interest in the vandalism case, but no charges were ever filed. We still have assets that feed him bits and pieces that he weaves into an ever more elaborate scenario. We are watching him closely, and if you hear anything of interest we will look to hear from you. Thank you very much, and the happiest of the Holiday Season to you and your family.

Sincerely,

Thomas Shively
Maj. USAF
S. & T. Group

1 Atch
1. Copy DD 214

for a few seconds, there resulted a drastic change in the behaviour of the detected targets... [During the first lock-on, at 0:13 hrs.] their speed changed in a minimum of time from 150 to 970 knots [170 to 1,100 mph and 275 to 1,800km./hr.] and from 9,000 to 5,000ft [2,700m. to 1,500m.], returning then to 11,000ft [3,300m.] in order to change again to close to ground level."

Explanation – Angels and stars!

The Electronic War Center (EWC) of the Air Force undertook a much more detailed technical analysis of the F-16 computerized radar tapes.

Although it was conceded that many aspects of this case still remain unexplained, Physicist Professor Auguste Meessen and SOBEPS basically accepted the Gilmard-Salmon hypothesis suggesting some of the radar contacts were really *'angels'* caused by a rare meteorological phenomenon. This became evident in four lock-ons ...

> "where the object descended to the ground with calculations showing **negative** [emphasis added] altitude... It was evidently impossible that an object could penetrate the ground, but it was possible that the ground could act as a mirror."

Meessen explained how the high velocities measured by the Doppler radar of the F-16 Fighters might result from interference effects but points out however, that there is radar trace, for which there is no explanation to date. As for the visual sightings of this event by the gendarmes and others, Meessen suggests that they could possibly have been caused by stars seen under conditions of *"exceptional atmospheric refraction."*

Letter – Fact of fiction?

The website Pegasus Research Consortium (2014) outlines the events which took place in Belgium during the above dates, and reproduces a letter (previous page) endorsed with the reference number DD 214 written to (redacted) from a USAF Major Thomas Shively, in which the officer mentions approving intended disinformation through the tabloid media to deliberately explain away the recent UFO activity in Belgium as being terrestrial objects, or a street light! There is a reference to a Mr Cooper., whom we believe to be 'William Milton Cooper.

Triangular UFO photograph – a revelation

In April 1990, a photo of a triangular object, upon which three lights are visible at each corner, was taken by a Patrick 'M' from Petit-Rechain, not far from the city of Liège. Further enquiries revealed that Patrick had taken the photo from the small terrace at the back of the house he shares with his fiancé Sabine, during one evening in April (presumably 4th April). Sabine was letting the dog out into the backyard, when she spotted a series of strange stationary lights in the sky. She immediately

Glasgow Herald.

11 APR 1990

Flying saucer fever grips Belgium

From JOHN FRASER
BRUSSELS, Tuesday

BELGIUM has gone UFO daft with more than 700 sightings of a flying object which is larger than a house. Witnesses in the latest incident last weekend have included 18 gendarmes.

Two Air Force F16 fighters, were scrambled to investigate the UFO, but it was not detected by radar.

The interest in UFOs has become so intense that this weekend will see a special Easter vigil, with thousands of people scanning the skies for visitors from space.

Video film of the unidentified object has been screened on Belgian TV. It was taken by amateur photographer Mr Marcel Alfarino, 42, from the window of his house in the centre of Brussels.

"The first time I saw the UFO, we were watching TV at home, and went into the kitchen," he said:

"We saw bright lights outside the window. I called the police, but they arrived too late.

"The next time I was ready with my video camera at the top of the house.

"I spotted it at about 2am, coming from the South Station, with three bright lights. It made a hissing noise, but seemed to glide effortlessly.

"It was shaped like a grey metal triangle with three bright white lights, and little red and green lights at the back."

Eighteen Gendarmes have also confirmed the latest sighting of the UFO, which disappeared after two Air Force F16 planes were sent to investigate.

The Belgian Society for Studying Phenomena from Space is organising a weekend vigil for UFOs, in the hope that more film evidence can be obtained.

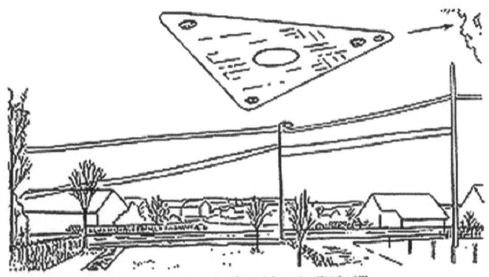

Fig. 2.40 - L'OVNI, tel qu'il a été observé par M.F., âgé de 12 ans, à Orena Rocmáis, le 3 novembre 1979 (voir p. 300).

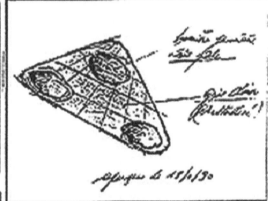

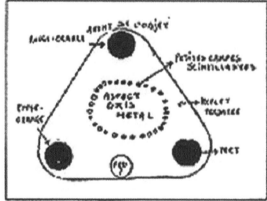

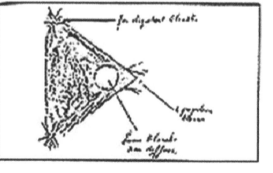

called out to Patrick, who was inside. He picked up his reflex camera, loaded with colour reversal film, and ran to the terrace – where he took two photos. Immediately afterwards, the lights began to move and then disappeared behind a neighbour's house.

A few days later, the developed slide film came back from the local photo shop. Much to their surprise the couple found that one photo had turned out perfectly clear, whilst the second showed nothing. The photo was kept in a drawer until photo journalist Guy Mossay, working for the country's major Press Agency – BELGA, picked up the story.

Patrick Ferryn, head of SOBEPS

It was examined by SOBEPS – the Belgium UFO Organisation, who claimed this picture was genuine, although the full name of the person involved was kept confidential. It was first brought to the notice of the public by a reporter for RTL – one of the country's most popular TV channels, who contacted SOBEPS to what appeared to be a spectacular piece of new evidence, following further reports of UFOs seen over Belgium airspace since late November 1990.

Photograph offered for sale

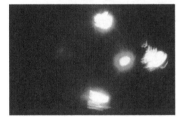

According to Mossay, the witness/photo-grapher had contacted him at his office in an attempt to sell the original slide and collect some money for his upcoming wedding (rumours have it that between 250 and 500 Euro was paid). Patrick 'M', however, claims it was one of his colleagues from work who had approached Mossay. He insists that he himself never got any money for the slide, but had only lent it to Mossay. Whatever the truth, Mossay got hold of the original and secured its copyright through SOFAM – a Belgian collective for visual arts authors that collects and redistributes royalties. Thinking it would be a good idea to exploit this rare piece of evidence in the media, MOSSAY mailed copies of it to *BELGA*

Patrick 'M'

and to various newspapers, magazines and TV stations, including *RTL*. The first to publish the slide was the French journal – *Science et Nature*. One by one the rest of the media followed and it did not take long before the Petit-Rechain photo started its march across the world.

On the 15th June 1990, a photograph was taken of an alleged black triangular UFO, at Wallonia, Belgium, by S. Henrardi, but rather oddly, it was not released until 13 years later. This is identical to the one as used in Wikipedia, although the author was not named.

The 'flying triangle'

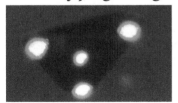

By the end of 1991, the Petit-Rechain photo had become an icon of a new type of UFO: the Flying Triangle (or simply 'FT', as ufologists like to call them). Despite the copyright and a substantial fee charged to use it, the photo ranks among the most published UFO photos ever. Endorsed by scientists and military officials, the slide acquired the best status possible in the field.

Ret. Major General Wilfried De Brouwer, Chief of Operations of the Belgian Air Force at the time of the wave, holds up a page with computer-enhanced images of the Petit-Rechain slide.

How it was hoaxed

Then, in a news item broadcast by RTL on 26th July 2011, exactly one month before a completed *History Channel* documentary about the Belgium UFO sightings was screened, Patrick 'M' confessed that the photo he had taken 21 years earlier was merely part of a prank he had concocted with a friend from work. In subsequent interviews, Patrick revealed it was his friend who had cut out a 60 to 80cm wide triangle from a piece of Styrofoam whilst he himself had squeezed four flashlights in the model, painted the middle one red with a marker, and suspended the lot with the help of a couple of wires and a kitchen stepladder. A dozen photographs were then taken. The whereabouts of the others is not known and, with all due respect, no time should be wasted trying to track these down.

(Sources: lestransformationsobservations/ovnilanguedoc.canalblog.com)

Explanation – Mass delusion!

In 1992, about three years after the first sighting, which occurred on 29th November 1989, in Eupen, Belgian, sceptic Marc Hallet wrote an essay about the Belgian UFO wave, criticizing the work done by the SOBEPS: *La Vague OVNI Belge ou le triomphe de la désinformation*, arguing that this UFOlogical organisation was spreading disinformation into the media.

Marc Hallet's thesis is that the Belgian UFO wave was mostly a mass delusion, boosted by the work done by the SOBEPS. This mass delusion would have followed Philip J. Klass's law:

> *"Once news coverage leads the public to believe that UFOs may be in the vicinity, there are numerous natural and man-made objects which, especially seen at night, can take on unusual characteristics in the minds of hopeful viewers. Their UFO reports in turn add to the mass excitement, which encourages still more observers to watch for UFOs. This situation feeds upon itself until such time as the media lose interest in the subject, and then the 'flap' quickly runs out of steam."*

In 1993, Pierre Magain & Marc Remy published an article in *Physicalia Magazine*, in which their conclusions do not match those from the SOBEPS. They also state that the Belgian UFO 'wave' would be better studied by people in the human sciences than by physicists.

Explanation – Helicopters, car engines, or strong wind!

In *The Belgian UFO 'wave' of 1989-1992 – A Neglected Hypothesis,* Renaud Leclet & Co. discuss the fact that some sightings can be explained by helicopters. Most witnesses reported that the objects were silent. This report argues that the lack of noise could be due to the engine noise in the witnesses' automobiles, or strong natural wind blowing away from the witnesses.

Authors:

The famous UFO photograph now lies tarnished by the admission of its owner, Patrick 'M', of it being hoaxed. We believe it was constructed from descriptions of UFO activity over Belgium during that period of time; ironically, there were many other occasions when similar (if not identical) craft were seen, particularly during the mid to late part of the 1990s. The reader will learn of many such examples as we continue our journey.

The commonality between the heavy UFO activity over Belgium, with the previously forgotten sightings over Essex, UK, faithfully recorded by Ron West and his colleagues, involving three separate *'globes of light'* forming a triangle in the sky, cannot be ignored.

David Marler – 'Triangular UFOs An Estimate of the Situation'

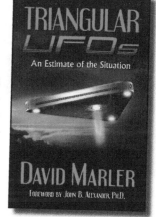

As we were in the process of completing the work for this month in December 2014, we were contacted by David Marler who has served as Field Investigator and State Section Director for MUFON. Currently he is an independent UFO researcher, and lectures on the UFO subject both on the radio and to live audiences. He has an extensive library which covers the last 65 years and has written a book (which he is sending us a copy) entitled *Triangular UFOs An Estimate of the Situation*. We look forward to reading the book soon, and congratulate him for his efforts – which have earned him high praise from those veterans within the UFO fraternity.

---

*SOBEPS – Patrick Ferryn (born in 1946, in Belgium) is a former photographer. He is now head of a company involved in video-conferencing, audio-visual for corporate and production of documentary films. He has been interested in the UFO phenomenon and lost civilizations since the early sixties. Patrick is co-founder of SOBEPS, with Lucien Clerebaut (1971), and of KADATH – Chroniques des Civilisations Disparues, with Ivan Verheyden (1973). SOBEPS is an acronym for Société belge d'étude des phénomènes spatiaux (Belgian society for the study of space phenomena). It was a UFO investigation group, famed for its investigation of the black triangle incidents in Belgium, known as the 'Belgian Wave', in 1989 and 1990.

The society was formed in 1971 and had 700 registered members before the end of the year. It was hosted in a small office room owned by its general secretary, Lucien Clerebaut, and its main activity was the publication of a magazine, Inforespace, in 1972. Membership rose to 1,750 in 1976, and Clerebaut purchased a building in Anderlecht for the society the same year. However, its popularity then started to decline, with a drop in membership down to 500 members in 1985; Inforespace went from a publication rate of six per year, down to only two per year, but in November 1989, a 'wave' of UFO sightings struck Belgium, bringing the SOBEPS into the mediatic spotlight. It received hundreds of testimonies and collaborated with the Belgian Air Force on a fruitless UFO hunt in April 1990. Due to financial difficulties, the SOBEPS dissolved on the 31st December 2007, and the COBEPS (Comité Belge pour l'Étude des Phénomènes Spatiaux or Belgian Committee for the Study of Space Phenomena) was formed to continue some of the SOBEPS's activities. (Source: Wikipedia)*

David Marler – UFO researcher and author of 'Triangular UFOs An Estimate of the Situation'.

'Behold A Pale Horse' – Milton William 'Bill' Cooper

Milton William 'Bill' Cooper (May 6, 1943 – November 6, 2001) was an American conspiracy theorist, radio broadcaster and author, best known for his 1991 book *Behold A Pale Horse*, in which he warned of multiple global conspiracies, some involving extraterrestrial aliens. Cooper was also described as an HIV/AIDS denialist, and a "militia theoretician". Little is known about Cooper's background and education, beyond the information supplied in his own accounts. Public records indicate a period of service in the US Navy, including a tour of duty in Vietnam with two service medals. He claimed to have also served in the US Air Force, as well as Naval Intelligence, until his discharge in 1975.

Cooper claimed *"an elaborate conspiracy theory that encompasses the Kennedy assassination, the doings of the secret world government, the coming ice age, and a variety of other covert activities associated with the Illuminati's declaration of war upon the people of America"*.

UFOs, aliens and the Illuminati

Cooper caused a sensation in UFO research circles in 1988 when he claimed to have seen secret documents while in the Navy, describing governmental dealings with extraterrestrial aliens – a topic he expanded on in *Behold A Pale Horse*. (By one account he served as a 'low level clerk' in the Navy, and as such would not

Milton William 'Bill' Cooper

have had the security clearance needed to access classified documents). UFOlogists later asserted that some of the material that Cooper claimed to have seen in naval intelligence documents was actually plagiarized verbatim from their research – including several items that the UFOlogists had fabricated as pranks.

Don Ecker – 'UFO Magazine'

Don Ecker of *UFO Magazine* ran a series of exposés on Cooper in 1990. Cooper linked the Illuminati with his beliefs that extraterrestrials were secretly involved with the US government, but later retracted these claims. He accused Dwight D. Eisenhower of negotiating a treaty with extraterrestrials in 1954, then establishing an inner circle of Illuminati to manage relations with them and keep their presence a secret from the general public. Cooper believed that aliens *"manipulated and/or ruled the human race through various secret societies, religions, magic, witchcraft, and the occult"*, and that even the Illuminati were unknowingly being manipulated by them. Cooper described the Illuminati as a secret international organization, controlled by the Bilderberg Group, who conspired with the Knights of Columbus, Masons, Skull and Bones, and other organizations. Its ultimate goal, he said, was the establishment of a New World Order. According to Cooper the Illuminati conspirators not only invented alien threats for their own gain, but actively conspired with extraterrestrials to take over the world.

James Forrestal

Cooper believed that James Forrestal's fatal fall from a window on the sixteenth floor of Bethesda Hospital was connected to the alleged secret committee Majestic-12, and that JASON advisory group scientists reported to an elite group of Trilateral Commission and Council on Foreign Relations executive committee members who were high-ranking members of the Illuminati. Cooper also claimed that the *Protocols of Zion* was actually an Illuminati work, and instructed readers to substitute 'Sion' for 'Zion', 'Illuminati' for 'Jews', and 'cattle' for 'Goyim'.

President John F. Kennedy assassination

In *Behold A Pale Horse*, Cooper asserted that President John F. Kennedy was assassinated because he was about to reveal that extraterrestrials were in the process of taking over the Earth. According to a 'top secret' video of the assassination that Cooper claimed to have discovered, the driver of Kennedy's limousine, William Greer, used *"a gas pressure device developed by aliens from the Trilateral Commission"* to shoot the President from the driver's seat.

The Zapruder film shows Greer twice turning to look into the back seat of the car; Cooper theorized that Greer first turned to assess Kennedy's status after the external attack, and then to fire the fatal shot. Conspiracy theories implicating Greer reportedly 'snowballed' after publication of *Behold A Pale Horse*. Cooper's video purporting to prove his theory was analysed by several television stations, according to one source, and was found to be *"... a poor-quality fake, using chunks of the ... Zapruder film"*.

As Cooper moved away from the UFOlogy community and toward the militia and anti-government subculture in the late 1990s, he became convinced that he was being personally targeted by President Bill Clinton and the IRS. In July 1998 he was charged with tax evasion; an arrest warrant was issued, but Cooper eluded repeated attempts to serve it. In 2000 he was named a 'major fugitive' by the US Marshals Service.

(Source: Wikipedia: Milton William 'Bill' Cooper)

War hero

Other searches on the internet reveal a different picture of this man. It is said that he grew up in an Air Force family and as a child lived in many different countries, graduating from Yamato High School in Japan, which no doubt influenced his views on the world, in contrast to his American counterparts. He served with the Strategic Air Command, United States Air Force, and held a secret clearance working on B-52 bombers, KC-135 refuelling aircraft, and Minuteman missiles. William received an Honorable Discharge from the United States Air Force in 1965.

Military service

William joined the United States Navy, fulfilling and serving aboard the submarine USS Tiru (SS-416), USS Tombigbee (AOG-11), Naval Support Activity Danang RVN, Naval Security and Intelligence Camp Carter RVN, Danang Harbor Patrol RVN, Dong Ha River Security Group RVN, USS Charles Berry (DE-1035), Headquarters Commander in Chief Pacific Fleet, USS Oriskany (CVA-34). Cooper was a member of the Office of Naval Security and Intelligence serving as a Harbor and River Patrol Boat Captain at Danang and the Dong Ha River Security Group, Cua Viet, Republic of Vietnam and was awarded several medals for his leadership and heroism during combat, including two with 'V' for Valor. He served on the Intelligence Briefing Team for the Commander In Chief of the Pacific Fleet. William was the Petty Officer of the Watch and designated KL-47 SPECAT operator in the CINCPACFLT Command Center at Makalapa, Hawaii. There he held a Top Secret, Q, SI, security clearance.

First Class Petty Officer

William Cooper achieved the rank of First Class Petty Officer, QM1, E-6 after eight years of Naval service, and received an Honorable Discharge from the United States Navy on 11th December 1975. He then attended Long Beach City College, where he picked up an Associate of Science Degree in Photography. He founded the Absolute Image Studio and Gallery of Fine Art Photography in Long Beach, California.

Executive Director of Adelphi Business College

William Cooper held the position of Executive Director of Adelphi Business College, Pacific Coast Technical Institute, and National Technical College. Mr Cooper was the National Marketing Coordinator for National Education and Software.

Produced several documentaries

He produced several documentaries, covering subjects such as the Kennedy assassination and secret black projects that have built flying disc-shaped craft. William was an internationally acclaimed radio personality, broadcasting the *Hour Of The Time* on WBCQ worldwide short-wave 7.415 MHz, from 10pm until 11pm, Eastern Standard Time (0300 to 0400 UTC) Monday through Thursday nights.

Family life

William Cooper lived in Arizona, formerly with his Chinese wife Annie, daughters, Dorothy (Pooh), little Allyson and their dogs, Sugarbear, and Crusher. In March of 1999, William sent his family out of the United States for their security.

5th November 2001

On 5th November 2001, Apache County sheriff's deputies attempted to arrest Cooper at his Eagar, Arizona home, on charges of aggravated assault with a deadly weapon and endangerment stemming from disputes with local residents. After an exchange of gunfire, during which Cooper shot one of the deputies in the head, Cooper was fatally shot. Federal authorities reported that Cooper had spent years evading execution of the 1998 arrest.

Robert Martinez

According to the Apache County Sheriff's office, William Cooper was fatally wounded during a late night gunfight. Contrary to what was reported earlier, it was not a SWAT raid but a simple confrontation between police and Cooper. One Apache County deputy, Robert Martinez, was critically wounded in the exchange. [Some sources claim the officer sustained two shots in the head]. Deputy Marinez had served as a law enforcement officer for four years, and was serving as a tactical officer at the time of the shooting. He was 40 years old and had served as a United States Marine during Operation Desert Shield and Desert Storm, and was married with three children.

Sheriff's report

According to the Sheriff's report, several deputies were positioned outside the Cooper residence to serve a warrant for Aggravated Assault and two counts of endangerment. Cooper had stated numerous times in the past that he would not surrender to law enforcement via his website and shortwave radio. At approximately 12.15pm, after leaving his residence in a vehicle, the report states that Cooper confronted plain clothed deputies, a short distance away.

> "As Cooper drove back to his residence, deputies attempted to stop him using a fully marked patrol vehicle to block the driveway. Cooper refused to stop or comply with verbal orders by the deputies."

Cooper then drove around the patrol car to evade the arrest, and tried to run over one of the deputies on the way back to his house. Cooper was then followed a short distance, where this time he was confronted by uniformed deputies.

> *"After refusing once again to comply with the deputies orders, Cooper exited his vehicle and began running towards the house, firing shots with a handgun at the deputies."*

When Deputy Martinez took a head shot, officers returned fire, the report said. (Cooper was shot four times, according to the post-mortem later carried out). According to the Sheriff's office, *"the surgery on Martinez went well, but the condition is still critical"*. (Some sources say that he died). Cooper had spent the last month challenging the government's claims about what caused the destruction of the World Trade Center on 11th September.

Authors:

The only comment we would like to make with regard to the version of events, as above, is that as far as we know, he only had one leg (the other prosthetic) which would prohibit being able to run quickly, one would presume. He had, according to the post-mortem, six penetrating and three perforating gunshot wounds to the head, torso, and extremities. In addition, he had blunt impact injuries to the head and extremities.

Many years ago, we heard a tape-recording outlining the hypotheses of Mr Cooper with regard to the extraterrestrial presence on the planet and of their collusion with Governments, amongst many other claims. I have to say that we found it chilling in its implications and frightening to listen to. This was not the sort of material one would disseminate amongst people, some of whom (particularly younger ones) could have been severely traumatised by what they heard; others may disagree. We cannot even be sure that the letter signed by USAF Major Thomas Shively is authentic, although one would not be surprised if it was; on the other hand it seems strange that serious admissions like this, regarding covering up UFO reports, should be made available to public scrutiny all these years later. If the document is genuine, then surely the officials involved should share some responsibility – albeit indirectly – for the violent actions of William Cooper!

We cannot find any trace of a Major Thomas Shiveley on the Internet at this current time, and have our suspicions about the authenticity of this letter.

Condolences

Our condolences go to the family of William Cooper and also the Sherriff's deputy for their tragic loss. Ironically, history records much about Mr Cooper but very little about the Mr Martinez. Mr Cooper's book which is advertised for sale on Amazon (2014) contains 79 mixed reviews.

Dr. Edgar Mitchell

Ironically, in recent years, Dr. Edgar Mitchell – whom I (John Hanson) had the pleasure of meeting – has publicly expressed his opinions that he is *"90 per cent sure that many of the thousands of unidentified flying objects, or UFOs, recorded since the 1940s, belong to visitors from other planets"*.

Dateline NBC conducted an interview with Mitchell on 19th April 1996, during which he discussed meeting with officials from three countries who claimed to have had personal encounters with extraterrestrials. He offered his opinion that the evidence for such *"alien"* contact was *"very strong"* and *"classified"* by governments, who were covering up visitations and the existence of alien beings' bodies in places such as Roswell, New Mexico. He further claimed that UFOs had provided *"sonic engineering secrets"* that were helpful to the US Government. Mitchell's book, *The Way of the Explorer,* discusses his journey into mysticism and space.

In 2004, he told the *St. Petersburg Times* that a *"cabal of insiders"* in the US Government was studying recovered alien bodies, and that this group had stopped briefing US Presidents after John F. Kennedy. He said: *"We all know that UFOs are real; now the question is where they come from?"*

Haunted Skies co-author John Hanson seen here recently with Dr. Edgar Mitchell

On 23rd July 2008, Edgar Mitchell was interviewed on *Kerrang Radio* by Nick Margerrison. Mitchell claimed the Roswell crash was real and that aliens have contacted humans several times, but that governments have hidden the truth for 60 years, stating: *"I happen to have been privileged enough to be in on the fact that we've been visited on this planet, and the UFO phenomenon is real."* In reply, a spokesman for NASA stated:

> *"NASA does not track UFOs. NASA is not involved in any sort of cover-up about alien life on this planet, or anywhere in the universe. Dr Mitchell is a great American, but we do not share his opinions on this issue."*

Ex-Canadian Defense Minister, Paul Helyer

In early September 2005, Paul Hellyer made headlines by publicly announcing that he believed in the existence of UFOs. On 25th September 2005, he was an invited speaker at an Exopolitcs conference in Toronto, where he told the audience that he had seen a UFO, one night, with his late wife and some friends. He said that, although he had discounted the experience at the time, he had kept an open mind to it. He also said that he started taking the issue much more seriously after watching ABC's *Peter Jennings' UFO Special*, in February 2005

Watching Jennings' UFO special prompted Hellyer to read US Army Colonel Philip J. Corso's book – *The Day After Roswell*, about the Roswell UFO Incident – which had been sitting on his shelf for some time. Hellyer told the Toronto audience that he later spoke to a retired US Air Force General, who confirmed the accuracy of the information in the book. In November 2005, he accused US President George W. Bush of plotting an "Intergalactic War". The former Defense Minister told an audience at the University of Toronto:

> *"The United States military are preparing weapons which could be used against the aliens, and they could get us into an intergalactic war without us ever having any warning . . . The Bush Administration has finally agreed to let the military build a forward base on the moon, which will put them in a better position to keep track of the goings and comings of the visitors from space, and to shoot at them, if they so decide."*

APRIL 1990

3rd April 1990 (UK) – Yellow *'ball of light'* seen over Essex

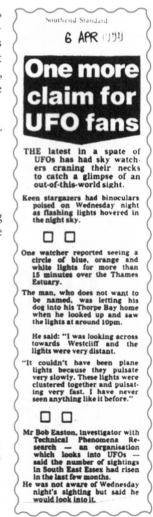

AT 8.20pm, Mrs C. Collins (54) from Maplin Way, Shoeburyness, Southend-on-Sea, was letting the dog outside, when she saw a yellow-orange 'ball of light' hovering approximately 2,000ft over the Thames Estuary, about half a mile away. She watched it for 10 minutes, at which point it took off, heading eastwards, at terrific speed. She went in to tell her son, but discovered that he had been watching it from the bedroom window. The incident was reported to Ron West.

Enquiries made with Southend Police and Airport, met with a negative result.

5th April 1990 (UK) – Yellow *'ball of light'* over Essex

At 3.30am, housewife Janet Wall (39) of Arnold Road, Dagenham, was finding it difficult to sleep. She got up to look out the window, when she saw, in the clear night sky:

> *"...a large yellow-orange moon sized object, moving over rooftops, across the roadway, about 100ft away from me, travelling very slowly."*

Southend Standard

6 APR 1990

One more claim for UFO fans

THE latest in a spate of UFOs has had sky watchers craning their necks to catch a glimpse of an out-of-this-world sight.

Keen stargazers had binoculars poised on Wednesday night as flashing lights hovered in the night sky.

☐ ☐

One watcher reported seeing a circle of blue, orange and white lights for more than 15 minutes over the Thames Estuary.

The man, who does not want to be named, was letting his dog into his Thorpe Bay home when he looked up and saw the lights at around 10pm.

He said: "I was looking across towards Westcliff and the lights were very distant.

"It couldn't have been plane lights because they pulsate very slowly. These lights were clustered together and pulsating very fast. I have never seen anything like it before."

☐ ☐

Mr Bob Easton, investigator with Technical Phenomena Research — an organisation which looks into UFOs — said the number of sightings in South East Essex had risen in the last few months.
He was not aware of Wednesday night's sighting but said he would look into it.

7th April 1990 (UK) – Triangular formation of lights over Essex

Whilst it appears the same object was seen by the previous two witnesses, one may consider that there may well be a connection with what was sighted on the 7th April 1990, by Thomas Queich (60) of Salisbury Avenue, Westcliff-on-Sea.

Thomas was looking out of his window, at 9.55pm, when he saw three lights, forming a triangle, moving very slowly across the sky, at about 10mph, heading towards him. He said:

> *"As they neared the house, they stopped in mid-air for a good five minutes, before moving again – heading eastwards. Suddenly, they picked up speed and were gone out of sight. I estimated they were at a height of 4-5,000ft and about half a mile away from me."*

7th April 1990 (USA) – Diamond-shaped UFO seen

At 11.45pm, two people were travelling by car on Blackiston Mill Road and Clarksville Road, near Route 1-265 at New Albany, Indiana, when they noticed two large objects hovering silently in the air, low down, showing two bright lights. Its shape resembled a large diamond.

> *"The underneath of the object seemed to have some sort of structure or windows. During the incident the car radio was changing stations arbitrarily and giving off static."*

Five minutes later it moved away.

(**Source:** NICAP Jim Delehanty & Mike Baker)

Light sparks UFO alert

Reading Evening Post. 9 APR 1990

A MYSTERIOUS light in the sky across Berkshire has sparked a UFO alert.

Three people across the county claim sightings in the early hours of the morning—on the night of the Harvest Moon.

Karen, a housewife from Test Close in Tilehurst, who doesn't want her full name disclosed, told the Post of her mystery encounter.

"I was moving around downstairs at about 1am and I turned around to see a green light through the curtains.

"I didn't have my contact lenses in so I went up to the window but it seemed to shoot right into the woods.

"My husband was wondering if it

By DAVID WILLIAMS

might have something to do with his computer. We've got a new computer and have connected it to loud speakers in the living room.

"At about midnight we were tapping on the keys to try and make the computer "talk" on the speaker."

On the same evening Hazel Green, one of Karen's neighbours saw a white light shining through her windows.

Hazel said: "I didn't think about it until Karen just told me. I thought it must be a car headlight when it came

in . . . but the light shone in the front of the house from the wrong angle."

Now Thames Valley Police have revealed that a woman from Hare Hatch near Twyford called at 2.20am on the same night.

Segeant Gordon Sinclair said: "We had a call from Hare Hatch when a person reported seeing a round object which appeared to be trailing fire and heading towards Reading.

"We didn't have any further reports and we think it might possibly be a shooting star. We have had similar reports coming after parties when people use laser lights so it may be connected with that."

Wrexham Evening Leader

−3 MAY 1990

UFO ALERT AS FLASHING LIGHTS BAFFLE EXPERTS

A MAJOR UFO alert involving police and scientists at Jodrell Bank was sparked when a man saw flashing lights in the sky.

Factory owner Rod Watson, 30, could not believe his eyes when he spotted flying coloured discs surrounding his house.

About six blue, green, and red discs lit up the sky as he gazed through binoculars in the early hours of the morning.

Rod, of Church Lane, Backford, near Chester,

phoned airports and weather centres to see if they had sighted the UFOs.

He then phoned Chester police station, who sent two officers to investigate but they were also unable to identify the objects.

Helicopters

Rod said: "A plane had been circling the house and I looked out of the window at 2am to see what it was doing.

"As it passed I saw red,

green, and blue lights flashing in the sky. They were like huge helicopters and at first I didn't believe what I was seeing.

"Then I looked out of the window again and there were more of them."

The policemen contacted their HQ to ask for assistance from Jodrell Bank space scientists.

Weather experts at Liverpool and Manchester airports were unable to explain the sightings, but a coastguard said they were metereorites.

8th April 1990 (Tasmania) – Bright *'green light'* seen

Mrs Cullen had been to visit her sister, following the birth of a new child in the family. They talked from midnight until after 3.30am – then Mrs Cullen set off home in her 1978 Toyota (a drive of some 15 minutes to her home, at Midway Point). The night was calm and fine, with some clouds.

Just after Cambridge, the highway heads north-east as it approaches the intersection with Acton Road. Mrs Cullen noticed, in front of her, to the right, a very bright *'green light'*. This *'light'* moved across the sky to her left (north) seeming to move over the Cambridge Airport area of the Tasman Highway. As she approached closer it returned, or bobbed back to the right (front) again. The road at this stage runs just south of east, at which point she noticed a car in the far distance and increased her speed up to 100kph, as she felt a little disturbed by the *'light's'* presence and did not want to be alone.

She later reported that she did not notice the movements of the *'light'*, because she tried to put it to the back of her mind – although she recalls the flashing light and lights at Hobart Airport, and the *'green light'* through the trees as she passed the Tasmanian Golf Club. The other car was still well ahead, but she was catching up to it. The course of the

Midway Point.

road at this point now heads north-east, before swinging north over the rise into Midway Point. Mrs Cullen remembers seeing the *'light'* out over the water as she drove up to the intersection ahead, at which point she caught up to the car in front – an old-style utility, with a white canopy.

To the right of the intersection was a service station with a large driveway cover. The bright mass of *'green light'* suddenly seemed to move up towards the service station, now increased in size.

> *"The 'green light' seemed to have a shape in the middle, of which I could only see the left-hand end – a level top, with a sloping left edge. It seemingly came over the road and above my car on the right side. The other car was turning off to the right, up a side street. The object appeared to veer away to the right and was out of sight towards the north-east. I quickly drove home."*

(Source: TA 1990-016)

141 UFOs reported by Canadians in 1989

Unexplained flashing lights and strange circles in the ground are spotted in Quebec, a saucer zooms over houses in Newfoundland and a diamond-shaped object zips through the Manitoba sky.

Throughout Canada people saw at least 141 unidentified flying objects last year, according to what's being touted as the country's first national survey of UFO sightings.

Chris Rutkowski, a Winnipeg researcher put together the survey from reports submitted to private investigators, police and the Ottawa-based National Research Council, which supplied two-thirds of the material for the study.

More than half the reports didn't have enough information to evaluate properly and one third had probable explanations, said Rutkowski, who has a

degree in astronomy and is president of the Winnipeg branch of the Royal Astronomical Society of Canada.

Of the rest, seven sightings were stamped as solidly unknown, meaning they were seen by several people and investigated by the police and NRC, without any explanation being found, he said.

He related three such incidents.

EVENING HERALD DUBLIN 11/4/1990.

14th April 1990 (UK) – Lights over the Thames Estuary

Silver UFO

At 11.30am, on the same day, a resident in Lucas Road, Grays, was in his front garden when he saw a bright silver object moving in the sky, over the A13, which he presumed, initially, was a child's silver helium balloon, heading eastwards towards Stanford-le-hope.

> *"It then turned a sharp right in the sky – which was most unusual – at the speed of a light aircraft, and at a height I estimated to be 25,000ft. Ten minutes later it was out of view."*

Over County Lough

At 4.30pm, a *'flying saucer'* – some 30 to 40ft in diameter – was reported to have circled the village of Carlingford, County Louth.

The object appeared as if to land, at one stage, but then took off, frightening a horse – which required veterinarian treatment.

According to local chemist – John O'Callaghan, the object was lit-up with orange lights that changed to blue as it went nearer to the ground, before changing to red as it headed away. Another man – Eamon Thornton – said the radio in the truck whined badly while the UFO hovered overhead.

Once again, we can see an object whose similarities with so many reports previously given, showing three vents or apertures on its outer surface, cannot be ignored. Was this the same UFO seen later, over Essex?

ADSCENE
-Canterbury, Kent-
13 APR 1990

Policeman spots UFO

A 'UFO' was spotted above Thanet last Thursday night. A police spokesman described it as green with a yellow tail, and said that no-one from military or civil aviation authorities could account for it.

"It's a real mystery," said the spokesman. "Usually some organisation or other will come up with an identification – but not this time."

The UFO started its journey along the north Kent coast at Margate – near to a site where circles in the corn were reported last year.

Researcher Richard Andrews who is writing a book on the phenomena of corn circles and their connection with UFO sightings, said: "We are getting nearer and nearer to solving the riddle of the circles and establishing a connection with 'lights in the sky'.

"It is important for serious researchers to disassociate these reports with little green men. The lights are not necessarily physical objects – we have established a connection with phenomena such as ball lightning and found a link with residue energy found at the site of the circles of crushed corn. "However at the moment nothing is proven."

YELLOW ADVERTISER
-Colchester-
27 APR 1990

Waggly UFO report

EIGHT people in the Southend area reported seeing what they believed was an unidentified flying object on Easter Saturday night.

Four people in Southend, three from Leigh and one from Canvey rang the East Anglian UFO and Paranormal Research Association's hotline to say they had seen a large, oval dull red-coloured object flying above the River Thames from Southend towards Shell Haven.

Observers said the object "waggled" in flight, was saucer-shaped and about 40ft in diameter, flew at about 500ft and was visible for about 10 seconds.

One estimated its speed at around £1,000, said Sheridan Lane, investigator with EAUFORA. The association will investigate the sightings, she added.

UFO hotlines are 01 594 4797 or Basildon 286079.

Southend Standard
20 APR 90

Orange and saucer-shaped

UFO experts are investigating eight sightings of a hazy, orange saucer-shaped object which shot along the Thames from Southend towards London at around 1,000mph at midnight on Saturday.

Eight witnesses rang the East Anglian UFO Para Research Association to report the sightings of the 50 feet diameter orange object around a quarter of a mile up in the sky.

If you saw it, the hotline for sightings is 0268 286079.

MYSTERY over Co Down — Carlingford pharmacist John O'Callaghan says he took this picture of a UFO last week.

At Southend, Essex, an orange saucer-shaped object was seen moving over *The Thames*, heading towards London, near midnight.

Eight people rang the East Anglian UFO & Paranormal Research Association 'hotline' to report sighting the 50ft diameter UFO, which was seen to '*waggle*' in flight, moving at a height of some 500ft.

(**Sources: Ron West/***Southend Standard,*** 20.4.1990 – 'Orange and saucer -shaped'/***Yellow Advertiser,***
Colchester, 27.4.1990 – 'Waggly UFO report'/***Irish Independent,*** 19.4.90 – 'UFO visitation dazzles village'**)

2004 – Sighting of a UFO over Ireland

During a search on the internet to trace a better image of the UFO photograph, as taken in 2014, we came across an interesting sighting on the Top Secret website, which took place in 2004, and felt it was worth bringing to the reader's attention, especially as the witness was Miles T. Johnston, who is known to us personally.

A huge shuttle-type space plane was sighted over Ireland on 27th April 2004, by Miles Johnston, at 8.30pm, travelling west to east and took eight seconds to travel directly overhead, to where it disappeared in the evening sky above Greater Belfast, Ireland.

Miles:

"I had hoped to have a computer version of this, but the pencil line drawing is what I have. I hope it has enough detail, if not the drawing, the text notes that come with it. The map is approximate. It could be a few degrees off either way, but the basic direction from west to east, disappearing from the low sun angle over the high sky above Belfast, is right. We viewed it from 900ft above sea level, on a high hill at Lough More, Co. Monaghan, while servicing my 160ft pirate radio tower (We joke and call it Alien Mountain, as we have a few odd things go on up here) so we were looking up at the time.

At 8.30pm on Tuesday, 27th April 2004, the sun was still above the horizon at that time of year, but quite low, and setting more north-west than due straight west. The colour of the main underbelly was blued by the atmosphere, which indicates its height was high. It was dull grey, gun grey. Some vestiges patterning/vehicle construction marks, gave me the impression to me it was a man-made advanced shuttle. The twin tails appeared very small from the angle of view, but appeared to be just above the dark black rectangular engine bay. It is possible there were no tails – that this white upper section was the rear of the main upper body. There were no engines visible, no nozzles – just a jet black rectangular engine, or vent port. No vapor trail was visible at all. The white nose implies it does not have a re-entry heating problem that the shuttle has. The front of the wings looked curved and protected in some way – not totally dissimilar to a shuttle wing, but much thicker and extending almost to the very nose. No flaps or aileron sections were noticed. I did not have enough time to observe this. After five seconds went by, I went to get my camera, just 2ft away, but it was gone by then over Greater Belfast.

That's about it. It really moved through the air effortlessly. It was about the size of a British 1p, or US penny, at arm's length. (My arm is about 30ins from finger to neck.) I have put a typical passenger jet and its vapour trail in the same scale as we saw this. We had scattered cloud, and this was well above the clouds, in a band of clear dark blue sky, directly above us.

It was very high from us. Even if it was 10,000 ft, it would be five or 10 times bigger than a 747. As I suggest, it was far higher. It really is an enormous craft. I hope that this is of value. It sure as hell tells me they (us) are flying a very heavy duty off planet bound vehicle that means business – perhaps an Alternative 3 vehicle?

Regards, T Miles Johnston

Dave Gilham (left) seen with T Miles Johnston

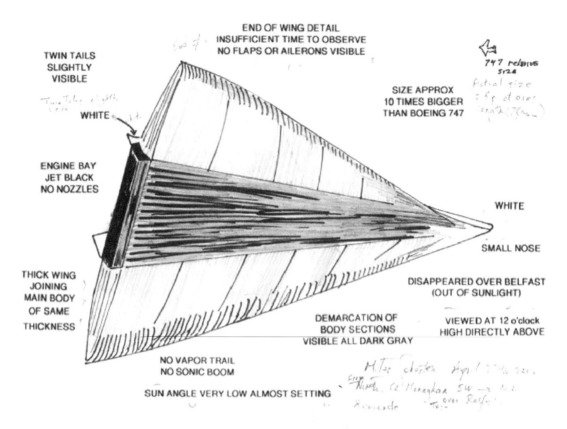

TWIN TAILS
SLIGHTLY
VISIBLE

END OF WING DETAIL
INSUFFICIENT TIME TO OBSERVE
NO FLAPS OR AILERONS VISIBLE

747 relative size

SIZE APPROX
10 TIMES BIGGER
THAN BOEING 747

WHITE

ENGINE BAY
JET BLACK
NO NOZZLES

WHITE

SMALL NOSE

THICK WING
JOINING
MAIN BODY
OF SAME
THICKNESS

DISAPPEARED OVER BELFAST
(OUT OF SUNLIGHT)

DEMARCATION OF
BODY SECTIONS
VISIBLE ALL DARK GRAY

VIEWED AT 12 o'clock
HIGH DIRECTLY ABOVE

NO VAPOR TRAIL
NO SONIC BOOM

SUN ANGLE VERY LOW ALMOST SETTING

15th April 1990 (Australia) – Cigar-shaped UFO seen

At 4.05am, Peter Pasini, from Townsville, Queensland, UFOR was watching Venus rise from the east, when he saw a cigar-shaped object, with white and red pulsating lights, to the south. It hovered and then disappeared into the night sky; five minutes later, a dark cloud was observed in the direction where the object had hovered.

15th April 1990 (USA) – Silvery dome-shaped object seen

A South Chicago, Illinois, young man was driving his car near the intersection of South Chicago Avenue and Commercial Avenue, at.7.30am, when he sighted a silvery object

hovering in the sky through the windshield (windscreen), which he described as being: *"...silvery, oval on the bottom, with some sort of round dome on top, making a whooshing sound."*

About a minute later the object disappeared, leaving the man with a headache, nausea and neck pain, after the incident.

(Source: NICAP, F. Bruno Molon)

UFOs reported over Belgium

It appears that in addition to the events which took place around the Essex area, during the first few months of this year, there was another 'wave' of UFO activity around Belgium. The events there captured the attention of the media, following a special Easter watch, organised by Belgium's Society for the Study of Space Phenomena, with observers at 20 vantage points and the Belgian Air Force providing radar back-up.

On the 16th April, scientists and observers took to the sky in aircraft, looking for any sign of UFOs, after reports of a luminous object had been sighted. On this occasion nothing was seen.

Financial Times – London.

18 APR 1990

Flying triangle has Belgians going round in circles

THE BELGIAN air force has been on alert for three nights running, writes Lucy Kellaway. Two Hawker Siddeley aircraft equipped with infra-red cameras and sophisticated electronic sensors have been patrolling the skies. Down below, the Belgian police force has kept a constant watch, helped by more than 1,000 concerned civilians. Along the border with Germany, 20 lookout posts have been set up. Their target: an Unidentified Flying Object.

Since December, there have been 800 reported sightings, and even though some resemble a lamp-post more closely than a UFO, many of the others are being earnestly examined by

SOBEPS, the Belgian Society for Studying Spacial Phenomena.

More surprising is how seriously the army is taking the whole thing. For the time being it says it is viewing the matter as a "technical curiosity" as the intruder has shown no aggressive signs. Should it turn nasty, it will be a different matter altogether.

The Easter operation was meant to be a world first, a confrontation between earth-bound defence forces and a UFO. The world's television crews camped out on a chilly Ardennes airfield to get the first pictures.

But the event made rather poor viewing. Several times the UFO was 'seen'

from the ground, but each time the aircraft got there too late, in one case missing the mystery intruder by just three minutes. To make matters worse, the cloud was low, the weather changeable, and the UFO tended to hover just above the rooftops, too low to be confronted by an aircraft.

The pilots, sworn to secrecy until the Defence Ministry has had time to watch the video evidence, seemed to have little to report, and could not confirm rumours of all kinds of irregular blips on their radars.

Far from declaring the operation a failure, the UFO-obsessed Belgian media appear more convinced than

ever that there is something odd hovering over the peaceful countryside of Wallonia. Scientists on the ground appear in the past few days to have produced a clear image of the object, which is said to correspond to the reports of eyewitnesses. It is a triangle 30m-50m in diameter, with red, green and white lights at the corners, 10 times brighter than any star. It has a convex underbelly and makes a sharp whistling noise.

Belgium may not quite yet have found its UFO. But it has found a nice new use for its air force now that its services are needed less and less by earthlings.

MOD letter

In a letter declassified by the MOD, in February 2010, sent to them by the Public Relations Officer at the Belgium Air Force, we learn, quote:

"Relating to your questions, I can confirm that two F-16s were scrambled on March 30 1990 as a reaction to both visual and radar observations.

The scramble was co-ordinated with and authorised by the Sector Commander of the NATO Air Defence System."

(Source: DEFE 24 1966/*Eastern Daily Press*, 16.4.1990 – 'UFO fever'/*Glasgow Herald*, 11.4.1990 – 'Flying Saucer fever grips Belgium')

Eastern Daily Press – Norwich.

16 APR 1990

UFO fever

BELGIUM is gripped by flying saucer fever, with lookout teams spending Easter weekend hunting for unidentified flying objects. UFOs have been reported in the south of the country over the past four months. Belgium's Society for the Study of Space Phenomena organised a weekend watch with observers at 20 vantage points and the Belgian air force providing radar back-up. Early yesterday 10 scientists and observers took off in a plane to search the skies for an hour after reports of a luminous object. They found nothing. "But that doesn't mean there wasn't anything," a spokesman said. The watch goes on until tomorrow.

18th April 1990 (USA) – Spherical UFO seen

A man driving in Milton, Florida, at 11pm, reported having sighted a spherical UFO, approximately 1,000ft away, estimated to be about 20-45ft in diameter. It then appeared to pace his automobile, appearing to change shape as it did so. It was last seen descending below the Escambia Bay Bridge. (**Source: MUFON Field Investigation files, case 900818**)

18th April 1990 (UK) – Cylindrical object over Essex

Another witness to something unusual seen in the Essex skies was Mrs Sheridan Lane from Boxted, Colchester. She later joined Ron West's UFO Group as his Public Relations Officer. Although we had never met Sheridan, we had read much about her and the role she played within the organisation, which included tape-recording members of the public, who had sustained all manner of strange experiences. She had a very cultured accent and described herself as a psychic and author. Her writing was in a most unusual style of very tall letters. This appeared to be her trademark. Prior to joining the East Anglian UFO & Paranormal Research Association, Sheridan experienced a sighting which took place at 1.40am, while at her home address.

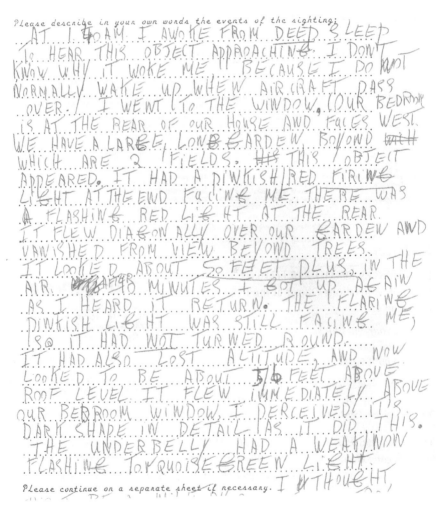

On its return journey it flew so low it looked ready to impact / would our roof. Flew directly over me – ie our / bedroom window. Flew diagonally 1.40 am Teusday April 18th 1990. Returned to fly over our roof 1.50 am.

Flashing pinkish/red light. Flashing pinkish/red light. Front view. Rear view. Flashing red light.

Under / Belly / view. Weak torquorse/green light. Non Flashing. Object was dark / grey or black. An unusual / distinct engine Tone.

20th April 1990 – Alan Godfrey describes his UFO close encounter

21st April 1990 (UK) – UFO lectures held at Bradford Central Library

Abductions were the theme of the UFO talk held at Bradford, on this day, organised by BUFORA member – Philip Mantle. Speakers included John Spencer, who is involved with the Mutual UFO Network. This was also the launch day for a new magazine, entitled *The UFO Debate*, edited by local UFO researcher – David Barclay. Also present was Andy Roberts – author and editor of the northern-based periodical *UFO Brigantia*. (**Source:** Philip Mantle/*Heckmondwike Reporter, Yorkshire, 19.4.1990 – 'Kidnap by Aliens top UFO agenda')

> **Halifax Courier & Guardian**
>
> **20 APR 1990**
>
> ## Close encounters
>
> A FORMER policeman will tell thousands of viewers about his close encounter with aliens in Todmorden in a live TV programme tonight.
>
> Mr Alan Godfrey will describe how he was beamed up into a spaceship on getting out of his patrol car in Burnley Road, Todmorden, on Granada Television's "Up Front" at 10.30pm.

25th April 1990 – East Anglian UFO & Paranormal Research Association

The Association's spokesperson – Sheridan Lane, claimed that sightings in Essex had reached a record 400 during the previous 12 months, and that a seminar would be held at Grays Central Library, on the 25th. – Tickets £1.50 at the door.   (**Source:** *Yellow Advertiser*, **21.4.1990** – 'Essex is visited from Space')

25th April 1990 (Australia) – Pulsating yellow light

A woman from Cando, Queensland, was awoken at 2am in the morning by the sounds of agitated dogs and cattle. An hour later, she was awoken again and saw a very *'bright light'* moving through trees. The *'bright light'* dimmed and lines of yellow light were seen blinking. Although it was a cold night, a hot breeze coincided with the dimming of the top white light. There was a swishing sound and shafts of blue light were observed. It is alleged that the witness may have sustained missing time, although we do not have any further details of this. (**Source:** A 1990-034)

27th April 1990 (UK) – Jellyfish UFO over Taunton

Mrs Eileen Manders of Treborough Close, Taunton, Somerset (the widow of an army officer) wrote to us, in 2007, about what she had experienced on the 27th April 1990, when aged 72. Eileen, formerly from Mauritius, had this to say:

"At 2.40am I was awoken by something, but what? Then my little Yorkshire terrier began frantically clawing at the duvet cover and making a pitiful whining noise. I thought he wanted to go out, and went to pick him up. As I live in an upstairs flat, he couldn't go down the stairs on his own.

Somerset County Gazette, Taunton.

‹ 4 MAY 1990

I WAS SHAKING FOR HOURS, SAYS TAUNTON PENSIONER

Eileen (72) tells of UFO sighting

By CARRE DUNN

STRANGE red lights have been spotted hovering over Taunton homes — and pensioner Eileen Manders believes visitors from another planet might be responsible for the phenomenon.

Mrs Manders, aged 72, of Hope Corner Lane, saw the "unidentified flying object" outside her home at 2.40 am last Friday.

"My little Yorkshire Terrier started whining, so I got up to see what was wrong," she said. "Through the bathroom window I saw a strawberry red light.

"I went into the bedroom, where the windows were open, and from there I heard a terrific crackling noise, like a fire. I was frightened to death."

She told the *County Gazette* she saw a blood-red ball in the centre of the strange light, a bit like a setting sun. "It was gyrating," she said, "and hovering as if it was

trying to get down."

Mrs Manders said the light came so close that she thought it must have dropped down somewhere in Taunton. But after watching the fiery ball for six or seven minutes she saw it disappear into the distance.

Throughout the whole episode her Yorkshire Terrier stayed in his bed, hiding away in fright.

"All I could think was that it was something from another world,"

said Mrs Manders. "I was shaking for hours and couldn't get to sleep."

The next morning she telephoned the police, who suggested she may have seen a flare. "But I can't think that a flare would do that," she said.

And she was not the only one to see the light. An 85-year-old neighbour said she saw a glow coming through her curtains, but thought it was someone using a torch to search for a cat.

Tony Dodd, director of research and investigations at Quest International, runs a 24-hour hotline for

UFO sightings. He said a similar "light" had been sighted at Bristol in the same week.

"This is a fairly common phenomenon," he said. "We're getting quite a lot of information about this sort of thing at the moment. UFO sightings throughout the country and Europe have increased dramatically."

But he stressed that sightings could not be recorded by Quest International until detailed investigations had been carried out. Anyone with information is asked to contact Mr Dodd on 0756 752216.

As I got out of bed, I realised his frantic efforts to wake me up were not as a result of a call of nature but due to fear. I looked around, seeing the whole room was flooded with a very bright – almost too bright to look at – strawberry pink light. I could also hear what sounded like a crackling noise and thought to myself that the flat was on fire, and decided to get out. I ran into the lounge and bathroom and realised there was no smoke or flames. I pondered if it could have been the flat below me, but was then stunned to see the strawberry light was outside the window. The noise then increased in sound; it was getting closer to me and I looked out, transfixed, to see this 'pulsating pink thing' slowly coming into view.

I felt sick with fear and terrified, and could only watch as this enormous pulsating and glowing pink jellyfish-shaped object passed through the sky over the top of the roof – a mere 30-40ft away. It was about 4ft in diameter and gave out no heat whatsoever. It seemed alive – that's the only way I can describe what I saw – as opposed to any machine."

Mrs Manders stood there for over five minutes, mesmerised, until the object had disappeared into the distance, and then went to check on the dog – which was still whining pitifully. Shock then came over her and she stood still, once again, trying to control her shaking. A short time later she made herself a cup of coffee and recovered somewhat.

The next morning, she rang the police at Taunton. A policewoman told her that she had probably seen a flare in the sky and not to worry!

Eileen:

"I had never seen anything like that before in my life and regard her offered explanation as being rubbish."

She rang the *Somerset Gazette* and asked them if they had received any reports of unusual objects. They told her that they had not. (**Source:** Personal interview/Tony Dodd, Quest/*Somerset County Gazette*, 4.5.1990 – 'I was shaking for hours, says Taunton Pensioner')

27th/28th April (UK) – Crop circles discovered, Denbighshire

Three circles in the crop were found on land at Voel Farm, near Llanfair, belonging to Mrs Pat Coulson and her husband, Derek. Each was 10-12ft in diameter – one slightly smaller than the others. The outlines had a distinct edge, which was about a foot wide, and they were arranged in a triangular pattern, four or five yards apart.

(Sources: Mrs Margaret Fry, Contact International UFO/*Denbighshire Free Press*, 1.6.1990 – 'Strange Circles found on Denbigh Moors Flying Saucer Mystery'/*Denbighshire Free Press*, 29.6.1990 – 'Evidence that UFO may have visited hill farm'/*North Wales Pioneer*, Colwyn Bay, 'Scorched circles: Expert will probe farm UFO link'/ *Rhyl & Prestatyn Visitor*, 7.6.1990 – 'Grass rings fuel flight of fancy')

Somerset County Gazette, Taunton

11 MAY 1990

Further sightings reported in UFO mystery

FURTHER reports have been coming in from Taunton residents who claim to have seen a great ball of fire hovering over their homes.

Pensioner Eileen Manders, aged 72, last week told the *County Gazette* of her terror at seeing a blood-red ball gyrating outside her window at 2.40 am on Friday, April 27.

And Tony Dodd, of Quest International, who runs a 24-hour hotline for UFO sightings, appealed to readers to get in touch if they had seen anything unusual.

Since then he's had reports of two more sightings, at 2 am and 2.30 am the same morning. He told the *Gazette*: "There's a lot more to this than meets the eye."

In one incident a man saw "a huge ball of red light hovering over fields at about 30ft". The object started moving erratically before gliding away into the distance.

Another man was woken by his dog barking, and found it cowering under a bed.

And in a further incident, believed to have happened the same morning, a woman and her son also reported seeing a huge red ball of light in the sky over Taunton.

Mr Dodd said the RAF confirmed that objects had been tracked on its radar equipment at the time the incidents happened.

He said: "I think this is just the tip of the iceberg. I am certain there are a lot more people who haven't yet come forward."

Anyone with information is asked to contact Mr Dodd on 0756 752216.

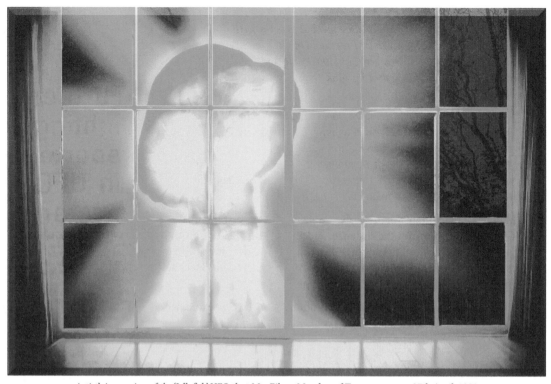

Artist's impression of the 'Jellyfish' UFO that Mrs Eileen Manders of Taunton saw on 27th April, 1990.

MAY 1990

1st May 1990 (UK) – Saturn UFO over Cheshire

AT 10.15pm, an object – described as creamy-white in colour, circular in shape, with a dome on top – was seen moving across the sky over Runcorn, by a cyclist returning home. He said:

"It was lit-up by a luminous light and travelling at tremendous speed in a sort of bobbing movement, but following a straight line, heading towards Frodsham."

(Source: *Runcorn World*, Cheshire – 'Alien UFO over Runcorn')

Alien UFO over Runcorn

World exclusive by Carla Flynn

AN alien UFO was spotted flying low over Runcorn this week.

It was seen by a man cycling home to Murdishaw from a friend's house at 10.15pm on Tuesday night.

The man, who wants to be known as Tony, said of his bizarre experience: "It flew past right in front of me. It really took me by surprise.

"I've been spotting aircraft for years and I know this definitely wasn't any kind of aeroplane.

"It didn't travel like ours, it didn't look like one and it was certainly going far too fast to be one."

Tony described the UFO as circular in shape with a dome on top. He said it was a white, creamy colour and was lit up by a luminous light.

"The nearest comparison I can think of is that it looked like the planet Saturn," he said.

"It was travelling at a tremendous speed and in a straight line but with a sort of bobbing movement. It was also very low or appeared to be very low.

"It was also silent. There was no noise coming from it at all and it was heading in the direction of Frodsham."

Before his strange encounter, Tony said he had always kept an open mind about alien spacecraft.

"I know thousands of people have said they have spotted UFOs in the past but I certainly believe in them now.

"People may think I'm crackers, but I know what I saw."

Tony also said it was travelling on the same flightpath aircraft take to Liverpool Airport.

"They must have picked it up on their radar," he said.

But a spokesman for Liverpool Airport told the World they didn't pick up anything unusual and declined to make any further comment.

Tony points out where he saw the UFO.

– Cheshire –
- 4 MAY 1990

2nd May 1990 (Australia) – Paced by a UFO

Mr Stanford – a truck driver for 20 years – reported having been followed by a bright star-like object, for over four hours, while driving between Yelarbon (West of Warwick) and the Logan Motorway, in Brisbane. He described it as the circumference of a pencil, held at arm's length. On three occasions, Mr Stanford stopped his vehicle to observe the object, which remained at a constant 45° elevation in front of the vehicle. During the sighting, lasting between 2.30am and 6.45am, the object was seen to change sides several times. Mr Stanford lost sight of the object near Cunningham's Gap, due to fog, but saw it again on the downward leg of the journey. This time the object was much higher up. The object was observed until sunrise in Brisbane.

(Source: QA 1990-031)

3rd May 1990 (UK) – UFOs over North Wales

As the UK experienced a heatwave, sightings of UFOs were reported over Cheshire, Merseyside, and North Wales. Some of the objects were later explained away as being meteorites, activated by the abnormal weather!

The objects were described as looking like large helicopters, flying at high altitude, surrounded by blue, green, red and orange lights; on other occasions one object, surrounded by four similar objects, was seen. It appears the phenomena were first spotted at 1am over Backford, Cheshire, followed by numerous calls made to the coastguard station at Formby. One of the witnesses was Rod Watson (30) of Church Way, Backford. He said:

Stoke on Trent Evening Sentinel.

- 7 MAY 1990

UFO sighting leaves 'plane spotter baffled

By Kathy Evans

TAXI proprietor Rod Watson is planning to enlist the help of scientists at Jodrell bank following a midnight close encounter with a UFO.

Mr Watson was trying to follow the path of an aeroplane with binoculars when an explosing ball of colour caught his eye.

He said: "I got out my binoculars to follow it, when I suddenly saw what I though was a very bright star.

Baffled

"It was very large, and made up of shades of red, green and orange — rather like a multi-coloured football.

"Then I noticed there were quite a few of them and I called the police."

Phone calls to Manchester Airport, and the meteorological office failed to unravel the mystery.

Mr Watson of Backford in Cheshire, said: "I'm very cynical about UFO's but this has really baffled me.

"One explanation is that they could have been meteorites, but I think there were too many."

Astronomy expert Mrs Michael Pace, who's based at the Newchapel Conservatory, in Kidsgrove, said: "It could have been the planet Jupiter because it is very low in the sky at the moment.

"Atmospheric haze tends to distort colours and give planets shades of colour."

A spokesman for the London Airport Traffic Control Centre said: "We have had an amazing number of reports of UFOs this year, which have turned out to be laser beams being used at lightshows or major events."

"A plane had been circling the house at 2am. I looked out to see what was going on and saw what looked like balls of green, red and blue, wobbling lights, about the size of helicopters. I called the police; two officers arrived, and were amazed at what they saw."

Weather experts were unable to offer any explanation to the police and public, many of whom rang Jodrell Bank. (**Source:** *Chester Tonight*, 3.5.1990 – 'UFO lights spark fears of invasion'/*Wrexham Evening Leader,* 3.5.1990 – 'UFO alert, as flashing lights baffle experts')

CHESTER TONIGHT – 3 MAY 1990

UFO lights spark fears of invasion

BRITAIN'S heatwave brought fears of an alien invasion to Cheshire and North Wales early today.

Police and coastguard stations were inundated with scores of reports of brightly-coloured flying saucers.

A group of mysterious highly-coloured objects were spotted flying high over Cheshire, Merseyside and North Wales.

Cheshire Police patrols verified the sightings and made immediate checks with the Manchester Meteorological Centre.

But the alien spacecraft turned out to be meteorites activated by the abnormal weather.

Experts said today that when viewed with the naked eye they would look like large helicopters, but flying high and surrounded by green, blue, red and orange lights.

UFO spotters would see one main body surrounded by a group of four smaller objects.

Sightings began shortly after 1am today, with the first call coming in from a puzzled taxi proprietor at Backford, near Chester.

And then the coastguard station at Formby reported calls flooding in.

Circling

A spokesman for Cheshire Police said: "It is easy to understand why people thought they were looking at UFOs."

Rod Watson, 30, of Church Way, Backford, rang police after spotting the UFOs. "They looked like balls of green, red and blue, wobbling about like helicopters."

Two officers were sent to investigate.

"The male constable didn't believe me even when he saw them himself, but the woman PC was amazed," he said.

● At 3am tomorrow, a comet will shoot across the north-east corner of the sky.

4th May 1990 – (Belgium) – Disc-shaped UFO

At 10.20pm, a witness from St. Georges, in Belgium, sighted a silent disc-shaped object – showing lights strong enough to illuminate the surrounding area – hovering above a yard, one meter off the ground.

(Source: *FSR*, December 1990)

7th May 1990 (UK) – Mystery light over Worcestershire

At 4.15am, Bill Moore of Lyttleon Avenue, Tardebigge (just outside Redditch, Worcestershire) was looking through his window, when he noticed a vivid bright *'light'*, high in the sky, over Stoke Prior.

"It then appeared to travel across the sky on the horizon towards Barnt Green, where it climbed higher, before heading back towards the south; it looked like a motorcycle light, moving fast down the road. I rang the police and contacted two radio hams on my CB in the Gloucester area. They told me they could see it as well."

Inspector Bob Dibble, of Bromsgrove Police, confirmed three police cars had been sent to Tardebigge, near to the Church, but found nothing.

(Source: *Bromsgrove Advertiser*, 10.5.1990 – 'Police alert over UFO'/ Personal interview)

Rochdale Observer, Lancs

!12 MAY 1990

Dont't feel silly, there are UFOs

THE only mystery about the Shawclough UFO sighting is why the gentleman phoned the police instead of the local UFO group, and why he felt silly about it.

If he or the police had bothered to inform us we could have told them a lot more about it that air-traffic control.

Perhaps a bigger mystery is why Greater Manchester Police is the only force I know of which does not co-operate with its local UFO authority.

Delay in getting this information might have resulted in us not getting a clear picture of the events. As it was, we already knew of similar sightings in the area from the nationwide UFO network.

UFO research is a complex,

complicated business, not made any easier by people refusing to do the obvious and refusing to accept that this planet is being visited regularly by creatures of a superior intelligence.

Phoning the police is pretty pointless. Doing so only contributes to the Government's cover-up.

I said twelve months ago, when the Rochdale group was reformed, that the Rochdale public had to "use it or lose it".

When police co-operation, press coverage and the attitude of the general public is much better elsewhere, it makes you wonder if we are wasting our time in Rochdale.

As a matter of interest, there was no more meteor activity this

last week than in any other April/May period. To involve the Met office is such matters is just a tool the Government uses to confuse the public and cloud the issue.

All sightings should, in the first instance, be reported to the Rochdale group (tel 54583 or 625028). More information can be got from Rochdale library.

If the gentleman concerned wishes to ring me in confidence it would be appreciated. I assure him he was not on his own in seeing his UFO that night.

M R JONES.

Rochdale UFO
Research Group,
Croft Square,
Smallbridge.

8th May 1990 (UK) – Triangular UFO over Essex

At 2.30am, Mrs Sheridan Lane was to witness further examples of UFO activity when she was awoken, and on going to look out of the window, saw:

> "...a triangular, black object, flying through the sky, about 70ft off the ground, moving very slowly. It was the size of a large aircraft and had white lights on it. I could hear a low humming noise. Within 30 seconds, it was out of view."

Sheridan gives this date on the UFO sighting report, but refers to the middle of May on the illustration she provided. This means we should not rely on this as being the actual date, taking into consideration the following sighting – which took place a short time later. Unfortunately, we are unable to trace Mrs Sheridan Lane, who we understand now lives in France.

BROMSGROVE ADVERTISER

10 MAY 1990

Police alert over UFO

BROMSGROVE police made an early morning May Day call to Tardebigge on Monday after a Charford man reported seeing a UFO flying over the area.

Mr Bill Moore, aged 71, of Lyttleton Avenue, was peering from his landing window shortly after 4.15am waiting for the dawn chorus to begin when he saw a vivid bright light high in the sky over Stoke Prior.

Mr Moore said: "I saw this brilliant white light which at first didn't seem to be moving.

"I woke my wife Barbara to come and take a look through the binoculars.

"The light then appeared to travel across the sky on the horizon towards Barnt Green, where it started climbing higher before heading back towards the south."

Mr Moore said he was convinced it wasn't a balloon, aeroplane or a star he'd seen. "It resembled a motorcycle light coming towards me fast down a road," he said.

"I rang the police then contacted two breakers in Gloucester on my CB radio who told me they could also see the object quite clearly from there."

He said: "It remains a mystery. I had always treated UFOs with a little scepticism. I now feel there is something I know nothing of, but about which I would like to know more.

Inspector Bob Dibble

of Bromsgrove police confirmed that three vehicles had been sent to Tardebigge in response to Mr Moore's sighting of the UFO over the church, but said they could find no evidence.

Jacko's wacko on UFOs

ODDBALL superstar Michael Jackson is convinced there are little green men in space—and is building a landing pad to welcome them.

The multi-millionaire singer claims space aliens told him in a dream they wanted to contact him.

So he has had plans drawn up for a giant UFO landing pad in the Nevada desert, says the magazine National Enquirer.

Mystery light over Yorkshire

At 2.44am on 8th April 1990, two police officers were on patrol at Madeley, near Huddersfield, West Yorkshire, when they saw a circular object, with flashing blue lights, flying over the M6 Motorway close to Walton's Wood, Madeley, at an estimated altitude of 5,000ft.

(Source: Gary Heseltine, PRUFOS)

16th May 1990 (UK) – Orange light paces motor vehicle, Essex

At 8.50pm, Carole Martin (40) was driving home through Birdbrook, Essex, when she saw:

> "… a saucer-shaped object in the sky in front of the car. It seemed to keep pace with me for about two miles. When I turned into Station Road, the lane where I lived, it disappeared."

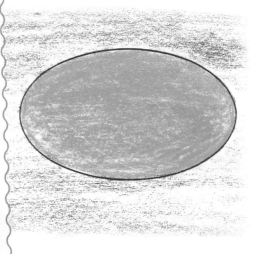

19th May 1990 (USA) – Bomerang-shaped UFO

At 4.35am, a Warrior Alabama man was driving to work when he sighted a boomerang-shaped object, with a fan tail, approach from the front, hesitate, and then pass 15-20ft over his truck, at a leisurely speed.

> "It had six big lights in front. I watched it until it was lost from view amid the rooflines in the vicinity."

The UFO apparently overflew a shale strip mine in the area. (**Sources: Todd Pierce, Field Investigator, MUFON field investigations database, case 900708**)

21st May 1990 (USA) – Delta-shaped UFO seen, showing three lights

At Trenton, New York, a family were on their front porch, at 9pm, with the family dog, when they saw a boomerang-shaped object move slowly over their house, at treetop level. A humming sound (low hum, generator hum, and rushing sound – like a jet pack) was heard. According to Joan Woodward, Animal Reaction Specialist, the house was described as wooded. Three adults, aged (41), (50) and (24) – all with high school education – sighted a dark boomerang or delta-shaped object, with large steady white lights at its three corners. Swirling or pulsating lines of smaller lights were seen on the bottom. The object approached haltingly and passed slowly over the house. A fourth son and a neighbour were also alerted to the object. No physiological effects were reported but the mother was described as *"in hysterics"*. The object reportedly manoeuvred over a neighbour's property for four hours or more, until the witnesses stopped watching and went to bed. (**Source:** *MUFON UFO DATABASE*, **Portion of Reports from the Files at MUFON Headquarters, July 1999, Sequin TX, CD-ROM, Case Log #930506E by Keith Conroy**)

23rd May 1990 (UK) – *'Flying saucer'* over Portsmouth

At 4.50pm, Robert Walker, Simon Ingate, and Christopher Martin – students at Portsmouth Polytechnic – were enjoying a spell of sunshine, playing cricket in the rear garden of their student accommodation at

42 Grayshott Road, Southsea. Robert was the first to see what looked like a black inverted soup bowl, speeding across the sky, and alerted the others – who watched it before eventually disappearing behind houses.

Five minutes later the UFO reappeared, reversing back along its original path. By this time Robert had picked up his Miranda FM/2 camera from indoors, and took three photographs before it disappeared, using Kodak 200 35mm colour film, speed 100/200.

Whilst the image is thought-provoking and similar in description to so many other sightings of UFOs, we should treat this at face value – understanding there was a suggestion that the students had used the UFO sighting to avoid taking examinations. Was this scurrilous information, or did they manage to capture a unique photograph of a UFO? Unfortunately, without being able to have the negative examined professionally, it would be impossible to conclude anything. However, we did examine the photo using various filters on the PC, which failed to reveal any threads or lines used to hang the object on, although there was some surface debris on the photo itself, consistent with age.

(Source: Nicholas Maloret, WATSUP)

Mysterious light baffles students

by GEOFF NAISH

THREE trainee teachers who spotted a mystery light over Exmouth at the weekend have asked if anyone can explain exactly what it was they saw.

The three students at Rolle College reported the UFO sighting to Exmouth police but checks with coastguard and other authorities have failed to come up with an answer.

Coincidentally, police all over the Westcountry received numerous calls at the weekend after what is thought to have been a meteor was reported to have "scorched" across the night sky before coming down with a "bang" in Bridgwater Bay.

○ Falling

The Exmouth students say the strange moonsized orange ball of light they saw was moving East to West and falling towards Lyme Bay off Exmouth — the wrong direction for the Bridgwater reports.

First year B.Ed. students Lee Jones, 19, from Weston Super Mare, and Mark Marsden, 20, from Sussex, were watching a video with fellow third-year American exchange student Stephanie Glover, 20, in a ground floor flat at Kingsthorpe Hall of Residence, Rolle Road, at 9.45 pm on Sunday evening.

They said their attention was attracted to the strange light in the dark night sky through the seaward facing window of the flat.

"We saw this light like an orange ball moving very slowly across the sky from our left to right. We saw it go down very, very slowly then go out of sight below the trees on our horizon," said Mr Marsden.

"It was like nothing we had ever seen before. We went down to the beach to see if something had come down in the sea but we could see nothing and two people we spoke to who were walking their dogs along the seafront said they had seen absolutely nothing," he added.

The three have been the subject of some attention from fellow students since reporting the sighting and would now like to know if anyone else saw anything or can explain what the mystery light was.

WESTERN MORNING NEWS 20.06.90

Rob Warner. 23. May. 1990

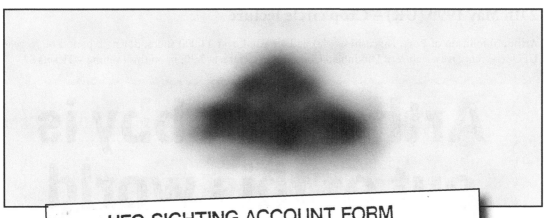

UFO SIGHTING ACCOUNT FORM

SECTION A

Please write an account of your sighting, make a drawing of what you saw and then answer the questions in section B overleaf as fully as possible. Write in **BLOCK CAPITALS** using a ball point pen.

MYSELF AND SIMON INGATE (25) BOTH STUDENTS AT PORTSMOUTH POLYTECHNIC WERE PLAYING CRICKET IN THE BACK GARDEN OF OUR LODGINGS AT 42 GRAYSHOTT RD SOUTHSEA PORTSMOUTH AT APPROX 4.30PM. CHRIS MARTIN ALSO A STUDENT CAME HOME AND JOINED US. AT APPROX 4.50PM CHRIS WAS BATTING, WHEN SUDDENLY HE NOTICED SOMETHING UNUSUAL IN THE SKY (SOUTHERLY) HE DREW OUR ATTENTION TO THE OBJECT. AT WHICH TIME I RAN INDOORS AND GRABBED MY CAMERA. I TOOK A PHOTO AS IT WAS JUST ABOUT TO DISSAPEAR NORTHERLY OVER THE ROOFTOPS. ONCE DISSAPEARED IT WAS APPROX 5 SECS WHEN IT REAPPEARED TRAVELING IN THE OPPOSITE DIRECTION. ONCE AGAIN IT DISSAPEARED OVER THE ROOFTOPS. APPROX ANOTHER 5 SECS PASSED WHEN WE ONCE AGAIN SAW THE OBJECT THIS TIME IT WAS IN A WESTERLY POSITION. I ONCE AGAIN TOOK A PHOTO OF THE OBJECT. IN ALL WE SAW THE OBJECT FOR APPROX 15 SECS AND OF WHICH I TOOK 3 PHOTOS IN ALL. WE LATER REPORTED OUR SIGHTING TO A LOCAL FREE NEWSPAPER CALLED STREETLIFE

Please continue on a separate sheet if necessary.

DRAWING*

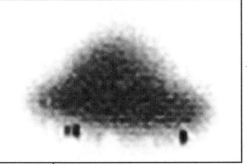

*If preferred, use a separate sheet of paper.

Your full name (Mr/Mrs/Miss/Ms) ....

.... Age 22

Address 42 GRAYSHOTT ROAD

SOUTHSEA PORTSMOUTH

Telephone No (.........) .... (STD ....)

Occupation during last two years ...... STUDENT ......

Any professional, technical or academic qualifications or special interests

COMPUTER SCIENCE DIPLOMA

6 A LEVELS. 2ND DEGREE STUDENT

Do you object to the publication of your name?
*Yes. *Delete as applicable.

N2

Today's Date 31/6/90

Signature ....

Published by the British UFO Research Association (BUFORA LTD.) for the use of investigators throughout Great Britain. Further copies may be obtained from BUFORA Research Headquarters., Newchapel Observatory. Newchapel, Stoke-on-Trent, Staffs., England

Form R1

24th May 1990 (UK) – Crop circle lecture

Arthur Tomlinson of Bury, Lancashire, who had amassed over 14,000 slides, during a period of 36 years UFO research, gave a lecture at Dukinfield Community Centre, at 7.30pm on this evening – Tickets £2.

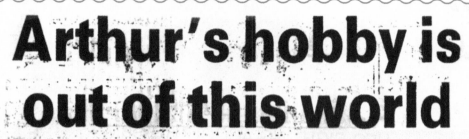

Arthur's hobby is out of this world

IF you fancy an evening that's literally out of this world — complete with photographs of aliens from space — then Dukinfield community centre is the place to be tonight (Thursday).

One of the country's top flying saucer experts, Arthur Tomlinson of Bury, will be giving a lecture on his 36 years of detailed investigations into the

phenomenon of Unidentified Flying Objects.

He told the Advertiser that he's in no doubt whatsoever that aliens have visited this planet —

and he reckons he's got the proof to convince the most sceptical of doubters during his two and a half hour talk covering all aspects of the phenomenon.

Mr. Tomlinson says he's got photos of flying saucers and other types of space craft, copies of top secret documents from around the world discussing various encounters with UFOs, over 14,000 slides showing various aspects of the phenomenon — as well as photos of aliens themselves.

He's been investigating into the subject for 36 years, during which time he's had several 'close encounters' with extra-terrestrial visitors, and made hundreds of interviews with other people who have seen UFOs.

Among these is a Yorkshire policeman who claimed to be abducted by a flying saucer — who Mr. Tomlinson and a colleague interviewed under hypnosis.

He also reckons that American army chiefs have actually tried to rebuild a crashed UFO and drive it, and have probably had meetings with aliens keen to talk to the superpower leaders.

His lecture in Dukinfield Community Centre starts at 7.30 p.m. and costs £2 — get there early because there's not likely to be much space inside — or call 766 4560 to reserve a seat.

THE ADVERTISER
-Ashton-
24 MAY 1990

Arthur Tomlinson

24th May 1990 (USA) – Boomerang-shaped UFO

In North Huntingdon, a 35-year-old woman was walking her dog at about 11pm, on a clear night, when she noticed the dog had become still and quiet. Looking up she saw a boomerang-shaped object approach, hover, and accelerate away. Although the object was silent, the woman felt a vibration.

Joan Woodward, who investigated this matter, tells of a black-surfaced *'boomerang'* with bright white lights, seen by the witness approaching from the south-west, at less than 500ft altitude. At its nearest approach, it was estimated to be less than 500ft away in horizontal distance. The *'boomerang'* hovered about 150ft from power lines and then accelerated away to the north-east. The shape was described as a fat boomerang, with inverted curvature of the base (bottom). Numerous bright lights on the forward edge of the wings were noted to dim and then to brighten.

(Source: *MUFON UFO DATABASE*, **Portion of Reports from the Files at MUFON Headquarters, July 1999, Sequin TX, CD-ROM, Case log 900704, by Wayne Willis and Stan Gordon.**)

May 1990 (UK) – *'Flying saucer'* over M5

During the same month, holidaymakers Linda and David Biggs from Newport, Gwent, were on their way to Cornwall and travelling along the M5, near Taunton, when they saw a saucer-shaped object hovering overhead.

> *"It was as big as a three terraced houses, with a dome on top and a long elliptical light at the front. Inside the light were two even brighter ones – like car headlights. We saw one of them move to point downward to the ground, allowing us to see it underneath – which was a flickering blue and white. The outline was as clear as a bell. None of us panicked. We were too stunned."*

Other reports included a huge, stationary, orange-red object, observed hovering over a field at around midnight, seen by a coach load of people travelling between Dunkeswell and Taunton, and a disc-shaped object with *'legs'*, and red flashing lights, which shot across a Taunton resident's garden, at 8pm.

25th May 1990 (UK) – UFO over Tipton

Ray Brown, with a Degree in Structural Engineering, was working for a 'Black Country' developer, in May 1990, working on wasteland next to the old Tipton Gasworks, in Alexandra Road – which involved clay capping certain areas where toxic chemicals had built-up into unacceptable levels, from strip mining ground worked back in the early part of the 20th Century. As part of this clean-up operation, huge concrete floors left over from demolished factory buildings were blasted and then broken up by smashing them with a huge demolition ball, operated from a crane, powered not by modern hydraulics but diesel.

For reasons that have never been established, some time during the afternoon, the jib of the crane raised itself, stretching the steel cable until it snapped, causing the gantry to buckle and crush the cab below it. Fortunately, nobody was inside this cab at the time.

Ray:

> *"The incident with the crane was totally inexplicable. I cannot understand what forces could have raised the jib up. Something even stranger was to take place, when as I was in the process of leaving the site, at 4.30pm, I noticed three objects moving against the wind over Merry Hill. Puzzled by what these objects could be, I stood watching and then realised they were approaching the construction site, by which time I could make out what looked like three grey coloured 'spheres' in a triangular formation, rotating as they moved across the sky over nearby fields. Suddenly they*

stopped, completely motionless in the air, approximately 20ft above my head. I stood not knowing what to do. I glanced at my watch to record the time and examined what looked like weathered 'spheres', without any sign of seams or joins. The 'sphere' at the back, making the point of the triangle, moved downwards – now forming three horizontal 'globes'. I sensed that I was being watched, or evaluated, in some way. I moved slightly to one side, so did the objects. I moved the other way and they followed suit, as if copying my actions. I pondered on what to do again, trying to make sense of the situation. I could see that they were real, as they cast a shadow onto the ground. I bent down to pick up a piece of broken brick to throw at them. In a split second, they vanished in front of me. I scanned the sky and was amazed to see what looked like the heat waves given off by an aircraft shimmering in the sky, moving towards Dudley Castle."

Reported to the Birmingham UFO Society

Ray told us that the sighting had lasted 17minutes and that he had reported the matter to the Birmingham UFO Society, run by Rob and Marilyn Aldworth (Marilyn was to tragically commit suicide some years later) and that within 24 hours of the incident taking place, he began to itch and noticed a strange rash covering most of his body, apart from the face, hands and back. During conversation with him about this rash, he became quite emotional and unbuttoned the front of his shirt, revealing that his arms and chest were covered with red, scaly, patches, diagnosed as Psoriasis – (a condition that can appear anywhere on the skin,

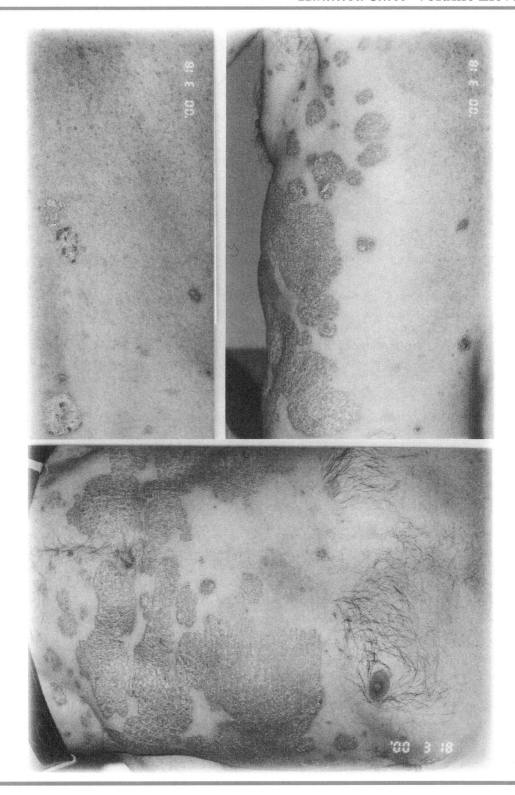

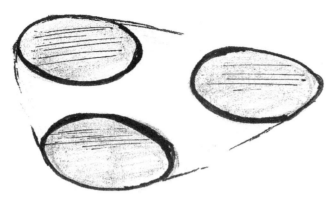

usually starting off as small red spots, before eventually forming circular or oval patches, 50-75 millimetres across).

Contrasting reports

It is always of value to check the area out to ascertain whether in the interim years similar objects have been seen, especially in view of the seriousness of what happened to Ray Brown. In November 2010 *The Daily Mail* reported on one such incident over Tipton, presented typically 'tongue in cheek', borne, no doubt, in our opinion, from poor education of the chosen subject – an inability to come to terms with the phenomenon itself and a wish to entertain rather than alarm its readers. Nothing appears to have changed over 60 years!

'Mysterious 'Dudley Dorito' UFO spotted over UK skies for the third time in three years' – this was the banner grabbing headline of *The Daily Mail* on the 17.11.2010 along with a photo of the triangular UFO, as alleged, over Belgium. Quote: *"You've heard about flying saucers – but how about a flying crisp? A UFO which resembles a popular salty snack has been spotted in the skies over Britain for the third time in as many years. The space invader, dubbed by locals the 'Dudley Dorito', was sighted over the Midlands. In the latest sighting of the 'extraterrestrial tortilla chip', quality inspector Munesh Mistry, 21, spotted the triangular object in the skies above his home in Tipton, West Midlands, at around 10.15pm on Sunday."*

Mr Mistry, who spotted the object with his friend Neil Martin, also 21, said:

> *"We saw this amazing fast-moving and silent craft in the shape of a triangle, made up of what appeared to be three lights, fly across the sky at a mind-boggling speed. At first it looked like three birds flying in unison – then, when seeing the triangle shape, we both were amazed and immediately discarded that explanation."*

He added they promptly logged onto the internet and saw previous sightings online and added,

> *"We wondered if there were any other reports of a similar sighting, as we are both convinced that what we saw was either a spy plane, being used by the military – if not, in my opinion, it is hardcore proof that it is an extraterrestrial spacecraft."*

12th March 2010 – UFO over Dudley Castle – From Birmingham UFO Group

On 12th March 2010, at around 4.10pm in the afternoon, witness 'PJ' was near the entrance of Dudley Castle, with his girlfriend, taking a look at the meerkats in the zoo area. It was a cold and cloudy day. 'PJ' noticed that the meerkats were acting strangely, making noises and all looking up into the sky. He looked up to see what they were looking at and noticed an unevenly-shaped black object. It was almost directly overhead and appeared to be quite high up. Dudley Castle is one of the highest points of the West Midlands, and it was at much higher altitude, so 'PJ' is not sure it would even have been seen from normal ground level. He estimates it was about the size of a car – though this was hard to judge. It initially appeared to be stationary, but then slowly began moving to the left.

Sighting Analysis – Dave Hodrien

"The object that 'PJ' and his girlfriend saw was certainly interesting. It is clearly black or dark in colour, with curved edges. When I first saw the photos I thought it may have been a home-made solar airship, made out of one or more black bin bags; these heat up in the sun and once the air inside them is hot enough, rise into the sky. However it could not have been one of these, because it was cloudy and cold. I feel the most likely explanation for the object was a black or dark coloured Chinese lantern that had been set off in the daytime. Because it was still light, it is probable that the flame within it could not be seen from the ground and would not cause the object to glow. I am certain of this as I have seen lanterns lit in daylight before, first-hand. From the initial zoomed view of the object, a flat edge can be seen at the lower left. The shape of the object is that of a Chinese lantern, with the flat base widening out into a rounded balloon-like shape. I believe the object was tilting, probably due to air currents. In the first photo it can be seen at a heavy tilt, revealing the flat base edge. The second zoom shows the object more at a diagonal, and the third with it upright and smaller as it is gaining in altitude. Case solved? Maybe, but I do find it interesting that the meerkats appeared to be aware of the presence of the object and acting unusually towards it. If it was simply a lantern or balloon, surely they would have ignored it?"

(Source Photos: Copyright Dave Hodrien, BUFOG, 2010)

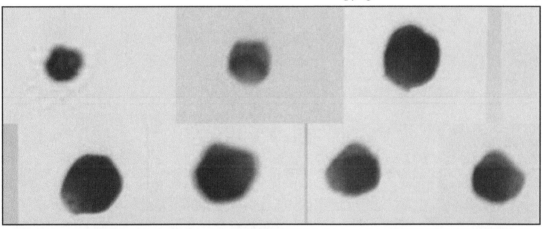

Dudley Castle

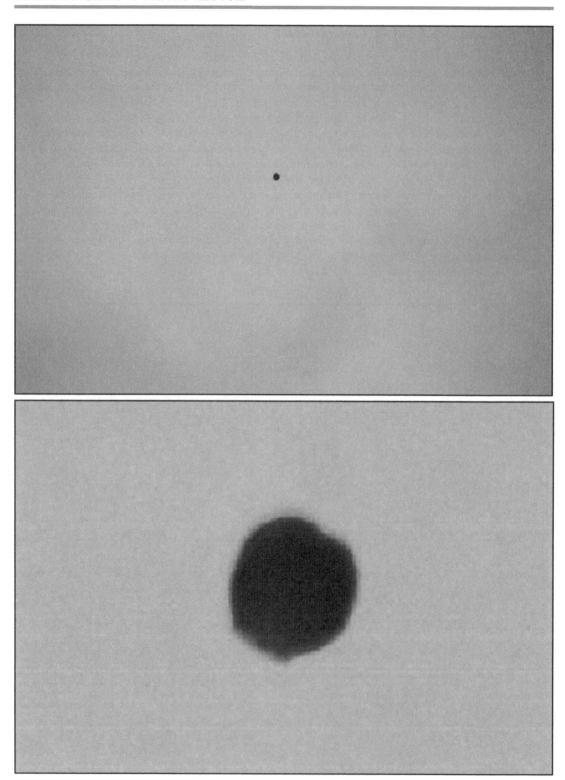

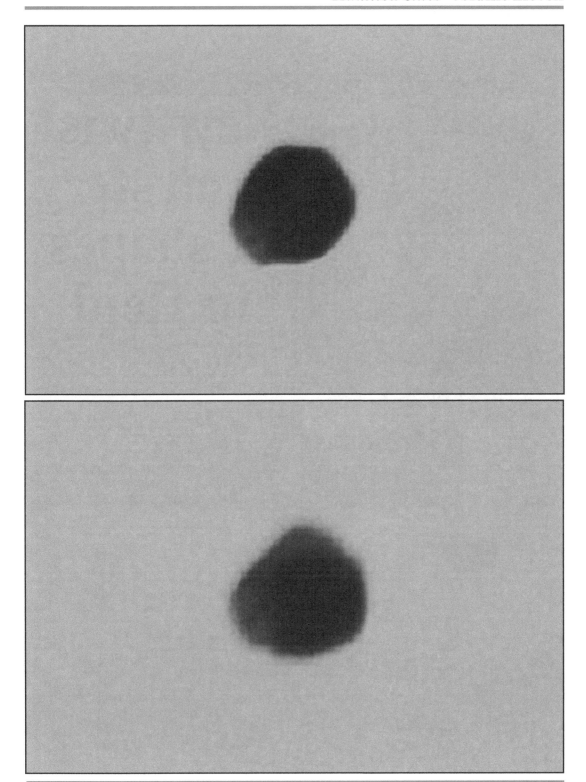

Southern Evening Echo.

3 0 MAY 1990

Cameras could capture the secret of the crop circles

New twist to mystery of shapes in field

CIRCULAR MYSTERY: Pat Delgado investigates the latest series of flattened crop shapes (inset) which have appeared in a field near the Devil's Punchbowl.

Report by Emma Corlett

THE discovery of a formation which breaks all the rules has added a further twist to the mystery of the crop circles.

Two geometrically perfect circles of flattened crops have appeared in a field near Winchester — but the latest find has thrown any theories of a vortex back into the melting pot.

The new formation of oblong shapes is set to capture the imagination of many visitors to the field off the A272 near the Devil's Punchbowl with its peculiar features and enormous size.

"There has been this theory about whirlwinds, but this ridicules the whole idea because here we have long rectangles," said Alresford man Pat Delgado, who has made numerous studies and written a book on his findings.

The 46m long crop formation consists of a huge circle with a rectangular shape attached. At the end of the "box" is an adjoining smaller rectangle with a curved end.

At the tip, a few feet away, is a smaller circle with the unripe crop flattened into perfect spirals swirling in a clockwise direction.

Either side of the main rectangular body area are pairs of long thin rectangles, with comb-shaped edges.

Many people have blamed UFOs or publicity-seeking vandals for the mystery rings experienced worldwide. But they have also captured the attention of scientists, astronomers, engineers, teachers and doctors.

● Research for unravelling the mystery could take a step forward next month with the planned installation of 24-hour surveillance equipment at one of the known formation sites in Britain.

35

MAY 30th 1990, LONGWOOD ESTATE, NEAR WINCHESTER, HAMPSHIRE.

Found on the 30th May, Two striking formations appeared here within one week, first was a three ringed circle, Then on June the 6th, again it was a three ringed circle, but with a difference. It consisted of two split rings and a complete annular ring encompassing the whole, the whole circle measured over 29 meters. The outer ring was clockwise swirled, the next ring was anti-clockwise, the next ring was swirled clockwise, and the inner circle was clockwise.

Then on June the 26th.........

29th May 1990 (USA) – Evansville, Indiana

At 9.45pm, an employee of ˙Evansville Regional Airport contacted Francis Ridge – a Field Investigator for NICAP – after having been contacted by people, who told of sighting a 'stingray' craft at low altitude. The craft was described as silent and moving at a steady but slow pace – much like a helicopter – and displaying approximately 15 yellow, green, and red lights, at an estimated height of 200ft over a populated area, heading in a West to East direction. It then turned South on a curved flight, before disappearing from sight two minutes later.

(Source: MUFON, Indiana, Fran Ridge)

30th May 1990 (USA) – Calumet City, Indiana

At 10.15pm, a 39-year-old mother and her two sons, aged 10 and 12, were relaxing in their home when they sighted an unusual object hovering over a house across the street, described as a 30ft, domed, grey disc, less than 100ft away, around 50ft off the ground, for seven minutes. The object had what appeared to be bright white windows around its circumference, which *'were wider at the bottom than at the top'*. Inside the bank of windows, a dark line appeared to be rotating. On the base of the silent object could be seen a foggy or fuzzy white glow. The UFO then drifted slowly away to the south-west and then left rapidly, going through various green, red, and yellow colour changes, before being lost to sight. It was claimed that a dog was affected by the incident, but recovered the next day. The sighting was corroborated by a Burnham police officer, who called around to the woman's house that night. It shouldn't come of any surprise to discover the younger boy complained, the following morning, of having had a dream about UFOs. One cannot help but speculate if there is more to this mater than we will ever know.

(Source: NICAP Field Investigator I. Bruno Molon)

˙Evansville is located 125 miles west of Louisville, Kentucky, in the far south-west corner of Indiana. The Evansville Regional Airport (EVV) includes a Public Safety Department in charge of fire, crash rescue security and EMS medical protection, throughout the facility and airfields. Each shift – six firefighters and their full-time chief – train and stand ready for any aircraft or public safety incidents.

JUNE 1990

2nd June 1990 (UK) – Three *'lights'* seen

BRIGHT white *'lights'* were seen hovering in the sky over Canvey, by local resident – Denise Radley, at 10.20pm.

"They looked like car headlights. They came towards me out of the sky – two big white beams. They sort of hovered for a while – then went over the houses and away. We saw a red light behind it. It resembled an upside-down saucer. I have never seen an airplane that hovers like that, silently."

Local UFO researcher – Ron West – confirmed he had received at least six similar reports to this, over Canvey, for the same date.

(Source: Ron West, East Anglian UFO & Paranormal Association/
Somerset Standard, Frome, 7.6.1990 – 'Upside-down saucer UFO alert')

6th June 1990 (UK) – Triangular UFO over army base, Essex

At 10.30pm, Carl Jefferson (17) of Layer Road, Colchester Road, Essex, was driving home with his friend, Gary Fisher (22) in his Ford Fiesta car, down Boudicca Way, towards St. Michael's Army Estate. Through the windscreen they saw three orange lights in the sky, fairly high up, forming a triangular shape. In front of the orange lights were a number of blue ones, around what looked like thousands of tiny portholes – none of which were flashing but completely still.

Carl:

"The object appeared to descend out of the clouds, before levelling off and heading towards the Mersea area, about a mile away, at which point we lost sight of it due to trees obscuring our view. We last saw it over the army estate. We decided to go and have a look for it and drove through a thick mist, which had built up in the area. After having checked out the Colchester area, we stopped at the army ranges in Abbotts Road. We were surprised to see the beam of two searchlights switch on from the army ground and move backwards and forwards across the sky, as if looking for the UFO. At this point I left the scene and dropped Gary off at home, before making my own way home, arriving there at 12.30am."

Interview conducted, 24th July 1990

The investigator – Desmond Stacey – had this to say, following his interviews with Carl:

"This is one of the most intense investigations I have ever dealt with and been involved during the last 16 years. I was impressed with what Carl told me and I believe his version of events. Carl took me out in his car and showed me the route taken by him and where the UFO was seen from.

HISTORY MYSTERY

with RICHARD HOLLAND

THE mysterious circles of scorched grass found on a farm on the Denbigh Moors recently has sparked a great deal of talk about UFOs.

Most people assume that the Unidentified Flying Object phenomenon is a recent one, dating from the Flying Saucer craze of the 1950's, when everyone was urged to "keep watching the skies," but in fact UFO-type sightings date back many hundreds of years.

In Welsh tradition they are called tân-we, a "fiery web". The tân-we is described as a "straight and long" light in the night sky which moves in a straight line for three or four miles, lighting the air around it and the ground beneath it.

"When it falls to the ground" — states an old account — "it sparkleth and lightneth all about." They tended to descend on the land of recently deceased persons.

On December 20, 1661, a woman travelling over a common at the village of Weston in old Montgomeryshire fell off her horse in terror at the sight of a "blazing star, which she and six men with her ● sometimes white and sometimes red,

with a tail like an arrow, which seemed to hang just over their heads."

Another UFO landed at Buckley in the 1880's. A fierce dispute had erupted over wages in the Buckley Collieries, and the miners went on strike. So poor did these miners become that they were forced to take up poaching to find food for their families.

Hovering

A group of miners were poaching on land near Padeswood one moonless night when they suddenly felt as if they were being watched. One chanced to look up, and there, hovering above them, was a large, purplish red luminous ball.

They dived for cover and hid under a hedge. Eventually, they raised their heads to take a look, just in time to see "a swirling ball of smoke, with small tongues of flame issuing from the base" ascending into the heavens.

Several weeks later the miners plucked up the courage to revisit the site of the landing, and there they found a circle of scorched grass, just like those found on the Denbigh Moors. There are several people living in

Buckley today who can remember their grandparents recounting this story to them as first-hand witnesses.

The mysterious circles are interesting in that not so long ago country folk would have described them as "Fairy Rings", believing them to be impressions caused by round dances performed by the Fairies at night.

Fairies and UFOs are sometimes linked. A folk tale from the Penrhyndeudraeth area tells of a man watching the descent of "a brilliant meteor" followed by a "hoop of fire." Out of this hoop stepped two little people. They began to dance and were soon joined by other small folk, and they all danced in a ring.

This is just a smattering of old accounts of what we today would call a "Close Encounter." Perhaps one day the mystery of UFO sightings will be solved, but until then — Keep Watching The Skies!

Richard Holland is the author of Supernatural Clwyd; the Folk Tales of North-East Wales published by Gwasg Carreg Gwalch at £4.50.

The locality is a military one, on a large scale, and I learn that some cars had been stopped and the occupants questioned by the military."

Gary was interviewed and he confirmed having seen the object in the sky and that it had three lights, which *'rounded off'* all the corners of the 'triangle'. He described the mist as being unusual and straddling the top of the hill.

Strange vivid dream

When Carl arrived home, he made his way to bed and went to sleep. The next morning, when he awoke, he remembered having had a vivid dream, in which a strong light lit-up the interior of the bedroom.

"I saw my body disintegrating into small oblong squares, accompanied by a strange noise. I then found myself outside the house, next to two people who were not human. Close by, above me, at rooftop level, was a dark, round craft, from underneath which was a thick red beam of light. The next thing was that I found myself back in bed with the red light over me – like a powerful jet of warm water, washing over my head, neck and shoulders. I became frightened. The jet then changed to pink, giving a stronger sensation, and I woke up."

Further Interviews with Carl, 11th August 1990

Desmond spoke to Carl again and learned that the size of the object was estimated to be 300yds by 150yds, with a height of 150yds. The two *'beings'* that he saw in the dream were described as:

"...the tall one had a black beard and our colour skin; the other was shorter and was matt black over his body. They didn't try to communicate with me – that's all I can remember about them."

The object he saw while outside, in his *'dream'*, was much smaller than the one he had seen.

"It had two globes – one on either side of the light. The bottom of the craft was light grey, and it was soundless."

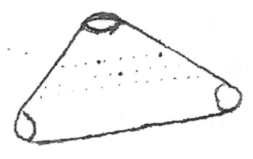

One senses that there is far more to this matter than we shall ever know. We cannot say that any Alien abduction took place in this instance, but would be surprised if it had, bearing in mind the circumstances concerned. We know that many people are unaware they have sustained an experience following a UFO sighting, because of suppressed memories. While the circumstances of this sighting may suggest something far more serious took place, we cannot prove it but we should be concerned as to what lies behind these manifestations and for what purpose?

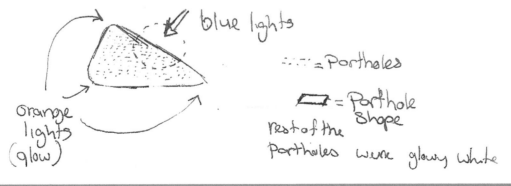

Same date

On the same date, housewife Mrs Kay Marsh (39) of Rise Park, Romford, Essex, happened to look through the window, at midnight, when she saw three red, white and blue, indistinct lights, hovering about 300ft above rooftop level in the sky.

> *"Two were close together. I called my sons Steven (15), Anthony (12), and daughter – Lisa (10), to come and have a look."*

The objects then shot away, 10secs later; one headed northwards, the other (two?) southwards. The family contacted Ron West. He sent Mr Trowbridge to interview them about what they had seen.

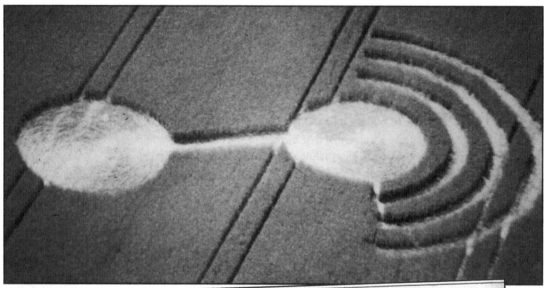

42.

JUNE 6th 1990, LONGWOOD ESTATE, NR WINCHESTER, HAMPSHIRE.
This one has been named 'THE PHOENOX' it was formed in wheat. Notice it has what we call the Dumbell shape, but now has three semi-circles

and not the troughs or boxes.

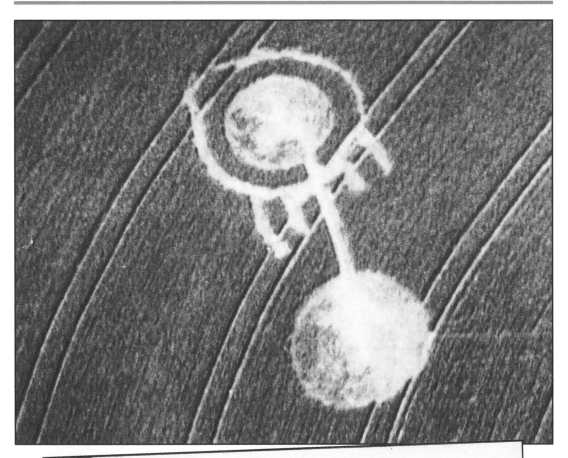

43

JUNE 1st WEEK, 1990. HAZELEY FARM FIELDS.

Another different formation had appeared here. Notice a it has the dumbell shape, one of the circles has an outer ring. It also displays a beak-like appearance from the air and the four fingers have a similarity to jellyfish or octopus tentacles.

7th June 1990 (UK) – Three lights over Birdbrook

8 JUN 1990

STRANGE SIGHTINGS REPORTS ... AND THE 'CORN CIRCLE'

Mystery of the UFOs

SOMERSET is in the middle of a "UFO flap" — reports of strange phenomenon are flooding in faster than anywhere else in the country.

Sightings recently reported in the *County Gazette* brought a storm of interest from Taunton residents, and Quest International investigator Tony Dodd has been inundated with telephone calls.

And the latest reports have coincided with the discovery of a huge "corn circle" on the Nynehead Road, about 1½ miles from Wellington.

Mr Dodd said: "There's no question about it — the sightings are definitely related. Now all we need to know is why the 'flap' is happening."

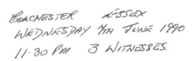

By CARRIE DUNN

On the M5 near Taunton holidaymaker Linda Biggs, of Newport, Gwent, was amazed to see a UFO hovering overhead as she travelled down to Cornwall with her family.

She described a saucer-shaped object about as big as three terraced houses, with a dome on top and a long elliptical light at the front.

She said: "Inside that light were two even brighter ones like car headlamps. We saw one of them move to point downwards towards the ground. Underneath the object was blue and white, and there was a sort of flickering. It was definitely a UFO."

Linda, 32, was with husband David, 38, and children Sarah, eight, and Jenny, six.

She said: "The outline was as clear as a bell. None of us panicked, we were just stunned by what we saw."

■ OTHER recent UFO sightings include one by a coachload of 13 people travelling between Dunkeswell and Taunton.

They reported seeing a huge stationary orange red ball of light hovering over fields at around midnight.

■ IN THE Wellington Road area of Taunton a resident saw a disc-shaped object with legs and red flashing lights shoot across his garden hedge at about 8 pm.

■ AND a resident around Greenway Road, Taunton, saw an orange red light suddenly come down from the sky and start hovering erratically over the sports field before disappearing into the distance.

It was in the middle of this spate of sightings that walkers discovered the "corn-circle" near Wellington.

The large flattened area surrounded by upright corn resembled similar bizarre and unexplained circles spotted in Taunton and Wiltshire last summer.

Mr Dodd is asking anyone with details of corn circles or strange flying objects around Taunton to contact him on 0756 752216.

BLACHESTER ESSEX
WEDNESDAY 7TH JUNE 1990
11·30 PM   3 WITNESSES.

8th June 1990 (USA) – Navarre Beach, Florida – UFO display

At 11.30pm members of the Bridges family observed a cluster of 20-30 lights that appeared to below over the Gulf of Mexico, about ten miles away from their home. These lights were seen to join together in a circular orbit and then shoot out in many directions. Some of the paths were jagged, with sharp turns and abrupt stops, while others were smooth stops. The UFOs would then regroup and repeat the process randomly. Another group of about 20 people, who were visiting in rental units, also saw the display – which was over in 30 minutes.

(Source: Rex Salisberry, *Gulf Breeze Sentinel,* Gulf Breeze, Florida, 14.6.1990)

11th June 1990 (UK) – Crop circles discovered at farm near Bickington

At 8am, Mrs Marlene Huggins – then landlady of the 'Dartmoor Halfway House, which lies on the Newton to Ashburton Road – happened to look outside, when she noticed a large *'circle',* accompanied by seven smaller ones, in the top corner of a field belonging to Little Chipley Farm.

Her husband, Barry, telephoned farmer's wife, Lyndi Westcott, and discovered, through conversation, that Lyndi's father, Fred, had driven past the field at 5am and hadn't noticed anything untoward.

Other witnesses included Tony and Elizabeth Callard of Broadpark, Bovey Tracey, who run Old Well Trees & Shrubs business with their partner, Mike Ware, in a field on the opposite side of the main road. The matter was reported to Ashburton Police, who then contacted the Cornish UFO group. They visited the location and expressed an opinion that the *'circles'* were not man-made, although invariably others suggested it was either the landing of an alien spaceship, practical joke, or a plasma vortex. (**Source:** *Mid-Devon Advertiser,* 15.6.1990 – 'Corn Circles baffle experts')

Mid-June 1990 (Tasmania) – Motorist encounters UFO

A man was driving home alone on a rural road in Sandfly, Tasmania, at 11pm, when he sighted a very bright white oval shape to the right of him. He stopped the car when level with the larger than Moon-sized object – now motionless in the sky – which he estimated to be 90 metres in height. Within a short time the object was seen to depart south-west, at speed. (**Source:** TUFOIC)

15th June 1990 (USA) – Apports of stones & poltergeist behaviour

The small hamlet of Centrahoma consists of a scattering of small houses and trailers, clustering around a tiny post office in south-eastern Oklahoma – an area known as Little Dixie, thanks to its strong Confederate connection during the Civil War. During 1990, this otherwise unremarkable place on the map, with then a total population of 150, was the subject of persistent attention over a four-year period, involving the levitation of stones and other household objects.

'Now the Dartmoor Halfway Inn. Closed until further notice, 2014

DAVE RUDLING

ROUND FIGURE: The mysterious big circles at Bickington

Circles 'caused by whirlwind'

A RARE weather condition caused perfect circles thought to be made by a UFO in a South Devon cornfield, an expert said last night.

Leading physicist, Dr Terence Meaden, said the mysterious circles at Little Chipley Farm, Bickington, near Newton Abbot, were made by a kind of tornado.

The eight symmetrical shapes were spotted in a field near the Dartmoor Halfway Inn on Sunday morning.

Robert Moore, a colleague of

Dr Meaden, said the circles were formed by a type of stationary whirlwind called a plasma vortex.

He said the phenomenon was first discovered in the early 1980s by Dr Meaden and the Circle Effect Research Establishment in Wiltshire.

There was a large circle, about 40 feet across and seven of about 10 feet.

Mr Moore said: "It's a lot more credible than the UFO theories. No one has seen a UFO near

these circles but there have been sightings of the vortex happening."

He said research had been done into other circles found in crop fields in the West Country over 10 years.

Farm owners Fred and Lyndi Westcott believed the shapes were the result of a practical joke.

Mrs Westcott said: "This is amazing. It seems it would have to be a joke."

Similar incident – Birmingham, UK

The series of incidents that occurred appears to have parallels with the stone throwing phenomena at Washwood Heath, Birmingham, UK, which began in 1981 (previously published in *Haunted Skies* Volume 9). The West Midlands Police spent some years painstakingly keeping observations on the three houses concerned. Despite the army being called in to analyse the trajectory of the stones, which continued to fall, nobody was ever caught. Taking into consideration previous incidents we had covered, where outbursts of paranormal activity (some

would refer to as examples of poltergeist behaviour) were reported to have taken place following the digging up of an ancient funeral urn and other ancient relics, we speculated on whether any association could be made between the continuing fall of stones and the discovery that the rear garden path of the middle house, which attracted most of the attention, was paved with old gravestones. Although there had been no physical disturbances to the stones themselves, which had been there for many years, we wondered if there had been some natural movement in the ground that had disturbed the ground and orchestrated the activity to begin happening.

Don Ramkin of HPPI – Apport of stones and a green toy elephant!

Oddly we were to see for ourselves other examples of apports of stones during many excursions to Rendlesham Forest, Suffolk. In addition to this, according to Don Ramkin – a friend of ours from Bexleyheath, London, who is a member of a Kent-based paranormal group – was to witness the fall of a green plastic toy elephant, which fell onto the ground. More from Don and his interesting group in due course, as they have themselves encountered similar incidents which befell the inhabitants of Centrahoma, during their investigations into the paranormal.

Begins with falls of stones

On the 15th June 1990, Centrahoma family Bill and Maxine McWethy – together with their 18-year-old daughter, Twyla, and her baby, Desireé – sought relief from the hot temperatures by moving their chairs into the front yard, hoping for a breeze.

Without warning, a single stone flew out of the darkness and struck the side of the house – then another stone came, followed by a third,

propelled out of the darkness by an unseen hand.

"Stop it!" Mr McWethy yelled, rising from his lawn chair.

More stones quickly catapulted from the darkness beyond the yard.

Bill and Maxine McWethy

Many more follow during the next 24 hours

The McWethys, only mildly annoyed at this stage, sought refuge inside the house – assuming it was local kids playing a prank – but the stones kept on coming, one every few minutes. Some were as small

Desireé Bell

as a thumbnail, others the size of a golf ball. To the McWethys' amazement the attack continued for 24 hours, even breaking some windows. As Centrahoma was too small to have a police station, Mr McWethy and his neighbours tried to investigate the cause of the phenomena, but they could find no source for the stone-throwing.

The next night, just as they were beginning to relax, the stone-throwing began again. The attacks continued, on and off, straight through June and into July. Still no

Brenda Bell

thrower could be caught. Eventually it began to dawn on the family, and the town's residents, that it might be *'a spirit'*. All doubt about it being a non-human agency was removed one July night when close on 50 people gathered at the McWethys' house, trying to catch the culprit.

Stones marked with nail varnish

Someone had a good idea. They marked some of the stones with nail polish and tossed them out into the dark in different directions. Within minutes they came sailing back. Someone else had an even better idea. They threw the marked stones into a nearby pond. Within moments they came flying back . . . wet.

August 1990 – The police became involved

By the middle of August, the family – now frightened – contacted the office of the Coal County Sheriff.

Deputy Bill Ward Jr. arrived in his patrol car, but before he could even get out of his car he came under a fierce barrage of stones. He managed to get out and search for the miscreant, but found no-one. Unable to explain the cause, he left. The family again called the sheriff, requesting that he put in an appearance. He reportedly said:

"If there's nothing I can see to shoot, I'm not coming."

Coins thrown at family

Maxine and her daughter, Twyla, were sitting in the front yard, one hot night, when they were subjected to a pelting – not of stones but coins: pennies, nickels, dimes, and quarters. A few days later, Maxine and a friend walked into the tool shed at the back of the house and were hit by a potentially dangerous 'wave' of screws, nails, and other metal bric-a-brac. They ran back outside, screaming. Even more disturbing was the sound of someone or something in the darkness of the tool shed, tapping away on an old typewriter.

November 1990 – Activity now inside the house

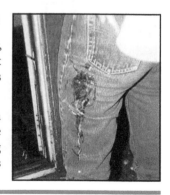

In November, the weather forced the family indoors. To their horror, whatever had been throwing the stones followed them inside – now not just throwing rocks and coins but bottles, eggs, and whatever odds and ends happened to be lying around.

The McWethys say that although these things were obviously pilfered from around the house, when they were thrown they seemed to simply materialise in mid-flight. The family would enter empty rooms to find that something had stripped the bed-clothes off the beds and draped sheets and blankets over two or more chairs to create makeshift tents.

Family contact newspaper for help

Seeking answers, the McWethys appealed to the *Coalgate Record Register*, the local newspaper. Two reporters were dispatched, one of whom – Helen Langdon – later admitted that the trip to the McWethys was accompanied by a certain amount of sniggering at the supposed ridiculousness of the story they had been sent to cover.

Stones thrown at the reporters

No sooner had the two reporters arrived than Mrs McWethy appeared on the porch, excitedly urging them to *"get in here, now!"* The two reporters scurried into the small white-frame home. Bill, Twyla, and Desireé, were already in the kitchen. The floor was covered with small stones. Instantly an attack of stones began from all directions at once, focusing on Twyla. The reporters, aghast, closed all doors leading into the kitchen and checked for holes in the ceiling and floor. The rocks continued zooming around the room for 45 minutes – like popcorn kernels exploding.

Helen Langdon, shocked and frightened, and suddenly feeling a need for spiritual comfort, asked aloud if this manifestation could be *"of God"*. Immediately the stones focused on her, assailing her from all directions. They all moved into the living room and *'it'* followed them. Helen sat on the couch next to Twyla. She noted in a few minutes that when Twyla stood up, stones had seemingly formed under where she was sitting. Twyla also said that when she woke up in the morning, there were often stones in bed with her. There was no doubt that Twyla was the focus of the phenomenon.

High-pitched noise

Twyla and her mother began hearing a high-pitched *'pssst'* sound around the house. The sound then resolved itself into a voice. Following a short report on the local public television station in Oklahoma City on the incidents, Peggy Fielding – a writer from Tulsa – and her colleague, contacted the McWethys and arranged to visit their home.

Ghost had popped to town – be back shortly

They arrived at the house on Saturday, 16th July. Upon entering the kitchen they were accosted by a number of people, who had spent the previous night in the house to experience the ghost. These were not members of the family and told the two women the ghost was still around and that it had slapped them, pushed them, pulled their hair and scratched them the night before. In fact, they said that it had just gone into town with Twyla and would be back in a few minutes *"You'll hear it. It makes a sound."*

Mrs McWethy welcomed the two women warmly and assured them that Twyla would be back in just a few minutes, accompanied by the poltergeist.

The spirit identifies himself as Michael Dale Sutherland

One of those present was an amateur investigator of psychic phenomena – Shirley Padley – who said she had tape-recorded the ghost. She played a tape of a high-pitched metallic sound (not human) that did, indeed, seem to be saying, *"This is Michael."*

"That's what he calls himself", she said. *"Michael Dale Sutherland."*

Twyla, Billy Joe Mc Wethy (hidden in back), Bill, Kim, and Bill's nephew Randy Baldwin

Shirley Padley

Shirley Padley had originally gone there to do a story with a television crew from a local station. She left thinking it was a hoax, because the sound the ghost made was just too strange. Later, she returned and became convinced. She said she had searched all through the southern United States for paranormal phenomena, but had found nothing real except this.

"There was a ghost. It threw things, it attacked people, it talked and it would be back in a few minutes. On top of that, the place had an electromagnetic atmosphere you could drive a nail into, it was so thick. It felt like being in the presence of a large, silent, invisible generator."

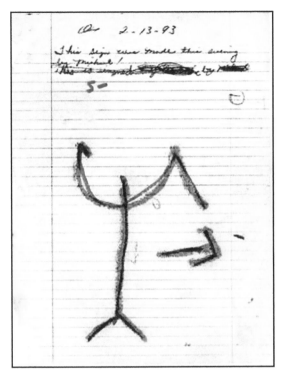

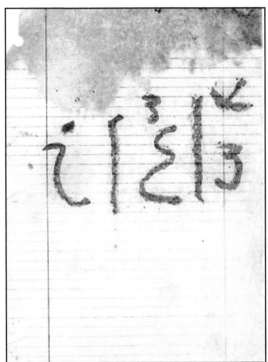

Some of the 'symbols' drawn with lipstick by the entity.

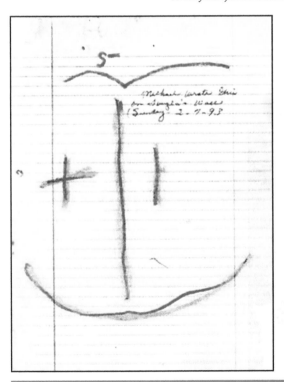

Desireé with spirit

Parakeets painted by entity

Mrs McWethy:

"Oh, he did that; he threw food colouring all over them. He warned me the night before. He said, 'I'm going to paint your birds'. I heard them squawking this morning. He'd thrown food colouring from the kitchen on them."

Peggy Moss Fielding was in the kitchen.

"I called out, 'come in here'. I hear him! The ghost had apparently arrived a few minutes in advance of Twyla. I could hear a high-pitched mewling sound – like a cat, only different. It was roaming around the house, from room to room, one minute seemingly next to us and the next minute far away in one of the bedrooms."

Heather Bell (back), Desireé Bell and spirit (left)

Mrs McWethy said: *"He usually picks out somebody to pick on."*

"What makes him pick out one person?" she was asked.

"He can tell who is the most scared", she said.

Is it an alien being?

Twyla came into the house (now aged 22). She sat down wearily at the table and I introduced myself.

"What is this thing?" she was asked. *"We could hear it mewling in a nearby room."*

"I think it's an alien", she replied. *"I really do. Once he took me to a field and showed me a place where all the grass had been pressed down, like something had landed there."*

"...A spaceship?"

She replied, *"He says he's from Saturn"*, she said, *"...and that he got left behind"*.

It then mewled from the living room.

Witnesses, Kim and Steven Carrell

"Of course, he lies a lot", Mrs McWethy added. *"He followed me home one time. He draws things with lipstick on the mirrors around the house, too … symbols. Some of them … we don't know what they are. This one we found in a book. It's the symbol for Saturn."*

They showed some copies of symbols the poltergeist had allegedly drawn. One was the astronomical sign for Saturn.

Peggy Moss Fielding, passed away in 2014

Peggy Moss Fielding is an Oklahoman who spent several years outside the USA in Cuba, Japan, and the Republic of the Philippines. She lived in Tulsa, Oklahoma, where she was a full-time writer of both fiction and non-fiction and taught writing, part-time, at Tulsa Community College. Fielding has published hundreds of articles, short stories, and several non-fiction books, which include contemporary and historical novels. She often spoke at Writer's Conferences and Seminars across the United States and belonged to Romance Writers of America, The Author's Guild, International Women's Writing Guild, Oklahoma Writers Federation, Inc., Oklahoma Mystery Writers and the Tulsa Night Writers.

Peggy and three other ladies wrote a book called *Chick~Lit for Foxy Hens*; it was only natural to give them the moniker of 'Foxy Hens'. There were

Peggy Moss Fielding

four more Foxy Hens books written with various contributing authors. Peggy specified she didn't want a big funeral but instead wanted her friends to gather together to tell stories of her life, antics, and what she meant to us. She also assisted Barbara Bartholic, a UFO Investigator, to write her book.

Barbara Bartholic, UFO investigator passed away in 2010

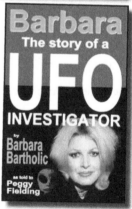

"My research began with hosting the Heaven's Gate people before they were Heaven's Gate. I went on to work for seven years with Jacques Vallée. He was portrayed as the French scientist in the movie, 'Close Encounters of the Third Kind'. Vallee and I travelled around the US and around the world researching cattle mutilations, UFO sightings and abductions."

(Barbara died on the 10th November 2010 from a stroke, aged 71)

Authors' comments

We were not there. We cannot even image what the family and the others that came to investigate had to endure. We have tried, to the best of our ability, to record what took place from what is available on the internet. We were unable to speak directly with Barbara and Peggy, as they had passed away. We emailed the Sheriffs department, hoping that they might be able to put us in touch with Bill Ward Jnr., and are awaiting a reply. We also left an email messages with Helen Langdon.

The sheer scale of frightening behaviour reported by the witnesses is difficult to comprehend in the cold light of day, when rationality and logic take over.

It is always easy to 'write-up' about incidents like these unemotionally when you weren't there. For those that were, how do you come to terms with attempting to understand the complexities of something that is normally invisible but adopts a humanoid shape when caught through the lens of a camera? So many questions and so few answers!

In folklore and parapsychology, a poltergeist (German for 'noisy ghost') is a type of ghost or other supernatural entity supposedly responsible for physical disturbances including loud noises and objects, such as everyday household items, being moved or thrown through the air. In addition to this, people have reported being physically assaulted in a variety of ways that has included being pinched and bitten. They have been traditionally described as troublesome spirits, who haunt a particular person instead of a specific location.

Such alleged poltergeist manifestations have been reported in many cultures and countries, including the United States, Japan, Brazil, Australia, and most European nations, with early accounts dating back to the 1st Century. The truth of the matter is that we cannot actually identify the root cause of an apparent intelligence who selects certain people as a conduit for their 'displays'. One wonders whether we should feel animosity towards something judged by some as demonic in nature, or sympathy for a tormented spirit.

Over the years we had spoken to many people who had told of close encounters with UFOs and their occasional occupants. Quite often, depending on the severity of how exposed those people were to the fields of radiation given-off, this appears to dictate further sightings or manifestations to occur. Although some of the people that came to investigate the fall of stones and other strange phenomena have now passed away, it is important we ensure history remembers their courage and commitment.

Taking into consideration the highly respected views of Trevor James Constable, and the comments made by Dr. Josef Allen Hynek (The Center for UFO Studies), born 1.5.1910, died. 27.4.86, US Astronomer/Scientist, Scientific Adviser to three consecutive UFO studies, undertaken by the US Air Force – Project Sign 1947-1949, Project Grudge 1949-1952, and Project Blue Book 1952-1969. Josef was asked in 1976 how he would react to the suggestion that UFOs may originate from another space-time continuum or dimension. He indicated the ET hypothesis was 'naïve' and felt it was an unlikely explanation for a phenomenon which takes into consideration various factors, strongly suggesting a linkage, or at least a parallelism, with occurrences of a paranormal nature. He also pointed out those reported instances when distinct, different UFOs, will converge and fuse into one object (many examples of which will be found in our books) and remarked, *"I'm anxiously waiting for the curtain to rise and the next act to begin."*

Early 1990's – Police disturb ghostly man at scene of burglary – Manchester

Mark (Spike) Thornton, Ex Detective Sgt Greater Manchester Police, contacted us in 2013 about a strange incident which took place during the early 90's:

"I was teamed up with a colleague on the Sub Divisional van, coming to the end of a night shift on a lovely summer morning when we got a call that an elderly lady in an area called Bowden, had been

subject to an aggravated burglary, having been lead round her home for most of the night by a male at knife point. Obviously, we got there as quickly as we could and upon arrival I ran up the garden path arriving at the front door with my colleague Sue just behind. I noticed that the front door was partially open, so I started to open it, shouting that the police were here.

As I started to open the door, I heard a female voice shout, 'Come in, I'm in the back'. I then opened the door. The layout was a narrow hallway leading to a staircase about 20 feet in and to the left about 10 feet in was a doorway leading to a front living room. As you can imagine, 6.30am on a summer morning, the day was bright and warm and her hallway was fully illuminated. As the door opened I was shocked to see a white male, approx 6ft tall, short dark hair, wearing light coloured trousers and a dark brown shirt, maybe in his late 20's early 30's, walk quickly from the hallway into the front room. I didn't see him face on but caught his side profile as he walked into the room.

I immediately assumed the burglar was still present and ran in after him. I was no more than maybe two to three seconds behind him and as I ran into the living room, a room approximately 13ft by 13'ft with no other exits, there was absolutely no sign of him. I stopped dead in my tracks and have to say that the temperature in the room was decidedly cold, bearing in mind how warm it was outside. Sue arrived in the room behind me, asking me what I'd seen. I told her, not wanting to appear stupid, that I was just checking the room for the aggrieved party. She looked at me very intensely and said 'No way', she went on to say that it had been obvious from the way I had entered and that I shouted stop, even though I don't remember that, that I had gone in to get to someone. That I had followed someone rather than casually looking into a room to see if anyone was in there.

She asked me again what I had seen, so I told her. She looked me in the eyes and immediately offered to go and check outside for any signs of the offender. Although I was a little freaked out myself, I had to smile at how quick Sue left the premises. I went on to find the witness in the back of the house and we dealt with her as you do. Later on, I mentioned that I thought I'd seen the offender in the house as I entered but she confirmed that he'd left almost an hour prior to our arrival. She had been delayed in contacting us as the offender had locked her in an upstairs bedroom. She asked me to describe what I had seen and was actually smiling as she asked. I described the male to her and to my amazement, she simply said, 'Don't worry, that's just my guardian angel. How do you think I got out of a locked bedroom, to phone you in the first place'. As you can imagine, I felt as if someone had just walked over my grave!!!!!! Sue and I talked about the whole situation as we drove back to the nick. She was convinced that I had seen someone and I can only believe what my eyes showed me. Was it a ghost, a guardian angel or something else, I'll let you make your own decision?"

Brenda Butler's investigations into paranormal happenings

We should remember that Leiston, Suffolk, woman – Brenda Butler – was not only involved in the investigation of UFO activity but also in incidents of a paranormal nature. According to files kept by her and Ron West, we learnt of a number of matters brought to their attention during the 1980s.

The Black Horse Public House, Leiston

The inexplicable incidents included a horrible smell and difficulty with opening the cellar door, which was slammed shut by an invisible force, lights coming on of their own accord, and taps being opened, according to the then Landlord – Fred Hammond – at *The Black Horse Public House*, in Leiston.

In 1988, the new landlord – Larry Lamb, and his wife – told of hearing

Brenda Butler with long-time friend and researcher, Chris Pennington

strange footsteps echoing through the pub on a number of occasions. The pub is now under new ownership as an Indian restaurant, known as the *Kingfisher*. Oddly, there has also been similar phenomena reported taking place at the The White Horse Inn on Station Road, in Leiston, which is said to be haunted by a poltergeist. It is claimed terrified members of staff and guests alike witnessed bottles and glasses flying off shelves, and doors in the pub opening and closing on their own accord. Things got so bad that an exorcism had to be performed in the pub!

Haunted house – Romford, Essex, 1968

In December 1968, nursing auxiliary Carole Mason (44), and her husband, moved into Bovey Way, South Ockeden, Romford, in Essex. They were accompanied by their two young children – Sharon (3) and Steven (1). Carole learnt that the previous occupier, who had passed away, was an old gentleman that collected cycles – of which there were still some kept in the shed.

After settling the children down for the night, during the evening of the 20th of the same month, Carole began to relax. However, the peace was shattered at 8.30pm by the children screaming. Carole ran up to the bedroom and asked her daughter what the problem was. She was stunned when the girl told her:

"There was an old man stood at the end of the bed; he had a grey beard."

On another occasion Sharon was physically pulled out of the bed and her favourite 'comforter' – a teddy bear – was thrown across the room.

The manifestations continued with further reports of the *'man'* being seen in the room by the child. Carole also had an Alsatian puppy which refused to go up the stairs and seemed very agitated. Carole made some enquiries in the close locality and spoke to a neighbour. He told her:

> *"You will regret moving into that house."*

The sound of ghostly footsteps was also heard. Things became worse; Carole found her husband sat in the chair, he seemed very frightened. She asked him what the matter was. He replied:

> *"Look at the handset on the telephone mounted on the wall."*

She looked and saw it was swinging to and fro and that a heavy breathing noise could be heard coming from the receiver.

Carole:

> *"We heard glass smashing in the kitchen; the dogs hackles came up. We went into the kitchen but found nothing.*
>
> *A few days later my husband was making a cup of tea and I was sat in the lounge, when my husband shouted 'Come in', because he thought I was in the garden and had banged on the window. I awoke at 6am, to make the baby's bottle up, to find glass all over the draining board sink, window ledge, and even in the garden."*

Carole was unable to discover where the glass had come from, as there was no glass objects kept in the house. The local vicar was informed and came around, remarking on how cold the house was, but didn't carry out an exorcism. From the information contained in the written notes, submitted to Ron West by Mr Peter Oliver, who conducted an investigation, it appears that the family had enough and moved to St. Mary Grays. Interestingly, before they moved, they threw the cycles out from the shed – which seemed to resolve the situation, as the manifestations ceased.

19th June 1990 (UK) – UFOs over Suffolk

In the early hours of this morning, residents of Newmarket reported having sighted strange luminous objects in the sky. One of them was Steven Milne of Tunbridge Close. He was out at 1.30am, when he saw:

> *"...strange green lights in the sky; there was a block of three going around in circles across the sky".*

At 2am, Clive Humphries and his sister, Camilla, saw the same phenomena in the sky over Freshfields, Newmarket. Enquiries were made with Mildenhall Airbase. However, they denied any knowledge. One explanation for what was seen was laser lights being used to celebrate a 'May Ball', somewhere!

(Source: Ron West/*Newmarket Journal*, Suffolk, 19.6.90 – 'Lights in sky spark UFO mystery')

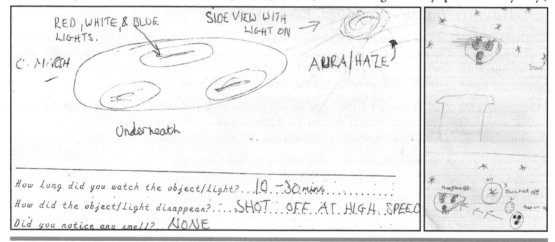

Western Evening Herald – Plymouth. 25 JUN 1990

Mystery circles in a field of cereals at Bickington

Crop of theories over circles

Amateur investigators in the Plymouth area still believe UFOs may be responsible for mysterious crop circles found in South Devon despite conceding that the latest discovery may be a hoax.

The new circles were found on a farm at Bickington, just off the A38 on the road to Newton Abbot on Saturday and were similar in shape to those found earlier at nearby Chipley Farm.

Although many believe the Bickington circles were the work of pranksters there is still argument over how the ones at Chipley Farm were created.

The latest findings has opened up the long running debate over how and why the circles, which have been found throughout Devon and Cornwall, were made.

UFO investigators from the Plymouth area who have inspected the new circles still believe UFOs are the believable answer to the question.

Bob Boyd of the Plymouth UFO Research Group said: "I don't believe it could be anything meteorological like a whirlwind that has cause it. That is stretching the imagination more than the UFO theory.

Lawrence Harris, chairman of Plymouth's Astronomical Society believes the circles were the result of air being blown through a narrow wind tunnel between two hillsides.

21 JUN 1990 Newmarket Journal. Suffolk

Lights in sky spark UFO mystery

NEWMARKET star-gazers could not believe their eyes when they saw what appeared to be unidentified flying objects hovering in the sky above the town in the early hours of Tuesday.

Stephen Milne, of Tunbridge Close, Burwell, was arriving home at around 1.30am when he saw what he described as "strange green lights in the sky".

"I was looking towards Cambridge and there were four lights that went together in a block and then went round in circles.

"I thought it might be lights from a fair but as far as I know there wasn't one on. Lots of people saw it," he said.

The lights were also seen by Clive Humphries, of Freshfields, Newmarket, at around 2am.

"There were four green lights, like disco lights. They kept splitting up and then going together again, just hanging in the air. My sister Camilla and some of my friends saw them as well," he said.

USAF Mildenhall spokesman Frank Randall confirmed the lights had nothing to do with base activities.

"We had no traffic in the air at that time on Tuesday as we close down from 10pm to 6am. Our midnight shift reported no unusual sightings in the area," he said.

■ The latest theory is that rather than a visitation from an outer planet the lights were laser beams from May Balls at Cambridge Colleges.

26th June 1990 (Australia) – *'Light'* seen

At 10.43pm over Gympie, Queensland, three people saw an orange-red *'light'*, low in the east, at treetop level. It then moved across the sky at tremendous speed, heading north-west. When it reached the northern horizon, it suddenly performed an upward movement, then down again. It seemed to stop, then travel on until out of sight. (**Source: UFO Research, Queensland, Gympie Branch**)

CIRCULAR MYSTERY FOR UFO SPOTTERS

A GROUP of UFO enthusiasts have been left scratching their heads by a mysterious series of perfect circles staining a Norfolk road.

Members of the East Anglia UFO Research Group, founded five months ago in Lowestoft, are trying to find out what made four large circles along a stretch of country lane near Hingham.

The group's founder, Mr Derek Longman, has been to study the marks but said there was no obvious explanation for what caused them. But members of the group are keeping an open mind before leaping to conclusions, he added.

One theory they are investigating is that the marks are linked to the mysterious flattened circles of corn that have been appearing in fields since the early Sixties.

The group has contacted experts on the crop circles but they have been unable to come up with an answer to the puzzle.

"Personally, I think somebody made those marks but I cannot think how or think why," said Mr Longman.

The four perfect circles, which first appeared last October, cover almost the entire width of the road. Mr Longman said that although they look like tyre marks they do not overlap and seem to be a stain in the tarmac.

The group, which meets at the Forbes Alehouse in Oulton Broad, is keen to hear from anyone who has any idea about what caused the circles.

Passer-by John Rath examines the mystery circles which have UFO spotters puzzled

30/6/1990
EASTERN EVENING. ECHO

JULY 1990

3rd July 1990 (Australia) – UFO after-effects

AT 6.10pm, three people were surf fishing off the sunshine coast at Bokarina, when they noticed a large, bright, moon-sized light. The object remained stationary for several minutes, and then started moving towards the sea. All the witnesses felt physically affected, some nauseous.

(Source: UFO Research, Queensland [Sunshine Coast Branch])

5th July 1990 (UK) – UFO over Mansfield, Nottinghamshire

6th July 1990 (Australia)

A motorist at Wurtulla, Queensland, noticed a bright, low, hovering object, which looked like a street lamp, some 300 metres away and 150 metres up. As he manoeuvred his car for a better look, the object disappeared after some 15 seconds – as if *'switched'* off.

(Source: UFO Research, Queensland [Sunshine Coast Branch])

CHAD
-Mansfield-

25 JUL 1990

Did you see it?

Mansfield UFO Group would like to make an appeal to anyone who saw a strange object or lights on the 5th of this month in the Mansfield/Pleasley area between 5 and 6pm.

An object as yet unidentified was seen by a Shirebrook man who believes it must have been seen by someone else as it was daylight and quite busy at the time.

Anyone with information please contact Mansfield 632622 or 660796 after 5pm.

L. TRUEMAN.
6 West Hill Drive,
Mansfield.

10th July 1990 (UK) – UFO sighted over Leyton

WALTHAM FOREST, N.E. LONDON.
CHINGFORD. GUARDIAN FRI 13TH July 1990

Eerie encounter of the UFO kind

A MAN claims he came face to face with a UFO on Sunday evening as he stood in a friend's garden in Leyton. *

The 'close encounter' happened at around 6.30pm when he looked up from the garden in Vicarage Road and saw a small round object swaying to and fro in the sky above him.

The 'UFO' had red, yellow, and green lights, which were moving.

And another man in the same area claimed he "felt compelled to

Paranormal report by Kelvin Ross

look up" and also saw the object, which hovered above him for around 10 seconds.

The sightings have now sparked an investigation by the East Anglian UFO and Paranormal Research Group, led by Roy Lake.

And it is not the first time mysterious objects have been seen in the sky over Waltham Forest.

Ten years ago several Walthamstow residents reported seeing a "golden ball of fire" over the Priory Court area, and after that so many incidents were reported that Waltham Forest was called a "centre for UFO activity".

In 1973 a nine-year-old Chingford boy saw a plate-shaped glowing object as he walked home, and in 1982 a mystery light followed a couple through Walthamstow streets.

Now the UFO and Paranormal Group wants to hear from other local people who saw the same object on Sunday, or have had any other types of sighting.

If you want to contact the group call the UFO Hotline on 081 594 4797.

Southend Evening Echo – Essex.

13 AUG 1990

Researchers seek clue to power-cut UFO in the sky

UFO researchers are on the trail of two mysterious flying objects seen hovering around Twyford Avenue in Great Wakering, at the beginning of July.

In the first case a local woman spotted the object about 300 yards from her back door. It was circular with three lights and three brighter lights inside, and appeared at about 8.30pm on Friday July 6.

UFO investigators in South East Essex are convinced it is the strongest-ever sighting in the area. Power in the woman's house went off three times while the object hovered.

After it took off over her roof at a 90 degree angle, her power came back on.

Another UFO, this time a mass of bright lights, was also spotted off Twyford Avenue at around

8pm on April 16.

Now members of East Anglian UFO and Paranormal Research Association, which covers South East Essex, have launched a 24-hour phone hotline in a bid to find out more about the strange objects.

Club secretary Bernie Carr, of Hall Avenue, Aveley, said: "We want to find out as much as we can about this UFO because we know it wasn't a plane or wind balloon.

"It's the first case we've heard of where electricity has gone off and we would love to establish exactly what it is. That's why we've set up the helpline and are asking anyone who might be able to help to call."

The hotline number is 0375 373065 or you can phone Mr Carr on 0708 860363.

Early July 1990 (UK) – UFO with three lights, over Essex

12th July 1990 (UK) – *'Flying saucer'* over Wimborne

Mrs Sheridan Lane (The Pubic Relations Officer for Ron West's group) was to find herself the centre of UFO attention, at 11.20pm. She was in bed, at the

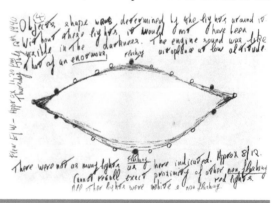

time, when she heard the sound of an approaching engine similar to that of a low flying plane.

As it seemed to be over the house, she went to the window and looked out. *"It was now about 80ft high over our garden. I was amazed and knew this was no plane"*, she said.

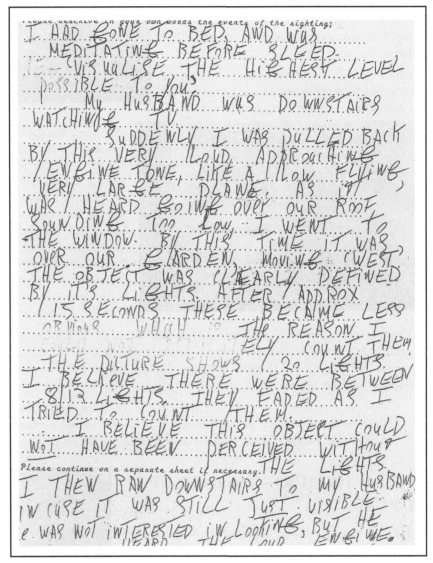

12th July 1990 (Australia) – UFO interacts with railway locomotive

At about 3.40am, fireman Fred Torre and engine driver Leo Sorbello, were in the cabin of a Babinda Sugar Mill Locomotive, travelling south between Strouds Nursery, Deeral and Harvey Creek. In a glimpse lasting one or two seconds, Leo saw an illuminated object move at high speed from the railway line to the right of the engine area. The whole front of the engine lit-up a reddish colour and Mr Torre called out to the driver (Mr Sorbello) *"Leo we're on fire!"*

Mr Sorbello immediately applied the brakes. As the locomotive was travelling at top speed (about 15mph), it took about 20 seconds and some 20ft before it stopped.

Mr Torre saw a glowing round object move from the front of the battery box and torque converter into the battery box – a gap of a little over three inches.

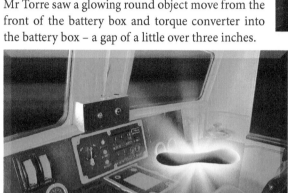

The object elongated itself, *"stretched out like chewing gum but didn't separate in two"*, to get into this space. Mr Torre said he does not know why but he got the impression that it was losing energy while it was trapped in this area. It didn't seem to have the strength to lift itself over the battery box and move away. The object then moved through one of the gaps in the engine floor, and struck one of the wheels. It turned red, *"glowed like a coal"*, and completed a full circuit of the wheel, before disappearing under the train – which then pulled up.

Mr Torre grabbed his torch and billycan and leapt out of the cab to try to capture whatever this thing was. He searched under the locomotive, the tracks around the locomotive and the surrounding area, for about 10 minutes, without success. He could have stayed longer, but the driver was becoming extremely agitated and so they went back to the mill.

> *"The shape of the object was round, with a definite edge. The shape changed when it squeezed through a gap of about three inches. It was approximately 1-2ft in diameter and its colour was pale, fluorescent, and moonlight in color – whitish-yellow – which changed to a reddish glow when it hit the wheels."*

13th July 1990 (UK) – Triangular UFO over Hull

The police were called after a woman resident of Hessle (south-west of Hull) and her 13-year-old son, told of sighting an object, at 11pm, with flames shooting out from the rear. Through binoculars she described it as being:

> *"...triangular-shaped when viewed sideways, with a squared rear end; it hovered for 30 minutes in the sky, before suddenly heading vertically."*

(Source: *Hull Daily Mail*, 14.7.1990 – 'UFO blazes into view over City')

13th July 1990 (USA) – Manchester, New Hampshire

At 7pm, a teenage girl reported having sighted a brilliant light from her bedroom window, rise up and hover over a swamp across the road from the house, a few hundred feet away. She realised this to be the forward light of a tapered cylindrical object, which then rotated to reveal its length enabling her to see square lights, or windows, equally spaced along the mid-section of its dark grey metallic surface. At one end was a horizontal cable; at the other end a red light. The object glided along laterally, until she lost sight of it behind a line of trees. (**Source: Dan Wright MUFON**)

14th July 1990 (UK) – UFO conference, Sheffield

– 5 JUL 1990   SHEFFIELD JOURNAL

I was kidnapped by an alien!

We're No. 1 for News

A WOMAN who claims to have been kidnapped by beings from another planet is coming to Sheffield to tell her story.

The International UFO Conference is being held in Sheffield at the Central Library on July 14 and 15.

Northamptonshire woman Elsie Orkinson, former head of a teaching centre and married to a police inspector at the time of her alleged abduction, is one of many witnesses giving first hand accounts.

Philip Mantle of the Independent UFO Network, who is organising the conference, said: "We will be breaking new ground.

"One of the Soviet Union's leading experts on UFOs Dr Vladimir Rubtsov will be at the conference.

"It will be the first time a Russian ufologist has ever spoken about UFOs outside of his own country.

"And we have one of America's top UFO speakers Budd

By ALAN CHARNLEY

Hopkins in Britain for the first time."

On show will be several photographs of spacecraft including one which has been tested at various places — including Kodak — to prove it is genuine.

Philip added: "The conference will be open to the general public and we are quite happy for sceptics to come along and listen to what is said.

"One of the highlights will be Elsie's account. She is an intelligent woman who insists she was abducted for a time by beings from another planet."

Philip Mantle,
Independent UFO Network

17th July 1990 (UK) – UFO conference, London

Camden & St. Pancras Chronicle
London

12 JUL 1990

Flying saucers

THE latest information about flying saucers and other unidentified flying objects will be revealed at a public meeting at 7pm next Tuesday (July 17).

American UFO expert Budd Hopkins will address the British UFO Research Association at the London Business School, Regent's Park.

17th July 1990 (Australia) – Queensland UFOs

At 5.10pm over Innisfail, Queensland, two policemen sighted an object:

> *"...like the flame from a Bunsen burner turned on its side, and approximately the same as the diameter of a full moon, move slowly across the sky. Three minutes later it was out of sight."*

(Source: *UFO Journal*, February 1991, p. 11)

Alice Creek – 5.30pm

A resident of Alice Creek observed a yellowish, shiny object, move across the sky in a west-north-west direction. In a few minutes it was out of sight.

6.15pm – Cairns

Forty-five minutes later, a man was sat at the Pier Shopping Complex, in Cairns, looking north-west, when he saw a bright orange object, leaving a trail, move across the sky, heading from south-west towards the north-west – gone in a minute.

7.25pm – Browns Plain, Brisbane

Wayne and Michelle – a young couple – arrived home. While Michelle was parking the car in the garage, Wayne saw a *'light'*, which descended through the sky in two to three seconds. The *'light'* stopped and started five times during its descent. A few seconds later, the *'light'* reappeared. By this time, Michelle had parked the car in the garage and had come outside. It then blinked red, blue and white, and moved away once again, before vanishing to a small point of light. Three or four seconds later, it suddenly reappeared (as if someone had turned on a large spotlight). When Michelle asked what it was, the object descended behind a house. A couple of seconds later, it reappeared again, moving back into the sky at a much slower pace than before. It moved towards them, passing over their home.

"The object was shaped like an aircraft, with no wings. It had a soft, blinking red light on its tail and lights on its underside. A whooshing sound, like a jet makes, was heard as it passed over us. We saw four lights on the underside of the object."

The object maintained its starting and stopping motion. As the couple ran to their backyard, its movement stabilised and it was last seen heading towards the direction of Brisbane.

7.50pm – Cairns

The activity continued with a sighting from the same locality – this time involving two painters, who, while packing up their gear, at 7.50pm, saw an enormous orange flame-like object, heading towards the Mareeba area to the north-west. It left a long trail in the sky and, even though they were looking towards the setting sun, the head of the object appeared to be silver in colour and was very brightly illuminated. The men took photos of the object, during the five minutes it took to pass overhead. The whereabouts of these photos are not known.

17th July 1990 (UK) – Budd Hopkins lecture, London

18th July 1990 (USA) – UFO over New Hartford, Connecticut

A woman was lying awake in bed, when she noticed bright flashing lights over her backyard. She went to the window and witnessed a small domed *'disc'*, hovering 100ft away, descending over the corner of the lawn. The object manoeuvred a few seconds without actually touching down. She noted it had flashing red, yellow and white, lights around its bottom rim. It then accelerated and was out of sight behind some trees in a second.

Two days later, a hired worker asked her about some strange material on the grass. She realised it was in the area of the sighting. After eliminating the local landscapers as responsible for an oily residue on the grass, she decided to report the incident.

(**Source: Randy Miles,** *MUFON UFO Journal,* December 1990, p.19)

---

18 JUL 1990   LONDON EVENING STANDARD

Aliens are taking our babies for a ride . . .

by Tim Cooper

ALIENS are abducting women and stealing their babies, according to a leading American authority on the subject.

Well, you don't need to lock up your daughters just yet, but the news was announced in all seriousness at the London Business School last night by Budd Hopkins, who has written two books on alien abductions.

There was no dissent among the 100 UFOlogists who crammed into a lecture hall in Regent's Park to hear and see the evidence.

Mr Hopkins, a painter-sculptor from New York, has spent the last 15 years studying the phenomenon of alien abductions.

He claims to have documented more than 300 individual cases, including pregnant women whose babies "disappeared" after their close encounters, confounding them, their gynaecologists and the fathers-to-be.

The victims are always, so far as one can gather, returned to terra firma after being whisked aboard alien spacecraft for a once-over by an ET GP.

They witness some strange sights—four ft aliens with grey skin and big black eyes, piles of extra-terrestrial corpses and even half-human half-alien crossbred babies. Once abducted, the victims are likely to be whisked into the ether again and again.

Mr Hopkins said he had never been abducted and had no such wish for himself or his family.

Children and young people seemed to be a particular target for the aliens, said Mr Hopkins, who showed slides to illustrate their experiences, including their impressions of the aliens they had encountered.

You had to admit they all bore an uncanny resemblance to each other. You also had to admit they looked like close cousins of the aliens in Steven Spielberg's Close Encounters Of The Third Kind.

As for his own opinions, Mr Hopkins displayed a reluctance to go on the record. "I don't think they come from Birmingham or Central America," he opined, adding, helpfully: "They come from somewhere else."

Wherever they do come from, he thought they proba-

Budd Hopkins: "I don't think it is an invasion"

bly had some kind of "genetic evolutionary problem" hence their eagerness to examine humans so closely and take our babies.

"I don't think it is an invasion," declared Mr Hopkins to the audience, members of the British UFO Research Association. "It could be some kind of infiltration. But I see terrible psychic damage coming in the wake of it.

"This phenomenon is very large worldwide. It is very upsetting. It has a very ominous quality.

"We are faced with something that deserves investigation, not ridicule."

DAILY STAR

THE PAPER THAT GIVES IT TO YOU STRAIGHT

THURSDAY, JULY 19, 1990

ALIENS 'SNATCH UNBORN BABES'

ALIENS are kidnapping babies for research, British UFO experts were warned yesterday.

They are even beamed up from the **WOMB**, baffling mums-to-be and gynaecologists. But they are almost always returned to Earth unharmed.

Some, though, are re-captured many times, so that alien boffins can watch how they grow up.

The astonishing theory comes from America's leading UFO expert, Budd Hopkins, who claims to have investigated more than 300 cases over 15 years.

Speaking at the London Business School, he told members of the British UFO Research Associa-

By NICK CONSTABLE

tion: "It could be some kind of infiltration.

"This phenomenon is very large worldwide. It's very upsetting. It has a very ominous quality.

"We are faced with something that deserves investigation, not ridicule."

19th July 1990 (UK) – *'Flying saucer'* over Wimborne

Electrician Graham Dodson was repairing a cable in a field near Wimborne, Dorset, during the afternoon, when he noticed a *'bright light'* similar to the evening star in the blue sky, about 45° off the horizon, which he presumed was sunlight reflecting off an aircraft. Ten minutes later, when he looked up again, it was still there. Curious, he went to the car and fetched a pair of binoculars and looked through.

> *"I was totally astounded to see, instead of a bright twinkling object, when viewed with the naked eye, a dark, round, inner core, with bright coloured shimmering lights rotating around its outer surface. I felt a shiver move down my spine and thought this was nothing constructed by human hands.*
>
> *I watched it for about 20 minutes, during which time it never moved – then it did, disappearing into the distance very quickly.*
>
> *After the sighting was reported in the local newspaper by my boss (who I told), I received a lot of 'stick' from my friends and colleagues, but I know what I saw."*

Air Traffic Control, at Bournemouth International Airport, suggested he might have seen a weather balloon, or a mirage caused by hot weather, as an explanation.

(Source: Personal interview/*Bournemouth Evening Echo*, 20.7.1990 – 'Close Encounter with UFO gives electrician a shock')

20th July 1990 (USA) – Pensacola, Florida

A retired navy pilot, and his wife, saw a huge bluish-white glowing orb in the sky over Pensacola, Florida, at 7.30pm. It was then seen to arc downwards and head away towards the direction of Pensacola Bay.

(Source: C. Joseph Barron, *MUFON UFO Journal*, December 1990)

22nd July 1990 (UK) – Glowing object over Peterborough

Peterborough pensioners – Dorothy Bird (71) and Anne Bingham (84) – were outside their home address at Stanground, Peterborough, when they noticed what they took to be a brilliant moon, shining in through the windows, at 6.45pm (unlikely to be the explanation, as the moon rises in the east).

Stoke on Trent Evening Sentinel

20 JUL 1990

Big rise in sightings of UFOs

By Andy Stanistreet

REPORTS of unidentified flying objects in South Cheshire and North Staffordshire have soared over the last 12 months.

Officials at the Cheshire UFO Studies Centre in Earle Street, Crewe, received 120 calls on their 24-hour hotline — an increase of 20 per cent.

Mystery

Most of the sightings concerned mystery lights in the night sky over the Crewe, Stoke-on-Trent and Stafford areas.

Investigations by experts from the centre have ruled out 95 per cent of the lights as UFOs — most of them being traced to aircraft or satellites.

But they are still engaged in a six-month inquiry after two separate callers reported a close encounter with a 35ft "bright object with a glowing centre" which landed in a field near Audlem — and then vanished.

Centre chairman Mr

Eric Morris said: "Most of the people who call us are genuine, and many are worried or frightened by what they have seen.

Strange

"After inquiries with the RAF, the Ministry of Defence, airports and interviewing witnesses, we can explain about 95 per cent of the strange things people see — but there are still the rest which remain a mystery."

The centre is to launch a magazine recording all its reports of UFOs, its investigations into each incident and conclusions.

On going outside they saw an object, the size and shape of a big red glowing colander, hovering in the sky. Five minutes later, it disappeared from sight. (**Source:** *Peterborough Evening Telegraph,* **24.7.1990** – 'Pensioners spot glowing red UFO')

Peterborough Evening Telegraph.

24 JUL 1990

1671

PENSIONERS SPOT 'GLOWING RED UFO'

A UFO sighting by two city women is being treated seriously by personnel at a local airbase, and will be reported to the Ministry of Defence.

Staff at RAF Wittering have taken details of the sighting by two shocked city pensioners, who watched spellbound as a luminous object hovered in the sky for nearly FIVE minutes.

And Flight Lieutenant Bob Chalmers, the base's community relations officer, said:

"We had a similar report of a red light in the sky about three years ago, and nobody can rule out something extraterrestrial being involved."

The two women, Dorothy Bird (71) and Annie Bingham (84), described the object as "the size and shape of a big red glowing colander."

They spotted it hovering in the skies while they were in the garden of Mrs Bingham's home in North Street, Stanground.

GLOWING

The amazing sighting comes as the mystery of strange crop circles — found all over Britain — deepens. Earlier this month mysterious circles appeared in a cornfield at Gedney Drove. Mrs Bingham said: "We saw a big red glow in the sky. We must have been watching for nearly five minutes, then it disappeared behind cloud."

Mrs Bird saw what she thought was a brilliant shining moon from her friend's window on Sunday. The two women then both went out into the garden and could see a round, red glowing light.

Mrs Bingham said: "We just stood speechless watching it. It could not have been the moon because it was only 6.45pm in the evening and the moon rises in the east."

● If you spotted the UFO or think you have seen one recently please ring the ET newsdesk on 555111 and tell us about it.

The nearest thing to the UFO spotted by Mrs Annie Bingham (left) and Mrs Dorothy Bird — a flying red colander. (Photo: 9007926/26)

23rd July 1990 (Australia) – Sausage-shaped object seen

A couple was travelling home to Camooweal from Mount Isa, at 6.35pm, when they saw a sausage-shaped object, which appeared to be about a foot long in the sky. It was displaying a number of green lights and one large, very bright, white light. They stopped the car to observe the object, and kept it in sight for five minutes, before it *'took off'*. It went down to a pinhead in one second before disappearing towards the Gulf, between Darwin and Normanton.

25th July 1990 (UK) – Cross-shaped UFOs seen

A housewife living in Wansford Road, Woodford Green, in Essex – previously married to a RAF fighter pilot for 35 years, during which time she had lived on various airbases – was waiting for the dog to come back inside, at about 1.30am, when she noticed a shooting star, which was followed by a misty ribbon of cloud, prominent in the clear night sky just under the 'Plough' constellation.

> *"I was surprised to see in total seven bright lights of a pinkish-orange colour emerge from the 'cloud' one after the other. These then flew away towards the north-east direction. Each light was in the shape of a plus sign, or cross – the 'tail' being slightly longer that the remaining three 'arms'. Each 'cross' was quite chunky. As they moved away I heard a soft rhythmic whirring noise – like a steady gentle wind with a continual beat to it. As they moved away it was as if space itself came alive; the blackness had a depth to it and was like a liquid."*

The witness contacted the Civil Aviation Authority, who informed the MOD, and was later sent some forms to fill in. (**Source: Roy Lake**)

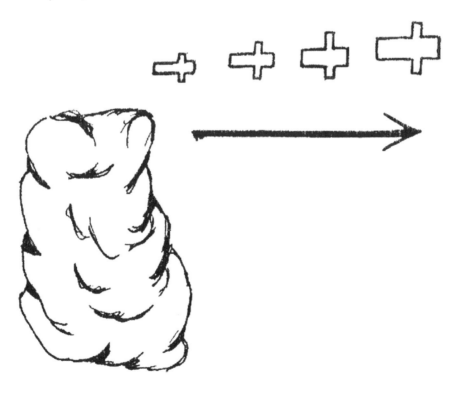

On the same date, 'an enormous round, shiny craft, glistening in the sunlight' was sighted in the sky next to a power cable, by delivery man – Peter Simpson – who was dropping off a parcel in Millgreen Road, Mitcham, when he saw the unusual object – which then disappeared, making a whooshing noise. (**Source:** *Croydon Post*, **Surrey** – 'Peters UFO encounter – UFO leaves ground traces?')

28th July 1990 (Australia) – Domed *'disc'* paces car

At Thornlands, Queensland, at 9.20pm, a motorist encountered a dome-shaped object, which *'buzzed'* his car. The man later developed conjunctivitis of the eyes following the encounter.

> (Sources: Keith Basterfield, UFO Research, Queensland;
> Timothy Good, *The UFO Report* 1992, p125)

Domed *'disc'* paces car

Another similar report was made over the same locality. Was there a connection? This one happened at 9.20pm and involved Mrs Amanda Green and her three children, who sighted a saucer-shaped object, with a dome on the upper structure, showing white and flashing red/green/white and yellow lights, in the sky to their left, as they drove through Thornsland.

Amanda:

> *"I drove quite near it to get home, almost passing underneath it. When I arrived home, the object was still visible. Hoping to get my husband out to see it, I ran into my home – only to find that, when we returned outside, it had vanished. The sighting was only five minutes, but the kids later complained of sore eyes."*

29th July 1990 (UK) – UFO display over Bicester

30th July 1990 (UK) – Oblong UFO seen over Stansted Airport

During the evening an object, described as oblong in shape, was sighted moving through the sky over Stansted. There were seven witnesses to this. One was an ex RAF serviceman, who was out fishing with his uncle by a lake, when he spotted something heading towards the airport from the South.

> *"It had an oblong front, was lit-up with searchlights, and flat around the back with two red lights to the rear; there was no engine noise. Despite the fact that it was just 200yds away from me, it remained motionless for about 10 minutes – then the lights went out and it disappeared."*

Bicester Advertiser – Oxon.

3 AUG 90

Lights in the sky

Strange lights in the sky have left a Bicester family feeling puzzled.

The Chambers family were at home in Kennedy Road, Bicester, around 11.30pm on Sunday night when they saw the mysterious lights rotating and pulsating in the sky.

Mr and Mrs Richard and Shirley Chambers, sons Danny and Sean, daughter Shirley and her boyfriend Dale Grant, all saw the lights.

An unnamed police officer who attended, and took a statement from the man, contacted Stansted Airport about the matter, and learnt from staff there that six other people had reported similar sightings.

A Ministry of Defence spokeswoman said:

> "The vast majority of reports we receive are very sketchy and vague. Only a handful of reports in recent years have warranted further investigation and none revealed any evidence of a threat."

30th July 1990 (UK) – Cylindrical UFO seen over Boscombe Down

Four members of a family from Hopton, Great Yarmouth, sighted:

> "...a red object with a rear light, apparently descending over farmland. The following morning a circular impression was found in the grass, surrounded by ten equidistant smaller circles."

(Source: Ivan W. Bunn/David Dane/*Eastern Daily Press*)

This would appear to have been the same evening when *"a cylindrical object, showing two large red lights at the top and bottom, with an orange light either side of the middle, making a heavy laboured noise"*, was seen by Porton resident Jane Manning-Philips, at 10.30pm, who watched it fly over Porton School, towards Highpost, and then around to Boscombe Down – where it disappeared from view.

(Source: *The Avon Advertiser*, Fordingbridge, 8.8.1990 – 'Did you see it, asks Porton Physiotherapist?'/Personal interview)

An appeal in the local newspaper attracted a reply from Mr J.V. King, who wrote to the *Avon Advertiser* on the 22nd August 1990, informing the readers of having seen an identical object, at 6.30am, at Salisbury, in May of that year, described as *"a glowing red object, seen to move backwards at an amazing speed."*

Crop marks found in fields

As we enter August 1990, we discover that a flurry of 'crop circles' were brought to the attention of Ron West, who painstakingly captured many of them on photos following personal visits made. Sadly, some of the films were lost in the post. It would be impossible to record, chronologically, the many incidents involving these fascinating phenomena, which have always attracted the public's attention over the years. However, it would be a disservice not to publish the result of Ron West's research.

One wonders if there was a connection with what was seen by two children – Lucy Humphries and Debbie Stares – who were at Lawlinge Playground, in Essex – important enough to bring it to the attention of the local Press.

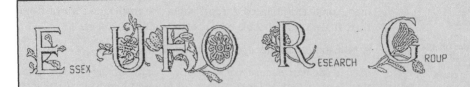

MINUTES OF PUBLIC MEETING HELD ON 3rd AUGUST 1990

STANWAY SCHOOL, WINSTREE ROAD, STANWAY, COLCHESTER

1)   Meeting opened at 7.25pm.

2)   Twenty three persons were present at the meeting, thirteen members
     and ten members of the public.

3)   Our Chairman, Ron West, opened the meeting and introduced the present
     members of the group. He also outlined the aims of the group and
     invited the non-members of the group to become members if they wished.

4)   The Chairman then invited Les Stacey, our President, to speak. Les
     thanked Ron for the time, money and effort that he had put into the
     group. Les also thanked his two sons, Clive and Peter, for their work
     in distributing leaflets and posters in the Colchester area. He also
     thanked all persons present for attending our first meeting. Les also
     mentioned apologies for absence received from Simon Poyser, Young
     Conservative's, Chelmsford and Adam Stacey.

5)   Les then handed the meeting back to Ron, who talked for the rest of
     the evening on various U.F.O. cases and 'Flying Saucers From The
     Earth's Interior.

6)   We then held a general discussion on the evening's events.

7)   The last twenty minutes of the meeting were spent in enrolling new
     members and the sale of Newsletters.

8)   Of the ten members of the public present, seven became members.

9)   The meeting closed at 10.00pm.

10) The next meeting is on Friday 17th August 1990 at Stanway School
     at 7.00pm.

     Signed.   Witnessed

AUGUST 1990

1st August 1990 – UFO over Long Eaton

A SILVER coloured UFO was reported over Totton sidings, at Long Eaton – and explained away!

Southend Evening Echo - Essex

−3 AUG 1990

Stargazer is transfixed by strange light

A SHOOTING UFO had a South East Essex stargazer reaching for the skies as a glowing white light zoomed across the night sky.

Garden centre supervisor Julia Diggines was walking home from work on Canvey when she spotted the single bright light hundreds of feet high.

The light, above King's holiday camp, sped along for some distance before changing direction in mid air.

Julia, 23, of Hart Road, Thundersley, was transfixed for minutes as the strange object lit up the skies.

She said: 'I didn't have a clue what it was. I didn't know whether it was a shooting star that had hit something and been forced to change direction.

"I have never seen anything like it."

The UFO sighting comes during a lull in reportings of unexplained objects.

In March UFO experts were flooded with calls of sightings of a white rotating light in the skies over Southend.

But since then little has been heard of out-of-this-world transport.

Mr Bob Easton, investigator with Technical Phenomenon Research which investigates sightings, said he had not had any other reportings of the unusual craft.

But he would speak to Julia and look into the matter.

A UFO sighting has been reported to Long Eaton police station.

A Long Eaton man insisted he saw a shimmering silver object hovering over Toton Sidings.

East Midlands Airport said they had no radar report of an unidentified craft — and suggest the object was a mischievously-designed hot air balloon.

LONGEATON HERALD

Maldon & Burnham Standard, Essex

2 AUG 1990

Strange landing

LUCY Humphries and I were watching the sky when something strange happened. A round thing came in to sight it was sort of red, orange, yellow it landed in a field.

We were so amazed we kept waiting and watching, but I forgot to mention that it was in Lawling playground.

Getting back to the story it seemed to be flashing and going up and down. We saw this thing go up in the sky then some back down again. We wish we had more proof but we have not. We thought this would be a good story — we think they might be U.F.O.s.

3rd August 1989 – UFO meeting

Essex UFO Research Group holds its public meeting at Stanway School, Colchester.

3rd/4th August 1990 – Corn circle discovered at Fordham, Colchester

AUGUST 4th 1990, FORDHAM PLACE FARM, FORDHAM, COLCHESTER, ESSEX.
This set of circles is called the Dumbell. It was reported to me
by Mr Ian Kedar, owner of the farm. As you can see there are two
circles joined to-gether by a 52 foot pathway. The overall length
was 128 feet 6 inches. Circle A, measured 38 foot 6 inches by 37
foot 6 inches. It had an off centre indentation. Measurements from
the off centre indentation were 18 foot 6 inches by 20 foot, East to
West and 18 foot 6 inches by 19 foot North to South. The corn was laid
in a clockwise direction, with no damage to the corn. This was
connected to a 52 foot long by 5 foot 10 inches wide pathway. The
corn in this pathway was laid in a North-Easton direction. This
then entered the second part of the Dumbell which measured 38 foot
6 inches by 39 foot. It also had an off centre indentation.
Measurements were 18 foot 6 inches by 20 foot East to West and 18 foot
6 inches by 20 foot 6 inches North to South. It also had a clockwise
swirl to the corn.

Case E/90/502.   Inv Les Stacey.   Fordham,
                            Ron West.   Colchester.

On Tuesday afternoon it was reported to me by a witness, living
in Fordham, that on Friday night she had been looking out of her
dining-room window whilst having tea (3rd August 90) at the corn-field,
there was a complete sea of corn moving slightly with the wind. But
on Saturday 4th August 90, whilst having breakfast, she noticed a
circle had appeared over-night. On investigating this circle, the
following details emerged: The field belonged to a Mr J Jinks of
Fordham Hall Farm, Fordham, Colchester. The overall size was 45 foot
north to south and west to east, with an off centre indentation.
This circle was made up of three circles:- Centre circle was 39 foot,
round, with the corn laid in a clockwise swirl, around this was a
further circle of standing corn 4 foot 8 inches wide, then beyond
that was a circle 1 foof 2 inches wide, with the corn laid in a
clockwise swirl, beyond that the corn wasstanding. There were no
tracks leading to the circle. The corn was bent over and not broken.

Diagram:-

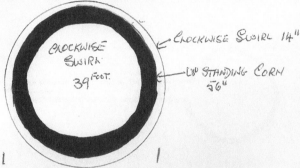

;;;

Case E/90/501.   Inv L.Stacey   Fordham.
                                      R.West.   Colchester.

On Monday the 6th August 1990, Les, Clive, Peter and myself investigated
a circle reported to us at Fordham Place Farm, Fordham, Colchester.
This circle in the corn was discovered on the 4th of August by the
farmer Mr Ian Kedar. There were two circles with a pathway joining
them together. The circles were not the same in size,,but both had off
centre indentations. The size of the circles were (A) 38 ft 6 inches
by 37 ft 6 inches, (B) 39 ft by 38 ft 6 inches, the pathway joining
the two circles was 52 feet long by 4 ft 4 inches wide. The corn was
laid in a clockwise swirl in both circles, the corn in the pathway
was laid in a straight line facing northwest.

Diagram of circles:-

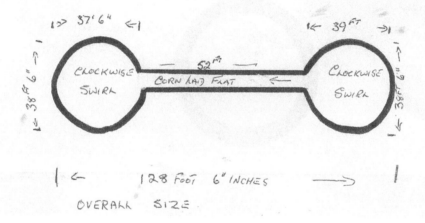

TUESDAY 7th AUGUST 1990 FORDHAM HALL FARM, FORDHAM, COLCHESTER, ESSEX.

This double ring circle was reported to us as having appeared during
the night/morning of the 3/4th August 90. The land belonged to a Mr
John Jinks of Fordham. Having obtained his permission. Les Stacey,
our president and myself entered his field to investigate the circle.

We measured a circle of 45 foot. It consisted of three circles in one.
The inner circle of clockwise swirled corn measured 39 foot in all
directions, but it had an off centre slight indentation. Measurements
of this were N to S 18 foot by 21 foot and E to W 18 foot by 21 foot.
Then there was a circle of standing corn measuring some 56 inches at
all points. Then there was a third circle of clockwise swirled corn
14 inches wide.

38.

Case E/90/504.   Inv Les Stacey,   Fordham,
                               Ron West.   Colchester.

On Wednesday the 8th August I was in a light aircraft taking photo's
of the Fordham circles when I noticed two other circles on the ground.
The following is the first of these circles which Les and I investigated.
This was the strangest of all the circles we had investigated so far.
I think the best way to put it to you is in the following diagram.
In our oponion this circle was not a hoax.

Diagram:

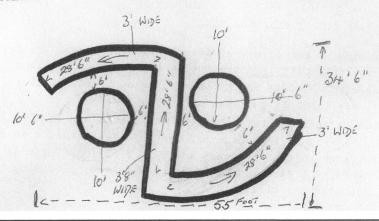

4th August 1990 (UK) – Noisy UFO over Norfolk

A member of a farming family at Knapton, near North Walsham, Norfolk, was disturbed by dogs, barking, and what sounded like a power saw cutting through timber. When they looked outside they saw a bright orange globe, covered in lights, rotating on its outer edge in the sky. The next morning they found the batteries in the tractor to be flat, along with the discovery of circular impressions in the nearby barley crop.

(Source: David Dane)

4th August 1990 – Crop circle found, Essex

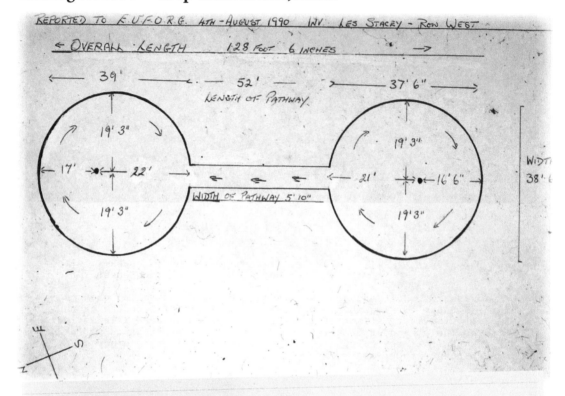

8th AUGUST 1990. LITTLE CLACTON, ESSEX.

This is a drawing of the circle at Little Clacton, Essex. The farmer not wanting the publicity, or, the public walking over his land, distroyed the circle before any photo's could be taken. However measurements were taken by me, they are as follows:-

The circle had an anti-clockwise swirl. From N to S was 36 foot 2 inches E to W 34 foot 6 inches. It had an off centre indentation, N to S 16 foot 6 inches by 19 foot 8 inches and E to W 15 foot 7 inches by 18 foot 11 inches. The farmer distroyed the circle by ploughing the section up that held the circle.

4th August 1990 (UK) – Was RAF jet intercepted by diamond-shaped UFO?

UFO BUZZED RAF JET

Secret memo sent to Cabinet over scare

BY **STEPHEN WHITE**
s.white@mirror.co.uk

A UFO report was taken so seriously it was passed to Cabinet ministers, it emerged yesterday.

Secret files released by defence chiefs show the sighting baffled experts.

They even had photos of the 75ft wide diamond-shaped object "buzzing" an RAF Harrier near the village of Pitlochry,

Perthshire, on August 4, 1990. Witnesses said it hovered for 10 minutes before zooming off at high speed.

The mystery – which remains unsolved – is detailed in a newly declassified MoD memo at the National Archives in Kew, West London.

In it, a Whitehall official admits bringing the case to the attention of ministers was "unusual" and requests drawings of the object, saying the "sensitivity of the material suggests very

special handling". Ex-MoD official Nick Pope said: "It was far beyond the most modern stealth aircraft being trialled at that time. The picture was assessed by our digital experts who concluded it was a real solid-structured craft.

"My opposite number in defence intelligence pointed his finger to the left and said, 'It's not the Americans', then to the right, saying, 'It's not the Soviets'.

"Finally he said, 'That only leaves...', and pointed his finger directly upwards.

PRICES TO GROUT ABOUT

▲ **SPEEDY** A sketch of the UFO that buzzed jet like one above

According to declassified files, released in early 2009 by the UK Ministry of Defence, we learn that the *Scottish Daily Record* newspaper was approached by two men [whose identities have never been released – at least to the public] and shown six photographs of a triangular object, seen hovering in the sky for about 10 minutes over the A9, at Calvine, twenty miles north of Pitlochry, underneath which were seen military aircraft making a series of low-level passes under the UFO, before it moved upwards, at great speed, and out of sight. [*The Scottish Daily Record* has never published these pictures.]

Sir Archie Hamilton

An MOD minute, prepared for the then Armed Forces Minister, Sir Archie Hamilton, dated 14th September 1990, states:

> *"Under-secretary of State (Armed Forces) may wish to be aware that the* Scottish Daily Record *may run a story regarding an alleged sighting of a UFO near Pitlochry [sic] in early August. Such stories are not normally drawn to the attention of Ministers and the MOD Press office invariably responds to questions along well-established lines, emphasising our limited interest in the UFO phenomenon and explaining that we therefore do not have the resources to undertake any in-depth investigations into particular sightings. The photographs show a large, stationary, diamond-shaped object past which, it appears; a small jet aircraft is flying. The negatives have been considered by the relevant staff that have established the jet aircraft is a Harrier (and also identified a barely visible second aircraft, again probably a Harrier) but have reached no definite conclusion regarding the large object."*

Dr. David Clarke

Dr. David Clarke – a university journalism lecturer and UFO expert – said:

> *"This is the most tantalising of all UFO reports. The files show that a year after the original photographs were taken, the MOD tasked experts to produce line drawings of the UFO, which would give officials an idea of scale. Even the creation of the drawings was shrouded in strict secrecy. One undated document suggests 'very special handling', because of 'sensitivity of the material'. It also orders 'minimum handling by listed personnel'."*

Freedom of Information request made

In a Freedom of Information request made to the MOD in respect of these photos, we were told quote:

> *"We have a record that two members of the public contacted the* Scottish Daily Record *newspaper to report a large diamond-shaped UFO hovering for about ten minutes, before ascending vertically upwards at high speed. The witnesses said that during the sighting a RAF aircraft, believed to be a Harrier, was in the area. The sighting was over Calvine, 20 miles North of Pitlochry, 4th August 1990. A number of colour photographs were taken and passed to the* Scottish Daily Record, *who in turn sent the negatives to the MOD. These were examined and it was considered the jet was a Harrier. No definite conclusions were reached regarding the large diamond-shaped object. Our records show that the negatives were sent back to the* Scottish Daily Record."

Nick Pope

Former MOD civil servant Nick Pope, who dealt with UFO reports, described the image as the *"most impressive"* ever shown to his department.

> *"The MOD has all sorts of equipment and expertise that we used to analyse and enhance imagery to tell whether there were any signs of fakery. This picture was assessed by our digital experts, who concluded it was a real photograph showing a solid-structured craft, which was estimated as being around 25m in diameter. There were no wings and no visible signs of any propulsion system. It was exotic and unknown in a way far beyond even the most modern Stealth aircraft being trialled at that time. I remember going to a briefing with the Defence Intelligence Staff, where the photograph was discussed. My opposite number in Defence Intelligence pointed his finger to the left and said, 'It is not the Americans', then to the right, saying, 'It is not the Soviets', and finally, he said, 'That only leaves...' and pointed his finger directly up.*

The photos were then sent to the Defence Intelligence Staff (DIS) who then sent them on to imagery analysts at JARIC (Joint Air Reconnaissance Intelligence Centre). Yet at the time, MOD hadn't even publicly acknowledged that there was any intelligence interest in UFOs at all. The whole situation was positively Orwellian. On the one hand, our line to Parliament, the media and the public, was that UFOs were of 'no defence significance'. We implied and sometimes stated that we didn't 'investigate' UFOs, but merely 'examined sightings to see if anything reported was of any defence interest' – as if the two were somehow different! I sometimes felt like Winston Smith, working for the Ministry of Truth. This was – literally – doublethink."

'UFO Data' magazine – 2007

This was not the first time Nick had mentioned this matter. In the edition of *UFO DATA*, published in July/August 2007, Page 34, 'The Nick Pope column' under the heading of 'The disappearing photograph', he refers to:

"Spectacular image of a UFO, a silver coloured craft – perhaps no more than a couple of hundred feet above the ground, if that. It looked diamond-shaped, but may have appeared triangular when viewed from underneath. This was something I'd come across in other investigations and was a feature of reports in the Belgian 'wave' and the Cosford incident. A colleague told me the story surrounding the image being taken; apparently the UFO had been seen near Pitlochry, Scotland, in 1990."

Book: 'Open Skies, Closed Minds'

Nick then outlines what he has said already with regard to the picture being removed from the wall by the Head of Division. In Nick's book – *Open Skies, Closed Minds* (Simon and Schuster Publishers, 1996, page 176) – he refers to the incident and discloses the photographs were sent to the *Scottish Daily Record* and the MOD, and dismisses any suggestion that the photos showed the top secret USAF Stealth aircraft, *Aurora*.

Questions raised in Parliament

"At some point in 1994, my Head of Division (a civilian, equivalent in rank to a one-star military officer, and long since retired) had somehow convinced himself that the craft was a secret prototype aircraft or drone – probably American. But in response to repeated sightings of triangular-shaped UFOs, capable of hovering and then accelerating away rapidly at high-Mach speeds, we'd just received assurances from the appropriate US authorities that the US wasn't testing anything like this over the UK. On the basis of these assurances, Defence Ministers had assured Parliament that no such aircraft/drones were being flown – so perhaps my Head of Division thought this was a lie and thought he was being loyal when, one day he took the photo away and locked it in his desk drawer. On the other hand, he was probably the one who drafted the Parliamentary assurances, so maybe he was just covering his back."

Martin Redmond, MP

Martin Redmond (MP for Don Valley, until his death in 1997) asked a question in the House of Parliament, along with various requests made under the FOI as to the whereabouts of this photo, but was told by the MOD that *'it could not be located'*.

Appeal for information – Who were the two men?

We emailed the Library in Perth, hoping that a search of the local newspapers – the *Perthshire Advertiser*, *The Courier* and the *Strathearn Herald* (on the dates given) might have contained some information relating to this incident – but there was nothing. We also emailed various newspapers in 2010, appealing for the men to come forward, but nothing was heard. What we found strange is why the two men concerned didn't contact another newspaper, following the newspaper's decision not to publish their photographs?

Were they warned off?

Despite the passing of nearly 20 years, these men have never come forward and contacted the media, wishing to bring the matter to the public's attention. Or were they warned not to? Whilst we have no qualms about accepting Nick Pope's opinion as to the validity of the genuineness of the photo, we felt unprepared to accept these were genuine without at least identifying (1) The person that carried out the photographic analysis (2) what were his qualifications? (3) The precise nature of the work carried out? (4) Did the MOD interview the men who had taken the photographs, if of course, they even existed in the first place?

Scottish Daily Record

One is bound to wonder about the role played by the editor of the *Scottish Daily Record* newspaper, who it is alleged interviewed the men from that office. On what grounds did he decide these photos were not to be published, and why did he send them to the MOD? Why has he never spoken out since (as far as we know) about this matter, and why is it that on another occasion, the *Scottish Daily Record* – when presented with photos taken by Ian Macpherson on the 19th February 1994, showing a UFO over Craigluscar Reservoir, near Dunfermline – not only sent his photos to the MOD but published them (albeit blown up and fuzzy) in an edition of their newspaper, on the 28.2.1994 – 'Is it a hubcap, a hoax or UFO?' – (in contrast to the local newspaper, the *Dunfermline Press*, who published a clear photo showing far more clarity)

No conclusions can be reached

In view of the lack of information available surrounding the circumstances in which these photographs were taken, followed by their subsequent examination by the MOD and the identities of the persons responsible, how on earth can we form any conclusions as to their validity at this present time?

We sent recorded delivery letters, with stamped-addressed envelopes, to the newspaper editor at the *Scottish Daily Record*, in 2010, asking them for any comment, but like the emails sent previously, they never replied – which makes one wonder what they have to hide? (**Source: Dr. David Clarke, PRO, reference Nick Pope. DEFE 24/1940/1 - page 114-DEFE 31/179/1 - pages 157-8-DEFE 31/180 – pages 55-57-DEFE 31/180/1 - pages 37-38**)

Nick Pope – Rendlesham files inadvertently destroyed

"What happened next? The suspicion was that someone had shredded the photo, but whatever the truth of the matter, it was never seen again. The same thing had happened with some Defence Intelligence Staff files on the Rendlesham Forest UFO incident that it turned out had been inadvertently destroyed and I was in the same position again: I think some people thought I'd put all this stuff through the shredder myself, but I promise I didn't. This was some years before the UK got its Freedom of Information Act. At the time, shredding the photo – if that's what happened – would probably have been a legitimate (albeit unfortunate) action. If such an action happened post-FOI, and was a deliberate attempt to circumnavigate the Act, it would have been illegal."

'Open Skies, Closed Minds'

"Ufologists first came across this story in 1996, when I mentioned it briefly in my first book, Open Skies, Closed Minds. *The story broke in the media in March 2009, when the MOD released the third batch of UFO files to the National Archives, as part of the wider program to declassify and release the entire archive of UFO files. As I'd worked on MODs UFO project, had been involved in the release of the files and was the media's 'go-to guy' for anything on UFOs, I was asked about the matter by numerous media outlets. A detailed article on this story ran in* The Scotsman *and on the* Sky News *website – though many others covered the story too."*

Witnesses never came forward

"The story received further publicity in 2012, with coverage in the Huffington Post *and the* Scottish Daily Record *– as well as* The Sun *– which continues to champion the UFO issue. Despite the various media interviews that I did on this story, and associated public appeals, the witnesses have never come forward. Neither has anyone at the* Scottish Daily Record *(or any other Scottish newspaper) come forward to say that they worked on this story back in 1990. Understandably, this has generated a few conspiracy theories. I wonder if the truth is a little more mundane. In their desperation to acquire the photos/negatives (and maybe kill the story), maybe DIS staff somehow tricked the journalist into handing over all the material and never gave it back. If the journalist hadn't briefed the editor, he may have stayed silent out of embarrassment. Similarly, maybe the witnesses were told that it would be better if they didn't discuss what they'd seen and took this as a threat. The MOD files that contain documents relating to this case have been released and are available at the National Archives, though MOD says that no trace has been found of the images, aside from one poor quality photocopy of a line drawing that was done as part of the original MOD investigation."*

CASE K/90/002 - MR JOHN JINKS FORXXXX XXXXXXXX
COLCHESTER ESSEX REPORTED TO E.U.FO.R.G AS HAVING BEEN FORMED DURING
NIGHT OF 3RD/4TH AUG 90

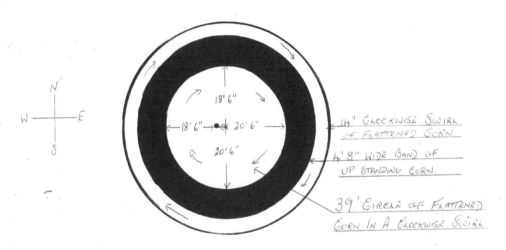

N
W — E
S

18'6"

18'6" • 20'6"

20'6"

1H" CLOCKWISE SWIRL
OF FLATTENED CORN

4'8" WIDE BAND OF
UP STANDING CORN.

39' CIRCLE OF FLATTENED
CORN IN A CLOCKWISE SWIRL

A PERFECT CIRCLE 45 FOOT WITH AN
OFF CENTRE INDENTATION.

INVESTIGATORS.

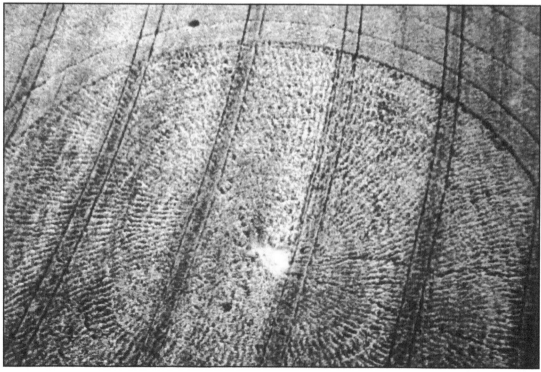

6th August 1990 (UK) – Triangular UFO over Essex

At 10.15pm, Richard Lyon (19) of Rowhedge, in Essex, was walking home along Pit Road – a tree lined road with several bends, and a water tower and pond.

> *"I felt something moving above me and looked upwards to see three red lights, set in triangular formation, moving overhead. The light in the middle was flashing and they were heading westwards. I went home and told my mother, Carol, what I had seen. She then accompanied me outside where, after gaining some height, we looked out and saw the lights still moving westwards – until we lost sight of them as they headed over the river, near Wivenhoe woods."*

(Source: Ron West/Desmond Stacey)

8th August 1990 (UK) – Crop circle found, Little Holland, Essex

Ron West:

> *"This drawing of the circle at Holland-on-Sea is identical in all aspects to the circle at St. Osyth – the same measurements, swirl, and indentation. The photograph was lost by Kodak."*

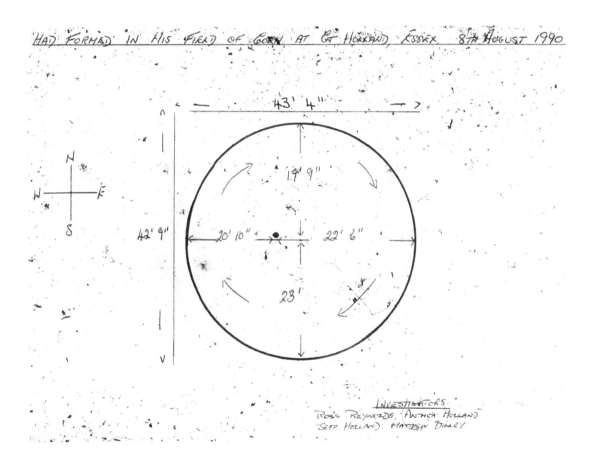

WEDNESDAY 8th AUGUST 1990. Gt HOLLAND, ESSEX.

Mr Lawrence, the farmer who owned a field at Gt Holland, reported to me that a circle had appeared in his corn field, during the evening morning of the 6th/7th August. On entering his field I found a circle of clockwise swirled corn measuring 43 foot 4 inches N to S and 42 foot 9 inches E to W. It had an off centre indentation which measured N to S 19 foot 9 inches by 23 foot, and E to W 22 foot 6 inches by 20 foot 10 inches. This circle appeared within a short distance of private houses and a roadway. On checking at all premises, nobody had seen or heard anything during the 6/7th August.

8th August 1990 (UK) – Arthur Tomlinson lectures at Macclesfield

- 8 AUG 1990 MACCLESFIELD EXPRESS ADVERTISER

Ready to prove the existence of UFO's

By BERYL BUTTERWORTH

THE EXISTENCE of flying saucers could be proved tonight at Townley Street School.

A man who believes that aliens from outer space are not science fiction will be giving a public lecture at the school. He is Arthur Tomlinson, who told the Macclesfield Express: "I am here to inform the public about what is going on in an effort to get public pressure eventually to expose it all."

To back up his belief, Mr Tomlinson has more than 150 slides, top secret documents released under the Freedom of Information Act in the USA, data on UFO crashes, photos of aliens and post-mortem reports on aliens from crashes.

● There have been local sightings. In 1966 a Macclesfield policeman, Colin Perks, was checking shop doors behind the Rex Cinema at Wilmslow when he heard a high-pitched whine and saw a UFO, shaped like a three-tier cottage loaf, stationary, 35 feet up about 100 yards away. After about five seconds, without changing its sound, the object moved rapidly away and passed out of sight.

● An Alderley man photographed a UFO in the 1960s and Mr Tomlinson says he found other reports that moved from Alderley to Ashton-unde-Lyne. There have been nine other seperate sightings.

● In September 1982 a pensioner saw a saucerlike object twinkling in the sky above the Hanging Gate pub at Sutton. Among other local people who saw it were several in the Bollington area.

Case E/90/503.   Inv R.Reynolds.   Gt Holland.
                        R.West. S. Biggs   Clacton on Sea.

On Wednesday 8th August 90, It was reported in the "Evening Gazette"
that a circle had been found at Gt Holland, Ross and myself went to
the sight and found out the following information.
The circle was on a Mr Lawrence farm at Gt Holland, Essex. We found
a circle 43 foot 4 inches by 42 foot 9 inches, with a clockwise swirl
with an indentation off centre. All the corn was up-standing around
the edges of the circle and no tracks lead across. All houses in the
area were checked, nobody had seen or heard anything.

Diagram:-

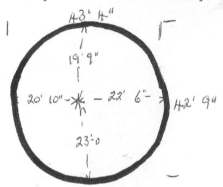

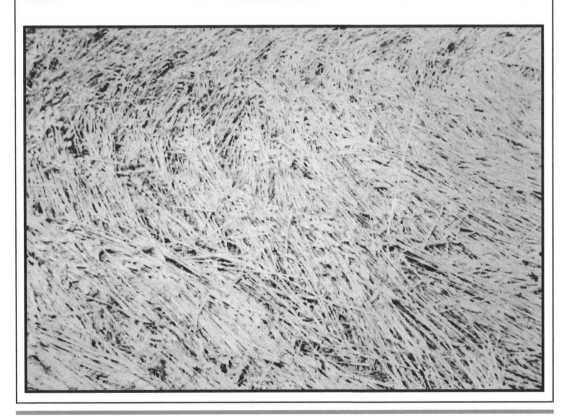

8th August 1990 (UK) – Crop circle found, Little Clacton, Essex

10th August 1990 (UK) – Triangular UFO over Essex

John Hayward (58) and members of his family were stood outside the family mobile home at Meadowview Park, St. Osyth Road, Clacton, Essex, at 11.30pm. It was a cold, clear, dry sky, with a light wind.

John:

> *"A large triangular object was seen stationary in the sky. There was a light at each corner and a small red pulsating one behind the lead one. We watched it for 10 minutes, until it began to get smaller and lost from sight."*

Crop circle found, Great Dunmow, Essex

Ron West:

> *"This circle was found at St. Dunmow, in Essex. It is identical to the circles located at Holland-on-Sea and St. Osyth – the only difference being is that it had a clockwise swirl. Photograph lost by Kodak."*

11th August 1990 (UK) – Crop formation found at Winchester

AUGUST 11th 1990. BARNFIELD NR CHEESEFOOT HEAD, WINCHESTER,
This was the last double pictogram formed in 1990. Notice that the
circlemakers ever inventive, have created "HORNS" at each end.

12th August 1990 (UK) – Crop marks found, Earls Colne

Ron:

"I was driving along the B1088 road, when I spotted it. This one was a perfect circle. Measurements were North to South, 28ft 6ins, and East to West, 28ft 6ins. It also had a centre indentation, with a clockwise swirl. Photograph lost by Kodak."

AUGUST 12th 1990. EARLS COLNE, ESSEX.

This is the second formation I found during my air trip. This is a
treble ringer. It was a perfect circle measuring 46 foot in all.
It consisted of a circle of 30 foot 6 inches in the center, followed
by a ring 6 foot 6 inches of standing corn, then a flattened circle
1 foot 3 inches wide, followed by another 6 foot 6 inches of standing
corn, followed by a further 1 foot 3 inches of swirled corn. All
swirls were in a clockwise direction. There was also a center
indentation.

Diagram:-

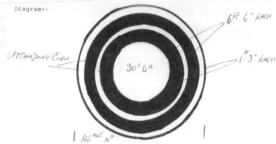

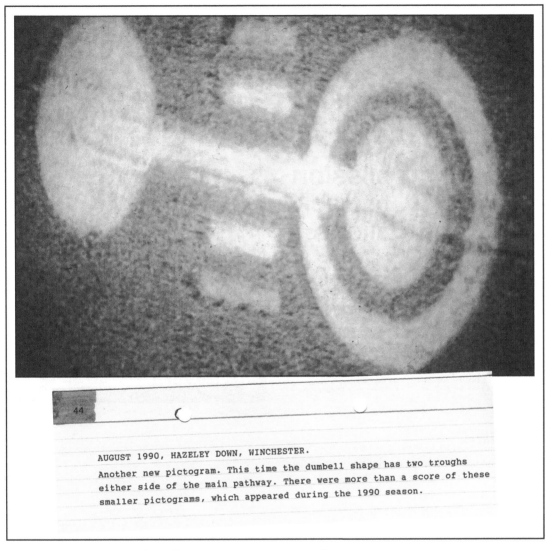

44

AUGUST 1990, HAZELEY DOWN, WINCHESTER.

Another new pictogram. This time the dumbell shape has two troughs either side of the main pathway. There were more than a score of these smaller pictograms, which appeared during the 1990 season.

12th August 1990 (UK) – UFO over Barnsley

Lesley Horner (37) was out walking his dog, during the evening, when he saw a flickering orange-white light in the sky over the town centre. Explanation: According to Leeds Weather Centre, it was a weather balloon.

(Source: *Barnsley Chronicle*, 12.8.1990 – 'Flying object')

13th August 1990 (UK) – UFO seen over Scotland

Mrs Morag Agnew was driving her family home to Twyholm, along the A762, at 10pm, when a shiny silver object passed quickly and silently in front of the car. Her daughter Kelly (8) also witnessed it. Her other daughter Jody (7) caught only a brief glimpse, while the brother Danny (4) slept through the incident.

(Source: *Galloway News*, Scotland, 16.8.1990 – 'Family's close encounter near Laurieston')

IS THERE ANYBODY OUT THERE . . ?

Mission to track aliens

TWENTY years ago six local people started a mission to hunt down UFOs. ⬤ ermined to beat the boffins at finding the answer to strange sightings and visitations, possibly by aliens from other planets, they armed themselves with a battery of UFO-seeking equipment.

And today from the headquarters of the Extra-Terrestrial Society — an old farmhouse between Whittlesey and Benwick which has been converted into a tracker's delight of paraphernalia — British Telecom engineer and part-time UFO hunter, Robin Lindsey has reached the conclusion: There's nothing out there — so far!

Nobody's more disappointed than Robin and his pals ... but they plan to keep on searching, just in case.

"We will carry on because it is interesting. We are doing original research which no-one has ever done before, we are constantly monitoring the atmosphere for changes in wind patterns and t⬤srature changes. Unexpect⬤ movement in these areas could indicate a UFO presence," said Robin, who spends his days making sure that earthbound communications go smoothly.

The Extra-Terrestrial Society may be small but the members are proud of their development

over the years from the early days in a rusty old caravan, with a car battery for power, to the farmhouse where their gear includes seismographs, microvariators, recorder charts, gauges and thermometers.

And all this complex equipment Robin, of Station Road, Whittlesey, reads every week on his visit to change the recorder charts to check that men from Mars haven't visited in the meantime.

"There are a lot of people who talk about seeing green men but we are seriously looking — we are trying to do things properly ."

Selkirk

In the same month, John Hay – living in a cottage at St. Mary's Loch, Selkirk, Scotland, with his small son, aged 11 – told of looking through the window above the attic bedroom, at 8am, when he saw:

> "...a totally silent 'craft', flying through the sky overhead, on what was a beautiful morning. It looked a bit like a rugby-ball, with pointed ends and stubby wings on the side. My son was awake and also saw it. We agreed that it was flying at about 400ft, heading in a north-easterly direction, bearing in mind the problems associated with trying to relate to something seen in the sky. The 'craft' was pale greenish in colour, showed no visible markings on its outer surface,and left no vapour trail or exhaust."

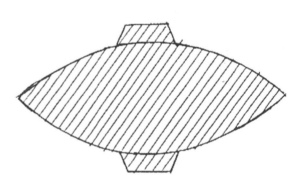

NE ◄

VIEW OF OBJECT FROM UNDERNEATH.
(OR PLAN VIEW)

15th August 1990 (New Zealand) – *'Flying disc'* seen

At 1am, a motorist was driving on an open straight piece of road in the country, through Twizel, South Island, when he noticed an orange glow that suddenly appeared in the rear view mirror of the car, about 1km behind the car, at ground level. At first he thought it might have been a farm homestead, with the lights on, but was then aware that the orange glow was following behind the vehicle.

> *"I thought it must be another car behind me, but what was strange about it is that the glow first appeared just out of nowhere on a straight piece of road, and if it was a car then it must be travelling at some speed as I was expecting it to catch up to me soon. I drove on for a further five minutes or so, but the 'lights' just stayed at the same distance behind me. After this amount of time I thought nothing of it and was sure it must be a car behind me. When I looked up into the rear view mirror of the car, there I saw it, about 40-50 metres behind the car and between 10-20 metres above me. This was no car."*

15th August 1990 (UK) – Triangular UFO over Essex

Seen by Timothy Sparkes (26) of Burrs Road, Clacton, at 6.20am, while on his way to work, heading eastwards, apparently just over rooftop level.

16th August 1990 (UK) – Triangular UFO over Yorkshire

'Three strange lights, forming a triangle' were seen in the sky over Stainland, Yorkshire, at 5am on 16th August 1990, by residents Ronald Farrar and his wife, Muriel. (**Source:** *Halifax Courier and Guardian*, **16.8.1990** – **'Lights in the sky mystery'**)

Mid-August 1990 – Bob Taylor plaque to mark landing of UFO

In the middle of this month there was considerable interest displayed by the Press, with regard to the placing of a plaque commemorating the landing of a UFO at Dechmont Woods, Scotland, by forester Bob Taylor, in 1979.

Scotsman – Edinburgh. **10 SEP 1990**

Plaque will mark Livingston's first close encounter of the third kind

237+

THE first plaque to be erected in Britain to commemorate an alleged UFO landing is to be unveiled later this year in Livingston, 11 years after the report.

It will be mounted on a cairn marking the spot where Bob Taylor, a foreman forester employed by Livingston Development Corporation, claimed to have stumbled across a silver spinning-top-shaped craft standing in a clearing and was attacked by two "strange creatures" before he

managed to stagger to his home a mile away in Broomieknowe Drive, Livingston Station.

The decision to give official recognition to the incident at Dechmont Law in November 1979, follows an approach to the LDS by Strange Phenonema Investigations (Scotland) and has been welcomed by UFO enthusiasts who regard Mr Taylor's experience as a very well-established and intriguing case.

Gordon Davis, the corporation's technical director, who is in charge

BY GORDON DEAN

of the project, said that visitors to the town often asked where the landing occurred and visited the spot.

He said that the case was still very fresh in a lot of people's minds. "A colleague was recently on holiday in America. When he said he came from Livingston, the Americans remarked that it was where the UFO landed, so the

incident is also internationally known."

Mr Davis said that the wording on the plaque would not say that something actually happened but that something was suspected of having happened. It will read: "This is the site referred to in Arthur C Clarke's *Mysterious World* which describes an encounter between a forestry worker out walking and what apeared to him as an Unidentified Flying Object."

Arthur Clarke is a leading authority on UFOs. The director said that while some people might claim that Mr Taylor imagined it all, one element that could not be explained were the marks, regular in pattern, and deep, that had been left behind with no tracks into the area and no tracks out.

Jenny Randles, director of investigations with the British UFO Research Association, said: "By erecting this plaque Scotland is certainly establishing a precedent

– 5 NOV 1990   Scotsman – Edinburgh.

Search for twilight zone trouser clue

237+.

A RETIRED West Lothian forester who claims to have seen a UFO is to have his trousers examined by psychics. The trousers, which have already been forensically examined by the police, were supposedly ripped and torn by extra terrestrial machinery.

Robert Taylor's world-famous close encounter came one sunny November morning 11 years ago when he was routinely checking a wood at Dechmont Law near Livingston. Coming to a clearing, he was confronted by a 30ft high object with portholes. It was silvery-grey but intermittently translucent.

Two round, spiky objects, which Mr Taylor described as being like Second World War sea mines, dropped from the craft and rolled towards him. They stopped either side of him, emitting a smell so pungent Mr Taylor passed out.

When he awoke, his dog was barking wildly, his body was bruised and his trousers torn. Too weak to stand, he

crawled to his van but crashed it into a ditch. Eventually, he staggered home and his wife raised the alarm.

An intensive police investigation followed. MI5 were rumoured to be involved. Mr Taylor, who is teetotal, was closely questioned. Police found depressions in the ground exactly where he said they had been and no official explanation has ever been offered for the incident.

The trousers, meanwhile, became an object of international fascination, as Ron Halliday of the organisation Strange Phenomena Investigations explains: "They travelled across the world, to the US and Japan, and eventualy ended up with the Yorkshire UFO Society. Recently we asked them to pass them back to us so that we can do psychometric tests on them."

Although the trousers have been manhandled by many around the world, Mr Halliday is confident that Mr Taylor's experience in them was so strong that a

psychic could examine them and pick up clues as to what may have happened.

"The trousers have been well examined but nobody has tried this before. Psychics can pick up something like a clock — or a pair of trousers — and give you a history of it."

Mr Taylor, now 72, and living in retirement in Perthshire, was surprised to learn that the trousers still existed. He said: "I thought these trousers were gone forever. I can't see psychics making anything of them. The police must have examined them as far as possible at the time."

Mr Taylor, who had no interest in UFOs or the paranormal before his disturbing experience, said he could never forget what happened.

Meanwhile, Livingston Development Corporation are to put up a plaque to the Dechmont Law incident. The plaque will be erected by workers on the Government's Employment Training scheme, better known as ET.

-2 NOV 1990 LOTHIAN COURIER

Aliens secret held by — Bob's trousers!

2374

PSYCHICS could solve one of the world's best known UFO mysteries...

By examining a West Lothian man's old, torn trousers.

But while that idea has not impressed Bob Taylor, he did reveal some startling news — a new UFO puzzle has landed on his doorstep.

In November, 1979, ex-forestry worker Bob claimed to have had a close encounter in a hillside wood near Livingston.

Part of his story centred around rips on the trousers he was wearing at the time.

The idea to have psychics examine the trousers came when three research groups — Scottish Research Into UFOs, Strange Phenomena Investigations and Scottish Earth Mysteries Reasearch — held a meeting at East Calder Community Centre last Friday.

Organiser Ron Halliday said: "We still have the trousers Bob was wearing and we're planning to carry out a psychometric exercise on them."

According to Bob's story, he stumbled across a flying saucer in a clearing.

While he watched the craft, two objects shaped like sea-mines fell from underneath it and rolled up to him.

Bob lost consciousness and when he came to, there were rips on each side of his trousers.

"The tears could indicate that Bob was lifted up in some way," said Ron. "What we're hoping is that the psychics just might pick up something to explain exactly what happened."

This week Bob was sceptical about the idea when he spoke exclusively to the Courier from his retirement home in Blairgowrie, Perthshire.

"I haven't heard anything about the trousers since the police took them away for forsenic tests 11 years ago," said Bob.

"But the UFO people can go ahead with whatever they think best."

LOTHIAN COURIER - 3 AUG 1990

CLOSE ENCOUNTER

Robert Taylor

THE NEWS that Livingston Development Corporation are to place a plaque in a West Lothian wood to mark a UFO sighting is somehow unlikely to raise as many eyebrows as Bob Taylor's story did 11 years ago.

For on the cold, bright morning of November 9, 1979, the blockbuster sci-fi movie "Close Encounters of the Third Kind" seemed to turn into hair-raising reality for the Livingston forestry worker.

His claims fascinated UFO experts, inspired an intensive police investigation and, according to some, even attracted interest from MI5.

Reports by Dave Cowan

At the time, Bob was described by a senior police officer as a trustworthy, respectable citizen, unlikely to make false statements.

And if "Close Encounters" had grabbed the nation's imagination it had passed over the quiet, teetotal countryman — he didn't believe in UFOs.

But when he recounted a story which could have come straight from that film's script, he said simply: "It was a spaceship."

Bob's account started with his setting out to check the woods at Dechmont Law.

Whatever happened next reduced him to a man who staggered home pale and hoarse with torn trousers and muddy clothes.

Bob said he had parked his van and approached a clearing, where he saw a stationary object in front of him. It was 30 feet high, and changing between being coloured grey and tranclucent, as if it was flashing. There was a flange round the middle upon which antennae were attached and it had round portholes.

Having watched the object for some time, Bob said he saw two devices like wartime mines — round with short spikes — suddenly fall from the "craft" and roll quickly towards him.

They stopped alongside him, one to his left and one to his right.

A strange choking smell came from the globes and Bob passed out. When he regained consciousness, his dog was barking wildly and he was so weak he couldn't walk.

Having crawled to his van, Bob ran it into a ditch as he tried to turn the vehicle. He then staggered to his house at Broomieknowe Drive, Livingston, slumped into a chair and told his wife what had happened. She phoned the LDC who told the police.

Until other forestry workers and detectives arrived at the clearing, Bob's story remained totally uncorroborated. Yet what was found next has never been explained.

Several marks were discovered on the ground that might have been made by the leg struts of a machine weighing several tons. If they were just tracks, why did they just start and end, leading nowhere?

Bob's story was not taken lightly. Forensic scientists checked his clothes, the police contacted Edinburgh airport and asked if anything had shown on radar that day — but everything drew a blank.

Scientists suggested that Bob had witnessed ball lightning. That might explain what he saw but how did the tracks appear?

And there was al gossip speculating that the dastardly Soviets might have been involved — hence the MI5 rumours.

However, one thing at least is certain.

That small plaque will mark one of Britain's most unearthly mysteries.

PLAQUE TO MARK UFO SIGHTING

A MYSTERIOUS incident in West Lothian which captured headlines worldwide is to be marked in a very down-to-earth manner.

Eleven years ago, forestry worker Bob Taylor found himself in the international news after claiming that he had a close encounter with visitors from outer space.

And, after a suggestion by UFO experts, a plaque is to be fixed on the woodland site where Bob said he saw a spaceship in November, 1979.

Livingston Development Corporation bosses liked the idea from Strange Phenomenums Investigations Ltd who, along with like-minded organisations and boffins across the world, continue to be fascinated by Bob's story.

He claimed that he stumbled across a flying saucer in a clearing in woods on Dechmont Law, Livingston.

An in-depth investigation held by the police unearthed nothing to prove or disprove Bob's account.

Scientists speculated that Bob encountered ball lightning, but, that failed to explain strange tracks that police found in the clearing.

And with UFOs back in the news — thanks to suspicious goings-on in English cornfields — the LDC has decided to persuade tourists to boldly go where few tourists have gone before.

LDC technical director Gordon Davis said: "The plaque will be produced by us with words based on Arthur C. Clark's book "Mysterious World".

"It will say something like: 'This is where a forestry worker said he saw something which appeared to him to be a UFO.'

"We think it's necessary to mark the site because of the numbers of people that are coming to Livingston looking for it. The tourists interest in this sort of thing is quite wide," Mr Davis concluded.

Indentation left a scene of encounter

Investigator Malcolm Robinson

Cumberland Evening News – Carlisle.

2 4 AUG 1990

My close encounter with UFO – hotel boss

A CLOSE encounter with an unidentified flying object has allegedly occurred in West Cumbria. Roy Daugherty, chief executive of the Westland Group which owns Workington's Westland Hotel, claims to have spotted a large ball of light hovering yards away from the hotel.

He said that he 'had been sober and stressed: "I am not a 37-year-old UFO crazy.

"It was a great big mass of light and it pulled down from the sky in front of me."

Roy had taken his dog for a walk at about 2.30am on Wednesday when the encounter occurred.

"It hovered there for about half a minute and I just kind of froze looking at it and so did my dog.

"It seemed like it was looking at us and then pulled off horizontally at great speed."

He described the object, which was shrouded in light, as a rounded structure some 60 to 80 feet wide, hovering about 80 feet off the ground.

He added that it had no windows.

"I wasn't frightened more interested in what it was and what it was

.Roy Daugherty
. . . close encounter.

doing and the feeling that it was looking at me," he said.

American-born Mr Daugherty said that his dog had been sick afterwards and he was so shaken that he had been forced to take the day off work.

● Police said they had no reports of UFOs in the area, while the RAF would not reveal any details of flights over West Cumbria.

22nd August 1990 (UK) – UFO over Workington, Cumbria

West Cumbrian businessman Roy Daughtey – Chief Executive of the Westland Group, was out walking his dog, at 2.30am, when a *'mass of light'* – described as a rounded structure, some 80ft wide – descended from the sky and hovered about 80ft above the ground, close to the Westland Hotel.

Roy stood watching the *'light'* – until it took off, 30 seconds later.

(Source: *West Cumberland Times*, 24.8.1990 – 'Ball of light over Workington Hotel')

23rd August 1990 (UK) – UFO over Southend

14 SEP 1990   YELLOW ADVERTISER –Colchester–

2379

Cash reward is on offer for a genuine UFO pic

by Steve Hart

THE gauntlet has been thrown down to find hard evidence of UFOs.

Following years of alleged sightings of strange lights in the sky and rumours of alien beings with big eyes abducting humans, for experiments — the ultimate proof is now being sought.

A cash reward has been offered for a picture of an extra-terrestrial craft. Peter Oliver, chairman of the East Anglian UFO and Paranormal Research Association said his committee had not yet decided the amount of the cash award.

Mr Oliver was speaking last week amid claims of further UFO activity in Southend, Great Wakering and Rochford.

He said: "The picture of a UFO will have to be one-hundred-per cent though. All pictures will be thoroughly checked and faked pictures won't stand a chance.

"If we receive a picture that interests us we will want to see the negative."

He added: "People should not be worried about telling us of sightings or contacts with alien beings. All reports are treated in strict confidence — names and addresses of people who report sightings to us are never revealed."

On Thursday, August 23, two young brothers reported seeing a bright light from their bedroom in St Edmunds Close, Southend, at about 12.45am.

Mr Oliver said: "The boys should down to their dad and rushed outside to get a better look at

the craft, but it had disappeared."

He said the boys described the UFO as a large orange coloured light with a smaller white light travelling down the object. It was moving northwards.

If you have a picture of an extra-terrestrial space craft, send it to Skywatch, Yellow Advertiser, Acorn House, Basildon, Essex, SS14 1AH, with your name and address and, if possible, daytime telephone number.

We will forward your pictures to Mr Oliver.

29th August 1990 (UK) – 'X'-shaped UFO seen over Colchester

At 9.30pm, Jeremy Hardy (8) of Defoe Crescent, Colchester, was out playing with his friends on skateboards at the recreation ground, near Cants Rose Fields nursery. He and his friend – Terry Jenkins – happened to look up into the sky as it was getting dark, and saw:

"...an object in the shape of an 'X', which displayed about 14 lights. On one line of the 'X' were some red lights, flashing on and off. The other lights were white. We then ran home and told my Mom what we had seen."

(Source: Ron West)

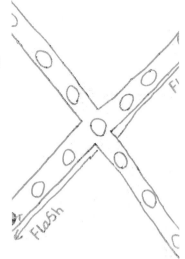

31 AUG 1990   Essex Chronicle, Chelmsford

Tank shape UFO

ESSEX Unidentified Flying Object researchers are investigating reports that a tank shaped craft, about 150ft diameter has been spotted on three separate occasions over the county.

One of the sightings was reported by two police officers in the south of the county.

The hovering object had five square red lights.

Two other sightings in different areas of the county also reported a tank shaped craft.

Essex UFO Research Group is holding a meeting on September 7 at the Quaker Meeting House, Church Street, Colchester. All are welcome. If anyone wishes to report sighting they can contact Les Stacey on 0206-211442.

Summer 1990 (UK) – Close encounter, Hampshire

Following an appeal in the local newspaper, Steven Beiderman from Fordingbridge, Hampshire, contacted us with regard to a strange experience which befell him in summer 1990.

"At the time I was driving along the B7073 road, near Godsill, when I saw an object resembling a Victorian sponge cake, covered in lights, pass overhead, making a low buzzing noise, heading towards the New Forest. When I arrived home I found out that I was unable to account for two hours of missing time. When you asked me if I had noticed anything unusual after the event, I can't remember anything specific, although during a visit to my optician, a few years later, he asked me when I had surgery, as he could see scarring on the lens of my eyes – presumably to have corrected a vision defect. When I told him I have never had this sort of surgery, he referred me to a consultant, who examined me and was just as baffled as I was when I told him I had no knowledge of any surgery on my eyes."

(Source: Personal interview)

UFO paces car

John Turvey, from Evesham, wrote to us with regard to what he experienced while driving towards Bredon, Worcestershire, during summer of 1990.

"It was a particularly fine dry evening, at the time, when I noticed a curious 'light' appearing and disappearing between the trees and hedgerows – as if pacing the car from one side. This went on for several miles, until whatever it was rose up vertically into the sky, at tremendous speed, and was soon just a tiny speck of light in the starlit sky."

The next day he eagerly scanned the local newspapers, hoping to find other reports of a UFO being seen – there was nothing. When he tried to tell people what he had seen, they laughed.

18 OCT 1990   WEST NOTTS. RECORDER

Have you had a close encounter?

2374

New group probes reports of UFOs

A BULWELL man has started an association for research into unidentified flying objects.

Postman Anthony James is eager to hear of any serious sightings of phenomena so he can compile and investigate the reports.

By Lynette Tasker

His interest in UFOs was sparked off by a library book back in 1973.

Since then he has researched the subject further and was prompted to form the East Midlands UFO Research Association after attending a seminar at Manchester last year where an American nuclear physicist said not enough people were investigating.

"More than 90% of reported objects in the sky can be identified, such as aircraft, planets and weather balloons," said Anthony.

"About five per cent of sightings cannot readily be explained and it is these that we are interested in."

In an effort to identify these, weather stations, airfields and airports are contacted.

"Many people have sighted UFOs but don't bother to report them because of the fear of ridicule or they don't know who to report them to."

Anthony will categorise any findings into nocturnal lights and daytime discs and close encounters of the first to fourth kind.

His first compilation is a close encounter of the first kind seen by his brother Mark and his mother.

Six years ago they claim to have seen an object hovering in the sky while walking along Saxondale Drive.

It travelled at 20mph, had white, blue and orange lights and was about 30ft long.

Circle

Anthony is also anxiously awaiting details about findings of a crop circle in the recent Operation Blackbird.

Scientists from Britain, America and Canada used £1m surveillance equipment on a field in Wiltshire.

"A fake circle appeared and then the operation was kept very quiet," said Anthony.

But via a telephone conversation with one of those present, Pat Delgado from the Circle Phenomena Research Group, Anthony learnt that what is believed to be a bona fide circle appeared.

"Pat was very reluctant to give details so I am trying to find out more from the Japanese crew who were there."

Diverse weather conditions can spark off bright lights and objects that look like UFOs. One such example is a cloud shaped like a flying saucer. And stars are sometimes mistaken for UFOs.

Anthony is well aware of tricks by hoaxers. One fake object in the sky was exposed after the photograph was computer analysed, revealing a piece of wire attached to it.

If anyone believes they have had a serious sighting he can be contacted on 275623.

● Anthony James

SEPTEMBER 1990

1st September 1990 (UK) – UFO sighted

WICKFORD man John Westgarth, and his wife, Doris, sighted a mysterious pink cigar-shaped *'mass of light'*, hovering over their house, which they said was *"undoubtedly one of the strangest things we have ever seen"*.

(Source: Technical Phenomenon Research Group, Billericay/*Billericay Recorder*, Essex, 7.9.1990 –
'UFO sighted hovering in the night sky')

4th September 1990 (UK) – *'Flying saucer'* over Essex

A 44-year old lady, of Sudbury Road, Castle Hedington, was awoken at 2am by a soft humming noise. She went to the bathroom and drew the curtains, when she was astonished to see:

"...a large, fiery saucer-shaped object, motionless in the sky. I let the net curtains drop down and made my way to the bedroom, where I collected my glasses. When I returned to the bathroom and looked out there was nothing to see."

She was not the only one to sight something unusual. Mrs Doris Thirlwell (74) of Avon, was another witness.

6th September 1990 (UK) – Close encounter, Dorset

During our occasional talks on the UFO subject, we met James Millen – a likeable man, whose enthusiasm knew no bounds! James, then the editor of *Rapport* – a 'Witness Support Group' magazine, devoted to people who had experienced close encounters, including allegations of abduction, had himself experienced a number of strange sightings – one of which took place on

114 SEP 1990

OAP queries: 'Did anyone else see UFO'

by Ann Shaw

MRS Doris Thirlwell doesn't want anyone to think that at 74 she has 'lost her marbles' but she believes she may have seen a UFO above her Acre Court flat.

Her sighting, through binoculars — of a 'funny shaped star', with bright lights around its elongated shape which came nearer and nearer without a sound as she stood on her second floor balcony — happened at nearly 10pm on 4 September. It disappeared after a red droplet detached itself from the main body.

"I'd like to know if anyone else saw anything that night. I did not believe in UFOs but now I am beginning to wonder. I've told the warden of the flats and the police and they are all very sceptical but I told them I have my full faculties and I know what I saw. In other words, I have not lost my marbles.

"Hitler did not frighten me and I had enough of him in the London blitz.

"This did not frighten me. It was magnificent."

6th September 1990. On this occasion, James and his wife – Pamela – were camping in a field overlooking Chesil Beach, when James got up to go to the toilet just before 3am.

> *"On my way back to the tent, I saw a bright light in the sky and then the appearance of eight golden 'balls of light' in the sky. I called Pamela to come outside to have a look, and went to fetch my camera. The next thing I knew was that it was 5.30a.m and we were back in the tent.*
>
> *A strange substance resembling lime mortar was found lying on the floor, the following day. I discovered, as time went on, that I had memory flashbacks of being in this white room, lying on a bench, with 'figures' standing around me. There were other 'figures'; some were tall, others short."*

James told us that the incident was reported to Nick Pope, at the Ministry of Defence.

James Millen

7th September 1990 (USA) – Culvar, Indiana

Two young women were in a car parked in a driveway, with the engine running, at 8.30pm. One of the girls was looking up at the stars, when she sighted an octagonal object passing over the car from the rear to the front. [This was the third report of an octagon in Indiana]. She pointed it out to the other girl, at which stage both girls became frightened and started crying. The object – about the size of a car – was described as:

> *"...dull grey, with pairs of red, blue, green, or clear lights, set onto each corner. The bottom of the object was dented inwards; I noticed lines on the inside. It was about the length of a telephone pole above the car. The car engine was running, so I couldn't hear any noise. It moved about the speed of an escalator."*

The girls started to get out of the car to get a better look, when the object disappeared before they could even shut off the engine.

> *"It went a little way in front of the car and vanished, and was only in view for a minute."*

(Source: MUFON, Indiana, Field Investigator Roger Lamberson and Mr K.O. Learner)

Harry's close encounter

Harry Deemer prepares for another night's star-gazing.

13th September 1990 (UK) – UFO, showing three lights, seen over Basildon

At 8.30pm, Mr P Gibson (36) – a fire officer with the local authority – was watching TV at his home address in Grapnells Vange, when:

> "I noticed what I first took to be something on fire, stationary in the sky. It appeared to consist of three different lights – red, blue, and green – the red light being most dominant. I called my wife and family to come and have a look at it. As the evening wore on, it moved further away and was out of sight. We kept it under observation for about an hour."

AN AMATEUR astronomer claims he has seen alien life zooming over the skies of Poole.

Pensioner Henry Deemer was star-gazing when he spotted a bright, white light speeding over his Green Road home.

When he went outside to investigate, the light all but disappeared, leaving a pink glow on the end of it.

Henry, 64, claims it wasn't a shooting star, a plane or that it had anything to do with the Bournemouth Festival of Lights laser show.

The retired factory cleaner said: "I was up in my attic just after 11pm

BY ANDY NICHOLLS

and saw with my naked eye this huge light, moving fast across the sky.

"It was just like a star. I couldn't get it into focus with my telescope...I dashed outside to see a pink light at the end of it and then it vanished. It was heading towards Wareham.

"It was definitely an alien craft from outer space. I have never seen anything like it before."

A spokesman for the festival of lights said their show ended at 10.30pm. No spokesman for Hurn Airport was available for comment.

4 SEP 1990 — Bournemouth Evening Echo

Oxford Mail.
15 SEP 1990

UFOs – myth or much more?

2314

SUBTITLED UFOs — A Modern Myth, Phantoms Of The Sky (Robert Hale, £12.95) will be of interest to ufologists and general reader.

David Clarke and Andy Roberts chronicle a sort of summary of ufology over the 50 years or so of its existence, drawing no hard and fast conclusions but debunking a few myths along the way.

Here's a rational-looking account of a subject that has so little solid substance.

DAN RICE

GLOUCESTERSHIRE ECHO - CHELTENHAM.
11 SEP 1990

UFO — or was it just a touch of the moon?

2374.

A BAFFLED Leckhampton man has seen the light — but he's still very much in the dark.

The skywatcher spotted a mysterious amber glow hovering in the sky when he was walking his dog in a field about 100 yards from Daisybank Road.

"I was looking across the town and suddenly this very strong amber light appeared. It would have been somewhere over Pilley Bridge. It was very, very bright."

"It moved very slowly towards me," he said. "There was a movement of air, but the light did not keep on a constant path.

"Then it stopped and kept still, went off to a pinprick, then disappeared altogether."

This ethereal experience lasted about 30 seconds.

"I am not suggesting it was a UFO. I am sure it can be explained rationally. But I am curious to know what it was," says Ferret's informant who, understandably, does not wish

Police said they had no reports of any mysterious lights being seen in the sky that evening.

Ken Sheldon of Cotswold Astronomical society reckons the only logical reason for the mystery light is the moon rising: "If he was looking towards the north east he could easily have seen a full moon rising into mist, which could have given an orange glow."

Explanation by way of UFOs and little green men are definitely out, he says.

More than one

"As with all UFO events, if there is one, several people normally report it.

"Whenever it happens there is usually more than one."

Ken says he hasn't experienced anything like it himself, and refuses to accept UFO theories until proved otherwise.

"I have heard about people seeing strange objects and strange lights. Until I see something I cannot explain I shall continue to look for a

19th September 1990 (UK) – Strange lights seen over Cambridge

At 7.25pm, Mr C. Massey (38) was out walking with his girlfriend, at Wandlebury Hill – an Iron Age hill fort – when they sighted two *'lights'*, hovering silently above trees, some 80ft up in the sky, about two miles away.

Mr Massey tried to film the objects but was initially prevented from doing so, due to a flock of sheep that surrounded them. However, he managed to take some film of other *'lights'* in the sky, after the first two moved away and out of sight, northwards.

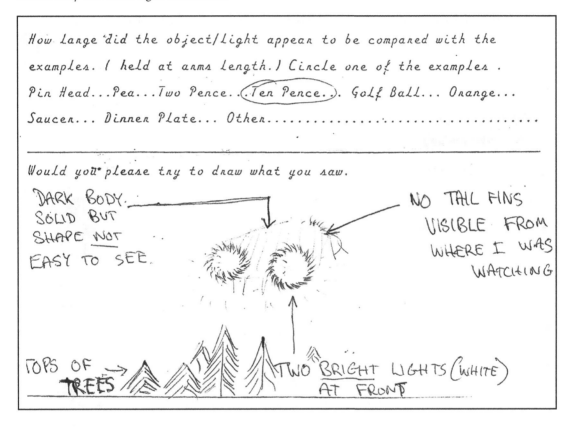

21st September 1990 (UK) – *'Flying saucer'* over Essex

At 10pm, Shirley Teresa Haynes (36) of Wellesley Road, Clacton, was walking to the off-licence to purchase some cigarettes, with her son – Stuart (13) – when they saw:

"...a dark object high in the sky, between houses opposite, covered with flashing lights, like diamonds, creating an impression of moving anti- clockwise in flight, heading towards Jaywick."

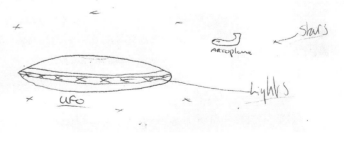

23rd September 1990 (UK) – Was this space debris?

At 10.30pm, Dorothy Softly (48) of Sawbridge, Hertfordshire, was at her home address, with her husband, when they saw:

> *"…an extremely bright 'light' zooming across the sky, heading in a South to West direction, before disappearing. It was far too big to have been a shooting star".*

25th September 1990 (UK) – Diamond-shaped UFO seen, Essex

Window dresser Deborah Jones (37) was driving to Ipswich from Kirby Cross, with her husband and two sons. Just after Manningtree Bridge, near to the Brantham Bull public House, one of her sons who was with her brought his mother's attention to something he could see glinting in the sky.

Deborah:

> *"As we continued on our journey, the road opened up and we all saw the object – which resembled a squashed silver diamond, with the top half revolving, as it headed along the side of a field. It then flew over a tractor and we saw the driver look up to see it. It then flew parallel to us for about 10 miles, at a speed of 60-70mph. As we began to see the chimneys of Ipswich Docks, it suddenly accelerated at tremendous speed, veered to the right, and shot out of sight."*

Derby Evening Telegraph.

22 SEP 1990

2374

Ben exposes UFO truth

by Neil Kerr

BUG-EYED monsters from Mars spotted in a Derbyshire field have been identified — as red-faced photography student Ben Meakin.

Investigators from two <u>UFO</u> societies went on inter-galactic alert when mysterious strobe-like lights were filmed by a Kilburn family earlier this week.

But the Close Encounters investigation was called off when 17-year-old Ben admitted: "It was me using a flash gun with a photographic experiment."

Techniques

Ben, a student at South East Derbyshire College at Heanor, had been testing photographic techniques near his home on Derby Road, Lower Kilburn, helped by his 19-year-old brother, Tom.

The pair had set up a camera with the lense shutter open, and then dashed around the field letting off a normal flash unit to see what the affects would be.

But as the bright lights illuminated the field, Melvern Pearson was alerted to the unusual phenomena by his daughter Marie (16).

And they used their family video recorder to tape the unusual flashing lights which mystified everybody, including police who investigated the incident.

When Ben learned his experiment had sparked off speculation of UFOs in the area he contacted the police — and brought everyone back down to earth.

27th September 1990 (UK) – UFO sighting over Church Stowe

Elsie Oakensen, from Church Stowe, was to find herself witnessing another example of UFO activity – this time, whilst driving homewards.

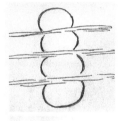

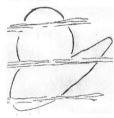

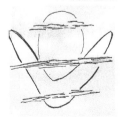

"It was a dark night, with no stars or moon visible, when I noticed something resembling four vertical moons, each one separated by a narrow strip of cloud in the sky. After continuing my journey along the A5, I noticed the four 'moons' were now compressed downwards, forming a pear shape. By the time I reached the top of Church Stowe, the image had changed again; it now looked like an orange-yellow 'ball of light', with a 'tail' on each side. Within minutes it had rolled over with the 'boomerang' pointing to the right – looking like an arrowhead in the sky."

Flying saucer was overhead then everything went pitch dark

ELSIE Oakerson was enjoying her lunch-break from work when she felt a strange tightening sensation around her head. It only lasted a few minutes and she soon forgot it.

But while driving along the A5 four hours later, she saw brilliant red and green lights near her Northampton home.

"At first I thought it was a low-flying aircraft," Elsie, 61, says of the experience two years ago.

"Then as I got closer I saw it was a dumb-bell shaped object which was about 100 feet above the road and 50 feet wide."

As Elsie drove underneath it, she felt compelled to stop but the road was too busy.

"I looked back and saw that the green lights had started to flash."

Suddenly she found herself sitting in complete darkness in her car, which had ground to a halt.

"It was only about 5.30pm but I couldn't see a thing," she says. "Then a flash of white lights revealed that I was about 50 yards further on.

"I felt no fear, I was absolutely fascinated by the whole experience."

The darkness faded and Elsie found herself another 30 yards down the road, this time in normal daylight.

"I had travelled nearly 100 yards without even starting the car," she says.

Elsie then continued on her journey without further incident. But two hours after she arrived home she felt another tightening sensation around her head. Some time later, Elsie decided to undergo hypnosis — but this time there were frightening results.

"I felt the tightening sensation again and saw the lights," she says.

"Then this ghost-like being came towards me. I was so terrified by it that the UFO experts had to bring me out of hypnosis."

Since then, Elsie has managed to steer clear of strange encounters.

"I've met about 15 other people who have had similar experiences to mine," she says.

"It's very reassuring to know that others have gone through the same thing."

Patricia Mee is just one such person. She has been hearing voices and seeing strange visions since she was just five years old.

Patricia, who lives in Manchester and works as a personnel manager for a video company, believes there is someone watching over her. But instead of being frightened by such a thought, she feels comforted. "It's reassuring to know someone is looking after me."

When Patricia was younger she was embarrassed to tell people about the things she had seen — at one point she thought she was mentally ill.

"I thought I was going insane but I couldn't tell anyone for fear of being ridiculed," she says. "Now I just accept it."

● *For more information, contact BUFORA, 1 Woodhall Drive, Healey Lane, Batley, West Yorkshire, WF17 7SW, or call the UFO hotline on 0898 654 637.*

ELSIE'S UFO CONFIRMED

'I saw spacecraft too'

EXCLUSIVE

by Paul Green

AN ALIEN spacecraft really DID fly over the Daventry area 18 years ago!

Georgina Laurie of Flore has broken nearly two decades of silence to confirm she saw the UFO which Elsie Oakensen of Church Stowe has always insisted abducted her.

And now the *Daventry Express* is challenging anyone else who saw something strange that night on November 22, 1978, to come forward and tell the truth.

During Elsie's famous incident, she drove under a silent 100ft long object hovering above the A5 near where she lives. She arrived home 15 minutes later than normal, and believes she was abducted.

Elsie always knew that Georgina had seen the craft – but respected her wish not to be identified. Georgina said: "My husband had his own business at the time and was worried that people would think I was a crank, and wouldn't use his firm. But I don't care what people think now."

She was travelling on a back road between Preston Capes and Woodford Halse at 7.15pm – two hours after Elsie saw the craft.

"As I started to come out of a T-junction there was a white light shining down in the trees," Georgina recalled.

"The car started to play up and changed it into second gear. The thing moved across the road. There was a red light and a green light, which were both static. Then it just went."

She said her three passengers at the time later forgot the sighting, and she has now lost contact with them.

"It was silent and made me feel funny. It must have been fairly big because of how far apart the lights were," said Georgina.

Both women will be appearing on the television programme Strange But True in the autumn to tell their stories.

Elsie has written a book about the abduction One Step Beyond which is on sale at Daventry Bookshop. She said: "Talking to Georgina was just like listening to myself, so many things were similar. I never thought I would find anyone else that would say they saw it. I knew other people had seen something, but they didn't want to talk about it."

● Did you see anything that night? Ring Paul Green in confidence on 01327 703383.

● Comment – page 6.

UFO spotters: Elsie and Georgina   Picture: James Robbins (96JUN73DC)

DAVENTRY EXPRESS opinion

YOU might believe that all this talk about alien abductions is a load of old nonsense (see our front page story). But for Elsie Oakensen, it is deadly serious stuff.

For the past 18 years, she has had people laughing at her behind her back because she has been brave enough to stand up and be counted. Remember, this all happened in the days before The X-Files television programme made it acceptable to talk about unexplained phenomena.

Now Georgina Laurie has decided to go public with her version of what happened that night in November 1978. She hasn't just made it up, because Elsie has known about her for years.

There must be other people still around today who saw some of the strange things that happened that night.

In the Daventry Weekly Express of November 24, 1978, founding editor Walter Green (no relation!) wrote a story about a mysterious giant triangular shape which was seen over Long Buckby.

That happened three days before Elsie and Georgina's sightings... could all the sightings be the same craft? Perhaps we will never know, but if you saw anything slightly strange that night, pick up the phone and give us a call – because the truth is out there!

Paul Green

(handwritten: 22. 11. 78)

(handwritten, circled: LIBRARY FIND ADDRESS)

Later that evening, a large boomerang-shaped object, estimated to be over 200ft in size, was seen moving silently across the sea at Clacton, in Essex, by a woman walking her dog, who described it as *"having one large white light to the front and centre, with four smaller white lights on each side".*

The following diagrams are as drawn by the witnesses:-

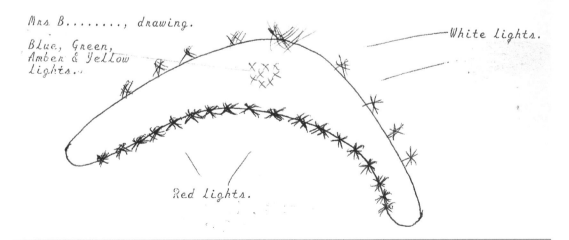

Mrs B........., drawing.

Blue, Green, Amber & Yellow Lights.

White Lights.

Red Lights.

<u>U.F.O REPORTS</u> .

The most exciting report from the public since our last newsletter (issue number 4). Is as follows:
Mrs B........
September 27th, 1990, 10.45 p.m. whilst walking her dog along the sea-front at Clacton on Sea. Noticed a large 'boomerang' shaped object, moving slowly and quietlt over the sea, running parallel with the coast (or seemed to be). Mrs B........ estimated the object to be approximately half a mile out to sea and about 1,000 foot high.
It had one large white light to the front and centre with four other smaller white lights on each side of the centre large light. After the object had passed ahead of her. Mrs B........ noticed approx eighteen red lights to the rear of the craft. Mrs B........ also noticed an array of other lights to the middle of the object, colours included, Blue, Green. Amber and Yellow glows. The sky seemed dark and no stars seemed to be about. it also seemed to be very quiet with no cars or other people about (that is strange for that time of night). The length of the sighting lasted three minutes. The object was moving from East to West. (Walton on Naze to Point Clear). Mrs B........ estimated the object size to be over 200 foot.

* * * * * * *

Bolton Journal
27 SEP 1990

Circle into space

23.74

MEMBERS of Heaton Book Circle will be exploring one of the intriguing mysteries of space when their new year gets underway next month.

Author Peter Hough, chairman of the Manchester UFO Research Association, will be exploring the question 'UFOs, Myth or Reality?' in a slide presentation.

The lecture, at Heaton Library on Monday, October 8, starts at 7.45 p.m. Admission is free and it is open to non-members of the Book Circle.

There's still time to catch the models of a fairground engine and horse-drawn carts on display at Farnworth Library, Market Street, Farnworth.

The models, in oak, mahogany and steel have been lovingly worked by former engineer Mr L. Tatlock who lives at Clifton Court, Farnworth. He worked for many years at Henry Crossley Packings, a local mill.

The models will be on show until the end of December.

OCTOBER 1990

3rd October 1990 (UK) – Three lights over Colchester

HELEN Robinson (30) was letting the dogs out into the back garden, at 11.15pm, when she saw:

> *"...three 'blobs' of light in the sky, forming a triangle. I called my husband, Harold. He came out and took some photographs. A few minutes later, they were out of view."*

Several photos were taken, but their whereabouts are not known. (**Source: Ron West**)

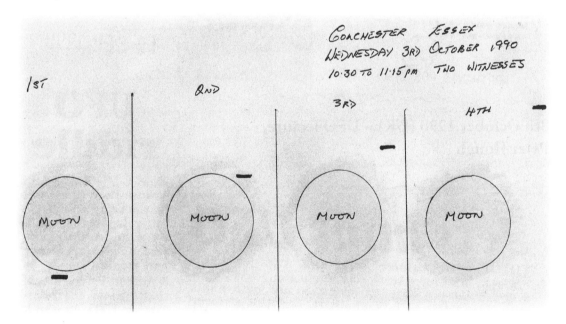

3rd October 1990 (USA) – UFO over Indiana

At 8pm, three people – including a Mr Flagg – were outside Argos Poplar Grove Church, looking up at the sky, when they saw a *'triangle'* with white lights on its corners, which appeared to be moving silently through the air, with its flat-side forward. (**Source: MUFON Indiana, Field Investigator – Norma Croda**)

Diamond-shaped UFO (UK) seen over Rollright Stones on Autumn Equinox

UFO mystery

A COUPLE claim they saw a UFO hovering over them while camping out one night last week.

Wolf Fernandez and his girlfriend Kirsty Berry, both of Cloutsham Street, Northampton, say the black, diamond shaped craft appeared as they lay in their tent by the mysterious Rollright Stone Circle near Banbury on the Autumn Equinox.

Mr Fernandez, 27, said: "At first I thought it was a plane, but it had lights all round the side and then it began to wobble about the clouds.

Slow

"It was really low and virtually stopped right above us then it just turned left and went away dead slowly. It made a noise like a generator, but really loud.

"Someone said it could have been one of those stealth bombers, but I know it wasn't. A stealt bomber wouldn't have lights all over it. I'm sur what I saw was a UFO."

NORTHANTS POST 05.10.90

8th October 1990 (UK) – UFO lecture, Peter Hough

Jets hunt UFO

THE Belgian airforce scrambled two jet fighters — to hunt for a UFO. Last night top brass threw a veil of secrecy over the operation and both pilots were forbidden to talk about it. But the airforce admit they found nothing. For the UFO — triangular with three bright lights — appeared to black itself out and disappeared with incredible acceleration. This year alone there have been more than 10,000 reported UFO sightings — mostly in French-speaking Wallonia.

Bolton Evening News

18 SEP 1990

UFO riddle

■ MEMBERS of Heaton Book Circle will be exploring one of the intriguing mysteries of space when their new season gets underway next month.

■ Author Peter Hough, chairman of the Manchester UFO Research Association, will be exploring the question "UFOs, Myth or Reality?" in a slide presentation at Heaton Library on Monday, October 8.

DAILY TELEGRAPH 13.10.90

Belgian UFO spotters are 'left seeing stars'

By Adrian Berry, Science Correspondent

THOUSANDS of Belgians have reported UFO sightings unaware they are looking at the planet Mars, a British astronomer said yesterday.

More than 2,600 people claim to have seen a strange triangular object with three huge lights hovering in the night sky. Pilots of two F-16 fighters, scrambled to investigate, reported that it accelerated away from them as they approached.

But Ian Ridpath, editor-in-chief of Popular Astronomy magazine, claimed the alien presence was nothing more than an illusion created by Mars, now unusually bright and close to the Earth, and certain stars.

"I don't want to say anything rude about the ignorance of Belgians, since people in many countries have mistaken Mars for a UFO," he said.

"What they are seeing is almost certainly a triangle in the night sky in the constellation of Taurus formed by Mars and two other bright stars, one of which is probably the bright orange star, Aldebaran, 65 light years away.

"The description by the fighter pilots of the object accelerating away is exactly consistent with what a planet or a star would appear to do. This illusion has been the cause of thousands of false UFO sightings.

"Next month, Mars will be even brighter, and for this reason National Astronomy Week is being held to educate the British public about the night sky and ensure they don't make idiots of themselves like the Belgians."

Other astronomers agree that people need educating, noting that, during blackouts at the time of the 1972 miners' strike, dozens looked at the stars and demanded to know why "those people" were still getting electricity.

Jimmy Carter, the former US President, once mistook the bright planet Venus for a UFO, and during the war several pilots tried to chase the two planets, thinking they were enemy aircraft.

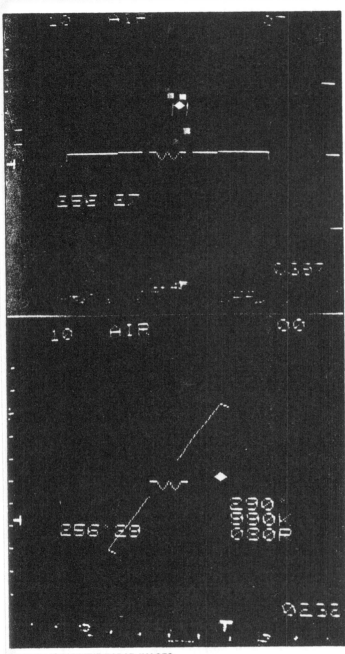

HOW TO "READ" THE RADAR IMAGES

Tʜᴇꜱᴇ photographs are extracted from the radar recordings of the *F-16s* sent up in pursuit of a UFO during the night of March 30/31, 1990. The two pictures formed on the screens with an interval between them of some seconds. On the first photograph the successive previous positions of the UFO are shown by small squares. The pilot having locked-in his radar onto the intruder, the symbol representing the UFO has now become a diamond-shaped lozenge. The small vertical lines framing it indicate that the pilot has signalled to his computer the target to be pursued, and the radar will henceforward stay automatically directed onto it. In the centre of the picture the "W" indicates the axis of the flight-path of the *F-16*, with its course, 256° 29 (west/southwest) indicated below. The lines on each side of the "W" represent the artificial horizon. The word "AIR" at the top-centre of the screen means that the radar is programmed for an air-to-air search, namely the detection of everything at an altitude of over 200 metres. The UFO is at a height of 2,000 metres, recorded at the top-right of the photo by the figures 07 (7,000 ft.). *The full video sequence shows that the UFO then dives towards the ground in one second.*

In the second picture, the figures 00 (top-right of the screen) show that the UFO is below the height of 200 metres. The line of the artificial horizon falls away; the aircraft starts to bank to the right in order to line up on the diving UFO. The column of figures beneath the diamond lozenge gives the speed of the object in knots, or 1,830 kms./p.h. (Mach 1.5)!

Finally, the 08OR indicates the nature of the target in coded language. This figure indicates that the target corresponds to no known identification.

The UFO went through the sound-barrier without producing any bang. In one second, it will be lost for the pilot.

FURTHER BRITISH PRESS COMMENT ON THE "BELGIAN WAVE"

By Gordon Creighton

As we indicated some time ago in our discussions of the Soviet reports of 1989 about UFO sightings and UFO landings, the journalists of the English-speaking world dealt with the problem by wrapping it up in a fog of general buffoonery which is so far unparalleled. If time and space permit we intend in due course to supply a detailed analysis of this remarkable operation.

Not too much has been said yet in Britain about the Belgian affair. *"Mum"* is clearly the word on *that!* But Britain's *Daily Mail* of October 11, 1990, has given us a nice piece in the buffoon tradition, with the buffoon headline carefully selected so as to cast ridicule on the entire report:-

HOW THEY TOOK THE NEWS FROM MARS TO GHENT

Daily Mail Reporter

Have the lords of the universe chosen their first colony on Earth? If they have, their subject people could be ... the Belgians.

The question is exercising the minds not only of the Belgian scientific establishment but also of the air force and police.

UFO freaks can forget all that stuff about flying saucers, according to a series of sightings over the tiny country more often concerned with eating, drinking, and minding its own business.

The mysterious visitors are appearing in flying pyramids.

Belgian police have logged more than 2,600 sightings of a triangular object, with three huge lights, hovering in the night sky — including reports from at least 20 of their own gendarmes. And UFO-spotters are euphoric after the latest sighting was apparently backed up by the Belgian Air Force's own radar log.

According to a physicist at Brussels Free University, Professor Léon Brenig, two *F-16* fighters scrambled from Ghent after reports from the public of another UFO.

He says their radar locked on to an object which accelerated away before they could see it.

The pilots have been forbidden to say anything. But Air Force Colonel Willfried De Brouwer, in charge of an official investigation into the incident, admitted: "They are convinced it was something special".

Professor Brénig, formerly an unbeliever, now claims to have seen a UFO himself.

He is hoping the analysis of photographs and radar echoes of earlier episodes will be ready this week and will be discussed at a gathering of the country's scientists later this month.

He is also arranging a UFO hunt for members of the Belgian Society for the Study of Space Phenomena, with the backing of the Belgian Army and Air Force, he says.

"No country has ever taken UFO sightings so seriously", he said. "I am a sceptical man, but I feel that something is happening which is very strange ..."

A DRAMATIC AND FULMINATING SOLUTION!

By Gordon Creighton

Only two days later (October 13, 1990), after all the hours that we had put into reporting and translating these stories from Belgium, we find, in one of Britain's most prestigious newpapers, the *Daily Telegraph*, the authoritative report which has finally put paid to all our nonsensical efforts over these past forty years in attempting to pander so much rubbish about so-called *"flying saucers"* and *"UFOs"* and so on.

Already, as our readers will be aware, we had seen, in the summer of 1990, the announcement from BUFORA, the world's leading authority on all these matters, that all UFO research was now at an end, and that all so-called "UFO reports" and "flying saucer reports", and all tales of close encounters with alien beings, have been conclusively and effectively explained away as due to the simple phenomenon of *plasma vortices*. (This ruling has received the official *imprimatur* of J. Randles, the leading world authority in all these questions and Britain's only professional writer since Wm. Shekspir).

(Inevitably the startling news puts the future of such a journal as ours in much jeopardy, and we shall shortly be discussing the problem of whether we ought to pack up or, conceivably, find some other theme on which we might continue to pontificate.)

We give below the all-important press item from the London *Daily Telegraph* of October 13, 1990, in which, as readers will see, Mr Adrian Berry, Britain's top scientific writer, rallies to the support of Mr Ian Ridpath, Britain's most distinguished living astronomer, in giving the true explanation for the absurd stream of tales that have been coming out of Belgium for almost a year past. In this particular case, admittedly, it seems that the ridiculous error has been due to the simple misinterpretation of an *astronomical* phenomenon (to wit the planet Mars) and not due to the misinterpretation of a *plasma vortex* phenomenon, but that does not alter the fact that the daft lunacy of thousands of simple-minded Belgian citizens — not to mention the daft lunacy of some of the top officials of their much-vaunted Belgian Air Force — now stands plainly revealed for all to see. (Incidentally, we here in Britain have the Belgians among our Allies in NATO! And — horror of horrors — NATO actually has its *Headquarters* in Belgium — of all places! The mind boggles at the depth of the dangerous incompetence which this scandal has now revealed. What can be the possible use of such nincompoops as this Belgian Air Force within NATO? Surely all of us who are concerned about the future of NATO and of Western Europe will feel eternally indebted to Messrs Adrian Berry and Ian Ridpath for having prised the lid off such a veritable can of worms!)

Here is their Report:-

DAILY TELEGRAPH, October 13, 1990 (page 7).

BELGIAN UFO SPOTTERS ARE 'LEFT SEEING STARS'

by Adrian Berry, Science Correspondent

THOUSANDS of Belgians have reported UFO sightings unaware that they are looking at the planet Mars, a British astronomer said yesterday.

More than 2,600 people claim to have seen a strange triangular object with three huge lights hovering in the night sky. Pilots of two *F-16*, fighters, scrambled to investigate, reported that it accelerated away from them as they approached.

But Ian Ridpath, Editor-in-Chief of *Popular Astronomy*, claimed the alien presence was nothing more than an illusion created by *Mars*, now unusually bright and close to the Earth, and by certain other stars.

"I don't want to say anything rude about the ignorance of Belgians" — he said — "since people in many countries have mistaken *Mars* for a UFO .

"What they are seeing is almost certainly a triangle in the night sky in the constellation of Taurus, formed by *Mars* and two other bright stars, one of which is probably the bright orange star *Aldebaran*, 65 light-years away".

"The description by the fighter pilots of the object accelerating away is exactly consistent with what a planet or a star would appear to do. This illusion has been the cause of thousands of false UFO sightings."

"Next month, *Mars* will be even brighter, and for this reason NATIONAL ASTRONOMY WEEK is being held to educate the British public about the night sky and ensure that they don't make idiots of themselves like the Belgians."

Other astronomers agree with Ian Ridpath that people need educating, noting that, during blackouts at the time of the 1972 miners' strike, dozens of people looked at the stars and demanded to know why "those people" were still getting electricity.

Jimmy Carter, the former U.S. president, once mistook the bright planet *Venus* for a UFO, and during the war several pilots tried to chase the two planets, *Mars* and *Venus*, thinking they were enemy aircraft.

NOTE BY EDITOR, FSR

Our readers will no doubt recall with admiration the sagacity and skill displayed by Ian Ridpath a few years ago at the time of the absurd story about a UFO having been seen in Rendlesham Forest, Suffolk. It was he who solved the matter by pointing out that what had been seen by the American Commanding Officer and other U.S.A.F. officers was simply the Orford Ness lighthouse flashing through the trees. These American imbeciles, some of whom had already been stationed there for months or even several years, had not even noticed the lighthouse until that evening, and did not even know that it was there! So naturally the poor fools concluded that it was a "UFO"!

Belgian air force put on UFO alert

From JOHN FRASER in Brussels

Yorkshire Post 11/10/90   2528

THE Belgian air force has scrambled two fighters to intercept a triangular UFO with three huge red lights.

Military officers have refused to give details of the night-time UFO search, and the two pilots have been told not to talk about it. But the air force admits it found nothing, because the craft appeared to put out its lights and zoom away at an incredible speed.

While many people regard the issue as a joke, it has puzzled many experts. There have been more than 10,000 reported UFO sightings in Belgium this year alone.

The air force has even put two planes — a C130 troop carrier and an Icelander reconnaissance aircraft — at the disposal of Belgium's Society for the Study of Space Phenomena. For four days the two planes, equipped with infra-red cameras, flew up and down the country with the UFO hunters on board, but again the only results were a crop of jokes in the Belgian Press — mainly in Dutch-language publi-

cations mocking French-speaking "UFO freaks".

The sightings and photographs taken by witnesses are now being analysed by computers at the Royal Military Academy. Experts at the Free University of Brussels are also making a study of radar-echoes picked up by two F16 jets.

Prof Leon Boenig, who is in charge of the research, said: "I am a sceptical man, but I feel that something is happening which is very strange. There have been too many sightings — 10,000 at least this year — and 80 per cent of them concern a triangular-shaped object.

"There have been reports from people in all social classes, from countesses to dustmen. More than 100 of the people concerned were policeman — there was even a Flemish tax inspector who saw a UFO from his garage near Liege.

"People lose their fear of seeming ridiculous when a solid, respected citizen like that is a witness."

Yorkshire Post 12/10/90

Fresh sighting in UFO hunt

From JOHN FRASER in BRUSSELS

BELGIAN UFO hunters were yesterday investigating a new sighting of a triangular object, which has made thousands of appearances in recent months.

They are trying to discover whether a colony of men from outer space has chosen their country to establish a new home.

The latest sighting of the triangular object was reported by a motorist near the Belgian-Luxembourg border.

"He was driving his car down a road when he saw some lights and thought there was an accident," said Belgium's chief UFO hunter, Mr Lucien Clerebaut. But when he drew closer he observed a huge triangular object at least 100 metres long.

"It was hovering several metres above the ground in a field by the road. There were green and red lights. Then it rose slowly to a height of about 50 metres before extinguishing the lights and accelerating away out of sight."

The motorist reported his experience on Mr Clerebaut's answerphone at his home in Brussels.

"The same night we had at least a dozen calls from several parts of the country, including Flanders," Mr Clerebaut said.

So far this year, there have been around 10,000 sightings of UFOs over Belgium, but no positive proof of what the triangular-shaped object can be. It has been spotted on air force radar, but the mysterious craft sped off when fighter jets were scrambled to intercept it.

Meanwhile a word of caution has come from Prof Leon Brenig, a physicist at Brussels Free University. The professor, who is analysing the witnesses' reports with computers, said: "I have some information that the object could be an ultra-secret new US plane."

UFO scramble

JET fighter pilots scoured the skies in vain after thousands of Belgians reported seeing a triangular-shaped UFO with three huge lights.

10th/11th October 1990 (USA) – UFO display, Monterey, Indiana

At Skibo Minnesota, formations of white objects, with red and green lights, were seen in the sky that alternately hovered and darted around. They were also tracked on radar. (**Source:** *UFOE II*, Section IV)

The following day, at 9pm, a delta-shaped object was sighted in the sky, near Grissom Air Force Base, Indiana by two people. It passed right over them, at around 500ft, with no sound. The object was described as:

> *"Three white border lights, set in a triangular pattern, base moving forward! The rear light was trailed by a faint white light blinking every once in a while. Inside the triangle there were many red, green and blue, smaller lights."*

> (**Source:** MUFON, Indiana, Field Investigator – K.O. Learner)

11th October 1990 (UK) – UFO seen over Yorkshire

A terrified motorist from Stalybridge, Yorkshire, contacted the Uppermill Police on this day, after having sighted what he referred to as *"a large saucer-shaped object, with flashing white lights"*, while driving over Saddleworth Moor, near the County boundary, on the Holmfirth road, at 9.45pm. According to the unnamed man, a large spotlight was also shone onto his car. The description also matched at least two other reports made from the same area.

> (**Source:** *Oldham Evening Chronicle*, 12.10.1990 – 'Alert on reports of UFOs')

---

12 OCT 1990

Alert on reports of UFOs

THREE separate reports of a flying saucer hovering above the moors had police in Saddleworth and West Yorkshire on the alert last night.

A 27-year-old Stalybridge man was shaking uncontrollably when he reported the UFO to police officers from Uppermill.

He saw the object earlier as he drove into Yorkshire and, as he returned, it shone a spotlight on his car, close to the county boundary on the Holmfirth road.

Large

His description of a large, saucer-shaped object, with flashing white lights, matched two independent sightings in West Yorkshire.

One was given by a woman who regularly travels the road and both sightings were within 45 minutes.

The moors have been the location for a substantial number of intermittent UFO reports over the past 20 years.

Aviation authorities were not aware of any craft in the vicinity around the time of the sighting, from 9 45 p.m.

13th October 1990 (UK) – The *Today* Newspaper – We are not alone! 'Kerb crawlies'

THE UNKNOWN

★ ★ ★ ★ TODAY Saturday October 13 1990 **23**

Driving home we saw strange lights

The craft hovered by nearby trees

Six robots were looking at us

The three of us now realise . .

WE ARE NOT ALONE

FANS of world-famous novelist Whitley Strieber were stunned when he revealed that his best-selling book Communion was based on a personal close encounter with aliens.

Strieber recalls how he woke one night to find a small but menacing creature in his bedroom.

"It had a rounded hat on, with its two sharp rim that jutted out about four inches, two dark holes for eyes and a black downturning line of a mouth that became an O. I was simply terrified," he says.

Later, the author claims, he was spirited away to a strange chamber where aliens operated on him.

Now Hollywood has made a film — Communion — based on his terrifying ordeal, starring Christopher Walken and featuring a soundtrack by Eric Clapton.

But it's not only Strieber who has had such otherworldly experiences. Thousands of people claim to have made contact with aliens. Here five of them describe their eerie encounters with visitors from another world.

KERB CRAWLIES: Rosemary met aliens on the A5

MIND PROBE: Christopher Walken is wired up and his brain probed by alien abductors in the film Communion

Haunted Skies comment:

What an offensive picture, inferring an association between a highly respectable woman – well-known to the authors – and some form of illegal activity.

Rosemary and her two friends, one of whom was Val Walters, endured a very strange experience which took place in 1983 – a matter that has been published in a previous volume of *Haunted Skies*. Such is the price of courage for reporting something which many treat with disbelief!

Rosemary Hawkins

Valerie Walters

News of the World, June 5, 1983

Did it happen ?—Three women who say they were kidnapped by UFO

CLOSE ENCOUNTER AT THE SHAMROCK CAFE

STRANGE red and white lights hovered overhead as three women drove home from their weekly night out.

Mysteriously, their car came to a halt outside the Shamrock cafe on the A5 in Shropshire, though the driver had her foot hard down on the accelerator.

Then the lights suddenly vanished and the trio rushed excitedly to a nearby police station, where they reported a close encounter with a UFO.

But that was when they noticed that something even stranger had happened. The drive to the police station should have taken five minutes. Instead it took twenty-five.

Only now, with the help of hypnosis under the strictest supervision, has an explanation been found for those missing twenty minutes. And it is amazing.

Gruff

Lights

Bed

SPECIAL REPORT by KEITH BEABEY and PIPPA SIBLEY

HYPNOTISED: Val

KIDNAPPED: Valerie and Rosemary, the UFO victims.

THE SPOT where a UFO captured the women

TERRIFYING: Artist's impression of the scene aboard the spaceship ... the aliens examine one of the women

Victims' view of the ship

UNCANNY: Under hypnosis, the three women produced remarkably similar drawings of the space

14th October 1990 (UK) - UFO over Essex

At 2.30am, housewife Natalie Lawlor (23) of Elm Grove, Great Clacton, in Essex, was sat downstairs, when she heard what sounded like something moving about outside. She went upstairs to the front bedroom and looked out.

Following her interview with members of Ron West's UFO Group, she wrote this account of what she and her father - Keith - saw, hovering over Holland Road. Keith described is as being a yellow pear-shaped object rather than triangular, and attempted to chase it, but lost sight of it near the seafront.

Summary of events.

Please describe in your own words the events of the sighting;

I was sitting downstairs in the living room, & I kept imagining things jumping about outside. I kept thinking that I have to look out, but could not go out. Then I went upstairs into my bedroom at the front of the house and saw the object straight away. It was gold colour and shaped as page 4. It shrunk back to a dot & gold clouds appeared either side; at the top. The object then appeared again fully, and the clouds became thin wavy gold lines. The object then disappeared with gold lines still there, the underneath where the object was or would have been 2 oblong shapes appeared (as on p4, ⊥) like so. There were lights on it red, green & maybe blue, very faint. It then went away, and the object appeared again with the thin gold lines. It slowly disappeared until the gold lines were left. Then slowly they disappeared. I think the object look something like this altogether [drawing] the object being a dome type thing of light and the oblong around the bottom.

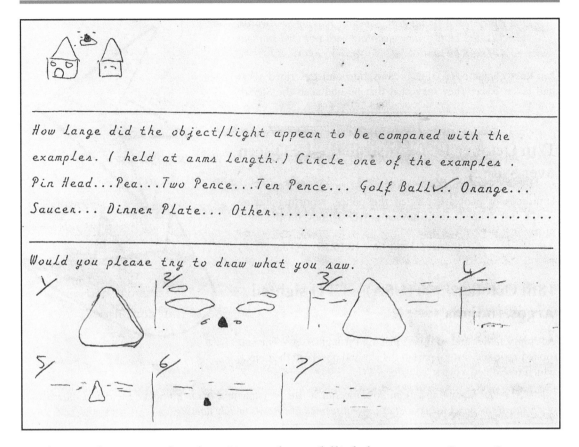

How large did the object/light appear to be compared with the examples. (held at arms length.) Circle one of the examples.

Pin Head...Pea...Two Pence...Ten Pence... Golf Ball✓. Orange...

Saucer... Dinner Plate... Other.............................

Would you please try to draw what you saw.

14th October 1990 (UK) – Cigar-shaped *'light'* seen over Scout Scar

At 10.30pm Chesterfield, Derbyshire, joiner – Roger Hadley – was driving along the A591 Kendal Bypass, towards the M6, with two others and his daughter, Sharon, when they noticed a cigar-shaped *'light'* in the sky.

> *"It looked like a fluffy light, about 30ft across, inside a cloud of steam or mist. It seemed to move about inside the 'cloud' in a left to right, then up and down manner. The shape seemed to change at one point, from cigar to spherical. We stopped for five minutes to watch it."*

The police, at Kendal, confirmed they had received a report of a UFO seen over Scout Scar, at 10pm, but suggested that it might have been people out looking for foxes, with powerful lights!

(Source: Personal interview/*Westmoreland Gazette*, Kendal, 19/10/1990 – 'Night lights may be UFOs')

16th October 1990 (UK) – UFO over Essex

RAF serviceman Michael Ross – now in his 80s, from Basildon, in Essex – sighted an unusual display of coloured light, swirling around the sky over the town, at 11pm.

> *"I picked up a pair of binoculars and was astonished to see the effect was being created by a UFO, performing random gyrations across the sky – a bit like a firefly.*
>
> *I continued to observe it until midnight, when I then saw two parallel 'globes of light' appear from*

the east – as if in tandem – before moving westwards, towards the 'craft' – now gleaming with reflected sunlight – out of sight by 1am."

Mr Ross contacted a UFO organisation and described what had taken place. They suggested that he had seen the Stealth Bomber!

17th October 1990 (Australia) – UFO seen over Sydney

Hundreds of people contacted the police, reporting having seen a disc-shaped object hovering over Sydney, on the early morning.

(Source: *Daily Star* 18.10.1990 'G'day ET!!')

18th October 1990 (USA) – UFO sighted, Argos, Indiana

At 7pm, a father and son were driving through Argos. The son looked up in the eastern part of the sky and observed the object, which resembled a black *'bow tie'*.

"At first I thought it was an airplane, but it was very low and made no noise. The object moved slowly; its speed varied and at times it seemed like it was merely floating."

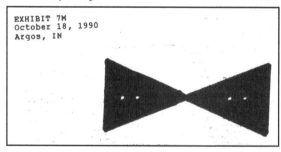

EXHIBIT 7M
October 18, 1990
Argos, IN

It was seen to descend to about 500ft in altitude and range. One side of the object showed two green lights – the other two, red lights. It was last seen heading away westwards. The UFO was viewed with binoculars at some point, for approximately 15 minutes.

(Source: MUFON, Indiana, Field Investigators – Lamberson and Learner)

19th October 1990 (USA) – Mysterious lights seen over Plymouth, Indiana

At 11.25pm, two people were driving home through the east side of the town, when they observed some strange lights, which passed over their car and then hovered in one place for a while, at only 50-75ft way from them. Initially, although frightened, they became curious and turned-off the car radio and rolled down the window. They saw an unusual configuration of red, white, and green lights, hovering silently in the sky. From the side, a domed dark top portion, showing a large white light, was seen centered underneath. Inbetween the dark top and the white light was a small red light.

"The bottom view looked like a bell-shaped pattern, with the red light in the lead and a green light at the rear."

The object was seen to head eastwards and then make a 'U-turn' and appear to land. Five minutes later it was spotted in the east, and seemed to be moving with them, before growing fainter over the next 15 minutes, before disappearing from view.

(Source: MUFON Indiana, Field Investigators – Lamberson and Learner)

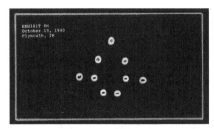

24th October 1990 (USA) – Silver *'disc'*-shaped object over Kentucky

At 2.45pm, a lady in a 12th floor office, at Louisville, observed a stationary, silvery, flat-bottomed *'disc'* below her level, against a backdrop of trees. About 20ft in diameter, its only feature initially was an upturned rim. The object began moving slowly upward and away in an arc, and then proceeded back and forth in half-circle paths, alternately displaying its black underside while continually moving farther away. The witness was joined by a second woman, then a man, who alone saw a second object – boomerang-shaped – merge with the first in the distance. About two miles away, the objects suddenly disappeared from view. Duration: 10 minutes. (**Source:** MUFON)

25th October 1990 (UK) – Mysterious force field encountered at Bristol

26 OCT 1990   BRISTOL JO.   AL

Experts investigate youngsters' UFO encounter with yellow peril

Bubble trouble

2374

EXPERTS are to investigate astonishing claims by two ten-year-olds that their game of flying saucers turned into a close encounter with a real UFO.

Youngster Kelly Broom told this week how she threw a frisbee towards her friend Rachel Stewart... and it hit a "force field" and zoomed back at her.

The scared youngsters tried to run home but were caught inside a mystery yellow bubble. They were hurled to the

Exclusive by Morag Massey

ground by a "shock" and lay there shaking with fear.

"We were really, really scared," said Kelly from her home in Walker Close, Downend.

"It was like an enormous bubble. We couldn't get out," she said. "It felt like we were suffocating and we thought we would die."

Kelly and Rachel were playing last Thursday afternoon in a field near Downend sports centre. The friends

held hands until they managed to break through and run home.

"It was difficult explaining it to people afterwards because it sounds so unreal," said Kelly.

Kelly's mum Tanya was convinced her daughter was telling the truth. She visited the field to try and work out what had happened.

"Kelly swore on her family's life she was telling the truth. I believe her," said Tanya.

"It must have been a UFO force-field. I'm relieved they managed to escape," she said.

29th October 1990 (USA) – Triangular UFO sighting over Argos, Indiana

During the evening, a married woman was at her home address; her son and husband were outside. An object was seen approaching from the east, which was originally thought to be an airplane, but as it moved silently closer, a triangular pattern of red and green blinking lights underneath the object were seen.

The husband ran into the house and asked his wife to come out. The object, showing two bright lights on the rear and estimated to be 1,000 feet away from the family, appeared to be white and shiny, with a rounded *'nose'*, and was kept under observation for about four minutes, before it tilted to the right and turned north-west.

(Source: MUFON Indiana, Field Investigator – K.O. Learner)

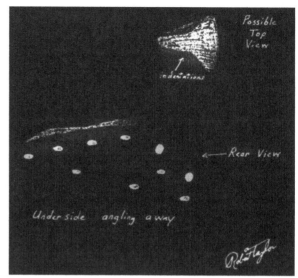

27th October 1990 (UK) – Red *'disc'* over Essex

Rosalyn Reynolds was driving home, at 12.30am, from Point Clear. When near to St. Osyth village, she saw:

> *"…two long red lights, swooping towards the vehicle at an angle to us. I called for Mark to stop and he did. I wound the window down and then this black 'disc' swooped towards us, at tremendous speed. It then swung silently, almost on the spot, at a 45° angle, before flying away towards woodland on our left.*
>
> *It had two very long cherry-red oblong lights, which gave the appearance of being on the side of a 'disc'-shaped object, which I estimated to be 2-300ft across."*

28th October 1990 (UK) – UFO over Essex

Mrs P. Bailey (57) – a housewife, from Wickford – was driving her white Mazda van along the A12, at 6.30pm, in October 1990, accompanied by her young son, after having been to see her mother in Rainham. The route back involved Hornchurch, Harold Hill Hospital, and then on to the A12.

> *"As we neared Mountnessing roundabout, along the old Roman road, we noticed a bright 'light' in the sky and wondered what it could have been. When we reached the traffic island, we were shocked to see what I first took to be a big black Harrier jet aircraft, hovering low in the sky, showing a powerful spotlight. I then realised I had never seen anything like this before in my life. I stopped for a better look but couldn't see anything, due to my vision being blocked by trees, so I turned around again – at which point it appeared to be circling in front of us and at one stage stopped in mid-air over the roof of a nearby house. Moments later it moved away and out of sight."*

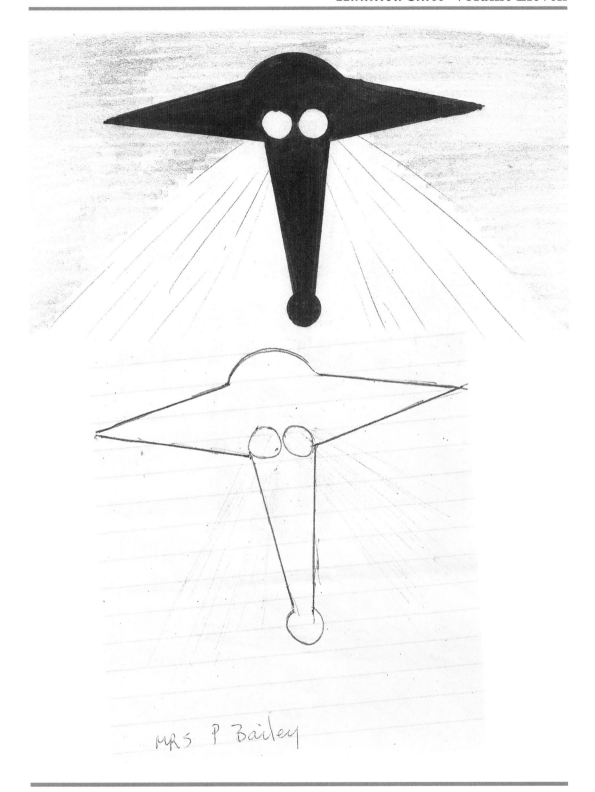

31st October 1990 (UK) – UFO sighting over Margate

6 NU. 1990 Thanet Times, Margate.

Couple spooked by close encounter on the planet Thanet

ARE ALIENS SPYING ON US?

Stars in their eyes — Tracey Render and Paul Cowell

TT2140/23

Exclusive report by Alison Terry

FLYING saucers may be spying over Thanet! It's not a Hallowe'en joke, but a real possibility if a weird sighting by a Thanet couple has an extra-terrestrial explanation.

Strange goings-on were seen in the sky over Kingsgate by a number of spooked locals in the early hours of Wednesday — which just happened to be Hallowe'en morning.

Several people say they saw lightning coming out of clouds, but Paul Cowell is sure he saw seven separate UFOs.

Puzzled Paul said: "I saw seven separate bundles of flashing lights go into a black shape in a cloud over the Captain Digby pub.

"If I have cracked, then I've cracked, but I have never seen anything like it before. It sounds absurd, but I know what I saw."

And Paul is sure the Government knows there is something going on in the skies, but has covered it up with warnings of freak weather conditions that did not happen.

"If I had only seen one of these things, I would have thought it was a helicopter. But there were seven of them. It was a very exciting experience, but shocking," he said.

A spokesman for RAF Manston said: "We cannot shed any light on the matter, so to speak. We did have a helicopter flying that night, but much earlier on. It is

nothing to do with us."

Paul and his girlfriend Tracey Render were watching the lightning from their house in Kingsgate, when they saw the spooky spectacles.

Paul said he saw the strange lightning, lighting up the clouds, making them gold in colour. Then he spotted a little mass of lights, similar to a star, travel forward and go into the black

shape. This was followed by six others.

"The lightning was coming out of the clouds. It was like a signal and then these things came in. I was shocked," he said.

"There was no way that black shape was a cloud," said Tracey. "I know what I saw, but I expect some people will think I'm mad."

The next morning Paul called Invicta Radio to see if

anyone else had seen the weird spectacle. Several people called to say they had seen the lightning coming out of the cloud, but no one had seen the curious clusters that went into it.

"I still can't believe it," Paul said. "I wanted to call someone to tell us we were not hallucinating. I have a strange feeling it is going to happen again tonight. I just wish I had a video camera."

Spy on our sexy Hallowe'en page 3 girl

Isle of Thanet Gazette, Margate

-2 NOV 1990

UFO report at bay

2374

FREAK lightning and seven flashing lights were sighted over the Captain Digby pub, Kingsgate, in the early hours of Wednesday.

Paul Cowell, manager of In The Red cafe, Margate, said he watched dumbstruck as the lights disappeared into a black shape in a cloud. He said he had never seen anything like it before in his life.

A spokesman for RAF Manston ruled out the possibility of helicopters. "It is nothing to do with us, so I can't throw any light on the matter, so to speak," he said.

NOVEMBER 1990

1st November 1990 (UK) – Half-moon-shaped UFO seen

AT 6.57pm, Christopher Richard Winter (57) – a civil/marine engineer by profession, who had seen service in the RAF – was in Firwoods Road, Halstead, in Essex, exercising the dogs near Stones Farm.

"I spotted a 'light' over Monks Wood, but continued on my journey. It then changed to dirty orange and then red, before growing smaller and disappearing from view, westwards. Compass bearing 200°SSW, heading westwards 270° laterally."

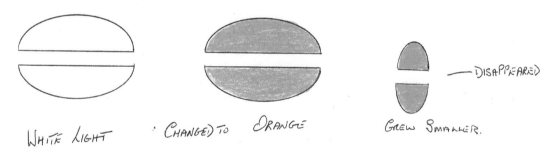

3rd November 1990 (UK) – UFO sighted over Essex

5th November 1990 (Genoa) – British pilot sights UFO

At 6.03pm, Captain Mike D'Alton was on a night flight from Rome to London, flying over Genoa, Italy, in a Boeing 737.

> *"A UFO appeared on our right-hand side... we were travelling at Mach point 8. It went into our 12 o'clock position and accelerated away.*
>
> *Another two Tornados saw it. In all my 23 years of flying, I've never seen a craft operate anything like this."*

According to flight chief steward – Bob Parkhouse:

> *"The UFO was moving from left to right across the horizon. It was a sight I'd never seen before!"*

Captain D'Alton would also state, later, that he was convinced of the extra-terrestrial origin of the object, because of its tremendous speed and agility. The UFO made no sonic boom, though travelling above the speed of sound. It also made manoeuvres beyond that of our current technology will allow. The sharp turns, at great speeds, that the captain witnessed, would have ripped any pilot to shreds.

The sighting was corroborated by the captains of two other Tornados in the vicinity, but nothing was seen by air traffic controllers.

The object was described as a silver '*disc*', with three faint points of light in arrow formation, and a fourth light behind it. Captain D'Alton said the object was visible for about two minutes over Genoa.

> *"I've never seen anything like it before and can't explain what it was. My co-pilot and I called in two cabin crew to see it and then it went out of sight. Ground radar couldn't pick it up, so it must have been travelling at phenomenal speed."*

(Source: *Sunday Telegraph*, London/Sunday Mail, Glasgow, 11th November 1990)

Sunday Telegraph –

11 NOV 1990

Pilot gets flying visit from UFO 2374

A BRITISH Airways pilot who has been flying for 23 years is convinced he saw a UFO this week. Captain Mike D'Alton, from Storrington, West Sussex, said the bright object must have been travelling at a phenomenal speed.

He described it as silver disc with three faint points of light in arrow formation in front and a fourth light behind it. It was visible for two minutes while his Boeing 737 night flight, from Rome to Gatwick was over Genoa.

Sunday Mail, Glasgow

11 NOV 1990

Airline pilot spots UFO

2374

A PILOT who has been flying for 23 years is convinced he saw a UFO last week. British Airways Captain Mike D'Alton said the bright object must have been travelling at a phenomenal speed.

He described it as a large silver disc with three points of light – in arrow formation – in the front, and a fourth light behind it.

"I've never seen anything like it before and can't explain what it was," said the 42-year-old West Sussex flier.

He said it was visible for about two minutes over Genoa, during his Boeing 737 night flight from Rome to Gatwick.

"My co-pilot and I called in two cabin crew to see it and then it went out of sight.

"Ground radar couldn't pick it up, so it must have been travelling at phenomenal speed."

Captain D'Alton said he has told the UFO Society Research Association about the mystery object.

Sunday Express **11 NOV 1990**

I saw UFO, says pilot

2374

A BRITISH Airways pilot who has been flying for 23 years claims he saw a UFO last week. Captain Mike D'Alton described it as a large silver disc travelling at high speed with faint points of light at the front and back. He and his crew saw it for about two minutes when his Boeing 737 was over Genoa during a night flight from Rome to Gatwick.

5th November 1990 (UK) – *'Flying triangle'* over Essex

At 10.30pm, Crystal Levesley of Wivenhoe, Colchester, was returning from an evening walk with her daughter, exercising the family dog, when they saw a large white *'light'* high in the sky. Crystal rushed in to fetch a pair of binoculars and, looking through them, saw three white lights forming a triangle. *"It then moved away; as it did so I saw a long hazy outline with a small green light at the rear."*

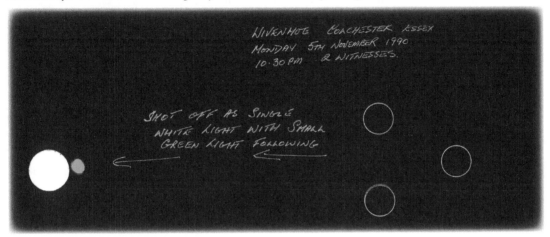

6th November 1990 (Australia) – *'Delta'*-shaped UFOs sighted

At 11.30pm, over Deniliquin, south of New South Wales, a *'delta'*-shaped object was reported to have hovered and manoeuvred about in the sky. Then two of the objects were seen; one landed in a field, and the other buzzed a car. Both UFOs were completely silent.

(Source: Timothy Good, *The UFO Report, 1992*, p. 138)

6th November 1990 (Belgium) – Further reports of UFO activity

ALERT OVER UFO

PARIS: Police in France, Italy, Switzerland and Belgium were inundated with calls yesterday about mystery shapes in the sky from orange balls and triangles to light clusters. But one UFO spotters club said: 'It was probably a satellite.'

Daily Star – London.

- 9 NOV 1990

UN-COMMON MARKET UFOs

SPACE experts said yesterday it was too soon to dismiss UFO sightings over Europe as a meteorite shower.

The triangle of moving lights was seen gliding silently across the sky by thousands of people in France, Belgium, Germany, Switzerland and Italy.

French experts who have been ordered to investigate the unidentified flying objects were amazed by the number of similar reports.

The Toulouse-based space boffins said they were puzzled because pilots reported the luminous shape moving parallel to the ground.

"This would suggest one or several self-propelled objects," a spokesman said yesterday.

"It could have been a meteorite," he added.

"But it could also have been aircraft or some other natural phenomenon."

7th November 1990 (Canada) – UFO display

A woman sights something strange in the sky, while swimming in the rooftop pool of her downtown Montreal hotel. It was described as a round, metallic object, projecting a series of brilliant light beams. She tells the lifeguard, who calls the hotel security guard. He contacts the police and a journalist from *La Presse* newspaper. The R.C.M.P, the Military, and even NASA, are called in. The aerial phenomenon lasts almost three hours, from 7.20pm to 10.10pm. The incident sparks sensation, due to the excellent documentation and the large number of very reliable witnesses. Some theorise that it is nothing more than the result of Northern Lights, dismissing the possibility of a UFO sighting. The event caught the attention of Bernard Guénette – a UFO researcher in Montreal.

Dr. Richard Haines

In 1992, Guénette and Dr. Richard Haines – a former NASA scientist – published a 25-page report on the sighting. The report concludes that *"the evidence for the existence of a highly unusual, hovering, silent, large, object is indisputable."*

It suggests some sort of huge physical object, about 540 metres wide, caused the lights but fails to identify its origin.

11th November 1990 (UK) – UFO over Essex

At 7pm, Mr P. Lumley of Point Clear, St. Osyth, Essex, was walking across a field, when:

> *"I saw, in the clouds, a very strange looking cloud – like cotton wool, or misty halo, around it – moving in an anticlockwise direction. Every now and then it glittered with what looked look sparks. It was a dark night and I walked up to the sea wall and looked out towards Brightlingsea, wondering if there was something out there that could be causing it. There was a dim moon to my right, and after watching the phenomena for a while I decided to return home."*

(Source: Ros Reynolds/Ron West)

13th November 1990 (USA) – Cluster of strange lights over Indiana

At 9pm two women were driving on US 35, at Logansport. The passenger alerted the driver that she had been watching something, and pointed into the sky. The driver said:

> *"I looked out of the passenger window and saw (100) bright lights going in sequence, one at a time, from right to left. As they lit up farther to the left, the ones on the right glowed to a red. It was the most beautiful thing I've ever seen. It moved in front of our car, across the road, then back in front of our car.*
>
> *It seemed weightless. It began to move east, at approximately 40-50 mph, and kept in front of us and to the right. We lost sight of it when we turned south, but found it again on Chase and Perrysburg Road (or at least what we thought was the same object). It was blinking red, green; white just above (maybe 15-20°) the horizon. It hovered for around 5-10 minutes, about 100ft off ground, approximately 200yds from us at its closest point."*

Was it sheer coincidence that approximately seven aircraft (jets) were observed in the area, during the sighting?

(Source: MUFON Indiana, Field Investigators – Roger Lamberson and K.O. Learner)

18th November 1990 (UK) – UFOs sighted over Somerset

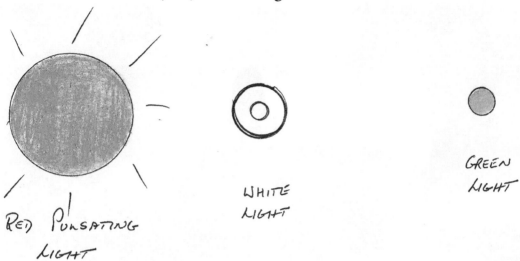

RED PULSATING LIGHT

WHITE LIGHT

GREEN LIGHT

20th November (UK) – UFO sighted over Essex

21st November 1990 (UK) – Report of alien abduction and rape

Kent housewife Maria Ward (33) – whom we met during a visit to the Wiltshire area, in the late 1990s – was to suffer a degrading experience, after claims of being abducted by an alien species. It began, according to Maria, after an intense light flooded into the room at 3.17am.

> *"I made my way to the landing. As the light went out I saw a ray of light on the wall, followed by a voice saying 'follow the light'. I then felt a sensation of being lifted upwards, and remember looking down at my feet and seeing the trees, garden, and rooftops".*

Into the Corridor

> *"My next recollection was being in a corridor and hearing the sound of shuffling feet, followed by the appearance of three little beings, about 3-4ft tall. They had large heads, a thin opening for a mouth, and were hairless and naked."*

They grabbed her by the elbows and led her along a corridor to a room where she was laid on a metal-like table, smelling something that reminded her of rotting leaves. Maria alleges the *'beings'* carried out experiments on her, before being joined by another taller alien. They were prodding and poking her, very quickly.

> *"...then a further 'being' appeared, even taller, about 5ft, milky-white in colour; his eyes were boring into me and I could feel he was reading my thoughts. It was like being raped mentally, forcing me to relive memories – everything stored in my mind, including emotions."*

Pinning her down, two of the smaller *'creatures'* held her head and inserted probes into her nose, while a third placed a triangular-shaped probe, with a light on the end, into her head, behind the ear, causing pain so excruciating that she thought she was going to die. Her next recollection was of having something done to her womb.

"I could feel something wriggling around inside me, like a worm. The next thing I knew was being in bed (at 4.26am) covered in blood. My feet were dirty and there was blood on the pillow and on my nightdress. My nose was bleeding and there was bruising around my thighs. Around my navel was a circular wound, which was seeping blood."

Maria was rushed to her local hospital, where doctors treated her for bruising on her thighs, hair pulled from the roots, and serious injuries to her private parts.

Comment by the doctor

According to Maria, a doctor's note commented:

"I have never seen these types of injuries and can find no logical cause for them".

Medical staff believed she had been raped and urged her to tell the police, but thought it pointless, under the circumstances, and denies the suggestion made to her, later, that it had been a dream.

On the lecture circuit

Maria has lectured at various UFO Conferences about her experiences. We would have liked to have asked her a number of further questions about the incident, especially one as private and sensitive as this, but without being able to obtain sight of the medical notes pertaining to her proscribed treatment at hospital, felt we could not take the matter further as we have lost touch with her, but hope that she may feel inclined to contact us in due course as we would like to obtain further details regarding medical notes and other documentary evidence.

(Sources: numerous/including *Sunday News and Echo*, Manchester, 1.3.1993 – 'Aliens tried to kidnap us'/ *Leeds Weekly News*, 8.10.1992 – 'Something strange is going on')

22nd November 1990 (UK) – Boomerang-shaped UFO

A *'boomerang-shaped object, showing nine lights and a larger white light at the front edges'*, was seen by security guards at St. Osyth, heading eastwards over Clacton.

At 2.30am, a triangular object was sighted passing through the sky, close to Clacton Pier, at an estimated height of just 50ft, by two women, walking along the Clacton seafront.

> "We could see yellow, blue, and green lights, about the centre of the craft, with a mass of red lights at the rear; it was moving slowly. We thought it was going to crash into the sea; we heard no noise. We estimated the size of the object to be 4-500ft long. I saw what appeared to be an opening near the centre of the object; it wasn't an opening, it might have been a bulge." (Source Bill Eden, Essex UFO Group)

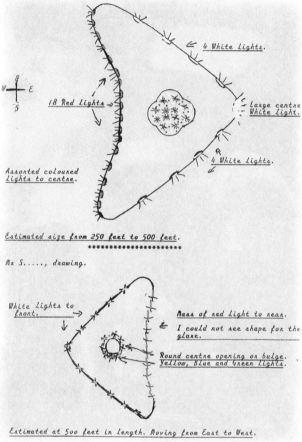

4 White Lights.

18 Red Lights →

Large centre White Light.

4 White Lights.

Assorted coloured lights to centre.

Estimated size from 250 feet to 500 feet.
****
Mr S....., drawing.

White lights to front. →

Mass of red Light to rear.
I could not see shape for the glare.
Round centre opening or bulge.
Yellow, Blue and Green lights.

Estimated at 500 feet in Length. Moving from East to West.

November 1990 (UK) – UFO over Ledbury, Gloucestershire

Gerry Wheatley was working for Pete Randall Flooring, Ledbury, laying a new concrete base at MSF Farmers', Ledbury (now the County Store) on what was a beautiful evening, with a clear sky.

> "As we worked, the occasional aircraft flew over quite low down. Being well acquainted with aircraft identification, I was able to distinguish what types of aircraft they were. At 11pm, I was on the way back to the caravan – in which we stayed while on site, about 100ft away from the car park. I glanced back. Pete was finishing off the bay in the doorway. As I turned around I was astonished to see an orange 'ball of light' across the hedgerows, about three-quarters of a mile away, then it extinguished from view. I rubbed my eyes, wondering whether I was seeing things, and started walking back towards Pete – but my curiosity aroused, I tuned around and saw what looked like a low cloud of mist hovering above the tops of trees. Inside the 'mist' was a pulsating light, which increased in brightness – as if someone was operating a switch. Pete appeared next to me, shouting out 'what the hell is that?' Suddenly there was a terrific flash of light and a cone-shaped object shot upwards into the sky and out of sight, in seconds, leaving a glowing vapour trail behind it. We were so excited that we had a drive around, but saw nothing else. The next morning I told some of the other men what we had seen. They laughed at us and made cryptic comments about 'little green men', so I kept my mouth shut." **(Source: Personal interview)**

25th November 1990 (USA) – UFO sighted over Milton, Florida

At 12.40pm, a Navy technician sighted a dull silver-grey wingless fuselage, flying from north to south at airliner speed.

(Source: Paul Ferrughilli, *Computer Catalogue of UFO Reports*, 1988-94)

Bobby dazzled

People 18.11.1990

UFO experts are investigating sightings by police of a strange object with blue and white lights over Somerset. London air traffic control say there was a "blip" on their radar at the time.

24th November 1990 (UK) – Fireball seen

28th November 1990 (UK) – UFOs over Swindon

A cluster of mysterious lights were seen circling over the town, between 8pm and 10.30pm, as a result of which over 150 people contacted the police and local newspapers. On this occasion an answer was found. It was the searchlights used to commemorate the opening of Cairo's night club!

(Source: *Swindon Evening Advertiser*, 29.11.1990 – 'Illuminating mystery rings bells')

–Plymouth–

25 NOV 1990

Strange lights from above

UFO Experts are investigating reports of strange lights in the sky over the West Country, early yesterday.

A police inspector saw what he believed was a meteor over Henlade near Taunton at 2.45 am, it exploded and lit up the sky with blue and white lights.

Police officers in Bridgwater also reported seeing the phenomenon travelling from south to north and disappear over the Bristol Channel.

The strange light was also seen by a Taunton milkman who saw a white object with a tail in the sky over the River Parrett at Bridgwater.

Coastguards checked the area but failed to find anything.

The air traffic control centre at West Drayton in London say there was a blip on their radar screen at the time of the sightings.

---

29 NOV 1990   Swindon Evening Advertiser – Wiltshire.

Illuminating mystery rings bells

Startled families feared a close encounter was imminent with a suspected UFO circling around Swindon last night.

They could see a cluster of mysterious rotating lights in the night sky.

As the hours wore on the lights seemed to hover over the town. The switchboard at Swindon police station received 150 calls from worried and disbelieving people seeking an explanation for the phenomenon.

The Evening Advertiser was also deluged with calls from residents

convinced that someone, or something, from outer space was about to land in their street.

One caller described the eerie white lights as like something out of the film Ghostbusters.

But the mystery was not a UFO piloted by aliens wanting to make contact with the Earth after all – just powerful searchlights raking the sky to let the world know about the coming opening of Cairo's nightclub, at Shaw Ridge Leisure Park, West Swindon.

The club was delighted with the interest in the town caused by their publicity stunt.

"I think it is fascinating," said club spokesman Ian Freeman. "I think if a UFO was around it would probably come to Swindon. It is one of the nicest towns I have been to."

The lights were flashing between 8pm and 10.30pm.

Tonight they will be flashing again to mark the club's official opening celebrations.

29th November 1990 (USA) – Pyramid of lights seen over Carbondale, Illinois

At 10.30pm, the chairman and chief executive officer of Freeman United Coal Mining Co. – Lincoln Roan – was alerted by his 24-year-old daughter, Kelcy, who burst through the door of their home and told him she had seen some weird lights.

Lincoln:

> "All I can say is that I've never seen anything like it before. They were shining almost like reflected light, and they looked to be moving at a very high rate of speed. I still seek a logical solution."

Kelcy was returning home from Carbondale and had turned onto Grant City Road, east of Carbondale, from Illinois 13, when she saw a pyramid of lights looming over her parent's house. She wasn't the only one to see the phenomena; about 15-20 other cars had also pulled up. Several people had got out of their vehicles and were watching the object, which was pyramidal, showing two white lights on either side. The *'pyramid'* was then seen to head towards Kelcy's direction, silently through the sky, but turned sharply and moved away into an east to west direction. (**Source: MUFON**)

1990 (UK) – Triangular objects seen at ground level, Tamworth, Staffordshire

Something far more down-to-earth but even more intriguing took place during the same year, according to Christine Collesby – a local historian from Tamworth, Staffordshire, who was out walking with her husband, Trevor, near the local golf course, along an ancient track-way.

> *"We heard what we thought was probably a duck or an animal, moving about in the undergrowth, followed by a bird fluttering in the air – obviously disturbed by something. We looked closer and were astonished to see two misty 'triangles', about 5ft in height, moving along the ground in a bobbling or shuffling motion, creating an impression that they were dancing. They snaked in and out of the trees, before suddenly stopping and 'melting away' in front of our eyes".*

DECEMBER 1990

SOMEWHAT as a contrasting footnote to the spectacular sighting involving Bob Taylor, way back in 1979, was another strange report which took place on the 10th January 1967. Wallie Barnett (77) – a retired teacher – was then living on a farm on Route 2, about twelve miles from Point Pleasant, West Virginia. At 10.30pm Wallie heard the beagles dogs barking and went out to investigate. Mr Barnett made his way to where the kennels were kept, behind the house, close to a thinly wooded slight ravine. He saw a large light on the summit of the hill, which then descended and moved slowly towards the ravine.

> *"It was the size of a Volkswagen car and appeared to have windows on it, which were brightly lit. As it got close to the ground, the lights went out. There were two four inch red lights on the front of the thing, which stayed on. As it approached closer, I saw many small white lights darting out from the object and then returning to it, as if they were doing a square dance."*

The object came down slowly and silently into the ravine, its lights swirling around, about 60ft away.

Mr Barnett paused, and then slid out of view behind a chicken coop. He ran over to have a look, but there was nothing to be seen.

A few days later, a County preacher and his entire congregation saw a large red fireball rushing past the church, travelling at ground level, about two miles from where Wallie's farm was situated. We cannot say whether there was any connection with the sort of object seen by Bob Taylor, but felt there were similarities in the descriptions given. (**Source: John Keel**)

14th December 1990 (UK) – Object seen

Mrs Brenda Trowbridge of London Road, Marden Ash, Ongar, awoke early at 6am.

> *"It was a frosty morning and there had been an unusual crescent-shaped moon, with the shaded area quite prominent. Suddenly an object, which I first thought was a shooting star, appeared to leave the moon and shoot away out of sight."*

16th December 1990 – Lights seen over Stratford-upon-Avon

Strange lights in the sky

STRATFORD UPON AVON HERALD 21.12.90

MYSTERY lights in the sky above Stratford have left police baffled.

They were called out on Sunday morning when a woman living in Loxley Road reported seeing a string of light appear in the sky shortly after hearing two explosions.

The police force helicopter searched the area and extensive inquiries were made but both failed to uncover any clues.

"The woman was in her kitchen when she heard a loud explosion and looked out of the window," said Insp John Bloxham.

"She heard another explosion and saw a big flash of light in the sky and a long string of smoke with three lumps in it, believed to be towards the direction of the Welcombe Hills.

Concerned

"We were rather concerned about this because we are aware that quite often a number of light aircraft are around and so scrambled the Warwickshire Constabulary helicopter. We sent various police cars out and talked to quite a number of people but couldn't find anyone who had seen or heard anything."

Police called off the search after checks with civil and military authorities confirmed that no aircraft were missing.

Police received a second call from a woman living on the Tiddington Road the next day, Monday. She also had heard an explosion and saw what she described as a 'flash' in the sky, but hadn't reported it immediately.

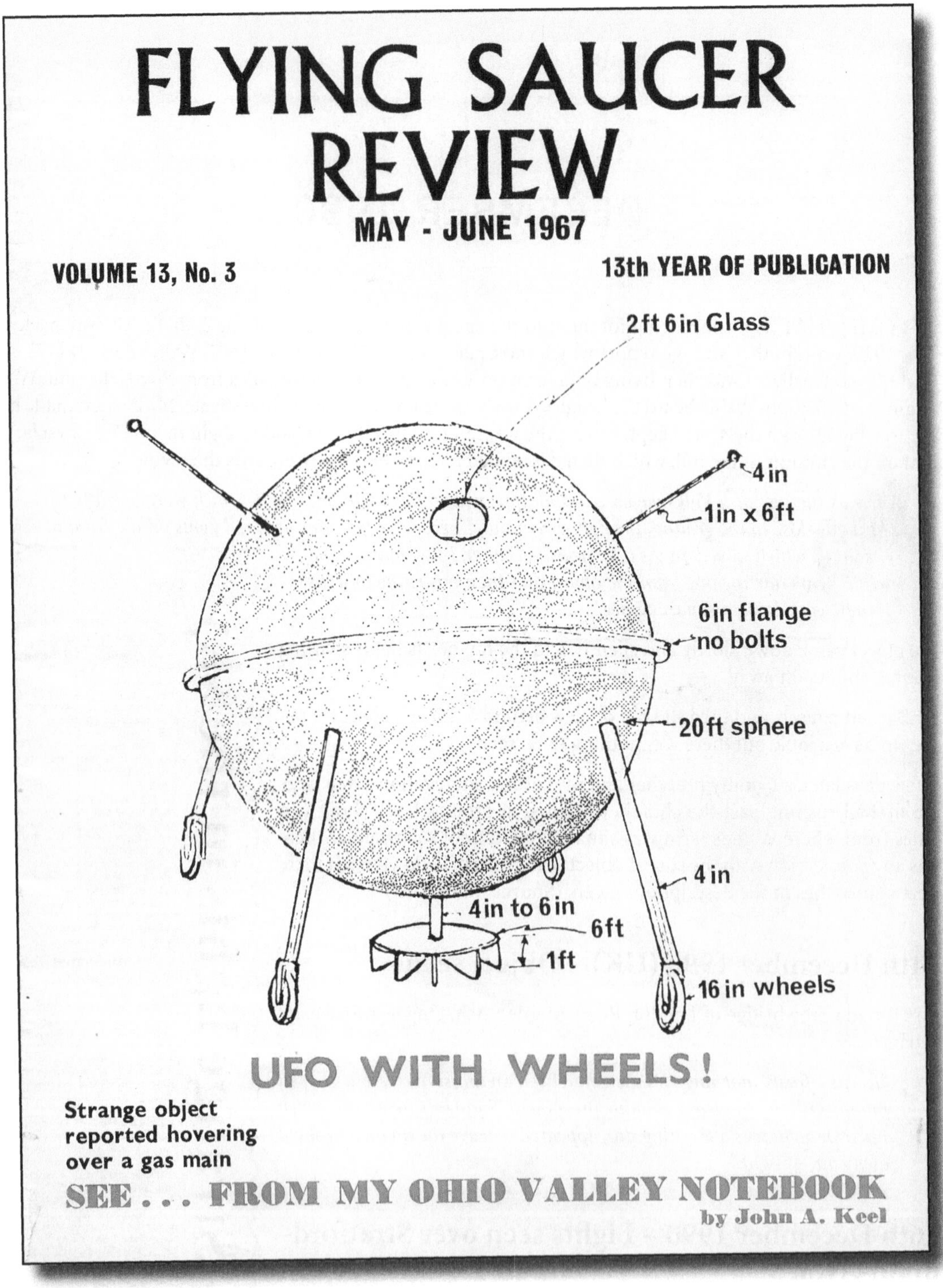

FLYING SAUCER REVIEW

MAY - JUNE 1967

VOLUME 13, No. 3   **13th YEAR OF PUBLICATION**

2 ft 6 in Glass

4 in

1 in x 6 ft

6 in flange
no bolts

20 ft sphere

4 in

4 in to 6 in

6 ft

1 ft

16 in wheels

UFO WITH WHEELS!

**Strange object
reported hovering
over a gas main**

SEE... FROM MY OHIO VALLEY NOTEBOOK
by John A. Keel

17th December 1990 (UK) – UFO display

At 10.50pm, Alan Shepherd (58) of Hartland Road, Reading, Berkshire, went to let the dog out.

"I noticed a red light, high in the sky below cloud cover. The dog went out. I followed him and went to have a look at the 'light'. Suddenly it shot away at speed towards the east, and then stopped about a 1,000ft away. It then hovered there for at least five minutes, changing colour to yellow as it did so, and then began to move towards the house. The dog ran into the house, clearly agitated.

I stood there and saw it change to a saucer-shaped object, some 100ft up in the air. The 'saucer' took up a position over the bungalow and then turned right and moved up to about 500ft in the air. After a few minutes it shot off at terrific speed, towards the north-west direction and disappeared into clouds completely silent."

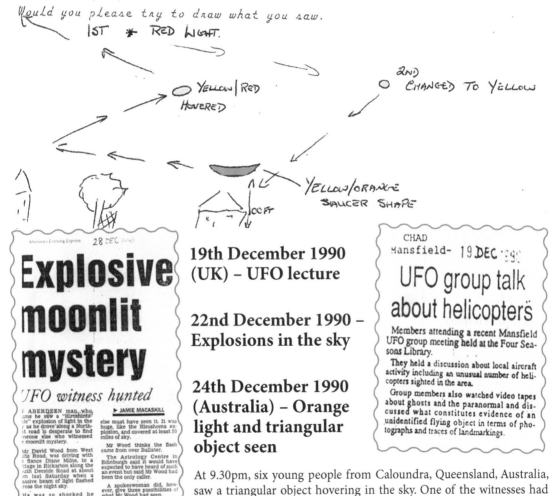

19th December 1990
(UK) – UFO lecture

22nd December 1990 –
Explosions in the sky

24th December 1990
(Australia) – Orange
light and triangular
object seen

Explosive moonlit mystery

UFO witness hunted

► JAMIE MACASKILL

ABERDEEN man, who claims he saw a "Hiroshima-like" explosion of light in the sky as he drove along a North-east road is desperate to find someone else who witnessed the moonlit mystery.

Mr David Wood from West Cults Road, was driving with his fiance Diane Milne, to a cottage in Rickarton along the South Deeside Road at about 8pm last Saturday when a massive beam of light flashed across the night sky.

He was so shocked he immediately stopped his car and switched on the radio "... need he would hear of some terrible tragedy in the des over the North-east.

But he heard nothing and after phone calls to a number of sky watching institutions is still mystified but is convinced others will back up his story.

else must have seen it. It was huge, like the Hiroshoma explosion, and covered at least 50 miles of sky.

Mr Wood thinks the flash came from over Ballater.

The Astrology Centre in Edinburgh said it would have expected to have heard of such an event but said Mr Wood had been the only caller.

A spokeswoman did, however, give three possibilities of what Mr Wood had seen.

"We have heard of incidents like this and there are three trains of thought. One is it is a meteor burning up as it enters the earth's atmosphere. The second is a UFO."

But she added ominously: "Sometimes it is seen as a prophecy of war, which is chilling considering the Gulf situation."

CHAD
Mansfield– 19 DEC 1990

UFO group talk about helicopters

Members attending a recent Mansfield UFO group meeting held at the Four Seasons Library.

They held a discussion about local aircraft activity including an unusual number of helicopters sighted in the area.

Group members also watched video tapes about ghosts and the paranormal and discussed what constitutes evidence of an unidentified flying object in terms of photographs and traces of landmarkings.

At 9.30pm, six young people from Caloundra, Queensland, Australia, saw a triangular object hovering in the sky. One of the witnesses had this to say:

"My cousins and I were playing handball on the driveway, when suddenly the whole sky was a bright orange colour. I remember looking down the street and seeing all the houses

and a church, like it was daylight; the sky was so bright. The man across the road was looking at us and pointing up. I looked up and could not believe what I was seeing. About 50 metres directly above us was a triangular-shaped object. On each point it had green lights and the bottom surface was swirling with lights going around and around; it was just sitting there, watching us. We were screaming out to our parents and, with that, it shot directly up into the sky at speeds I had never seen before, and the sky quickly went back to black within seconds – then it was gone."

The group ran upstairs to their parents and, to this day, still cannot understand how they did not see how bright it was outside.

The man across the road confirmed to the parents what happened.

According to the unnamed witnesses, one of the younger brothers suffered nightmares for many months later, following the event.

UFO & Crop Circle Conference – Quest International

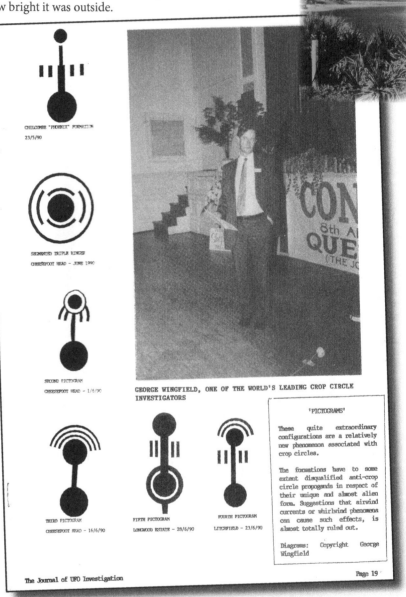

CHILCOMBE "PHOENIX" FORMATION 23/5/90

SEGMENTED TRIPLE RINGS CHEESEFOOT HEAD – JUNE 1990

SECOND PICTOGRAM CHEESEFOOT HEAD – 1/6/90

THIRD PICTOGRAM CHEESEFOOT HEAD – 16/6/90

FIFTH PICTOGRAM LONGWOOD ESTATE – 28/6/90

FOURTH PICTOGRAM LITCHFIELD – 23/6/90

GEORGE WINGFIELD, ONE OF THE WORLD'S LEADING CROP CIRCLE INVESTIGATORS

'PICTOGRAMS'

These quite extraordinary configurations are a relatively new phenomenon associated with crop circles.

The formations have to some extent disqualified anti-crop circle propoganda in respect of their unique and almost alien form. Suggestions that airwind currents or whirlwind phenomena can cause such effects, is almost totally ruled out.

Diagrams: Copyright George Wingfield

The Journal of UFO Investigation   Page 19

Conference 90' Review

Mark Birdsall

Quest International's hurriedly arranged northern UFO conference took place on the 22nd September in Leeds, and we were delighted to see so many of our subscribers at the event. With only some six weeks to prepare, the majority of the 102 people thoroughly enjoyed themselves.

The event – dubbed, **'UFO & Crop Circle Conference'** offered our subscribers an ideal opportunity to review and discuss the most fascinating occurrences pertaining to both subjects.

One pleasing aspect for the organisers, was the fact that many of our researchers and subscribers travelled great distances to Leeds on a bleak and rainy day. Mr Higgins from Scotland chose to make the long journey south, and countless others travelled hundreds of miles north – our thanks to them all. Disappointing was the lack of media exposure which surely dented the final attendence figure. Nevertheless, British UFO researchers from a variety of regional groups were represented, including Roy Lake and colleagues (East Anglian UFO Research organisation), members of the successful Bristol QUEST team, and a number of Lancashire and Midlands research groups.

The organisations research packages sold extremely well, and the two large display rooms were well received. Linda Howe's, 'A Strange Harvest' also caught the attention of many persons.

Many of those attending were particularly interested to learn of the recent investigation into the crop circle phenomenon, designated 'Operation Blackbird'. The project – which spanned some three weeks had been plagued by controversy from day one, but leading researcher, **George Wingfield** made certain that this years patterns, researches and theories, were placed firmly in perspective.

Allied by a variety of recent slides, Mr Wingfield carefully provided a detailed look into some of the most amazing circles to have appeared on these shores. To compliment some breathtaking photographs, we had the added bonus of a second projector showing graphic displays of 'pictograms', some of which can be seen in this review.

Pictograms represent a relatively new and bizarre twist in the continuing 'advancement' of the crop circle enigma. The giant formation found at Alton Barnes on the 12th July 1990, received widespread publicity. The array

of circles 'double' and 'triple ringers', conjured up all sorts of questions.

There was never any doubt about the way in which Wingfield dismissed those who contest the formations are the result of natural phenomena, but throughout the sixty minute talk, his argument was meticulously linked to a very sound scientific appraisal. Quite frankly, no one had ever seen anything like it.

George Wingfield was making his second appearance at a QUEST conference, and unlike 1989, which was incidentally, his first public talk, he spoke with a fluency which even established lecturers' could not hope to beat. Perhaps this was due to the fact that he believed in his research, a situation sadly lacking in some anti-circle researchers who have niether the tact, nor scientific qualifications which allow them to make conjectural statements. This has led to bitter 'fighting' between the two factions, and has only increased the puzzlement for an already confused public.

There was no mistaking either, his anguish in respect of the absurd hoax which was generated on the first day of 'Operation Blackbird'. For the first time, we saw clear photographs of the circles and the 'harsh' manner in which they were hoaxed. Game boards of a demonic nature and wooden crosses were clearly visible lying in the centre of the crudely produced circles. No denying, that this action had dented the chances of public and perhaps 'political' respect. Who had conceived this brainless action, which provided a marker for hilarity in the British press?

Like Quest International, Mr Wingfield had learned of a sinister attempt to ridicule the investigation before it had a chance to succeed. **"Evidence suggests it was the Army,"** he said. Intrigued by this not-so-amusing act, Wingfield sought other pieces of candid evidence which would hopefully cloak the debunking 'ghosts'. Crop circles were captured in the making, although only a poor photograph portraying small almost insignificant markings was shown. And unknown to many, was the subsequent mutilation of a white horse close to the scene of the 'watch'. UFOs... demons... or another attempt to blight the operation?

Real impact was generated by the 'pictograms' which are beginning to appear more frequently; and in relation to this remarkable phenomenon, many questions from our subscribers were fired at the speaker. A message perhaps?

The Journal of UFO Investigation

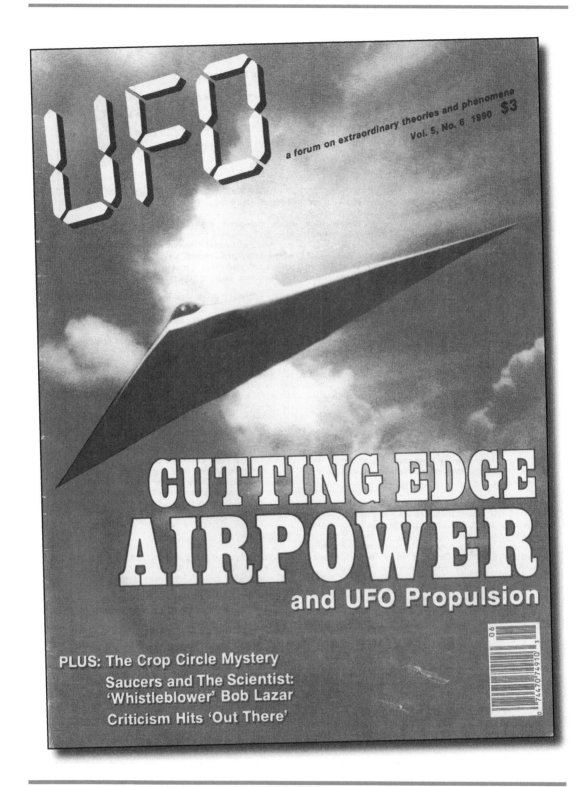

UFO

a forum on extraordinary theories and phenomena

Vol. 5, No. 6 1990 $3

CUTTING EDGE AIRPOWER

and UFO Propulsion

PLUS: The Crop Circle Mystery

Saucers and The Scientist:
'Whistleblower' Bob Lazar

Criticism Hits 'Out There'

PART 2

1963-1964

3rd January 1963 (USA) – Lights seen in the sky

AN object, larger than a star, was seen stationary in the sky, displaying six to eight red lights, over Western Rootstown. Rootstown Township is one of the eighteen townships of Portage County, Ohio.

(Source: *Beacon Journal,* Akron, Ohio, 3.1.1963)

7th January 1963 (Australia) – Silver *'light'*

Between 11am and 3pm, a slow moving silver *'light'* was seen over the Bass Strait, Victoria.

8th January 1963 (UK) – Object in the sky

At 5pm, Beccles ambulance driver Alfred Crisp, and his attendant, Charles Bennett, were driving towards Hulver Street, Norfolk, along the B1127, near a local lake, when they noticed a long, dark object, motionless in the sky. Suddenly, without any warning whatsoever, it shot off across the sky at speed.

(Source: Ivan W. Bunn, *'Lantern'* series)

17th January 1963 (USA) – Five objects

Five ascending objects, resembling rockets, were seen over the Grayland area of Washington.

24th January 1963 (USA) – UFO seen

At Lexington, Kentucky, a post office safety engineer sighted a round object, travelling east to west, and a delta-wing aircraft north to south. The UFO's line of flight intersected the aircraft path at right angles.

(Source: Bluegrass, NICAP)

28th January 1963 (USA) – Elliptical object

At 10.30pm, an elliptical object was seen in the sky over Seattle, Washington, changing colour from green to others – believed to have been a meteor. (**Source:** *Post Intelligence,* **Washington, 29.1.1963**)

28th January 1963 (UK) – Cigar-shaped UFO

At 5.20pm on the same date at Shilton, Coventry, England, Mary Sharp and her mother sighted a yellow-orange cigar-shaped object, showing four portholes, lying on the ground. It left a short time later and headed away, at speed, towards Rugby. (**Source: Bob Tibbitts, CUFORG**)

5th February 5th 1963 (USA) – UFO over missile site-aircraft scrambled

At 11.45pm, following a report of a yellow-white glowing UFO, about 3ft in diameter, seen over a missile site at Charlottesville, Washington (located in west Central Virginia, approximately 100 miles south-west of Washington DC) aircraft were scrambled to respond. It appears that a pulsating yellow '*light*' was also seen to manoeuvre around their plane, by a private pilot and a newsman passenger.

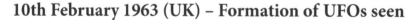

6th February 1963 (USA) – Pilot sights UFO

A pilot of a C-46 aircraft was flying 15 miles south-west of Montebello on a 40° heading, at 12am, when the pilot sighted a large, round, very bright star-like object at the one o'clock position, at 3-5° above the horizon. The object appeared to vary in size during observation, and gain in elevation to 15-30° above the horizon. The object was last sighted at 3-5° above horizon at the 4-5 o'clock position. The length of the observation was approximately 45 minutes. (**Source: Dan Wilson**)

10th February 1963 (UK) – Formation of UFOs seen

Retired psychiatric Staff Nurse Bill Cassidy, from Eccleston, Lancashire (in his 70s) contacted us in 2006, after reading an appeal made by us in the local newspaper, requesting any information on UFOs seen in the locality.

Bill told us he was living in a flat, overlooking wasteland near to an old coal tip. While looking through the window, at midday, he saw five objects, heading across a blue sky, on what was a cold day – cold enough for the *River Mersey* to have frozen over.

> *"As they approached closer, I was able to see they were silver metallic 'saucers' in appearance. The 'craft' on the outside of the formation was much smaller than the one in the middle. I shouted to my wife. We watched in stark disbelief, as they moved overhead, at a height of about 300ft off the ground. We rushed to the other side of the house and saw them heading towards RAF Burtonwood Airbase – then closed. My wife rang the* Liverpool Echo, *who contacted the MOD. They were told we must have seen weather balloons, released from Preston!"*

(**Source: Personal interview**)

15th February 1963 (Australia) – Domed UFO over Victoria

At 7am Charles Brew and his 20-year-old son, Trevor Brew, were at work in the milking shed on their farm, 'Willow Grove', near Moe, Victoria. It was daylight, but rain clouds lay overhead.

Object appears in the sky

Charles Brew was standing in an open area, with a full view of the eastern sky, when he saw a strange object appear and descend very slowly towards the milk shed. As it did so, livestock in the area – which included a pony and nearby cows and two farm dogs – fled in fear. [A local newspaper was to later report that the cows turned somersaults, which the Brews' later denied]

UFO hovers over farm

The UFO descended to a height of about 30 metres, hovering over a stringy-bark tree, and was described as being:

> *"…about eight metres in diameter and three metres high. The top section appeared to be a transparent dome of a glass-like material, from which protruded a two metre high mast or aerial. The 'aerial' appeared to be as thick as a broom and resembled bright chrome. The top portion of the 'disc' itself was battleship grey in colour and appeared to be of metallic lustre. The base or underside*

section glowed with a pale blue colour and had 'scoop-like protuberances around the outside edge'. This section rotated slowly at about one revolution per second".

Rotated slowly

This spinning motion apparently caused the protuberances to generate a swishing noise – somewhat like a turbine noise – that was clearly audible not only to Brew but also to his son, Trevor, who was located inside the shed, near the operating diesel-powered milking machine units.

Strange sound heard

Charles Brew felt his eyes were drawn towards the object *'as though beams of magnetic current'* were between it and him. He also experienced a peculiar headache, which came on with the approach of the object. After hovering for a few seconds the object began to climb, continuing on its westward course and passing up into the cloud deck again. Trevor did not see the UFO, but confirmed the unusual sound – like a didgeridoo or bull-roarer [aboriginal artefacts which can produce pulsating, wind-rushing noise].

15.3.1963 – *The Wimbledon Borough News*, London, reported on a gleaming silver, circular object, seen in the sky over Wimbledon Common on this date.

Royal Australian Air Force sends investigators

Flight Lieutenant N. Hudson and Squadron Leader A.F. Javes, of the RAAF, interviewed Mr Brew. While impressed with his credibility, the weather at the time of the sighting – heavy continuous rain, with very low cloud and poor visibility, and with a fresh wind in an easterly direction – seems to have led them to consider that it might have been a tornado!

Explained away as a tornado!

On 6th March, Dr. Berson and a Mr Clark – Commonwealth meteorologists – were interviewed to ascertain if clouds could produce this type of phenomenon. They agreed that tornado conditions could cause this effect. According to them, the only difference in Brew's report was that the object moved from east to west, because in all their previous reports of this nature have been from west to east. [Mr Brew stated that the wind was fresh, from an easterly direction.] However, a meteorological report states that wind was westerly at eight knots. Despite this lack of rigour in determining how relevant their hypothesis was, the RAAF officers' report concluded:

> *"There is little doubt that Brew did witness something, and it is most likely that it was a natural phenomenon. The phenomenon was probably a tornado. There was no reported damage along its path; therefore, one could assume that it was weak in nature."*

The Department of Air responded to a civilian UFO group enquiry about the incident, with the following statement:

> *"Our investigation and enquiries reveal that there are scientific records of certain tornado-like meteorological manifestations, which have a similar appearance in many ways to whatever was seen by Mr Brew. The information available is such, however, that while we accept this is a possibility, we are unable to come to any firm conclusion as to the nature of the object or manifestation reported."*

The official sighting summaries removed any such doubt. By then, the 'possible cause' was listed as 'a tornado-like meteorological manifestation'.

Dr. James McDonald visited Charles Brew during his 1967 Australian trip, interviewing him at the site of the 1963 incident. McDonald concluded:

"Like that of many other UFO witnesses, it is extremely difficult to explain in present-day scientific or technological terms."

Summary of Unidentified Aerial Sightings reported to Department of Air, Canberra, ACT, from 1960

Despite the extraordinary nature of the 'Willow Grove' incident, and the high level of official interest in it, the sighting was listed in a subsequently released *"Summary of Unidentified Aerial Sightings reported to Department of Air, Canberra, ACT, from 1960"* as having a possible cause of *"tornado-like meteorological manifestation"*. Are we really expected to believe that what the men saw was a tornado?

If the illustration (which is shown here) is typical of a tornado in action, then this would suggest that the thousands, if not millions, of other cases involving similarly described objects, reported all over the world, is the answer to the UFO phenomena! This is in our opinion a preposterous explanation. As we have said before, all the authorities have to do is supply an explanation – no matter how ridiculous it is – purely because the majority of people will accept it as a rational answer without question, knowing that UFOs cannot exist.

(Sources: *Auckland Star*, 16.2.1963/*Australian Flying Saucer Review*, No. 8, June 1965/*FSR*, 29.5.1961/
Bill Chalker, 1996/NAA File series A703)

21st February 1963 (USA) – *'Globe of fire'* strikes car

A motorist was driving his car through Belgrade, Montana, at 2.30am, when his car was struck by a strange *'globe of fire'*, and several people called the authorities to report they had been awakened by a peculiar object crossing the sky. (**Source:** *Magonia 565*)

27th February 1963 (USA) – Crescent-shaped UFO seen

A large crescent-shaped object, with what appeared to be portholes set into its structure, was seen over Modesto, California, by seven people, who told of watching it descend to about a 1,000ft and project a bright beam of light, before moving away. (**Source:** *Anatomy of a Phenomenon*, Jacques Vallee)

28th February 1963 (USA) – Smoke rings seen

A number or mysterious *'smoke ring'* cloud effects were seen in the sky over Northern Arizona, which, according to *Science* – the American association for the advancement of Science – was unprecedented in years of sky watching. (**Source:** NICAP)

February 1963 – Royal Navy and UFO seen entering Arctic Ocean

A contingent of the Royal Navy's North Atlantic Fleet was participating in exercises off Norway.

At 3.15am, between Spitzbergen Island and Norway – 30-50 miles off the Norway coast – an object was tracked on the ship's radar, at 35,000ft, and then by sonar after it entered the water. It was then tracked at 50ft below the surface and continued into deep water at a range of 20,000yds. The radar signature indicated it was 100ft-120ft in diameter. The object was also tracked by other ships and the order was issued for the fleet to execute an evasive 'Z' pattern manoeuvre. Jets were scrambled. The duration of the alert was at least 15-20 minutes. (**Source:** *MUFON Journal*, 1984)

Editor
DAVID WIGHTMAN

Volume 9 No. 4
March   1963

URANUS

CONTENTS

Britain re-enters the Space Race
The Ice Age Cometh?
Halley's Comet and the Chronology of
    the Bible Lands
A Forgotten Method of Producing Power
Space Science Graduates
Satellites in Orbit
Low Temperature and Vacuum Physics and
    Man in Space
Metals Cold Weld in Space
Space Jottings
1962 In Retrospect
More on "Hydronautics"

Subscription Rates:
    Six Issues
    14/- or $2.00

Published every
    second month.
Post Free 2/6 or 40c.

MARKHAM HOUSE PRESS LTD., 31 KINGS ROAD, LONDON, S.W.3.

6th March 1963 (USA) – Bright flash

At around 10.37am, a bright flash was observed by numerous witnesses from Louisiana to Texas. One report said a large bright flash was seen 20 miles north of Barksdale Air Force Base. It was also seen by two light aircraft and a SAC Bomber. Another report stated that there was on observation of a bright flash and metallic falling object, 40 miles north-north-west of Chennault Air Force Base, at 10.55am.

(Source: *McDonald list*, Dan Wilson)

8th March 1963 (UK) – Two *'discs'*

Over Wallsend, Northumberland, two grey-blue *'disc'*-like objects were seen in the sky, joined by what looked like a tube. (**Source:** *Evening Chronicle,* 21.3.1963)

11th March 1963 (USA) – UFOs sighted

Just after 8pm, a brilliant light was seen heading westwards over Oahu, Hawaii, leaving a trail observed by many people.

Two National Guard pilots, flying jets about 40 miles west of Honolulu, reported the UFO was *"much higher"* than their altitude of 40,000ft and moving *"very fast"*. (At 7.28pm, a newsboy, in El Sobrante, California, saw two oval-shaped yellow lights pass over the San Francisco Bay area, from North to South, travelling at high speed.) (**Source:** NICAP)

18th March 1963 (UK)

Over Blaydon, Durham, during the afternoon, a round object was seen in the sky, projecting rays of light. (**Source:** *Evening Chronicle* 29.3.1973)

18th March 1963 (USA) – Did UFO cause missile to change direction?

A strange object was sighted over the Atlantic coast of Florida a few moments before a Minuteman missile launched from Cape Canaveral, which then veered off course and had to be destroyed.

(**Source:** *UFO Investigator,* **March-April 1963, page 4** – 'UFO SEEN AS ROCKET VEERS OFF COURSE')

We were to come across many other instances involving interference with Top Secret facilities by UFOs. An illuminating letter is shown from Pat Delgado, about what he witnessed while at Woomera Rocket Station, Australia, during the early 1960s.

P.Delgado
4.Arle Close
Alresford
Hampshire SO24 9BG.

John Hanson
P.O.Box 6371
Birmingham   31 January 1998.
B48 7RW.

Dear Mr.Hanson

Thank you for your letter containing your enquiry about my
association with sightings of apparent UFOs at Woomera,
Australia, missile range in the early 60's.

The range is situated in South Australia. It is over a thousand
miles long across unoccupied desert and was at that time used for
testing rockets and missiles. They were fired from the head of
the range where the instrumentation building was situated. This
building contained all the necessary electronic equipment to
track and trace the flight and path of all vehicles and missiles
being tested.

My job was to operate and maintain a group of large plotting
tables which drew traces of every missile flight, and these
flights varied greatly in height and distance.

To make sure no aircraft strayed into the firing zone before and
during firings a very strict radar surveillance was kept in
operation. If the radars detected any form of air intrusion
during critical time periods, officials in the instrumentation
building were alerted and took whatever action was deemed
necessary.

The radars would be surveying mostly down range and it was on two
occasions that we were alerted that unidentified objects had
appeared down range at a high altitude. The objects were
described as being one large one from which several smaller ones
were emerging. The small ones would fly around in various
directions and then return to the larger craft then this would
move off rapidly and disappear. Of course, these incidents would
constitute a hazard and must have been the subject of an official
report.

All details of missile range activities would have been
communicated to the H.Q. of Weapons Research Establishment in
Salisbury, near Adelaide.

Woomera, situated where it is, in the South Australian desert,
is the perfect place for observing the skies, especially at
night. Numerous times I have watched stars set on the far distant
horizon, the air is so clear. A place where you can be treated
to a display of meteorites most nights, as well as seeing

unidentifiable lights and flashes in the sky.

As well as the official reports of UFOs there were of course
many unofficial ones as seen by Woomera residents and by truck
drivers travelling to the place across the desert at night, some
drivers claimed to have been paced by them.

The well documented Nullabor Plain UFO encounter took place
south west of Woomera and when you look at a map of these places
you can see the vast thousands of square miles of desolation
where mysterious incidents can occur and I am sure they often do.

I hope this satisfies your request.

Kind regards and good luck with your endeavours.

Pat Delgado

You may use this article in your book.
Thank you for crediting it and/or SAE

19th March 1963 (New Zealand) – UFO leaving Earth!

The *New Zealand Herald* told of a mysterious star-like object, discovered by the radio telescope at Parkes, New South Wales, which has baffled Australian and American astronomers. The object was recorded as moving away from Earth at a speed of 30,000 miles per second.

26th March 1963 (USA)

At 11.40pm, Mrs D. Wheeler and Claudine Milligan from Naperville, Illinois, saw 6-8 red *'balls'*, arranged in a rectangular formation in the sky, which changed into two objects with lights, by the end of the sighting.

(Source: Berliner)

26th March 1963 (Australia)

A moon-sized object was sighted moving across the sky over Ballarat, New South Wales.

28th March 1963 (UK) – Incident at Norwich

Norwich resident – Miss I. Duffield – was sitting near the Britannia Barracks,

Norwich, with her boyfriend, at 8pm, when a van pulled-up. Two men alighted, and proceeded to set up a tripod on the ground. From out of the tripod came a yellow and red light which shot up into the sky, moved over the barracks, and disappeared. A second light then came out of the tripod, at which stage the couple – now feeling rather frightened – decided to leave.

The next day, they read in their local newspaper that similar lights had been seen over the town, the same evening.

Britannia Barracks,

Was this some exercise involving the discharge of flares, or is there a more mundane explanation? Enquiries with the MOD and the local newspapers failed to obtain any explanation.

(Source: *Norwich Evening News*, 30.3.1963)

1st April 1963 (UK) – UFO reported

Over North Shields, Northumberland, a straw-coloured object was seen moving through the sky over North Shields, at 11.20pm. (**Source:** *Orbit*, **Feb/March 1963**)

4th April 1963 (UK) – Arrowhead UFO

At 10.30pm, a silver shining object, resembling an arrowhead, was seen over Blackburn, Lancashire, by Tom Leaver of Norfolk Street, Mill Hill, in Blackburn.

> *"I had been watching television and went out to fetch some coal. I saw an object, shining like silver, travelling across the sky very fast. I was facing south at the time. I watched it for about a minute, as it flew west to east passing under the moon."*

The matter was reported to the police and MOD, who were unable to offer any explanation.

(Source: *Blackburn Evening Telegraph*, 5.4.1963)

4th to 7th April 1963 (USA) – 'V'-shaped formation

At 9pm, seven or eight lights, in a 'V' formation, were seen moving through the sky over Santa Barbara, California. The following day, at 7.30pm, east of Barstow, a number of strange luminous glows were reported in the sky. During the night of the 5th, what looked like a dirigible was seen moving over the Arizona desert. On the 5th and 6th April, a number of glowing fireballs were sighted between San Diego to San Francisco. At 2am on 7th April over Hollister, California, bright red *'balls of light'*, trailing smoke, were reported.

8th April 1963 (UK) – No comment from RAF Boulmer!

Mr Peter Finlay – an engineer from Stakeford, Newcastle-upon-Tyne, was driving between Rothbury and Whittingham when he noticed, through his windscreen, an object reminding him of *"a black wagon wheel"* moving across the sky, at a height of approximately 800ft, and two to three miles away. *"Minutes later a RAF Jet shot across the sky."*

Mr Finlay rang the Duty Officer at RAF Boulmer, to report the incident, but was told by the man that *"he was not prepared to comment on the matter"* (**Source:** *Newcastle-upon-Tyne Journal, 9.4.1963*)

UFO over Wales (UK) – Multiple lights seen

On the same day, Miss Susan Mitchell of Wilmslow, Cheshire, was walking along the promenade at Cricieth, Wales, with her companion. They were looking out to the south-west part of the sky, at 9pm, just after the sun had set, when they saw:

> *"...a very steady brightness – quite large. It appeared to be drifting slowly across the sky. Suddenly, a smaller light detached itself from the main one and fell behind, disappearing from view. Then the main object ejected further lights at one or two second intervals, until there was fifteen of these lights in the sky, which themselves disappeared from view. A short time later, the main object itself inexplicably vanished from view."*

(**Source:** *UFOLOG*)

13th April 1963 (UK) – Silver UFO

Blackburn resident – Mr T. Reade – was walking along Westgate, Blackburn, at 9.25pm, when he saw:

"...a silver-like object flying across the sky, at great speed, just under the moon, heading in a west to east direction; at 9.30pm, it was out of sight."

14th April 1963 (UK) – Formation of objects

As twilight fell over Cambridge, at 7pm, a string of between five and nine flame-coloured objects were seen stationary in the sky – one behind the other – forming a curve. Eight seconds or so later, they vanished from sight. (**Source: Isle of Wight UFO Society**)

18th/19th April 1963 (Tasmania) – UFO Display

Over Woodsale, Tasmania, a number of revolving objects, flashing brilliant red and green lights, were seen crossing the sky during the night. (**Source:** *Launceston Examiner*, **19.4.1963**) At 7pm on the 19th April, similar objects were seen until 10.30pm. (**Source:** *Launceston Examiner*, **20.4.1963**)

19th April 1963 (UK) – Oblong-shaped UFO seen over the sea

Mr A.J. Rawden (35) of High Street, Ryde, Isle of Wight, was looking out to sea, at 7.15pm, from Ashey Down, when he saw:

"...a whitish coloured area, oblong in shape, motionless in a belt of sea mist, between the sea and a brilliant sunlit sky. I watched it until 7.45pm, when it faded away".

(**Source: Kath Smith, Isle of Wight UFO Society**)

28th April 1963 (UK) – Saucer-shaped UFO seen

At 4.am Mr and Mrs L. Greenhaigh of Essex Avenue, Haywood, Lancashire, was awoken by the sound of an engine approaching,

"...like the sound of a rocket engine, accompanied by the brightest light we have ever seen".

They ran to the window, presumably thinking it was an aircraft in distress, and were astonished to see ...

"a saucer-shaped object, so close it almost touched the roof; it illuminated the bedroom as it went by. The light seemed to be projected downwards – nothing upwards at all. It swerved away and hovered in mid-air over a partly built house across the road. About 10 minutes later, it descended as if landing."

The couple waited and heard the engine noise again, some 10 minutes later, but saw nothing else, and then went back to bed.

(**Source: BUFORA**)

29th April 1963 (UK) – Two cylinders seen

At 10.45pm, over the Isle of Wight, a cigar-shaped UFO was seen 55° off the horizon, by a Mrs Spanner and her daughter.

> *"At 1am, a small red light came out and headed off north-east. Through binoculars, two long narrow cylinders – vivid bright green in colour – showing a brilliant red light at the forward end, could be seen – like two cigarettes, held together – which slowly moved out of sight."*

(Source: *UFOLOG*/Personal interview, Eric Spanner)

3rd May 1963 (UK) – Object over Warwickshire

At 9pm, a dark stationary object was seen in the sky over Alveston, Warwickshire, ejecting a grey vapour.

(Source: Cheltenham Flying Saucer Group)

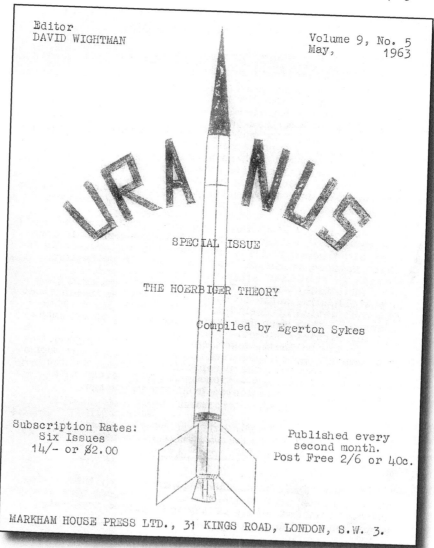

452

5th May 1963 (USA) – Flashing UFO

During the late afternoon, an object was seen in the sky showing flashing red and white lights, apparently hovering over Mount Zion, Wisconsin. (**Source:** *The Dial, Boscobel,* **Wisconsin, 9.5.1963**)

7th May 1963 (USA) – Strange fall from the sky

On the 7th May 1963, there was a fall of flimsy gossamer-like material over Picayune and New Orleans. Was this angel hair? (**Source:** *Times,* **Picayune, New Orleans, 8.5.1963**)

15th May 1963 (New Zealand) – Red *'light'* seen

The Mount Gambier Police were contacted by a number of people who reported being followed, for several miles, by a bright red *'light'* which changed to white. (**Source:** *The New Zealand Herald,* 22.5.1963)

19th May 1963 (USA) – Spectacular sighting of UFO

The Reverend Father R. Dean Johnson – Priest, in charge of All Souls Episcopal Church in Waukegan – and his wife, was driving on the western edge of ˙Waukegan, heading south on Green Bay Road – Highway 131, which runs parallel to Lake Michigan.

At 10.15pm, Dean noticed a stationary bright white light in the south-east direction and called his wife's attention to it. She thought it may have been a floodlight, some six or seven miles out, over Lake Michigan, maybe 2,000ft or more high.

Dean:

> *"The light appeared to be getting smaller, so we reasoned it was moving away from us and was merely giving an illusion that it was stationary. Moments later it changed course, moving south-west, as we continued south. As it came closer it looked like a huge, somewhat elongated, floodlight."*

At this point Mrs Johnson exclaimed, *"It's on fire"*, sparking fears that it was an aircraft in distress. The couple looked upwards again and saw a pulsating or flashing light, moving across the sky in a steady pattern.

By this time the object was over northern Waukegan and descending as it did so.

A 'craft' with square windows is seen

> *"After having driven another five miles, we were then close enough to see it was not a single light but windows, showing the interior of a 'craft'. These windows then became more distinct and were, in fact, square. The entire object looked oblong, with two windows on separate levels – like the fuselage of a double-decker airliner, with the nose and tail chopped off square. There were no wings or navigation lights."*

Dean drove another half mile and stopped the car.

At this point the object passed overhead, causing them to get out of the vehicle, allowing them to see:

> *"...a drum-shaped object with vertical sides, in profile oblong. I estimated it was 2-300ft above us, 80ft in diameter, and 15ft high. The entire 'craft' revolved counter-clockwise, at one and a half revolutions per second. It was moving at about 40mph. The windows – some 3ft across – were evenly*

˙Waukegan is a city and the county seat of Lake County, Illinois, United States. As of the 2012 census estimate, the city had a population of 94,267. It is the ninth-largest city in Illinois by population. It is the fifth-largest city on the western shore of Lake Michigan, after Chicago, Milwaukee, Green Bay, and Kenosha.

spaced all the way round the two levels. On each level there was a section which either had no windows or else a compartment not illuminated, that is in one position. The upper left windows were dark, and the lower right also. As the 'craft' revolved 180°, there were illuminated windows the full width of both levels. Hence from a great distance, as the 'craft' revolved, it alternately illuminated its full width and then only partially, which gave it the accordion effect."

The couple got back into their car and continued southwards. They noticed a stalled car on the road ahead of them, which was being looked at by three men who were oblivious of the presence of the 'craft' above their head.

Several other users of the road did see it, however. A car load of young men went past shouting, *"Look at that flying saucer"*, and pulled off to get a closer look. The mysterious 'craft' was then seen to continue towards the south-west for about another mile, before turning south-east, passing over Green Bay Road and over North Chicago and onto the lake, moving in a zigzag pattern, gaining altitude – now over *Lake Forest* – before being lost from view.

Media not interested!

One cannot praise the good Reverend enough for an excellent account, which is most informative.

Not surprisingly, his attempts to gain Media attention for what was, after all, a 'close encounter with a UFO' were fruitless, despite contacting someone from the *WKRS Radio Station* at Waukegan, who came to see him and tape-recorded his account of the sighting. Not one word (as far as we know) was ever aired by either the radio station or its affiliate – the *Waukegan News Sun*.

Dean published their account in the Parish paper, when he discovered that several of his parishioners had also seen a similar object, just before an electrical storm had moved in off the Lake, two weeks later.

(**Source:** Frank Edwards, *Strange Fate*)

20th/21st May 1963 – UFO seen over the Atlantic

Although the witness was unable remember the exact date which was estimated to be the first or second week in May 1963, it appears bearing in mind her visit to Canada that it may have been approximately the date as above.

A married woman from Hertfordshire contacted Gordon Creighton (Editor of *FSR*) with a very interesting story to tell, while flying over the Atlantic during May 1963. At the time, she was working for NATO as an English language secretary. On the day in question she was one of a party of 50 NATO personnel, en route from Canada in a DC8, which appeared under military control rather than civilian.

"We took off from Orly Airport, Paris, some time after 10am, and were told that the flight to Ottawa would take about seven hours. As there were only 50 of us, the plane was relatively empty. I took a window seat on the port side (left) near the wing. The other two seats in my row remained empty throughout the flight. As NATO personnel we were, of course, all known to each other and very much a family group. The weather was beautiful and the captain announced that we would be flying at 36,000-38,000ft.

Gigantic cigar shaped object seen

After lunch had been served, I sat enjoying the view. I was reaching down for a book from my holdall when I was astonished to see, below the plane, something dark and absolutely tremendous that stood out in vivid contrast to the brightness all around.

I pressed close to the window in disbelief and saw, almost beneath the DC8, a gigantic dark grey 'torpedo'-shaped object.

It was utterly unlike anything I had ever seen before in the whole of my life. It looked like it was made of steel. No portholes or windows were visible, no wings or projections – nothing but the long perfect torpedo form with its bullet-shaped head and the rear end, which was cut-off squarely. It was well below us, maybe 2,000 metres, but I had no way of being able to gauge this or to estimate the size of the thing.

By now a swathe of tiny clouds was beginning to pass over it, though it remained visible through them for a few seconds before being lost from view.

I decided – as none of the people aboard appeared to have seen it – not to say anything, knowing they would only laugh at me."

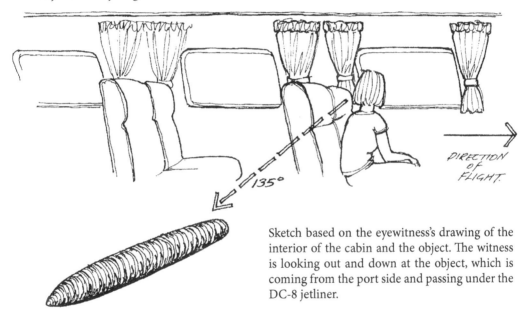

Sketch based on the eyewitness's drawing of the interior of the cabin and the object. The witness is looking out and down at the object, which is coming from the port side and passing under the DC-8 jetliner.

Aircraft begins to move up and down violently

"I sat thinking about what I had witnessed, for about 30 minutes or so, when suddenly, the aircraft started to shudder and pitch up and down violently, which I presumed was the result of air pockets, but never as bad as this before. The passengers sat there petrified, silent, and white faced.

At some point I stood up and went to look for the stewardess, shouting 'I'm scared. What's going on?' I lifted a curtain in front of what appeared to be a sleeping berth and found the stewardess, with her hands covering her eyes and in a state of distress. I went back to my seat after being unable to arouse her, despite the motions of the aircraft and claps of thunder heard. I noticed I was bathed in perspiration, although my light dress was dry.

I made my way back to the stewardess's position but she had gone. I hammered on the cockpit door and shouted 'what was happening', as by now I was really frightened. The second stewardess appeared and looked at me as if I was mad, and then announced 'ladies and gentlemen, do not be alarmed – the cabin is being depressurized'. Shortly afterwards, the captain made the same announcement."

The witness wondered if her experience had been caused by the depressurization of the aircraft, but is at a loss to understand the behavior of the stewardess and why nobody else saw the UFO, especially the crew.

NATO Meeting

An examination of the NATO meetings, held at Ottawa from the 22nd to 24th May 1963, revealed the following matters were discussed:

Berlin – Cuba – Laos – Disarmament – Political Consultation – Organization of nuclear forces assigned to SACEUR – Balance between conventional and nuclear arms – Defence problems of Greece.

(Source: Gordon Creighton, *FSR*, Vol. 27, No. 3 Nov. 1981. Reprint Volume 46/4, winter 2001)

Summer 1963 – 'Flying cigar' over Tramore, Co. Waterford (Ireland)

Could there have been a connection with what Susan Bissette, from Tramore, County Waterford, sighted while watching a local rugby match from the back garden of her house, in summer 1963?

> *"I saw what I took to be a small cigar-shaped aircraft, hovering silently off the ground, about 100ft away. It had a red fuselage, with silver patches over the body, and I estimated it to be about 9-12ft in length. I wondered if it could have come from the nearby airbase. Suddenly, it dawned on me that this was no aircraft. It had no windows, or wings. How could it stay upright? I directed my husband's attention towards it. Seconds or so later, it made a sharp right-hand turn, and accelerated – like a rocket – over the horizon."*

When Mrs Bissette telephoned the airbase to report the matter, they suggested she must have been drinking!

(Source: Personal interview)

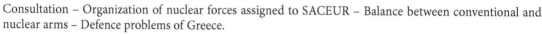

20th May 1963 (New Zealand) – Motorist followed by UFO

A youth – driving between Glencoe and Mt. Gambier, near the Victoria border – saw an object at the side of the road, which he first thought was a truck or bulldozer. When about 20 yards away, a *'bright light'* came on and dazzled him.

> "I pulled up; the object moved across the road and I speeded up. The light suddenly shot straight up into the air and hovered above the car while I drove underneath. Although I was driving at 50-60mph, the light followed me."

21st May 1963 (UK) – UFO sighted

At 9.15pm on 21st May 1963, a brilliant golden coloured object was sighted in the sky over Cross Lane, Bobbington, in Cheshire. It was then seen to carry out a number of movements, including climbing and hovering. (**Source:** *The Liverpool Echo & Evening Express* 22.5.1963)

22nd May – (UK)

Seven members of the Bebbington 1123 Air Training Corps sighted something unusual in the sky, also at 9.15pm. One of them – Cadet Warrant Officer, Jeffrey Green – described what happened:

> "I should imagine it was at an altitude of about 50,000ft – possibly more. It seemed to hover, and then disappeared very quickly – too fast to be an aircraft. As it went from sight, it seemed to be climbing in a westerly direction – quite unlike anything I have ever seen before in aircraft recognition classes."

(**Source:** *The Liverpool Echo*, 22.5.1963)

23rd May 1963 (USA) – Blue *'disc'* seen

Over Sunnyvale, California apparently at tree-top height a blue coloured disc was seen in the sky hovering and circling slowly, before rising vertically and then disappearing from sight. (**Source: NICAP Subcommittee.**)

29th May 1963 (Australia) – UFO sighted from observatory

An unidentified flying object, orange in colour, was sighted at 6.58pm by Professor B. Bok – director of the ˙Mt. Stromlo Observatory – and two colleagues.

> "It was self luminous and not glowing from reflected rays of the sun, orange-red in colour, and headed in a west to east direction, passing almost directly over the observatory. It could not have been a meteor, because it was far too slow and left no trail. It was below light cloud and didn't lose its brightness in the minute we watched it. It might have been a satellite; if so, it wasn't one normally seen at Stromlo. It appeared at the wrong time and glowed far too brightly for a normal satellite."

The CAA confirmed no aircraft were logged in that locality at the time of the observation.

(**Source:** *The New Zealand Herald*, 31.5.1963/The News, 30.5.1963)

---

*The first telescope installed at Mount Stromlo was the Oddie telescope, which was installed on 8th September 1911. The building housing this telescope was the first construction funded by the Commonwealth Government in Canberra. In January 1913, the first telephone was connected to the Queanbeyan telephone exchange. Mount Stromlo was devastated by the Canberra bushfires of 2003. The fire, fuelled by the pine plantation that covered the mountain, destroyed or badly damaged much of the observatory and water treatment plant. Road access is via the Cotter Road on the south side and Uriarra Road on the east and north. The summit is reached by a road joining Cotter Road, just outside Duffy. (**Source: Wikipedia, 2015**)

31st May 1963 (Atlantic) – Tracked on radar

At 2.03pm local time, three radar tracks were detected at a speed of 1,400mph, by airborne radar, at location given as 44North and 49West. There was no visual sighting, although the targets were indicated at ranges of two, three and a half, and five miles. Two of the targets were following identical paths – three minutes later they were gone.

6th June 1963 (UK) – Lantern in the sky

At 11.40pm an object – resembling a *'lantern, hanging in the sky'* – was seen over Whyteleafe, in Surrey, by Mrs Phyllis Watters, who watched it for 30 minutes, before it gradually moved away into the distance.

(Source: *Coulsdon & Purley Times*, 14.6.1963)

Between 3rd and 8th June 1963 (UK) – Dome-shaped UFO

Isle of Wight resident – Doreen Waddell – had just finished feeding the swans off The Solent, at Gurnard Bay, one afternoon, when she saw . . .

> *"a dome-shaped object, motionless in the sky, opalescent or translucent in appearance, shimmering as it caught the rays of the sun. It then moved away in a straight line, towards the direction of Portsmouth. I felt a great sorrow as it left, feeling that nothing else seemed as important."*

(Source: Kath Smith, Isle of Wight UFO Society)

9th June 1963 (UK) – Lights spilling out

At 11.10pm, a luminous object was observed in the sky, over Chelmsford, by Mr H. Cafferata and his friends – Mr and Mrs Alan Woods. They saw it for a period of between 10-15 minutes.

> *"The object was first seen at an angle of 60° elevation, and then changed course gradually, by as much as 45°, taking a wide curving path to the east, until lost from view at an elevation angle of about 30°. While travelling along this course, it seemed to vary in speed considerably, sometimes appearing to move very slowly; at other times, very quickly. Relatively small 'lights', or luminous objects, were seen emerging from it, one after the other, about five or six in number, which moved away and out-of-sight."*

(Source: Mr H. Cafferata, and Mr and Mrs Alan Woods)

9th-15th June (New Zealand) – Cigar-shaped UFOs reported

(Source: *Hawkes Bay Herald Tribune*, 19.6.1963)

16th June 1963 (New Zealand) – Two UFOs seen

A college student from Palmerston North City sighted two brilliant lights descending through the sky in a zigzag fashion.

> *"They then hovered stationary for about five seconds, in front of me, before suddenly moving away at high speed, upwards, at approximately a 45° elevation, and disappeared."*

(Source: NICAP Adviser – Harold H. Fulton)

Doreen Waddell's report

UFOLOG

REF NO 8/11

I.S. ISSUE NO

witnesses: ..I was alone..........

Please write your story below, and make a drawing of what you saw, if you can;
then post this form back to us in the enclosed stamped addressed envelope.

The afternoon was hot and the sky very blue except for one or two fleecy clouds. After feeding the swan that frequent the shores of The Solent, I paused to admire the beauty of the surroundings, before returning a few yards to the beach-hut hired for a week at Gurnard Bay. Looking up at the sky I was amazed to see a large, noiseless object that appeared to be hovering high in the sky. Compared with the small, fleecy clouds it was of quite another "substance". I would describe it as translucent, opalescent, shimmering looking more the colour of silver as it caught the rays of the sun and the background of blue sky emphasized this.

So far as I could judge without binoculars it was circular & dome-shaped, like nothing I'd ever seen before. It appeared to hover, then to move in a straight line in the direction of Portsmouth. This of course, may have been the effect of fleecy cloud moving west while the object still hovered, but I did not see it disappear. As I was experiencing a great sorrow at the time, nothing else seemed important to me then.

The following month I read in the paper of the Charlton Crater and thought it not unlikely that I had been gazing at a Flying Saucer, my interest was aroused when attending an advertised open meeting of I.W.F.O.I.S much later.

(Continued overleaf if necessary)

Here a film was shown and after the film a few slides and I was surprised to see a coloured picture of the very scene (plus UFO) I had witnessed at Gurnard, only the person who took the photo called it "The Sunset" and I think must have taken it later in the day as there was more glow in the sky. This is my reason for interest in the investigation.

Doreen P. Waddell.

35th April 1964.

18th June 1963 (USA) – UFO over Niagara Falls

Over Niagara Falls, New York, an unidentified object, flashing various colours, was seem moving around erratically for over two hours. At about 10pm., the UFO moved from west to east, reversed its direction, and then headed back west. Later, it headed south-east, rising higher in the sky. Local astronomers and airport officials could not account for the object. (**Source: NICAP**)

19th June 1963 (USA) – Silver light

An unidentified white light was observed descending through the sky over Burlington, Massachusetts, changing colour. As it did so, it finally appeared silver. It then circled the area, before disappearing behind objects on the horizon. (**Source: Walter N. Webb – Boston NICAP Adviser**)

UK – Spinning UFO

A spinning object, showing white light, was seen in the sky over Newton Heath, Manchester.

(Source: *Manchester Evening News*, 19.6.1963)

21st June 1963 (USA) – Grey UFO seen

Over Chicago, Illinois, a student saw a grey, apparently spherical, UFO with a central row of yellow lights, at low altitude in the sky. The object made a '*sizzling sound*' as it moved eastwards, then turned sharply and disappeared to the north. (**Source: NICAP report form**)

23rd June 1963 (USA) – UFO shaped like two soup bowls

At 1am an object, described as about 30ft in diameter, shaped like two soup bowls, one on top of the other, connected by a rim, were seen hovering over power lines at East Weymouth, Massachusetts, 300ft away from the observers, making a buzzing or roaring noise. A few minutes later it moved away and out of sight.

(Source: *UFOs: Interplanetary Visitors*, by Raymond E. Fowler)

26th June 1963 (USA) – UFO sighted

At East Weymouth, Massachusetts, during a summer heat-wave, Ebrico and Janet Gilberti were finding it difficult to get to sleep.

Around midnight they heard an ear piercing, vibrating, roaring noise, and rushed to the window to look out to see a large object, showing two glowing orange lights, some 300ft away, affixed to what resembled two greyish bowls, or hamburger buns, on top of the other.

The next morning Janet telephoned South Weymouth Naval Air Station, to report the matter. They confirmed that they had no aircraft in the area and would ring her back. Of course, they never did!

(Source: Raymond Fowler)

Pine Crest, California – Four UFOs

Four glowing greenish objects, with halos, were observed by a technician and numerous others. Three of them moved to the west direction and were approached by a similar object from the west. The fourth object stopped and hovered as the three approached, split formation and continued west. The fourth object then continued east. (**Source: NICAP Subcommittee**)

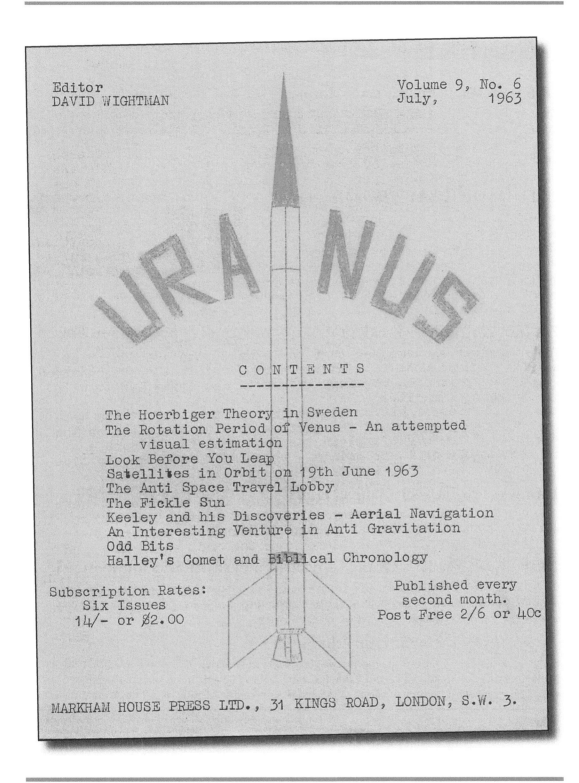

Editor
DAVID WIGHTMAN

Volume 9, No. 6
July,   1963

CONTENTS

Subscription Rates:
  Six Issues
  14/- or $2.00

Published every
second month.
Post Free 2/6 or 40c

MARKHAM HOUSE PRESS LTD., 31 KINGS ROAD, LONDON, S.W. 3.

27th June (UK) – Shining object sighted

A shining balloon-shaped object was seen moving against the wind over Flamborough Head, Yorkshire.

(Source: *The People*, 28.6.1963)

28th June 1963 (Australia) – Motorist chased by UFO

The Willaston Police reported an incident which took place at 9.30pm, involving a complaint by a motorist, who informed them that he had been chased by a UFO – described as having a concave top and flat base – before heading off into the night, at fantastic speed. On the same day there was a sighting of an oval object, which hovered at about 150ft in the sky over Royton, Lancashire. (**Source:** *Oldham Chronicle*, 29.6.1963)

2nd July 1963 (USA) – *'Blimp'* reported

At Tucson, Arizona, a large *'blimp'*-like object was reported in the sky. Was there a connection with the nearby ˙Davis Monthan AFB Titan II Missile site – home of the 390th Strategic Missile Wing, consisting 18 Launch Facilities around the Tuscon area. We were to come across many incidents, both in the UK and the USA, involving the presence of UFOs seen over military installations and power sources.

7th July 1963 (UK) – Freak thunderstorms . . . did sheep go missing?

Freak thunderstorms, were reported over Dufton Fell, Westmoreland. Two craters found, diameter of 200ft, with depth of 2-3ft, end of same the month, by farmers Bill Richardson, of Ghyll House, Dufton, and John Rudd, of Dufton Hall. According to some reports, it is alleged forty sheep were found to be missing; others told of a similar occurrence that took place over 50 years previously. (**Source:** *ORBIT/Yorkshire Post*, 1.8.1963)

9th July 1963 (UK)

11.10pm – A luminous object, ejecting smaller ones, was seen over Chelmsford, Essex.

10th July 1963 (USA) – Object lands

At Fern Creek, Kentucky, a cigar-shaped object was seen in the sky, which discharged a small *'disc'*-like object that was seen to land. (**Source:** NICAP)

10th July 1963 (UK) – Orange object seen in sky/marks found in field

On July 10th 1963, according to the village policeman – PC Anthony Penny – who made his report after returning from holiday, an orange object was seen to flash through the sky and vanish near the field where strange marks had been found.

Marks found in the crop Edinburgh

On the same day, many miles to the north, two star-shaped craters were discovered in a field belonging to Mr James Brown, at Middle Moneynut Farm, Edinburgh. They had a diameter of 16ft, a depth of 2-3ft and were 12ft apart, with 12 channels, varying in length of up to 44ft, radiating outwards. Around the craters,

---

˙Davis–Monthan Air Force Base is a United States Air Force base located within the city limits approximately five miles (8.0 km) south-southeast of downtown Tucson, Arizona. It was established in 1925 as Davis-Monthan Landing Field. The host unit headquartered at Davis–Monthan is the 355th Fighter Wing assigned to Twelfth Air Force, part of Air Combat Command (ACC). The base is best known as the location of the Air Force Materiel Command's 309th Aerospace Maintenance and Regeneration Group (AMARG), the aircraft boneyard for all excess military and government aircraft. (**Source:** Wikipedia)

large blocks of earth had been scooped from the ground and scattered over an area of 40 yards. The police and bomb squad arrived, but found nothing. The site was later visited by Frank Satterthwaite, Bill Muir, Miss O' Harrow and Harry Lord, all members of the Tyneside UFO Society, who concluded, *"an unknown object had landed, causing the craters",* discounting any possible hoax.

(Source: *Orbit, The Journal of the Tyneside UFO Society* – May/June/July, 1963)

The Tyneside UFO Society investigate

The Tyneside UFO Society, which included Harry Lord, from many years ago, William Muir, Alfred Miller, and Mr and Mrs John Leslie Otley, published a number of early UFO magazines, entitled *ORBIT*, during the 1960s.

What better way could there be of showing our appreciation for the efforts made by them to preserve this early, important social history, by presenting the relevant pages of Volume 5, No. 2, which covers the Societies investigation into seven possible landings of UFOs during 1963.

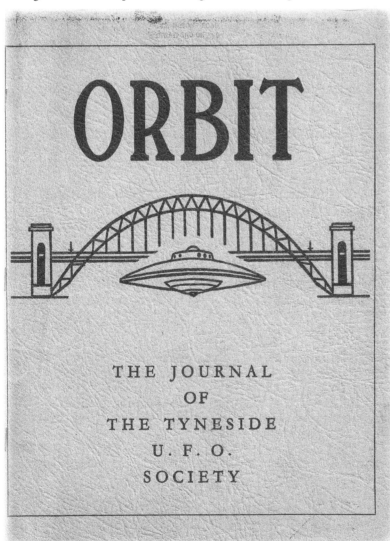

Alfred Miller,

John Leslie Otley

Mrs Jean Otley

E D I T O R I A L.

So far as ufo researchers in Great Britain are concerned, the year 1963 will probably always be remembered as "Crater Year." Certainly no aspect of 'Saucer' activity has ever before attracted quite so much press publicity and in only a few weeks there was a tremendous amount of speculation and comment on these mysterious events in the majority of the British daily newspapers.

Circumstances appeared to decree that 'The Wiltshire Crater' should be responsible for most of the conjectures concerning the origin and reason for the strange visitation. But with the publication in this issue of Orbit of the results of the TUFOS investigations in Scotland and Westmorland it will be seen that a definite pattern of incidents seems to have taken place.

Despite the volume of radio and press reports, however, it is doubtful whether the average person has been impressed by the evidence of visitation by alien space-craft. As usual it is only the ufo enthusiast, with all the facts available to him through 'flying saucer' literature, who can appreciate the facts.

There have been many reasons given, in the past, for the strange behaviour of the press, in regard to ufo activity. Politics, economics, the work of the 'silence group', government orders - all these have been held responsible for the lack of ufo news in the press. Any of these may in fact, be true. But one fact remains - the British Craters excited press curiosity and comment to a degree never shown before.

And what do they do - these people with the means and literary ability to put facts before the general public? In practically every one of the scores of reports on this matter there has been no attempt to publish carefully considered opinions or even to treat the subject with gravity and seriousness. Always the jest, the suggestion that some Cosmic Comic Opera was being played out in our heavens, never the report, well-informed through study, of the ufo subject.

It is indeed time that the Press awoke to its responsibilities in this matter. It has the means and power to seek and receive at the top Governmental level answers to the ufo mystery. Many of us suspect that governments do know what is behind the advent of these extra-terrestrial craft. The world's editors and journalists have a heaven-sent opportunity to report the truth.

May they soon return to the standards of honest, factual reporting upon which journalism supposedly is based.

ooooooOoooooo

(2)

THE BRITISH VISITATIONS AND CRATERS.

SEVEN POSSIBLE LANDINGS.

Report by

Harry Lord.

Towards the end of June and all during July the saucers became the big news story they deserve to be. Not since 1952 has there been such excitement in this country. Radio, TV and newspapers have been busily recording events which were little short of sensational. So much has happened that it is extremely difficult to sort it all out. If I were asked to put it in a nut-shell I would say that at least two carrier ships travelled over parts of Britain carrying out a survey by sending down objects, some of which appear to have landed. I suspect that one covered south England and the other Northern England and parts of Scotland. The two main rendezvous points appear to be the Solway Firth and mouth of the Thames.

A study of sighting reports during the period indicates that UFO's from the one over Southern England may have caused the craters at Charlton, Wiltshire and possibly the one at Southampton, whilst the carrier seen near the Isle of Man on July 28th and 30th may have been responsible for the craters at Middle Moneynut, East Lothian; Dufton Fell, Westmorland; Flamborough Head, Yorkshire; Sanquhar, Dumfriesshire; and Southerness, Kirkcudbright.

As the Charlton episode has been well covered by "Flying Saucer Review" Vol.9 No.5 and Luforo Bulletin Vol. 1V No.3, I propose to concentrate on the events in the north which have been investigated by our Society.

It should be mentioned that the Charlton Crater remains unexplained. It was not caused by a bomb or meteorite. This has been proved. The possibility of a hoax is ruled out because of the tremendous amount of labour which would have been necessary involving elaborate equipment and many men. The last I heard was that the Farmer, Roy Blanchard, is still convinced that an unidentified flying object landed on his field and took off again.

THE MIDDLE MONEYNUT CRATERS.

The first indication that strange things were happening in the north came when a report of craters appearing on ground at Middle Moneynut Farm appeared in the press. On July 10th, Mr James Brown, a 62-year-old farmer, found two craters on a hillside of his farm. They were star-shaped, irregular in outline with a diameter of 16ft. and a depth of 2 to 3 ft. They were 12 feet apart with 12 channels varying in length up to 44 ft. which radiated out from them. Around the craters large blocks of earth had been scooped from the ground and scattered over an area up to 40 yds. from the craters. There were also a series of square holes 1ft. wide and 2 ft. deep around the craters. These were situated at the ends of the channels.

Farmer Brown mentioned the discovery to his wife, family and neighbours but nothing was done about it until they heard of the happenings at Charlton on TV. They then decided to tell the authorities and the police came to investigate. An Army bomb disposal team followed but could find no metal of any kind or other unusual phenomena. The craters remain a mystery.

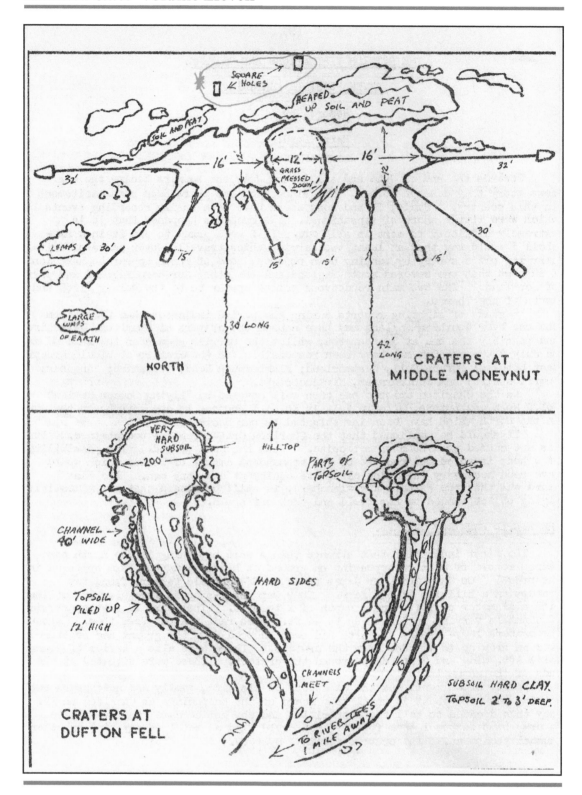

CRATERS AT MIDDLE MONEYNUT

CRATERS AT DUFTON FELL

(4)

TUFOS INVESTIGATION.

On the 4th August, six members of the Tyneside UFO Society journeyed from Newcastle to Middle Moneynut to investigate the site. They were: Frank Satterthwaite, Stewart Stevens, Bill Muir, Miss Laurenson, Miss O'Harrow and myself. After much discomfort due to rain and mist we finally found the craters the next day. We were immediately impressed with what we encountered even though many people had been there before us and trampled over some of the evidence.

In appearance the craters were very much like the reported description and our own measurements were similar to those of the police which appeared in the reports. The following details not included in the original reports were noted: (1) The soil and grass between the two craters had been pressed down to a lower level than the surrounding area. It was about 2 inches lower and suggested to us that a very heavy object had been in contact with the ground at this point. (2) The two longest channels were very thin, shallow and irregular as though a flexible, pointed instrument had scraped the top of the soil. Our conclusion was that some object had first "touched down" at the extremities of these two channels and then settled heavily where the craters were situated, throwing huge clods of soil and peat forwards.

We were all of the opinion that some unknown object had landed there causing the craters. As there was no trace of metal or other material to be seen we could only assume that the object went straight upwards when it left. The ground was undisturbed outside the perimeter of the squarish holes. This defeats any theory that a hoax had been tried because an enormous amount of labour would habe been necessary involving much equipment which would have left tell-tale marks. The cost of the operation would have been enough to make it a very extravagant hoax!

THE DUFTON FELL CRATERS.

At the end of July yet another set of craters appeared. These were giant-sized and were found on the slopes of Meldon Hill, Dufton Fell, Westmorland. Local shepherds were mystified.

Mr. W. Richardson, who owns the land, thinks there may be a connection between the craters and the fact that 40 sheep are missing from his flocks. The craters are a short distance from each other and linked at one point. The larger of the two measures 60 yards across and is 2 ft. deep. At the point where they are joined, large sods have been torn up, some of them 10 ft. across. From here a channel has been cut down the fellside to the River Tees, almost a mile away. It has not been revealed when the craters were formed but it is known that a freak thunderstorm occurred there on July 7th, a short time before their discovery.

TUFOS INVESTIGATION:

On August 11th, the same TUFOS members, with the addition of Andrew Steele and Miss E. Lambton, visited the craters on Meldon Hill, part of Dufton Fell, Westmorland. We found them very different to those at Middle Moneynut. These craters were gigantic!

At the top there was this huge, almost circular depression about 200 ft. in diameter and 2 to 3 ft. deep from which all the topsoil, peat and heather had disappeared, leaving only the clay, subsoil, looking as if it had been scraped clean by a bulldozer. The lower end of the crater narrowed to form a ravine. On each side of this the earth was piled up to a height of 10 to 12 ft. as though shoved to the sides by tremendous force.

To the right of the larger crater (facing uphill), about 50 yards away and slightly lower down, there was another crater, slightly smaller and with a similar ravine leading from it. The two ravines then joined up lower down the hill to

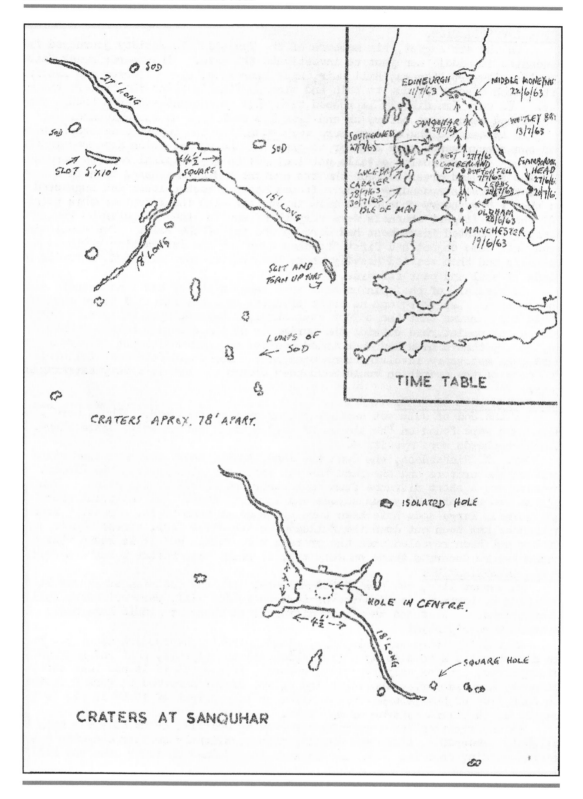

TIME TABLE

CRATERS APROX. 78' APART.

CRATERS AT SANQUHAR

(6)

form a Y-shape. The ravines were about 40 ft. in width and where they joined the bottom of the Y-shape twisted down into a natural gully which carried on for about a mile to the river. Giant clods of peat, some as big as a car had been carried down the ravines either to be heaped up at the sides or carried into the river. There was evidence of a terrific torrent of water having raced downhill carrying all before it.

As the topsoil of this hill was saturated with constant rain we formed the opinion that nature had been partly responsible for the phenomena and indeed, the people of the district are firmly convinced that the freak storm did it. However considering the circular craters and the fact that none of the rest of the hill had been disturbed we feel that this is inconclusive. Why should these two particular spots be damaged alone? It seems more likely that some other agent such as a heavy object may have landed here, caused the disturbance of the soil and consequently caused a natural landslip.

As the largest crater was completely denuded of topsoil and the second one less so, it is possible that both craters could have been made by one object bouncing, making the large one first.

THE SANQUHAR CRATERS.

On August 2nd. the first reports appeared of craters at Sanquhar, Dumfries. An official from Eskdalemuir Observatory visited the site during the last week in July to examine these mystery craters. They had appeared on the hillside at Tower Farm, occupied by the noted sheep breeder, Mr. Gavin Hendrie.

When Mr. Hendrie discovered the holes, he notified the police, who called in bomb disposal officers. But mine detectors failed to find any trace of metal, and the officers could offer no explanation.

There were two craters about three yards apart and linked by a furrow a foot deep, and the holes themselves are about 6 ft. in diameter. The observatory official, after a minute inspection declared that the craters had been caused by "a powerful light.ning stroke" going into the ground and converting moisture into steam, which in turn burst the ground upwards.

TUFOS INVESTIGATION.

Only one member of TUFOS went to Sanquhar to investigate. He was Mr. Frank Satterthwaite who reports:

"I saw the two craters at Sanquhar, the first being about 10 yards from the road. There is a definite pattern about both of them. The first was roughly an oblong, 5ft wide by 3 ft with 2 channels leading from opposite corners up to 16 ft. long. The channels were about 6 inches deep and the grass on each side of the channel was cut for about 6 inches. You could lift the grass up just like skin. In the middle of the first crater was a round hole about 9 inches deep. There was a square hole about 3 yards from the channel. I asked a local shepherd if he thought the crater could have been made by a practical joker, but he would not agree with this idea and was unable to offer any explanation.

The second crater lay aproximately 26 yards away from the first. It was about 4 ft. square and up to 12 inches deep. There were two short channels and one long one, approximately 24 ft. long. Turf from the craters was spread about all over the place. I could not see any spade marks."

OTHER CRATERS

We have received reports that craters have also appeared at Southerness, on the southern coast of Kirkcudbright, Apparantly they appeared about the same time as those at Sanquhar. There is also a report of craters at Kirkconnel though the latter may refer to those at Sanquhar as both places are very close together. We have not yet been able to visit Southerness bu t may do so soon.

(7)

THE FLAMBOROUGH HEAD CRATER.

A crater was also discovered at Flamborough Head on or about July 20th. This was in a 20 acre field and was 10 ft. in diameter. The surrounding grass was dead and blackened. Explosive experts travelled there to try and explain it without success. It was hastily suggested that a bolt of lightning ignited a small pocket of natural gas in the soil. The Daily Express, July 22nd, stated that the experts would be offered plenty of advice and suggested explanations from the people of Flamborough (pop 1,325). Heading the list is the theory that the crater was caused by something from outer space. The village policeman Ronald Taylor said "I thought of a meteorite. It does not look like an explosion although the soil has been scattered over 20ft."

Mrs. Hood, wife of the farmer on whose land the crater appeared thought there might have been an explosion. "But if so," she added,"the shell must have been more than a foot below ground because we touched nothing when we ploughed."

The coastguard said: "We are nearest and we never heard an explosion". Other theories are that subsidence caused the 2ft deep crater or that someone is simply playing tricks. But the thought that Flamborough finds at once most appealing and most appalling is that the answer lies not in the soil - but in space.

THE POSSIBLE PATTERN.

As there were frequent reports of UFOs over Britain during the time of the craters a general idea of the complete operation can be partly deduced by studying the following time table of events:

June 19th - Newton Heath, Manchester. The Manchester Evening News on June 19th reported that a schoolboy called his mother to come out and see a rainbow. He then saw an object in the sky. "It was oval-shaped and spinning round. There was a white light on it, and it passed overhead towards Clayton." It made no sound and was as big as an aeroplane.

June 22nd - It was probably on this day when the Moneynut Craters appeared because both the farmer and wife say that there was a "bang" heard between 5.a.m. and 6.a.m.

June 27th. - Flamborough Head, Yorks. The People. June 28 reported that a shining object in the sky had holiday makers mystified for hours at Flamborough Head yesterday. Coastguards decribed the object as balloon shaped and almost transparent. They said it was moving against the wind.

June 28th - The Oldham Chronicle of June 29th reported that a group of Royton people recently saw a "flying saucer". It was oval-shaped and hovered silently 150 feet above their heads for 15 minutes then it glided over a hospital towards nearby playing fields. It was a very bright object with something spinning above it.

July 7th - The craters at Dufton Fell may have occurred on this date as the farmer's wife days there was a freak thunderstorm then.

July 10th - The Middle Moneynut craters were discovered by Farmer Brown.

July 11th - The day after the discovery of Farmer Brown's craters in the Lammermuirs six people say they saw a flying saucer high in the sky above Edinburgh. It was observed for about 10 minutes. It was shaped like two saucers, one on top of the other and had a hump on top. It was dark underneath and greyish-white on top. There was no sound and the object seemed to gyrate.

July 13th - Whitley Bay, Northumberland. Mr. Walker of Whitley Bay claims that the day before the crater was discovered at Charlton he saw a large, white, shining orb flying over his home. It moved due east at 12,15 a.m. moving towards Tynemouth at 2.a.m. over the sea. There were very strong sound vibrations and he

(8)

saw a smaller object orbiting around it. The date of this sighting is doubtful.

July 20th - Flamborough Head craters found on this day.

July 24th - Leeds, Yorkshire. Flying Saucer seen by group of schoolboys. They saw it hovering over Roundhay Park woods at 8.45.a.m. on their way to school. It was a silver-grey object, circular, with a "cockpit" on top and it made a buzzing sound.

July 27th - West Cumberland.(Dis.tington, etc.) A tumbler-shaped object was seen in the sky over West Cumberland at night. It was glowing brightly in the northern half of the sky and was under observation for a period of nearly three hours!

July 27th - The craters at Sanquhar and Southerness were reported on this day (B.B.C. Scottish News 6.15.p.m.)

July 28th - Mr James McGill, on holiday at Luce Bay saw an unusual object in the sky east of the Isle of Man. It was stationary.

July 30th - Mr. McGill again saw the object east of the Isle of Man. This time three lights appeared to emerge from the main one, and then return. Probably the most important sighting among the above is the last one, this appears to have been a carrier craft. The objects which came from this object may have landed at Southerness (on the Solway), and at Kirconnel and Sanquhar.

Then there is the sighting at Flamborough Head about three weeks before the craters were discovered. There appears to be a good connection here. Another close connection appears to be the saucer seen at Edinburgh, not too far from Middle Moneynut and close in time.

Let us assume that the carrier craft was moving about northern England and Scotland releasing UFOs of various kinds, each having a particular function. By plotting the course of this object using our time table, the picture would look something like this:

The operation would begin at Manchester on June 19th. The next event is the crater at Middle Moneynut three days later followed by a UFO sighting five days later at Flamborough Head and then another one at Oldham the next day. It is quite possible that the carrier followed a triangular course over a period of nine days because it is well known that these craft are never seen to travel at speed. It is the saucers and other types which fly at fantastic speeds.

There are two points to note at this stage. (1) A direct flight from Manchester to Middle Moneynut would pass directly over the Dufton Fell area. (2) A freak whirlwind occurred at Thirsk, Yorks., on June 25th, leaving a mile long trail of wreckage. Buildings were flattened and cars hurled into the air to drop yards away. Although Thirsk is not in line with Moneynut and Flamborough, it is possible that after travelling southwards towards Thirsk, the object then turned left towards Flamborough.

After the sighting at Oldham on June 28th, the craters appear at Dufton Fell nine days later and four days after this an object is seen at Edinburgh. Once again it is noticed that Dufton Fell is in the line with Oldham and Edinburgh. Two days later a sighting occurs at Whitley Bay, Northumberland followed by the discovery of the crater at Flamborough Head a week later. After this we get the sighting of a saucer at Leeds four days later. Again we notice that Whitley Bay is in direct line of flight from Edinburgh to Flamborough Head.

After the Leeds sighting there appears to have been a deviation across country to West Cumberland where the tumbler-shaped object is seen three days later. The supposed object is now nearing the Solway Firth and heading towards Southerness and Sanquhar where craters are discovered at this time. The next day the carrier is seen with UFOs going in and out of it. This appears to be the rendezvous point and time for departure. No more incidents have since been

```
                                    (9)
reported.
        An alternative to this idea is that the carrier "anchored" over the Solway
and remained there during the whole operation, sending out UFOs to the different
points to perform a particular duty and then return.




    References:         Hull Daily Mail July 20; Daily Express July 22,23;
                        Scottish Daily Express July 25; Daily Record July 25;
                        The Scotsman July 25; Scottish Daily Mail 25,27;
                        Glasgow Herald July 25; Yorkshire Post July 25;Aug 1;
                        Northern Echo July 25; The Guardian July 30;
                        Cumberland & Westmorland Herald Aug.3;
                        Berwickshire News July 30; Dumfries News July 28;
                        Scottish Farmer Aug3.
```

10th July 1963 (UK) – Marks found in farmer's field

On the 18th July 1963, following an article published in the *Daily Express*, relating to a mysterious hole found in a farmer's field in Charlton, Mr Charles Stickland (Editor of *LUFORO* magazine) made his way to the area, accompanied by Mr Nigel Stephenson, who later wrote an excellent description of what they found:

"The place is a field at Manor Farm, Charlton, Wiltshire, a little to the east of Shaftsbury, Dorset, owned by farmer, Roy Blanchard. When we arrived on the 18th, Captain John Rogers – head of the Bomb Disposal Squad – was in attendance. He confirmed they had been called out on the 10th July. The field is divided into two crops – barley and potatoes. The site is on the boundary between the two crops; the measurements are probably close to the original, but bear in mind that others had visited the site before we had arrived, and may have disturbed it to some extent. The central hole was about 5ft across and 3ft deep. It was not completely empty but had some loose rocks in it and was situated in a shallow depression – 8ft in diameter, not more than three or four inches below the surrounding ground – and from which the potato plants had disappeared. In the barley were three gaps which did not extend to the boundary of the planted area. When they were discovered, all of the barley had disappeared and only loose soil remained. The cutting in the potato ridges was very ill-defined by the time we had reached the site; only a few potato plants were seen within a roughly circular area of about 12ft radius from the centre. The Bomb Disposal Squad continued their examination of the site until the 25th July, when their metal detectors picked-up an object subsequently identified by the British Museum as being an 'iron pan' – a hard cement-like layer made-up of iron hydroxide, as a result of chemical reaction caused by water percolating through the uppermost layer of the soil, which could not have caused the hole and markings."

No Bomb found

Some people suggested the crater had been caused by an unexploded wartime bomb. But the Army bomb disposal squad determined there was no bomb, or remains of any meteorite, Major H. P. Qualtrough from Horsham Bomb Disposal Unit pointed out those six men had been deployed for ten days on this task.

Dr Randall

A rather curious character by the name of Dr Randall, who claimed to be an Astro Physicist, informed the Press that the crater had been formed by a flying saucer from Uranus! The Press reported the Dr's claims, and so fuelled speculation about the strange nature of the crater. Questions about the crater were raised in the House of Commons, it was concluded that as it stood the business could not be entirely explained.

It was a flying saucer!

Roy Blanchard was convinced there was only one explanation as to the crater's origin, a flying saucer! He admitted:

> "I didn't actually see it, but what else could it have been? Obviously some craft from outer space, since it sucked out my barley and potatoes when it took off."

THE ARMY DON'T DIG IT

DAILY MIRROR 25-7-63

MYSTERY holes in the ground at opposite ends of Britain were baffling Army bomb-disposal experts and police last night.

In WILTSHIRE, four sappers and a sergeant dug yesterday in a potato-and-barley field belonging to farmer Roy Blanchard, of Charlton.

They were trying to find out what had caused a shallow crater 8ft. in dia-meter and marks on the ground.

In EAST LOTHIAN a squad of police from Edin-burgh helped three Army bomb-disposal experts to investigate two shallow craters 16ft. in diameter on lonely Lammermuir Hills.

There, great lumps of earth had been scattered more than 40ft. from the craters. And there were channels up to 44ft. long radiating from them like spokes of a wheel. After a day's digging all the ex-perts found . . . nothing.

Later, an Army spokes-man called for " a note of sanity," and said : " We do not support any Spaceship theory."

But two M Ps. Mr. Roy Mason (Lab., Barnsley) and Mr. Patrick Wall (Cons., Haltemprice, Yorks.), have put down Commons ques-tions asking if flying saucers are involved.

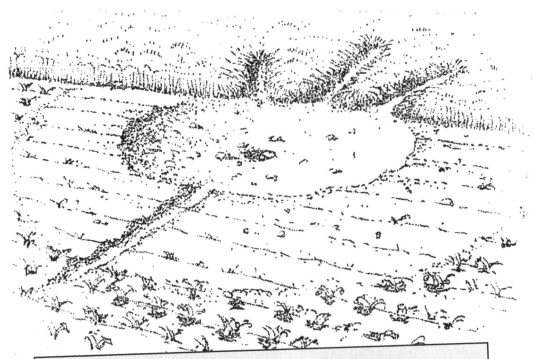

NEWS FLASH: by F.W. Smith.

The Society has recently contacted the elusive Dr. Robert Randall who appeared on the Charlton 'crater' scene in July, 1963. It will be remembered that Randall, having made some extraordinary statements, disappeared mysteriously and left intense speculation rife among the national press and populace. The Daily Mail, which refused later to go back on its word, published a hoax 'confession' that put the dampers on Randall's Uranian spaceship. The letter they would not print is by the 'confessor' himself and can be read in either the Autumn BUFOA journal or the Nov/Dec. issue of Flying Saucer Review; the 'hoaxer' is one John Southern.

Dr. R.J. Randall, Ph.D., M.A.S.O. (qualifications are genuine and can be looked up in appropriate registers) has now re-appeared and published a report containing his story of the Charlton and other craters. The main substance of the report is his alleged contact with a dying spaceman on a Scottish moor. It is an intriguing document, but we do not wish to pass any comment at this stage and suggest that interested readers should send 2/6 for their own copy to:

Dr. R.J. Randall, 4, Sidbury Hill Ave, TIDWORTH, Hants.

IWUFOIS are hoping to invite Dr. Randall to the Isle of Wight to give members a first hand opportunity to talk to him.

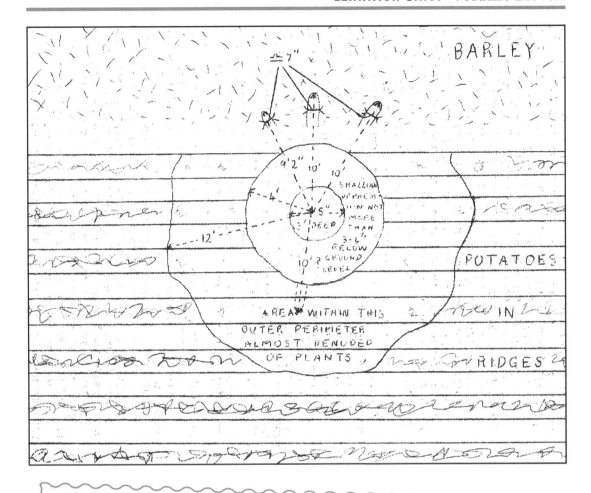

Green men? THAT hole was dug by earthling hoaxers

By GERARD KEMP

A MAN claimed yesterday that he helped to dig the mystery hole in a farmer's potato field, which some said was caused by a flying saucer.

TV repair man Mr. John Southern, 37, laughed at stories of green men from outer space. . . .

The hole was dug at dead of night by ordinary pale-faced earthlings using old-fashioned shovels, he said.

Mr. Southern, of Tokyngton avenue, Wembley, added: "I cannot give the names of the two men who pulled the hoax with me."

For ten days after the crater was discovered at Mr. Roy Blanchard's farm near Charlton, Wiltshire, an Army bomb disposal unit investigated the hole with mine detectors and spades.

A science-fiction writer identified the hole as marks caused by a flying saucer which had force-landed then flown off. Sightseers poured in.

Then the Army emerged to the statement: "With a tinge of regret, we announce that the mysterious hole . . . has yielded nothing more dramatic than a half-pound lump of matter which appears to be a meteorite."

Stories

Now doubt is cast on even that crumb of consolation for the star-gazers and flying-saucer fans.

Mr. Southern said: "The two men who pulled this hoax also did the crater that appeared in Scotland.

"One of them is dead 32 and works in TV; the other is a Leeds-born student at present in London.

"I write short stories in my spare time. Haven't had any published yet. Only a manual on How to Play the Guitar.

"I was writing this television play and showed it to my friend in TV. It was called The Big Hoax and dealt with mysterious craters that appeared overnight. My friend said: 'Let's see if it could be done.'

"With the student, we met in a Wembley cafe and planned the whole thing.

"My wife Phyllis was on holiday with our 11-year-old son Christopher so she wasn't in on it at all. When she got back I told her about the hoax.

"We had planned a third crater up near Cambridge. We even went up to do it but the weather was so bad we packed it in. We left the shovel and spade outside the gate of Madingley Farm on the Haddingham road."

Last night Major H. P. Qualtrough, of Horsham Bomb Disposal Unit, said: "We had six men working on this crater for ten days. They could have been on much more important work."

Genuine

"If it's a hoax I'm prepared to laugh with the next man. We often get hoaxed. Nearly always in Cambridge rag week. We just accept it in good grace.

"All I can say is that at the time this appeared to be quite genuine."

But farmer Blanchard said: "I don't believe this story that the whole thing was a hoax. I think anyone who believes it was a hoax is being hoaxed."

FLYING SAUCER REVIEW

SEPTEMBER—OCTOBER 1963

VOLUME 9, No. 5   **9th YEAR OF PUBLICATION**

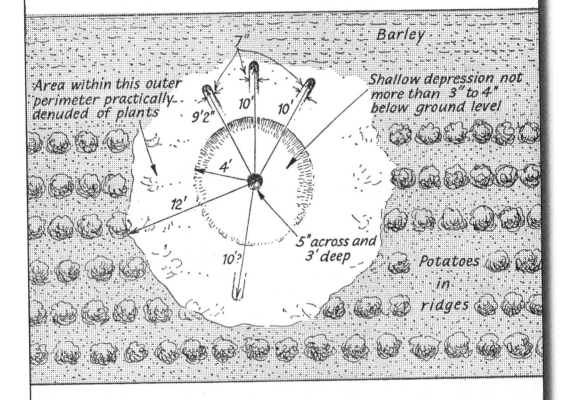

THE WILTSHIRE CRATER
FULL INSIDE STORY

11th July 1963 (UK) – UFO sighted

At 3am, Captain Cornelius Buck – resident of Rownhams Mount (North of Southampton) – was awoken by the sound of dogs, barking frenziedly.

On looking out of the window, he saw a curious glow over the roof of one of the wings of the house, and thought a fire could have broken out.

> *"I then became aware that the light was coming from above. Glancing upwards, I saw what looked like a blowlamp, with a flame directed downwards, giving off an orange glow, surrounded by what appeared to be clouds of smoke. After a short time, the orange glow turned to bluish-white, and the whole contraption appeared to go straight up."*

(Source: Norman C. Toogood)

Edinburgh

On this date a spinning object *'like two saucers with hump on top'* was seen over Edinburgh.

(Source: *Scottish Daily Mail*, 27.7.63)

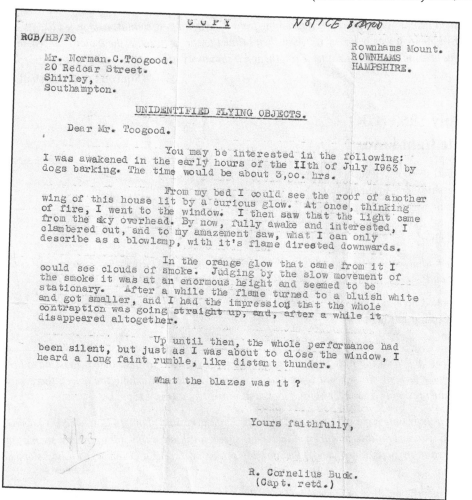

13th July 1963 (UK) – Red *'light'* in the sky

Mr C. Palmer from Rainville Road, Hammersmith, London, was driving home with his sister and brother-in-law, Mr F. J. Andrews, along the A30, and stopped for rest between Crewkerne and Shaftesbury at 1.45am.

"We were looking at the moon, which had just risen, when my brother-in-law called my attention to a strange 'light' he could see, a short distance below the moon. We got out of the car and watched it head towards the north, appearing as a red flashing light. It appeared to change direction, three times."

(Source: LUFORO, No. 3, June/July/August 1963)

14th July 1963 (UK) – Cigar-shaped UFO

At 3am, Frank Selwood of Parkstone, Dorset, awoke and looked out of the bedroom window. He saw,

"towering over a large gasholder at the rear of the house, a huge cigar-shaped object, as big as four terraced houses, about 300ft up in the air, showing an intermittent flashing wavy blue-green light. I could hear a quiet sort of whistle coming from it, and flapping sounds. It sounded like its engine (or whatever it was) running rough. It then seemed to spring into life, the motor changed, and the lights became continuous along its length, and it shot away towards the west at a fantastic speed."

(Source: Frank Marshall, BUFORA)

Would you please try to draw what you saw.

16th July 1963 (UK) – White light lands

Stephen Earl (59) of Wisbech, Cambridgeshire, employed by Brooks Farm, was with his son (10) catching rabbits. His son asked his father,

"What's that white light dad?"

Stephen looked up and saw an object descending through the sky at an angle.

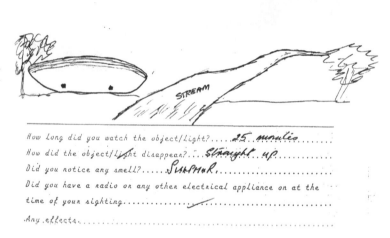

How long did you watch the object/light?..... 25 minutes ....

How did the object/light disappear?... Straight up...........

Did you notice any smell?..... Sulphur.......................

Did you have a radio on any other electrical appliance on at the time of your sighting...................................

Any effects...

"It then landed in the next field, close to a stream. I thought, at first, that it must have been a helicopter or light aircraft, but there was no sound. We stood watching the object; there was no movement coming from it, or lights. I looked at my watch; it was 9.15pm.

After a short time it glowed white and then lifted off the ground about 15-20ft, where it hovered in the air. Suddenly it shot upwards, at incredible speed, until just a tiny dot in the sky, seconds later. I looked at my wristwatch; it was 9.40pm. My son looked at his and remarked it had stopped at 9.17pm."

We believe that the location of the incident was The Avenue, Madingley, Cambridge CB23 8AD.

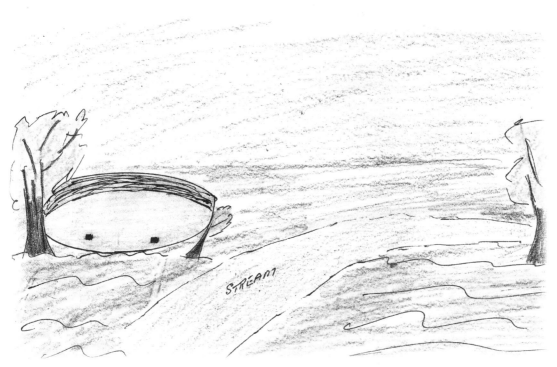

*Brooks Farm, Wisbech, Cambs
16th July 1963   9-15 pm*

STREAM

17th July 1963 (USA) – Shaped like a watermelon

An object, shaped like a watermelon, was seen over Clinton, Ohio, at 9pm. At 10.10pm, still in the same State, over Mansfield, a bright white *'light'* was seen moving rapidly across the sky. Another report was made at 11.15pm over South Akron, Ohio, of an elongated object seen changing shape and colour from yellow to white, as it headed across the sky.

18th July 1963 (USA) – US Air Force converges on UFO

At Sunnyvale, California, a technical writer for United Technology Centre saw a *'disc'*-shaped UFO hovering in the sky. He exposed 8mm colour film of the object, using a 36mm telephoto lens. (A few frames of the film were submitted to NICAP, but the image is too small to show detail).

When four jet interceptors converged on the UFO (three from the west and one from the east) it drifted westwards, tilting back and forth, *"then pulled up in a short arc and shot up out of sight in an estimated three seconds."* (**Source: Report via Bay Area NICAP Subcommittee**)

20th July 1963 (USA) – UFO sighted

At about 7.50pm, a shiny silver object was observed hovering at high altitude over Springfield, Illinois. It was seen to move up and down, back and forth, but remained in the same area of the sky. As dusk fell, the object (now resembling a bright star) began to move across the sky, picking up speed, before disappearing into the distance. (**Source: NICAP report form**)

20th July 1963 (UK)

At Flamborough Head, Yorkshire, a hole – 6ft in diameter and 12-18in deep – was found with radiating cracks. (**Source:** *BUFORA Journal,* **summer 1963**)

22nd July 1963 (UK) – Landed UFO

At 8.30pm, schoolboys – William Holland, Paul Lightfoot and Keith Kerfoot from Parr, St. Helens, in Lancashire – were playing on the nearby tip.

They noticed a shining, spinning object, descending from the sky, which came to a stop approximately 70ft above their heads. William said at the time:

> *"It had a red flashing light and was spinning. It stopped dead, and the red light went out. Something slid back and what looked like a periscope came out, swivelled, pointed at us, and went back inside the object, which then shot upwards into the sky and vanished into a strange coloured cloud, a few seconds later."*

We traced two of the boys concerned, and spoke to them regarding the incident, after launching an appeal for any other witnesses to come forward, but no additional information was forthcoming.

'Flying saucer' seen

At 9pm on the same date, Mr and Mrs C Dickenson (41) from Crutches Lane, Strood, Kent, was watching television in the kitchen of their bungalow, when she became aware of her husband gazing intently up into the night sky. She asked him what he was looking at, and he replied, *"A flying saucer"*.

She said:

"I thought he was joking, and looked out and saw a pale yellow dome-shaped object, surrounded by an orange glow, moving northwards across the sky, over the end of the new M2 Motorway. It was very high up, but there was no mistake about what it was. It's funny, but when the subject has come up before, we used to laugh at people who had seen 'flying saucers'."

(**Source: Anglo-Polish UFO Group/Isle of Wight UFO Society**)

On Monday, 22nd July 1963, my Husband and I were watching T.V. in the kitchen of our bungalow. My Husband was sitting side-ways on to t window, whilst I had my back to it. I noticed that my Husband was staring up at the sky and when I asked him what he was staring at, he said he was watching a flying saucer. I thought he was joking but he told me to hurry and look or I should be too late. I immediately turne round and was just in time to see the unfamiliar object. The time was approximately 9.00 p.m. This object was dome shaped – pale yellow in colour – and I say surrounded by an orange coloured glow, altho my Husband said he did not notice the glow particularly. However, we both agree on the colour of the actual object. My Husband saw it for a few minutes whilst I saw it in the last remaining seconds. The directio of the flight was North from Strood end of the New Motorway – the M2. I am sorry we can give no details of the direction of wind but no doubt the Met. Office can furnish you with this information. The elevati above the horizon about 30 degrees. The assessment of speed is rather difficult as it did not appear to be moving – it just decreased in size. There was no deviation to left or right. If it was moving, then it must have been going away from us in a straight line. If there was any sound from it, we should not have heard it, as e had the T.V. set switched on. As far as we can remember, the day had been a fine one. There was wispy cloud in the vicinity but not in this particular area where we sighted the U.F.O. The sky was very blue which is what made my Husband look up at the sky in the first place. The size of the objec was about ¾ – 1 " in length (in perspective) but I am sure you will agree that it is most difficult to give a really accurate estimate here.

My Husband and I both think that this object must have been travellir at a terrific rate and a long way up, hence its rapid decrease in size. One has only to compare it with a Jet Aircraft which in spite of its high speed, is still visual for some time after it has passed overhead.

Lastly, I should like to say that although I would admit that I have quite a vivid imagination, my Husband most certainly has not. He is a very "down-to-earth" person and very sceptical usually about suc matters as Flying Saucers, – in fact in the past we have both laughed a people who have claimed to have seen such things. My imagination was not working overtime that night however – we both now we had witnes something different – something which we just cannot find any reasonabl explanation for.

At 10.45pm an object, shaped like an inverted dessert dish, with three tiers of lights – yellow, orange, and red around the outside – was seen crossing the main Cheltenham to Evesham Road, in Gloucestershire, at a speed of about l00mph, heading north-west. Another report told of a similar (if not same) object seen over Hinton on the Green, Worcestershire, at 10.45pm. (**Source:** *Gloucestershire Echo*, 23.7.1963)

24th July 1963 (UK) – *'Spinning top'* UFO

At 2am, a UFO – described as looking like *"a gigantic spinning top, with a shimmering gold centre, red top and blue/green base"* – was seen by Mr Robert Armitage, the Manager of a petrol filling station at Accrington, Lancashire. He said:

> *"It was a clear night when I saw the object stationary in the sky, east, towards Burnley. Suddenly, it arced across the sky towards Bacup, stopped, and began to shimmer. I watched it for about 15 minutes, as it flew silently across the sky. It was a beautiful thing to look at."*

Staffordshire

At 8.45am, a silver-grey, buzzing, circular object was seen, with what looked like a *'cockpit'* on top, flying through the sky over Staffordshire. (**Source:** *ORBIT*)

A short time later a silver-grey circular object, showing a *'cockpit'* on top, was seen over Roundhay Park, Leeds, in Yorkshire, making a buzzing noise.

25th July 1963 (UK) – *'Flying saucers'* seen

Seven silent objects, showing pale orange lights, were reported flying through the sky over Anchorsholme, near Blackpool, at 12.50am. (**Source:** *West Lancashire Evening Gazette*, 8.8.1963)

Scotland – *'Flying saucer'* seen

At 9.45am, Councillor John Gallagher from Calder Avenue, Coatbridge, was on duty at Whifflet North signal box, Coatbridge, when he noticed an aircraft heading towards Renfrew.

> *"Just as it disappeared, a 'flying saucer' came into view, which stopped and hovered over the town centre, at a height of about 100ft, before heading to the north side of the parish church. When I looked back again at 10am, having attended to a passing train, it was nowhere to be seen."*

(**Source:** *Scottish Daily Mail*, 1.8.1963)

Roslyn, Midlothian – Two *'flying saucers'* seen

The same day, doctor's wife – Ruth Scott from Roslyn, Midlothian – was in the garden, with her son, Simon (10) and university student, Ben Oddotte, when Simon drew their attention to something in the sky.

> *"It looked like two saucers, one on top of each other, with a hump on top, a dark underneath and grey top, travelling south."*

Edinburgh – *'Flying saucer'* seen

A similar object was seen over Clermiston, Edinburgh, by Elizabeth Potts and her two children.

(**Source:** *Scottish Daily Mail*, 27.7.63 – 'We saw flying saucer over City, say six'/*Scottish Daily Mail*, 1.8.1963 – 'Councillor logs a flying saucer')

Walsall, Staffordshire

At 11.30pm, *"a large, flashing, stationary red light"* was seen over Walsall, Staffordshire

(Source: *Wolverhampton Express & Star*, 1.8.63)

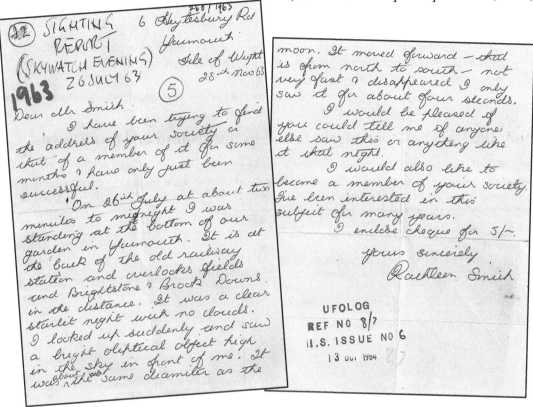

27th July 1963 (UK) – *'Tumbler'*-shaped UFO seen

A mysterious-shaped object was seen in the night sky, over West Cumberland, by Leslie Rae – a youth employment worker, at Workington – who was a fellow of the Royal Astronomical Society. A short time later, Distington Cumbria , resident – Harry Stalker, sighted, along with a number of friends, *"a tumbler-shaped object in the sky, for over three hours."* (**Source:** *The Guardian*, 30.7.1963/ *West Cumberland Times*, 3.8.1963)

UFO seen over Worcester

Donald Lloyd and his wife, from St. Andrew's Road, Malvern, had just retired for the night when the bedroom became lit-up with a powerful light, despite the curtains being drawn. The couple looked out and saw a large ball-shaped object over the Old Hill Callow End direction.

> *"It moved towards Malvern in an arc and disappeared in a south-easterly direction. Just before it went, the light tuned orange. We saw it again about 45 minutes later, this time coming from the Old Hill direction, before it turned northwards – gradually diminishing as if climbing at speed, an angle of 45°. After it had gone, there was a sound like the noise of a powerful jet."*

(Source: *ORBIT*)

28th July 1963 (UK) – Green UFO with aerial seen

At 8.35pm, over Providence Lane, Long Ashton, Bristol, a green oval object was seen. The witnesses were John White and Howard Williams (19).

Builders' labourer, Howard said:

> *"It had an aerial and made a whistling noise – like tuning a radio. It came from the direction of Weston-Super-Mare and flew at 100ft above the top end of the lane, near Long Ashton Golf Course, before rapidly climbing out of sight, two minutes later."*

(**Source:** *Bristol Evening Post*, 29.7.1963 – 'Riddle of a Saucer')

July 1963 (UK) – *'Ring'* marks found in the ground at Afton Downs

Isle of Wight resident Kathleen Smith, her son Clive and nephew John were out walking in Afton Down when they came across some strange marks in the ground. Here is what she had to say about it in a letter sent to the Isle of Wight UFO Society.

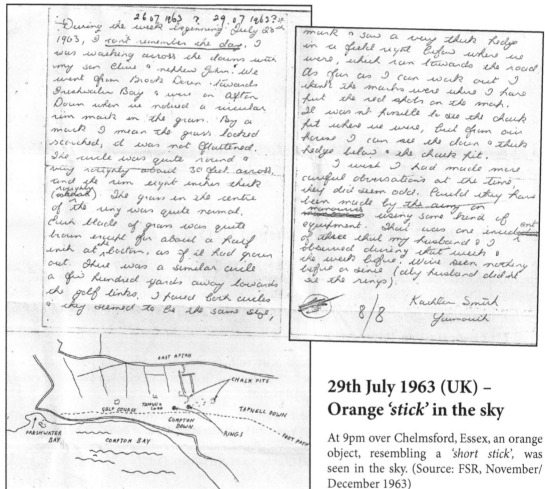

29th July 1963 (UK) – Orange *'stick'* in the sky

At 9pm over Chelmsford, Essex, an orange object, resembling a *'short stick'*, was seen in the sky. (Source: FSR, November/ December 1963)

Also on this day, a glowing object was reported crossing the sky, at speed, over Bristol, during the early morning and night-time – later explained away as being a weather balloon on fire!

(Source: *Worcester News & Times*, 30.7.1963)

30th July 1963 (UK) – Three objects seen

At West Huntspill, Somerset, just after midnight, a large, oval, glittering, quivering *'light'* was seen in the sky, by local resident Alice Chiswell with a stream of red and orange light falling away from it, *"Quivering like a jelly"* followed by an early morning sighting over Woolacombe, Devon, when three bright orange objects were observed.

(Source: *Burnham-on-Sea Gazette & Highbridge Express*, 1.8.1963/*North Devon Journal Herald*, 1.8.1963)

During the same morning, three strange *'lights'* were seen moving over the Isle of Man.

A bright orange object was reported over Woolacombe, Devon. (**Source:** *North Devon Journal*, 1.8.1963)

Nottingham – Mystery 'light' seen

At 2am, Edward O'Dowd (29) was out fishing at Trent Bridge, Nottingham, with his two brothers – Peter (22) and Barry (15) – when they saw a 'light' in the sky.

> *"It came at a fast speed and appeared to disintegrate. About 15 minutes later, we saw the same thing; they were not very high. We do not believe it was a shooting star, meteorites or satellites. We have seen plenty of those."*

(Sources: *Nottingham Evening Post & News*, 31.7.1963 – 'Sky light mystery over City')

Clacton-on-Sea

On or about the 31st July 1963, Frank Pearson from Wallington, Surrey, was enjoying a week's holiday at Clacton-on-Sea, and lying on the beach at 6.30pm, looking upwards, when something over the sea caught his attention.

> *"It wasn't very big and moved slowly across the sky. I watched it, trying to make out what it could be, but it was quite a distance away – roughly the size of a sixpence. It then moved in a swaying motion and came to a stop – now much lower, over the sea. As it sunk lower, it resembled an aircraft without wings – then it rose upwards into the sky and*
> *headed off over Clacton, where I lost sight of it. I decided to go in for tea. When I came out, at 7pm, I could see it again in the sky."*

The following day, Mr Pearson learnt (through newspaper reports of UFOs that other people had sighted) of a similar object over the Clacton area. (**Source: Isle of Wight UFO Society**)

31.7.63

UFOLOG REF Nº | 8/6

AERIAL PHENOMENA SIGHTING REPORT

TO BE COMPLETED BY WITNESS

NAME ..... FRANK PEARSON ..... DATE Tuesday 6th October 196?

ADDRESS .. 111. BLENHEIM GARDENS Wallington. Surrey AGE IF UNDER 21 34 (?!!)F

LOCATION OF SIGHTING (GIVE MAP REF IF KNOWN)

CLACTON - ON - SEA · ESSEX

DATE OF SIGHTING (ABOUT) 31st Auley · 1963 ..... TIME OF DAY 6.0 PM. TILL 7.0 PM.

DESCRIBE BRIEFLY THE WEATHER CONDITIONS "A LITTLE Cloudy AT THE TIME".

"IT HAD BEEN A WARM AND SUNNY DAY". (NOT MUCH WIND). = BUT WAS EAST)

FOR HOW LONG WAS THE OBJECT IN VIEW? CLEAR VIEW FOR 10 MINUTS .... (ONE HOUR)

WERE THERE ANY OTHER WITNESSES? . HoliDay WITNESSES "yes" BUT NO ADDRESSES

WERE ANY PHOTOGRAPHS TAKEN? .. "NOT THAT I KNOW OF" BUT REPORT IN EVENING PAPERS NEXT DAY

I HAD ONE WEEKS HOLIDAY FROM WORK; PLUS ONE DAY FOR THE AUGUST BANK HOLIDAY.

THE WEATHER WAS VERY GOOD UP TILL THE END OF THE WEEK. NO CLOUDS. SUN ALL THE WAY

IT IS RECKOND, THAT THE WIND FROM THE EAST. IS FAMOUS AT CLACTON - ON. SEA AND IT

WAS SO ON THIS DAY, AND ALL THE WEEK. NOT MUCH WIND BUT VERY PLEASANT. THEN ABOUT. 6.

ON THE DAY FOR THIS REPORT, I WAS JUST ABOUT TO GO TO THE HOTEL FOR MY EVENING

MEAL, WICH WAS AT 6.30 PM. FOR BY THIS TIME EVERYONE ON THE BEACH SEEMED TO BE

GOING HOME (OR FOR A MEAL). I WAS LYING FLAT ON MY BACK "LOOKING UP AT THE

SKY (I HAD MY RADIO ON) A FEW CLOUDS WERE PUSHING ALONG THE SKY FROM THE

EAST. I THINK THEY WERE JUST EVENING CLOUDS. WHEN I SAW SOMETHING OVER

THE SEA UP IN THE SKY. SO I SAT UP AND LOOKED HARD AT IT. IT WAS NOT

VERY BIG, (AND NOT MOVING). ANYWAY I LOOKED AT IT FOR QUITE SOME TIME

THEN, IT CAME OVER FROM THE EAST VERY QUICK. AND SEVERAL TIMES SLOWLY

MOVING IN EACH DIRECTION BUT STILL MOVING OVER TO CLACTON. I LOOKED

UP AT SOME PASSERS BY (THAT IVE JUST SEEN AN OBJECT STOP IN THE SKY).

BUT THEY COULD SEE NOTHING. IT WAS A WASTE OF TIME, WHEN I LOOKED

AGAIN I WAS "DUMBFOUNDED" I TOLD A MAN TO KEEP THIS EYES OPEN OVER

THE SEA (HE COULD SEE IT) AND GOT VERRY EXCITED ABOUT IT; ((NOW THAT

- I THINK OF IT, I WAS A FOOL)) I SHOULD OF GET HIS ADDRESS"

PLEASE CONTINUE OVERLEAF OR ON ANOTHER SHEET IF NECESSARY

'V'-shaped UFO over Kent

On the same evening, an unidentified object – described as 'V'-shaped, *"like a shiny plastic triangle, with a red glow at the bottom, which was seen to change into a circular shape"* – was seen moving slowly across the sky, heading north to south, over Gillingham, Kent, at 8.30pm, before going upwards and out of sight.

Devon – Three 'lights' seen

Over Woolacombe, Devon, three bright orange objects were seen heading across the sky. (**Sources: North** *Devon Journal Herald*, 1.8.1963, *Chatham, Rochester & Gillingham News*, 2.8.1963 – 'Was it a 'flying saucer' over Medway towns')

1st August 1963 (UK) –UFO's reported over West Midlands

At 11.30pm, on the 1st August 1963, a mysterious red *'beam of light'* was again seen in the sky over Walsall, West Midlands, by Mr E. Dunn and Mr G. Cope, who called the police. Following the attendance of an officer, the two men told him:

> *"It was flying at about 600ft and circled over the Beechdale Estate, three times, changing in colour from red, to blue and white, sometimes stationary in the air for a period of up to 20 seconds, before vanishing behind Bloxwich Fire Station."*

At 11.40pm, Mr R. Martin, from Rowan Road, Walsall, dialed 999, after seeing a strange object circling over the Bescot area. By the time a police officer arrived there was no sign of the UFO – which was explained away by the officer as likely to have been an aircraft! (**Source: *Walsall Observer*, 2.8.63**)

Diamond-shaped UFO seen

Schoolboy John Castelete (14) from Oakdale Road, Oxhey, was viewing the sky through his telescope, during the same evening, accompanied by his next door neighbor, Denis Haisman (14), when he saw something very odd in the night sky.

> *"It wasn't a 'flying saucer'. It was diamond-shaped, solid in the middle, and revolving in mid-air; it kept going bright and then dark. We watched it for two hours."*

(**Source: *West Herts. & Watford Observer***)

5th August 1963 (USA) – Motorist chased by UFO

After having been to the Kerasota drive-in cinema to see the 'Great Escape', Ronnie Austin and his girlfriend, Phyllis Bruce, from Fairfield, Illinois, were travelling home along Route 15, after having passed Mount Vernon Airport, when they noticed a dazzling *'ball of light'* hovering just above trees, towards the south-west direction. As they continued on their journey, the object appeared to be keeping parallel with them. Ronnie tried desperately to outrun the object, increasing the speed of the car up to 120mph, but to no avail – the object continued to keep up with them. When he slowed down the vehicle, so did the object – which, then appeared over the right-hand fender of the car. Suddenly it flew across the road, and upwards, where it rested briefly over a relay tower before darting across the road – now 200 yards in front of the car. After dropping Phyllis home, at Bruce Farm, Ronnie set off towards his own home, still being followed by the persistent *'light'*. When about a mile away, the luminous object faded to a dull orange and darted straight for the car, at tremendous speed but came to halt about 100ft, a short distance away, causing the car radio to erupt in a burst of static – the engine spluttering and almost cutting out, before running smoothly again as the *'light'* moved away – now dull orange. For almost three miles the *'light'* stayed with Ronnie, who arrived home and jumped out of the car, with the *'light'* apparently following him right up to the front door. Ronnie awoke the family and they all confirmed sighting the *'light'* – now stationary in the eastern sky, about 200 yards from the family farm. The family also awoke the next door neighbours – Mr and Mrs Dwight Withrow – who came out to have a look.

Police arrive

The police were called. The first to arrive at 12.45am was State Trooper Richard Gidcumb, of McLeansboro, and George Sexton, Marshall of Wayne City – then, a short time later, Deputy Lee, by which time the *'light'* was now resembling a bright star in the sky, remaining there until dawn.

Doctor S.W. Conarski attended and proscribed a mild sedative for Ronnie, who was very shaken by the ordeal. (**Sources:** *Chicago Tribune*, Undated/*Strangers from the Skies*, Brad Steiger)

Keenes Boy Chased Home By 'Flying Saucer'; Police Called!

WAYNE COUNTY PRESS. AUG 5-1963 MONDAY

BOY GIVEN SEDATION TO QUIET HIS NERVES AFTER INCIDENT.

An 18-year-old Keenes boy was chased home Sunday night by a flying saucer or some other unknown heavenly body!

The whole neighborhood out his way is talking about it.

The lad was so frightened he ran into his home, awakened his father and mother and when his dad saw it he ran inside for his shotgun. They wondered if it might be some invading force from Mars . . . or Russia.

Hid In Kitchen

When the father displayed his gun, the object seemed to move closer.

So the family ran back into the house . . . . gathered in the kitchen and turned out the lights.

Quickly they called police at Mt. Vernon. Fairfield police were promptly notified to keep watch. At first the police thought they were joking.

Deputy Saw It

6th August 1963 (UK) – *'Spinning top'* UFO seen

Robert Brown – a van boy with Smiths Bakeries at Hawkhill, Edinburgh – sighted a silver coloured object, resembling a child's spinning top, with a flat bottom, hovering over the city, at 4am, accompanied by *"a strange wheezing noise"*, before going out of sight, a few minutes later.

(**Source:** *Evening Despatch*, 6.8.1963 – 'Another saucer seen in Edinburgh')

Sanford, Florida (USA) – UFO display

Orville Hartle – Chairman of the LaPorte, Indiana NICAP Subcommittee – was on a brief visit to Florida, when he sighted a UFO. Orville then obtained a full report with signatures of 13 additional witnesses. The object was first seen in the north-west sky as a red, then white, moving light. To the west, the star-like light hovered, and then moved south. To the south, the object began a series of gyrations and pulsated on and off, visible intermittently. It moved up and down, back and forth, once emitting a flare of greenish-white light.

7th August 1963 (USA) – Diamond-shaped UFO seen

At about 9pm, Chauncey Uphoff and Mike Hill, from east of the Fairfield area of Illinois, heard the dogs barking and went out to investigate. They saw a yellow-orange diamond-shaped luminous object in the south-west sky, at about a 1,000ft altitude, moving silently eastwards. This was joined by a pinpoint of white light, moving from south-east to north-west, and climbing, making what appeared to be a drumming sound. As it neared the first object, the latter blinked out. When the pinpoint of light disappeared to the north-west, the diamond-shaped object reappeared as dim grey to the south-west, manoeuvring towards the two men to the south, at about 45° elevation. The object then turned south-east, making a 'U'-turn or loop, now appearing on edge with a tail or trail, changing colour to orange – then brilliant blue and white, before finally disappearing in the south-east direction. (**Source:** NICAP)

7th August 1963 (UK) – UFO seen over Wolverhampton

Bilston Grammar schoolboy – Peter Jones, was in Parkfield Road, Ettinghshall, at 10.30 pm., with three other friends, when they saw an object, slightly smaller than the moon, changing colour from red to pink to white, occasionally ejecting a bright rocket like trail, travelling towards Bilston. (**Source:** *Wolverhampton Express & Star*, 8.8.63, "Thing' in the sky')

Central Illinois (USA)

At night-time, five people observed a luminous source flying slowly over the railroad tracks, heading west, then north, before appearing to land in a wooded area. (**Source:** *Magonia 576*)

9th August 1963 (USA) – UFO follows car

At Mt. Vernon, Illinois, Former Mayor – Harry Bishop – observed a large, bright red oval *'light'*, which appeared to be 300 or 400ft high in the sky, *"about the size of a washtub"*, at 10.10pm. It followed a car along Centralia Road. When the car stopped, the driver jumped out and looked upward. The UFO stopped and hovered, then moved away at right angles to its original course, at a high rate of speed. It seemed to be making a light whirring sound.

Bishop estimated that the *'fireball'* was in sight for from 10-15 minutes.

August 1963 (USA) – Mel Torme witnesses UFO display

Mel Torme Reveals for the First Time . . .

I Saw a UFO Put On a Dazzling Aerial Ballet

Singer Mel Torme reveals for the first time that he saw an incredible UFO whose dazzling "aerial ballet" and "impossible turns" left him with little doubt that the craft had come from another world.

"I'm a pretty tough cookie to fool," said the performer, recalling his dramatic sighting over New York City. "I have a pilot's license, and believe me, never in all my hours of flying have I seen anything in the air capable of maneuvering at the speed this baby traveled.

"It was a hot, humid day in August 1963. I was up late working on an arrangement to a new song. Around 2 a.m., I went out to walk my dog, and almost immediately my attention was diverted in the general direction of the East River.

"There — drifting out of the blackness of space — was this glowing red object."

At first, recalled Mel, the strange object "was barely a speck against the sky." Then, as it moved to a position almost directly overhead, Torme said he was able to see a form behind the glowing light.

"I could see a strange saucer-shaped craft," he revealed. "The UFO was up around 5,000 feet, just looking down at me. It was unlike any aircraft I am familiar with — and I know them all!"

Suddenly, the UFO took off in a southerly direction. "It moved quickly — faster than my eyes could follow. Then a fraction of a second later, it came to an abrupt halt.

"It stopped dead on a dime as if it had run into an invisible obstacle. Then it start-

MEL TORME
"Whoever was on board must have had flesh made out of steel."

ed doing 'figure 8' maneuvers and 'loops.' It put on a real show, darting back and forth — as if performing an aerial ballet.

"Its 'impossible' right angle turns literally defied the laws of aerodynamics."

Mel said no human could have withstood the tremendous G-forces created by the rapid acceleration of the craft. "Whoever was on board must have had flesh made out of steel."

After 5 minutes. the UFO "zipped away," says the singer, who added that in all likelihood it was a ship from another world. "Descriptions from other observers of similar craft leave little doubt in my mind that this is what is most commonly referred to as a 'flying saucer.' "

— EDWARD SIGALL

12th August 1963 (UK) – UFO hovers over power station

A pear-shaped object was sighted over several towns in the Black Country area and was seen hovering over Birchills Power Station, dropping smaller *globules of light* from it before moving away. According to the police at Walsall, other reports were received by them of similar accounts, including sightings of *'strange lights'*, over the town and an orange *'light'* seen hovering over Birchills and Ocker Hill Power Stations by Walsall residents, Kathleen Edwards and Raymond Laban. (**Source:** *Wolverhampton Express & Star*, 13.8.63/ UFOSIS/Alan Poyner)

One of the witnesses was Mr S. J. Day, who was in his garden in Highfield Road, Dudley, at 10.26pm the same evening, when he saw:

> *"...a bright pear-shaped white light (blue at the bottom) which appeared to be dropping other white lights. I counted eleven of these and of the eleven five were double lights.*

They were in the sky for about a minute and a half and then they all disappeared but, suddenly, a bright flash lit-up the sky and they were back, followed by a dull bang in the sky a few minutes later."

UFO seen over Wolverhampton

Another witness was Wolverhampton bus inspector – John Challenger, of Gibbons Hill Road, Sedgley. At 10.24pm, he was walking along the main Wolverhapmton road, towards his house, with other members of the family, when they saw a large white light, under a cloud, which appeared to drop smaller lights from it. He was astonished to discover, when he arrived home, to learn that his daughter had seen something similar on Saturday night, the 10th August. (**Source:** *Wolverhampton Express & Star,* 13.8.1963)

13th August 1963 (USA) – Landed UFO

Near Ellsworth, Maine, a family and their housekeeper observed an elliptical object – apparently on the ground adjoining Molasses Pond – for more than an hour. Lights were visible along its length and, occasionally, rays of light shone upward from each end of the object.

(**Source: Witnesses interviewed by Walter N. Webb – NICAP Adviser**)

Honolulu, Hawaii – UFO seen

While on holiday in Hawaii, chemist – Dr. Richard Turse from Princeton, New Jersey – saw a round red object in the sky pass overhead, at great speed, heading south-west to north-east, at about 11.30pm, which was seen to make two sharp turns while in flight.

17th August 1963 (UK) – Three flashes of light seen

On the 17th August 1963, three flashes of light lit up the night sky over Bilborough, Nottingham. These were followed by *"two beams of light"* seen to cross each other's path, and the appearance of an *"orange disc",* sighted rushing headlong across the sky, according to Mr Ronald Atkin, who was stood with two other men when the incident took place. (**Source:** UFOSIS)

18th August 1963 (USA) – UFO sighted

At Fort Kent, Maine, a silvery *'disc'*-shaped UFO was seen by two young boys, passing from north to south, emitting a hum intermittently.

19th August 1963 (UK) – Glistening object

At 7.45am, David Anthony Mohan from Grantley House, Ackroyden Estate, Wandsworth, looked out of the window in the family's top flat, to see what the weather was like, when he saw:

"...something silver and glistening, travelling silently in a north-east direction; it passed high in the sky over the top of Timperley Court and seemed to be moving at about 60mph. It had a flat top – like a platform or deck. Underneath was a long object – like a wireless aerial sticking out. About seven seconds later, it disappeared behind a small cloud. I waited, but didn't see it again."

(**Source:** *Wandsworth Borough News,* 23.8.1963 – 'Was it a flying saucer object sighted over Ackroydon Estate?')

22nd August 1963 (UK) – *'Flying jellyfish'* UFO

Mr D. Evans – a Swansea Bank manager and ex-RAF Operation Control Officer – was returning home with his wife and friend, Mr King, after a visit to the hospital.

> *"I looked up towards Langland Bay Golf Club and saw this thing, which I thought was a very large flare – but it passed directly overhead, completely soundless and on a definite track, unaffected by the wind. There was a tremendous glow given off. It was the shape of a shuttlecock or jellyfish, and moved low and majestically through the air."*

Mr Evans then rang the police, who confirmed that they had received two reports from the public regarding this object. RAF Air Traffic Control, at Uxbridge, was contacted. They said they had no knowledge of any flares being discharged.

(Source: *South Wales Evening Post*, 23.8.1963 – 'Mysterious object is seen in the sky off Langland, large as a double-decker bus, with red-orange glow')

31st August 1963 (UK) – *'Flying saucer'* over Croydon

Mrs Marie Rodgers, ex-District Councilor for many years and still involved in the local community, spoke about an extraordinary sighting, which happened when she was living near to Mitcham Common, Croydon, Surrey.

> *"I was in the kitchen, when my son burst into the house and asked me to come and have a look at something strange in the sky. I went out with him and saw this dome shaped object, hovering over trees, at Mitcham Common. I stood there, mesmerized, looking at this thing, which reminded me of an upturned lampshade, with cavities below it. Suddenly, it pulsed with light, veered away, and was out of sight. I asked around, afterwards, if anyone else had seen it. They*

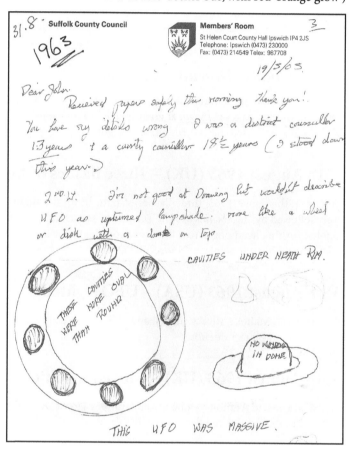

hadn't – which I thought very odd, as it had been a Bank Holiday, with crowds of people on the Common, including many police officers. I telephoned the Daily Mail *newspaper, who told me they had received a number of calls from the public about the UFO, and would get back to me. I'm still waiting for them to ring, over 45 years later!"*

(Source: Personal interview)

Croydon, Surrey, England 1915   © Copyright 2001 www.davidhadey.com

8th July 2006

Waveney MP Bob Blizzard has offered his congratulations and thanks to two Labour Party members in recognition of their efforts for the group, Waveney and the County. Brian Hunter and Marie Rodgers were presented with 'Outstanding Achievement' certificates signed by Prime Minister Tony Blair at the group's AGM. Brian served as the secretary agent for the Waveney Labour Party for 11 years and Marie was a former Chair of the Oulton Broad Labour Party. Both Marie and Brian have served as district and county councillors and as Chair of Waveney District Council. Brian was also Leader of Waveney District Council and Marie has represented various community groups and organisations, including police forums and Victim Support. Both have now retired from their roles and the certificates are recognition of their marvellous contributions. Mr Blizzard said: *"I am delighted to be able to present Brian and Marie with their certificates and thank them for the excellent service they have given the Labour Party in Waveney. This recognition is thoroughly deserved and I am particularly pleased the Prime Minister has added his own personal thanks to them both."*

Obituary 2011

We were sorry to hear that former County Councillor Marie Rodgers passed away on Monday 29th August 2011 aged 83. Marie was Labour Party Representative, elected on 15th October 1987 to the Pakefield Division, moving in 1993 to Lowestoft St Margaret's Division. During her time as County Councillor she served on nine committees and also served for a time as a member of the Police Authority. Marie stood down in May 2005.

6th September 1963 (UK) – UFO over power station

Southampton schoolboy, Michael Blake – a fifth former at Testwood School – was walking along Houndsdown Avenue, Houndsdown, when he noticed an oval red object in the sky, towards the south-east, at an angle of some 60°.

"As it descended, it oscillated from side to side, following an 'S'-shaped course, alternating in colour from dark to light red. After reaching a height of about 200ft in the air, it hovered over the electric power station, at Marchwood, three miles north of Hyde, enabling me to see a superstructure. I went indoors to tell a friend. When 1 came out, it had gone."

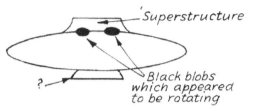

14th September 1963 (UK) – *'Flying saucer'* seen

An amateur astronomer from Goldthorpe (who had previously been sceptical about reports of 'flying saucers') was in his garden, intending to look at Orion, at 5am, when he noticed:

". . . a 'flying saucer' moving on a very low course, before disappearing in seconds over adjacent buildings. It was almost identical to what other people (whom I have never believed) described. It was spherical in shape, surrounded by a metallic 'tyre', and was spinning as it flew silently across the sky."

(Source: *South Yorkshire Times*, 5.10.1963)

Wolverhampton (UK) – Strange 'star'

Frederick Parker and his son, David, were looking at the planet Saturn, when they noticed:

". . . a 'star', moving westwards through the sky, before it then altered course to the east, stopped for about 20 seconds, and then continued its journey, before disappearing from view."

(Source: *Wolverhampton Express & Star*, 19.9.1963)

Susanville, California (USA) – UFOs over the forest

At 3.15pm, Mr E.A. Grant – a veteran of 37 years employment as a forest fire lookout for the US Forest Service – saw a round object in the sky intercept a long object, then either attach itself to the latter or disappear. (Source: *Project Blue Book 1963 Summary*, Berliner)

Southampton (UK) – Heart-shaped UFO

At 9pm on 14th September 1963, schoolgirl Vivienne Taylor was with her father when the couple saw a glowing bright red, oval object, heading north-westwards. It disappeared into a cloud – then emerged almost at the point where it had entered. It then travelled back along the direction from whence it had come, but now showing a heart or 'B'-shaped dark marking in the middle. The *'mark'* was not evident before the object entered the cloud.

15th September 1963 (UK) – UFO paces vehicle

Joan Allinson of Rosedale Lodge, Alnmouth, Northumberland, was driving home with her father and approaching Shilbottle, at 3.30am.

"We saw a golden pulsating object, about 24ft long, hovering in the sky at about a 1,000ft. It was crescent-shaped and had a golden halo around it.

It followed us for fifteen minutes and would, on occasion, dart towards us, stop, and then reverse direction. It always stayed on the offside of the car sometime ahead of us. It took me a week to recover from the shock of it all."

Ohio (USA)

At 6pm over Vandalia, Ohio, Mrs F. E. Roush saw two very bright gold objects – *"one shaped like a banana; the other, like an ear of corn in the sky"* – one was staying stationary; the other, moving from west to north.

(Source: Berliner)

Hampshire (UK) – 'Spindle' UFO

At 4.45pm the same day, James Poulton – a sixth form pupil, at Testwood School – was with his parents, sister, and brother-in-law, five miles north of Barton-on-Sea, Hampshire, when they noticed an object high in the air. It resembled a silver gyroscope, with a very thick spindle, showing prominent black spots, travelling at moderate speed. It appears this object was similar to that sighted by Michael Blake, on the 6th of September 1963. One is bound to wonder what the source of attraction was to this peculiar object? (**Source: Peter I. Kelly**)

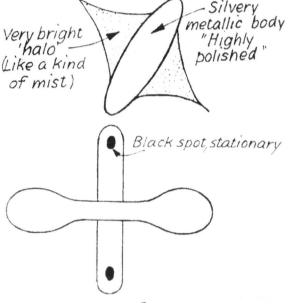

18th September 1963(UK) – UFO over Stafford

Frederick Taylor the proud owner of a telescope he had constructed himself was with his wife Ann and others at the family home when saw something unusual.

30-6-06. 18/9/63 5. Boons Grove
01785 257269   Moss Pit
                     Stafford ST17 9S

Dear Mr Holloway.
        With reference to our phone call this evening, I will certainly give you my experience of seeing a sighting on the evening of 18th September 1963 of something unusual in the sky.
        My late Husband Frederic made a 6" telescope - including making the mirror which took the best part of a year. He was very interested in astronomy

2
until we could see it no more. It obviously was not a plane, but I guess we will never know just what it was.
        I would be most interested to read of some of the sighting that you have a record of, thank you so much. I will keep your letter in case I do see anything mysterious.
        Sadly my Husband sold his telescope a few years before he died.
        Well Good Luck to you with

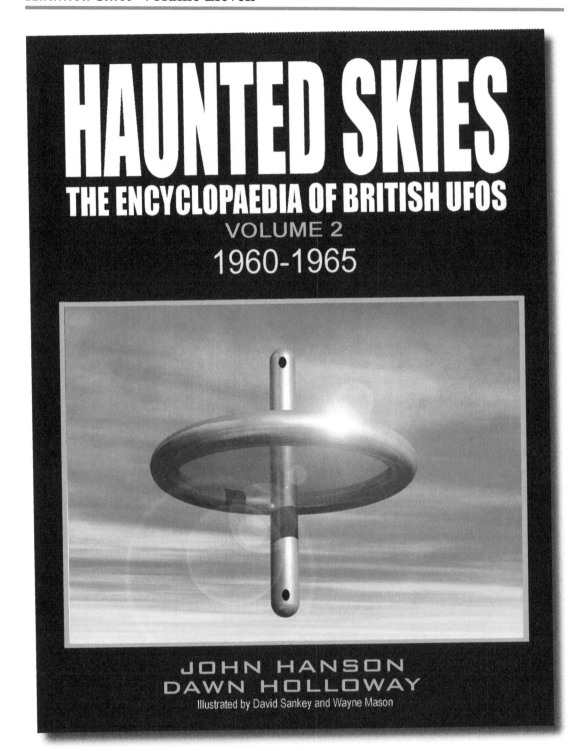

The Hampshire 'Spindle' UFO depicted on the cover of 'Haunted Skies' Volume 2

19th September 1963 (Canada) – Strange *'being'*

At 8pm, four children from Saskatchewan Canada saw a bright, oval object hover above a field and drop something. Approaching the site, they were confronted by a 3 metre tall *'man'*, dressed in *"a white monk like suit"*, who held out his hands and made unintelligible sounds. The children fled in panic, and one girl was admitted to the hospital in shock. (**Source:** *Magonia 581*)

20th September 1963 (USA) – Egg-shaped UFO

A rancher from Huntsville, Arkansas, sighted an egg-shaped UFO moving eastward, about 10° above the southern horizon. Through binoculars, a dark spot was visible near the top of the object. As it proceeded west, the UFO dimmed, turned orange, and then faded from view 10-15 minutes later.   (**Source:** NICAP)

Wonthaggi, Victoria (Australia) – TV interference

Following some interference on the TV reception, a resident went outside and saw an object hovering in the sky. This darted away at high speed. His was one of three similar reports made in the area.

26th September 1963 (USA) – *'Disc'* with bright spot

Sunnyvale, California. A police officer, and many other people, sighted a grey *'disc'*, with a central bright spot on it, moving on a westerly course, at high speed, across the sky. (**Source:** *UFOE*, VII)

27th September 1963 (UK) – Two UFOs

A resident, living near Manchester Airport, was awoken at 5am by a bright light and the sound of powerful engines. He jumped out of bed and saw:

> *"...a rapidly moving and very brightly-lit object dropping down through the sky. I thought it was a plane, crashing, but then it halted and hovered for a while, as if looking for something, and then began to move from side to side and dropped even lower. It was so bright the stars looked dim next to it.*
>
> *I roused another member of the family and we watched it. At 6am, aircraft from the airport began to take-off (as there is no flying during the night). By 7am, the object had disappeared from sight."*

(**Source:** *Manchester Evening News*, 1.10.1962 – 'Mystery of the thing in the sky')

Over Huddersfield UK

At 7.30am, ex-RAF employee – James Brooke of Lodge Road, Huddersfield – was in his garden when he saw:

> *"...two strange circular objects, apparently attached to each other, flying slowly across the sky, heading eastwards – like nothing I had ever seen before."*

(**Source:** *Huddersfield Examiner*, 27.9.1963)

Was there a connection with an object seen at 2.30pm over Worsley, by a couple, who watched a shining object for a few minutes, until it disappeared behind clouds?

September 1963 (UK) – Metallic object found

Mr Rumsey from Shanklin, Isle of Wight, sent Kathleen Smith, of the Isle of Wight UFO Investigation Society, an illustration of an object he found on a netball pitch. He told her:

> *"It lay in the centre of an arrow-shaped scorched or burned depression, about 1-2ins deep, 2-10ins long and approximately 5ins wide; the object looked like a piece of pipe with the end closed, and appeared to have a grey-copper coloured mottled finish – as if it had been red hot. It was heavier than lead and very hard."*

Mr Rumsey reported his find to the school and they contacted the police, who took it away. When Mr Rumsey telephoned them about the object, he was surprised when they told him that *"it may have been dangerous and has been destroyed"*.

2nd October 1963 (USA) – UFO tracked on radar and seen visually

In the Mediterranean, off the coast of Sardinia, at approximately 2am local time, radar operator Harry Allen Jordan, on the *USS Franklin D. Roosevelt* (CV-42), was on watch when he picked up a radar contact 600 miles down range at 80,000ft altitude. The object moved to 300 miles at 35,000ft and then to 10 miles range at 10,000-15,000ft. The object was tracked at speeds of up to 4,000mph and flew in a 'Z'-pattern, making right angle turns.

The officer of the deck was informed and awoke the captain, who ordered the scramble of two F-4 Phantom II jets. The object was moving closer to the ship and suddenly disappeared from the radar scope. The object reappeared and was getting closer to the *Roosevelt*. The object came to within several hundred feet of the ship, as at least 15 persons (with binoculars) watched the object hover for a moment. This was at approximately at 2.32am. The object then disappeared. (**Source: Dan Wilson**)

Harry Jordan

Harry Jordan served in the United States Navy aboard the destroyer escort *U.S.S Laffey*, destroyer *U.S.S. Loeser*, and the aircraft carrier *U.S.S. Franklin D. Roosevelt* CVA-42. He served in the Operations Intelligence Division on all three ships. His duties within O.I. Division were to display, analyze, report, and record radar, radio, and electronic emission data within the Combat Information Center. He was trained on radar and Electronic Counter Measure equipment for both passive and active systems at the naval station in Newport, Rhode Island in 1963.

Harry Jordan

Harry:

> *"I served two Mediterranean cruises aboard the* Roosevelt *during a period from 1962 to 1964. Upon discharge from active duty I was assigned to the Jones Point Naval Reserve Training Station*

in Alexandria, Virginia as an instructor. I trained enlisted as well as naval officers on the use of navigation equipment and reporting methods particular to radar intelligence. I served as a recognition expert. I could detect with various electronic equipment, air to surface contacts while at sea, on land or in the air. The equipment aboard the Roosevelt could detect surface or air contacts from 300 miles depending upon their height." (Source :Personal Interviews/Dan Wilson NICAP)

Manchester (UK) – UFO seen again

At 6.45pm, a resident of Audenshaw, Manchester, sighted a glowing object appear out of a cloud, hover for a while, and then climb back up into cloud. As it did so the light dimmed, enabling him to see a black oval object.

4th October 1963 (USA) – Triangular UFO seen

At 1pm, East Hartland, Connecticut State Representative – Mr L.B. Martin – saw a silvery, triangular object, with a row of black dots across the leading edge, moving across the sky at an estimated speed of 2,000mph. As it passed overhead, a flame-like tail was seen. (**Source: NICAP**)

Bedford, Ohio (USA) – Oblong light

At 3.32pm, schoolboy – R.E. Carpenter (15) – saw an intense oblong light, with tapered ends, surrounded by an aqua haze, which flashed and flickered while stationary in the sky. (**Source: Berliner**)

Cheadle, Cheshire (UK) – Spinning UFO

At 1.30pm, a coloured spinning object was seen hovering thousands of feet up in the sky, over Cheadle, giving out a white flash of light every few minutes. It was seen by Stuart Scully (then aged 13), who wrote a letter to the local newspaper. Similar objects were also reported on the 5th and 8th October, over Teesside.

(Source: *Manchester Evening News*, **8.10.1963 – 'Spinning mystery in the sky'**)

5th October 1963 (UK) – Bright glow

John Baker – a sixth form prefect at Testwood Secondary Modern School, Southampton – was fishing on the River Test, near Totton, at 11.30pm, with three friends, when they noticed an extremely bright glow towards the east, about three times the size of the sun, *"so bright, we had to look away. It resembled burning magnesium – then faded from sight."* (**Source: Peter I. Kelly**)

9th October 1963 (UK) – Golden UFO

A large gold or silver coloured object was seen at 8.46am, hovering over the Woodhurst housing estate, Birkenhead, at an estimated height of 500ft, by a number of people, including Mr Peter Robinson, who was taking his daughter for a walk, after breakfast. (**Source: *Liverpool Echo*, 19.10.1963**)

14th October 1963 (UK) – 'Ball of fire'

Housewife – Joan Child – was preparing breakfast at her Woodingdean home, at 6.45am, when she heard a *"whooshing"* noise – strong enough to rattle the windows in the house. Looking out of the window, she saw a '*ball of fire*' about 12ins in diameter, flashing past the house, a few feet off the ground. A search of the locality by Mrs Child and her neighbours, who came rushing outside, failed to reveal anything out of the ordinary.

(Source: Personal interview)

20th October 1963 (UK) – '*Wandering Star*'!

At 2am, Leeds housewife – Mrs M. Foster – happened to look out of the bedroom window and see "*a large star, blue-green in colour moving from side to side in the sky*".

She awoke her husband and the couple watched it for 20 minutes, until it disappeared from view behind a row of houses.

At about the same time (2am), Mr C. Lambert, from Ipswich, noticed:

"*...two objects at great height in the sky, one brighter or larger than the other, connected by a 'line', or something similar, weaving from side to side in level flight, circling, hovering and spiralling overhead, for about 10 minutes, before heading towards Ipswich*".

(Source: *East Anglian Daily Times*, 29.10.1963)

21st October 1963 (UK) – Orange '*discs*' seen

An identical object to that seen over Leeds, the previous day, was sighted over Harrogate, at 6.45am, by Mrs D. Cook. (Source: *Yorkshire Post*, 24.10.1963)

Later that evening, strange '*discs*' of orange light were seen by several people living in Bilborough, Nottingham, at an estimated altitude of between 8-10,000ft.

(Source: *Nottingham Evening Post*, 23.10.1963)

23rd October 1963 (USA) – Noisy UFO

At 8.35pm, several unnamed students from a college at Meriden, Idaho, saw an object – shaped like a circle from below and a football from the side – hovering low in the sky over the observers, making a deep, pulsating, loud, extremely irritating sound, before changing course to the south-west, when it was lost from view behind houses and trees.

(Source: Mary Castner/CUFOS/Don Berliner)

28th October 1963 (Australia) – Landed UFO with occupant seen

High school teacher Mrs E. D. Silvester from Norwood, Adelaide, was out driving, at 7.30pm, on the Salisbury-Elizabeth road, with her children – Michael (10), Alison (8), and Julie Anne (6) – when she saw an object land. Puzzled, she stopped the car in order to take a closer look.

She was stunned to see what looked like a man, wearing a type of helmet and what looked like a gas mask attached to it. About 40 minutes later, the object took off [presumably with its occupant].

Mrs Silvester later made drawings and a tape-recording for the vice-president of the Flying Saucer Research Bureau – Mr C.R. Norris.

(Source: Mr C.R. Norris, Flying Saucer Research Bureau/*Hobart Mercury*, 5.2.1963)

29th October 1963 (UK) – UFO over hospital

A highly polished object, silvery metallic in appearance, was seen hovering over Roundway Hospital, Devizes, during the early morning, by hospital orderly – Martin Tucker.

(Source: *Bath & Wiltshire Chronicle*, 29.10.1963)

31st October 1963 (Australia) – Glowing orange object

At 4.15am, bread delivery man – Jim Davidson (28) of Hagelthorn Street, Wonthaggi – was on his early morning round, when he saw a slight glow in the sky.

> *"It got bigger as it came towards me. When it reached me, it turned and took up my course. It stayed 100 yards ahead of me and about 80ft up in the air. It was 8-12ft long and glowed orange, except for two tail fin sections at the rear that glowed red. It was not metallic of any substance like metal – more like a cloud, but it wasn't one. I followed it for two miles. It gave me a fright when it moved across the road to my right and continued to pace me.*
>
> *The object moved further to the right, accelerated up a hill, and then began to descend. I stopped, now frightened, and remembered I had bread to deliver in Nyora, and drove on. The next time I saw it was when I looked out to sea and saw a moving orange glow, several miles out."*

Coincidentally, the same red glowing object was seen by bread delivery men – Frank Coleman (43) and Norman Veal (42) – also from Wonthaggi.

Sylvia Hutton

Miss Sylvia Hutton – Honorable Secretary of the Victorian Flying Saucer Research Society – carried out a full investigation into the incidents and then went to see her local Parliamentary member of the House of Representatives – Mr Donald Chipp. She asked him if a resolution could be passed at the present session of Parliament, into reported UFO activity, so that the matter could be fully investigated and the findings be made public.

Sylvia:

> *"In due course I received a reply from our Minister of Defence –* ˙*Mr Athol Townley – who said that the Government does investigate UFO reports and keeps in touch with other friendly Governments, but the Australian Government considers there is no reason for making statements to the public at this time."*

3rd November 1963 (USA) – UFO seen

Over Corona, New York, a Pan American Airways mechanic noticed a star-like object manoeuvring across the northern sky, at 1.30am. The light moved rapidly, slowed, and seemed to *"shudder"*, and then changed course by about 45°. Finally it made a 90° turn, accelerated, turned again, and disappeared from view.

(Source: Report obtained by New York NICAP Subcommittee)

˙Athol Gordon Townley (3rd October 1905 – 24th December 1963) was an Australian politician and Minister for Defence. Townley was born in Hobart and educated at Elizabeth Street State School and Hobart High School, and at Hobart Technical College. He qualified as a pharmaceutical chemist in 1928 and in 1930 found a job looking after quality control for a Sydney baker. In 1931, he married Hazel Florence Greenwood and they later moved back to Hobart where he formed a partnership with his brother, Rex that eventually owned three pharmacies. He joined the Royal Australian Navy in September 1940, and in February 1941, he was sent to England to train in bomb – and mine – disposal work. He returned to Australia and commanded the patrol boat *Steady Hour*, which assisted in destroying a Japanese midget submarine during the attack on Sydney Harbour in June 1942. He was put in command of the *Fairmile B* motor launch ML817 in January 1943, promoted to acting lieutenant commander in March, and was involved in the New Guinea campaign. (Source: *Melbourne Sun*, 21.9.1963/Sylvia Sutton, Secretary of Victoria Flying Saucer Research Society/ FSR, Volume 10, No. 2, March-April 1964/Wikipedia, 2014)

8th November 1963 (Australia) – Strange glow in the sky

At 7.50pm, Ted Colbert (22) – auction room clerk of Broome Crescent, Wonthaggi – and his fiancée, Jennifer Hughes (17), were driving along the South Dudley Road, half a mile from the Bass Highway, when they noticed a glow in the sky over South Dudley. Ted stopped the car.

He said:

> *"At first I thought a coal mine was on fire, but then saw the glow was moving slowly through the sky. I could see rays of light projecting from the top of it, and realised it was moving around the coast. We headed for Dalyston three miles away, but only saw a faint glow. We drove to Kilcunda and then made our way back to South Dudley, but by this time it seemed smaller and further away."*

12th November 1963 (USA) – Police chase UFO

Port Huron, Michigan: Deputy Sheriffs chased a low-flying UFO, which first appeared as a white flashing light. At times the object seemed to have a *"big divided window"* on it. When the UFO hovered, the deputies approached and flashed their squad car light. A flashing red light then became visible on the UFO. The object finally moved away to the north-west, making a motor-like sound. Other residents reported flashing lights and high-pitched or whining noises at the same time.

12th November 1963 (UK) – UFO like a falling leaf

At 3am, Mr Dennis Mackintosh – a teacher at Testwood Secondary Modern School – was driving through Chandlers Ford, Hampshire, when he saw a silvery object in the sky to the south-east.

> *"It appeared to be oval and was descending like a falling leaf. It then stopped in mid-air for a few moments, over what I believe were the railway works at Eastleigh. I then lost sight of it."*

UFOs over M6 Motorway

In 2009, we spoke to British UFO author Nick Redfern – now living in Dallas, Texas, – after having read his book, *Cosmic Crashes – The Incredible Stories Of The UFOs That Fell To Earth* (published by Simon and Schuster, in 1999), which included a chapter relating to his investigation into this incident, following his examination of the declassified file that contained over 60 pages. In correspondence with Flt. Lt. Stevens, on the 3rd January 1964, Wilfred Daniels, told him:

> *"On the 12th and 14th November (1963) last, there were UFOs over the M6 Motorway, at Warley, (my own sighting), and at Tittensor, Manchester, (lorry driver witness). There were two UFOs between Preston and Southport, on Wednesday, 12th November 1963."*

During the same morning police and coastguards were alerted, after bright lights that were seen to change colour and alter course, were observed in the sky over Southport, for nearly two hours. Local resident – Mr Tony Softly – claimed he had been chased by an object with spinning rings, while driving with friends.

(Source: *Daily Express* and *Daily Mail*, 14.11.1963 – 'Flying Saucer chases car!')

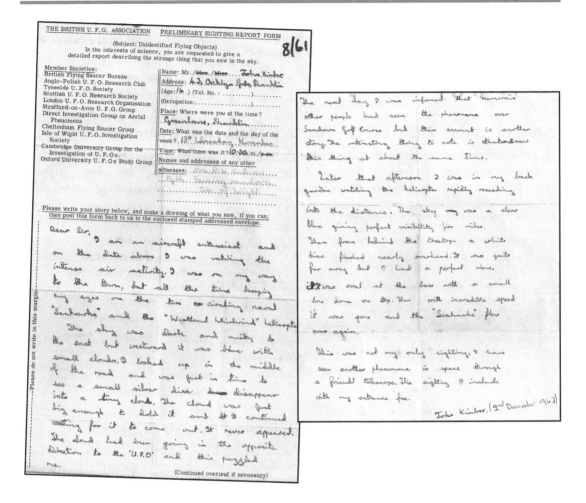

14th November 1963 (USA) – *'Disc'*-shaped UFO seen

A huge blue-green *'disc'* was seen hovering in the north-west sky over Carson City, Nevada, at about 4:45am, by Mrs Blanche Pritchett, who said she was listening to her radio when a bright light, shining through her drapes, caused her to look outdoors. As she watched the hovering object, her radio went off. A brilliant shaft of light from the UFO illuminated a hilltop. Suddenly the UFO blacked out and disappeared, after which the radio resumed playing. Other residents reported odd glows in the sky that morning.

18th November 1963 (UK) – Silver *'disc'* seen

Shanklin resident – John Kimber – was watching a number of Westland Whirlwind helicopters and Seahawks, flying over the Isle of Wight, at 10.30am. Weather conditions were described there being a dark and misty sky to the east, but blue sky, with small clouds to the west.

> *"I was just in time to see a small silver 'disc' disappear into a tiny cloud – hardly much bigger than the UFO. I waited for it to come out, but nothing appeared. The puzzling thing was that the 'cloud' had been moving in the opposite direction to the UFO."*

The next day, Mr Kimber discovered that a number of people had seen a similar UFO while on Sandown Golf Course. Incredibly, during another period of intense aerial activity over the island, he saw a small, white, dome-shaped, object appear in the sky during that afternoon.

"No sooner had it gone out-of-sight then the RAF Sea Hawks flew over, once again."

(Source: Isle of Wight UFO Society)

20th November 1963 (USA) – North Dakota close encounter

Two school girls from Neche North Dakota were on their way home along Highway 55 during the late evening, when they saw a UFO in the sky surrounded by light haze. Then a glowing bright orange oval shaped object shot across the front of the car and circled around the side before disappearing to the southeast.

Object drops into the sea (UK)

It appears that during the same day, off the coast of the UK, the crew of the 650-ton collier *Thrift* were heading southwards to Blyth, for a cargo of coal, with Captain J. Murray in charge, when a flashing *'red light'* was seen 15-30ft above the sea, about three quarters of a mile off the port side, by four of the crew, and then disappear into the sea. The captain alerted Stonehaven radio and commenced a search of the area. The ship was joined by lifeboats from Aberdeen and Gourdon Aberdeenshire. A RAF Shackleton also joined the search but found nothing.

Captain Murray:

"The light was heading north, silently. We had two radar contacts on our screen, but when we got to within a quarter of a mile of them they disappeared – as if something had sunk below the surface."

(Source: *Shields Gazette*, 21.11.1963)

27th November 1963 (UK) – UFO sighted

A silver *'ball of light'* was seen over St. Austell, Cornwall, at 5.45pm. A long, brightly-lit, stationary, object was seen in the sky over the Lizard Peninsular. A short time afterwards, it began to move across the sky in a series of *'stop and start'* movements, before being lost from view as it entered cloud. (Source: Tyneside UFO Society)

29th November 1963 (UK) – Object with three spikes seen

A shining object was seen by pupils at Cradle Junior School, Fforestfach, near Swansea, described as, *"looking like a hovercraft, with three spikes sticking out and a propeller turning around underneath it"*. Was this a man-made appliance or UFO?

Swansea (UK) – Shining UFO seen

A shining object was seen by pupils at Cradle Junior School, Fforestfach, near Swansea, described as:

"...looking like a hovercraft, with three spikes sticking out and a propeller turning around underneath it."

December 1963 (Australia) – UFO over Queensland

In December 1963, a married couple and their two children were out camping at Blythesday Crossing, Queensland. They were relaxing outside the tent, during the evening, when they saw a *'light'* in the sky, which they took to be the headlight of an approaching train. The *'light'* then began to move closer, at which point Mathew instructed his wife to put the children in the tent. Within seconds, the *'light'* – now a large round 'ball', with what looked like windows around it – was overhead. Their next conscious recollection was seeing the object leaving. The daughter complained of discomfort to the back of the head. How this was caused we do not know, but presumed it may have happened when she fell to the ground. The next day the husband went to pick up some supplies and was astonished to find, after purchasing a local newspaper, that many others had reported seeing what appeared to be the same UFO. (**Source: PRA**)

2nd December 1963 (USA) – *'Disc'*-shaped UFO seen

At the Grand Rapids, Michigan, a motorist stopped his car at a traffic light, at about 9.30am, when he noticed a strange object glittering in the sun.

The object tipped on edge and revealed a *"disc or pancake shape"*, before heading away at speed towards the south-east. (**Source: NICAP**)

6th December 1963(UK) – Large *'star'* seen

Mr H. J. Wells of Wroxall, Isle of Wight – a brick kiln setter by occupation – was waiting for a friend to pick him up for work, at 7am, when:

> *"I noticed what I took to be a large 'star' moving across the sky, travelling in a west from south-east direction. I waited, thinking it was going to 'shoot and disappear'. This didn't happen. It resembled a blazing 'ball of fire' – red-yellow in colour – which occasionally flashed a light, like that seen on an aircraft."*

Was this space debris, as opposed to any UFO – but, if so, why was it flashing?

(**Source: Letter to Fred Smith, Isle of Wight UFO Society**)

7th December 1963 (UK) – Fiery object seen

As a result of some publicity given to the UFO subject in the BBC Round Up programme, Newport resident – Mrs Monica Allpress – wrote to the Isle of Wight UFO Society about what she and her daughter, Sarah (11) saw, at 5.40pm, while visiting Farmer Alan Wood – then owner of Rookley Farm.

> *"Our attention was caught by a very large, fiery object, which shot across the sky, heading east to west, travelling parallel to the Earth, before inexplicably vanishing halfway across the sky. The shape of the object was vaguely reminiscent of an aircraft, with body and wings, but its edges were ragged, as fire might be. It looked like a cross between a meteor and aircraft."*

(**Source: Isle of Wight UFO Society**)

11th December 1963 (USA) – Over Oregon

At 7am, McMinnville, Oregon: Professor of mathematics and astronomy – Mr W. W. Dolan (also Dean of the faculty of Linfield College) saw a bright star-like light, hovering in the sky, which dimmed and moved about. (**Source: Don Berliner**)

12th December 1963 (UK) – Warbling UFO

Mr N. Sachs was walking his dog along the beach at Polperro, Cornwall, at 10.35pm, when he saw what he took to be a fireball dropping down through the sky. To his amazement, it stopped overhead,

> *"….making this warbling noise, flashing green and orange lights, before slowly rising upwards and disappearing from sight."*

(Source: British Flying Saucer Bureau)

14th December 1963 (UK) – Rectangular UFO

A huge cigar-shaped object, with lights streaming out of it, showing four rectangular dark patches on its body, resembling windows, was seen over Margate, at 11.35pm. **(Source: Cambridge University for the Investigation of UFOs)**

20th December 1963 (UK) – UFO seen

Julian Mills (7) was walking home in Hadley Gardens, Chiswick, as dusk fell, when he saw a huge strange object crossing the sky, described as showing six triangular pale yellow lights on its body. He called his mother, Connie, and sister, Ria (12), outside. They then alerted neighbours, while Julian telephoned Chiswick Police to report the matter.

Connie:

> *"It was making a droning sound – too large to have been an aeroplane. The neighbours were puzzled."*

(Source: *Brentford and Chiswick Times*, 27.12.1963)

21st December 1963 (USA) – Tracked on radar

At 12.21am, approximately 780 miles north-west of Honolulu, a MATS aircraft 21837, flying at 20,000ft, picked up an object on radar, apparently making passes at an estimated speed of 380 knots over the MATS aircraft. **(Source: Dan Wilson)**

24th December 1963 (UK) – Car battery drained by UFO

At 7.25pm, Mr Raymond Chandler of Mottram, Cheshire, was driving his Landrover, near Rowarth, in the Glossop area, when he saw a brilliantly coloured object hovering near his car. This frightened him, and appears to have been the cause of draining his recently purchased new battery. According to Mr Chandler, cows in the area were agitated and did not provide milk for a few days. **(Source: Nick Redfern)**

26th December 1963 (UK) – Did landed UFO create crop marks?

Following reports of UFOs being seen in the Essex area, Pauline Abbott (then aged 17) – a trainee riding instructor at the Ivy Chimneys Riding School, Epping – was exercising her horse, 'Leberstram', in the yard of the riding school, at 4pm, on a misty afternoon.

She heard a squelching noise coming from the nearby field, which she took to be a duck, quacking – then wondered if there was somebody in the field itself, and shouted out, *"Who's there?"*, but received no answer.

UFO seen on the ground

Pauline:

> *"I saw this thing on the ground. It was about 3ft high and 8ft wide, greyish in colour, with a glow coming from the one end. I sat on the horse, too frightened to move. Whatever it was took-off slowly and disappeared into the distance.*

When I later went to have a look in the field, I found a number of deep indented marks in the ground, approximately 8ft across, by 1.1/2ft deep, with four lines radiating outwards from the circular marks, and 'cup' marks at the end of each line."

Other witnesses are found

As a result of subsequent further publicity in the local newspapers, *The Times* and *Wessex Star* (3.1.1964), two girls contacted them to report having seen a dome-shaped shiny object in the sky, during the same morning.

Dr. D.G. Doel and his daughter, Diana, investigate

Fortunately, Dr. D.G. Doel, who was to become involved in a number of UFO investigations, during this period, heard about the matter and paid a visit to the area, together with his daughter, Diana (unaware of the incident until March 1964), where they met up with the owner of the riding school and Mr Banks, who then directed them to the riding stables where Carol Foster (18), Robert Ewing (13), and Pauline Abbot, were waiting.

Taped Interview

In a tape-recorded interview, the couple told of arriving at the stables at 8am on the 26th December – a dry but overcast day – when they saw an unusual object crossing the sky. They described it as being:

"...long and flat, with a dome-like protuberance, without visible windows at the end, silvery-white in colour, and bright. [Presumably, self-illuminating, as there was no sun.] When they took their eyes off the object to look around for any other witnesses, and looked back again, it had gone.

Dr. Doel then interviewed Pauline Abbot

She told of arriving at the stables at 4pm on the 27th, and riding the horse to the field concerned, when she heard a squelching noise. Thinking it was somebody walking through the mud (not forgetting the previous day's UFO sighting, which had been brought to her attention), she looked out and saw a peculiar object on the ground in front of her and shouted out: *"Mr Banks, there is a UFO in the field"*, describing it as . . .

"8ft long, 3ft high in the middle, tapering down to a point at each end, bright and white in appearance, despite localised misty conditions. Towards the left of the object was a feature that looked like a car windscreen, or panel, glowing much brighter than the rest".

After calling out, the object took-off in a shallow climb, where she lost sight of it as it passed behind a haystack.

The next morning, some of the occupants of the riding stables went to the scene and examined it, finding the previously described *'marks'* on the ground, *"as if a blunt knife had been dragged across the grass".*

John Cleary-Baker PнD. Editor, BUFORA Journal – His conclusion:

"...was possibly an aircraft, and that the later incident, involving Pauline, was a reflection of light", and suggested, *"the marks in the ground were lightning, striking the ground. The evidence of a single witness, described by a responsible person well acquainted with her as 'imaginative', is a somewhat precarious foundation on which to erect a narrative of a UFO landing. I will not go so far as to accuse this young lady of hoaxing, but I feel that a pennyworth of fact has been augmented by a pound's worth of invention. The evening was misty and a light reflection from a vehicle on the road nearby, distorted by a swirl of vapour, could afford a fanciful mind all the prerequisites for a UFO landing story. Miss Abbot's story impresses me as representing much ado about little."*

Is it any wonder that Pauline Abbot became the subject of much ridicule to the extent that she regretted intensely having ever reported the matter in the first place?

The reality may be quite different!

What happened to the material recovered from the scene? Was it ever analysed? Were any photographs taken? What were the views of the original BUFORA investigator – Mr Paul Webb? He attended the scene, and discovered a thick, silvery, slimy, deposit on top of a fence post, in *'line of flight'* identical to what was found on the ground where the object had landed. (**Source:** *BUFORA Journal*, Vol. 1, No. 1, summer 1964)

"I don't need a tonic," I said crossly, "and I *did* see a flying saucer."

"There aren't such things," said Pete scornfully. "You've been reading too many science fiction books."

"There *are* such things," I insisted, "I saw one. And I'll prove it to you." And without another word I began my investigation into the Flying Saucer Mystery.

Before I saw my flying saucer, I must admit that I never really believed in them myself, so I was rather surprised to discover that thousands of people all over the world claim to have sighted these U.F.O.s (Unidentified Flying Objects).

I paid a visit to Mr Waveney

This U.F.O. was seen in Pescara, Italy in September 1957.

trying to find out about us."

I asked Mr Girvan where he thought these space ships came from. "It's thought that they come from Venus or Mars," he said, "but, of course, we can't know for certain."

Paul Trent of Oregon snapped this disc-like object, which he describes as cruising silently through the sky, leaving no vapour.

I left Mr Girvan's office, feeling very excited, but slightly nervous, about the whole thing. I still wasn't quite sure how much I believed, so I set off to meet a girl who claimed to have actually seen a saucer on the ground.

Seventeen-year-old Pauline Abbott of Buckhurst Hill told me her story. "It was the week before Christmas," she began, "and I was at our local riding stables exercising a young German horse, Leberstram. The time was about four o'clock and it was a bit misty. I was just riding him back to his stable to feed him, when I heard a sort of squelching noise. At first I thought it was a duck quacking. Then I decided it must be somebody in the field. I called out 'Who's there?' but there was no answer.

Then suddenly I saw this 'thing' on the ground in the field. It was about three feet high and eight feet wide and was greyish-white in colour and rather shiny. Also, there was a kind of glow coming from one end."

Pauline borrowed my pencil and did a rough sketch of what she saw. (Fig. 1.)

I was almost mesmerized and just sat on Leberstram and looked at it. It was a bit like a dream. And as I watched, it took off very slowly and disappeared into the distance.

"I realized what it was because U.F.O.s had been sighted around the area, and I notified the local paper. But I didn't mention it to any of my friends, because I was afraid they would laugh at me and think I was nuts. Then, the next day, we found

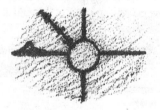

some strange marks on the ground which looked like this . . ." She did another quick drawing (Fig. 2), ". . . and I knew they had been left by the saucer."

She went on: "But even now I still get teased by people who read the reports. Bus conductors grin at me and say: 'Seen any flying saucers lately?' Nobody seems to take the subject seriously!"

I was impressed, and got in touch with the Ministry of Defence (Air) for their views. "Well, we haven't actually investigated this particular incident," a spokesman told me, "we only look into these sightings if we're asked to. And, over the last 12 years, 90 per cent of the U.F.O.s we've investigated have turned out to be weather balloons, aircraft,

Pauline Abbott points to the spot where she saw the flying saucer.

28th December 1963 (Channel Island) – Close encounter

Mr Colin Provest of Valongis, Alderney (one of the Channel Islands – a British Crown Dependency in the English Channel, off the French coast) was taking his dog for a walk, when he saw, by the light given-off by the full moon, a strange object approaching him. He described it as:

"…being 2ft in length, with a red sphere at one end and a yellowish-white tail, 18ins long, tapering to a point, with an attachment looking like a bomb's fin, slowly descending through the air, at an angle of 45°, some 40 yards away, 50ft off the ground".

(Source: *Space-link*, Vol. 1, No. 2, Mar/April 1964)

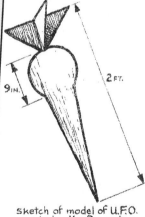

Sketch of model of U.F.O.
made by Mr. Provest.
ALDERNEY C. I.

December 1963 (New Zealand) – Ruby red UFO

Mr V. Burnett, of Ngongotaha, sighted something unusual at 10.15pm.

> *"Travelling slowly in an east-west direction, low down on the horizon, came a moon-sized, glowing, pulsating, ruby-red 'circle of light', composed of equal segments – the spaces between easily discernible. It moved at a leisurely fashion across the sky. While watching this ring-shaped object, I was amazed when it turned back along its track, made a slight detour to the left, and headed south over the town. It was a strange and beautiful sight – like a ruby bracelet against black velvet."*

1964

Project Blue Book

PROJECT Blue Book was one of a series of systematic studies of unidentified flying objects (UFOs) conducted by the United States Air Force. It started in 1952, and it was the third study of its kind (the first two were Project Sign (1947) and Project Grudge (1949). A termination order was given for the study in December 1969, and all activity under its auspices ceased in January 1970. Project Blue Book had two goals: To determine if UFOs were a threat to national security; to scientifically analyse UFO-related data. Thousands of UFO reports were collected, analysed and filed.

Condon Report –12,618 reports collected

As the result of the Condon Report (1968), which concluded there was nothing anomalous about UFOs, Project Blue Book was ordered shut down in December 1969 and the Air Force continues to provide the following summary of its investigations: No UFO reported, investigated and evaluated by the Air Force, was ever an indication of threat to their national security; there was no evidence submitted to or discovered by the Air Force that sightings categorized as 'unidentified' represented technological developments or principles beyond the range of modern scientific knowledge; and there was no evidence indicating that sightings categorized as 'unidentified' were extraterrestrial vehicles. By the time Project Blue Book ended, it had collected 12,618 UFO reports, and concluded that most of them were misidentifications of natural phenomena (clouds, stars, etc.) or conventional aircraft. According to the National Reconnaissance Office, a number of the reports could be explained by flights of the formerly secret reconnaissance planes U-2 and A-12; a small percentage of UFO reports were classified as unexplained – even after stringent analysis. The UFO reports were archived and are available under the Freedom of Information Act, but names and other personal information of all witnesses have been redacted. (**Source: Wikipedia, 2015**)

Black Vault website, 2015 – John Greenewald

In 2015, Project Blue Book files were made available on the Internet by 33-year-old television producer and UFO enthusiast – John Greenewald, who has been filing Freedom of Information Act requests for information on UFOs, and other topics, since he was a teenager. He now has a database of over 650,000 pages of declassified material in PDF format which can be searched by year or keyword. Some people seem to believe that most of the incidents reported to Blue Book can be explained away rationally as misidentifications of planets, or hoaxes, and that there are very few instances of interest, rather than genuine UFO sightings left unexplained. An examination of the colossal number of reports contained within the pages of the *Black Vault* for the 1964 period revealed, to some degree, occasionally the opposite, taking into consideration the difference between the official 'analysis' and information contained in the written statements or sighting reports filled out by the witnesses.

Each file contains an initial completed reporting 'card', containing simple details, recording details of the time, date, and nature of the UFO sighted – no doubt necessary to utilise some standardisation, in view of the enormous amount of documents received by Project Blue Book. The problem is that if one was to depend on the evidence presented by the information on the 'card', and its subsequent conclusions, one would believe the files had little to offer. However, examination of what some of the witnesses had to say quite often revealed a different picture!

6th January 1964 (USA) – *'Ball of flame'* seen

At 7.9pm over Crossville, Tennessee, a *'ball of flame'* (much larger than a meteorite) was seen heading through the sky shedding particles of light, until it was lost from view. Explanation: Meteor. (**Source: Project Blue Book, 10073**)

10th January 1964 (UK) – Holes found in field

On 10th January 1964, farmer Roy Peach of Puckwell Farm, Niton, Isle of Wight, was ploughing 'Ridges' – his 13 acre field – when he came across a hole, 15ft in depth by 2ft wide. An examination of the hole revealed that it turned off at a sharp angle. Thinking that it might have been caused by a Second World War unexploded bomb, he contacted PC William Donovan, from Ventnor Police Station, who arrived at the scene and then reported it to the Royal Navy Bomb Disposal Squad, who – after a preliminary examination of the scene – felt unable to commit as to any explanation. They later handed over the matter to the Army Bomb Disposal Squad at Horsham, who spent two weeks on the site, before eventually filling in the hole – now 20ft deep. (See Volume 2 of *Haunted Skies* for full 'write-up' and photographs of the scene).

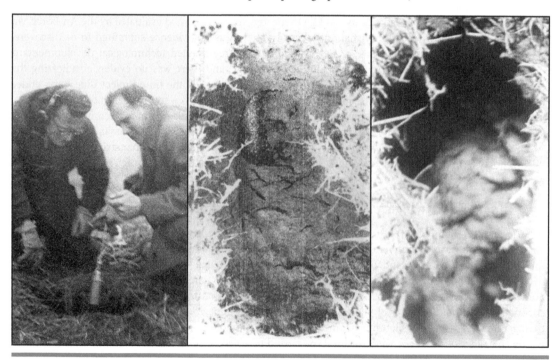

15th January 1964 (Australia) – Pencil-like UFO seen

People in several parts of Victoria reported seeing a pencil-shaped object in the sky. The witnesses included the Reverend R. Hillbrick, of Richmond, who saw it from Trafalgar. Mr H. Morgan, of Government Road, watched it for about 10 minutes, at 8pm. He said:

> *"I was in the Air Force for 25 years and it wasn't a plane."*

It was also seen over Phillip Island, by Mr J. Collins.

> *"It was a thin object, about 100ft long, and was moving slowly backwards and forwards across the sky, towards the west. From time-to-time, a white light flashed from its front."*

(Source: *Melbourne Sun*, 16.1.1964)

22nd January 1964 (USA) – Purple object seen

A light purple object, larger than a meteor, was seen entering the Earth's atmosphere at 45° elevation, heading south, at 10.15pm, by a military source; object then broke into five pieces at 10,000ft. The location was 31.35N-175.50W. Verdict: Meteor analysis not ruled out; however, there are more indications of satellite decay and the case is carried in that category.

(Source: Black Vault, WWW 2015/as above, Project Blue Book 10073 reference)

Over Lincoln Park, Michigan (USA) – Blue star

At 10.20pm over Lincoln Park, Michigan, an object – described as a blue star, moving around like a corkscrew, with whitish streaks in the sky – was seen over a period of some 35 minutes, when it then dimmed out. – Explanation: Insufficient details for evaluation.

At 11.34pm over Red Bluff, California, a circular white light, estimated to be 150ft in diameter, was reported over an 8,000ft mountain, at 10° elevation, for 15-20 minutes. Explanation: Venus.

(Source: Project Blue Book)

23rd January 1964 (Australia) – Lights in the sea

At Groote Eylandt, a group of lights was seen in the sea; in the middle of them was a shadow, which rotated clockwise, making the lights appear to pulsate. The compass aboard the boat went haywire. Unfortunately, we have no information as to the identity of the vessel concerned and names of the crew who witnessed the objects. **(Source: Ron West, UFO archives)**

24th January 1964 (USA) – Explosions in the sky

As twilight settled over the Idaho/Mexico area, the authorities were inundated by telephone calls from the public and the media, reporting what looked like explosions and various patterns in the sky. On this occasion it appears the answer was the launch of a Vandenberg missile. Apparently the explosion is due to natural phenomena, caused by the gradual lessening of density from the Earth to the outer fringes of the atmosphere.

(Source: Black Vault, WWW 2015 – Project Blue Book)

26th January 1964 (USA) – Car driver encounters UFO

At Moultrie, Georgia – a physics student, at Georgia Institute of Technology – was driving his car, at 7.30pm, when a dull red sphere rose up from behind trees, crossed the highway at low altitude, then turned and appeared to follow his car, before dropping back and heading towards the ground.

(Source: NICAP report form)

Yellow orange light seen

Also on this date a yellow-orange light was seen moving across the sky, between 11.25 and 11.35pm, by a witness from Gainesville, Florida. He wrote initially to NASA about the sighting; they forwarded the letter on.

27th January 1964 (USA) – Roman candle UFO

At 11.15pm, an object resembling a bright roman candle – greenish-blue in colour – was seen to fall beyond the horizon over Newtown, Ohio. Explanation: Meteor. **(Source: Project Blue Book)**

28th January 1963 (USA) – Rocket-like UFO

During the early morning over Bourbonnais, Illinois, an object described as resembling a rocket – amber in colour, with fins on the side, trailing blue flame – was seen for two minutes, at an elevation of 60°. The object was then seen to descend and straighten in flight. Explanation: Meteor. **(Source: Project Blue Book)**

29th January 1964 (Australia) – *'Glowing light'*

At 12.30pm, a *glowing light* was seen moving across the sky, over Melbourne.

3rd February 1964 (Australia) – Humanoid *'figure'* seen

At 2am, a woman living in Gum Creek, South Australia, awoke. On looking through the window, she saw a *'figure'* materialise as it descended through the air. (**Source R. Hall,** *Univited Guests,* **page 126**)

5th February 1964 (UK) – Rectangular UFO seen

At 3.24am, British Rail signalman – Gerard O' Flynn – sighted:

> *"… a long, silver, rectangular object (like a plank) projecting upwards at an angle in the sky, at an estimated height of two miles, which I thought was a jet fighter. Fifteen seconds later, it was gone."*

(**Source: DIGAP, Harry Bunting,** *UFOLOG*)

SECTION TWO   DIGAP SIGHTING FORM D.I.

(1) DATE OF OBSERVATION   5/2/64   TIME   3.24am   (PLEASE STATE HOW IT WAS DETERMINED)

(2) LOCATION OF OBSERVER(S)   South West
(PLEASE INDICATE THE DIRECTION OF THE   M/Cr.
OBJECT(S) INCLUDING ANY CHANGES BELOW, TOGETHER WITH THE POSITION OF ANY LANDMARKS AND MAIN ROADS). INDICATE NORTH.

(3) WEATHER AT THE TIME
    TEMPERATURE   MILD
    WIND DIRECTION & FORCE   Not Known
    TYPE OF CLOUD & HEIGHT   Hazy

(4) DURATION OF SIGHTING   15 Secs

(5) DID THE OBJECT(S) HOVER, SWAY FROM SIDE TO SIDE, FALL LIKE A LEAF, SHIMMER, ROTATE, OSCILLATE?

(6) COLOUR OF OBJECT(S)   Silver
    PLEASE STATE ANY CHANGE OF COLOUR DURING THE SIGHTING   NO

(7) DID THE OBJECT(S) MAKE ANY SOUND FOR EXAMPLE WAS IT LIKE A HUMMING TOP, A BEE, A PASSING TRAIN, A JET PLANE?   No Sound

(8) PLEASE SKETCH THE OBJECT(S)' SHAPE(S) GIVING ANY CHANGES DURING OBSERVATION (SEE SQUARE OPPOSITE).

(9) DID THE OBJECT(S) GIVE OFF SMOKE, LEAVE A TRAIL, OR DROP ANY ARTIFACTS, RESIDUE?   No

(10) ESTIMATED SIZE OF OBJECT(S), COMPARE WITH A SIXPENCE HELD AT ARMS LENGTH   HALF SIZE.

(11) ESTIMATED SPEED (m.p.h.)   NIL

(12) ESTIMATED HEIGHTH & DISTANCE   2 miles - 2 miles

(13) DID YOU OBSERVE THE OBJECT(S) WITH THE NAKED EYE, OR THROUGH SUNGLASSES, BINOCULARS, TELESCOPE, THEODOLITE, OTHER EYEPIECES, OR THROUGH A CAR WINDSHIELD OR A HOUSE WINDOW?   Naked Eye

(14) DID YOU OBTAIN A PHOTOGRAPH OF THE INCIDENT?   NO
    TYPE OF CAMERA USED, STILL/MOVIE
    TYPE OF FILM
    SHUTTER SPEED
    FOCAL LENGTH OF LENS
    SIZE OF APERTURE USED
    COLOUR OF FILTER USED
    CAN WE BORROW OR RETAIN THE FILM/NEGATIVE?

(15) ANY EFFECT ON THE FOLLOWING:-
    (a) TELEVISION RECEPTION?
    (b) RADIO RECEPTION?
    (c) CAR IGNITION SYSTEM?

(16) ANY OTHER POINTS NOT COVERED BY THE ABOVE QUESTIONS

I(WE) HEREBY STATE THE ABOVE IS AN ACCURATE ACCOUNT OF MY(OUR) OBSERVATIONS.
                    (signed)   G. O'Flynn

N

W   E

S

SKETCH OBJECT(S)

90° (Zenith)
75° 60°   45°
                30°
          15°

POSITION OF OBSERVER

5th February 1964 (USA) – UFO sinks yacht

This tells of a mysterious object that sunk a yacht, followed by the sighting of two objects over a 40 minute period in the sky over Montgomery, Alabama, one of which was larger and pointed on the top with a flat bottom. Strangely, once again, the time given is GMT, rather than local, which was 6.10pm. Explanation: Jupiter and Venus. (**Source: Project Blue Book**)

Object Sinks Yacht

The yacht, "Hattie D"—a converted Navy search and rescue craft, was struck and sunk on Wednesday, 5 February, 1964 by an unknown object about 25 miles off the rugged coast of Cape Mendocino, California. A Coast Guard helicopter, dipping between 30-foot-high waves, pulled a German shepherd puppy, nine crewmen, the Captain and his wife from the pitching deck of the yacht.

The "Hattie D" set out from Seattle on January 24, then after various stops, left Neah Bay, Washington on February 2 for California.

All eleven survivors insisted the yacht struck or was rammed by a "metal object." "I don't care how deep it was," said crewman Carl Jensen. "what holed us was steel and a long piece. There was no give to it all all." Jensen was referring to the 7,800 foot depth at the point where the sinking occurred.

We include this incident because it correlates with official and unofficial sightings of UFO in the ocean in recent years.

The same date records the sighting of a red cigar-shaped object, resembling a large star, with a trail like a meteor. This was seen by a highway patrolman (36) of the Oregon State Police, who was driving east of Corvallis, Oregon, at 2.29am. Explanation: Meteor. (**Source Project Blue Book**)

8th February 1964 (USA) – Egg-shaped UFO

A small circular or egg-shaped object, light red in colour, was seen moving in steady flight north to southwards through the sky over Albany, Oregon, at 11.45pm, by two observers at separate locations. One of the witnesses described it as having a pointed nose, with a glowing white flame. Ten seconds later it was out of sight. Explanation: Meteor.

(**Source: Project Blue Book**)

11th February 1964 (USA) – Eight UFOs seen

A total of eight, white oval objects, in a straight line, were seen in the sky passing over Brooklyn, New York, heading in a south-east direction, by a man walking home at 11.15pm. Explanation: Meteors.

(**Source: Project Blue Book**)

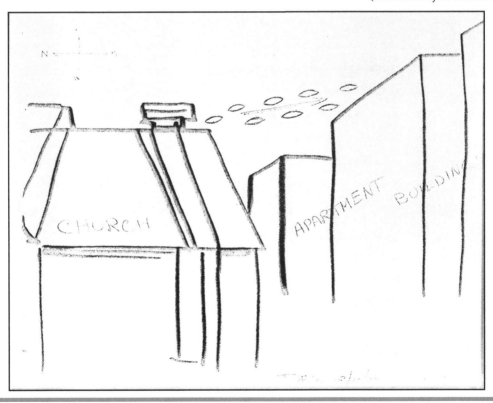

Brooklyn 30, N.Y.

February 12, 1964

Office of the Secretary of the Air Force
Washington 25, D.C.
Public Information Branch
Gentlemen;

On the night of February 11, 1964 I was walking home from a friend's house when I sighted what might have been a U.F.O. I was walking near a church behind which is a row of six story apartment buildings. At a minute or two before or after 11:15 P.M. I looked up and saw eight white objects travelling in a tight formation. Within a fraction of a second they passed XXXXXXXXX from over the edge of the church where I first saw them, to behind the apartment buildings. I ran to the corner of the block, in the direction the objects were travelling, just in time to see the XXXX objects disappear behind the apartment buildings across the street. Throughout all of this time the objects moved in a straight line toward the Southeast.

After this I ran to my home (half a block away) and drew the enclosed sketch. It is a representation of how the scene looked from where I first sighted the objects. The objects themselves were oval shaped and white. They seemed very slightly fuzzy around the edges as though they might be glowing. I could see no surface features. They were about three-fourths the XXXX diameter of the moon and almost as bright as the full moon. I heard no sound as they passed over. They didn't emit any engine noise or such

-2-

sound. The following morning, February 12, 1964, I called the Air Force In formation Service at PL-3-5609. IXXXXXXXXXXXXXXX I was told by the seargeant on duty that such matters were handled by your office and that I should write to you.

I would like to know if any other reports were reported at the same time. What sort of explanation can you suggest for this sighting?

I will be glad to supply any further information if necessary.

Thank you.

Very truly yours,

13th February 1964 (USA) – UFO sighted

A round object was sighted in the daylight sky over the junction of Sepulveda and Culver Boulevard, Los Angeles, at 12.20pm. It was seen to hover and turn in sharp circles, before moving away in a south-east direction. (**Source: NICAP**)

19th February 1964 (UK)/(Australia)

Mr L Henderson – a passenger in a DC3, returning to the UK from Germany, at 5.55pm GMT – was flying over the North Sea, above a solid layer of cloud extending to the horizon, when he sighted:

> *"...a dark grey, almost black, cylindrical object, inclined at a slight angle, appearing solid (although fuzzy in outline) and – apparently – below and to the left of the sun. Its size in contrast to the sun was approximately three times its length. At the base or lower end could be seen what looked like a small grey cloud. The object remained in this position for about five minutes. I moved my hand about, while observing to ensure this was not any reflection and asked the passenger, sat behind me, to confirm he could see it as well. At this point, the object started to move away to the left of the sun's disc, and also changing its angle until about horizontal, then appearing to fade away as it moved off at a tangent to the Earth's curvature – now appearing to be a quarter of the size of the sun's disc."*

(Source: *ORBIT*, November/December 1963; January 1964, Volume 5, No. 4)

On the same day at Gum Creek, South Australia, it is claimed that a male resident saw a UFO hovering over a nearby house. Inside the object was seen a *'man'*, standing at a wooden railing.

20th February 1964 (Australia) – UFO paces vehicle

At 6.17pm, a grazier was driving his car near Tilley Swamp, 30 miles north of Kingston, South Australia, when he heard a noise – like a high-pitched generator whine. He looked out and saw a large, silvery shadow, apparently travelling alongside the vehicle, *"at least three chains across (198ft). A couple of seconds later, it took off at incredible speed."* (**Source:** *Adelaide Advertiser,* **22.2.1964**)

20th February 1964 (USA) – Pulsating UFO

At 2.20pm a police officer (believed to be Mr Harrop) was entering the gate house at Defense Depot 5 in the Odgen area of Salt Lake City when he sighted a fiery object with a tapered tail ten times its length moving through the sky at 60 degress azimuth. It appeared to pulsate in flight before disappearing a few seconds later beyond the north ridge of Ogden Canyon. Explanation: Consistent with meteor analysis.

(Source: Project Blue Book)

20th February 1964 (UK) – Sighting by Mr Doodson (See opposite)

21st February 1964 (Australia) – Police sight UFOs

Two police officers from Adelaide, reported having sighted a bright *'globe of light'* zigzagging across the sky, during the early hours of the morning. At Mile End, South Australia, two 5ft in diameter *'discs'*, surrounded by a bright *'ring'*, were seen manoeuvring around the sky. Was this a display of UFO behaviour?

SECTION ONE

YOUR FULL NAME: MR./~~MRS./MISS~~   *Mr. Greenwood Doodson*
(BLOCK LETTERS PLEASE)
YOUR PERMANENT ADDRESS   *33, Church Street, Stalybridge, Cheshire*
TELEPHONE NUMBER
AGE   *52*
OCCUPATION   *Barber.*

QUALIFICATIONS (IF ANY)   /

IF AND WHEN IT IS DECIDED TO PUBLISH THE SIGHTING MAY WE DISCLOSE YOUR NAME AND
OCCUPATION?   *YES*

ANY OTHER WITNESSES   NAME(S)   ADDRESS(ES)
                             NONE

TOTAL NUMBER   *1*

HAVE YOU ANY EYE-SIGHT DEFECTS?   *none, but requires spectacles*
WERE YOU WEARING GLASSES AT THE TIME OF THE SIGHTING?   *YES*
HAVE YOU PREVIOUSLY SEEN A U.F.O., OR ANY UNUSUAL AERIAL PHENOMENA?   *NO*
OR SEEN EARTH SATELLITES? (WHEN)

HAVE YOU HAD ANY EXPERIENCE OF OBSERVING THE SKY? e.g. AS A MEMBER OF AN
ASTRONOMICAL SOCIETY?, OBSERVER CORPS.?   *NO*

DID YOU REPORT THE SIGHTING TO THE NEWSPAPERS?, METEOROLOGICAL OFFICE?, POLICE?,
WHAT WAS THEIR COMMENT?   *NO*

HAVE YOU ANY IDEAS OR THEORIES WHAT THE OBJECT(S) MIGHT HAVE BEEN?
Assumed it was a satellite.

NOW PLEASE TURN OVERLEAF AND COMPLETE SECTION TWO (IF YOU REQUIRE ANY HELP IN FILLING
IN THE FORM PLEASE CONTACT YOUR LOCAL INVESTIGATOR AT THE FOLLOWING ADDRESS, OR
TELEPHONE NUMBER.)

NAME

                             ADDRESS

TELEPHONE NUMBER

> **Mr. H. BUNTING, GRAD. I.E.E.**
> 34, BOWERFIELD AVENUE,
> HAZEL GROVE,
> STOCKPORT,
> CHESHIRE.
> TELEPHONE: POYnton 3956

continued overleaf:-

UFOLOG
REF No *26*
I.S. ISSUE NO *9*

23rd February 1964 (USA) – Golden *'ball of lights'*

At 9pm a *'golden ball of lights'* was seen heading across the sky at an estimated speed of 5000mph and height of 5-6000ft over Philadelphia, Pennsylvania. Explanation: The object which appeared to be 50 feet in diameter was later explained away as a meteor. (**Source Project Blue Book**)

26th February 1964 (USA) – Two lights sighted

At 9.15pm, two lights were sighted in the sky over the western horizon at Greenville, Ohio, sinking slowly for a period of 30 minutes, and were brought to the attention of Captain Farr, at Wright Patterson Air Force

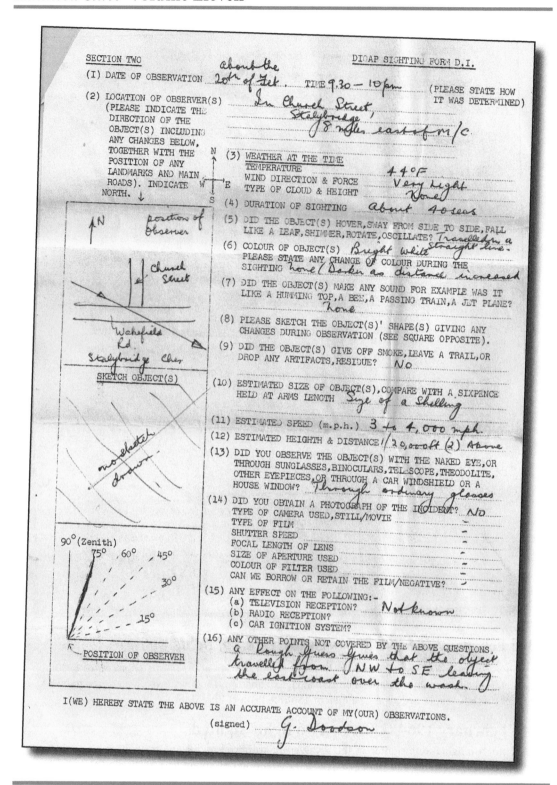

SECTION TWO   DICAP SIGHTING FORM D.I.

(I) DATE OF OBSERVATION *about the* 20th of Feb. TIME 9.30 – 10pm (PLEASE STATE HOW
                           IT WAS DETERMINED)

(2) LOCATION OF OBSERVER(S) *In Church Street,*
(PLEASE INDICATE THE   *Stalybridge,*
DIRECTION OF THE   *8 miles east of m/c.*
OBJECT(S) INCLUDING
ANY CHANGES BELOW,
TOGETHER WITH THE
POSITION OF ANY   (3) WEATHER AT THE TIME
LANDMARKS AND MAIN   TEMPERATURE   *44°F*
ROADS). INDICATE   WIND DIRECTION & FORCE *Very Light*
NORTH.   TYPE OF CLOUD & HEIGHT *None*

         (4) DURATION OF SIGHTING *About 40 secs*

         (5) DID THE OBJECT(S) HOVER, SWAY FROM SIDE TO SIDE, FALL
            LIKE A LEAF, SHIMMER, ROTATE, OSCILLATE? *Travelled in a*
         (6) COLOUR OF OBJECT(S) *Bright White* *straight line.*
            PLEASE STATE ANY CHANGE OF COLOUR DURING THE
            SIGHTING *None (Darker as distance increased*

         (7) DID THE OBJECT(S) MAKE ANY SOUND FOR EXAMPLE WAS IT
            LIKE A HUMMING TOP, A BEE, A PASSING TRAIN, A JET PLANE?
            None

         (8) PLEASE SKETCH THE OBJECT(S)' SHAPE(S) GIVING ANY
            CHANGES DURING OBSERVATION (SEE SQUARE OPPOSITE).

         (9) DID THE OBJECT(S) GIVE OFF SMOKE, LEAVE A TRAIL, OR
            DROP ANY ARTIFACTS, RESIDUE? *NO*

SKETCH OBJECT(S)

         (10) ESTIMATED SIZE OF OBJECT(S), COMPARE WITH A SIXPENCE
            HELD AT ARMS LENGTH *Size of a Shilling*

         (11) ESTIMATED SPEED (m.p.h.) *3 to 4,000 mph.*
         (12) ESTIMATED HEIGHTH & DISTANCE *1/ 20,000 ft (2) Above*
         (13) DID YOU OBSERVE THE OBJECT(S) WITH THE NAKED EYE, OR
            THROUGH SUNGLASSES, BINOCULARS, TELESCOPE, THEODOLITE,
            OTHER EYEPIECES, OR THROUGH A CAR WINDSHIELD OR A
            HOUSE WINDOW? *Through ordinary glasses*

90°(Zenith)
75° 60° 45°
    30°

         (14) DID YOU OBTAIN A PHOTOGRAPH OF THE INCIDENT? *NO*
            TYPE OF CAMERA USED, STILL/MOVIE
            TYPE OF FILM
            SHUTTER SPEED
   15°   FOCAL LENGTH OF LENS
            SIZE OF APERTURE USED
            COLOUR OF FILTER USED
            CAN WE BORROW OR RETAIN THE FILM/NEGATIVE?

         (15) ANY EFFECT ON THE FOLLOWING:-
            (a) TELEVISION RECEPTION? *Not known*
            (b) RADIO RECEPTION?
POSITION OF OBSERVER   (c) CAR IGNITION SYSTEM?

         (16) ANY OTHER POINTS NOT COVERED BY THE ABOVE QUESTIONS.
            a rough guess gives that the object
            travelled from NW to SE leaving
            the east coast over the wash.

I(WE) HEREBY STATE THE ABOVE IS AN ACCURATE ACCOUNT OF MY(OUR) OBSERVATIONS.
      (signed) *G. Dodson*

Base; he contacted Captain Quintanilla, who said he had seen them also, and that they were Venus and Jupiter.

1st March 1964 (USA) – UFO display

At Middleboro, Massachusetts, one or more objects were seen in the sky performing erratic motions, for almost two hours, by two teenage boys, one of whom was an amateur astronomer and presumably knowledgeable about the night sky. What was significant about this report was the statement made by the witness that, quote:

"At the time which the objects were about to leave, an airplane (it sounded like a double engine piston driven) with what at first appeared to be similar lights, could be seen coming from the NNE.

The information which I wish to give here is that at distance greater than the objects, the plane could be heard and its lights separated into ones which you know the positions of as well as anyone of aircraft. The objects could not be heard and their lights seemed to be from a single source; it seemed as one 'bulb' with a rotating tri-coloured globe of three sections – red, green, and amber – each of 120°. Occasionally, but not in any pattern, the red flash would be very bright (really it was not a red flash but the red sequence) – brighter than Venus at greatest elongation. I would like to stress that the moon glow did not necessarily mean the sky was hazy, which it wasn't, but that the object could be seen when near the moon and only then, since they were unlit except for the lights. I also feel that I should stress that when the single object was closest at 3,000ft, there was still no sound and the distance here is one I am very sure of – 3,000ft. There was no unusual activity in the sky, such as thunderstorms or such phenomena. The plane chasing (this is what it seemed to be doing) the last object chased it in a wide arc from NNE to West, through to the South-east, where they both disappeared over the horizon. The object did not increase speed to elude the aircraft and they stayed well in front of it. This may or may not be of any great importance, but the object seemed to halt its motion; it got either brighter or dimmer, and it has just occurred to me that the erratic side to side motions may actually have been the objects moving in a rectangular-shaped manoeuvre. Would you please give me the analysis of this sighting?"

Following investigation into the matter, USAF Colonel Eric T. de Jonckheere of Blue Book concluded:

"Misinterpretation of conventional objects; the duration of one hour and 41 minutes contains several sightings of multiple objects. No time motion sequence can be interpreted from the data presented. Some characteristics of balloons, aircraft, and astronomical bodies, are confusing. The duration of each object was omitted."

2nd March 1964 (Australia) – Silvery UFO seen

A long silvery object was sighted hovering in the sky over Grassmere, Victoria, South Australia. On the same date a white planet-like object, showing a bright light, was seen over Bridport, Tasmania. (**Source: Ron West – limited details only**)

4th March 1964 (Australia) – Silver *'disc'* seen

Three schoolboys at North Plympton, South Australia, reported having seen a silver *'disc'* in the sky, which remained motionless before flying away, a few minutes later. (**Source: Ron West**)

14th March 1964 (USA)

The pilot of a clipper aircraft, en route from Tokyo to Honolulu over the Pacific Ocean, contacted Air Traffic Control after he observed:

"A white domed-shaped 'cloud' appeared on the horizon, in front, in the north-east direction, at 1.16pm GMT. The 'cloud' appeared to be 15° wide and rose to 10° off the horizon. It was white and glowing. It rose rapidly in the air. After approximately two minutes, the top arc of the 'cloud' broke free of the horizon and became a white arc – like a rainbow – rising in the sky, followed by a thin tail. Below the tail was a white glowing 'ball', with a flashing light in the centre. The arc tail and light rose to 50° above the horizon and about 2o'clock from my position.

At this time the arc and tail disappeared but the flashing light continued to the south-west, until it passed below the horizon.

Duration of sighting: 15 minutes."

The pilot, who said he had seen three nuclear explosions previously in his service, remarked on the similarities between the appearances of the object, which resembled a mushroom cloud.

Oddly, while it was stated in the file that no missile testing had taken place in the area at the time, we learn that a missile was launched from Vandenberg, at 4pm, according to Colonel Fredricks, in reply to enquiries made by him at the time. (**Source: Project Blue Book**)

14th March 1964 (USA) – Triangular UFO sighted

At Silver Springs, California, a boy (aged 14½) sighted something unusual in the clear night sky, at 15° due west, at 1.42am, while plotting the paths of meteors for a school project, which he first took to be a satellite but felt this was not the case. He wrote to NASA, who forwarded his letter on to Andrews Air Force Base. A questionnaire was then sent to him by Captain Hector Quintanilla, USAF Chief, Aerial Phenomena Branch, on the 25th March. An illustration submitted by the teenager shows a grey triangular object, showing two lights on its body. (**Source: Project Blue Book**)

16th March 1964 (USA) – Six or seven objects sighted

At 5.6pm (GMT) six bluish-cream objects, forming an unbalanced formation, were seen crossing the sky at 55-60° elevation over Lakewood, California. Their speed was estimated as being 3,000mph, at a height of 10.000ft. In a few seconds they were out of sight. Explanation: Boloides or Meteor.

(**Source: Project Blue Book**)

16th/17th March 1964 (USA) – *'Flying saucer'* seen

Over Orange, Connecticut, an object – described as resembling a *'flying saucer'* and making a heavy buzzing sound, moving at low altitude – was reported. (**Source: Project Blue Book**) See opposite.

19th March 1964 (UK) – Pilots sight UFO

Pan American Boeing 707 airline pilot – Captain E. D. Morrison was en route from New York to London, with 42 passengers, and about 200 miles west of Land's End, when he noticed an object higher up in the

Peck Beck School
107 Grannis Road
Orange, Connecticut 06477
March 18, 1964

Dear Sir,

Two people in our class saw an unidentified flying object. Five other people in our community saw it also. It was seen Monday, March 16, 1964. Tuesday March 17, 1964 our class heard something and a boy in our class said it sounded like the object he saw. We have a book that shows and tells about flying saucers. One of the saucers in the book is exactly the same as the one they saw. It makes two noises that we know of. One is a heavy buzzing sound and the other sound was short and continuous. It wasn't a plane, helicopter, jet or satellite and flies at a low altitude. It wasn't flying at a high speed and the object seems to stay in one area. It has white, red, green and orange lights that stay on all the time. The night one person saw it four other people heard it.

The Yale Observatory spotted an unidentified flying object. We enclose a copy of the object. Please send us more information on the subject. Thank you.

sky, at 6.34am, while flying at 31,000ft. The object, which was seen by all on the plane, changed colour from blue to red-hot flame, leaving a white trail extending to about a 100ft behind it. At an estimated height of 80-100,000ft, it exploded in a great flash. The same phenomena were also seen by Captain R. A. Bothos, who was piloting a DC8 from New York with 77 passengers. This matter received much publicity, with suggestion of it as having been a rocket that had gone off course, which had been automatically exploded at a certain height. (**Sources:** *Manchester Evening News,* **19.3.1964**/*Evening Chronicle* – 'Jet pilots see mystery space object'/*Cork Evening Echo/Lancashire Evening Post*)

21st March 1964 (USA) – Photo of UFO

At 6pm, a photo was taken of a bright object in the sky over Roswell, New Mexico, heading northwards at 70° elevation, by a local resident, and submitted to the Air Force Weapon Laboratory Research and Technology, at Kirtland Air Force Base, by Captain Frederick Kruzel. This incident was brought to the attention of Project Blue Book. In a letter by Colonel Eric T. de Jonckheere we learn,

> *"Image caused by drop of some type of processing chemical on the film elusion during processing."*

Our Comment: This object was kept under observation for five minutes by the witness. The report attached is self-explanatory and describes the events leading up to the capture of the egg-shaped UFO on film. It seems odd that the witness was not shown the image on the film he took.

No doubt if he had, he may well have confirmed that this is what he saw as well!

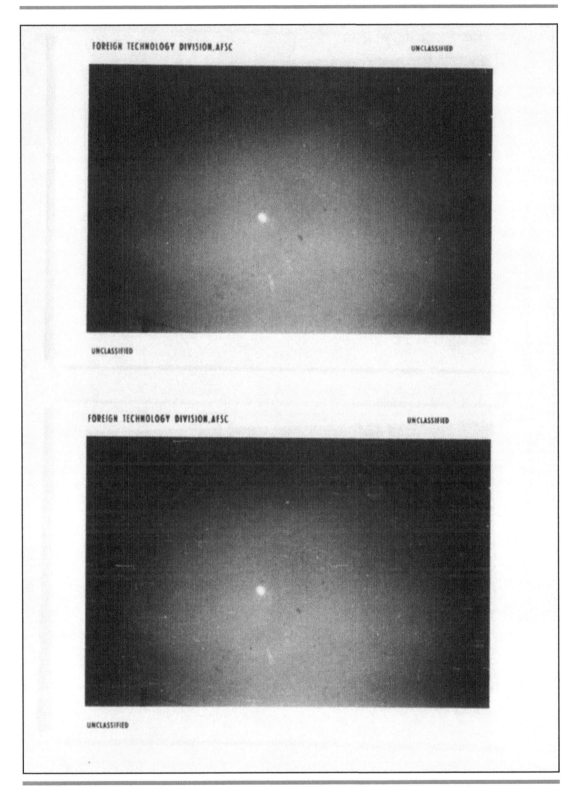

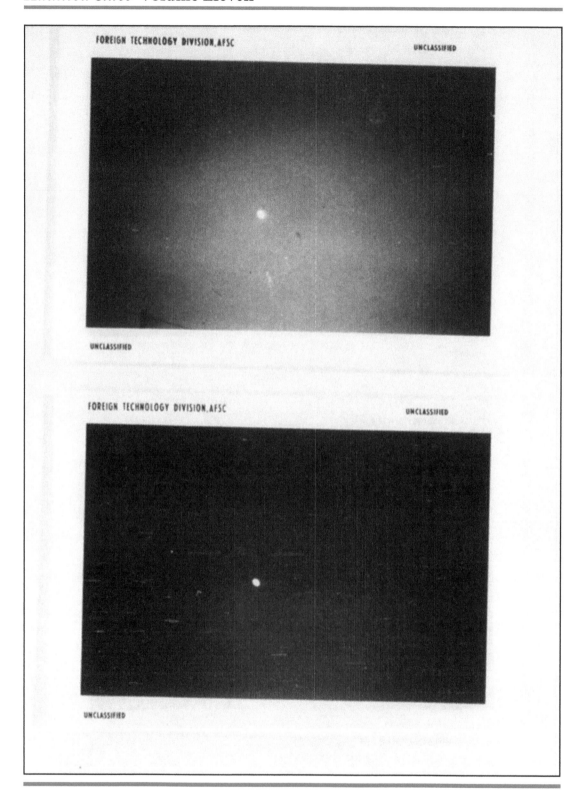

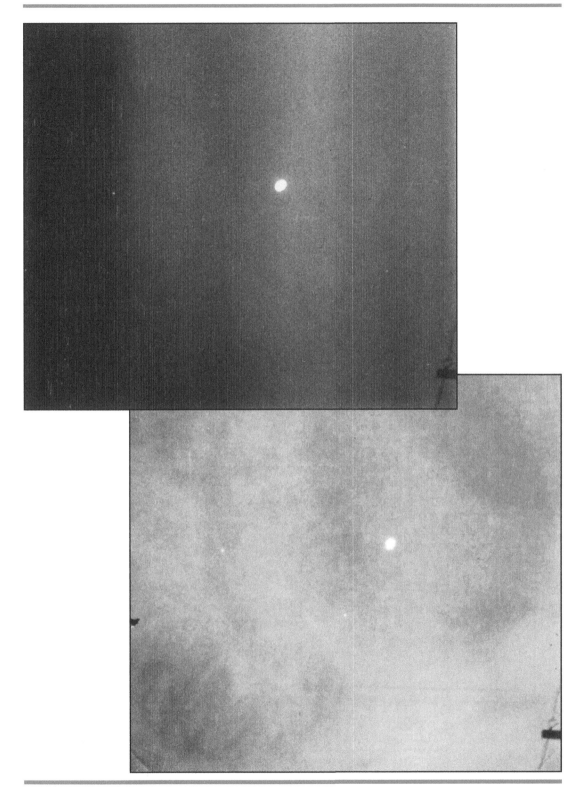

Page 7

34. Date you completed this questionnaire: _____ 2 _____ _____ Sept _____ _____ 1964 _____
Day   Month   Year

35. Information which you feel pertinent and which is not adequately covered in the specific points of the questionnaire or a narrative explanation of your sighting.

I AM UNABLE TO GIVE THE EXACT DATE BECAUSE IT WAS LAST SPRING. I DIDN'T REPORT THIS TO ANYONE BUT SIMPLY TOOK A PICTURE OF IT. CAPT. FRED KRUZAI HAPPENED TO BE A GUEST AT MY HOME & SAW THIS WHILE I WAS SHOWING SLIDES.

THIS PICTURE WAS TAKEN AT DUSK AFTER THE SUN WAS WELL SET BUT BEFORE THE STARS WERE OUT.

CAMERA — MAKE - TOWER 37
35 mm WITH AUTO ELE. EYE.
SHUTTER SPEED 1. 38
LENS - F. 45 mm
CAMERA SHUTTER SPEED SET AT $\frac{1}{250}$

Air Force Weapons Laboratory
Research and Technology Division
Air Force Systems Command
United States Air Force
Kirtland Air Force Base, New Mexico 87117

REPLY TO
ATTN. OF   WLF

SUBJECT   UFO

TO   FTD (TDA/Col McDavid)
Wright-Patterson AFB, Ohio 45433

1. An officer recently reporting into this base, Capt Frederic
J. Kruzel, has called my attention to the sighting and photographing of a UFO in Roswell, New Mexico. The photographer in
this case was standing in his yard in Roswell with a 35 mm
Japanese built camera snapping pictures of flights of birds
when he saw a UFO and photographed it. This was shortly before
the recent flurry of sightings in the Rio Grande valley a few
hundred miles west of Roswell.

2. Capt Kruzel saw the picture which appeared to be a metallic
oblate spheroid but he did not interrogate the photographer about
associated sounds, apparent speed, estimation of size, or other
particulars because he did not wish to plant any ideas in the
observer's mind in the event that an expert wished to interrogate
him later. Capt Kruzel plans to secure copies of this transparency.
If the UFO office is interested in following up on this matter,
I will be happy to send them the copies of the print when we are
able to secure them and put them in touch with Capt Kruzel.

FOR THE DIRECTOR

Francis T Bradley

FRANCIS T. BRADLEY
Colonel, USAF
Ch, Foreign Technology Division

M/R Telecon w/Col Bradley on 4 Aug 64. Will attempt to obtain photos
and forward to TDEW (Maj Quintanilla).

28th March 1964 (USA)

The sighting took place between 6.30pm and 9.15pm and involved two photographic students from Anselm College – Timothy Neil and David Van Buskirk. Three photographs were taken using a Crown Graphex camera, loaded with 4x5 films, speed 100 -F.4.5, on a tripod, from a 4th storey building.

(Source: Project Blue Book)

Silver object seen with a three ball landing gear

Mr Fred Steckling and his wife had just left a department store, at 3.20pm, when they were astonished to see a silver object, showing:

> *"...what looked like a three ball landing gear plainly visible; the craft was moving at a height of about 12,000ft, and out of sight within seconds."*

(Source: *The Little Listening Post*, Washington)

29th March 1964 (Atlantic) – Three green flares seen

At 2.17am the crew of a military aircraft sighted three green flares, fading into purple, heading 275°, flight level 9.5, at an elevation of 45° above the horizon. Seconds later they, were gone. (Source: NICAP)

2nd April 1964 (USA) – UFO takes off

At 8.45pm, an object – described as showing four *'Ferris wheel- like'* lights, with four huge red lights and other white ones – was seen near the ground, 300ft away, before taking off, to the consternation of a Monticello, Wisconsin, motorist and his passengers. Explanation: Unidentified. (Source: Project Blue Book)

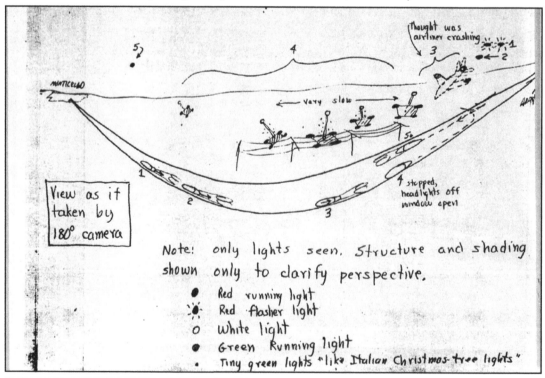

MONTICELLO, WISCONSIN

3 APRIL 1964

Observers were leaving Monticello and heading westward on County C Road toward the town of Argyle when at about 2100, they noticed two red blinkers in about the 11 o'clock position from the observers location. Their first reaction was that an accident had occurred and that there were police cars on a hill in the distance. Almost immediately, however, they recognized that the lights were too far above the ground for such a conclusion. It then appeared that an airliner was about to crash and that they were more or less on the direct line, even though the object was somewhat to their left. The car was stopped and headlights turned off so that the persons could observe the object.

As the lights came closer, it apparently slowed down to a hovering position right alongside of the car, but about 100 yards to the left of the road. At this time there were four red lights. The object went behind telephone poles and wires as it was hovering.

At no time were the observers able to see any body in the object or any superstructure. Only the fact that the lights maintained a geometrical relationship throughout the sighting led them to believe that the lights were indeed attached to a physical structure of some sort. A few times they gave the impression that the red lights did reflect dimly off a metallic surface.

The object then passed slightly to the rear at which time the driver started the motor, turned on the headlights, and drove ahead to turn around. As he turned around, he found the light pattern growing smaller in the east. The observers chased the objects but the attempt was futile, because the object disappeared into the distance. The total duration of sighting was somewhere between five and fifteen minutes.

COMMENTS

Considering the possibility of some type of aircraft being responsible for the sighting has to be ruled out since there was no noise heard at all by any of the observers, even though one of the windows was rolled down. According to the observers a helicopter couldn't be responsible for the sighting because the subtended angle was much too great to have been a helicopter over one hundred yards away. Also, no landing lights were used, and a helicopter that close to the ground would have landing lights on.

Scientific balloons, if they descend nearly to the ground, do not suddenly take off and rise rapidly as so reported by the observers. This tends to discount such a sighting. The weather was reported as being cloudy by the local weather bureau.

With the information available a conclusive explanation is lacking. This factor makes this case unidentified.

4th April 1964 (USA) – Mysterious images seen on TV!

A timekeeper from the Sheraton Belvedere Hotel, Baltimore, Maryland, was watching the Johnny Carson show on his TV, at 3.30am, when it appears he tuned the dial and saw strange saucer-shaped images forming on the screen. The images continued until 6am. Explanation: Interference, accompanied by imagination!

(Source: Project Blue Book)

9th April 1964 (UK) – UFO over Bedfordshire

An object – described as resembling a lamp, swinging in the sky – was seen over the north of Luton by at least three people.

Taxi driver, Mr John Hodges, was one of them. He had this to say:

> *"I was returning to Luton after dropping a fare off, at 10.30pm, when I saw a 'light' – like the headlamp of a car – in the sky. It then faded but came on again. I watched it and realised the fading effect had been caused by the object swivelling around in the sky. There were beams of light radiating from it. It was hovering over the Barton area and perfectly still. As I was driving towards Luton, hoping to find other witnesses, I saw Jack Foreman – who is ex-RAF, now a taxi driver – and stopped to show him the 'light' in the sky. He thought it was definitely strange and not an aircraft. The two of us retuned to the taxi rank and found another witness – William Hodges of Abbey Drive.*
>
> *We continued to watch it. All of a sudden it began to move like a pendulum, with a gentle swinging motion, until 11.45pm, when it headed away, northwards, and was lost from view as it dropped below the horizon."*

Daily Telegraph

The incident attracted the attention of the *Daily Telegraph*, who published their account in its edition of the 9th May 1964.

The Air Ministry wondered if it might have been a weather balloon, searchlight, or Venus. The spokesman said:

> *"I know people will laugh at our explanation, but it (Venus) does sometimes move in an extraordinary manner."*

10th April 1964 (USA) – UFO sighted, F16s scrambled!

Six to twelve objects were picked up by radar, 30 miles east, in the sky over Merced, California – moving at a height of between 60-90.000ft. F16's from Castle AFB were scrambled and although they achieved a radar lock, they were unable to keep the lock on. Two more aircraft were scrambled – this time equipped with high pressure suits as used on the U2s. Explanation: NORAD. It was a balloon, confirmed by pilots of U2.

(Source: Project Blue Book)

11th April 1964 (USA) – Fantastic sighting of UFO

A psychotherapist from New York was out with his wife and two children, enjoying a picnic supper on a hill, 1,800ft above sea level, about 10 miles north-west of Homer, New York, at 6.30pm. Several jet aircraft had gone over, leaving vapour trails which had quickly disappeared.

As he looked up into the sky, once again, he saw what he took to be a large jet trail, heading north-west to south-west.

Black spiral seen

"It was very white and wide and at the south-west end there was a break in the trail of about one mile; the next thing was a black spiral of what we took to be smoke appeared in the sky. The white trail seemed unusually wide for a jet trail, and the black portion looked very dark because of the setting sun behind the hill several miles away. The white vapour gradually drifted southwards, slowly disappearing. Everything up to this point seemed to be quite normal. Suddenly it occurred to me that the black spiral had moved to the west, while the white trail had drifted southwards. I picked up a pair of binoculars and looked through, when I was surprised to see wisps of smoke streaming out of the black cloud, almost boiling out."

Black spiral changes shape

"By now it (the black spiral) was slowly approaching the distant stratus cloud formation. Suddenly it changed from horizontal to a vertical position and resembled a smoking plane falling slowly through the sky, assuming a shape similar to banana. It stopped and hung there for two to three minutes, before slowly sinking into the clouds and then obliterated from view."

PHYSIOTHERAPIST
CORTLAND. N. Y.
February 23, 1965

Dr. J. Allen Hynek
Dearborn Observatory, Northwestern Univ.
Evanston, Illinois, 60201
Dear Dr. Hynek

Apparently our minds were operating on the same wave length last week, because at the time when you were writing your letter of February 18th, I was in the process of assembling the sketches and data and putting them together in a comprehensible form. I was honored to receive your telephone call and very pleased to discuss the sighting with you. I have re-read my letter to you for the first time since it was sent and realize that I contradicted myself in some of the details.

One point is that the jet trails actually appeared from West to East as stated in the letter and not vice-versa as stated in my telephone conversation. Since our conversation I have returned to the location of the sighting and as nearly as I can remember it to be find that the trail of the object was actually nearer the South end of Skaneateles Lake and not half way up as I stated to you. Further. I had also forgotten that I had mailed a copy of my letter to you to Stephen R. Putnam of Scituate, Mass, whose hobby is UFOs. However, I never heard from him and the only reason I wrote to him was that he had had an article in our local paper. Other than that I have discussed this matter only with close friends.

It is amazing what details one can forget in six months time and you caught me at a very busy time in my office so that my recall was not too quick on the matters we discussed. I am inclosing herewith seven prints of the sighting which my wife prepared from our description of the same describing it as nearly as we all can recall, together with a description of the same and I intend to return to the location to have photographs made for your reference.

In the event there is anything further wherein I can be of assistance to you in your research of similar situations, kindly advise and I will be very happy to do so. Thanking you very much for your interest herein, I remain,

Sincerely yours,

WSO:dd
Inclosures 8
Reg. Mail, RR

Another one appears!

"A few minutes later my daughter exclaimed 'there's another one', and pointed into the sky. This one was a horizontal pencil-shaped object; it was impossible to determine the length but it could have been as big as a submarine. It moved from the left of the horizon to the right. We couldn't agree whether this was the original object that had reappeared or another one. Then a flash of light came from the rear of it and it shot forward with incredible speed, for a distance of about five times its length, and halted in mid-air. The object became thick in the middle, showing a cloud of smoke coming from it, before shooting backwards as rapidly as it had gone forward."

Now saucer-shaped!

"Again it hovered but shortened its length until saucer-shaped, i.e. fat in the middle. From the saucer shape it became almost perfectly round – then slowly divided into two parts, one above the other, like a singe cell does under a microscope. The top object slowly became smaller.

As it appeared to fade off in the distance, the lower one headed downwards, at a 45° angle, towards where we had seen the banana-shaped one disappear. At this point it divided once again, but this time the bottom object assumed a vertical pencil shape while the top one faded away. The whole episode was over in 45 minutes."

(**Source:** *Anatomy of a Phenomenon UFOs in Space*, **Jacques Vallee/Project Blue Book**)

13th April 1964 (UK)

At 8.43pm, bus driver – Bob Fall – reported sighting a cigar-shaped object that crashed into the *River Lea*, at Walthamstow, cutting the telephone wires as it did so. The police made a search of the area and, after finding nothing, suggested he had seen ducks flying in a line! (**Source: Dr. Geoffrey G. Doel and daughter**)

17th April 1964 (USA) – Tracked on radar

At 7.22am, Aircraftman Edward Lowe – radar operator, at 858th RADRON, Fallon AFS, Nevada, picked up on ground radar two blips, in stacked formation, with rapid changes in altitude at 122° at 60,000ft, at 145 mile range. The motion was up and down. The length of the observation was one hour and 21 minutes, when the blips disappeared to the south-east.

(**Source: Dan Wilson,** *McDonald List*)

Seven flashing lights, at great height

At 8pm over Norfolk, Virginia, an object was seen passing through the sky at great altitude, showing seven powerful white flashing lights. This was seen by crew members of an Eastern aircraft en route from Miami to New York, who then radioed Air Traffic Control centre at New York. According to the unnamed crew, following what was believed to be some sort of *'blast'*, the object headed southwards. Explanation: Enquiries made revealed there had been no launch of any missile from Kennedy Space Center although it was considered there may have been connections with NASA activities. (**Source: Project Blue Book**)

18th April 1964 (USA) – Three *'stars'* seen

At 7.30pm, an object – described as *"three stars, forming a triangle"*, was seen passing through the sky over Manassas, Virginia. It appeared to be breaking up like *"a red spark that burned out"*. Initially it was seen as bright as a meteor over the eastern horizon, and rising in flight over duration of between five to eight minutes. Explanation: Likely to be connected with research activities from Wallop Island, or Radio Sonde train (balloon) from Washington DC, at 6.49pm. (**Source: Project Blue Book**)

21st April 1964 (Australia)

At Norseman, West Australia, a motorist claimed that he had been chased by a *'red light'*.

24th April 1964 (USA) – Police officer sights egg-shaped UFO

Sergeant Lonnie Zamora was chasing a speeding car due south of Socorro, New Mexico, on a clear sunny day, at about 5.45pm, when he:

"...heard a roar and saw a flame in the sky, south-west, some distance away - possibly a half mile or a mile."

Thinking a local dynamite shack might have exploded Zamora broke off the chase and went to investigate. Zamora struggled to get his car up the steep hill. Successful on the third attempt, he listened out but heard no further noise. For the next 10-15 seconds he proceeded west, looking for the shack whose precise location he was unable to recall.

Artist Karl Rajanen's rendering of the Socorro UFO Encounter of April 25, 1964.

Page 8-A ★ SAN ANTONIO EXPRESS — Thursday, April 30, 1964

Flying Object Expert Checks Into Reports

SOCORRO, N.M. (AP)—One of the things that bothers the scientist investigating New Mexico's unidentified flying object reports for the Air Force is the lack of mention of radar contacts.

"It's my understanding New Mexico is infested with radar equipment," said Dr. J. Allen Hynek of Northwestern University, an astronomer who is a special consultant to the Air Force. "I'm going to check to see if there have been radar contacts that might tie into these reports."

Hynek visited Wednesday the secluded hill where Socorro policeman Lonnie Zamora reported seeing an egg-shaped object fly away from a draw last Friday evening. Other reports have followed. The Socorro report and another at La Madera in northern New Mexico were similar in that state and military authorities confirmed a scorched area where the object was supposed to have landed, and wedge-shaped impressions

that appeared to have been left by some type of landing gear. Hynek would not offer an opinion on just what Zamora did see.

He said he had investigated many such sightings but "this is one of the clearest, no that's not the right word; just say it is one of the soundest, best substantiated reports as far as it goes.

"Usually one finds many contradictions or omissions in these reports," Hynek said. "But Mr. Zamora's story is simply told, certainly told without any intent

to perpetuate a hoax. The story of course was told by a man who obviously was frightened badly by what he did see. He certainly must have seen something."

Zamora's reliability as a witness was supported by Dr. Lincoln LaPaz of the University of New Mexico who has an international reputation in running down reports on fireballs and meteorites.

"I would first point out that we are not personally involved in the investigation of these unidentified flying objects," LaPaz said. "But I do want to say that I have had contacts with Mr. Zamora for 16 years in my work and he is a thoroughly dependable observer."

Hynek said he found little at the Socorro site.

"The area certainly has been thoroughly messed up by the tourists. There's nothing to see there now."

He said soil samples had been taken to "see if there are any particles in the ashes or at the site that might be foreign to this area."

He said the lack of radar contact reports bothered him.

"So often we have such a contact and then can trace the object to some natural paenomena or aircraft," he said.

The scientist also discussed the markings that Zamora said he saw on the side of the object, a red, inverted V with bars through it.

Hynek said that a report that the Air Force had asked Zamora not to discuss the markings was false.

ARTIST'S CONCEPTION—This drawing is an artist's conception of the unidentified flying objects seen in the last week in New Mexico. It was made from newspaper accounts of six persons who say they saw the craft.—UPI Telephoto.

Hynek tells it as it really was! ⇨

Notice that J. Allen Hynek, official USAF investigator said that Zamora told him the red emblem on the object was (as said in the turquoise rectangle, left) an inverted V with bars across it [actually three], as Hynek told me Zamora had said to him.

In that last paragraph at your left, I have underlined the word Air Force, because in saying *that*, Hynek was being absolutely truthful. How so? That is because it was Captain Richard T. Holder of the U.S. ARMY who advised Zamora not to divulge the actual emblem he had seen.

Ray Stanford, Author, Socorro Saucer in A Pentagon Pantry

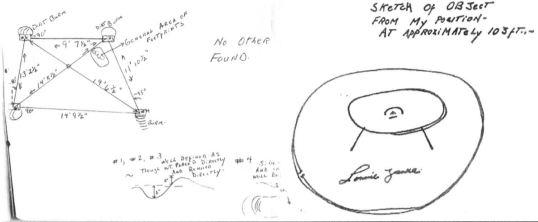

Shiny object seen

It was then he noticed a shiny object *"like aluminum; it was whitish against the mesa background, but not chrome, and shaped like a letter 'O', to the south, about 150-200 yards away"*. At first he took this to be an *"overturned white car ... up on its radiator or on the trunk"*, with two people standing close to it, one of whom then seemed to notice him and showed some surprise.

Lonnie:

> *"I only caught a brief sight of the two people in white coveralls beside the 'car'. There was nothing special about them. I don't recall noting any particular shape or possibly any hats, or headgear. These persons appeared normal in shape but possibly small adults or large kids."*

DECLASSIFIED
Authority NND 923007

OFFICIAL FILE COPY

JOINT MESSAGEFORM

SECURITY CLASSIFICATION: UNCLASSIFIED

SPACE BELOW RESERVED FOR COMMUNICATION CENTER

ZNR 30 JUN 64 15 33z
TOT – 30/1640Z

PRECEDENCE	TYPE MSG (Check) BOOK	MULTI	SINGLE	ACCOUNTING SYMBOL	ORIG. OR REFERS TO	CLASSIFICATION OF REFERENCE
ACTION ROUTINE						
INFO ROUTINE		X		AF		

FROM:
FTD, WRIGHT-PATTERSON AFB, OHIO

TO:
~~AFMDC, HOLLOMAN AFB, NEW MEXICO~~

~~INFO:~~ AFMDC, HOLLOMAN AFB, NEW MEXICO / RUWGBA

30-6562

UNCLAS/TDEW(UFO)

FOR MDG, INFO MDFC. REFERENCE TELECONS MR SEYEN, CAPT WEIMER AND CAPT QUINTANILLA, 24 JUN 64. CAPTAIN HECTOR QUINTANILLA, AO 2231554, WILL ARRIVE ON OR ABOUT 6 JUL 64 FOR MEETING WITH MDC COMMANDER. CAPT QUINTANILLA IS CLEARED UP TO AND INCLUDING TOP SECRET.

COORDINATION: *Walley E Kuntz* TDXS 30 June 64 DATE

SPECIAL INSTRUCTIONS

30 1526Z

DATE	TIME
30	1026
MONTH	YEAR
JUN	64

TDEW/UFO OFFICIAL FILE COPY

WRITER
SYMBOL: TDEW/UFO
TYPED NAME AND TITLE (Signature, if required): HECTOR QUINTANILLA, Jr Capt/mhs
PHONE 69216/66378 PAGE NR. 1 NR. OF PAGES 1
SECURITY CLASSIFICATION: UNCLASSIFIED

RELEASER
SIGNATURE: *David C. Blevins*
TYPED (or stamped) NAME AND TITLE: ERIC T de JONCKHEERE
COLONEL, USAF
DEPUTY FOR TECHNOLOGY AND SUBSYSTEMS

DD FORM 1 MAY 55 173 REPLACES DD FORM 173, 1 OCT. 49, WHICH WILL BE USED UNTIL EXHAUSTED

After stopping for a couple of seconds, Zamora approached in his car meaning to help, and radioed his dispatcher to advise him he would be getting out of the car to check a car in the arroyo. (A dry creek or stream bed-gulch that temporarily or seasonally fills and flows after sufficient rain.) Lonnie stopped his car, got out, and attended to the radio microphone, which he had dropped, and began to approach the object.

Approaching the UFO

Keeping the object in view he ran behind his car, bumping his leg on the rear fender and dropping his glasses, but continued running northwards away from the object, which was still near the ground.

> *"It was oval in shape – smooth, no windows or doors. I noted red lettering of some type. Insignia was about 2½ft high and about 2ft wide and was in the middle of the object, which still looked like aluminum-white."*

Roaring noise heard

> *"The object was still on the ground when the roar started. It began to rise to about the level of the car; say, 20-25ft. I guess about six seconds later, the object started to rise and I glanced back. I ran, I guess about halfway to where I ducked down – about 50ft from my car is where I ducked down – just over edge of hill. I guess I had run about 25ft when I glanced back and saw the object level with the car, and it appeared about directly over the place where it rose from. I was still running and I jumped just over the hill – I stopped because I did not hear the roar. I was scared of the roar, and I had planned to continue running down the hill. I turned around toward the object and at same time put my head toward ground, covering my face with my arms."*

Object moving away

> *Being that there was no roar. I looked up and I saw the object going away from me. It did not come any closer to me. It appeared to go in a straight line and at same height – possibly 10-15ft from ground – and it cleared the dynamite shack by about 3ft (shack about 8ft high). Object was travelling very fast. It seemed to rise up, and take off immediately across country."*

Radio's dispatcher

Lonnie picked up the sun glasses from on the ground and got into the car. He radioed Nep Lopez – the radio operator – to *"look out of the window, to see if you could see an object"*. He asked him, *"What is it?"*

Lonnie:

> *"It looks like a balloon. I don't know if he saw it. If Nep looked out of his window, which faces north, he couldn't have seen it. I did not tell him at the moment which window to look out of."*

Zamora went back to his car and contacted the Sheriff's office by radio and watched the object still moving away swiftly, without flame, travelling over the ground, showing no smoke trail. It cleared Box Canyon or Six Mile Canyon Mountain and then disappeared over the mountain.

Visits the scene – marks in the ground made by four legs?

> *"I went down to where the object had been and found, the brush was burning in several places. I heard Sgt. Chavez (N.M. State Police at Socorro) calling me on the radio for my location, and I returned to my car, and told him he was looking at me. Sgt. Chavez asked me what the trouble was, because I was sweating and he remarked on how very pale I appeared. I asked him to look at the burning brush. Sgt. Chavez and I made our way to the site and Sgt. Chavez pointed out the tracks. When I first saw the object (which I had first taken to be a car) I saw what appeared to be four*

legs of some type from the object to the ground. At the time, I didn't pay much attention to what it was. Thinking it may have been an accident, I hadn't paid any attention to the bottom of the object, slanted outwards to the ground.

The object might have been about three and a half feet from the ground at that time. I just glanced at it. Can't tell how long it was that I saw the object the second time – possibly 20 seconds – just a guess from the time I got out of the car, glanced at object, ran from object, jumped over edge of hill, then got back to car and radio as object disappeared.

When my radio microphone fell as I got out of car, at scene area, I heard about two or three loud 'thumps', like someone possibly hammering or shutting a door, or doors, hard. These 'thumps' were possibly a second or less apart. This was just before the roar. The persons were not seen when I drove to the location. Just before Sgt. Chavez arrived I got my pen and drew a picture of the insignia on the object."

Physical traces left behind

Some physical trace evidence left behind – burned vegetation and soil, ground landing impressions, and metal scrapings on a broken rock in one of the impressions – were subsequently recovered and analysed by investigators for the military, law enforcement, and civilian UFO groups. The event and its body of evidence are sometimes deemed one of the best documented, yet most perplexing, UFO reports. It was immediately investigated by the US Army, US Air Force, and FBI, and received considerable coverage in the mass media. It was one of the cases that helped persuade astronomer J. Allen Hynek – one of the primary investigators for the Air Force – that some UFO reports represented an intriguing mystery. After extensive investigation, the Air Force's Project Blue Book was unable to come up with a conventional explanation and listed the case as an 'unknown'.

Since the officer passed away on 9th November 2009, there have been allegations made that he was the subject of a hoax – and the object, some form of experimental craft being tested – which appears very unlikely.

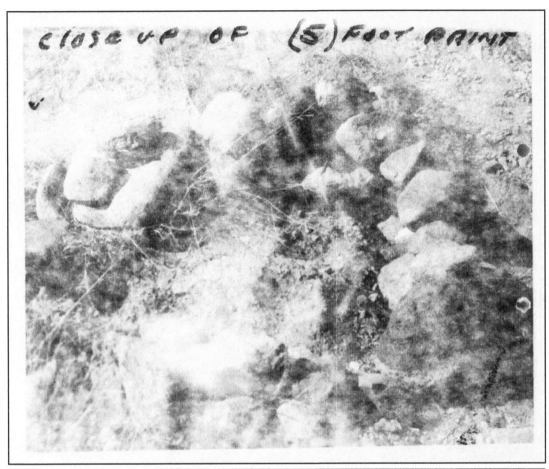

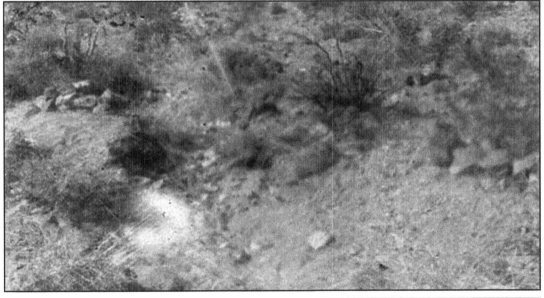

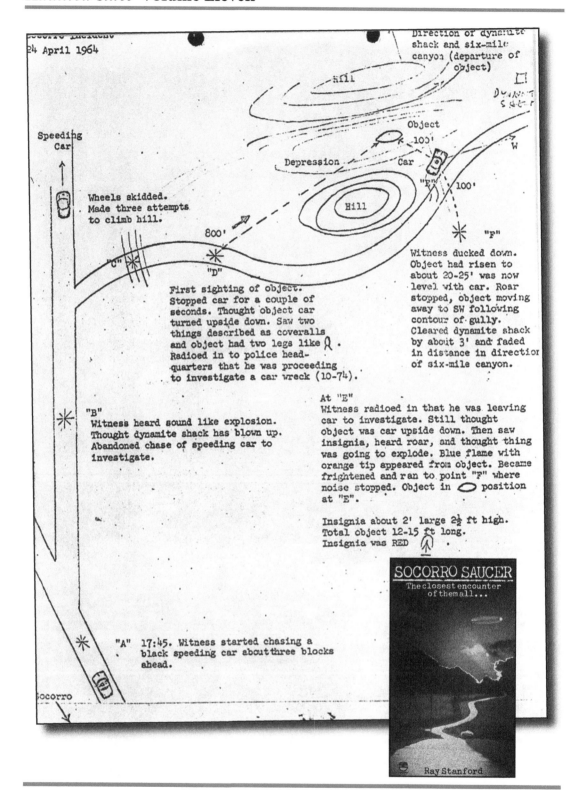

Socorro Incident
24 April 1964

Direction of dynamite
shack and six-mile
canyon (departure of
object)

Hill

Object
~100'

W

Speeding
Car

Depression

Car

"E"   100'

Wheels skidded.
Made three attempts
to climb hill.

Hill

"F"

800'

Witness ducked down.
Object had risen to
about 20-25' was now
level with car. Roar
stopped, object moving
away to SW following
contour of gully.
Cleared dynamite shack
by about 3' and faded
in distance in direction
of six-mile canyon.

"C"

"D"

First sighting of object.
Stopped car for a couple of
seconds. Thought object car
turned upside down. Saw two
things described as coveralls
and object had two legs like Ω.
Radioed in to police headquarters that he was proceeding
to investigate a car wreck (10-74).

At "E"
Witness radioed in that he was leaving
car to investigate. Still thought
object was car upside down. Then saw
insignia, heard roar, and thought thing
was going to explode. Blue flame with
orange tip appeared from object. Became
frightened and ran to point "F" where
noise stopped. Object in ⬭ position
at "E".

"B"
Witness heard sound like explosion.
Thought dynamite shack has blown up.
Abandoned chase of speeding car to
investigate.

Insignia about 2' large 2½ ft high.
Total object 12-15 ft long.
Insignia was RED

"A" 17:45. Witness started chasing a
black speeding car about three blocks
ahead.

Socorro

SOCORRO SAUCER
The closest encounter
of them all...

Ray Stanford

DECLASSIFIED
Authority NND 923.057

4/28

Defensor & Chieftain

PRICE 10c

d Since 1540 — Home of the Famed New Mexico Institute of Mining & Technology

Published Tuesdays & Thursdays in Socorro, N. M. 87801   TUESDAY, APRIL 28, 1964

Of UFO Landing Here Observed

City Policeman Zamora Reports Sighting Egg-Shaped Object and Views Take-Off; Tourist Sees Craft Just Before Landing

★

Santa Fean Reports Seeing UFO Landed North of Espanola

An unidentified flying object was reported to have landed and taken off near La Madera, north of Espanola, two days following the stop of a UFO in Socorro.

The evidence that Orlando Gallegos of Santa Fe reported was similar to that found in Socorro. He and his family went to visit his father, just north of La Madera, arriving about 12:30 a.m. Sunday.

Gallegos later told State Police he saw the object sitting on the ground in a gravel area when he went outside to chase away horses. He did not approach closer than 200 feet. He noticed a

(Continued on Page 4)

What appears to be substantial evidence of an unidentified flying object landing and taking off in Socorro has been observed.

City Policeman Lonnie Zamora, a highly reliable source, saw a four-legged, egg-shaped object, and two persons in a gully a mile south of the courthouse shortly before 6 p.m. Friday. He saw the object rise straight up and take off, and disappear beyond Six-Mile Canyon to the west. Some of the evidence of the landing and take-off remained in the gully. There were four shallow holes where the object apparently landed on its legs; there were burned greasewood and seared clumps of green grass; there were two round, very slight depressions. No footprints were found.

Zamora said he saw lettering on the side of the UFO, and he sketched the lettering on a paper sack after the object had taken off. He did not believe the lettering was in English and he observed no numerals as there are on known aircraft. Zamora said he was not at liberty to further describe the lettering.

Where UFO Landed in Socorro: State Police Sgt. Sam Chavez and Lewis A. Reddell, publisher of El Defensor-Chieftain, stand at one of the stone-circled depressions (arrow) made by a leg of an unidentified flying object which landed in a gully a mile from the courthouse last Friday. The arrow in left foreground points to another depression made by a leg. Near the center foreground are burned greasewood and clumps of grass. The person at the left also looks over the scene, which had not been trampled by the curious Saturday morning when his photo was taken.

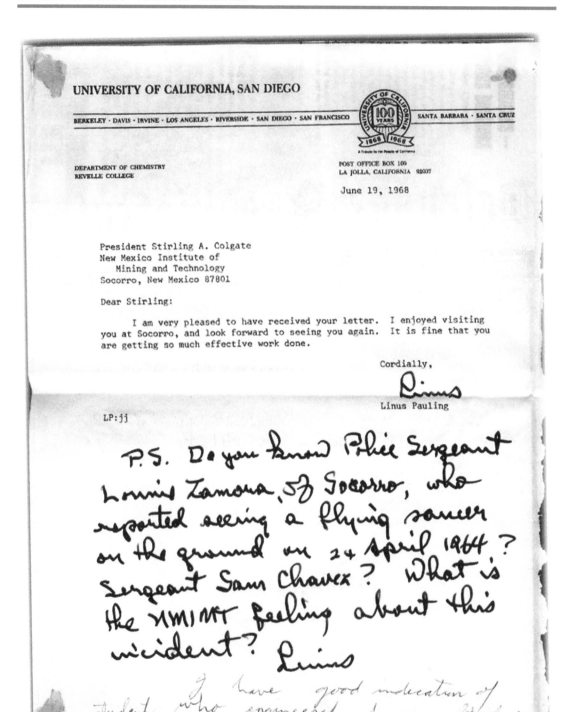

UNIVERSITY OF CALIFORNIA, SAN DIEGO

BERKELEY · DAVIS · IRVINE · LOS ANGELES · RIVERSIDE · SAN DIEGO · SAN FRANCISCO   SANTA BARBARA · SANTA CRUZ

DEPARTMENT OF CHEMISTRY
REVELLE COLLEGE

POST OFFICE BOX 109
LA JOLLA, CALIFORNIA 92037

June 19, 1968

President Stirling A. Colgate
New Mexico Institute of
    Mining and Technology
Socorro, New Mexico 87801

Dear Stirling:

    I am very pleased to have received your letter. I enjoyed visiting
you at Socorro, and look forward to seeing you again. It is fine that you
are getting so much effective work done.

                                          Cordially,

                                          Linus Pauling

LP:jj

P.S. Do you know Police Sergeant Lonnie Zamora, of Socorro, who reported seeing a flying saucer on the ground on 24 April 1964? Sergeant Sam Chavez? What is the NMIMT feeling about this incident? Linus

student who have good indication of engineered hoax. Student has left — cheers Linus

24th April 1964 (USA) – Close encounter with humanoids

Mr Gary T. Wilcox (27) who had spent three years in the Army – stationed in Germany as a sergeant in the Engineers, with an honorable discharge – was working on the family business 300 acre dairy farm in Davis Hollow Road, a few miles north-east of Newark Valley, Tioga County. He was spreading manure during the morning of the incident. Shortly before 10am, he decided to check out a field on a part of the farm which was surrounded by woods, in order to see if the ground conditions would allow ploughing.

Shiny object in the field

As he approached the field, about mile from the dairy barn, he saw a shiny object that he first took to be a discarded refrigerator. As he approached closer, he realised this was not the case and speculated whether it was the wing tank which had fallen from an aircraft. He came up to the object and later said:

> "It was shiny and looked like aluminum. It was about 20ft long, some 16ft wide, and shaped like an egg. I touched it but felt no heat. I couldn't see any doors or opening in it".

Two 'beings' appear from Mars!

> "Suddenly two human-like men appeared. They were about 4ft tall, and wore clothing that appeared not to have any seams, and were wearing what looked like a headdress with a full face hood; they had arms and legs but I can't say whether they had feet or toes. One of them said, in English, 'Do not be alarmed, we have talked to people before. We are from what you people refer to as planet Mars'."

PAUSE IN WORK — Gary T. Wilcox, 28, of Davis Hollow Road, Newark Valley, works in the barn on his 300-acre farm unperturbed by interest he roused with a report of talking April 24 with two Martians who, he said, landed in a spacecraft at a secluded spot a mile from his barn.

Was it a joke being played?

Gary's first reaction was to wonder if someone was playing a joke on him. Their voices seemed to come from their bodies, rather than the headdress covered heads. They expressed an interest in organic material, such as fertiliser, and why he was spreading it around the farm.

Gary:

> "The 'Martians' told me they grew food in the atmosphere but changes in the Universe were expected to create problems. They said they were visiting Earth to obtain information about organic material. They carried a tray filled with soil, and talked about space on their ship. I had difficulty in

understanding their explanations, but I do remember them telling me that they said they can only travel to the planet every two years and are presently using the western hemisphere, and expressed surprise that I had seen their craft. The two 'beings' said that astronauts from Earth would not be successful in space travel and would die after a year in space, because their bodies are not adaptable to such conditions."

They asked him if he had any organic material and he went to get a bag of fertiliser. As he did so the 'craft' took-off, making a noise like a car idling. There was no turbulence exhaust of fire or raising dust; seconds later, it was out of sight. Gary went to the barn and picked-up a bag of fertilizer, which he took to the spot in the field where the incident had happened, and left it there. The next morning it had gone.

Miss Priscilla Baldwin

This incident was brought to the attention of his mother, who treated it as a joke, but neighbour, Miss Priscilla Baldwin – a radar technician, during World War II – became interested.

"I was in the Air Force for three years and my career field was Aircraft Control and Warning. In my work I plotted UFO blips, as they were called at the time, on the radar screen in the control centre. Many times blips were not identified. The speed in most cases was unbelievable. However, I don't know if any of that was ever the reason for my interest or not, but I do believe it had a lot to do with it."

She sat with Gary on 28th April and took detailed notes of his experience.

On 29th April, she accompanied Gary to the site of the encounter – pictures were taken and rocks and leaves collected where the red dust had accumulated. (Recent rain had eliminated any evidence of dust.)

Sherriff George Williams

Miss Baldwin then contacted the Tioga County Sheriffs Department and Officer George Williams carried out an investigation on the 29th April and 1st May 1964. Since Wilcox did not want to interrupt his chores, Miss Baldwin took Officer George Williams up to the field where the encounter had occurred and was shown the location of where the red dust had been and bag of fertiliser left. Because of recent rain there was no evidence of any red dust. On 1st May, when they came back to the barn, Officer Williams asked Wilcox if he would be willing to attend Owego that evening to make a formal statement. He agreed and subsequently went to Owego, at 7pm. When Miss Baldwin stated that she had taken notes of her conversations with Wilcox, Officer Williams asked if he could borrow them. She gave these to the officer. On 7th May, she travelled to the Sheriff's Office and these notes were returned to her.

Officer Williams did note what he felt was a discrepancy in the account. Wilcox had driven to the site on the afternoon of 24th April with his tractor, to drop off a bag of fertiliser. On 29th April, he drove up to the same spot with his tractor, accompanied by Miss Priscilla Baldwin. Williams could not find a second set of tractor tyre marks when he came to the site with Baldwin, and Williams could not understand this. He also did not investigate for any depressions in the ground as evidence of the visitors taking earth samples. This piece of information was not conveyed to him at the time of his onsite examination, for some reason. Williams did give an assessment of Wilcox's character:

"He admitted that he drank a little but he was not drinking at the time of this reported incident. He also stated that he had some marital difficulty, but this did not encourage him to drink any more than he had been accustomed. This man does not appear to be unstable or mentally disturbed in any way. He is a hard worker. The complainant in this case says that she has no reason to doubt him."

Police report filed for investigation

After the police report was completed, Sheriff Taylor contacted the FBI office in Binghamton New York and the Boston, Massachusetts, Atlantic Coast Air Command. The Binghamton FBI office then contacted their superiors in Albany, who consequently contacted the Air Force. Although Hancock Air Force Base, Syracuse, claimed that the case was under investigation, Wilcox claims that the USAF never contacted him. Wilcox also claimed that officials from the Space Guidance Centre, in Owego, had paid a visit to the farm.

According to Mr Wilcox

FBI, or federal agents of some kind, visited the Sheriff's Office, and pointed out certain items in the story that should not be divulged. These items might alarm the public!

Gary also claimed that the Civil Defense checked a soil sample from the site for radioactivity. He received a letter, later, stating that the sample gave a reading of 1.5 roentgens with the plug out and 2.5 roentgens with the plug in. The reading should have been zero, with a reading of 3.5 roentgens considered contamination level. This statement has never been independently confirmed.

First newspaper reports

The first newspaper report came from the *Binghamton Press* and the *Owego Times*, dated 8th May 1964. The general viewpoint was one of disbelief, but also that the source of the story – Gary Wilcox – was someone of exceptional reliability.

Newark Valley's own newspaper, the *Tioga County Herald*, did not report the story until 15th May. The paper was run by a husband and wife team – Justine F. Brandes (editor) and Leon G. Brandes (publisher). Justine first became aware of the story from talk circulating in the local village. Her first reaction was to investigate, but thought she should ask the advice of a more experienced newspaper man. When they did publish the article she expressed great dismay over missing what was probably then the biggest scoop in the newspaper's history.

Examined by a psychiatrist

In 1968, *Dr. Berthold Eric Schwarz (who passed away on 6th October 2010) was then the Assistant Attending Psychiatrist at the Montclair Community Hospital in Montclair, New Jersey. He first learned about Wilcox's encounter with alien beings while studying a variety of UFO sightings that had occurred in Towanda, Pennsylvania.

On 18th October 1968, Gary Wilcox was psychiatrically examined in his home. His wife was interviewed as well. He also spoke to Wilcox's two brothers, Floyd and Barry, his mother, and Sheriff Paul J. Taylor. Another interesting contact was Vic Kobylarz – a neighbouring farmer and steelworker. Vic was a relative by marriage to Mrs Theresa Krajewski, who happened to be a friend of Dr. Schwarz. Vic spoke with Wilcox shortly after the UFO event.

---

*The sad news just reached us via Brent Raynes, author of Edge of Reality (Inner Light Publications).

Brent says: *"The passing of a true giant in the paranormal field. It is with genuine and deep regret and sadness that I must report the passing of a long-time and dear friend and colleague, Dr. Berthold Eric Schwarz, 85, of Vero Beach, Florida.*

Dr. Schwarz, a true giant in the field of ufology and parapsychology, passed away on Thursday, September 16. Born on October 20, 1924, in Jersey City, New Jersey, he engaged in private practice as a psychiatrist for nearly 25 years in Montclair, New Jersey, and then after moving to Vero Beach in 1982 continued for slightly over 20 more years. He leaves behind a grieving and loving wife of 55 years, named Ardis, and a son and daughter, Eric Schwarz and Lisa Ericson, as well as one granddaughter named Kristi In the fields of ufology and parapsychology, Dr. Schwarz had many friends. For this magazine he wrote many articles and put us in touch with many intriguing personalities, many of whom we interviewed for this publication."

According to his brother, Floyd, Wilcox had turned down a considerable sum of money from a leading national magazine for the publication rights to his story – this in spite of Gary not being especially affluent. He also refused payments for lectures of his experience.

Dr. Schwarz was extremely impressed with Wilcox's obvious background and evidence of stability, integrity, honesty, and intelligence.

(Sources: *Binghampton*, **New York Newspaper, 9.5.1964 – 'A Dairy Farmer's report of talking with two Martians who landed in one of his fields in a spacecraft has Tioga County aroused with curiosity'/***Syracuse Herald-Journal*)

Note: Wilcox did not learn about the Socorro landing, New Mexico, until 11th May, when Wilcox's father brought a newspaper clipping, describing the event.

Dr. Berthold Eric Schwarz

24th April 1964 (USA) – Red object seen

Over North Platte, Nebraska, a red object trailing what looked like *'lines'* was seen heading through the sky towards the north east by a 12-year-old boy and his friend, who were looking through a telescope when they saw the object. Explanation: Believed to have been a comet or meteor. (**Source: Project Blue Book,**)

[If this was the case then why did it return along the path taken 15 minutes later?]

26th April 1964 (USA) – Landed UFO?

At 1.30am, a ranger's son at Espanola, New Mexico, observed an object emitting flames and noise. His father sent him back to bed. The next morning, father and son went to have a look and discovered the grass was still smouldering and there were footprints nearby. The State Police and Kirtland Air Force Base were notified. It was claimed that there were similarities with the prints found at Socorro on the 25th April. Whether this deduction was made following the arrival of Air Force personnel from Kirtland is, of course, conjecture.

Landed UFO at La Madera

On the same night, according to The UFO Reporter, in its summer edition, we learn that Orlando Gallagos) (35) of Santa Fe, sighted an object similar to that involved in the Lonnie Zamora incident, at his father's home in La Madera.

Orlando was chasing away stray horses, at 12.30am, when he noticed an unusual *'craft'* on the ground in a gravel area, some 200ft away. He described it as being *"the length of a telephone pole, about 14ft in diameter; rings of blue flame came from jets underneath it"*. He tried to persuade his family to come outside and see it, but they were too frightened. The next morning a check of the locality revealed some disturbance.

Police attended – depressions found

State Police Officer Martin Vigil attended, and found that rocks within the centre of a charred area were cracked and a nearby bottle melted. Four depressions and unusual paw prints, resembling those of a mountain lion were seen. Explanation: Fire in dump. (**Source:** *Albuquerque Journal* **28.4.1964**)

28th April 1964 (USA) – Burned by UFO

At noon, Albuquerque, New Mexico children – Sharon Stull (10) and Robin Stull (8) – sighted an egg-shaped object, hovering near the Lowell Elementary School for about 10 minutes. Robin refused to look at the object and ran off. The object bounced up and down about three times in the sky and then left. Later, Sharon was treated for *'infra-red'* burns on her face. According to Police Lt. C. K. Jolly, the physician said he believed Sharon saw something and it had burned her. (**Source: Dan Wilson**)

Minot Air Force Base, North Dakota (USA) – Tracked on radar

An object was sighted by a civilian pilot, about 50 miles south of Minot Air Force Base, at 8.50pm. Ground radar then picked-up the object, which appeared as a light 3,000ft below the aircraft, flying at 7,000ft and apparently following the aircraft. Minot Air Force Base Ground Control reported a scope indication of an object at 160°, bearing 15 miles, moving outbound at approximately 25 miles from the station, orbiting in a five mile circle. The object then proceeded inbound to the station to approx 15 miles and disappeared from the scope. (**Source: Dan Wilson, Brad Sparks,** *McDonald List*)

29th April 1964 (USA) – Egg-shaped UFO lands

A group of teenagers claimed they had seen a glowing, egg-shaped, object land at night-time over Canyon Ferry, Montana. An examination of the area revealed four shallow holes, 13ft apart, forming an imperfect square. In the centre was a round mark, about 3ft in diameter, where the grass and prickly pear cactus was lightly scorched. (**Source: Project Blue Book**)

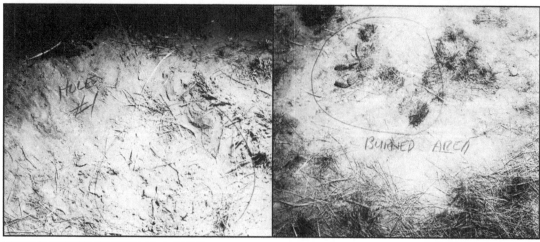

29th April 1964 (UK) – UFOs sighted over Warwickshire

Stephen T.K. Gingele wrote to Bill Dillon about a UFO sighting, which took place at 9.25pm.

55, Chadwick Road,
Falcon Lodge,
Sutton Coldfield.
Warwickshire.
2 May 1964.

Dear Mr. Dillon,

Thank you very much for sending me the Aerial Research Centre Newsletters, which I have found most interesting.

On 29 April 1964 I saw some strange objects in the sky, some of which resembled satellites, but I am convinced that they were not, as will be seen from my reports. I telephoned Mr. P. Davies on Thursday 30 April 1964, about the objects, and he told me to send full details to you.

Well, at 9.25 p.m. on 29 April 1964, after making my Variable Star observations, I noticed low in the western sky, about 20° above the horizon a fusiform shaped object, silver in colour, which travelled in a South East to North West direction. I asked my brother to keep an eye on it while I went into the house to get my telescope. When I returned I noticed that the object had stopped. I observed it

through my telescope, but because the object had been going away from me, it appeared only as a bright orange star with a glow around it. This may not have been the case however, because the object may have changed shape, but it was quite difficult to say. The object could be seen through my telescope for about 30 secs, before it mysteriously disappeared. The whole observation lasted three minutes, and observing conditions were excellent.

Two minutes later, at 9.30 p.m. I noticed another object similar to a satellite, which may have come from the part of the horizon where the other object had disappeared. Its course however, was somewhat irregular, varying from 30° above the horizon to 20° above the horizon. From when I saw the object till it disappeared, its course was in a North East to South West direction. Its colour was orange-yellow. The object could be seen for about three minutes.

The following is a rough diagram of the directions of the first and the second objects that I saw:

N.E-S.W.

30° Above horizon .... OBJECT II

OBJECT I
S.E. – N.W
DIRECTION

20° Above Horizon

DISAPPEARED
HERE

WEST HORIZON

As I was going in to tell my father what I saw, I noticed at 9.37 p.m. in the north sky, about 60° above the horizon an object that resembled a satellite, moving very fast in a North West to South West direction. At got to about 30° above the horizon it disappeared. This was probably due to it entering the Earth's shadow. The object was blue in colour, about as bright as a second magnitude star, and could be seen about 25 to 30 secs.

When I told my father that I had seen three satellite looking objects about every five minutes he became interested and decided to come out. Then at 9.44 p.m. we noticed the same or another object to the one which I had seen 7 mins earlier. It was identical to the other one, travelled

in the same direction, was the same colour and disappeared at 30° above the horizon. It could be seen for about 25 to 30 secs.

It was these two objects that puzzled me, because I have never known two satellites to travell in exactly the same direction and to be identical, and especially at an interval of only seven minutes.

As far as I know there was only one satellite that could be visible that evening. Echo II. & which is of a yellow colour and travells in a south to north direction. Therefore none of the objects could have been that satellite. I have in fact seen that satellite on many occasions.

I would be very grateful if you would write and tell me of some of your U.F.O. experiences.

Hoping to Hear from you soon,

Stephen T.K. Gingele

29th April 1964 (UK) – Shimmering *'disc'* seen

Local science teacher Patrick I. Kelly, of Testwood School, Southampton, was contacted by pupil David Lawrence, who told him that while watching a game of football on the 29th April 1964, he heard a woman asking her husband: *"What's that?"*, pointing upwards into the sky. Her husband replied, *"It's a cloud."*

David:

> *"I looked up and saw a small grey coloured regular cloud, moving across the sky. It was shaped like a 'disc' and shimmering. It then tilted and moved, increasing in brightness, until lost from view."*

30th April 1964 (USA) – UFO seen on the side of a hill

Motorist Gloria Biggs, her husband, and mother – Lorene Ayres, from Fontana, California, reported having sighted an object on a hilltop just off Highway 91, some 10 miles west of Baker, California – described as being smooth, brown and dome-shaped – which promptly vanished from view.

It is said that an examination of the area later revealed a large depression left in the ground.

(Source: *Salt Lake Tribune*, 30.4.1964)

UFO sighted

Mr and Mrs James Pace, accompanied by their two children – Suzanne and Michael – along with their neighbours – Mr and Mrs Robert Cameron, and their son, Kevin – were on the front lawn of the house at Green Rivers, Wyoming, when they saw an object in the sky. Through binoculars it resembled a shining round light, standing on edge like a silver dollar, very high in the sky. It hovered for half an hour, before being obscured by clouds.

Mrs Pace:

> *"The day before, when the kids were talking about 'flying saucers', I thought they were just making it up. I then read in the* Desert News *of reported 'saucer' sightings. I started questioning the children a little closer. I found out that children in the neighborhood and those attending Roosevelt Elementary School had reported seeing UFOs on Thursday evening."*

(Sources: James D. Wardle, Salt Lake UFO Council/*Salt Lake Tribune*, 1.5.1964/*Desert News*, 2.5.1964)

'Flying saucer' captured!

On this day, the news media was buzzing with rumours of a *'flying saucer'* having been captured and stored in a hanger at Holloman Air Force Base. Coral Lorenzen – author of the *Great Flying Saucer Hoax* and Director of the Aerial Phenomena Research Association (APRO) – telephoned Terry Clarke of KALG Radio, in Alamogordo (nine miles east of Holloman). He told Coral that he had been monitoring the range communication on that day, when he had picked up the following from a lone B-57 Bomber, flying a routine mission in the vicinity of Stallion Site, a few miles east of San Antonio, Northern Mexico: *"I've got a UFO."* The controller asked him: *"What does it look like?"* The pilot: *"It's egg-shaped and white."*

Minutes later, the pilot contacted the controller and said, *"It's on the ground."*

At this stage, photo crews were instructed to standby, just before radio communications ceased, and a security clamp down began. Coral was unable to establish what had occurred, but she did learn of a report by a security guard on the range, the same night, who spoke of seeing a UFO on the ground.

(Source: Coral Lorenzen, *Fate Magazine*, October 1964)

'Strange Fate'

In Frank Edward's book – *Strange Fate* – we read of the same account submitted by Carol Lorenzen, on page 140, except that it contains an additional three words, which may be judged as being of some importance… *"I'm not alone up here."*

The controller asks him: *"What does it look like?"*

The pilot: *"It's egg-shaped and white."*

The controller asks him: *"Any markings?"*

The pilot: *"Same as Socorro – I'm going to make another pass."*

This is followed by: *"It's on the ground."*

Strangers from the Skies by Brad Steiger also contains the account on page 71, which is identical, apart from the reference to Socorro. One then presumes this was perhaps wishful thinking by someone, although it would not have been Coral – that much we are sure.

1st May 1964 (USA) – Three objects seen

At 12.23am, a married couple from St. Louis, Missouri, reported seeing:

> *"…a scintillating object, showing rays brighter than a star, in the westwards direction, shining through treetops; it appeared to be 25ft off the ground. It faded as it moved west and was gone, an hour later. Another object was also seen resembling car headlamps."*

Explanation: Likely to be Venus and Jupiter. (**Source: Project Blue Book**)

North Carver, Massachusetts

At 1am, objects – described as consisting of a formation of three revolving beacons (red, blue and green) accompanied by three smaller ones trailing behind, similar to the larger formation – were reported south-west of Carver, at a height of about 5-6,000ft, by a local resident.

At 1.20am, following a call to the nearby airbase, a Homey 68 aircraft from Otis Air Force Base was instructed to look over the area, but failed to sight anything unusual. The witness on the ground confirmed the UFO was still there, with a second one due west of his position. Boston Search Control was contacted. They telephoned the local police, who attended at the scene and confirmed a visual but were unable to identify the objects. At 2.25am, the witness contacted the authorities to say there was now a third object – again confirmed by the police. As fog came down, a few hours later, the objects were lost from view. Explanation: Stars. (**Source: Project Blue Book**)

3rd May 1964 (Australia) – Glowing objects seen

At 6.5am over Canberra, New South Wales, a large glowing white object was seen in the sky, heading towards the north-east, in a wobbling movement – as if out of control. Next to it was a smaller object, showing a faint red light. At one stage both objects appeared to collide and bounce off each other.

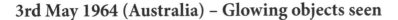

4th May 1964 (USA) – Bright spinning light seen

A bright light, described as the length of a plane, was seen moving through the sky, by twelve observers, at a speed of about 150mph, over Rolling Meadows Des Plaines, Illinois, at a height judged lower than a conventional aircraft. The illuminated object, heading in an east to south-west direction, was seen to revolve in flight for 10 seconds, before fading away four minutes later. (**Source: Project Blue Book**)

5th May 1964 (USA) – Marine flare or UFO?

Boise TV Stations were contacted by people reporting a bright red-orange UFO, seen moving slowly across the sky. This was later explained away as being a 20,000 candle power marine flare, launched in the sky on a 12ft parachute by a man over the Seamans Gulch area of the town. The man concerned later contacted Dwight Jensen, at *KB01-TV News*, to admit responsibility. It appears that this incident took place around 4.50am and that people had contacted the Sheriff's office at Boise, Idaho (who contacted Mountain Home Air Force Base), reporting seeing two large red *'balls of light'* in the sky – which appeared to be landing rather than falling – with flames shooting downwards. It appears a search was planned of the locality, the next morning, by Strategic Air Command Officers, although the results were no doubt not made available to the public, who had accepted the *'marine flare explanation'* – which, of course, it may well have been for all we know. (**Source: Project Blue Book**)

Cigar-shaped and 'diamond' object seen

On the same date, at 1.20am, UFO sightings took place over Houston Street, Savannah, Georgia, involving reports of an:

> *"...object resembling a silver dollar, showing four to five windows, with what looked like landing lights, moving at a speed of about 80mph."*

This was seen heading northwards, at a 45° elevation. Others living in Forsyth Park, Savannah, told of seeing a large bright centre light, with four to five smaller lights, in diamond formation, at 1.40am This one was seen heading silently across the sky, at 130mph, towards the south-west.

Interestingly an additional light was reported in the locality, veering south-east.

6th May 1964 (USA) – Aircraft debris found

On this date the owner of an Ohio farm, situated in Yellow Springs, contacted the USAF reporting that one of her employees had found two pieces of 4ft x 5ft green and yellow aluminium plate. This was discovered to be part of a crashed B-57, although the file contains no information as to the circumstances in which this aircraft came down and when. (**Source: Project Blue Book**)

7th May 1964 (UK) – *'Headlamp'* UFO

An object resembling a bright *'headlamp'*, with what looked like a single light on its side, was seen in the sky over Warden Hill, Luton, Bedfordshire, at 10pm, by members of the Payne family. They told of seeing it, *"swinging like a pendulum and apparently rotating in the sky, constantly dimming and becoming bright. When it appeared, a strong wind blew up."* (**Source: Aerial Research Centre, Luton**)

9th May 1964 (UK) – Oblong pattern across the sky

Somerset resident – Mr N.C. Toogood – was watching the sunset from his bedroom window.

> *"It was a clear night, and there were no stars visible. All of a sudden, a single white 'light' appeared high in the sky towards the south. After observing the 'light' for a minute, I realised it was slowly moving in an oblong pattern over the sky. Intrigued I picked up a telescope and noticed it wasn't wide at all, but long and very narrow – like an 'edge-on' disc, both points being bright red, with a yellow centre. It then vanished, but reappeared, 15 minutes later, heading slowly northwards, until lost from view."*

(Source: Isle of Wight UFO Society)

On the same day from Pascoe Vale, Victoria, Australia, was an account of two moving yellow lights seen moving around each other as they crossed the sky.

9th May 1964 (USA) – Daylight sighting of three large crescent-shaped objects

At 11.23pm, three objects were sighted over Chicago, Illinois, by an amateur astronomer, who wrote about the matter to Wright Patterson Air Force Base. The man concerned said he saw:

> *"...three light-green, large crescents, for a few seconds, travelling at high speed in an east to west direction, 40° off the horizon, south of where the Leo Constellation would be. Each object was about half the diameter of the moon, brightness third magnitude (dim but large), oscillating in size and colour slightly nebulous. The objects held a tight formation."*

(Source: Project Blue Book)

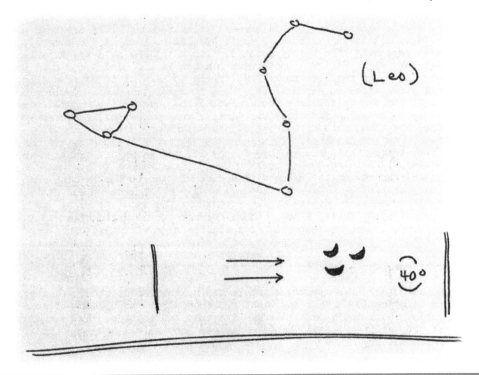

DEARBORN OBSERVATORY
NORTHWESTERN UNIVERSITY
EVANSTON, ILLINOIS 60201
16 November 1964

Major Hector Quintanilla
Foreign Technology Division
Box 9494
Wright Patterson Air Force Base
Dayton, Ohio

Dear Major:

As you see from the enclosed copy of the letter to Mr. ████ (case of 9 May 1964), I think it is quite likely that he saw after-images. I had quite a long talk with him on the phone, and he was most cooperative. He seemed to be quite impressed by the fact that we were interested in his case and said that he was honored that we were spending any time on it at all.

His story was still very much the same as he gave in the original report. Here are some of the highlights of our conversation:

He was most impressed by the oscillating motion of the crescents; he said it was "most fearsome," and he was both trembling and perspiring when it was over. I asked him to re-enact the time sequence and check it with his watch, and when he did so, he indicated the whole duration was three to five seconds. His original report, I believe (although I don't have it at hand at the moment), said something like twenty seconds, didn't it? He said the experience was very vivid," like a photograph planted in his mind." He said that ever since he has been pondering, trying to hand it on to something, but still finds no explanation. When I asked him what he would put up in the sky to simulate the situation, he said he'd put three moons as seen through a fog as he was particularly impressed by the motion the object had both across his line of sight and yet seeming to vanish in the distance. This seems to me very characteristic of an after-image: the more you try to see it, the faster it dashes away.

He said he was on the phone within five minutes to the Tribune and the Planetarium and sent a telegram to Sky and Telescope and, I believe, he also said to Wright-Patterson. He said the night was exceptionally clear, "one of those once or twice a year nights." So any question of searchlights against a high cirrus is out. He is convinced they were objects, and fearsome ones. The edges were fuzzy, and the whole objects were apparently of third magnitude. His eyes were dark-adapted.

He said they have mercury lights in the neighborhood, and another possible explanation is that he saw light reflected from the bottoms of some birds, but I don't particularly like that explanation. He said that as soon as it happened, he "immediately knew he had seen something extraordinary."

When he told me, however, that just before that he had been looking
at the setting dials of his telescope, illuminating them with a red
light, it seemed that we might have the explanation there, as you see
I have indicated in my letter to him.

So, all in all, the fuzzy edges, the greenish tinge, the faintness
of the object, the peculiar motion, and the fact that even looking at
a red light just before adds up, it seems to me, to the likelihood
that this was a subjective experience. Perhaps, he had been bending
over and suddenly straightened up. Anyway, I don't think we should
chalk this up to anything really out of the ordinary, and unless he
comes back with a very sharp and cogent denial, I think we might well
evaluate this as a subjective experience, possibly after-images
caused by watching a red light.

I'm working on the Altas, Mt. Vernon, and the ▮▮▮▮▮▮cases. I haven't
been able to locate the Northwestern student as yet. One final thing in the
▮▮▮▮case, it was he himself who brought up the suggestion that it might
have been caused by the red light. Usually when the witness brings up a
suggestion like that, it often means the he's pretty convinced himself
that that is what it was.

                    Sincerely,

                    [signature]

                    J. Allen Hynek

JAH:krf
enclosures

9th May 1964 (USA) – Three red lights seen

A boy (aged 14) from Huntsville, Alabama, was out during the late evening, when he saw three sharply outlined red objects moving behind cloud, similar to landing lights of an aircraft, about half a mile away. The illustration provided shows three lights, forming a triangle, heading westwards.

The witness writes of observing the lights moving over and, fetching a pair of binoculars, he saw:

> "...three round shapes, moving towards a cigar rocket-shaped thing, which intercepted the red lights. The cigar-shaped thing then shot upwards."

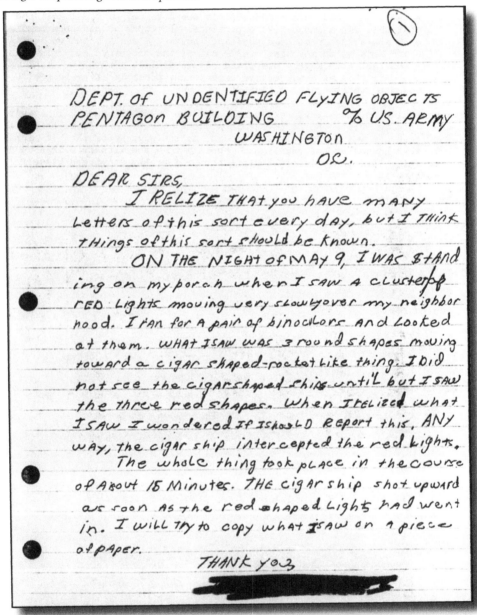

Explanation: Data presented conflicts with data presented in letter, confusing reports – possible a/c sighting, possible balloon observation, and almost anything else. (**Source: Project Blue Book**)

UFO display

During the evening there were multiple reports of lights and objects seen in the sky over Ashville School for boys, Ashville, North Carolina. Explanation: *"Imagination of the observers as adding to the misinterpretation of conventional objects, such as a/c and various stars/planets, the most prominent of which was Venus magnitude -4.2"*

(**Source: Project Blue Book**)

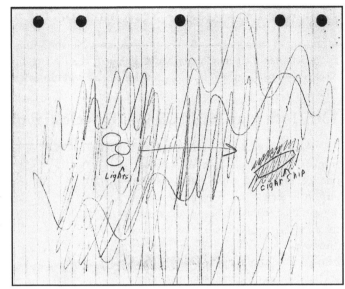

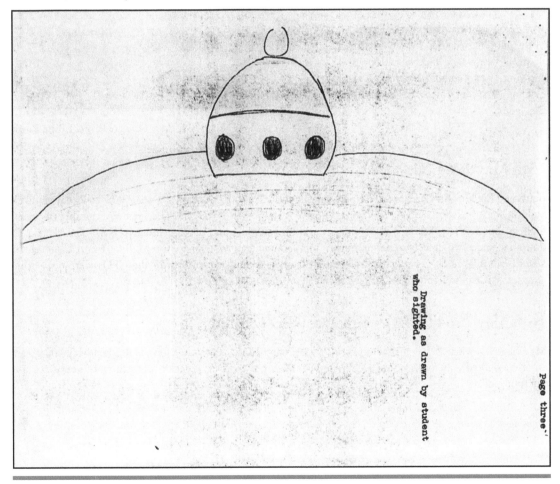

Drawing as drawn by student who sighted.

Page three

12th May 1964 (USA) – Searching for *'the monster'*

A number of farmers around the Smithfield area, North Carolina, began a search for what became known as *'the monster'* – a person described as being 7ft tall, leaving long footprints. This took place following the discovery of two pigs, a goat, and a cow, killed and partially eaten. (**Source:** *Evening Standard,* **13.5.1964**)

13th/14th May 1964 (USA) – Tri-celestial phenomena

An Apollo spacecraft was launched from White Sands, at 1pm. As dusk fell, one red, green and yellow light – like an airport beacon – was seen in the sky at 40° elevation to the left, below Venus, over the west edge of Carlsbad, New Mexico. They were last seen just above the horizon below and to the left of the 'Big Dipper' and kept under observation for two hours and fifty minutes.

At 2.25am unusual lights were also seen by the pilots of two aircraft, who described them as being pale blue in colour and showing *"a photo strobe-like light, north-east of Newman, Texas"*. Explanation: Betelgeux

(**Source: Project Blue Book**)

15th May 1964 (USA) – UFO display

Between 11.30am and 12.15pm, surveillance radar at the Holloman Range, as well as FPS-16 Radar facility at Stallion Site, tracked two objects in the area north of Stallion Site. The UFOs performed a number of precise flight manoeuvres, including side by side separation rejoining and other manoeuvres. An observer on the ground sighted two objects as being, *"brown and football-shaped, flying at low altitude, before disappearing behind buildings at the instrumentation site."* It is alleged that one or both of the UFOs were responding alternately with the standard FAA recognition signal. (**Source: NICAP**)

16th May 1964 (USA) – Box car UFO sighted

Mr Mitchell – a truck driver previously with the Coast Guard – was travelling along Highway 40, at 2am, when he sighted – 30 miles east of Heber City – a navy-grey colored object circling the mountains at about ten thousand.

> *"The object appeared round and somewhat flat – the size of a railroad box car – its edges glowing as if covered with a phosphorous coating. It rose to a height of about 15,000ft and emitted a noise like a jet engine – the noise decreasing as it headed away."*

(**Source: Project Blue Book**)

17th May 1964 (UK) – UFO causes damage

A UFO, described as *"16ft in length, showing two aerials, and a flashing red light, making a buzzing noise"*, was seen hovering over the garden of a house in Kirkby, Liverpool, on the evening, before taking-off over nearby rooftops, by Mrs Margaret McCutcheon and her son, Robert Hirst (13) – then living in Mottram, Liverpool. We traced Robert and spoke to him about the incident – a matter which still provoked great curiosity up to his death, some years ago.

We were also contacted by a relative of Robert, in 2009, who told us that *"trees and bushes in the back garden were discovered burnt after the UFO had left"*.

(Source: Personal interview/*Daily Express*, 8.5.1966/ UFOs over Kirkby, John Parkinson)

Illustration of the UFO sighted on the 17th May, 1964, by Robert McCutcheon.

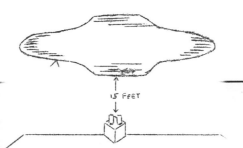

15 FEET

November – December 1964

Volume 10, No.6

Page 24

Flying Objects over Kirkby

From the Liverpool Echo, July 27: "Police checked reports of mysterious flying objects over the Kirkby Industrial Estate last night after a call from two watchmen. For three weeks 37-years-old John Parkinson and his mate Albert Sanderson have been keeping a careful check on the dazzling balls of light which they have seen hover above their hut in Lees Road and then flash across the sky.

"Nearly every night, say the men, they have watched the objects appear over the estate at about 11 p.m. and move around the sky at varying speeds, before they finally disappear in the early morning.

" 'We have told everyone including our family and friends, but they just laugh and shrug it off as though we had one over the eight,' said John of 7 Fern Grove, Princes Park.

" 'Last night there were six of these things, stopping and moving in the sky just as though they were being controlled. We coultn't stand it any longer and told the police so that they could see for themselves.'

"Mr. Sanderson also went to a nearby Birds Eye Food factory and told night security staff, who watched one of the objects moving down the length of Lees Road.

"The watchman and factory staff were not the only people to see the mysterious objects. Mr. Alan Cash of 6 Christowe Walk, Croxteth, with three friends, saw a strange light in the sky over East Lancashire Road, near Kirkby, about 11 p.m.

"During past weeks there have been numerous reports of unidentified flying objects sighted over the Merseyside area. Both the meteorological office at Liverpool Airport and Bidston Hill Obswevatory have received many calls from people claiming to have seen them.

"A police spokesman said that two men had been sent to the Lees Road area to investiga te, and so far as they could make out, while members of the public had definitely seen something, it was probably nothing more than a collection of ▓▓▓▓▓ bright stars."

Filed 28th Feb 65

Tipton, Indiana (USA)

At 10.15pm, citizens and police officers who were called to the scene (presumably following a report of a UFO) sighted a round, reddish object, hovering in the air; it then darted across the sky and appeared flattened while in motion.

UFO over Idaho

On the 17th/18th, an object was seen in the night sky over Grangeville, Idaho, for two nights in succession. Sheriff James Fuzzell was one of the witnesses.

> *"It looked like a street light but much bigger; there were people taking photographs of it. I looked through binoculars; it was oblong in shape and 8-10ft long. It moved back and forth and appeared to be near to Cottonwood Air Force Radar Station."*

Colonel Luif Zendegui – the Station Commander – was contacted. He confirmed that several of his men had reported sighting a bright object, *"...but what it was I don't know and neither do they. We are buffaloed. I have forwarded a report to a higher headquarters."*

18th May 1964 (USA) – Landed UFO near Salem, Oregon

Michael Bizon (then aged 10) living at Hubbard – a small town about 30 miles south of Portland, 20 miles north of Salem – went outside at 7am, to perform his morning task of turning the cow out of the barn. As he began to do this, he noticed she appeared very agitated.

On reaching the barn door, he noticed a bright silver object in the middle of the wheat field, about 6-8ft wide and 4ft high. There was a cone on the front and it stood on four shiny legs. It was making a beeping noise. It rose upwards, slowly – then, making a whooshing noise, shot upwards into the sky. His mother – Mrs L.M. Bizon – confirmed that her son came running into the house, very frightened. Michael asked her to go into the field. She refused and telephoned the Deputy Sheriff.

At 8am, the first person to arrive was carpenter – Ray Mortensen. He was told what had transpired, and carried out an examination of the field.

> *"The wheat was flattened out – like the petals of a flower – as if a terrific blast of wind had flattened it from the centre. It was even in all directions – not like an animal would trample and disturb the wheat. I saw three dinner plate size spots on the ground, at three locations, pointed out to me by Michael. The fourth mark was ill-defined, because it was on ground that a tractor had run over and made hard."*

At 8.30am, a Deputy Sheriff arrived and confirmed something had crushed the wheat and of finding three areas about 3ft apart that looked as if something had rested there. In the afternoon some officers from an air force base, called in by the police, arrived and spoke to the family about the incident.

(Source: *Portland Reporter*, 21.5.1964)

Mt. Vernon, Virginia

At 5.15pm, Civil engineer – F. Meyers – saw a small, glowing, white '*oval*', split twice after moving from the right of the moon (to the E, half moon phase, 115° azimuth, 48° elevation) around to the left.

(Source: Berliner)

At 10.15pm an army pilot reported having sighted a brilliant yellow-white light approaching Lawrence Airport, Massachusetts. It was then seen to turn 360° and shoot away at a speed estimated to be 1,000mph, without causing a sonic boom.

20th May 1964 (UK) – Rectangular UFO seen

Mr Alan Bissett, from South Harlow, was visiting the annual Pinner Fair, in Middlesex, when he noticed:

> "...a silver, rectangular-shaped object, resembling a helicopter blade, with a halo around it – unlike any helicopter I had ever seen, and at a height where a helicopter could not have operated".

22nd May 1964 (USA) – UFO seen again

The automatic tracking site, situated north of Stallion Site, Holloman, picked-up an object moving at a speed of 25mph, which came to within 3,700 yards of one of the installations. Clearly this was no aircraft or natural phenomena. As a result of these continuing incursions, the incidents were released to the Press on the 24th May, by Mr Lorenzen and Frank Edwards. On 25th May, Holloman Air Force Base released a Press statement through the Associated Press, claiming they were natural phenomenon, such as a dust storm, and that they had no knowledge of any visual sighting at Holloman or an egg-shaped object under guard in one of their hangers!

24th May 1964 (UK) – The 'Templeton' photograph

On a pleasant spring day, Carlisle fireman Jim Templeton – who had a passion for photography – was out picnicking with his wife and daughter Elizabeth (5) at Burgh Marsh, a local Cumbrian beauty spot separating England from Scotland. Jim took a photo of his daughter wearing her new dress.

When he collected the processed film the shop assistant said, *"That's a marvellous colour film, but who's the big fellow?"*

Jim was baffled until he took a close look at the photographs. On one print – apparently standing just behind his daughter's head – was a large *'figure'* dressed in a *'spaceman'* suit. Jim knew there had been no-one else around at the time he took the photograph – apart from two women, sat in the car, three or four hundred yards away.

Jim immediately had the negative tested by contacts in the police force and with the film's manufacturers, Kodak. Both said the image had not been tampered with and could not account for what the *Cumberland News* began to call the 'Solway Spaceman'.

The photograph was soon on the front page of the local newspaper and, within days, Jim and his daughter became media celebrities as the image was flashed around the world. However, the price of this involuntary fame and attention was high. Jim's daughter was taunted and bullied and he had to take his daughter out of school for a while because her nerves were suffering.

MOD contacts

The Ministry of Defence showed no interest in the incident until the *Cumberland News* contacted them for their possible explanation. The MOD said they would be pleased to analyse the photograph and asked him for the original film and camera for analysis, but Jim refused them permission.

Close up of the head of the 'spaceman'. Far right is a Photoshop 'unsharp' mask which shows 'artefacts' of the digital example available.

Received a visit by two men, dressed in black

Later that summer Jim was visited at the Fire Station by two men, dressed entirely in black and driving a brand new black Jaguar car – unusual garb and transport for the times. They asked to be taken to the place where the photograph was taken. Jim queried their identity and was shown a card bearing an official crest and the word 'Security'. They told him, *"We're from the Ministry, but you don't need to know who we are. We go by numbers."*

Jim noticed the pair referred to each other as *'nine'* and *'eleven'*. Their obvious lack of knowledge of the area and inability to pronounce local place names led Jim to conclude they were not local people.

Once they reached the marshes Jim said the following conversation took place:

"Pull up on here. Is this where the photograph was taken? Can you take us to the exact spot?"

Jim replied in the affirmative and showed them where the photo had been taken. One looked at the other, and the other looked at him and said,

"This is where you saw the large man, the alien?"

Jim replied, *"No, we didn't see anybody...I never saw anybody."*

The man thanked him and walked away.

In a somewhat bizarre conclusion to the encounter, the two men drove off, abandoning Jim to walk a mile to the nearest garage for a lift to Carlisle.

Jim Templeton never saw the mysterious 'Men in Black' again. (Jim Templeton died on 27th November 2011.)

26th May 1964 (USA) – Thin white UFO seen

At 7.43pm a RAF pilot, and ex-Smithsonian satellite tracker, saw a thin white ellipsoid-shaped object flying straight and level over Cambridge, Massachusetts. At 11pm over Pleasant View, Pennsylvania, the Reverend H.C. Shaw saw a yellow-orange *'light'* in a field, shaped like the bottom of a ball, and chased it down the road for two miles. (**Source: Berliner**)

At 9.34pm, a woman living one mile north of Eaton Rapids telephoned the police at Michigan, reporting a completely silent red rotating or flashing light in the sky, west of her house.

> *"It appeared to move back and forth between the stars, then stop for a second and move up and down."*

(**Source: Project Blue Book**)

30th May 1964 (USA) – Photo of UFO at New York's fair

May 1964 (USA) – UFO landing!

Established 193

Jan, 27, 19

MUNHALL, PENNSYLVANIA

Roofs & Gutters
Painting & Decorating
Furnaces & Air Conditioners
Ceramic, Vinal Tile Floors & Val
Hardwood Floors & New Stairways
New Windows, Doors & Trim
New Cabins & Cabin Sites

Kitchens
Sink Tops
Bath Rooms
Accoustic Ceilings
Siding, Awnings, Railings
Brick, Stone, Brick Crete Siding
Change Your Old House To A New
House By Modernizing

AerialPhenomenia Branch
(TDEW)
Wright Patterson AFB Ohia
45433

Dear Sir:

1964

I want to tell you about what I saw last may while plowing our land for
A garden.

I saw. A very bright light something that resembled a very large flores
light bulb, but much larger & brighter.

I heard A sizzling sound & saw this great lighted thing coming down on
angle from the sky at about 7Pm Day light. It came down from the north
east such as coming from Kane Pa to Sheakleyville Pa. directly over ou
farm house & over our maple tree I would say 50 ft in the sky & landed
our field below the old chicken coop.

It was about 6 to 8 ft long & about 6to 8" round from where I was stand
& very bright glow of blue white & like it was burning orange color on
bottom but it was much brighter than any shooting star I ever seen or a
other bright light.
A young man about 17yrs of age & myself ran down into the field then st
ped when it landed & retreated because we thought it might explode & we
may get hurt.

The next day we & some women friends walked over this land but we could
find anything. we either missed it or it burried itself or perhaps it v
A little farther on into our next filed at the angle it was traveling
very fast. Sunol Road. Deer creek towhship Mercer Co. P
farm & it was traveling due south towards Pgh Pa. I saw your article.
ress Special Writer . Sunday Press magazine.

Let us bid on your job before you let your contract. You will save enough to get a cabin site and a few paymer
on your cabin, Cabin sites, 3 miles from PYMATUMING PARK in the country with small creek. ½ mile from DEER PAI
Lots 50 x 100 - $295.00 up to $595.00. 3 miles from FRENCH CREEK and back waters of CONNEAUGHT LAKE. Back wat
for fishing and duck hunting. Lots 50 x 100 - $198.00 and up. $25.00 down, $20.00 per month.

BROCHURE SENT ON REQUEST

31st May 1964 (UK) – Three flashes seen

Schoolboy Keith Bell of Hopedene, Leam Lane, Gateshead, was at home making a cup of tea, when he sighted *"three luminous, egg-shaped, flashes"*, each of approximately three seconds duration. They were crossing the sky in an east-to-west direction, at 11.35pm. They were also witnessed by his parents, who were upstairs at the time. Unfortunately, as their view through the widows was restricted by frosted glass, they only saw *'flashes'*.

Other people living in the street nearby later complained of having heard an unusual humming noise, which continued until 1am. (**Source:** *Orbit*)

31st May 1964 (USA) – UFO display

During the late evening, Mr and Mrs. Nelson Rodeffer, of Colesville, sighted a brilliant *'star'* with reddish overtones, moving through the sky against a background of fixed stars in the northern sky.

> *"It made a sharp turn left, did a 'U' turn and began to zigzag, before halting and rocking slightly. Suddenly it shot upwards, at speed, and was gone 30 minutes later."*

The Rodeffers called the Goddard Space Centre, who confirmed it was not a satellite or weather balloon. The UFO was also sighted in Rockville by friends of the couple who were alerted at the time of the sighting.

Enquiries made revealed that, just prior to the sighting, other people living in the Coleville area had seen what they described as bright silvery objects, showing a green-blue hue flying at the speed of a jet. Through binoculars, *"a strange undercarriage could be seen."*

(**Source:** *Washington Daily News*, 6.6.1964)

1st June 1964 (UK) – Fiery object

A fiery white spherical object, about half the size of a full moon, trailing a *'streaky flare'* behind it, was seen moving in an arc across the sky over the Isle of Wight, in an east to south-west direction, at 9.30am, by Shanklin teenager – Richard Abell.

(**Source: Isle of Wight UFO Investigation Society**)

1st June 1964 (USA) – Two objects sighted

At 8pm, a round object, larger than any aircraft, was seen heading in a south-east to west direction across the sky over Chicago, Illinois, by a group of four people. Five minutes later, a second appeared following the same path.

(**Source: Project Blue Book**)

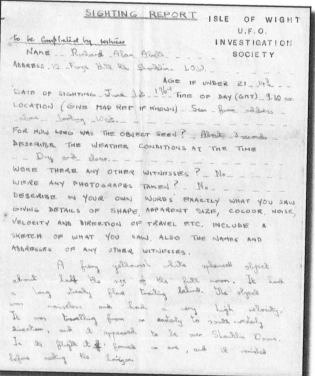

2nd June 1964 (UK) – Domed UFO with three legs; and occupants?

At 4.10pm, Raymond Varty, Jim Berry, Raymond Bell and Brian Powell, from Woodwynd Lane, Leam Lane Estate, Gateshead, reported having sighted . . .

". . . a silver, domed object, about the size of a dining table, with portholes around the top, with three legs, seen falling like a leaf through the sky and making a low buzzing noise, descending approximately 120 yards away from where we were stood".

Apparently Raymond's mother heard the object but did not see it. (**Source:** *UFOLOG*)

At 5.30pm, David Wilson (then aged 14) decided to walk down to Leam Lane Farm to collect some straw for his rabbits. When he arrived, he saw a group of about ten children, standing about 20 yards away from a hay stack, followed by the startling sight of:

"...six or eight small human beings on top of the stack; they were about two and a half feet tall and dressed in bright green suits. They appeared to be digging into the haystack, as if searching for something. Their hands seemed like lighted electric light bulbs".

David went home and told his parents what he had observed, and decided to make his way back to the scene, but was stopped by the farmer. David who told him that in conversation with another child she told him . . .

"she had seen a circular, silvery object, take-off from the ground in a spinning motion, giving off an orange glow".

Local headmaster – Mr M. Coates, of Roman Road Junior School – denied that he had called a special assembly of the children to discuss *'the little green men'*, or that he had told the children to keep away from the farm.

"There is no truth in these silly rumours", he said. (**Source:** *Newcastle Journal,* **9.1.1964 'Spacemen of Felling – 'Flying Saucers and Green Invaders have split whole neighbourhood')**

4th June 1964 (USA) – Burnt by a UFO?

Charles Keith Davis (8) was stood outside the door of Hobbs Laundry, Hobbs, Houston, with his grandmother – Mrs. Frank Smith – when she,

"...heard a strange sound – like something whizzing by real fast, and then I heard Charlie screaming; I turned around and saw Charles covered in black, with his hair on end and burning. I grabbed him and tried to smother out his hair."

A woman came rushing out of the laundry and poured water over Charles, who was taken to Hobbs Hospital with burns – caused, he said, *"by a 2ft long object, which spun like a top and made a whooshing noise."*

A doctor examined the boy and said that although Charles was in good condition, he had been burnt on the face by an open flame and was now bald. An investigation was launched by the police, who were unable to discover the nature of what it was that had caused the burns to the child.

(**Source:** *Houston Chronicle,* 4.6.1964)

5th June 1964 (USA) – Shimmering sphere seen

At 2am, the wife of Commodore's who was judged above average intelligence, was driving from the Air Force academy through Texarkana, Texas, accompanied by three cadets when a red shimmering half sphere object was sighted in the sky, about five miles away, at 5,000ft. Their curiosity aroused, the party stopped the car and got out. After getting back into the vehicle they drove at high speed, hoping to catch-up with it. As they approached closer, it suddenly flew away laterally across the sky. Dr Allen J Hynek wrote to the witness about this matter. In his letter he suggested she may have mistaken the crescent moon, and received an interesting reply, despite the official explanation given was they had seen the Moon! (**Source: Project Blue Book**)

UNITED STATES AIR FORCE ACADEMY, COLORADO

December 9, 1964

Dear Dr. Hynek:

In reply to your recent letter, I would be most pleased to furnish any information regarding the sighting in question. I must say it is a bit refreshing to make contact with someone who does not scoff at the possibility of "UFO's." After relating it to my family this summer and sensing their doubtfulness, I was inclined to forget the incident.

The time was about 2:00 A.M. June 5, 1964 about 25 miles west of Texarkana. There were two Air Force Academy cadets and my nine year old daughter asleep in the back seat. Another cadet was driving and I was sitting (awake) in the right front seat. I noticed the object first and mentioned it to the cadet at the wheel. He saw it and brought the car to a halt on the roadside. The object appeared at about 2 O'clock high, as pilots say. We were heading directly east and it was ahead, above and to the right slightly.

It appeared as a large luminous red-orange blob of fiery mass. There was a rolling over motion about it but you say only the bottom part of it if it was in ball form. It did not appear round as a ball or orange, it looked as a bright orange would if it was being turned over and over and the upper two-thirds of it were hidden.

We roused the two cadets asleep in the back seat and all got out and watched it as it appeared to hover. It was not a blinding light but a very intense reddish-orange coloration.

We returned to the car and proceeded to increase speed as if to get a closer look. The object appeared for perhaps 60 seconds to come closer and brighter in color and then it disappeared so quickly that you could not follow it with the eye or see any signs of a trail. It just vanished just as it had appeared.

We discussed this thing for a good hour among us. One cadet said maybe it was a weather balloon but none of us could imagine what it could be reflecting from to make it so brilliant. Another suggested a forest fire reflecting on low clouds, but there was not a fire in sight anywhere.

I have not seen or talked with the aforementioned cadets since that trip and can not say if they would want to put their impressions of it on paper or not, but they are all first classmen and pretty sharp boys and I'm sure no one can say that they or I just imagined it. There was a definite something there and I'm just as curious as the next person to get to the bottom of it.

UNITED STATES AIR FORCE ACADEMY COLORADO

Whenever your findings are published in book form, I would certainly like to read it. It must be a fascinating study and yet frustrating when an answer does not appear to be in sight.

I am so glad there were other observers along on the trip to see it. I have had quite a few fairly serious experiences with extrasensory perception and I'm afraid if I'd seen it alone, my family would be more or less tempted to call me a "witch."

Thank you for your letter, Dr. Hynek, and I hope I have been of at least a small bit of help.

Sincerely yours,

US Air Force Academy
Colorado

12th June 1964 (Australia/USA) – UFO over Dandenong & Ohio

Four people, from Belgrave South and Narre Warren North, were travelling home from Dandenong, at 5.55pm, in two separate cars. The driver of the first car was mechanic Robert Preston, accompanied by Jeannette Stephenson (17) of Emerald Road, Narre Warren, and Dorothy Murfitt (17) of Courtneys Road, Belgrave South.

Robert:

> "We saw a red light in the sky. It was stationary, so we pulled over and watched it for four or five minutes. Suddenly, it took-off like a flash across the sky. Dorothy

8 January 1965

Mrs.
U. S. Air Force Academy
Colorado

Dear Mrs.

This is in answer to your letter of December 9. Thank you for being so cooperative.

I am struck by one thing, and that is by a fact you failed to mention. Comparison with the almanac shows that the crescent moon was in the precise part of the sky you saw your crescent shaped object. It seems almost impossible that this could be so, but obvious mistakes are frequently made, and the moon, when rising, and viewed through scudding clouds and perhaps additional meteorological conditions, can fool people. We do have documented cases in which the setting moon has been the source of several UFO reports.

I'd appreciate you opinion on this, and, of course, if you saw the moon separately from this object, this could hardly be the explanation. The fact is, however, that the moon was in almost the precise spot you described. May I have your reaction on this hypothesis?

Sincerely yours,

J. Allen Hynek
Director

JAH:kr

wound the window down, but we couldn't hear any noise. It had a bright red light in the front and a dim white light on the rear; neither of them was flashing. It was about 800ft up in the air. It headed away, towards Melbourne, moving in a west to east direction."

Jeannette:

"I thought it was a helicopter, hovering in the sky. As we turned into Hallam Road, it came down towards us – then passed in front of us.

It appeared to be dome-shaped and travelling terribly quickly. It looked like a dinner plate turned upside-down on a table, but the bottom was slightly domed."

(Source: Sylvia Button, Victoria Flying Saucer Research Society)

Ohio sighting

On the same night, Richard Crawford – Chief of Police at Elmore, Ohio, located twenty miles south-west of Toledo – was driving towards the town, when he noticed a brilliant *'light'* off the side of State Route 51, and pulled the car over to obtain a closer look. Thinking he was looking at an illuminated blimp, Richard switched on his spotlight and aimed it at the *'light'* in the sky. He flashed twice. Immediately afterwards, the *'light'* flashed back twice, as if in response. Puzzled, he put it to the back of his mind and continued his night patrol. At 11.30pm, after checking the Harris Elmore School, he noticed the *'light'* again, which appeared to be closer to the ground. He flashed the spotlight at it – there was no response. The *'light'* then moved away, followed by a soft *'swishing'* sound. He then radioed his deputy – Carl Soenichsoen – who was also out on patrol, and arranged a rendezvous at a local food market on the outskirts of the town. When Richard arrived, Carl ran over to him and pointed at the *'light'* in the sky, which was now blinking at one second intervals. As the two men watched, the object began moving toward them, picking up speed. Crawford said:

"I'm going to notify the Highway Patrol. They have a plane; maybe they can figure this out."

While the Chief radioed the State Highway Patrol, Soenichsoen continued to watch. The object appeared to be just beyond the Ohio Turnpike – a distance of about a mile – and glowing in brightness and size.

From globe to 'V'-shaped

Suddenly, without warning, it gained speed rapidly and changed from a globe to a wedge or horizontal 'V'. *"Look at that!"* cried Soenichsoen.

It then changed course abruptly and headed south-west, passing about 500ft in front of the men. Both men saw clearly what now appeared to be a *'flying wedge'*. The upper part of the *'craft'* was about a third longer than the lower part; the lower part consisted of a series of closely placed lights.

No other lights were visible; neither man could see anything indicating additional structure. Whether the object had actually changed shape, the men could not say. The UFO headed away at a *'fantastic rate of speed'*, making a loud roaring noise – like a jet – and was out of sight in seconds.

Within minutes, two more officers arrived on the scene – one from Genoa, the other from the State Highway Patrol. The officer from Genoa had heard Chief Crawford's call. Both men, however, were too late; the object had disappeared over the horizon. The State Highway Patrolman immediately put in a call to the Toledo Express Airport, 10 miles west of Toledo, explaining what Chief Crawford and Officer Soenichsoen had seen, and asking for a radar check of the vicinity. The operator on duty reported the sky clear. He said:

"There's nothing in your area within a radius of 45 miles".

Either the object was too low, or it was miles away.

Interestingly, the Police Chief wondered if the UFO had been attracted to a local plant that produces ˙beryllium.

(Source: *FATE Magazine*, November 1964 – Richard D. Osborn/*Strangers from the Skies*, Brad Steiger, 1966)

Toledo, Ohio 43614
June 22, 1964

Dear Sir:

My name is ██████████ I am 22 years old and a
graduate of the University of Detroit. I work at Radio Station
WTOD in Toledo as ████████.

Leaving the station alone the night of Saturday, June 13,
1964, at about 9:15, one hour after sign-off, I observed three
strange objects in the air flying over the wheat field adjacent
to the station property. They were roughly 300 feet up in the air,
and moving away from me very slowly, at perhaps 10 miles an hour.
They had approximately the size and shape of the cockpit of a
helicopter, which I thought they were at first. I could see them
only by the light that they themselves gave off, so that I couldn't
tell for sure whether or not there was more to them than this
cockpit shape. The light diffusing fairly evenly from their
interior was white, and affixed to the side (apparently, of course)
was a red light which blinked on and off about once a second.
At first when they were pretty close, I heard a low rumbling as
if from a reciprocating engine, but possibly that originated from
some other source, such as the roadway. At greater distance,
though no more than 1000 feet, no sound was audible. I looked
for any green light there might be on the objects, but none were
to be seen. I was prevented from following them directly by the
waist-high wheat. After crossing a nearby road, they seemed to
hover over a barn. I started to move in closer for a better view,
skirting the wheat field, and when I was still maybe 500 feet from
them, they suddenly began to circle around a common point as center
in a plane parallel to the surface of the earth with a diameter of
revolution about equal to the width of the barn and at an extreme
rapidity. When I reached the barn, they had disappeared. It is
possible that the objects actually were parts of one single object,
the variation observed in the apparent distance between the things
then being explained as a change in viewing perspective.

If you wish me to complete some kind of form report, I would
be happy to oblige.

Sincerely,

˙Beryllium is the chemical element with the symbol Be and atomic number 4. Because any beryllium synthesized in stars is short-lived, it is a relatively rare element in both the universe and in the crust of the Earth. It is a divalent element which occurs naturally only in combination with other elements in minerals. Notable gemstones which contain beryllium include beryl (aquamarine, emerald) and chrysoberyl. As a free element it is a steel-gray, strong, lightweight and brittle alkaline earth metal. Beryllium is also a quality aerospace material for high-speed aircraft, missiles, spacecraft, and communication satellites.

13th June 1964 (USA) – Three UFOs seen

At Toledo, Ohio, Mr B. L. English – an announcer for radio station WTOD – told the listeners, at 9.15pm, of having seen three glowing white spheres, showing red on their sides, moving slow, hovering and then moving in circles very fast, making a low, rumbling sound. See letter on previous page. (**Source: Berliner**)

14th June 1964 (USA) – Was it ball lightning?

At 9pm at Dale, Indiana, a small basketball-sized object was seen to land in the backyard of Charles Englebrecht (18). The incident was later brought to the attention of NICAP Investigator William Powers of Unit No. 1 (Indiana) NICAP, who speculated that it might have been an example of ball lightning.

```
Information Only                                                  Dale, Indiana
Source:  American UFO  Committee Review, Vol 1, No 2, Sep 64      14 June 1964


        June 14: Dale, Indiana: About 9 p.m. Charles Englebrecht was watching
TV in his living room. Suddenly the TV set and lights in an adjoining room
went out and he noticed almost at once a luminous object outside the window.
He ran to the door to investigate, and saw a glowing object about the size of a
basketball land about 50 feet away. As he tried to move closer, he felt some-
thing like a mild electric shock and was unable to move forward. After about 2
minutes the UFO took off, emitting a whining sound. Holes, scorch marks and stains
were among the physical evidence left.
```

```
        SAUCER LANDING IN INDIANA: A sensational news report from Hunting-
burg, Indiana, dated June 14th, tells of a landing quite similar to the Glass-
boro, N.J. incident. On a farm two miles northwest of Dale, Indiana, a glowing
object  landed at about 9 p.m. one night,  and then flew away,  leaving behind
the smell of sulpher.  The UFO also left behind a burned spot, and three holes
or indentations in the ground,  approximately  a half inch deep each.  An Air
Force investigator came to the scene and interviewed Charles Engelbrecht,  the
18-year-old youth  who  witnessed  the landing.  The investigator  retrieved a
small piece  of metal  from the burned spot. When examined  under a jeweler's
glass, the metal appeared to be "grooved on the surface, like a walnut."
        The same UFO was seen in daylight,  several hours earlier,  by two
youths who were on a fishing trip southeast of Yankeetown, Indiana. The object
was traveling at treetop level,  and when it was within 200 yards of the young
men,  it veered away,  going out of sight  at the same level.  The UFO made no
sound, and appeared to be 10 or 15 yards in diameter. It was visible for about
ten minutes.  An unconfirmed report  broadcast by a local radio station stated
that the object hit a farmhouse in the vicinity,  causing a television set to
blow up.
```

```
                                    ...Lack of space prevents us from giving
details,  but we have recently learned of two more incidents in which physical
evidence was apparently left behind by  a flying saucer,  as in the Glassboro,
N.J. case. The first incident occurred near Connelton, Indiana, a few days af-
ter the sighting described in the middle of Page 23. No UFO was seen, but four
mysterious burned circles were found in a hay field  belonging to Mr. and Mrs.
James Stown. These were described  as "acid type burns."
```

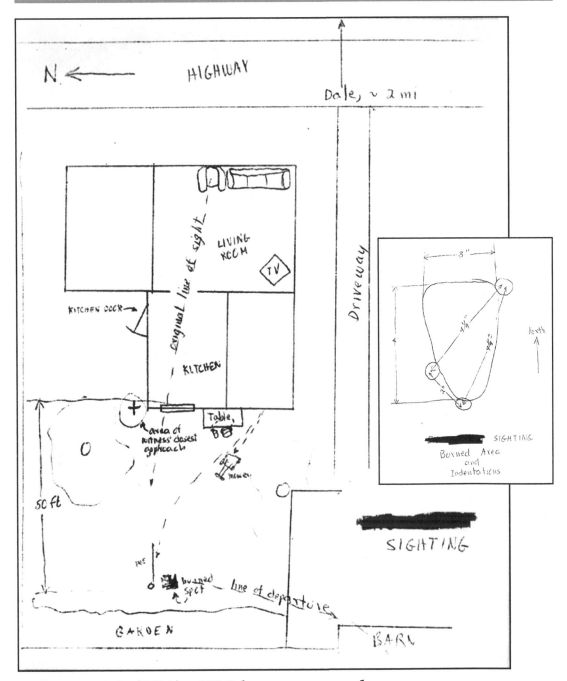

15th June 1964 (USA) – UFO hovers over yard

William Angelos (20) – a technical school student from Henry St Lynn, Massachusetts – was watching television at, 11.10pm, when he heard *"...a loud, throbbing noise, similar to a rough-running piston engine"*, outside his family's apartment. William immediately rushed to the door of the apartment, located on the ground floor and looked out into the courtyard, situated between three apartment buildings. He noticed a red light above the parking lot in the courtyard, and was astounded to see it was actually on the underside of a large, solid, plain object – hardly more than 20ft away from him.

Domed disc hovered in courtyard

> *"It was shaped like a disc, oriented in a horizontal position, flat on the bottom with a domed upper surface. When I first noticed it, the domed disc was approximately 12ft above the pavement, so that it was seen against the wall of the building on the opposite side of the courtyard. It ascended slowly in a nearly vertical climb toward the west-south-west and disappeared, at an elevation of 45°, after duration of at least a minute."*

NICAP Investigator – Walter Webb – discovered that several other neighbours had heard the loud sound; including Angelos' mother. At least one had seen the red light flashing through her window at approximately the same time Angelos reported seeing the disc ascending. Other neighbours reported having experienced television interference at the same time.

22nd June 1964 (USA) – Mushroom-shaped cloud appears over ocean

The New Orleans coastguard were contacted by the crew of a schooner in the Gulf of Mexico (Grid Reference 23.37N by 89.33W), who reported sighting a mushroom-shaped cloud, resembling an atomic explosion, at 6.47am, which rose to thousands of feet and lasted for 10 minutes. A search was made of the area by aircraft, but nothing else was seen. Suggested explanation: Munitions test at Elgin Air Force Base.

(Source: Project Blue Book)

24th June 1964 (UK) – Square UFO plotted on radar

A RAF Radar operator revealed the following:

> *"At 8.36pm a target was sighted at a range of 12 miles on a bearing of 130° magnetic. The echo had the appearance of several thin parallel lines of unequal length in the direction of movement, the lines being very close together and thinner towards the tail end. Its length was indicated at approximately eight miles and its speed at 5,400mph. The echo was observed out to a range of approximately 29 miles where, over a period of five seconds, it assumed zero velocity. It then changed aspect becoming square – its size approximately 1-2 miles. The echo remained stationary for almost 18 seconds. It then reversed course for four miles, veering off in an arc to north of radius five miles. Its speed now measured 450mph and the echo slowly became elongated at right angles to its course."*

(Source: Confidential to Fred Smith, editor of *Space-link*)

25th June 1964 (USA) – Three objects sighted and photographed

Jack Spiro (14), son of Mr and Mrs. Nathan Spiro of El Paso, Texas, was using his telescope when he sighted three 'V'-shaped objects in the sky – one glowing; the other two, dark ivory in appearance.

> *"It looked like a silver ice-cream cone, accompanied by two ivory objects."*

He took three colour photos using a telephoto lens, and sent them to Dallas for processing. When the film came back, the parents contacted Bigg Air Force Base and told them what had taken place. They sent a car to pick up Jack from school and took him to Fort Bliss Airbase, where the film was being analysed by technicians. Jack later told his parents that an ivory 'V'-shaped object had appeared on eight frames. Mrs Spiro then contacted the newspapers to report the incident, although it appears that Major Thornton – an Intelligence Officer – and Colonel William W. Saunders, pointed out that there was nothing but *"either an abrasion on the film, or a spot caused by processing".* Jack's mother told UFO researcher – Coral Lorenzen – of a conversation with Major Thornton, in which he had told her there had been something unusual on the film and appeared quite excited.

The incident was investigated by 95th Bomb Wing Intelligence – who concluded it had been a weather observation balloon, launched from El Paso Weather Station, 10 minutes before the sighting had taken place.

(Source: Project Blue Book/*Texas Times*, 27.6.1964)

Australia

On the same day, three newspaper boys from Relowe Crescent, Mont Albert, North Victoria – Terry Crowe (14) James Crowe (10) and Paul Hazelwood (12) – were amongst many people covering an area between Woomera to Melbourne, who reported sighting a large green *'light'*, which changed to red, as it hurtled across the sky at 5am. (Source: *The Reporter,* 24.6.1964)

26th June 1964 (UK) – 'Flying saucer' seen

At 2am, Mr Edwin Vipond and his wife, Elaine, licensees of the Moor House Inn, Seaton Burn, Northumberland, were asleep with the bedroom window open (as it was a hot night). They were awoken by a high-pitched buzzing, like a *'spinning top'*. The couple went to the window and looked out, seeing:

> *"...a pulsating, saucer-shaped object, ringed with electric blue light, moving up and down in the sky, heading westwards. Suddenly it shot upwards and out of sight."*

(Source: *Evening Chronicle*, 26.6.1964 – 'North couple report Flying Saucer')

Other witnesses were Mr M. Godfrey of 241 Wingrove Road, Newcastle-upon-Tyne, and Mr F. Fawcett of 5 Rectory Road, Gosforth.

The incident was later brought to the attention of Kath Smith, who for over 40 years ran the Isle Wight UFO Society. Sadly, she has now passed on. What a pleasure it was to meet her, some years ago.

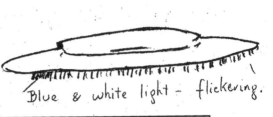

Blue & white light - flickering.

NO	DATE	TIME	MAP REF 78	DOCS
2/2	26/6/64	0200 hrs	239 738	CA

LOCATION: MOOR HOUSE INN, Seaton Burn, Northumberland

DETAILS: A buzzing noise, "like a destroyer's siren", was heard at approx. 0200 hrs. The witnesses saw a UFO surrounded by a pulsating electric blue light. Object seen for 3 or 4 mins. Remained stationery for that length of time. ①

WITNESSES: Mr & Mrs Vipond, Moor House Inn, Seaton Burn (+ 3 other) Northumberland.
Mr M. Godfrey. 241, Wingrove Rd, Newcastle on Tyne 3
Mr F Fawcet. 5, Rectory Tce, Gosforth N/land.

FLYING SAUCER REVIEW

September – October 1964

Volume 10, No.5

Page 18.

Sightings at Seaton Burn

From the Newcastle-upon-Tyne "Evening Chronicle" of June 26:
"Mr. Edwin Vipond, 'mine host' at the Moor House Inn, Seaton Burn, Northumberland, and his wife, Eileen, saw a flying saucer today.

" 'And before you make a crack about the beer being too strong,' said Mr. Vipond, 'let me say that we did not imagine this. It was quite definitely a flying saucer.' Mr. Vipond and his wife both saw the flying saucer – time: 2 a.m. today. "

"Mrs Vipond told the Evening Chronicle: 'It was a hot night and we had the bedroom window open. Then we heard this loud buzzing noise like the high pitched buzzing of a spinning top. It kept droning on and on until I went to the window to see what was causing it'.

" 'I looked up and there, high in the sky, was the saucer, ringed in an electric blue light. The whole saucer seemed to be pulsating up and down.' "

"Mr. Vipond, who joined his wife at the window, added: 'I could hardly believe my eyes. The saucer was moving in an East to West direction, then it shot upwards and out of sight.'

"The couple feel sure that someone else may have seen the saucer. Said Mrs. Vipond:- 'There was a lot of heavy traffic on the road for that time of the morning and someone must have seen it.' "

(Credit to Mr. Harry Lord.)

Salford, Lancashire – Saucer-shaped UFO

At 9pm the same date, John Chapman – a design engineer from Salford – happened to look through the window of his house. He saw a grey saucer-shaped object, with a domed top, crossing the sky at a height of about 500ft, approximately 5-10 miles away.

> *"It was heading in a south-easterly direction. The object moved under cloud and then into it. All of a sudden it reappeared, but flew away in the opposite direction."*

> (**Source: DIGAP, H. Bunting/***UFOLOG***)**

26th June 1964 (USA) – UFO sighted

At midnight over Huber Heights, Dayton, Ohio, an object – showing two blinking lights, one larger than the other, resembling a bright star – was seen moving at the speed of a transport aircraft across the sky, and disappeared from view at an elevation of 80°. (**Source: Project Blue Book**)

27th June 1964 (USA) – UFO metamorphosis

Over Clairton, Pennsylvania at midnight, a bright luminous spherical *'ball of light'*, showing what appeared to be some sort of antenna, rotating anti-clockwise in flight (three times the size of the sphere) sticking out from the object, at an angle of 30°, was reported. Suddenly, the sphere broke-up leaving a thick smoky vapour, followed by the appearance of three distinct objects which then changed into eleven *'discs'* forming a 'V' shape. (**Source: Project Blue Book**)

Over Forest Park, Ohio

During the same morning, three boys were camping outside near Cascade Road, Forest Park, Ohio. At 12.35am one of the boys – Mark Oakley – noticed a white *'light'* moving across the sky SSE to NNW, at about 40° elevation. It then changed its course from south-west to north-east, and disappeared over the horizon. The boys made their way back to Mark's house and telephoned the Forest Park's Police to report the matter. It appears that the police put them through to another department – who told them it was probably a rocket, launched by the Government. The boys pointed out the changes of direction and were told this was caused by humidity.

They retuned to where they had been sleeping out, and decided to continue observations. At 12.30am they saw another *'light'* moving in the same direction as the first. They telephoned the Forest Park's Police but by then the sky was clear.

They collected a camera and continued their night time vigil. At 3.50am they were rewarded by the appearance of a third *'light'*, which was moving in the opposite direction. A photograph was taken. However, its whereabouts are not known. Explanation: Echo 11 satellite. (**Source: Project Blue Book**)

Maupin, Oregon

Reports were also made of three bright blue objects seen heading across the sky at an elevation of about 45° the same morning.

This occurred at 450am, 5am and 5.10am. On the last occasion when it was seen, the object changed course about 5°. Explanation: Possibly meteors. (**Source: Project Blue Book**)

28th June 1964 (UK)

NO	DATE	TIME	MAP REF	DOCS
2/18	28.16/64	1245 hrs		C/A

DETAILS — A brilliantly lit circular UFO seen in a very clear sky for 5 minutes. Drifting S~N. Upper part had a bluish tinge while lower part was much brighter. No sound. Object seen through a small telescope.

LOC — Wingrove Ave, Newcastle on Tyne. ④

WITNESSES — Mrs. M.E. Godfrey. 241, Wingrove Ave, Newcastle on Tyne.

29th June 1964 (USA) – Motorist encounters UFO

Rancher George W. Rogers – then living in Spring Valley, near Ely, Nevada – was driving home with his brother, Bert, when they noticed a peculiar object in the highway ahead of them, situated beside the road and about 4ft from the ground. They first thought it was a jeep off the road; they soon changed their minds when it came up and over the road, resting briefly on what looked like a slender pedestal about 2ft long. By this time the men were now only a few feet away from the object, which they described as a pyramid-shaped top, with its point tapering down to the pedestal.

George:

> "I jumped out of the car and ran to touch it. As I drew near it made a loud humming noise and shot up into the air, at a height of 10ft, before coming back down onto the highway, about 5ft away from us. I approached it again, a few times, but it kept moving away."

A short time later it rose slowly upwards and headed-off in an eastern direction, before disappearing from view. (**Source:** *Ely Nevada Record,* 1.7.1964)

UFO interaction – burns sustained

During our research into the UFO subject, we were to come across many incidents involving not only damage to vehicles, caused through UFO interaction, but albeit rare reports of bodily harm to human beings. One such matter took place in the mid 1990s, when following the sighting of a UFO over the Avebury Stones, in Wiltshire (UK), the top of the car was later found to be burnt, and the witness threatened!

UFO swoops down over motorist

Wellford, South Carolina man – Beauford E. Parham – was returning home after a business trip to Atlanta, Georgia.

"I was travelling at about 65-70mph along Highway 59, at about 1am, when an object came hissing down and stopped in the air – like a humming bird – right over the car. As it did so, the engine of the vehicle slowed down. It resembled a giant top; the bottom portion seemed to be whirling in one direction and the upper part in the opposite direction. I could see what looked like fin attachments around its outer edges."

The UFO made three passes at the vehicle, first swooping down to pause in front of the headlights, and then whooshing over the top of the car, leaving behind an odour – like embalming fluid. The second time it followed Mr Parham for almost two miles, before it began its third dive – at which point he pulled over to the side of the road and turned off his lights. The object then shot away and disappeared from sight.

Mr Parham drove to Anderson Airport, where he told Albert Myrick – a Federal Aviation Agency employee – what had occurred. Albert examined the top of the car and noticed it was blistered and covered in oily spots. Mr Parham had burns on his arms which required dressing.

The Air Force launched an enquiry into the matter and concluded it had been ball lightning! Mr Parham rejected the explanation and pointed out that the radiator of the car had to be replaced, as it had been *'eaten away'*. Interestingly, he claimed that two days later (which would have been the 31st June 1964), he learned that a woman motorist also sustained third degree burns after being subjected to a similar incident to his, when grocery sacks in her car had caught fire. (**Source:** *Flying Saucers Are Hostile*, **Brad Steiger & Joan Whritenour/***South Carolina Independent*, **1.7.1964/***North Carolina Charlotte News*, **3.7.1964**)

29th June 1964 (UK) – 'Flying saucer' seen over Lancashire

John Chapman of Salford also saw something highly unusual and filled out a sighting report form. Unfortunately we have no further details of this incident.

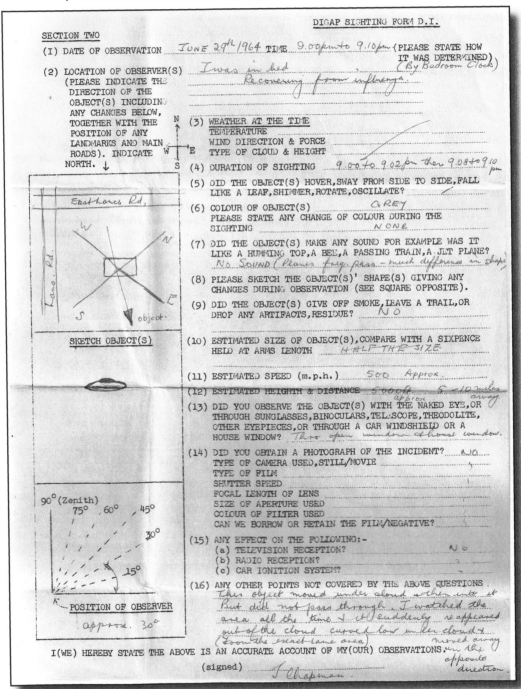

30th June 1964 (UK) – Orange *'light'* seen

Mr H. Pool (18) of 81 Plumstead Road, Kingstanding, Birmingham, was looking out of his bedroom window, at 11.20pm, when he saw:

> *"...a bright orange 'point of light' in the sky, towards the south-east, at about 25° elevation; it was moving west to east very fast. At first I thought it was the Sputnik – then realised this was not the case."*

Other witnesses were Mr and Mrs Hopcroft and their son – Michael – of Plumstead Road, Birmingham.

(Source: *UFOLOG***)**

1st July 1964 (UK)

At 2am, a bright yellow star-like UFO was seen moving north-east over Newcastle-on-Tyne, by Mr R. Mooney, Mr F. Thompson of Wallsend, Northumberland and Mr F. Alderson of Newcastle, before vanishing from sight. A few minutes later an intense white object appeared in the sky, heading south-west (possibly the same one returning?).

At 9.45pm, a thin grey line was seen to appear in the orange sunset over County Durham. It gradually grew thicker and changed colour to dark grey. Clouds were seen to move around it, but the object remained perfectly still. Two airplanes arrived and began to circle the sky. The UFO faded away but reappeared for a few minutes, before finally disappearing. **(Source:** *UFOLOG***)**

At 10.55pm a white *'disc of light'* – far larger than Venus – was seen moving through the sky against a strong wind, at an estimated speed of 7,000mph, heading east to west, over Newcastle-on-Tyne. **(Source:** **TUFOS)**

'Little green men' seen!

Thousands of children joined in a hunt after reports of *'little green men'* were seen at the bowling green, Jubilee Park, Jubilee Drive, and Liverpool.

(Source: *Liverpool Echo*, 2.7.1964**)**

It began when a group of schoolchildren told parents and teachers they had seen

NO	DATE	TIME	MAP REF Sheet 78	DOCUMENTS
2/1	1/7/64	0200	285643	CA

LOCATION :- C.A. Parsons, Walkergate, Newcastle on Tyne.

DETAILS :- A bright yellow starlike UFO. moving NORTH-EAST. Seen for approx. 10 secs, then it vanished. Three minutes later an intense white UFO was seen moving SOUTH-EAST WESTERLY direction at a very fast speed.

WITNESSES: Mr. R. Mooney. 41, Durham St. Wallsend, Northumberland. Mr. F.E. Thompson. 41, Strawberry Gdns. Wallsend. -"- Mr. F. Alderson. 433, Stonleigh Ave. Newcastle 12

NO.	DATE	TIME	MAP REF 78	DOCS
2/7	1/7/64	2145 hrs	325555	CA

DETAILS : A thin grey line appeared in an orange sunset. Gradually grew thicker and changed colour to dark grey. Clouds were moving around it but object was quite still. Two aeroplanes appeared and began circling. UFO faded away slowly. It reappeared after a few minutes and was watched for 3 minutes before it finally disappeared. Observer was facing NORTH-WEST

WITNESSES: Miss Margaret Haw. Penshaw, Houghton-le-Spring, Co. Durham.

NO.	DATE	TIME	MAP REF.	DOCS
2/6	1/7/64	2255	N/K	CA

DETAILS : Observers saw a disc of white light "bigger than Venus at its largest," moving EAST-WEST. Object was between observers and a high layer of cloud. UFO moved against the wind at approx 7,000 mph.

WITNESSES: Mr. & Mrs K. Offen.: Fawdon, Newcastle on Tyne. 3

'little green-skinned people', wearing white hats, in Jubilee Park, Jubilee Drive, in Kensington. The children's tales were naturally dismissed as immature imaginings – until adults also reported seeing strange things around Jubilee Drive.

Mrs Williams (63) was enjoying a cup of tea in the garden at her house in Edge Lane on the afternoon of the 1st July 1964, accompanied by her friend – Mrs Williams, and 67 year-old neighbour – Mrs Jones. While enjoying the hot afternoon, they became aware of an unusually loud chattering of magpies in the shrubberies at the bottom of the garden. Mrs Williams then recoiled in shock, because something surreal and a little frightening stepped out from the stark shadows and into the bright sunlight.

> "I saw a 'figure', about two feet in height or less, with pale yellow-green skin, standing there. 'He' wore a small white helmet – very similar to the safety headgear worn by modern cyclists – and was clad in a one-piece suit, which had reflective texture of plastic. The face looked human, but childish, and it was much smaller than a normal face."

Jubilee Drive

Mrs Williams saw as well, and let out a squeal of surprise; the little *'being'* turned and fled into the shrubs.

The women were too scared to investigate how the entity had gained entry into the garden at that time, but the next morning Mrs Jones brought her nephew and his Alsatian dog to the bottom of Mrs William's garden, and discovered a small opening in the fence where a rotten strip of wood had been broken. The nephew repaired the fence. He and his aunt noticed that the German shepherd dog was very uneasy while it was in the garden, and seemed to be able to see something they couldn't.

Janet Bord:

> "The city was an unlikely setting for a series of reported fairy sightings in the summer of 1964. Little green people, varying from three inches tall to garden gnome-sized, were being seen at night in the city's parks and golf courses, as well as at people's houses and flats. The excitement grew so intense when the reports were widely publicised, that on one occasion a crowd of people gathered near the bowling green in Edge Hill in August 1964, hoping to see fairies (or whatever they were) and had to be restrained by the police. Later the same year, a woman living in Wavertree claimed that three little men in green clothes had been sitting on her backyard wall, throwing stones at her dog, and other women saw them climbing a tree in Wavertree Park. These events demonstrate the difficulty the researchers sometimes have of easily distinguishing between reports of fairies, aliens and other non-human beings."

St. Chads

So convinced were local children that hundreds of them plagued the vicar of Kirkby (Rev. J. Lawton) by invading St. Chad's churchyard in search of the little people. At times the numbers were such that the police had to chase the children away. According to the *Liverpool Echo* (13th July 1964), scores of children began searching the churchyard at St, Chad's for leprechauns. After what was described as two days of hectic activity, which probably began on Friday, 10th July, relieved Rev. Canon John Lawton told the Echo's reporter on the night of Sunday, 12th July, that:

"...the children seem to have been convinced, at last, that there are no leprechauns".

Incredibly, during the same period, children had also searched the grounds of St. Marie's Roman Catholic School and Mother of God Church, Northwood, Kirkby.

The truths behind what exactly happened are unclear even today. It was not the first or last time we would come across instances of what appeared to be mass hysteria which swept the area, influencing children's minds. These all followed wild unsubstantiated claims which should have no place in today's modern society. However, once upon a time, we would have laughed at the very prospect that 'flying saucers' even existed, let alone they had occupants. (**Sources:** *Liverpool Daily Post*, July 1964/*Liverpool Echo*, 2.7.1964/*Kirkby Reporter*, 17.7.1964/*Echo*, 13.7.1964 – 'Little folk and Flying Saucers')

Leprechauns seen at Belfast

Although we cannot be sure of the exact date, we were fascinated to learn of yet another incident, involving a frenzy of excitement which swept the locality, after it was claimed a *'leprechaun'* had been sighted in Tamar Street, East Belfast, on or about the 10th September 1964. The fact that the culprit was later identified as six year-old Jimmy Hughes, playing in a derelict house, dressed as Robin Hood, who was chased away by police after fears for his safety, appears to have triggered off, once again, that insatiable 'spark' which ignited the population's imaginations and desire to descend onto the street, causing massive disruption. Ironically, the crowds that gathered there included many adults. The incident – which involved the attendance of the police and fire service – also attracted the interest of David Bleakley, labour MP for Victoria, who handed over a petition to Belfast Corporation, demanding action to keep the crowds and children away from the embankment and derelict houses. One senior police officer was quoted as saying:

"A grown man, cold stone sober, insisted to me he had seen a leprechaun!"

Was this the explanation?

In the 26th January 1982 edition of the *Liverpool Echo*, a man called Brian Jones – short in stature and pipe smoker – claimed that he was the *'leprechaun'* responsible for sparking off a wave of hysteria which swept the locality. He claimed that he had been seen by local children, wearing a red waistcoat, a pair of navy-blue trousers, Wellington boots, a denim shirt and a woollen hat with a red bobble on it, while tidying up his grandfather's garden in Edge Lane, which backs onto the park.

"I bounded into view, babbling made-up words; I jumped up and down, picked up turfs and threw them at the children. Not surprisingly, the children ran away in a 'blind panic'."

Over the course of the next few days further 'confrontations' took place between him and large groups of children, who came to see the *'leprechaun'* – actions which necessitated the intervention of the police. A similar bout of hysteria appears to have erupted several miles to the north-east of the city, in the overspill town of Kirkby, when *'flying saucers'* and *'leprechauns'* were reportedly seen by local children.

1st July 1964 (USA)

A family, who were on the way back from a camping trip to the High Sierra, were near Bridgeport, Mono County, California, at 9.30pm (latitude 38°, longitude119°) when they saw a bright object moving rapidly across the sky, heading in a north to south direction, followed by a smaller and much dimmer object. They wrote to NASA, who forwarded their letter on to the USAF. Explanation: Aircraft, or *"believed to be satellite by witness"*. (**Source: Project Blue Book**)

2nd July 1964 (USA) – Three objects seen

A family of five were outside their house, as dusk fell in Denver, Colorado, when they saw three pale green objects, *"similar in appearance to balloons or large bubbles, but much faster, like a string of beads"*, one behind the other, heading in an arc across the sky from the north-east to the south-west – gone in five seconds. Explanation: Probable Meteor. (**Source: Project Blue Book**)

Dayton, Ohio

As twilight fell at 9.55pm over Dayton, Ohio, a teardrop-shaped white *'light'*, showing green at the bottom, was seen moving across the sky from the direction of North, before being lost in the south. It was seen to pass close to the constellation of Polaris and near Arcturus.

3rd July 1964 (UK) – Massive star-like object seen

At 11.15pm, a massive star-like object, flashing intermittently, was seen travelling across the sky over Hunt's Cross, Liverpool.

According to the witnesses – a woman and her son – *"It was heading towards Runcorn, changing colour from brilliant silver to red, as if signalling".*

(**Source:** *Liverpool Echo*, 9.7 1964)

At 11.28pm, a similar object was seen from Birnham Road, Wallasey, Cheshire, by Mr and Mrs Oldrid. A few hours later, a mysterious bright *'star'* was seen at 2am, by Miss R. Broadbent of Stuart Road, Walton. It was low down in the sky, heading towards Aintree. (**Source:** *Liverpool Echo*, **6th, 8th & 9th July, 1964**)

4th July 1964 (UK) – 'Flying saucer' over Derbyshire

Two women were walking home from a Girl Guides meeting, late one evening, along the B6415 Bolsover to Renishaw Road, heading towards Mastin Moor, Derbyshire. It was a clear night, with many stars visible.

They had just passed the Woodthorpe turning, when they both had an inclination that something was going to happen. Nervously they looked around and then upwards, when they were surprised to see a saucer-shaped object in the sky.

"It had lights all around it and was almost overhead. The lights seemed to merge together, as if spinning, before moving away and out of sight."

(**Source:** *Ovni*, **March/April 2003, Omar Fowler, PRA**)

4th July 1964 (USA) – Red lights sighted

During a firework display over Clearwater, Florida, over 50 people wrote to the Air Force and other authorities, bringing their attention to the sighting of six red lights in the sky, at 8.30pm – (others spoke of three lights seen) – which were not believed to be associated with the fireworks display. According to the main card, as kept by Project Blue Book, the pilot of a light aircraft dropped five railroad flares into the sky, at a height of 10,000ft, and that the flares extinguished at 7,500ft. (**Source: Project Blue Book/***Clearwater Sun*, 6.7.1964 – 'Everyone baffled by red lights'/*Clearwater Sun*, 7.7.1964 – 'Air Force seeking photos of sky lights')

5th July 1964 (UK) – Two 'lights' seen

Mr John Eaves of Aintree, Liverpool, sighted two bright star-like objects heading in a straight line through the sky, from the direction of Liverpool to Preston, at 1.10am. Enquiries made later with Liverpool Airport and Bidston Observatory failed to explain what had been seen. (**Source: Isle of Wight Society/Liverpool Echo, 6.7.1964**)

6th July 1964 (UK) – Cigar-shaped UFO seen

At 8.50pm, Jean Jarvis from Holmefield, Heavitree, Exeter, was in her garden, talking to neighbour – Betty Leaworthy – when they noticed:

> "...a bright silver cigar-shaped object, moving silently through the air from the direction of the setting sun. It was so bright you couldn't look at it for too long. By the time we even thought about fetching a camera it had gone. This was no airplane. We are used to seeing them pass over."

Exeter Airport was contacted; they stated that there were no flights listed for that time. (**Source:** *Express and Echo*, 7.7.1964 – 'Uncanny object flew over, says Exeter women')

8th July 1964 (UK) – UFO sighted

At 3.40pm, Mrs Wendy A. Madge from Hayes, Middlesex, was sitting in Rosedale Park with friends, when their attention was directed to a minute 'circle of light' – almost a pinpoint in the sky.

> "At first I was unable to see it, because of its extreme height, but when my eyes became focused I could see it moving at high speed in a WSW direction. I thought it was a satellite – an idea quickly dismissed when it slowed down and stopped in the sky for about 30 seconds, before heading-off towards the south-west, where it disappeared behind cloud."

Liverpool

At 11.25pm, two bright star-like objects (one of them making a slow, jerky movement) were seen in the sky above St. George's Hall, Lime Street, Liverpool, heading towards the direction of Bootle.

11/6	8.7.64	23.25
Near St.George's Hall, Lime St., Liverpool.		
Two very bright star-like objects, thought too bright to be stars. One 'star' moved off towards Bootle with slow, jerky movement. Visible for 4 minutes. Report from Mr. R. Donnelly, a member of M.U.F.O.R.G and Mr. R.D. Hughes, Vice-Chairman.		

(**Source: Mr R. Donnelly and Mr R.D. Hughes, MUFORG/Flight International, 30.7.1964**)

8th July 1964 (USA) – Five *'lights'* sighted over 'classified' location

During night-time at ˙Killeen Airbase, Texas, (now West Fort Hood) three *'lights'* were seen in the sky, with two trailing behind the other – one white, the other an orange *'blob'*, heading in a west to east direction – by a motorist and his companions. According to three witnesses, the silent objects moved up and down in flight and occasionally halted in mid-air. They were kept under observation for some 20 minutes, during which time the orange and white one went out at 10 minutes duration. The observers were a party of 15 enlisted personnel from the base. They were Sergeant William S. Love, Security Police, Robert J. Halix, Fred E. Serra Jnr., Private First Class, Jonnie Belk, Larry M. Crawford, Fairley V. Halstead, Donald Lukaszewski, Jonnie D. Maraable Jnr., Bobbie O. Muncrief, Daniel A. Over, Ferdinand Paulch, Eugene R. Pierce, Billie E. Williams, Private Thomas Kitterell and Private Frank J. Veitch, Military Police Company C, Kileen Air Force Base. Explanation: Assumed to be helicopter activity. (**Source: Project Blue Book**)

10th July 1964 (UK) – Two *'lights'* seen

At 10.40pm, Mrs Reginald Smith from Blackheath, London, was driving home when she and her friends noticed two *'lights'*, motionless in the sky; one of them was glowing green. When she arrived home, she alerted her husband. The couple then watched, as the two *'lights'* headed away in what appeared to be a smooth and controlled manner. Mr Smith rang the MOD, who told him that they had received no other reports.

11th July 1964 (USA) – Two red *'lights'* seen

At 10.45pm, over Buckley, Illinois, two red *'lights'* were reported moving through the sky. They were seen by a family, driving home along Route 24, south of Piper City, who felt that they were not aircraft from their speed, distance apart, and behaviour. Explanation: Aircraft. (**Source: Project Blue Book**)

Cape Girardeau (USA) – Cone-shaped UFO seen by pilot

At 2.25am a pilot reported the sighting of a UFO to Cape Girardeau tower, whilst flying from Perryville, Missouri, to Cape Girardeau, Missouri.

The tower operator observed the object with binoculars and contacted Memphis, who in turn contacted Belleville, Illinois. Radar contact by the 798th Radar Squadron was made at a bearing of 152° at 85 miles. The altitude varied from 33,200ft to 8,900ft. There were apparently no aircraft in that area. The visual observation from aircraft and ground of the objects described them as shaped like a cone, or long rectangle, and the colour was intense white, orange or red. There were three objects seen, but never more than two at one time.

(**Source:** *McDonald list*/**Daniel Wilson, NICAP**)

˙Killeen Air Force Station came into existence as part of Phase III of the Air (ADC) Mobile Radar program. On October 20, 1953, ADC requested a third phase of twenty-five radar sites be constructed. It was constructed on the existing Robert Gray AFB to provide radar protection for the Fort Hood area. The 814th Aircraft Control and Warning Squadron were moved to Killeen AFS on 14 February 1957. It operated AN/FPS-20 search radar and AN/FPS-6 height-finder radars at the station, and initially the station functioned as a Ground-Control Intercept (GCI) and warning station. As a GCI station, the squadron's role was to guide interceptor aircraft toward unidentified intruders picked up on the unit's radar scopes.

In addition to the main facility, Killeen operated two AN/FPS-18 Gap Filler sites between April and December 1960: Schulenburg, Texas (TM-192B): - 29°45.42.N 096°55.51.WNormangee, Texas (TM-192C): - 30°59.39.N 096°06.48.W.

Killeen was inactivated 1st February 1961 due to budgetary cuts. Today most of the site is unused, but maintained by Fort Hood with most of the buildings being torn down. A radio tower is now on the site. The circular concrete foundation for the AN/FPS-20A search radar tower is clearly visible in aerial imagery. (**Source: Wikipedia 2015**)

Washington DC

Over Washington DC, as the sun set, an object – described as being brighter than Venus – was seen over a 15-minute duration and reported to the authorities, who suggested it was a balloon. Explanation: Aircraft.

At 11.27pm, a student – studying astronomy from Mankato College, in Minnesota – sighted:

> "…an object – like a satellite – passing through the gamma star Cygnus, and then the gamma star in Cassiopeia, before disappearing from view at 11.35pm."

He wrote to NASA, in Washington DC, who forwarded his letter on to the USAF. They concluded that it was not Echo 1 or Echo 2 satellite, but felt it might have been an aircraft or other satellite. (**Source: Project Blue Book**)

11th July (USA) – Glowing UFO over Louisiana

A woman living in New Iberia, Louisiana, was alerted by her grandfather, who told her he had been watching a *'star'* for an hour, which had then shot across the sky.

> "He showed me a star and that is what I thought it was. It had red, green, and white lights on it, and was doing some manoeuvres. I fetched a pair of binoculars and clearly saw the object. It looked like a glowing jet with green and red lights and was zigzagging up and down, back and forth in circles. On one occasion it looked as if it was going to crash when it headed downwards, spinning. Sometimes the red light would flare up brighter than normal. We watched it until 1.30am."

According to the witness, her grandfather had telephoned Lafayette Air Force Station – who told him it was a star. Explanation: Star or planet. (**Source: Project Blue Book**)

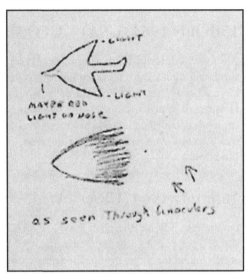

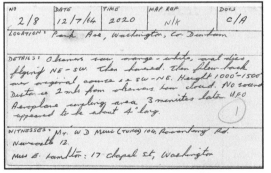

12th July 1964 (UK) – Orange UFO

An orange-white oval-shaped object was sighted over Park Avenue, Washington, County Durham, at 8.20pm, moving in a north-east to south-west direction. According to Mr William D. Muir – then a member of the Tyneside UFO group:

> "…the object flew back along its original course, at a height of 1,000-1,500 feet; a few minutes later, an aircraft appeared and circled the sky".

13th July 1964 (UK) – Black *'swishing'* UFO

Miss Louise Franklin saw what she described as *"a dull coloured black round machine, making a 'swishing' noise, showing a thin rod on top with a flashing small white light"*, heading North to South over Worthing, Essex, at 5.30pm – gone in a few seconds.

15th July 1964 (UK) – *'Cone'* UFO seen

Mr R.M. Glazier from Edgware, Middlesex, sighed something strange at 1.31pm.

> *"...of what appeared to be a star crossing the sky, followed by a similar object seen at 12.30am, 16th July 1964, which came to a sudden stop in the sky, before proceeding forwards in a sweeping 'S' movement, of flight. Through my 60mm. telescope, I managed to get a glimpse of what looked like a bicycle wheel."*

Later on that day, *"a brilliant, cone-shaped object, was seen hovering over the sea,"* about three miles west of Point of Ayr, by observers from Wallasey Coastguard Station, Cheshire, including Mr R.W Lambert, at 3.45pm. After five minutes, the *'cone'* inverted and moved out to sea, where it was soon lost from view.

(Source: Isle of Wight UFO Society, UFOLOG Information Sheet, No. 3, 9.9.1964, handwritten)

15th July 1964 (USA) – UFO showing three legs

An object – described as having three legs on the bottom, with lights that kept glowing and dimming, and was larger than a car – was seen hovering over Rio Americana School at Sacramento, California, east along the river near Fair Oaks Boulevard, by two students – one from Sacramento University, and the other from Hastings. It appears that the time of the incident was 7pm. When the investigators spoke to the female student, afterwards, she could not recall the sighting. It may well be that she did not and that another student was involved, who may well have not been interviewed. Explanation: Unreliable report. (**Source: Project Blue Book**)

16th July 1964 (USA) – White *'lights'* pace aircraft

On the 16th July, Northern Air Service Pilot – Mr K. Jannereth – sighted four white *'lights'* moving across the sky, in a stepped up echelon formation, while fifteen miles south of Houghton Lake. Two more were seen, which joined the larger group. They then closed-in on the aircraft and flew alongside it for five minutes.

(Source: *UFOE*, Section 111, Berliner)

Crescent-shaped object over San Antonio, Texas

A yellow crescent-shaped object was seen flying across the sky, which then spilt into two and rejoined itself while in flight. Explanation: Quarter moon. (**Source: NICAP**)

Conklin, Broome County, New York – creature seen

In the beginning of the afternoon, five young boys – Edmund (9) and Randy Travis (7), Floyd Moore (10), Billy Dunlap (7) and Gary Dunlap (5), were playing in an apple tree along Woodside Avenue, in a field two miles from their homes, when they noticed a strange dome-like object – like a car chromium bumper – resting in a field alongside of the road, partially hidden by tall weeds. They then heard some sounds similar to someone playing a penny whistle or kazoo, as if from a pipe – apparently coming from what they said was a *'creature'* in a tree, about 150 feet away.

Description

They described this *'creature'* as about the size of a small boy, 3ft tall, dressed in shiny black pants and a black short-sleeved shirt. Its face had a human-like appearance. A black helmet was seen on its head, with two antenna-like wires protruding from the top, and white wavy lines or a white lettering (unidentified by the children) across the front. A transparent plate or lens (part of the helmet) covered the eyes. The boys started throwing apples and stones at it but it was out of range. It continued to emit the weird noises. The *'creature'* then fell backwards out of the tree and appeared to fall slowly, or float, to the ground. It then headed toward the dome-like object and stepped on the top of it. The boys asked *'him'* if he needed help or water, but the same noises continued with no other response. At this point the children left and ran home.

Leaving the scene

Three of the boys ran to the Travis home, and told Mrs Edmund Travis they were looking for a jar of water for the *'spaceman'*. They said they could not understand what he said, but it sounded like he needed water.

The grandfather of these boys was sent after the other two boys. He met them along the way, walking home from the field, and questioned them.

At first the boys denied seeing a *'spaceman'*, for fear of punishment for lying, as they thought nobody would believe them. Later they admitted that they had seen it. Mrs Travis threatened to punish her sons if they did not tell the truth. They tearfully insisted they were not lying. The boys were then separated and required to tell what they had seen and, in tears, each told the same story. None of them retracted their original claims. After that, Mrs Travis said she believed the boys.

The boys then accompanied Mrs Travis to the field. The object and its occupant were gone, but they found a perfectly circular area where weeds had been flattened and bushes broken. The moss appeared dry and yellow, as if *"intense heat had withered it"* and two depressions were found outside the area, as though the object had been supported on legs. A newsman discovered a third depression later that day. The story then appeared in a local newspaper and was apparently investigated by ufologist Walter Webb, who found no ordinary explanation for the episode. (**Source:** *The UFO Investigator*, **NICAP, USA, page 6, August 1964**)

17th July 1964 (UK) – UFO over forest

At 6.45pm, Mr C. Wood from East Woodburn, Northumberland, was looking across the sky, towards the north-east, when he noticed:

> *"...a petal-shaped object (smoky grey in colour) apparently hovering over Harwood Forest, Bellingham; it disappeared and reappeared at least seven times, moving closer to me as it did so. Four minutes later it finally went."*

> (**Source:** *UFOLOG*)

NO	DATE	TIME	MAP REF	DOCS
2/11	17/7/64	1845		C.A.

DETAILS Observer was looking in a N.E. direction when he saw a blurred, circular, or petal shaped object – smokey grey in colour. The UFO appeared and disappeared seven times – each time coming closer to him. Seen for 4 minutes. 10° – 15° elev. Appeared to be over Harwood Forest.

LOC — Bellingham – Woodburn Rd, Northumberland

WITNESSES Mr. C. Wood, East Woodburn, Northumberland

17th July 1964 (USA) – UFO sighted over Ohio

The articles, (as shown), appeared in the *Lorain Journal,* on 20th July 1964, and documents an event with an illustration of a rocket ship-shaped UFO, seen by Lorain resident – Mr J. Richard Lukovics. A follow-up article, published on 21st July 1964, confirmed a number of other witnesses to the phenomena. However, the FAA declined to comment.

UFO Observers Agree On Sketch Given By Lorainite

By BILL WILGREN

The Journal newsroom received several phone calls yesterday afternoon on the unidentified flying object spotted here last Friday night.

All of the callers agreed that the picture published in The Journal yesterday was similar to the flying object that they saw.

After seeing the UFO, J. Richard Lukovics, 1203 E. Erie Ave., sketched the object and submitted his drawing to The Journal.

Among the callers yesterday was Mrs. Mary Churchill, 7231 Elyria Ave. She said she and a companion, Mrs. Irene Palmer, were driving on 28th St. and turned at Fulton Rd when she saw the object.

Mrs. Churchill said she spotted the round object with a great big fiery tail flying over the tall boom at Thew Shovel.

She asked Mrs. Palmer to look but it disappeared before she saw it. Mrs. Churchill said it went out like a light.

They turned around and went back to the spot to see if it was a reflection. They saw no visible sign of a reflection.

Mrs. Churchill said this is the first time she ever saw anything like this. "I'd still like to believe it was a reflection but after all the other people saw it, it made me stop and wonder. I'm convinced there was something there," she said.

Mr. and Mrs. Joseph Endrai, 1234 W. 29th St., said they were sitting near their garage when they spotted the same object.

Mrs. Endrai described the alarming sight as "round in front with a bright shining silver light." She said red flame or fire was coming out of the tail. It was no airplane, Mrs. Endrai noted.

Robert Uleski, 13, of 1410 W. 21st St., was sitting on his front porch Friday night when he saw it. He said it appeared in the middle of the sky and looked like a cone with fire coming out of the back. It was not very high.

A Federal Aviation Agency spokesman in Oberlin said that he had not received any reports on the object. Questioned about weather conditions Friday night, he said there were no atmospheric conditions present that would cause such a phenomena.

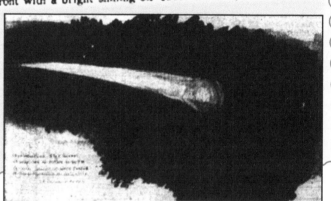

UNIDENTIFIED OBJECT—An unidentified flying object (UFO) was seen by several area residents Friday night. Larry Davis, 19, 706 E. 34th St., was at the home of his parents in Sheffield Lake when he spotted it. Mike Urgo, 24, 1925 E. 32nd was in Elyria when he saw what "looked like a rocket ship, real bright silver gray....there might have been fire coming out the back." J. Richard Lukovics, 1203 E. Erie, submitted his interpretation of the phenomena (above). He described it as "a circular shaped object with a heat trail approximately three times the diameter of the object in length that appeared to be traveling in an east to west direction in a descending path. The object was as visible as a low flying aircraft." Spokesmen at NASA, Cleveland, and the FAA, Oberlin, stated they had not received any reports of the object.

July 17, 1964
9:45 P.M.

On the night of July 17, 1964, my husband and I were
returning from the Sears store in Middleburg Heights (commonly
called Southland) via the Big Creek Parkway. It was a clear
hot night and we drove through the park at approximately 15
M.P.H. enjoying the cooler air. We were headed south nearing
the Whitney Road exit when my husband, pointing directly ahead
through the windshield, told me to, "look there!" I myself
did not see anything until he made a left hand turn onto
Whitney pulling off onto the shoulder of the road beside the
park sign. He opened the car door and got out standing on the
left side of the car. I, having on my lap our two year old
son, leaned out of the window, waist length, the baby excitedly
saying, "There's a skyrocket." On my right some distance above
the trees and telephone poles was an intensly bright (white hot)
oval shaped object. It seemed to hover, then dropping down
slightly, began to spin and change color from white to pink to
a glowing red. (like a coal on a cigarette being smoked in the
dark.) It shot up vertically. My husband seemed to sense this
object was going to "move out" and had gotten into the car again
telling me to keep it in view and direct him. There I was,
arm extended, sighting off the end of my forefinger through the
telephone wires, leaning out as far as I dared. We were then
travelling east. The object during its spinning seemed to have
diminished to one quarter of its size and in the sky appeared to
be as large as a red golf ball. I finally told my husband that
there seemed to be a vague elongated form (shadowy) surrounding
this red light. It was then we decided we were seeing a UFO,
not having given any thought to that conclusion beforehand. The
object made a left angle turn onto Pearl Road (USR #42) and we
tracked it approximately four miles when it suddenly v'ed out and
in again. We attempted a right turn losing it, when it resumed
its former course, and ascended vertically disappearing among the
many stars which were evident that night. While tracking this
unknown object we attained a speed of 55 M.P.H. It was several
days later that we both realised that we hadn't had one red
light to stop our progress and Pearl Road has many. Why?

Looking back and discussing this subject between ourselves, we also noted that there was no wind, there were no persons nearabouts on the ground in this area, my husband definitely
looked. This object had not been set off or sent up as would
have some gadget remotely controlled. There was no sound given
off by this object.

We knew we had witnessed some "unusual phenomena" to
put it mildly. Not knowing were to turn in order to find a
logical explanation, and being unable to pass it off, I finally
began a systematic search. On Sunday, July 17, 1964, I called
our observatory speaking with an unidentified gentleman who advised me that Mr. Snow, the director of the planetarium, would

-2-

assuredly be interested. I left our phone number but never receiving a return call gave that source of possible information
up as nil. Why?

On Monday, July 20, 1964, I called the U.S.A.F. Office
of Special Investigation and spoke with a very pleasant Inspector
General who asked me not to go into detail with him but rather to
write to A.T.I.C. Wright Patterson Air Force Base in Dayton, Ohio,
which I did later on July 26, 1964. (Sunday) .

On Thursday, July 23, 1964, I just happened to see a
Mr. Earle J. Neff featured on the Mike Douglass show. He was informing the public in regard to UFO sightings. I telephoned
Charles Tracy at the newspaper office immediately after the program and was advised to contact him, (Mr. Neff.) I did so. This
resulted in a meeting and we learned for the first time about
N.I.C.A.P. in Washington D.C. and various Ufology Projects.

On Monday, July 20, 1964, I also called N.A.S.A. and
was told no one there was qualified to discuss this type of phenomena.????

On Monday, July 20, 1964, I also called the Sattelite
Tracking Station. I was told we had in all probability seen a
bolide meteor. The gentleman went into the business of the dif-
fusion of gasses thereby creating the light intensity. He also
said that it was quite possible for a meteor to change its trajectory and defy earth's gravity. (?) That is not what the book
tells me.

July 17, 1964, (9:45 P.M.): At the same time the
██████████ were experiencing their sighting on Whitney Road, two
Parma residents spotted a large, high-flying, lighted white
object coming from the N.E. The object's steady flight to the
S.W. took it past the observers who saw it attain an angle of
55-60' elevation and to their left. (They were facing north.)
The object, as large as a dime, blinked every two seconds; an
intense bluish-white on a much less intense white. The object
was constantly illuminated.

In general its shape was round, maybe oval. The object
moved along steadily and swiftly, disappearing high in the S.W.
Duration two to three minutes, no sound, con-trails, ect., no
other lights. The weather--clear. Observed by Mr. and Mrs.
[morning.]

I was most grateful to hear from the Department of the
Air Force in Washington D.C. on September 3, 1964. I have filed
a written report as has my husband. Waiting....................

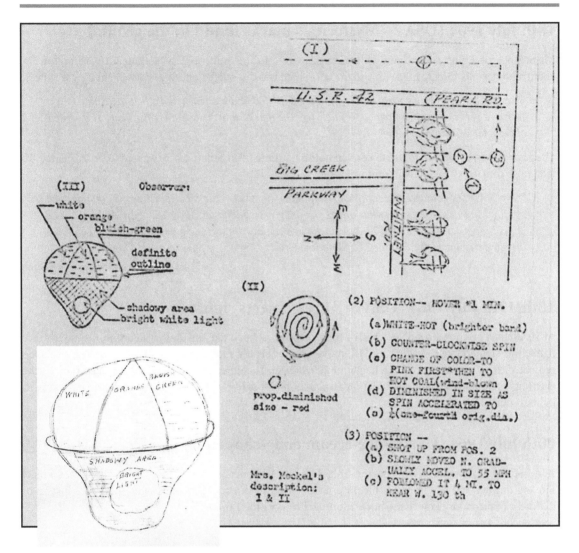

One of the witnesses was Andy Zirkle.

"I remember that night. I now live south, in West Virginia; I have family still up in Lorain. However, no-one has time to get the article for me that was in the Lorain Journal. I emailed the newspaper, but they said that they had lost all archives due to a fire. They advised me to go to the library and that the library would be able to locate the article."

A retired Unites States Navy gunner resident, at Berea, Ohio – was out driving with his wife, at 9.45pm, in Middleburg Heights, Cleveland, Ohio, when they sighted a strange *'teardrop-shaped object, showing lights on its body'* in the sky. Their curiosity aroused, they decided to try and follow the object, which then rose upwards and out of sight. In a letter sent to the USAF about the incident, the couple further described the object as having *"bands of colour on the upper part, with white, orange and bluish-green lights on the bottom, and a shadowy white light in the centre"*. See Project Blue Book images (above).

Explanation: Balloon! (**Source:** *Lorain Journal,* 20.7.1964)

18th July 1964 (USA) – Mysterious marks found in the ground

Mr S. Hopkins-Philip from Gainesville, Georgia, wrote to the Smithsonian Institute, in Washington DC, about a mysterious 15feet 'ring', with a slight 'tail', which was discovered on Mr and Mrs Paul Lee's front yard.

> *"Around the edges were several marks, evenly spaced and about an inch and a half in depth – marks such as a very large camera tripod would leave. The marks didn't fade in the rain. I enclose a sample of grass for your information."*

The grass was analysed and found to contain nothing unusual. The letter was forwarded to the Air Force. The letter also contained the following information:

> *"Several UFO sightings have been reported in our immediate area by local citizens. Although such sightings are described somewhat differently, they are similar to saucer-shaped objects – a little larger than a car – with red, white, and green lights. It always leaves a particular odour. In one case they declared they felt radiation."* Explanation: Grass.

(Source: Project Blue Book)

18th/19th July 1964 (USA) – Three objects sighted

At 10.48pm, a bright yellow object, with a tinge of silver (shaped like the bottom of an iron) showing three lights, was sighted over Washington DC, moving in an erratic motion towards the south-east, at a speed estimated to be 1,000mph and at a height of 200,000feet. The object had, in fact, been sighted the previous evening, heading in the opposite direction. Explanation: More likely to be a high flying aircraft in view of the lights. (**Source: Project Blue Book**)

20th July 1964 (USA) – Ice-cream cone-shaped UFO

At 9.45pm, employees working on the Thixol chemical plant, Brigham, Utah, sighted two grey objects moving through the sky in single file, in a north to south direction; seconds later, they were lost in the darkness. Explanation: Low flying birds. (**Source: Project Blue Book**)

Morrison, Illinois

A fiery light was seen heading through the SSE part of the sky, over Morrison, Illinois, at 5am, by USAF Airman First Class Lowell F. Buffett, 12284334, described as moving at an altitude of about 7,000feet, with an apex of light – the most intense portion at top, fanning out at the bottom.

Another witness

About a mile away, a motorist (a World War Two veteran) was driving eastwards along State Route 101, two miles west of Littleton, Illinois, at 4.45pm, when an object rose up in front of the car about a mile away.

> *"It was shadowy, cone-shaped, with reddish-purple fire jetting out from underneath."*

The man initially thought it was a rocket, with mixture too rich, because of the sparks coming out of the base. It then climbed to about 1,500feet, levelled off, made a sharp loop, and then climbed to 35,000feet heading eastwards, before disappearing in seconds. The *'rocket'* was shaped like an upside-down ice-cream cone, some 60feet in diameter. Explanation: Unidentified. (**Source: Project Blue Book**)

Member has selected the "All Others" tour. Travel of dependents and transportation of household goods to the oversea area during the assignment of sponsor to the station covered by these orders is prohibited. Travel of dependents and transportation of household goods to a designated location under the provisions of paragraphs 7005 and 8253, JTR is authorized. Transportation from such designated location is authorized only upon reassignment of the member to a new duty station.

unusual light in ESE sky approx 700 ft

At 0500, 20th July 1964 By airman named on Reverse side

I was on US Highway #30, 7½ m. west of Clinton, Iowa, Traveling East

Description as follows

MOST INTENCE ———— ← Apex

No Determate object was seen. Only The Light Ray

MOST INTENCE →

Trail of Ray

I stopped & cut off engine To check for a sound, & could Hear None

ITS direction of report was N.N.W. & Appeared To be Traveling in That same direction After about 45 sec. To 1 min The light faded out

Ardeall F Loffett, 12254334

USAF

% Illinois Headquarters
Selective Service System
405 East Washington Street
Springfield, Illinois 62701
22 July 1964

TO WHOM IT MAY CONCERN:

At about 4:45 a.m. on 20 July 1964 I was driving eastbound through a wooded area on State Route 101 about two miles west of Littleton, Illinois, when I noticed a shadowy cone-shaped object, with fire jetting out of the bottom, rise straight upward over the trees in front and to the right of me at a distance of possibly one mile.

My first thought was that it was a jet plane, then I decided it was a rocket powered cone-shaped object. I recall thinking that their rocket mixture was too rich as the sparks or flames were reddish purple. I then realized I might be looking at a "flying saucer."

As I continued driving eastward the object climbed to about 1500 feet and leveled off, coming directly toward me. At that moment it reminded me of a large sunflower with yellow petals sticking out all around it; I was looking at its front side and the petals were the rocket sparks fanning out around the edges. This lasted only a second or two, then it made a sharp loop upward and almost reversed its course, leveling off at about 3500 feet and heading almost due east. It was as if the operator had gotten his bearings. The sparks from the rocket now turned a bluish yellow, making a ball of fire, and in a very few seconds it was completely out of sight.

This flying object, as I saw it, was shaped like the cream of an ice cream cone with the rockets where the cracker part is. I would guess it was about 60 feet in diameter. I have drawn the attached sketch to show how the object looked to me in the various positions in which I saw it. I cannot say whether it was ascending from the ground at the moment I first saw it or whether it may have been flying at tree top level when I saw it making its flight straight upward.

The sky was clear and still dark, although it was beginning to turn gray in the east. I was alone in my car. There was no other traffic on the highway in that vicinity. My car windows were up because of the cool weather and I heard no unusual sounds. The whole incident as described above probably took no more than one minute.

21st July 1964 (USA) – Spate of UFO reports, UFO display!

The State Police at Lansing, Michigan, were contacted by members of the public, reporting UFOs being sighted during the early morning, from around 1.14am to 1.50am. (Many reports told of erratic motions in the sky by white lights, sharply outlined and bevelled.) According to Major Hector Quintanilla Junior, it was aircraft on special night photographic missions with their landing lights on. Apparently the aircraft were using a generator, which makes a shrill sound of a higher intensity than the aircraft engine, and was flying at 500feet.

Surprisingly, he said, in a letter to the Lansing Police:

> "We have not established the origin of these flights; however, many of the missions have a security classification on, due to the equipment operational matter and product of the work being performed".

Explanation: Aircraft! (**Source: Project Blue Book**)

Waldorf, Maryland

At 3.30am, two objects were seen in the east of the bright moonlit night sky, moving erratically at an elevation of 30°, travelling westwards. They were observed for almost two hours, and disappeared as dawn came up. The illustration provided by the witnesses shows two oval objects, with vapour above them – one of which was seen to move in a triangular motion across the sky – the other rectangular.

Explanation: Atmospheric conditions! (**Source: Project Blue Book**)

During the same night, retired USAF Intelligence Sgt. Charles E. Peterson – who had himself been involved in dealing with reports of UFOs from members of the public, during the early 1950s, prior to retirement –

was lying on his back, looking up into the sky north of Yachats , Oregon, when he saw:

> "...*a bright object slightly below the moon, and 45° above the horizon. It was the same size as a star, but bluer and brighter.*
>
> *It rose against the face of the moon, turned half left, and headed up the coast in a northerly direction. It paused briefly and then continued on its journey.*"

Explanation: Likely Echo 11 satellite. (**Source: Project Blue Book**)

23rd July 1964 (UK) – Glowing UFO with windows

At 1am, Mr William Elrick and his wife, of Uddington, were returning home from holiday, driving along the moors between Rochester and Jedburgh, when:

> "...*we saw a bright object approaching from the north, which we took to be an aircraft. As it came level with us, we saw it had no tail, nose, or navigation lights, and was aglow with lights that seemed to shine from the inside, and had about four or five windows*".

At 10.20pm, Mr F Coulson from Elsdon, Northumberland, sighted a small object – like a pale star – circling the sky in a clockwise fashion.

.NO	DATE	TIME	MAP REF	DOCS
2/16	23/7/64	2220		C. A.

DETAILS — A small object, like a very pale star, was seen circling 6 or 7 times in a clockwise direction. It was very fast and very small.
The observer has been watching similar UFOs, every night for the last 4 years.

LOC — Elsdon, Northumberland   ④

WITNESSES — Mr. F. Coulson; Blaxter, Elsdon, Northumberland.

On the same date, at 12.50am (excluding the time differential) a resident of Sayre, Oklahoma, saw a '*light*' moving in the western part of the sky, while sat in his front yard. He thought it was a satellite, but became curious about its erratic motions, which included it appearing to stop and hover while in flight.

In a letter written to the USAF, the man said:

> "*It stopped and changed direction towards the Earth, as if losing altitude. It then stopped again and changed course to the north-east, before stopping due east.*"

Explanation: Echo 1 satellite. (**Source: Project Blue Book**)

During the same evening, a grey spinning object was sighted moving across the sky, at a speed estimated to be between 400mph and 1,000mph, over Coudersport, Pennsylvania, for a period of 15 seconds.

24th July 1964 (Australia) (USA) – Tracked by radar

A formation of white objects was seen crossing the sky over Longreach, Queensland.

At 4.26am, Tower operators at Langley AFB, Virginia, sighted multiple brilliant round objects in the sky through 7 x 50 binoculars. They were also observed on radar by the GCA operator. The sighting was described as four objects 1½ minutes in trail, followed by two objects 1½ minutes apart, and three to four minutes separating the two formations. The objects appeared as large as a silver dollar, held at arm's length, and resembled burning magnesium. No sound was heard. The objects were observed to the south of the field at a 75° angular elevation. (**Source:** *McDonald list*, **Dan Wilson**)

24th July 1964 (USA) – Egg-shaped UFO

A luminous egg-shaped object was seen at a height of 20,000feet, over a C130 Hercules aircraft at Lakewood, Arkansas, ten miles west of Little Rook Air Force Base, during the afternoon. The object – estimated to be a quarter of the size of the aircraft – split into two. One part then broke into two – one piece disappeared from view; the other headed towards the south-east, five minutes later. Explanation: Balloon, or sunlight reflecting off aircraft. (**Source: Project Blue Book**)

25th July 1964 (USA) – Two UFOs sighted

At 3.15am, two objects were seen in the sky over Fort Huachuca, Arizona. The first one was initially thought to be the satellite Echo 1, moving in a south to north direction; the second one appeared and seemed on a collision course with the first but then turned eastwards, changing course several times as it did so.

It then appeared to land on Laundry Ridge on the Mustang Mountains, some 40 minutes later. Explanation: First object satellite, second one a balloon! (**Source: Project Blue Book**)

26th July 1964 (UK) – Six UFOs reported

A spate of UFO activity occurred at 11pm over Lees Road, Kirkby Industrial Estate, Liverpool, when *"six dazzling balls of light"* were seen hovering and flashing across the sky in a display – attracting the attention of the workers, who telephoned the police.

Two of the witnesses, night watchmen – John Parkinson and Albert Sanderson – claimed that it was a *"regular occurrence"*.

By the time police arrived there was nothing to be seen. The officers suggested the men had observed *"a collection of stars"*.

A number of people who telephoned the Meteorological Officer at Liverpool Airport and Bidston Hill Observatory, to report seeing UFOs, were also told by the police that *"they had seen a collection of bright stars"*. (**Source:** *Liverpool Echo*, **27.7.1964**)

~~11~~/9	26.7.64	23.00

Lees Road, Kirkby Industrial Estate, near Liverpool and East Lancashire Road, Kirkby.

Six dazzling balls of light hovering and flashing across the sky. Several night workers in factories on the Estate said objects were "stopping and moving in the sky just as though they were being controlled." Police spokesman said two men had been sent to area to investigate, but it was probably no more than a "collection of stars." Report from "Liverpool Echo", 27.7.64. Witnesses:
John Parkinson, 7 Fern Grove, Princes Park, Liverpool.
Alan Cash, 6 Christowe Walk, Croxteth, Liverpool. Albert Sanderson, no address yet.

26th July 1964 (USA) – Objects sighted

At 10pm over Cresco, Iowa, 10-12 white objects were seen heading in a staggered formation across the sky, in a straight trajectory north to south direction, under cloud cover, and on edge of a thunderstorm area. No sound heard, trail or exhaust seen. They disappeared over the horizon, ten to fifteen seconds later. Explanation: Flight of birds. (**Source: Project Blue Book**)

Marietta, Ohio (USA)

At 8.55pm, a crescent-shaped object was reported in the sky over this location, faster than any satellite, moving silently at a height of 100,000feet, at 30° elevation, according to the witness.

27th July 1964 (USA) – Sphere showing three beams of light

Norwich, New York, resident Mr Louis Daubert – an engineering supervisor by occupation – was on his way to pick up his daughter, Norma, from a Girl Scout camp, at 7.30pm, when he saw a strange object, hovering 50 feet over a field near the town of Sherburne. He stopped his car, to obtain a closer look, and saw a stationary aluminium sphere with a fluorescent luminous ring which emitted three beams of very bright light, before it took off, flying away at high speed. (**Source:** *UFOE Section V*/**Vallée,** *Magonia,* **618/Unknown newspaper – 'Glowing UFO seen by Norwich man'**)

Defiance, Ohio

At Defiance, Ohio, a boy (aged 11) and his parents reported having sighted an object they described as being:

"...like the points of a pin, with streamers".

A short time later, four other residents from the same community sighted a ball-shaped object, with a pale blue centre, in the sky.

28th July 1964 (USA) – Cone-shaped UFO seen

At 10.30pm, a former Navy pilot and another man, working in a field at Lake Chelan, Washington, saw an intense cone-shaped light project up from the ground to a similar light in the sky, alternating on and off. A round, aluminium-looking object, about 30 feet in diameter, with a red and white light, then appeared and descended to the ground. This was accompanied by a strong whistling sound, like a small jet, followed by high-pitched voices heard – similar to children playing. Before this object took off, a low-flying Jet circled its position. The densely wooded area was explored by helicopter and on foot, a few days later, by Sheriff Nickell and a USAF officer – but nothing was found. (**Source: Vallée,** *Magonia*, **619**)

29th July 1964 (USA) – *'Ball of fire'* seen in the sky

At Livingston, Montana, a semi-transparent object, *"like a big ball of fire"*, was seen in the sky. According to the female witness, it was too bright to look at for any period of time and resembled *"a washing machine lid"*. As dawn approached, it rose upwards and out of sight.

On the same date, over Washington, Missouri, was a report of two objects seen east of the Milky Way, at 10.25pm. They were first seen over the south-eastern horizon, travelling towards the south-west. Explanation: Aircraft! (**Source: Project Blue Book**)

30th July 1964 (UK) – Glowing object

At 2am, Mrs Catherine Walsh from Pelsall, West Midlands – unable to sleep – was looking out of her bedroom window, when she saw,

> *"...a blue, yellow and green, oval-shaped, glowing object"*, *heading across the night sky.*

(**Source:** *Walsall Observer*, 7.8.1964)

Late July 1964 (USA)

It was reported that Jack Hall – a resident of Flemington, New Jersey – was driving home, late one night, when he saw a glowing object in the sky, followed by it landing in a nearby field. He stopped the car, got out, and approached the field. When about 500 feet away, the egg-shaped object – some 10 feet in circumference, with a glow emanating from underneath it – began to move towards him. Jack panicked and ran away. His wife and daughter were inside the house and, although they did not see the UFO, they did see a strange glowing light shortly before Jack arrived home.

The State Police were contacted and made a search of the locality, but found nothing untoward.

1st August 1964 (Australia) – A bright object, with a glowing tail, was seen over Onslow, Western Australia.

1st August 1963 (UK) – UFO sighted

At 1.40am, a very bright object was seen to come down in the sea over Govey Pier, Jersey, by local resident – Miss McLoud – who was then living about half a mile away from the pier. Another witness may have been Terrence Bradley.

UFOLOG REF N° 8/36.

AERIAL PHENOMENA SIGHTING REPORT

TO BE COMPLETED BY WITNESS

NAME: TERENCE BRADLEY ___ DATE 28/9/64

ADDRESS 56 LINDEN RD NEWPORT I.W AGE IF UNDER 21 ___

LOCATION OF SIGHTING (GIVE MAP REF IF KNOWN)
DUTCHMAN HOLE N° ATHERFIELD (SOUTH WEST COAST OF I.W)

DATE OF SIGHTING SAT 1ST AUG 64 ? TIME OF DAY 22·15 HRS

DESCRIBE BRIEFLY THE WEATHER CONDITIONS CLEAR STARLIT NIGHT

FOR HOW LONG WAS THE OBJECT IN VIEW? 10 TO 20 MINS

WERE THERE ANY OTHER WITNESSES? YES

WERE ANY PHOTOGRAPHS TAKEN? No

WOULD YOU PLEASE DESCRIBE IN YOUR OWN WORDS EXACTLY WHAT YOU SAW, GIVING DETAILS OF COLOUR, SHAPE SIZE (COMPARED WITH A THUMBNAIL OR SIXPENCE HELD AT ARMS LENGTH) DIRECTION (WITH REFERENCE TO ANY NEARBY FEATURES ie. CHURCH STEEPLE, TREE, HILL, ETC.) SPEED OF TRAVEL (APPROX) AND IF POSSIBLE THE NAMES AND ADDRESSES OF ANY OTHER WITNESSES. A SKETCH OR DIAGRAM OF THE OBJECT AND ITS MOVEMENTS WOULD BE OF VALUE.

LIKE A MEDIUM SIZE STAR TRAVELLING IN A ERRATI
ZIG-ZAGING ~~~~~~ COURSE FROM SOUTH-WES
TO NORTH EAST.

2nd August 1964 (Australia)

A yellow-orange coloured object, resembling a rocket, about 50 metres long, with what appeared to be windows in the side, was seen in the sky over Wittenoom Gorge.

2nd August (USA) – Three 'lights' seen

During the late evening, three dull white 'lights' were seen directly overhead in the sky over San Jose, California, moving in a south to north direction, estimated to be about a quarter of the moon in size and between 2-3,000 feet in height. The witness rejected any suggestion that he had seen an aircraft or weather balloon. They were observed for two minutes, before being lost from view. Explanation: Probably aircraft. (**Source: Project Blue Book**)

3rd August 1964 (UK) – Shining *'disc'*

Between 8 and 9pm, a white shining *'disc'*, with sharp edges, was seen by Monmouthshire man – Andrew Wooldrige – and his brother, who were driving along the A470 road in the Brecon area, when they saw it,

> *"...shooting across the sky and stopping in mid-flight – then became lost from view as we went past the sides of a mountain."*

DATE. 3rd Aug. 1964.   3/8/64

TIME. Between 20.00 and 21.00 hrs.

LOCATION. Between Brecon and Merthyr Tydfil.

The witness was travelling along the A470, and just before the intersection with A4059 noticed a white shining disc, 1" at arms length, with sharp edges. Seen facing East through the open window of a car, it appeared stationary but then shot across the sky and again stopped. It was in view for about 7 mins. before being obscured by a mountain. At one point it passed through a cloud estimated to be fairly low and about a mile away. It was evening and there were a few clouds in the sky.

4th August 1964 (UK) – *'Flying disc'* with red light

At Dumfries, "a bright circular 'disc', with a flashing red light on top, making a queer noise", was seen passing through the sky, by two men, at 6am. It then apparently settled on a distant hilltop, over Longwood, outside Dumfries.

(**Source:** *UFOLOG*, Issue No. 7, 21.10.1964/*Dumfries and Galloway Standard*, 8.8.1964)

5th August 1964 (UK) – Three lights, forming a triangle

Mr and Mrs Hurst were watching TV at their home address in Dalton, near Huddersfield, Yorkshire, when they were astounded to see:

"...three orange lights, forming a triangle – one of which appeared to be revolving – moving slowly across the sky."

(Source: *Huddersfield Examiner*, 5.8.1964/*UFOLOG*, Issue No. 2, 31.8.1964)

Three Orange Lights.

This sighting and the very sensible comments that accompany it were taken from the 'Huddersfield Examiner' for August 5: "Unidentified objects in the sky for which no apparent logical explanation can be found fascinate the mind of modern man. In these times, when lunar travel is 'just around the corner' rather than the mere product of some author's fertile imagination, it is easy to let one's thoughts run riot and envisage all sorts of weird contraptions hurtling around our planet through the night sky.

"And so the reports come in from people who are convinced (and not having seen what they have seen we can but believe them) that they have seen objects in the sky, and I have just heard from Mr. and Mrs. A. Hirst, of 5 Kelvin Avenue, Dalton, who tell me of one "thing" which they spotted recently.

Mrs. Hirst said that they were watching television when, through a crack in the curtains, they saw three orange lights - they dashed to the window and there were the lights, floating slowly across the sky. They noticed that the lights formed a triangle, and one of them appeared to be revolving.

Could it be no more than a common or garden plane ? No, because 'the thing' whatever it was, was moving silently (and completely silent jets have yet to be put in the air). Gathering speed, it moved from a southerly direction gravitating to the east and disappearing.

"It was more like a helicopter than anything else, but there was no noise". Mrs. Hirst told me. Her husband thought that it was rather like a "buzz-bomb" from the last war - but one without the 'buzz'!"

REF. No.	DATE	TIME (G.M.T.)	MAP. REF.	DOCUMENTS.
17/2	4/5 Aug? 64	Evening	-	-

LOCATION. 5 KELVIN AVE. DALTON. NR HUDDERSFIELD. YORKS

DETAILS.
WHILST WATCHING T.V. THREE ORANGE LIGHTS WERE NOTICED THRU' A CRACK IN THE ROOM CURTAINS. THE WITNESSES ON DASHING TO THE WINDOW SAW THE LIGHTS MOVING SLOWLY ACROSS THE SKY. THE LIGHTS FORMED A TRIANGLE AND ONE OF THEM APPEARED TO BE REVOLVING NO NOISE ACCOMPANIED THE LIGHTS THE OBJECT OR OBJECTS MOVED FROM A SOUTHERLY DIRECTION GRAVITATING TO THE EAST AND THEN DISAPPEARING
INFORMATION TAKEN FROM 'HUDDERSFIELD EXAMINER'. THIS REPORT IS BEING INVESTIGATED.
WITNESS: MR + MRS. A. HIRST.   UFOLOG.

DATE: 1964 August 6th..   TIME: 2350 (on 6th.) till 0005hrs.(7th).

LOCATION: 99a, Musters Rd., West Bridgford, Nottingham.

DATA: Witness first saw object through room curtains. Went outside to watch
watch its slow progress across the sky. Witness described it thus: " If
it had stopped it would have looked just like a star." As it passed due
South point it appeared to "go round" something in its path, thus:

← E   ↑ S   W →   direction of travel.

The object was at a maximum elevation of about 60°. It disappeared before
reaching the horizon, probably into haze from the town and street lamps.
Object appeared definitely high up. Object was due South at midnight
because witness heard the nearby clock strike at that moment. The object
was much brighter than the other stars. It seemed to have a "swirl" in it
as if it were spinning.

WITNESS: Mrs. E. Page of above address.

COMMENT: This is a typical distorted description of Echo I, whose time of
flight that night was from midnight to 0.18 a.m., rising WSW, max.
elevation 65° in the South, and setting in the East. There might appear
to be a time discrepancy but further investigation showed that the church
clock has not been always reliable. The movement of the object "around an
obstacle" is a typical optical illusion, especially with satellites
against a black back-ground. Despite the obvious nature of this sighting
the description of the witness is interesting in being typical of the many
exagerations people are capable of........beware the unwary investigator!

6th August 1964 (UK) – Was this a Cosmos satellite?

Doctor M. Carter of Corton Road, Lowestoft, was visiting Mr and Mrs Neal of Wegnall Mill, a quarter of a mile south from Presteigne, Powys, when they sighted a bright light moving overhead, in irregular surges of movement, travelling one degree of 'arc' in three seconds, which was later suggested *"may have been"* the Polyot 2 or Cosmos 36 satellites, according to the Isle of Wight UFO Society.

7th August 1964 (UK) – Seeing things!

At midnight, Colin Reed and Paul Joy of All Saints Crescent, Hastings, sighted an object, *"resembling a cottage loaf, black or dark red in appearance, with beams of light projecting from the top and bottom"*, moving across the sky, a few hundred feet away from them, heading towards the south-east. They reported the matter to the police, who suggested they were *"seeing things"*. (**Source:** *UFOLOG*, 12.4.1965, Issue 14, Kath Smith)

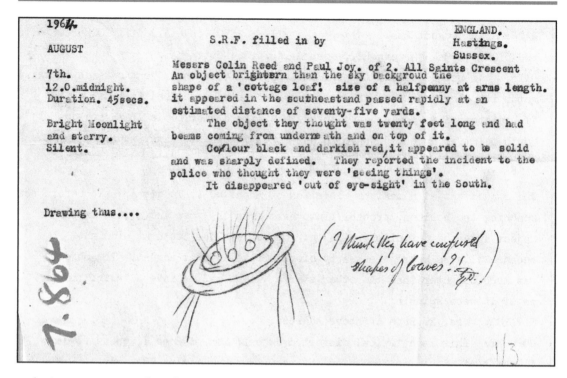

1964

AUGUST

7th.
12.0.midnight.
Duration. 45secs.

Bright Moonlight
and starry.
Silent.

S.R.F. filled in by

ENGLAND.
Hastings.
Sussex.

Messrs Colin Reed and Paul Joy. of 2. All Saints Crescent
An object brighter than the sky backgroud the
shape of a 'cottage loaf' size of a halfpenny at arms length.
it appeared in the southeast and passed rapidly at an
estimated distance of seventy-five yards.

The object they thought was twenty feet long and had
beams coming from underneath and on top of it.

Colour black and darkish red,it appeared to be solid
and was sharply defined. They reported the incident to the
police who thought they were 'seeing things'.

It disappeared 'out of eye-sight' in the South.

Drawing thus....

(I think they have confused shapes of leaves?)

8th August 1964 (UK) – More people seeing things!

A yellow/white oval object was seen hovering over Wellington Road South, Stockport, by housewife – Ruby Roe – at 1.30am this morning.

Cheshire UFO

At 3am, Mr Ernest David Hopkins from Hazel Grove, Macclesfield – an aircraft engineer by occupation – was driving his 1961 Ford Zephyr, accompanied by his wife and two sons – Christopher and Mark – on their way back from a holiday in Cornwall. They noticed a *"brilliant pure white light"* at the side of the road in front of trees.

As they turned into the junction with the A34 Wilmslow Road/A536 Macclesfield Road, they were surprised to see that the glowing object was now following. After keeping pace with them for nearly an hour, at 50mph, it suddenly shot up in into the sky and disappeared from sight.

(Source: DIGAP, Harry Bunting, *UFOLOG*, Issue No. 9, 5.11.1964)

9th August 1964 (UK) – Triangular UFO

In the early hours of this morning, a brilliant neon red light was seen hovering in the air, at a height of approximately 2,000feet, over Arun, Littlehampton, Essex, by local men – Brian Mills, P. J. Homer, and Mr Smith – who were out fishing on West Works Pier, close to the English Channel.

In a letter written to Kath Smith, of the Isle of Wight Society, Brian described what happened.

"After setting our eyes on the object, it appeared to be in two halves; the top corner triangle having

a more intense glow than the lower crescent, seen for approximately two minutes. The object then enlarged slightly for a few seconds. We immediately switched off our torches. It appeared to come towards us, but then altered its direction northwards toward Arundel, for a second or two, and then faded away completely before reappearing, a few seconds later, still heading towards the North. After 30 seconds, it changed direction and headed towards Bognor Regis; five minutes later, it faded away.

We returned to our fishing, facing directly westwards where we thought it had gone. Within two to three minutes, it reappeared above the skyline at Bognor. By 4.40am, it was no longer visible."

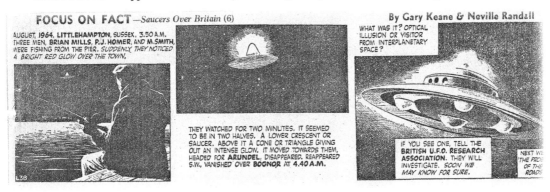

Over Hove (UK)

The same object appears to have also been seen by Mrs R Baker, from Hove, who sighted what she described as:

"...a bright neon red 'flying saucer', travelling through the sky over the Downs, during the early morning – its red lights blinking on and off while it hovered or stalled between Hove and Brighton railways stations."

Nottingham (UK) – Yellow *'disc'* seen

At 10.13pm on the same date, Mr M. Harrison from West Bridgford, Nottingham, was outside looking for the Perseid meteor shower, when he noticed an object in the sky to the north, described as being:

"...a large yellow 'disc', flying at a height of 150feet – north to east. As it went into the distance, I saw it roll from side to side; a few seconds it had gone."

(Source: William Blythe/*UFOLOG*, Issue 2, 31.8.1964/Isle of Wight UFO Society/*Evening Argus*, Brighton, 14.8.1964 – 'What a relief to see flying saucer report')

Birmingham, West Midlands (UK) – *'Flying saucer'* seen

Frank Peake from Hollywood, near Birmingham, West Midlands, contacted us after a newspaper appeal, with regard to what he saw many years ago. At the time, he considered it important enough to record in his personal diary – still available for scrutiny, over 35 years later.

"I was walking along Broad Street, Birmingham, past the Hall of Memory, at 8.15pm, when I was stunned to see a light-coloured grey/silver object, with a dome or conning tower on its top, darting in and out of broken cloud over where a rainbow had formed. I watched as it stopped and started in the sky, at a height of about 5,000feet, approximately a quarter of a mile away. When I arrived

home I eagerly read the newspapers, believing hundreds of people must have seen this object in the sky. There was nothing – apart from a report, a few days later, of a UFO sighted by three schoolboys from Sutton Coldfield, who said they had seen a UFO land and take-off from a wooded area in the nearby park."

10th August 1964 (USA) – Red light approaches runway

At 5.16am, Aircraft Commander Captain B.C. Jones and navigator 1st Lt. H.J. Cavender were in a parked USAF C-124 transport plane, on Wake Island, when they saw a red blinking light approach the runway, stop, and make several reverses, before flying away. (**Source: Berliner**)

12th August 1964 (New Guinea) – Unusual light seen

At Kavieng, Papua, New Guinea, an unusual white *'light'* was seen moving across the sky.

12th August 1964 (USA) – Crescent-shaped UFO

At 5am, an object – described as resembling a burning haystack, crescent in shape – was seen in the sky over Brekkens Corner, Montana, by a motorist and his companions. The motorist stopped his car and went to have another look – by which time the object was now oblong, rising in the sky, and orange in colour. The UFO stayed in the area until 6.15am, when it moved away slowly – southwards. Explanation: Moon. (**Source: Project Blue Book**)

14th August 1964 (UK) – Dozens of lights seen

At 4.45am, *"a perfectly round shape, containing dozens of lights inside"*, was seen in the north-east part of the sky, by Mr and Mrs Cyril Harry of Caerwent, Monmouthshire. It appears that the same object was also seen by another Newport couple, at 5am, who said:

"It was as brilliant and three times the size of a star. At 6am, it disappeared behind a cloud."

NO	DATE	TIME	MAP REF	DOCS
2/17	14/8/64			

DETAILS

A bright circular disc with a red flashing light on top was seen by two men. It appeared to settle on a distant hilltop. It made a queer noise as it passed. "It looked just like one of them flying saucers. We were terrified" said one of the men

LOC — Longwood (outside Dumfries) on the Dalbeattie Rd.

WITNESSES — NOT. KNOWN
Investigators proceeding
Reported in Dumfries and Galloway Standard 8/8/64

15th August 1964 (USA) – Bullet-shaped UFO

At 1.20am, a New York resident – Mr S. F. D'Alessandro – saw a 10 feet x 5 feet bullet-shaped object, with wavy lines on the rounded front part, and six pipes along the straight rear portion, making a *'swishing'* sound as it passed through the sky, causing his dog to growl. (**Source: Berliner**)

Yosemite National Park, California (USA) – Three UFOs seen

At 8.15pm, Mr E. J. Haug – of the San Francisco Orchestra and Conservatory of Music – and C. R. Bubb – High school teacher – was camped out at Benson Lake, Yosemite.

"At 8.15am, we were by the side of the lake when we heard the sound of rushing air, and were surprised the branches on the trees didn't move – then we heard it again and looked up to see three objects, heading east to west across the sky at incredible speed – gone in seconds.

In the brief moments that I observed them, I was able to clearly see the three bright silvery objects moving on a parallel course but at variable forward speeds. As one of them moved ahead of the other two, there was an adjustment and they would line-up for a moment, before another would get ahead – then the adjustment would be repeated."

Explanation: Unidentified. (**Source: NICAP**)

17th August 1964 (Tasmania)

A blue coloured object was seen in the sky, moving around in circles, before being lost from view.

17th August 1964 (UK) – UFO sighted

DATE: 1964 August 17th..   TIME: 11.44 p.m. B.S.T..

LOCATION: 23, Highfield Rd., West Bridgford, Nottingham,

DATA: Witness was out looking for meteors when he saw a reddish light about above him. At first he thought that it was a meteor, but a second or so later he saw that it had a definite shape. At this point it was about 30° East of the vertical, and was about ½° across (see drawing) (size is the same as the full moon).

The object continued to the horizon of house roofs opposite (elevation 4°) and seemed to rise slightly and to turn South.

The movement was undulating and it appeared to be moved by the wind (which was strong and from West to East). The height was low, colour reddish, no noticeable noise, and the outline was slightly fuzzy. The object was faint

WITNESS: Master C. R. Kitchin (17) of above address.

18th August 1964 (UK) – UFO display

A mysterious flying object was seen over Newport, at 5.20am, by Mrs B. Byron, who was looking out over the docks and Channel, when she saw a *'bright light'* appear in the sky. Strange tiny *'spots of lights'* were reported being seen travelling through the sky, at fantastic speeds – by many people (including the local post of the Royal Observer Corps) – high in sky over the Cheviots, above the small village of Elsdon, and were seen to change direction at impossible angles, sometimes flying in formation. (**Source: John Ogilvy/***News Daily,* **20.8.1964)**

18th August 1964 – UFO sighting by pilots over Atlantic

At 12.35pm over the Atlantic, some 200 miles East of Dover, Delaware, USAF Major D.W. Thompson and First Pilot Lt. J.F. Jonke were flying a C-124 transport airplane (No.31007) with the 31st Air Transport Squadron, 1607th Air Transport Wing, out of Dover Air Force Base, at 9,000feet and 200mph true airspeed, when they saw a large, round, blurred or diffuse edged, red-white luminous object, on a collision course with the C-124 from ahead and about 500 feet below. A collision was averted when the pilot took evasive action by turning from a 260° heading to 340°; the object made a right turn and disappeared. (**Source: Berliner/ NICAP**)

Denver, Colorado

At 2.45am on this date, an egg-shaped *'light'*, with a flashing *'head'*, was seen over Denver, Colorado, travelling across the sky at an angle of 45° off the horizon. The *'light'* was seen zigzagging at first, before heading in a north to south direction. At one stage, it was seen to halt momentarily in the sky. Explanation: Aircraft. (**Source: Project Blue Book**)

19th August 1964 (UK) – Objects over Birmingham

At 10.35pm, Mr and Mrs Derek Samson from St. Margaret's Road, Olton (just outside Birmingham) were in their garden when they saw what they took to be a satellite, heading south-west to south-east.

> *"Suddenly another brilliant object appeared and overtook the first one, which halted in mid-air for a short while, before gaining speed and moving direction – now due south."*

(Source: Derek Samson)

Above: Derek Samson and wife

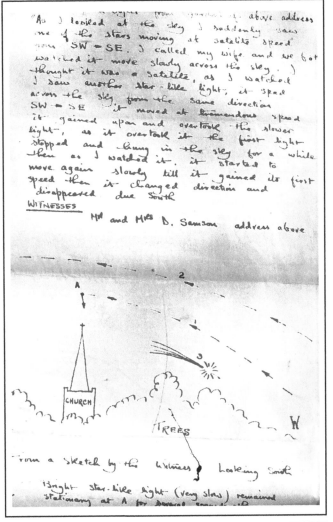

20th August 1964 (Australia) – Explosion heard

An explosion was heard – apparently coming from the sky – over Turner Station, on the Ord River. This had been preceded by a *'silver spot'*, or *'track'* seen in the sky. (**Sources: Unknown**)

21st August 1964 (UK) – *'Flying saucer'* seen

Eric Bridge – a Company Director, from Macclesfield – was out, trout fishing, as dusk fell at a dam, situated between Macclesfield and Leek.

> *"It was 9.15pm when I first saw this object, over Rudyard. It veered to the right and started to approach my position, allowing me to see a large half-round contraption along the outer edge, with an orange coloured rim. There was a quadrant on it, and lights kept going on and off. I thought it was looking for a place to land. I was shaking like a leaf and telephoned the police, who contacted the Manchester Evening News."*

(**Source:** *Daily Express*, 22.8.1964/Harry Bunting, DIGAP, Issue 7/*Manchester Evening News*)

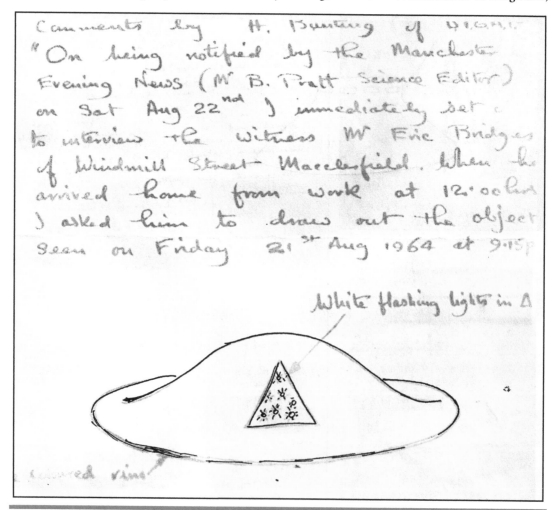

Saucer-shaped UFO seen

At about the same time, schoolgirls – Loraine Cunningham (11) and Julie Powell (16), from Brocklehurst Avenue, Macclesfield – sighted a silver, saucer-shaped object, with what looked like aerials at each side, flying through the clear night sky at a height they estimated to be only a couple of hundred feet.

> *"It was rotating very fast and then stopped, turned on its side, and headed off towards the direction of The Hollies – and gone in two minutes."*

(**Source:** *UFOLOG*, 21.10.1964)

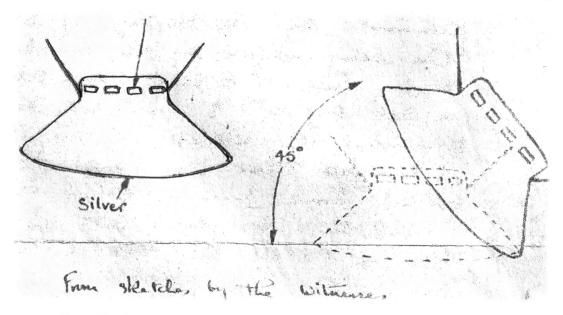

Yellow 'disc'

At 9.47pm, members of the Gingele family found themselves witnessing further examples of UFO activity when, while standing outside their house at Chadwick Road, Falcon Lodge, Sutton Coldfield, they saw a yellow '*disc*', described in size as being, *"small – but larger than Venus in comparison – moving across the sky. As it approached closer, the yellow changed to red. Behind it was a smaller, fainter, yellow light. We watched it for two minutes, until it was out of sight."*

(**Source:** *UFOLOG*, Issue 5, 28.9.1964)

UFO sighted

At 11pm an object, resembling *"a large electric light bulb, with frosted glass, seven or eight times the size of a sixpence (as seen from the ground)"*, was seen flying through the air at the height of nearby flats in Nicholson Avenue, on the junction with Queen's Drive, Macclesfield, by William Cumberlidge.

(**Source:** DIGAP, Harold Bunting)

Moses Lake, Washington

According to Project Blue Book, this was the date when seven photographs were taken of a UFO landing spot. See following images from Project Blue Book.

22nd August 1964 (UK) – *'Ball of light'* seen

A shimmering small *'ball of light'* was seen in the sky over Heaton Moor, Stockport, heading towards the direction of Reddish, at 3.10am, by Mr Harrison, who reported it being motionless in the sky for seven minutes, before disappearing from sight.

23rd August 1964 (UK) – Black cross-shaped UFO seen

At 4.30pm, black cross-shaped object was seen motionless in the sky over Mobberley, Cheshire, by Mr A. M. Johnson, at an estimated height of l,000ft, and two miles away; ten or fifteen seconds later, it vanished from view.

(**Source: Harry Bunting, DIGAP**)

25th August 1964 (USA) – Dome-shaped UFO seen

At 9.30pm a silvery object, showing a central dome on top, with red and white lights on its rim, was seen *'fluttering'* off the ground at Church Field, Littleton, Massachusetts, accompanied by a soft roaring sound; the object then shot away, at high speed.

One hour later, a silvery object, about 20ft in diameter, showing a central dome on top and a glowing white rim, making a whining noise, was seen hovering below treetop level near a power substation, close to a rest home at Lynn.

26th August 1964 (USA) – Large red *'star'*

At 9.20pm a glowing object, resembling a large red *'star'*, was seen in the sky over Melrose, Massachusetts. Through a 2.4inch telescope, at 35power, it was seen as about a third of a degree in diameter, and looked like a red pulsating ellipsoid, showing a red-orange halo.

27th August 1964 (UK) – Blinding light

At 3.50am, Mrs Kathleen Shard from Woodford, near Stockton, was awoken by flashing lights. Rushing to the window, she looked out and saw *"…this huge blinding light, apparently coming towards me. It then receded, but approached again and vanished seconds later"*. (**Source: Harold Bunting**)

Later the same day, at 8pm, a curious white object was seen moving over Low Fell, Gateshead, heading south to north.

NO	DATE	TIME	MAP REF	DOCS
2/19	27/8/64	20 00		C. A.

DETAILS — Silent, white high flying object seen directly overhead. No noise, no vapour trails, no wings. Flying South to North on a straight course.

LOC — Home i.e. Low Fell, Gateshead, Co. Durham. ④

WITNESSES — WISH TO REMAIN ANONYMOUS

Unidentified Flying Objects and other types of unexplained Aerial Phenomena.

It will be of great help if you give accurate and detailed information on your sighting of _____ *Thursday 27th Aug. at 10 mins to 4 am*

Please return this form as soon as possible to the above address.
THANK YOU FOR YOUR HELP AND CO-OPERATION.

SECTION ONE

YOUR FULL NAME: MR./MRS./MISS   *Kathleen Shand*
(BLOCK LETTERS PLEASE)
YOUR PERMANENT ADDRESS   *address as above*
TELEPHONE NUMBER
AGE
OCCUPATION   *Housewife*

QUALIFICATIONS (IF ANY)   *Some nursing certificates also Domestic Science C.G.L.I. (City & Guilds London)*

IF AND WHEN IT IS DECIDED TO PUBLISH THE SIGHTING MAY WE DISCLOSE YOUR NAME AND OCCUPATION?   *not answered. not keen.*

ANY OTHER WITNESSES   NAME(S)   ADDRESS(ES)

not (But mentioned it few hrs later at breakfast.)

TOTAL NUMBER   *1*

HAVE YOU ANY EYE-SIGHT DEFECTS?   *Long Sight.*
WERE YOU WEARING GLASSES AT THE TIME OF THE SIGHTING?   *NO*
HAVE YOU PREVIOUSLY SEEN A U.F.O., OR ANY UNUSUAL AERIAL PHENOMENA?   *NO*
OR SEEN EARTH SATELLITES? (WHEN)   *NO*

HAVE YOU HAD ANY EXPERIENCE OF OBSERVING THE SKY? e.g. AS A MEMBER OF AN ASTRONOMICAL SOCIETY?, OBSERVER CORPS.?   *NO*

DID YOU REPORT THE SIGHTING TO THE NEWSPAPERS?, METEOROLOGICAL OFFICE?, POLICE?, WHAT WAS THEIR COMMENT?

HAVE YOU ANY IDEAS OR THEORIES WHAT THE OBJECT(S) MIGHT HAVE BEEN?   *As Jodrell Bank is so near I thought something was photographing it*

NOW PLEASE TURN OVERLEAF AND COMPLETE SECTION TWO (IF YOU REQUIRE ANY HELP IN FILLING IN THE FORM PLEASE CONTACT YOUR LOCAL INVESTIGATOR AT THE FOLLOWING ADDRESS, OR TELEPHONE NUMBER.)

NAME   ADDRESS

TELEPHONE NUMBER

Mr. H. BUNTING, GRAD. I.E.E.
34, BOWERFIELD AVENUE,
HAZEL GROVE,
STOCKPORT,
CHESHIRE.
TELEPHONE: POYnton 3956

continued overleaf:-

UFOLOG
REF NO 3/9
H.S. ISSUE NO 6
16 OCT 1964

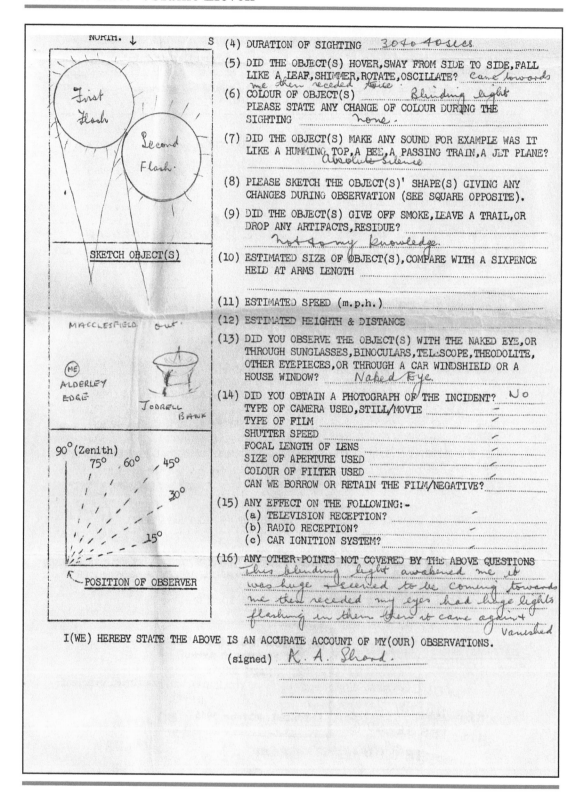

NORTH. ↓   S

First Flash

Second Flash.

SKETCH OBJECT(S)

MACCLESFIELD   out.

(ME)
ALDERLEY
EDGE

JODRELL
BANK

90° (Zenith)
75°   60°   45°
              30°
           15°

POSITION OF OBSERVER

(4) DURATION OF SIGHTING   30 to 40 secs.

(5) DID THE OBJECT(S) HOVER, SWAY FROM SIDE TO SIDE, FALL
LIKE A LEAF, SHIMMER, ROTATE, OSCILLATE?   Came towards
me then receded twice

(6) COLOUR OF OBJECT(S)   Blinding light
PLEASE STATE ANY CHANGE OF COLOUR DURING THE
SIGHTING   none.

(7) DID THE OBJECT(S) MAKE ANY SOUND FOR EXAMPLE WAS IT
LIKE A HUMMING TOP, A BEE, A PASSING TRAIN, A JET PLANE?
Absolute silence

(8) PLEASE SKETCH THE OBJECT(S)' SHAPE(S) GIVING ANY
CHANGES DURING OBSERVATION (SEE SQUARE OPPOSITE).

(9) DID THE OBJECT(S) GIVE OFF SMOKE, LEAVE A TRAIL, OR
DROP ANY ARTIFACTS, RESIDUE?
not to my knowledge.

(10) ESTIMATED SIZE OF OBJECT(S), COMPARE WITH A SIXPENCE
HELD AT ARMS LENGTH

(11) ESTIMATED SPEED (m.p.h.)

(12) ESTIMATED HEIGHT & DISTANCE

(13) DID YOU OBSERVE THE OBJECT(S) WITH THE NAKED EYE, OR
THROUGH SUNGLASSES, BINOCULARS, TELESCOPE, THEODOLITE,
OTHER EYEPIECES, OR THROUGH A CAR WINDSHIELD OR A
HOUSE WINDOW?   Naked Eye.

(14) DID YOU OBTAIN A PHOTOGRAPH OF THE INCIDENT? No
TYPE OF CAMERA USED, STILL/MOVIE
TYPE OF FILM
SHUTTER SPEED
FOCAL LENGTH OF LENS
SIZE OF APERTURE USED
COLOUR OF FILTER USED
CAN WE BORROW OR RETAIN THE FILM/NEGATIVE?

(15) ANY EFFECT ON THE FOLLOWING:-
(a) TELEVISION RECEPTION?
(b) RADIO RECEPTION?
(c) CAR IGNITION SYSTEM?

(16) ANY OTHER POINTS NOT COVERED BY THE ABOVE QUESTIONS
This blinding light awakened me it
was huge + seemed to be coming towards
me then receded my eyes had huge lights
flashing in them then it came again +
Vanished

I(WE) HEREBY STATE THE ABOVE IS AN ACCURATE ACCOUNT OF MY(OUR) OBSERVATIONS.

(signed)   K. A. Shand.

USA:

At 10pm, a bright glowing yellow *'ball'*, about 10ft in diameter, was seen crossing the highway in front of a motorist at Littleton, Massachusetts, which then rose slightly to clear the top of a nearby hill.

During the same date, eight photographs of UFOs were taken over Hondo Air Force Base, Texas.

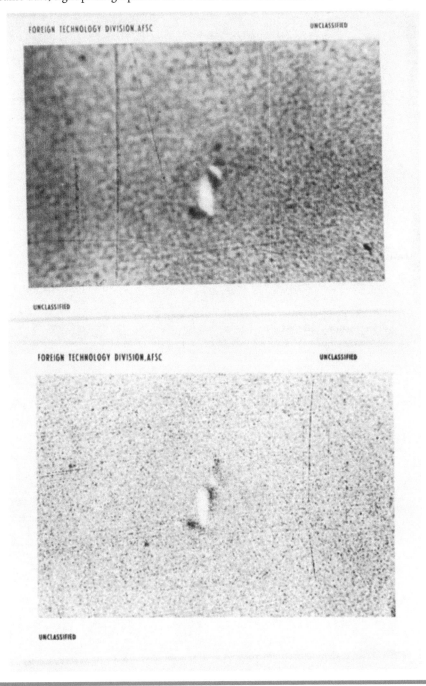

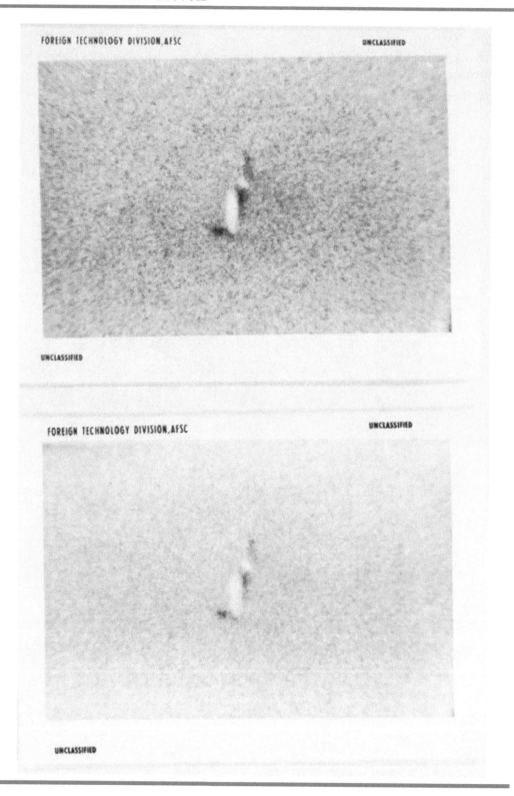

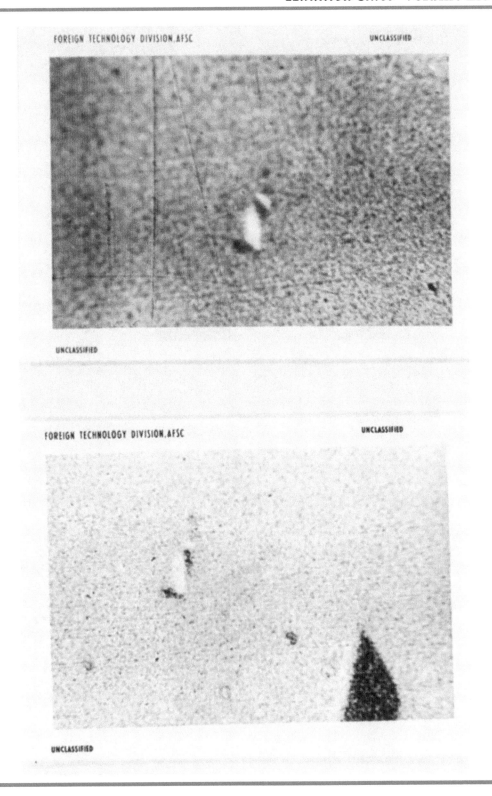

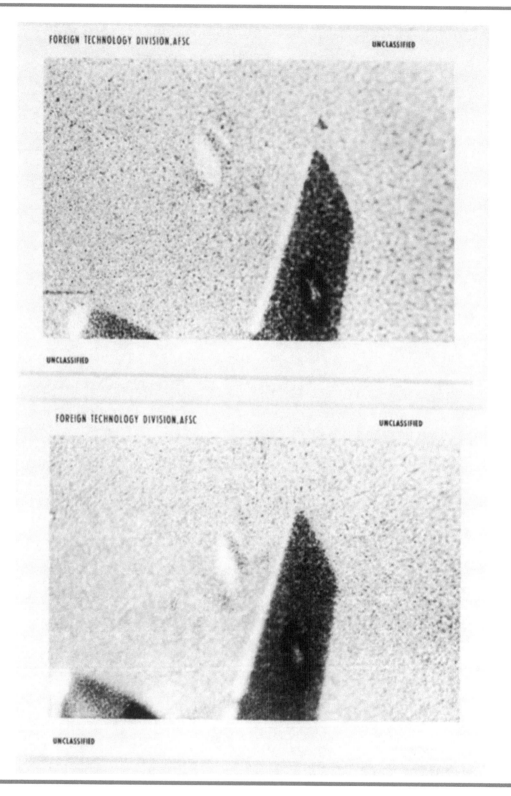

30th August 1964 (USA)

An oval UFO was photographed by Rick Blevins over Seville, Ohio.

(**Source: Brad Steiger and JoanWhritenour,** *Flying Saucers Are Hostile,*1967)

30th August 1964 (UK) – Glowing sphere seen

NO	DATE	TIME	MAP REF.	DOCS
2/20	30/8/64	23.45.		C.A.

DETAILS: A sharply defined, orange-red sphere appeared for approx. 10 secs. It was flickering and pulsating. Travelled a short distance then disappeared. Direction was SE to N.W. Could it have been a fireball?

LOC At. home

WITNESSES R. Murray. 48, Wingrove Ave, Fenham, Newcastle on Tyne

31st August 1964 (UK) – Three *'windows of light'*

At 9.10pm, Mr Frank Borrows and his wife of Chorlton-cum-Hardy, near Manchester, sighted an object in the sky travelling at fantastic speed, from north to south, rushing past an aircraft which had just taken off from Manchester Ringway Airport.

At 11.05pm, Mr and Mrs Hankinson of the Queensway, Heald Green, Cheshire, sighted what appeared to be

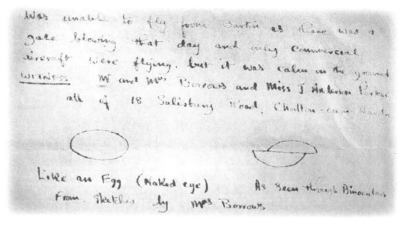

two *'lights'* following each other across the sky, heading north-west to south-west, at considerable height. They were judged far too fast to be satellites and were out of sight 30-45 seconds later. (**Source:** *UFOLOG*, No. 6, 13.10.1964)

At 11.10pm, Mr Borrows sighted a second object appear in the sky, described as:

> *"...resembling a wasp in shape, with lights on the front – so strong they would have blinded you had it been lower. It had three windows on the side facing me, lighting up the interior. My compass went*

wild as it passed overhead, at a speed much faster than an aircraft. I estimated it was probably at a height of some 3000ft."

Mr K.K Armin also saw it. He was living in Stockport, Cheshire. He wrote to the MOD and this was their reply:

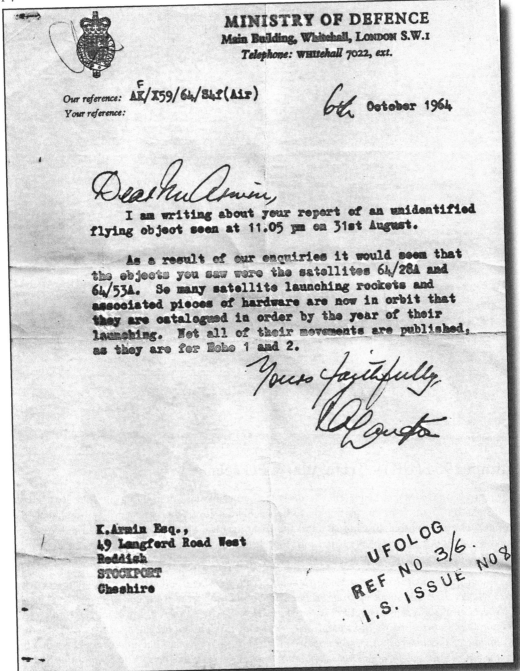

MINISTRY OF DEFENCE
Main Building, Whitehall, LONDON S.W.1
Telephone: WHITEHALL 7022, ext.

Our reference: AK/X59/64/84f(Air)
Your reference:

6th October 1964

Dear Mr Armin,

I am writing about your report of an unidentified flying object seen at 11.05 pm on 31st August.

As a result of our enquiries it would seem that the objects you saw were the satellites 64/28A and 64/53A. So many satellite launching rockets and associated pieces of hardware are now in orbit that they are catalogued in order by the year of their launching. Not all of their movements are published, as they are for Echo 1 and 2.

Yours faithfully,

K.Armin Esq.,
49 Langford Road West
Reddish
STOCKPORT
Cheshire

UFOLOG
REF NO 3/6.
I.S. ISSUE NO 8

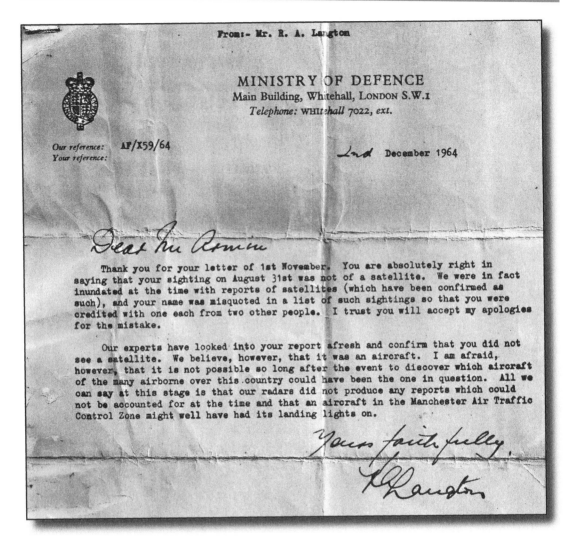

From:- Mr. R. A. Langton

MINISTRY OF DEFENCE
Main Building, Whitehall, LONDON S.W.1
Telephone: WHItehall 7022, *ext.*

Our reference: AF/X59/64
Your reference:

2nd December 1964

Dear Mr Armin

Thank you for your letter of 1st November. You are absolutely right in saying that your sighting on August 31st was not of a satellite. We were in fact inundated at the time with reports of satellites (which have been confirmed as such), and your name was misquoted in a list of such sightings so that you were credited with one each from two other people. I trust you will accept my apologies for the mistake.

Our experts have looked into your report afresh and confirm that you did not see a satellite. We believe, however, that it was an aircraft. I am afraid, however, that it is not possible so long after the event to discover which aircraft of the many airborne over this country could have been the one in question. All we can say at this stage is that our radars did not produce any reports which could not be accounted for at the time and that an aircraft in the Manchester Air Traffic Control Zone might well have had its landing lights on.

Yours faithfully,

K Langton

Autumn 1964 (UK) – Triangular UFO seen

In autumn 1964, Mrs Mabel Leigh Till – a designer by occupation, then living in Stoke Road, Baddeley Green, Stoke-on-Trent – was just getting off to sleep, at about 1am, when she heard a noise like an electric motor. It was most unusual, bearing in mind the rural location of the property concerned. After getting dressed, she went out into the back garden and stood listening. There was nothing to be seen, or heard – just the glow of lights from a nearby town on the horizon.

> *"Suddenly, without warning, a black triangular craft, showing a solitary red light, approximately 35-40feet in length, swept up from behind a line of damson trees at the end of the garden (some streets away) and slowly moved over the house, clearing the TV aerial. It was dark metallic grey in colour, showing streaks in its paintwork – as though a coat had been applied too thickly. In the middle of the underneath were a number of curious square panels, illuminated by one panel in the centre – the colour of red hot metal but not metallic, more like Perspex in composition. A bar of brighter orange light moved along the panels in numerical order, 9-12, at 3½ second intervals.*

There was no sign of any portholes, or openings, although when the craft went across the lane, I noticed an oval-shaped light at each tip, magenta in colour, inside a hollow channel. The motion of the craft was accompanied by a gently singing purr, like that given off by a small electric motor, the tone being 'G' natural."

(Source: Jackie Hepworth/Gordon Creighton, *FSR*)

'Mrs Till – according to her life-long companion, Jackie Hepworth (to whom we spoke) – was a woman of considerable artistic skill. Sadly, she has now passed away, but should be congratulated for her excellent description of the UFO – meticulously written down after the event – allowing us the opportunity to see for ourselves something which cannot be explained away rationally. One also speculates on the significance of this UFO and the 'wave' of sightings that were to strike England and Europe, a quarter of a century later. Mabel may be gone, but her sighting will survive.

Mabel Leigh was one of the great designers of the art deco period. She attended the Burslem School of Art from a young age, where Gordon Forsythe was Principal. Her first job was at Cauldron Pottery, where she remained until financial difficulties at the Pottery led to her move to Shorter & Sons. Her talent was quickly recognised there, and she was given her own studio and four assistants. She stayed at Shorters for two years (1933 – 1935), until leaving to join Charlotte Rhead at Crown Ducal. During her time at Shorters, her designs were influenced by the patterns and colours from the Middle East, Africa and Central America, the range she produced being known as Period Ware.

Mable Leigh married John Till in 1939, and became Mabel Leigh Till.. She spent most of her time as a freelance designer, mainly in the design and production of bathroom tiles. She retired to Wales in the late 1960s, where she continued to create art. Her work is unique – a remarkable woman, whom we never had the pleasure of meeting, but one thing is assured this lady, had an eye for detail!

Close encounter with landed UFO

Joan Vincent, who has served in Local Government in a variety of positions, including Chairwoman of the County Planning Office – a long-standing Borough Councillor and Governor of her local school – decided to pluck-up the courage and tell what she and her husband Roy saw, over 40 years before, in the Karslake area of Cornwall, during the autumn of 1964.

"We read about some students from Fowey College, who reported having seen 'flying saucers' over Carloggas Downs, and decided to go out and have a look for ourselves. After driving for a short time, we stopped at 5pm in Karslake, where we scanned the surrounding skies, hoping to see something. Ten or fifteen minutes later, the whole of the open countryside was enveloped in brilliant light. Startled, we stood there trying to identify the source of this light, and realised it was coming from a field behind a hedge, about 50 yards away from our position."

Joan Vincent

Dome-shaped object on the ground

We walked over and peered behind the hedge, and were flabbergasted to see a large dome with an upper surface that appeared to be translucent – like glass – with a lower solid body, grey or green in colour, about six feet in length and three feet in height. Unfortunately, as our view was restricted by another hedge, we were unable to determine whether the 'craft' was actually resting on the ground, although it appeared that way. We could see what looked like a large cabinet, with dials inset around the outside, and what looked like portholes. At this stage, I felt frightened and asked Roy to take us home. We decided to keep quiet, knowing we would be the subject of ridicule."

THE TRUTH IS OUT THERE

LEFT: Vernon Salmon's drawing of the object he is convinced was a UFO. RIGHT: Joan and Roy Vincent (below) drew this flying object they saw one night over the clay district.

"Maybe one day we shall all agree what it was we saw," Mrs Vincent said this week.

Orange ball in sky was not from Earth

by IAN SHEPHERD

[newspaper body text partially illegible]

Flying saucer like the ones in films

[newspaper body text partially illegible]

UFO ailments

We asked Joan if she had noticed any unusual medical symptoms that had occurred after the UFO experience. She told us about a small lump on her right leg, out of which – to her horror – grew something resembling a blade of grass that could only be cut off using scissors. Despite seeking medical advice over the years, the condition remained undiagnosed until it stopped growing, leaving a small scar.

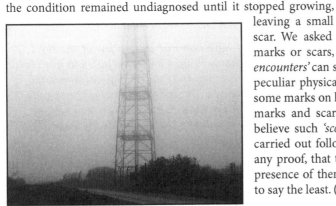

Carloggas Downs

We asked her if she had discovered any unusual marks or scars, following the event, knowing that *'close encounters'* can sometimes seem to result in all manner of peculiar physical ailments. She confirmed she had found some marks on her leg identical in size and depth to other marks and scars brought to our notice by people who believe such *'scoop marks'* are evidence of alien surgery carried out following *'abduction'*. We cannot say, without any proof, that these marks are caused by aliens, but the presence of them following a UFO encounter is puzzling to say the least. (**Source: Personal interview**)

We salute the courage of people like Joan, who, knowing the likelihood of ridicule being aimed at her, at least recognises the importance of bringing this to the public's attention. If she was the only one, well, that would be different – but of course she is one of thousands that have experienced something similar.

Joan:

> *"In 1981 I was elected. I stood against three men and won by just over 100 votes – which was a surprise. I didn't think for one minute that I would win; I was thinking more about using it as experience to get elected to Restormel."*

She went on to become a well-respected member of both the County Council and local Council.

Joan:

> *"I have always had the desire to help other people in the area and there have been some big events which have happened over the years.*
>
> *There were the plans for a nuclear power station at Luxulyan, many years ago, which we campaigned against, and we have worked successfully to get improvements in the china clay areas as well. It has been very enjoyable. The thing I enjoyed most was being chair of planning that I was for nine years. During that time we set up the minerals panel and created links with the industry for the good of the area. The restoration of Caerloggas Downs is a good example – the industry wanted to tip in more on top of there, but I just felt that was terrible so we worked to see what we could do to improve it. After a lot of meetings, they did re-profile it. There are a lot of habitats down there and that has come back now. People walk their dogs and enjoy the countryside, so it was worth it."*

Prince Charles

During her time as a councillor, Mrs Vincent has also had the privilege of meeting many people who visited the county. She said:

Roy and Joan Vincent

> *"I have met such a wide variety of people over the years, including government ministers who have come down here or who I have met in London.*
>
> *I have also met quite a few of the royal family. Prince Charles was hilarious when I met him, and Prince Philip was wonderful as well. The first time I met the Queen was at the Royal Cornwall Show and told me she didn't like to see caravans by the sea!"*

In 2014, while reviewing this incident for Volume 11, we telephoned Joan – now 14 years on from the last contact with her – and were saddened to learn that Roy had passed away seven years ago.

1st September 1964 (Australia) (UK) – Pilots sight two UFOs

The First Officer on an Ansett flight (Melbourne-based Australian Airline) en route from Melbourne to Canberra, near Holbrook, sighted two silver objects.

> *"One appeared approximately 3,000ft above the aircraft, dead ahead; the other, much higher, at the one o'clock position. Both appeared as solid silver ovals, i.e. no wings."*

Their sighting was later explained away as being either aircraft, or refraction of light.

(Source: NAA file series A703/*Project 1947*, Keith Basterfield)

Isle of Wight (UK) – *'Circus ring'* UFO

At 9.30pm, Mrs B Morris of St. Mary's Place, Ryde, Isle of Wight, sighted:

> *"…a bright pulsating red object, resembling a circus ring, about 45ft in circumference, showing double blinking lights on one side, moving through the night sky, flying along a straight line from the direction of Cowes to St. Catherine's Point. Five minutes later, it had gone from view."*

(Source: *UFOLOG*)

2nd September 1964 (UK) – Rotating UFO

At 8.50pm, *"a red-orange flickering light, rotating around its central axis"*, was seen moving no more than a few miles per hour across the sky, over Hollins Farm, Macclesfield, Cheshire, heading towards Macclesfield, by Elizabeth Astle, (aged 16) and her friend, Gillian Bailey of High Street, Macclesfield. (**Source: DIGAP/ *UFOLOG*, Issue No. 6, 13.10.1964**)

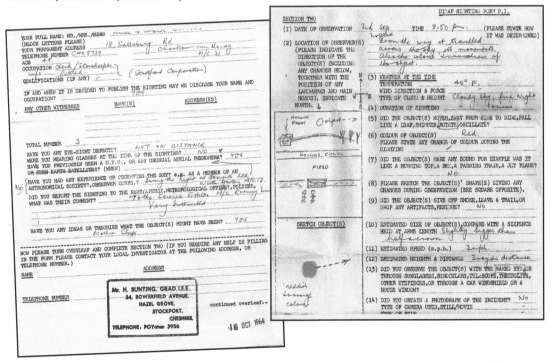

4th September 1964 (USA) – Did a UFO land in Glassboro, New Jersey?

It is said that hundreds of people made their way to an oak forest near Glassboro, New Jersey, on 6th September, to look at a circular clearing of charred earth, following a report of a red glowing object seen to land in the forest, two days previously. It began on the Saturday night (the 4th September) when Mr Ward Campbell of 30, Selsea Drive, Glassboro, called the police after his two sons – Ward (11) and Don (8) – told him of having been approached by a man (aged about 20) who told the boys he had seen a glowing object land in the forest. The police took samples of earth and other material, which was sent to McGuire Air Force Base for examination.

```
                              9▓▓▓▓▓▓▓▓ne
                         Bloomfield, Connecticut

                                              9 Dec 64

Major Maston M. Jacks
USAF PIO, Pentagon
Washington, D.C.

Dear Major Jacks;

Thank you very much for your letter, and enclosure, of 24 November 1964, in answer to
my UFO questions.  I was interested to see that the Air Force still carries the report
from Socorro as unsolved, particularly since a recent letter from Dr. Donald Menzel
to me carried a contrary opinion.  Although he admits that he had not seen "any de-
tailed information" about the Socorro report, he flatly came out that it "was prob-
ably a hoax or a delusion."  I sent him a copy of your fact sheet but as yet he hasn't
commented on it.

With respect to the "hoax" conclusion on the Glassboro, N.J. sighting, I am now in
possession of a NICAP report on that sighting.  In it, they quote at some length two
tree experts who examined the leaves of trees in the area, as well as other
vegatation, and gave it as their opinion that the "singe" damage done precluded
a hoax by youngsters.  They stated that leaves were recovered from a 40-foot oak and
that other damage done to trees would have required the use of machinery - one injury,
they stated, "was not inflicted by any known type of tool."  Might I ask if you all
have queried these men or looked into this aspect of the report at all?  Or are you
basing your "hoax" conclusions solely on the evidence of a few footprints and bits
of tin foil which could well have been made (or dropped) by persons visiting the site
before your people arrived?  It is my understanding that several days elapsed between
the time of the initial report and the visit by an Air Force investigator.

"ith respect to your statement that the Air Force "still maintains the responsiblity
for investigating UFOs", might I enquire as to why Westover AFB, in the case of the
Shutesbury, Mass. sighting covered in my 14 Nov 1964 letter, stated that they were
referring the information to the FAA for further investigation?  Seems strange to me.

And might I also ask if your office has received and evaluated THE UFO EVIDENCE, a re-
port published last summer by NICAP?  I understand that it is heavily documented and
relates a number of sightings made by pilots, astronomers, missile engineers and many
other reputable, technically trained personnel.  It would seem from the data presented
there that a substantial case has been made for a more scientific and open investigation
of UFOs than has been made in the past.

I shall be interested in your comments.

                              yours truly
```

29 December 1964

Dear Mr. ▮▮▮▮▮▮:

This is in reply to your letter of December 9.

The Air Force conducts a scientific investigation of UFO sightings. In fifteen years of research, no evidence has been found to support the contention that UFOs are extraterrestrial objects under intelligent control. Thousands of UFO observations have been determined to be a misinterpretation of conventional or natural objects.

The Socorro, New Mexico, sighting is still unsolved. However, no evidence was found which indicated that the vehicle was from outer space. Since we cannot find the pilots who were flying the vehicle, the case will remain unsolved. The lack of radiation and the speed of the vehicle indicate that the craft had not experienced any space residency.

The Glassboro, New Jersey, report is definitely a hoax. The investigation was conducted by several officers from McGuire AFB. After the investigation, the officers determined that the reported sighting was a hoax and that no additional investigation was necessary. Photographs of the area revealed that only one bush was broken. This could easily have been done by applying weight or any other object to the top of the tree.

The newspaper you forwarded on the Shutesbury, Massachusetts, sighting of 14 November 1964 indicates that the object observed was an aircraft. The spokesman from Westover AFB Information Office probably had FAA check for aircraft under their operational control, since all civilian flights are under their jurisdiction. This officer had checked for military aircraft and determined that none were operational in the area. His check with FAA was a routine procedure for evaluating sightings attributed to aircraft observation. Since this report was not forwarded to Wright-Patterson from Westover, we can assume that the aircraft was identified by FAA; therefore, no UFO report was submitted. The object was not an unidentified flying object but an aircraft.

Broken limb on a tree and imprint at the site

5:9:64

Air Force Probes Glassboro area for signs of Flying Saucer.

In a clearing among tall oaks in the Glassboro, N.J. area on Sept. 5 a circle of ground about 20 feet was found that appeared to be scorched by intense heat. The area was discovered after reports of an unusual red glow in the sky over the woods.

In the centre of the circle was a conical hole 30 inches across the top and more than 2 ft deep. 11 4-inch holes were gouged around the main holes forming a 25 foot triangle enclosing the others.

Bits of metal and what appeared to be sand that fused into glass were found in the big hole. Tops of nearby trees were said to be scorched.

After an investigation by 3 Air Force intelligence officers ATIC believed the entire incident was a hoax created by teen-agers in the area. But Glassboro Patrolman Robert Toughbill said "Its possible that it was a hoax but if it was I'd like to know how it was done." (INTERPLANETARY NEWS SERVICE. V.2.N.5: 1965). P. 40.

Another witness was Mr Richard L. Gaskill. He described the area as being about 12 miles south-east of Philadelphia. On a visit to the location, Richard recovered some metal particles from the centre hole and noted that there were, in fact, three small holes made in the earth.

Mr Gaskill – whose account was published in the *BUFORA Journal* (Volume 1, No. 2, Autumn 1964) – obtained samples for analysis, which were sent to a Mr G. Elliot [whose credentials are not disclosed]. His report identified the material as:

Four main components – namely, two metals, charred carbonaceous material and a little soil.

1. The first metal was aluminum, in the form of a badly crumpled foil with a slightly oxidized or dirty surface. The foil was about 0.0015-5-0.002 inches thick, when smoothed out. There were three large pieces and a few smaller fragments of this metal, which appeared reasonably pure from normal chemical test.

2. The second metal was tin, in the form of fused pieces of no defined shape. There were three pieces of tin somewhat smaller than the aluminum pieces and distinguishable by their brighter slightly yellowish tint, compared to the grey of the aluminum. The metal appeared to be pure, with the exception of a small trace of lead by normal chemical test.

3. The black material was well carbonized wood of twigs, probably heated in a very restricted supply of air, to give a charcoal containing little organic matter.

4. The sample contained a few small lumps of soil, with normal composition, containing a fair amount of siliceous matter, a little carbonate, a little pyrites, etc.

It was considered that the aluminum foil may have been a wrapper from chocolate or cigarette packet, and that it hadn't been in the soil for long.

Molten tin had been found at the scene, following a UFO incident in Brazil on the 13th December 1954, when the object had dropped a liquid substance. Whether this was the case at New Jersey, no-one can say.

This version of events seems in conflict with another account, which tells of a pair of teenagers from Glassboro, New Jersey, who was approached by two strangers – Nordic looking, with long, blonde hair – who showed them the landing site of an unidentified flying object. (The boys said they never actually saw the craft on the ground, but did see a red light descend and ascend nearby.)

Investigators from the local police department, the US Air Force, and NICAP, discovered several pieces of physical evidence at the site, including a 28 inch circular crater, surrounded by 11 nearly equidistant disc marks – which was suggested to be a hoax, although this has never been proved.

Cisco Grove, California – UFO landing

Donald Schrum (28), and his friends, were out hunting in an isolated area of Placer County, when he became separated from his companions. At sunset he decided to sleep in a tree for the night. Later he saw a white light zigzagging at low altitude and, thinking it was a helicopter, jumped out of the tree and lit fires to attract its attention. The light turned toward him and stopped about 50-60 yards away. The object's strange appearance frightened Schrum, so he climbed back up in the tree.

Humanoids appear

After a while, two humanoids and a robot-like creature approached the tree. From then on Schrum was in a state of siege, as the beings tried to dislodge him from the tree. At one point a white vapour emanated from the robot's mouth and Schrum blacked out but woke up again nauseous, and began lighting matches and throwing them down to frighten the humanoids away, at which point they retreated.

Robot knocked backwards!

Finally he shot an arrow at the robot; when it hit, there was an arc flash and the robot was knocked backwards. This was repeated two more times, and the humanoids scattered each time. A second robot now appeared and a vapour again rendered Schrum unconscious. When he awoke, he discovered that the two humanoids were climbing up the tree toward him, so he shook the tree and threw things down at them to ward them off. The same actions were repeated all night. Near dawn, more beings approached and *'large volumes of smoke'* drifted up and he blacked out. He awoke hanging from his belt and the creatures were gone. Later, when reunited with his companions, Schrum found that one of the other hunters, who also had got lost and separated from their camp, had seen the UFO.

(Source: *Strange Effects from UFOs*/NICAP, 1969, page 17)

6th September 1964 (UK) – Rugby ball UFO

Schoolboy P. McCourt of West Bridgford, Nottingham, reported having seen:

> *"...a silvery oval-shaped object – like a 'metallic' rugby ball – flying through the sky, at a height of 500ft off the ground, about two miles away, heading in a south to north direction, at 5.50pm."*

Was this a balloon, reflecting sunlight? One was released from Hucknall Weather Station at 6pm, everyday, to check wind speed. If so, perhaps the time noted by the witness was incorrect.

(Source: *UFOLOG*, Issue No. 6, 13.10.1964)

Over Lancashire (UK) – Conical UFO

At 11.30pm, an object – described as resembling a conical sea buoy, with lights that changed from red, to green and white – was sighted by Mrs Ivy Harrison, SRN, and her husband, Percy – a plant supervisor of Salford, Lancashire. Investigations carried out by the Isle of Wight UFO Society revealed the object was seen to *"silently hover and rotate, presenting what looked like a hard blue exterior through binoculars."*

(Source: *The Daily Express*, 8.9.1964 – 'The star that wasn't what it seemed')

On the same evening, amateur astronomer – Mr R. Glass – was observing the Cygnus constellation, when he noticed *"a foggy white object, flying in a zigzag across the sky, heading north-east"*, which he thought might have been a meteor – until he focused on it and saw a blurred cigar-shaped object that changed from an *'on edge'* view to vertical. He believes the object was outside the Earth's atmosphere.

(Source: Personal interview)

DISAP SIGHTING FORM D.I.

SECTION TWO

(I) DATE OF OBSERVATION _6th Sep. '64_   TIME _11.30pm._   (PLEASE STATE HOW IT WAS DETERMINED)

(2) LOCATION OF OBSERVER(S) (PLEASE INDICATE THE DIRECTION OF THE OBJECT(S) INCLUDING ANY CHANGES BELOW, TOGETHER WITH THE POSITION OF ANY LANDMARKS AND MAIN ROADS). INDICATE NORTH. ↓

At Home in bedroom, (Going to Bed)
65° N.W. Fixed between chimney stacks
Lost after about 20 mins moving north
very slowly behind chimney.

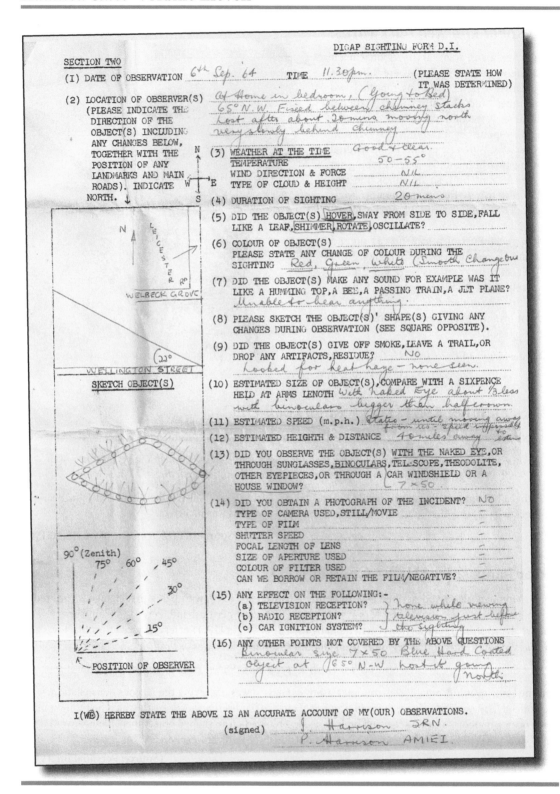

SKETCH OBJECT(S)

(3) WEATHER AT THE TIME _Good & clear._
TEMPERATURE _50-55°_
WIND DIRECTION & FORCE _N.il._
TYPE OF CLOUD & HEIGHT _N.il._

(4) DURATION OF SIGHTING _20 mins_

(5) DID THE OBJECT(S) HOVER, SWAY FROM SIDE TO SIDE, FALL LIKE A LEAF, SHIMMER, ROTATE, OSCILLATE?

(6) COLOUR OF OBJECT(S) PLEASE STATE ANY CHANGE OF COLOUR DURING THE SIGHTING _Red, Green, White (Smooth change but_

(7) DID THE OBJECT(S) MAKE ANY SOUND FOR EXAMPLE WAS IT LIKE A HUMMING TOP, A BEE, A PASSING TRAIN, A JET PLANE? _Unable to hear anything._

(8) PLEASE SKETCH THE OBJECT(S)' SHAPE(S) GIVING ANY CHANGES DURING OBSERVATION (SEE SQUARE OPPOSITE).

(9) DID THE OBJECT(S) GIVE OFF SMOKE, LEAVE A TRAIL, OR DROP ANY ARTIFACTS, RESIDUE?   _No_
Looked for heat haze - none seen.

(10) ESTIMATED SIZE OF OBJECT(S), COMPARE WITH A SIXPENCE HELD AT ARMS LENGTH _With naked Eye about 3 less_
with binoculars bigger than halfcrown.

(11) ESTIMATED SPEED (m.p.h.) _Static - until moving away_
from us - speed impossible

(12) ESTIMATED HEIGHTH & DISTANCE _40 miles away to est_

(13) DID YOU OBSERVE THE OBJECT(S) WITH THE NAKED EYE, OR THROUGH SUNGLASSES, BINOCULARS, TELESCOPE, THEODOLITE, OTHER EYEPIECES, OR THROUGH A CAR WINDSHIELD OR A HOUSE WINDOW? _7 × 50_

(14) DID YOU OBTAIN A PHOTOGRAPH OF THE INCIDENT? _NO_
TYPE OF CAMERA USED, STILL/MOVIE _-_
TYPE OF FILM _-_
SHUTTER SPEED _-_
FOCAL LENGTH OF LENS _-_
SIZE OF APERTURE USED _-_
COLOUR OF FILTER USED _-_
CAN WE BORROW OR RETAIN THE FILM/NEGATIVE? _-_

(15) ANY EFFECT ON THE FOLLOWING:-
(a) TELEVISION RECEPTION?   } _none while viewing_
(b) RADIO RECEPTION?   } _television just before_
(c) CAR IGNITION SYSTEM?   _the sighting_

(16) ANY OTHER POINTS NOT COVERED BY THE ABOVE QUESTIONS
Binocular size 7×50 Blue Hard Coated
Object at 65° N-W lost it going
north

90°(Zenith)
75° 60° 45°
30°
15°
POSITION OF OBSERVER

I(WE) HEREBY STATE THE ABOVE IS AN ACCURATE ACCOUNT OF MY(OUR) OBSERVATIONS.

(signed) _J. Harrison JRN._
P. Harrison AMIEI

10th September 1964 (UK) – *'Flying saucer'* seen

A *'flying saucer'* was seen by hospital worker Elgar Thomas, of Lower Crumpsall, Manchester, who said:

> *"Before I lost sight of the object, it stopped and then shot even further skywards and disappeared; it was about three times the size of an aircraft, without wings."*

> (Source: *Manchester Evening News*, 10.9.1964)

10th September 1964 (USA) – Cedar Grove, New Jersey

At 7.09pm, chemist – Mr P.H. DePaolo – reported having sighted four white lights, three to four feet apart, heading through the sky northwards, for 45 seconds, until out of view.

11th September 1964 (UK) – Two orange *'flashing lights'*

A *'flashing light'* was seen in the sky over Huddersfield Road, Halifax, at 11.25pm, by Trevor and Doreen Whittaker.

> *"It was bigger than a star, moving from north to south in the eastern sky. On going outside to have a look with binoculars, we saw it was two orange flashing lights, one above the other, the lower being smaller than the above."*

The sighting was the trigger which led to Trevor developing a keen interest in the UFO subject, and after joining BUFORA, he was to investigate a number of sightings in West Yorkshire during the 1970s.

12th September 1964 (UK) – Red *'ball of light'* seen

Mr E Ford of Southsea, Hampshire, was scanning the sky for the Echo 2 satellite, at 3.48am, together with Mr C. Lucas and another colleague.

He was stood at the main gate at Hilsea Depot (old ordnance depot) opposite Old London Road, Portsmouth, when they saw what looked like:

> *"...a small, dull red 'ball', travelling along a flat trajectory from the south-west direction – heading quickly towards the north-east.*
>
> *As it approached closer, we saw it was emitting a bright red light every few seconds. At 3.54am, it had gone."*

> (Source: *UFOLOG*, John Feakins)

14th September 1964 (UK) – Rotating UFO

At 5.15pm, Mrs Ann Powell and her daughter, Ann, saw a silver rotating object speeding across the sky, travelling towards Belle Vue, Manchester, from the direction of the Ringway. Within seconds, it became lost from view. (**Source:** *UFOLOG*, **Issue No. 6, 13.10.1964**)

15th September 1964 (USA) – Six photos taken of a UFO over Baton Rouge

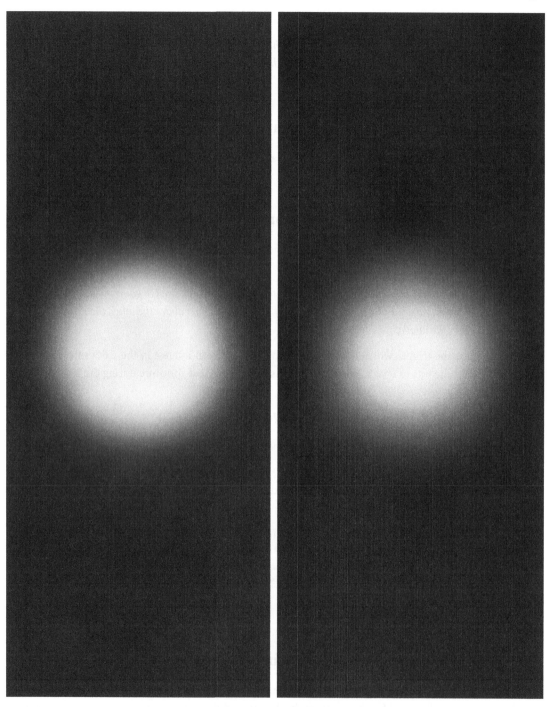

Two enlargements from the original Baton Rouge photographs

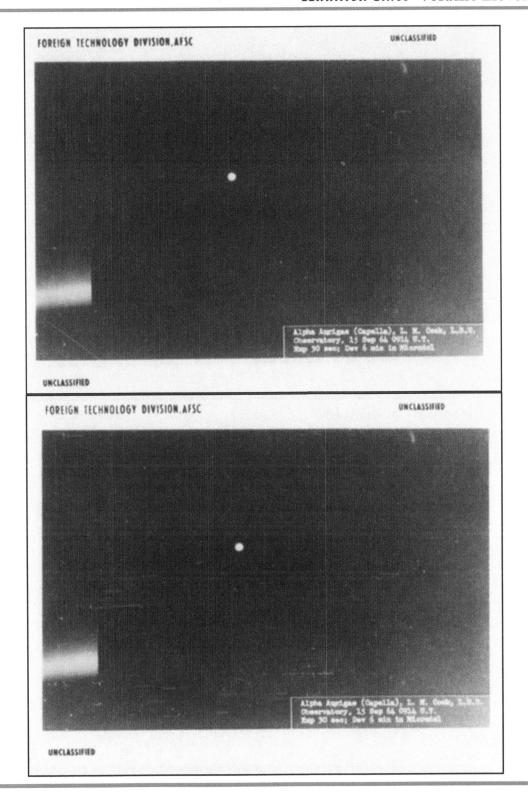

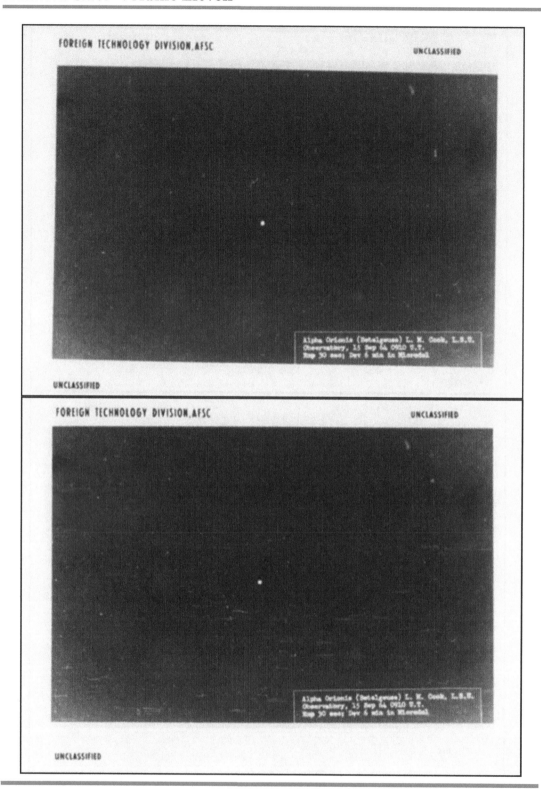

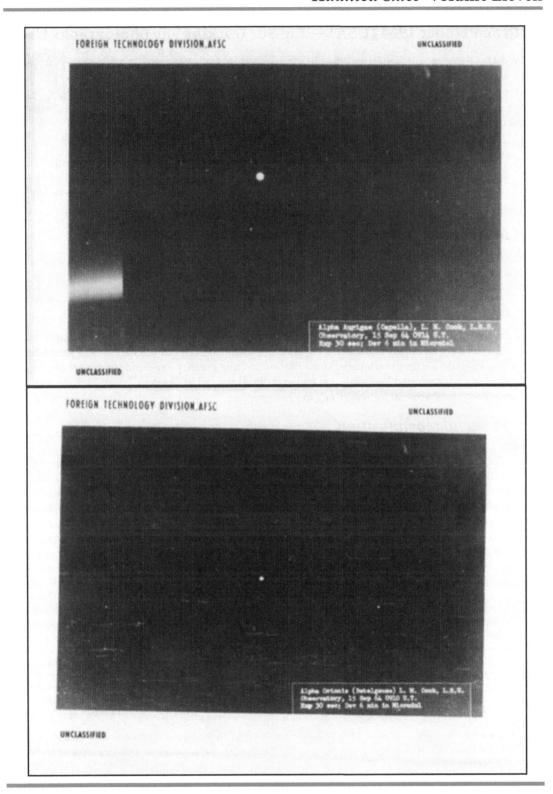

15th September 1964 (USA) – *Big Sur tracking site photographs UFO

Retired USAF Lieutenant Robert Jacobs, PhD has served in academic roles, including university professor, Journalism and Broadcasting. He was the first Air Force officer in the photography career field, to be awarded the Air Force Guided Missile Insignia; the Missile Badge and had a very interesting story to tell about what he witnessed, while on duty at Vandenberg Air Force Base, in 1964.

Robert Jacobs:

> *"I have been a participant in an official United States Government-ordered UFO cover-up. I've been ridiculed by some of my colleagues in academia because, in 1982, I wrote an article about this cover-up and it appeared in* The Sceptical Enquirer. *It was not my intention to become a tabloid writer then or now."*

Missile Launched

To the best of his recollection the date of the event was believed to be either September 2nd, 3rd, or 15th, 1964, and involved the launch of an Atlas missile. He says:

> *"It was an Atlas-F, as I recall strongly, but it may possibly have been an Atlas D. The flight was in support of the Nike-Zeus objectives."*

Nike Zeus was one of the United States' projects to develop an anti-missile missile. This particular mission was part of a test of an enemy radar-defeating system, which had been put together by Kingston George – the project engineer for the experiments. At the Big Sur tracking site they were ready to go as the countdown from Vandenberg progressed loud and clear on the radio. At the call of *"ignition, lift-off"*, all cameras rolled and scanned to the south-east for something to photograph.

Powerful magnification

Robert:

> *"The magnification of the Boston University Telescope was truly impressive. The exhaust nozzles and lower third of the Atlas missile literally filled the frame at this distance of over 100 nautical miles. With one tracking mount operator on azimuth and one on elevation working completely manually, it was not easy to keep the image centered in the early stages of flight. As the nose-cone package approached T + 400 seconds, sufficient angle of view had been established that we were literally locked down with the whole in-flight package centered in the frame. No one on the site was watching the screen by this point. Our mission to provide the engineers with a side look at three stages of powered flight had been accomplished and we were a very happy bunch, congratulating each other and letting the film run out in the 35mm motion picture camera focused on the Kinescope.*
>
> *I took the cans of exposed film and headed down the coast to Vandenberg and our laboratory. Processing of the film would occur that night and the results would be ready for viewing the next day."*

"'Big Sur" is derived from the original Spanish-language "el sur grande", meaning "the big south", or from "el país grande del sur", "the big country of the south". This name refers to its location south of the city of Monterey. The terrain offers stunning views, making Big Sur a popular tourist destination. Big Sur's Cone Peak is the highest coastal mountain in the contiguous 48 states, ascending nearly a mile (5,155 feet/1571 m) above sea level, only 3 miles (5 km) from the ocean. The name Big Sur can also specifically refer to any of the small settlements in the region, including Posts, Lucia and Gorda; mail sent to most areas within the region must be addressed "Big Sur".

According to the list of missile launches found on Wikipedia for 1964, these are the 'failures' which occurred at Vandenberg AFB: 3rd April 1964 (Atlas F) – Stuck valve – engine failed to start.8th October 1964 (Atlas-Agena D SLV-3) – engine malfunction. (**Source: Wikipedia, 2015**)

MANSMANN RANCH
5716 E. JENSEN

Peter Bons
'73 Jensa St Apt E

~March 8 1983

Dear Peter:
Your letter relates your background and
interest in the sciences most involved in UFO research.
I wish I could be more helpfull to persons like you on
Lee and his group. Our meeting was exciting in exchanges
of information and very pleasant. However how much information
was gathered to determine the exact items being held by
those with a need to know, and "their" or the "identity" thereof
is or was meager. My "defran" was complete so gave them whatever
information I could. Dr. Rob. opened a pandoras box and in the
last few months I have very bombarded with phone calls and letters. I
try to answer the sincere ones.

First the Enquirer story time except the date was
1964 I was in Vietnam in '65. Telescopic photography of that
magnitude makes sizes undeterminable, we knew the missile
size but could not compare since we did not know how
far from the missile the "object" was at time of beam
release. Moncurvarability was also at question for the
same reason. Propulsion was plasma like but not
probable. In such gravity; plasma induced speed and maneuverability would
not seem possible. From clearity, action and situation

in the film.

the assumption was, at that time extraterrestrial.
Details would be sketchy and from memory. the shape was
a classic disc, the center seemed to be a raised bubble,
not sure any posts or slits could be seen but was
stationary, or moving slightly—floating—over the entire
lower saucer shape which was glowing and "seemed"
to be rotating slowly. At the point of beam release — if it was
a beam, it, the object, turned like an object required
to be in a position to fire from a platform ... but again
this could be my own assumption from being in aerial
combat. Assumptions are easy where unknowns are evironment.
There is one thing going on which may bring more to
light soon. Howard University is into computer scanning
for extraterrestrial signals from world wide information
gathered from great amounts of data, good scientific data.
      "Wish I could be of more help. Maybe sometime
you will be in ▆▆▆▆ and can stop by. I go to Stanford U.
periodically so call first.
              Best of luck on your research

                                    Cusmann
                                    Jeb

Mr. Lee M. Graham

Dear Mr. Graham:

1-30-1983

The Enquirer story is true except the year was 1964 not 1965. The camera system we used was capable of "nuts and bolts" focus from a point seventy miles from any object being tracked so the photos were readable. I was not then nor am I now able to relate any "conclusions" or "facts" that were captured on film. However I do have some deep concerns about information, so vital now to the future of mankind, falling into the wrong hands at the wrong time. A case in point, We had the "secret" information on "the Bomb" and the future of mankind was protected, up to now, of its further use by U.S. Also the fallout development of super weapons have been accomplished by U.S. And the answer to our successes has been more and bigger bombs built from our secrets which fell into the wrong hands because someone else found and released our secrets to those who have no concern over the future of mankind, only of their own. Haunting their development of gas as a weapon of war is also proof of their _love_ of _others_. Lee, what I am getting at is that from all of my projects and research I have come across many instances where small groups of selected persons are working on items far advanced from any published data yet can be imagined

1.121

Can you see why this country would be selected for communication from other worlds? Can you see why some areas are kept secret to prevent further desmigration of mankind? And can you see what would happen if the information 'discovered' fell into the wrong hands and was used against, not for mankind? We the U.S. have had such secrets in our hands and have proven our dedecation to preservation. Thats why you have uncovered so much information from U.S. but not all.

I would like you to touch base with two people. One a writer like yourself, doing work for Omni and others. You might like to compare notes on a one for one basis. The other a specialized technician like yourself, who I call "the Devels Advocate" will bend your ear about me, his theories on UFO's and 4th Dimention probibilitess and where and when we may gain the knowledge I'd intended to give us to fill up the Void we have never used of our brain. #1 Eric Mishora, Omni 617-332-0207 Home or # 213-853-7779 Office & #2 Tom Bosker. (also a sci-fi writer) 5015 W. Agusta Circle, Glendale Arizona 85308.

Lee keep me posted on your progress I can do two things one let you know if you are getting worm, and to Verify whatever I can. Sincerly

MANSMANN RANCH

May 6, 1987

Mr. T. Scott Crain, Jr.
Mutual UFO Network

Dear Scott:

A reoccurence of cancer, a very bad farming situation and the resultant financial problems that needed immediate attention, precluded the possibility of my involvement in any but priority duties. Therefore, your July 30, 1986, letter is in a box with many others that need to be addressed, researched, answered and sent.

I am still in the midst of this battle, so my reply will be short.

The events you are familiar with had to have happened as stated by both Bob Jacobs and myself because the statement made from each of us after 17 years matched. What was on the film was seen only twice by Bob Jacobs, once in Film Quality Control and once in my office at the CIA attended showing. I saw it four times. Once in my own quality control review and editing for the General and his staff; once in review with the Chief Scientist and his assistant; once for the Commanding General with only one of his staff; and the fourth time with the Chief Scientist, his assistant, the three government men and Bob Jacobs.

I ordered Lt. Jacobs not to discuss what he saw with anyone because of the nature of the launch, the failure of the launch mission and the probability that the optical instrumentation (the film) showed an interferance with normal launch patterns. Now for your questions:

1. The object was saucer-shaped. (Dome? Don't remember.)
2. Do not know the names of the CIA personnel.
3. Only assumptions from the seriousness of the situation.
4. I was ordered not to discuss any of what was seen or discussed during the screenings. I only passed my order, as the ranking optical instrumentation officer, on to Lieutenant Jacobs. There was no one else involved.
5. No film was ever released from our archives without a signature. I even signed out film when we had launch showings to VIPs in the General's office on short notice. However, I released the film to the Chief Scientist over <u>his</u> signature, then they departed.
6. The articles in the Enquirer and OMNI on my part and the statements made by both Dr. Jacobs and myself were factual. The statements you referred to that an "Air Force spokeman said, 'there <u>is</u> nothing on the film and that the rocket did hit its target," <u>makes</u> no sense. This means the film is available and the records of the launch and the results are also available. If the Air Force spokesman did review a close-dated launch and saw nothing, it could not have been the launch that perpetuated such quick security action.

(continued next page)

Page 2 - T. Scott Crain, Jr. - 5/6/87

7. Further? If the government wishes to withold such vital information which most certainly relates to our basis Star Wars research, then this information must be protected.

Working in special projects my entire Air Force career from the earliest airborne radar in WWII, Air Defense Systems during the Korean War, Airborne Reconnaissance Ssytems during the Cold War, Photo computerized systems of unprecedented utilization and intelligence fathering during the Vietnam conflict, (therefore a veteran of four wars and more combat area time than most), I may be over protective of our security.

I can only say in regard to your research that in all my activities to date, indications point to one fact...the information gathered from space is very favorable to our side.

Sincerely yours,

F. J. Mansmann, ScD.

The men in grey

The following day, Robert was back at his desk, enjoying the feeling of accomplishment from the Big Sur expedition, when he was called by Major Florenz Mansmann, who asked him to come right away to his office at the Headquarters building. When he arrived, he found a movie projector set-up in the office, and a group of people waiting.

Among them were (as he recalls) two men in plain grey suits, who spoke little and watched him intently as the lights were dimmed and the film played on a bright screen. (Mansmann has since stated that there were actually three men present.)

Robert:

"It was a surprise and a delight for me to be seeing the kinescope recording from Big Sur, after all the months of planning and weeks of work. I was quite amazed and very pleased with the quality, especially at the distance involved, as we could make out quite plainly the separated nose-cone, the radar experiment and the dummy warhead, all sailing along beautifully about 60 miles, straight up from planet Earth and some 300 to 500 nautical miles down range."

January 14, 1985

Florenz J. Mansmann

Dear Florenz,

I suppose you've seen the followup article which appeared in the January issue of <u>OMNI</u> Magazine under the "Anti Matter" section. Once the cat is out of the bag, it keeps on mewing it seems!

Lee Graham has sent me a package of his investigations which include two letters from you: one to him and one to a Peter Bons. I have read them with some fascination and not a little trepidation. They reveal a good deal more about that fateful piece of film than even I knew. It appears you did a good deal of analysis on it at the time.

I've pursued some research and investigation into the UFO phenomena ever since leaving the big blue womb of the Air Force. That incident seems to have set off an unquenchable thirst for more information about our possibly interstellar visitors. One of my more delightful encounters was with Dr. Fred Cranston. At the time I was teaching at Cal State Humboldt. Fred was a professor of Physics there, having first been one of the developers of the hydrogen bomb. He retreated to teaching, much as I did, in a fit of conscience, hoping to do something more meaningful with his life. He had been an investigator and speaker on UFO's for several years when I met him. His files and our many conversations set me on the side of the "true believers" once and for all!

Unlike Lee Graham, I am not a "buff". My research and thinking about the problem have been quiet and quite personal for the most part. The article in <u>The Enquirer</u> was originally intended for <u>OMNI</u>. It was written in a more articulate and academic tone. They rejected it, of course, as being "unsubstantiated". As a poor teacher in an impoverished state, I then sold it to <u>The Enquirer</u> to pay a few bills. I want you to know that I had no idea that it might prove quite so explosive, nor that it was quite as "real" as it turned out to be. The ridiculous style in which <u>The Enquirer</u> rewrote it is also quite an embarrassment to me! I also want you to know that, even after 17 years, I would never have written the piece had I known that it might still be "classified" somehow. It seemed pretty blase and even ridiculous to me at the time I wrote it, considering how much more meaningful "secrets" during my tenure in the service are now public knowledge.

2.

I have followed the announcements and pronouncements by folks like Carl Sagan with avid fascination. Between the lines, even in popular "fictions" like "E.T." and "Close Encounters of the Third Kind", one can certainly draw the conclusion that contact of SOME kind has taken place. The reports of McDermott and others of our astronauts are striking, especially in later retractions and denials of the "bogeys" and "UFO'S" in near space by public officials. The steady and continuing investigation of near space by our "friends" in the Soviet Union indicates more than a passing fancy on their parts, I think.

Therefore, I find interesting your comments on the relative benifecence of the U.S. versus the "wrong hands" people. As an American who, like you, has seen and experienced something of the last forty years, I would like to believe that we are "pro-mankind" and that any communications of higher technologies with concomitant improved destructive powers would be shared with us and no one else. We were, after all, at the end of WW II, the ONLY country with "the Bomb" and the ability to deliver it on target and at will. Had Stalin gotten that power, we would doubtless no longer be here to write letters or articles. If we were, we'd be speaking Russian! So, we were the first nation ever to have the sheer technical ability to conquer the planet and we did NOT do so. That's terrifically good for us as a people to have done, I suppose! Perhaps the recognition of our good will in rebuilding the war-torn Earth also counted in our favor.

Philosophically, however, I have to wonder at our arrogance in assuming that if contact from interstellar intelligence HAS taken place, that it has only taken place with us. The technology to which you and I were witness, the technology recorded on that few feet of film, indicates orders of magnitude from our relatively primitive efforts in 猸 mechanics, propulsion and possibly quantum physics as well. Such intelligence might be suspected to regard us as little more than savages: ALL of us on this planet. I might even in my more retrospective moments, regard that beam of light..no, THOSE BEAMS of light on our film as a WARNING. A shot fired across the bow, so to speak, of our nuclear silliness ship. I have a true account, told me by another former Air Force guy of a VERY close encounter in 1957 at one of our SAC bases in the Atlantic. I'll relate it to you in person one day, I hope.

Lee Graham tells me that the Air Force now denies that there even existed a "telescope site" from which to shoot such film. You and I know it was there. I have a photo of us/smiling at the radio device I designed to send timing signals up there from Vandenberg. I got the Missile Insignia for that one. You and I also know that the same site exists today on Anderson Peak. From it we see the shuttle enter California airspace! The Air Force can ONLY deny things, it seems. And, like the Russians and the Nazis, when they deny the truth and then the truth comes out in public, how can they expect our citizens to have trust and confidence in the institutions we have erected to serve us?

3.

Given that, as you put it to me at the time, "this never happened" [referring to the record of the UFO on film], it's not surprising that Lee Graham can't get verification of it from the Air Force or the Freedom of Information Office. When Lee Graham tells me in a letter that you confirm the story but are "reluctant to make any inquiry...for fear of reprisal from the agency that appropriated the film", I shudder in my boots. I have an old, rusted, bent key. I picked it out of the dirt at Dachau. An historian friend of mine affirms that it was used to, most likely, to open the hot oven doors at that awful place which consumed so many of my people who were afraid of "reprisal" from their government. Over two decades after the filming of a "warning shot", must we still fear "reprisal" for seeking answers to what may be the innermost secrets of the cosmos itself?

I'm only a humble school teacher and alfalfa farmer in Wisconsin. I could disappear tonight. Only my fiance, my dog and a few close friends would notice. Because I am an American, I don't fear such "reprisal", however. Perhaps it is because I am a very naive American? Perhaps it's because our government has done such a very good job of making "nut-cases" out of anyone who reports a UFO that my credibility is shot and nobody cares what I say anymore.

Certainly there are a large number of "fringies"; true deluded or psychotic people who have climbed aboard the UFO bandwagon, claiming daily free rides to Venus and elsewhere to give their impotent lives some notoriety and meaning. The media have had a lot of fun propagating their stories at the expense of those of us who investigate in good faith and natural curiosity at a most peculiar and potentially exhilarating phenomenon or set of phenomena.

And all of this leads me to question; why all of this idiotic coverup? They are here, aren't they? We know it. The Russians know it. The South Africans and Pakistanis know it. Every kid in the third grade knows it. Reagan with his "Star Wars" nonesense knows it. So what's all the "fear of reprisal" business. Steven Spielberg told us all about it, for God's sake. Do we have to hear it at Disneyland?! Do guys like Lee Graham have to ferret out the truth to convince their buddies that they aren't nuts?

O.K. So, maybe we've found out a few trivial bits of this and that which might be useful in the national defense and deserve to be classified somehow. But where's the harm in letting everybody in the great news that the universe is alive with other intelligence and that we are not bound for eternity all alone anymore? It's the best damned thing since Christmas and a few nurds in secret rooms don't deserve to keep it all to themselves.

It would be great fun to sit down with you sometime and talk and howl at the moon and the great spinning discs and faces on Mars and beyond. Maybe I'll be out your way this summer.

Best regards,

Bob Jacobs

UFO appears on film

As they neared the end of the film, Mansmann said, *"Watch carefully now, Lieutenant Jacobs".* At that point a most remarkable vision appeared on the screen. An object flew into the frame from left to right, approached the warhead package and manoeuvred around it. The *'thing'* flew a relative polar orbit around the warhead package, which was itself heading toward the South Pacific at some 18 thousand miles an hour!

Four bright flashes

It was seen to emit four distinct bright flashes of light, at approximately the four cardinal compass points of its orbit. These flashes were so intense that each *'strike'* caused the Ionic tube to *'boom',* or form a halo, around the spot.

Warhead malfunctions – Domed UFO seen

Following this remarkable aerial display, the object departed the frame in the same direction from which it had come. The shape of the object was of a classic 'flying saucer'. In the middle of the top half of the object was a dome. From that dome, or just beneath it, seemed to issue a beam of light which caused the flashes described. Subsequently the warhead malfunctioned and tumbled out of sub orbit hundreds of miles short of its target.

The lights came on

Major Mansmann said: *"Lieutenant Jacobs were you or any of your people fooling around up there at Big Sur?"*

Robert: *"No sir, I answered honestly, shaking with excitement."*

Major Mannsman: *"Then tell me ... what the hell was that?"*

Robert: *"I looked Major Mansmann straight in the eye and said, 'It looks to me like we got a UFO'. There was a stifling silence among the men in grey civilian suits, who continued to stare at me. Major Mansmann gave them what I can only describe as a 'let me handle this' look."*

Cover up begins

Major Mannsman: *"Let's just say it never happened. You are to say nothing about this footage to anyone. As far as you and I are concerned, this never took place, you understand?"*

Robert: *"I looked at the men in the grey suits. They were not smiling. I felt hot and anxious. I was sweating badly. I think I just sat for a minute looking blankly at Major Florenz Mansmann. I had just seen the most fantastic event of my life. It etched a path in my memory as deep as the one put there almost a year earlier, when President John F. Kennedy had been shot to death in Dallas. I wanted more than anything to see it again, to study it under a magnifier, to analyse the pictures frame by frame."*

Major Mansmann smiled. *"I don't need to remind you of the seriousness of a security breach, do I Lieutenant?"* he asked.

Robert: *"No, sir."*

Major Mansman: *"Good."*

He walked Robert to the door and then said, *"What you just saw did not take place – it never happened."*

Robert: *"I looked at him once more. Something flickered deep in his eyes as he again looked at the men in grey, then back to me, and said,*

"...but, if at some time in the future..." [Authors: presumably inferring a promise to divulge further information]

Major Mansmann said finally: *"If you are pressed by someone about this and you can't get out of answering, just tell them it was flashes from laser tracking, OK?"*

Robert: *"With that, I was ushered out the door and into over a decade of silence on the subject. Never mind that, in 1964 we did not have laser tracking, nor did we or any other power on Earth have spacecraft capable of flying circles around a sub orbital capsule. I tried to sublimate the whole incident out of loyally and respect for Florenz Mansmann, whom I liked a great deal."*

1973 – Discussed on radio station

During a late night talk show which he hosted in Eureka, California, in 1973, Robert outlined tentatively, some small details about the incident.

The response was almost as astonishing as had been the event itself. His program director – Richard Van Pelt – came forth to tell his own tale of a 'close encounter' which happened to him while he was an Air Force Security NCO in Iceland, 20 years earlier.

Conclusions

Robert:

1. *"What we photographed that September day in 1964 was a solid, three-dimensional, intelligently-controlled flying device.*

2. *It emitted a beam of energy, possibly a plasma beam, at our dummy warhead and caused a malfunction.*

3. *This 'craft' was not anything of which our science and technology in 1964 was capable. The most probable explanation of the device, therefore, is that it was of extraterrestrial origin.*

4. *The flashing strikes of light we recorded on film were not from laser tracking devices. Such devices did not exist then, aside from small-scale laboratory models.*

5. *Most probably the Boston University Telescope was brought out to California specifically to photograph this event, which had been prearranged. That is, we had been set-up to record an event which someone in our Government knew was going to happen in advance.*

6. *What we photographed that day was the first terrestrial demonstration of what has come to be called SDI or Star Wars. The demonstration was put on for our benefit for some reason by extraterrestrials. It is this aspect of the event, not merely the recording of another 'flying saucer' which caused such consternation both on the part of Major Mansmann, when he told me it never happened, and on behalf of the government in its two and one half decade cover-up of the event and the record we made of it."*

[Before Mansmann's death, 40 years after the actual event, it is said the Major confirmed the UFO incident in writing.]

Denial that he ever served!

"It is this defense-oriented aspect of the case which has caused investigators to run into stone walls in trying to track down my story. The Air Force has alternately denied that I was ever an officer, that I was ever stationed at Vandenberg, that I was OIC of Photo-optical Instrumentation in the 1369th Photographic Squadron, that there was a tracking site at or near Big Sur, California, that an Atlas-F, or for that matter, any other missile was launched on or about the date or dates I reported."

Kingston George

According to Kingston 'King' George – the project engineer for the experiments – it is claimed that he had identified the object as nothing to do with UFOs in an article by the *Skeptical Enquirer* Winter 1993, pp180-187.

> *"The Air Force obtained some unusual photography while experimenting with very sensitive optics equipment during ICBM launches on the West Coast nearly 30 years ago. Three years ago, in an article titled 'Deliberate Deception The Big Sur UFO Filming' (Jacobs 1989) one of the members of the experimental team claimed that the objects observed were beyond normal technical explanation and implied that the government had been communicating with aliens from outer space.*

Specifically, he claimed that the team had photographed an intelligently controlled flying device. He asserted that it emitted a beam of energy, its capabilities were beyond the science and technology of our time, and it was therefore probably of extraterrestrial origin. He concluded that we had knowingly photographed a . . .

> *"demonstration . . . put on for our benefit for some reason by extraterrestrials. I was the project engineer for these experiments. This article is intended to provide a more rational account of the sightings of September 1964 and to supply firsthand facts that should loosen any attachment the uninformed might have to Bob Jacobs' version."*

Kingston said:

> *"Over the period of 30 days, from 31st August to 30th September, during which the Boston University telescope was ready to film launches, eleven flights were made from Vandenberg."*

Robert Jacobs:

> *"Unfortunately, it is not clear whether Kingston George was privy to the screenings of the Big Sur film which recorded the UFO. I suspect that he was one of those to whom Mansmann has admitted showing the film and that documentary evidence states clearly that a missile did malfunction during the test period."*

Freedom of Information requests – There were no launches!

Bob was disappointed to discover that no verification of this incident could be obtained following FOIA requests and his own military records everything except the specific launch and the fact of its having been filmed. Incredibly he was even told initially that no launches had taken place, then an acceptance there were launches but no malfunctions. From official unclassified Air Force documents in Bob's possession he was able to confirm the following information regarding mission malfunction.

Robert Hastings – author of 'UFO's and Nukes'

One man that conducted a thorough investigation into this matter was Robert L Hastings – author of *UFO's and Nukes*.

He was born on 6th May 1950, in Albuquerque, New Mexico, at Sandia Base, where atomic weapons were engineered. His father, Robert E. Hastings, retired in 1967 with the rank of (USAF) Senior Master Sergeant. In 1966-67 the Hastings family was stationed at Malmstrom AFB, Montana, during one peak period of UFO activity at nearby Minuteman nuclear missile sites. In March 1967, Hastings witnessed five UFOs being tracked on radar at the base air traffic control tower. He later learned that these 'unknown targets' had been manoeuvring near ICBM sites, located south-east of the base. This experience ultimately led to his decades-long research into the UFO-nukes connection. Hastings received a BFA in Photography at Ohio University, in 1972, and worked as a photographic technician at Northern Illinois University for eight years. In 1981, after conducting numerous interviews with former and retired US Air Force personnel regarding their knowledge of nuclear weapons-related UFO incidents, Hastings ventured out on the college lecture circuit to speak about the US government's cover-up on UFOs. To date, he has appeared at over 500 colleges and universities in the US, as well as Oxford University in England. In 1986-88, Hastings retrained in Electron Microscopy at San Joaquin Delta College in Stockton, California, and received a certificate in Materials Science Applications. Between 1988 and 2002, he was employed as a laboratory analyst by Philips

UFOs and Nukes

EXTRAORDINARY ENCOUNTERS
AT NUCLEAR WEAPONS SITES

Robert Hastings

Robert Hastings:

"Perhaps most disturbing of all, in his latest article in Skeptical Inquirer, *George writes that 'Bob' Jacobs concocted the UFO story and, elsewhere, calls it a fabrication. This is libellous, given that he is accusing Dr. Jacobs of fraudulently attempting to hoax a non-existent incident. Can George prove these accusations? What evidence would he be able to present in a court of law to support his claims?"*

Spoke to Kingston George in 2003

Robert called George in January 2003. He told him: "I don't know why [Jacobs] carries on like that. He's gotsome other motive than truth, I can guarantee you that!" Robert asked George whether he meant that Jacobs was lying about the UFO encounter to make money by publishing the story. He replied: *"Either that, or he has totally gone off the edge"*

Robert Hastings:

"So, according to Kingston George, Bob Jacobs has either lied about the Big Sur UFO Incident solely to benefit financially, or he is psychologically unstable. Well, Mr. George, all of your baseless, actionable charges have been duly noted by Dr. Jacobs. Given his standing as a tenured academician, with a professional reputation at stake, your accusations may reasonably be construed as attacks on his integrity and/or competence. So, the question remains: Is Kingston George merely in deep denial or is he knowingly disseminating disinformation — assisted by long-time Sandia Labs PR Specialist Kendrick Frazier — to hide the enormity of the Big Sur case as it relates to US national security and the now well-documented UFO-Nukes connection? Regardless, as the documentation referenced in this article attests, the September 15th, 1964 incident, bravely divulged by Jacobs and Mansmann, was certainly not the only occasion when a UFO was observed and/or tracked on radar during one of the US military's missile launches."

Date given of 22nd September 1964

In both of his articles for *Skeptical Inquirer,* Kingston George claims that the date of the test launch was 22nd September 1964. However, he has never provided any documentation as to how he determined that that date and no other was the actual date of the filmed launch first revealed by Jacobs in 1982. Importantly, George claims that he viewed the film of the same launch mentioned by Jacobs *'a few weeks'* after it was shot (note this delay – it is important) and clearly saw the deployed radar-defeating decoy warheads flying near the actual dummy warhead – the very decoys he assumes Jacobs mistook for the UFO. However, Major Mannsman identifies the date as the 15th September 1964.

Tracking down the missing film

Robert:

"With regard to getting a copy of the film, Eric Mishara, Lee Graham, T. Scott Crain, Jr., and others have tried to trace it and run into a wall of futility. I don't believe that anyone can succeed in getting the film, because its existence will have been completely expunged from the records by now. Finally, if the government did officially classify the film either back then or subsequently, then perhaps there were/are compelling reasons for it to have done so. As the B-2 'Stealth' Bomber has now been unveiled publicly at last, we can contemplate the rationale for having kept it 'classified' for so long. At some point, when no harm can come from the information, perhaps the film for which I was responsible that long ago September day in the cool, clear mountains of Big Sur will be made public, along with the possibly awesome technological power which the images recorded on it represented."

(Source: *MUFON UFO Journal*, Issue No. 249)

Note: We checked the Project Blue Book files and found a report of something unusual at Stead Air Force Base, Nevada, for the 22nd September 1964. It involved a bright blue fluorescent vapour seen rising from south to north in the sky, at an angle of 45degrees, moving at excessive speed.

Another witness told of seeing an object heading in a southerly direction, which appeared to blow up. Two objects were also referred to as resembling reflected chrome with red glows at their tail end. It was determined that the object(s) were in fact an Atlas D Missile, launched at 6.08am. According to the list of launches for the 15th September 1964, there was one Atlas D 'butterfly net' – no indication that it malfunctioned.

20th September 1964 (UK) – Luminous *'disc'* over Bletchley

At 11.20pm, schoolboy Martin Page from Bletchley, Buckinghamshire, happened to look out of his bedroom window.

"I saw an elliptical, luminous white object, divided by a straight line, with a number of 'dots' along its length, the bottom part of which was rotating.

It was tilted (as shown in the sketch) and was heading in the direction of north-west from south-east.

(Source: *Bletchley Evening Gazette/ Isle of Wight Society*)

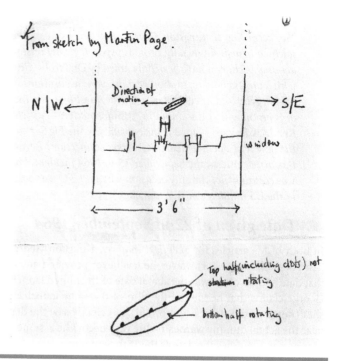

21st September 1964 (UK) – Silver *'disc'*

At 3am, *"a silvery oval 'disc of flickering light', as bright as a car headlamp, occasionally stationary for a short period"*, was seen towards the north-east over Beeston, Nottingham, by Miss S. Hind and her sister.

(Source: Isle of Wight UFO Society)

22nd September 1964 (UK) – UFO display

An intermittent light, flashing red and green, *"under some sort of apparent control"* was seen over Wilmslow, Cheshire, at 9.15pm, by members of the Powers family. After an hour, the size reduced to that of a star in visual image.

A white light was seen circling the sky over Bletchley, during the same evening, *"as though it was fixed to the edge of something rotating, before heading off west towards the direction of Stony Stratford, at great speed – still rotating."* (**Source: Isle of Wight UFO Society/***Bletchley Gazette***)**

23rd September 1964 (UK) – Flying 'disc'

At 8.30pm, Carol Leonard of Portfield Close (12) and Elizabeth Wood (13) of 4, Police Houses, Broughton Road, Buckingham, Bucks, saw a bright yellow-white object, hovering above the skyline. They called Elizabeth's mother, who alerted the neighbours. The object began to head westwards across the sky, maintaining the same elevation and moving through 80 degree of arc, before being lost from view about a minute later. It reappeared, a short time later, and was seen to move back along its path. It repeated this movement several times over the half an hour it was kept under observation.

Incredibly, the family sighted a similar UFO over the next three nights, at about the same time.

At 9pm a *'disc'*-shaped object, showing red and green lights, was seen in the sky over Leicester Road, Salford, occasionally halting in mid-flight, before being lost from view. (**Source:** *UFOLOG*)

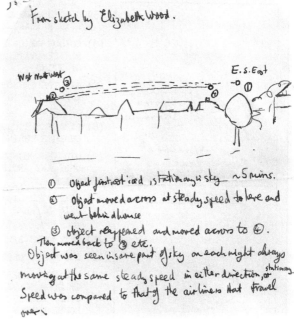

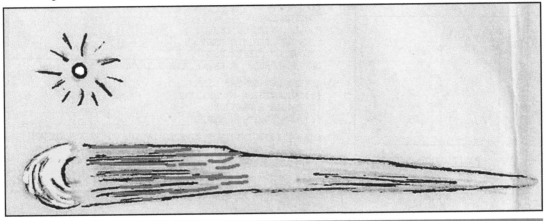

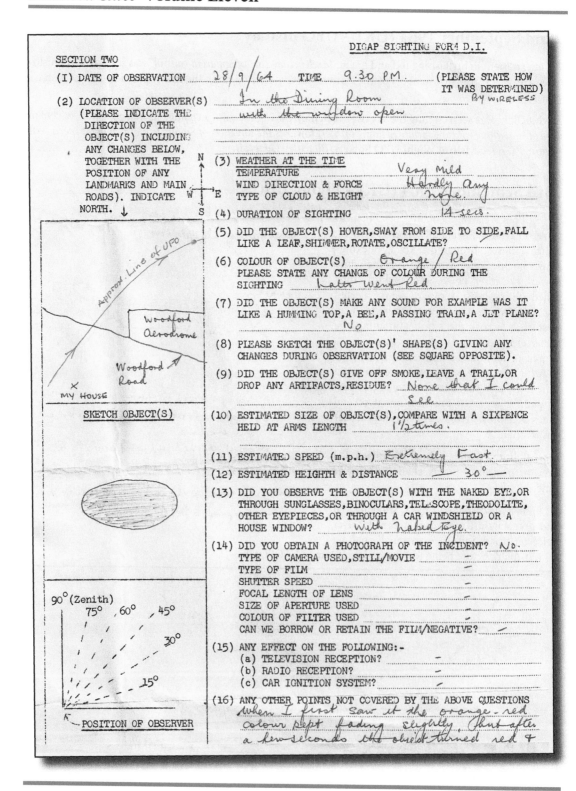

DIGAP SIGHTING FORM D.I.

SECTION TWO

(1) DATE OF OBSERVATION 28/9/64 TIME 9.30 P.M. (PLEASE STATE HOW
IT WAS DETERMINED)
BY WIRELESS

(2) LOCATION OF OBSERVER(S) In the Dining Room
(PLEASE INDICATE THE with the window open
DIRECTION OF THE
OBJECT(S) INCLUDING
ANY CHANGES BELOW,
TOGETHER WITH THE
POSITION OF ANY
LANDMARKS AND MAIN
ROADS). INDICATE
NORTH.

N
W E
S

(3) WEATHER AT THE TIME
TEMPERATURE Very mild
WIND DIRECTION & FORCE Hardly any
TYPE OF CLOUD & HEIGHT none.

(4) DURATION OF SIGHTING 14 secs.

(5) DID THE OBJECT(S) HOVER, SWAY FROM SIDE TO SIDE, FALL
LIKE A LEAF, SHIMMER, ROTATE, OSCILLATE?

(6) COLOUR OF OBJECT(S) Orange / Red
PLEASE STATE ANY CHANGE OF COLOUR DURING THE
SIGHTING Later went Red

(7) DID THE OBJECT(S) MAKE ANY SOUND FOR EXAMPLE WAS IT
LIKE A HUMMING TOP, A BEE, A PASSING TRAIN, A JET PLANE?
No

(8) PLEASE SKETCH THE OBJECT(S)' SHAPE(S) GIVING ANY
CHANGES DURING OBSERVATION (SEE SQUARE OPPOSITE).

(9) DID THE OBJECT(S) GIVE OFF SMOKE, LEAVE A TRAIL, OR
DROP ANY ARTIFACTS, RESIDUE? None that I could
see.

(10) ESTIMATED SIZE OF OBJECT(S), COMPARE WITH A SIXPENCE
HELD AT ARMS LENGTH 1½ times.

(11) ESTIMATED SPEED (m.p.h.) Extremely Fast.

(12) ESTIMATED HEIGHTH & DISTANCE 30°

(13) DID YOU OBSERVE THE OBJECT(S) WITH THE NAKED EYE, OR
THROUGH SUNGLASSES, BINOCULARS, TELESCOPE, THEODOLITE,
OTHER EYEPIECES, OR THROUGH A CAR WINDSHIELD OR A
HOUSE WINDOW? With naked eye.

(14) DID YOU OBTAIN A PHOTOGRAPH OF THE INCIDENT? No.
TYPE OF CAMERA USED, STILL/MOVIE
TYPE OF FILM
SHUTTER SPEED
FOCAL LENGTH OF LENS
SIZE OF APERTURE USED
COLOUR OF FILTER USED
CAN WE BORROW OR RETAIN THE FILM/NEGATIVE?

(15) ANY EFFECT ON THE FOLLOWING:-
(a) TELEVISION RECEPTION?
(b) RADIO RECEPTION?
(c) CAR IGNITION SYSTEM?

(16) ANY OTHER POINTS NOT COVERED BY THE ABOVE QUESTIONS
When I first saw it the orange-red
colour kept fading slightly. Then after
a few seconds the object turned red &

SKETCH OBJECT(S)

Approx. Line of UFO

Woodford
Aerodrome

Woodford
Road

× MY HOUSE

90°(Zenith)
75° 60° 45°
30°
15°
POSITION OF OBSERVER

28th September 1964 (UK) – Orange object

At 9.30pm, a bright orange-red object was seen silently crossing the sky over Woodford Road, near Woodford Aerodrome, Stockton, Cheshire, by John Stott, aged 15. (**Source: Harold Bunting, DIGAP/***UFOLOG*, **Issue 6, Isle of Wight UFO Society**)

30th September 1964 (UK)

A sharply defined flickering red-orange sphere was seen over Newcastle-on-Tyne, at 11.45pm. Was this a fireball? Our enquiries revealed another report on the same day, involving a star-like object seen heading over Bletchley, before disappearing behind a block of nearby flats. (**Source:** *UFOLOG*)

October 1964 (Australia) – Triangular UFO

Four employees at the NASA site, Wallops Island, reported having sighted a triangular object moving in over the base, which was seen to execute a 90 degree turn in the sky.

October 1964 (UK) – Cross-shaped UFO sighted

A brilliantly-lit 'T'-shaped UFO was seen in the east of the sky over Oldham, Lancashire, between 11.00-11.30pm, by retired postmaster – Mr Thompson Brown of Prestwick, Lancashire. He saw it with his wife, and described the object as:

> "...*changing colour from white to green at times, and hovering at an estimated height of under 2,000 feet. I had seen the same object three weeks previously, and believed it to be an aircraft used for carrying out some sort of check of TV and wireless apparatus.*"

Incredibly, Mr Brown reported having sighted this object nightly, for over three weeks, prior to the 17th October, when it moved from its regular position in the sky towards the south, at 11pm. This spurred him to write to the local newspaper, appealing for any other witnesses to the phenomenon. He said:

> "*It would be interesting to learn what the brightly illuminated object, seen nightly and fairly high in the sky, looking eastwards from Prestwick, was. The object appears to be in the form of a cross, or part of one, and illuminated stationary.*"

Was it an early appearance of the 'Flying Cross' – a UFO that was to plague the skies of the UK in the autumn of 1967? (**Source: Harold Bunting, DIGAP**)

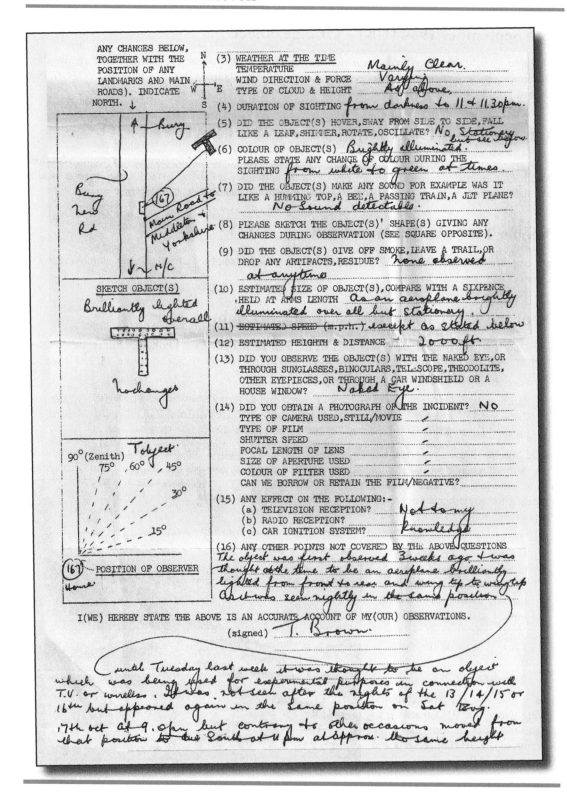

ANY CHANGES BELOW, TOGETHER WITH THE POSITION OF ANY LANDMARKS AND MAIN ROADS). INDICATE NORTH. ↓

N W E S

SKETCH OBJECT(S)

Brilliantly lighted overall

no changes

90° (Zenith) — 75° — 60° — 45°
30°
15°

T object

(167) POSITION OF OBSERVER

House

(3) WEATHER AT THE TIME — TEMPERATURE *Mainly Clear.*
WIND DIRECTION & FORCE *Varys*
TYPE OF CLOUD & HEIGHT *As above,*

(4) DURATION OF SIGHTING *from darkness to 11 + 11.30pm.*

(5) DID THE OBJECT(S) HOVER, SWAY FROM SIDE TO SIDE, FALL LIKE A LEAF, SHIMMER, ROTATE, OSCILLATE? *No, Stationary but see below.*

(6) COLOUR OF OBJECT(S) *Brightly illuminated*
PLEASE STATE ANY CHANGE OF COLOUR DURING THE SIGHTING *from white to green at times.*

(7) DID THE OBJECT(S) MAKE ANY SOUND FOR EXAMPLE WAS IT LIKE A HUMMING TOP, A BEE, A PASSING TRAIN, A JET PLANE? *No Sound detectable.*

(8) PLEASE SKETCH THE OBJECT(S)' SHAPE(S) GIVING ANY CHANGES DURING OBSERVATION (SEE SQUARE OPPOSITE).

(9) DID THE OBJECT(S) GIVE OFF SMOKE, LEAVE A TRAIL, OR DROP ANY ARTIFACTS, RESIDUE? *None observed at anytime.*

(10) ESTIMATED SIZE OF OBJECT(S), COMPARE WITH A SIXPENCE HELD AT ARMS LENGTH *As an aeroplane brightly illuminated over all but stationary.*

(11) ~~ESTIMATED SPEED (m.p.h.)~~ *except as stated below*

(12) ESTIMATED HEIGHTH & DISTANCE *2000ft.*

(13) DID YOU OBSERVE THE OBJECT(S) WITH THE NAKED EYE, OR THROUGH SUNGLASSES, BINOCULARS, TELESCOPE, THEODOLITE, OTHER EYEPIECES, OR THROUGH A CAR WINDSHIELD OR A HOUSE WINDOW? *Naked Eye.*

(14) DID YOU OBTAIN A PHOTOGRAPH OF THE INCIDENT? *NO*
TYPE OF CAMERA USED, STILL/MOVIE
TYPE OF FILM
SHUTTER SPEED
FOCAL LENGTH OF LENS
SIZE OF APERTURE USED
COLOUR OF FILTER USED
CAN WE BORROW OR RETAIN THE FILM/NEGATIVE?

(15) ANY EFFECT ON THE FOLLOWING:-
(a) TELEVISION RECEPTION? *Not to my*
(b) RADIO RECEPTION?
(c) CAR IGNITION SYSTEM? *knowledge*

(16) ANY OTHER POINTS NOT COVERED BY THE ABOVE QUESTIONS *The object was first observed 3weeks ago + was thought at the time to be an aeroplane brilliantly lighted from front to rear and wing tip to wing tip as it was seen nightly in the same position.*

I (WE) HEREBY STATE THE ABOVE IS AN ACCURATE ACCOUNT OF MY (OUR) OBSERVATIONS.
(signed) *T. Brown.*

until Tuesday last week it was thought to be an object which was being used for experimental purposes in connection with T.V. or wireless. It was not seen after the nights of the 13/14/15 or 16th but appeared again in the same position on Sat Nov. 17th oct at 9.0pm but contrary to other occasions moved from that position to due South at 11pm at approx. the same height

2nd October 1964 (UK) – UFO and RAF jets

At 5.35pm over Heaton, Newcastle-on-Tyne, a metallic object was observed hovering in the sky, visible for two minutes, followed by the arrival of two RAF jets, seen to close in on the UFO – which shot away westwards. (Source: *UFOLOG*, Issue 7, 21.10.1964)

POST CARD
THE ADDRESS TO BE WRITTEN ON THIS SIDE

UFOLOG
REF NO. 2/23
I.S. ISSUE
5

OBJECT LOOKED LIKE THIS.

NO.	DATE	TIME	MAP REF	DOCS
2/23	2/10/64	1735		C.A.

DETAILS — A bright disc seen hanging motionless in sky. for nearly 5 mins. Then 2 RAF jets appeared – bearing down on UFO. The jets were quite close when UFO moved slowly in a Westerly direction. Aeroplanes changed to an interception course but UFO flew off and left them "standing"

LOC — Walking south from Parsons Works in Heaton, Newcastle.

WITNESSES — Mr. G. Hastings, Heaton, Newcastle on Tyne 6

3rd October 1964 (UK) – 'V'-shaped formation

3 10 64

DATE: 1964 October 3rd..   TIME: 10.30 p.m. B.S.T..

LOCATION: 6, Cromford Rd., West Bridgford, Nottingham,

DATA: Just after 10.30 p.m. witness saw at about 70° elevation a group of white dots arranged in two V-shaped formations - seven or eight in each formation - exact number unknown. Each dot was very small and appeared to be slightly elongated in the direction of travel. All were of the same brightness - approximately same as 2nd. magnitude star.

Objects first seen in the S.W.. They then quickly crossed the sky near the zenith and went off in a North-Easterly direction. Witness lost them in the haze of lights over Nottingham at an elevation of 15°. Sighting lasted only about 3 seconds. Witness could hear no noise from the objects.

At first the formations appeared thus:

After passing the zenith, the formation became straggley - rather in the manner of birds in formation - thus:-

But they quickly regained the original formation.

One V occupied about 5° arc.

All the lights were visible all the time, none appeared to have gone out.

The formations showed no sign of perspective as they approached the horizon.

WITNESS: Master M. Harrison (17½) of above address.

COMMENT: Telephone calls to the following places brought no further light on the origin of the two formations, and no possible suggestions as to where they could have come from:-

    (a) Hucknall Met. Office.
    (b) R. A. F. Newton, East Bridgford.
    (c) Derby Municipal Airport.
    (d) R.A.F. Syerston.
    (e) R.A.F. Syerston Officer's Mess.
    (f) Royal Canadian Airforce Langar.
    (g) The Nottingham Guardian Journal and Post had heard nothing, took the storey down at length and don't seem to have used it (shame!).

The Defence Ministry is being tackled for a possible explanation.

4th October 1964 (USA) – UFO photographed

A UFO was photographed over Karona Beach Park, Oahu, Hawaii. Blue Book decided, after professional examination, that they were gouges in the film emulsion. Apparently the object was not seen when the photograph was taken. This appears to have been the case.

Owego, New York (USA) – Strange lights seen

At 8.45pm, a motorist driving through countryside in Owego, New York, saw an object above woods, some 200 yards away, showing a flashing red light on top, with three white lights underneath, about 15 feet long, heading in an east to west direction, at about 60mph. It was last seen turning northwards, before being lost from view. Explanation: Possible aircraft. (**Source: Project Blue Book**)

7th October 1964 (UK) (USA) – UFOs and mysterious beam seen

At 5.40pm, Mr and Mrs T. Moore from Brockton Crossroads, near Stafford, sighted a pulsating golden-yellow ball-shaped *'craft'*, heading eastwards, showing two distinctive *'bumps'* underneath it. When they arrived home and put the TV on, it showed a split picture and the radio apparently gave-off a high-pitched humming noise. (**Source: Wilfred Daniels**)

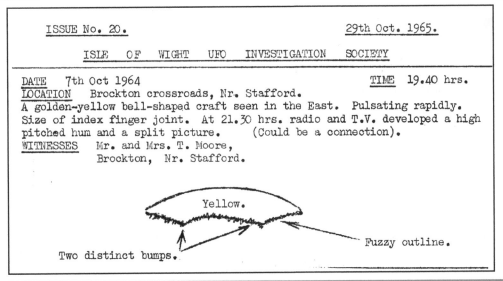

At 9pm a Kahoka, Missouri woman went outside onto her porch and glanced upwards, when she saw what she first took to be the moon, slightly towards the north-east direction.

> *"I opened the screen door and took off my glasses and it was still there. It looked like an electric light pole reaching from the Earth to the Moon. For fear of imagining it, I ran to a neighbor's house and a teenager came out and was as amazed as I was. At 9.30pm the light had gone, the sky was black and there was no sign of the Moon."*

The next day the woman went to her newspaper office -the *Gazette Herald* – and was astounded to discover that their switchboard had been flooded with calls. Some people suggested it might have been a barge; others, surveyors working west of Kahoka.

> *"I did not see the Moon. I saw bear-shaped clouds, floating around the cantered light. On one occasion the cloud looked funnel-shaped."*

The women wrote to J. Edgar Hover at the FBI Headquarters, in Washington DC, about the incident.

(Source: Project Blue Book)

10th October 1964 (UK) – Golden UFO

At 11.30am, *"a golden coloured metallic object, resembling a dinner plate in appearance"*, was seen flying slowly across the sky over Testwood, heading towards the Southampton direction. It was witnessed by Mrs G. Worthington and her daughters – Jane and Sandra. The object then moved from the vertical position, showing what appeared to be a dome-shaped superstructure.

At 10.30pm the same day, *"a clearly defined triangle of blue light"* was seen in the sky slightly north of due east, over Lyndhurst, by Totton Grammar schoolboy – David Demant. (Source: Peter J. Kelly)

11th October 1964 (USA) – UFO seen following jet fighters

At Brockton, Massachusetts an engineer, and others, observed a dome-shaped object following jet fighters. The UFO shot straight up and out of sight. (Source: *UFOE*, Section IV)

12th October 1964 (UK) – Pink *'discs'* seen

At 9.30pm, a loud humming noise was heard over Whitehall Road, Gateshead, Newcastle-on-Tyne, by Arthur Toogood. He rushed outside, just in time to see *"two pink 'discs' – like full moons – one bigger than the other"* pass overhead. A neighbour – Mrs Olive Turnbull, living in Bewick Road – also sighted the objects. The matter was later brought to the attention of the Acklington Meteorological Officer, who suggested *"they had seen a shooting star in the vicinity. Looked at from an angle, it may have seemed strange"* – an explanation which cannot be taken seriously!

NO	DATE	TIME	MAP REF	DOCS
2/22	12/10/64	2130hrs		

DETAILS — A loud humming noise was heard and on looking outside they saw 2 pink discs like full moons, one bigger than the other

LOC — Gateshead on Tyne.

WITNESSES — Mr. A. Toogood, Whitehall Rd, gateshead. Mrs. O. Turnbull, Bewick Rd, Gateshead.
INVESTIGATIONS PROCEEDING

19th October 1964 (UK) – Burnt by UFO

Mr G. Morton-Sooley was cycling home near Emneth Tunnel, Wisbech, at 9.40pm, when he saw green, red, and yellow lights, moving horizontally across sky. He was hit by something which burnt its way through six layers of outer clothing and left a small burn mark on his skin. (**Source: Cambridge UFO Group**)

CUGIUFO now (1965 Jan 13) have Mr. Sooley's raincoat, jacket, tie, andpullover, which he sent us quite voluntarily when we asked him for details of his sighting or rather experience.

Initial examination reveals the following:

Raincoat: A rectangular burn hole, 2" x 4½", major axis 60° to verticle, sloping down from wearers right to left. Top button burnt on one corner.

Pulover: Rectangular hole, 6" x 2", axis vertical, centred over wearer's solar plexus.

Tie: Synthetic fibre, nylon (?) (being checked), melted in lower right hand corner of wide end.

Jacket: Rectangular hole, 4" x 2", axis as in raincoat, situated at base of lapels.

Burn passed through two layers of raincoat, one layer jacket, ditto pullover, clipped the tie and according to Mr. Sooley, went through shirt and vest as well. That is six layers of clothing.

21st or 22nd October 1964 (UK) – Cross-shaped UFO

Southampton housewife – Mrs Evelyn Vickers – wrote to Fred Smith of the Isle of Wight UFO Society about what she witnessed, between 6-7.30pm.

> *"It was an oval-shaped object, quite large in size, through the centre of which ran a long cross. Both the 'cross' and the 'oval' were pink – as if the setting sun had etched the peculiar pattern in the sky. I was impressed. I called the neighbours to witness it."*

22nd October 1964 (UK)

At 8.05pm, a silver sphere – twice as bright as Venus – was seen descending through the sky over Heaton, Newcastleon-Tyne, by Mr W.J. Dunbar, before changing course at a sharp right-angle and disappearing behind the moon. (**Source:** *Cambridge University Group Investigation of Unidentified Flying Objects*/Isle of Wight UFO Society)

REF.	TIME	DATE	G. R.	DOE
2/70	22.20hrs	16/12/64	—	—

WIT. Mrs. J. Stephenson. Low Fell, Gateshead.

LOC. 3 Sheriff Hill Gateshead.

DETAILS 10 people saw a RED, pear shaped object hanging stationary in the sky. No sound. After a few moments the object faded away.

M/C Evening News.   24/10/64   28/10/64

Riddle of the Night Sky.

Strange objects in the night sky – two
luminous round objects, each with a faint
aura of light underneath – are reported to
have been seen in the upper part of Frodsham
, Cheshire.

A spokesman at the Jodrell Bank observatory
said nothing unusual had been noticed

MUFORA notified   H.B. DIGAP
& investigating

NO	DATE	TIME	MAP REF	DOCS
2/27	22/10/64	2005 hrs		C A

LOCATION
ROTHBURY TCE, HEATON, NEWCASTLE ON TYNE, 6

DETAILS
A silver sphere, as bright as Venus but
2½ times its size. Moved down towards
EARTH then cut off at rt. angles maintaining
a constant speed. Then it disappeared
into a cloud near the moon.   (PTO)

WITNESSES
MR. W. J. Dunbar } Newcastle upon Tyne.
MISS P. Donkin

24th October 1964 (UK) – Domed UFO

At 10pm, British Rail worker Robert Britland – then living at Helsby, Cheshire – noticed a revolving *'red light'*, hovering approximately 600 feet in the air, towards Frodsham Marshes.

> *"I could make out a big saucer shape, with a dome on top. It made off toward the south-westerly direction."*

25th October 1964 (UK) – Red revolving light

The following evening, Robert noticed a wide beam of light appearing over the top of Helsby Hill, at 10.45pm, stretching out to the horizon, which became thinner in the distance towards the direction of Liverpool.

> *"About five minutes later, a red revolving light – like the one on Saturday night – passed overhead. As it did so, the beam of light cut out, almost creating the impression that the red light was utilising, or feeding off, the beam in some way."*

(Source: *Runcorn Weekly News*)

UFO over Somerset

Shortly before midnight, Sheffield coal merchant James Sharman, Walt Depledge and two friends, were out night fishing in Somerset, when an object with a dazzling *'red-light'* appeared overhead, illuminating the landscape and frightening a herd of cows in a nearby field, before accelerating and vanishing from view.

(Source: *UFOLOG/Daily Express*, 25.10.1964 – 'The one that got away')

EXTRACT FROM "DAILY EXPRESS" 26/10/64

THE ONE THAT GOT AWAY   -   A FLYING SAUCER

Four anglers spoke with relief last night of the one that got away.

The men from Sheffield and Accrington said of the "thing" hovering 12 ft above the silent waters of Kings Sedgemoor Drain in Somerset:-

"It must have been a flying saucer". Within seconds of seeing the mystery object, a half crazed herd of cows stampeded towards them. Said one of the anglers, coal merchant Mr. Jim Sharman, 21, of Jefflock Road, Sheffield "We saw a red light approaching up the drain. It was just like the red light on an aircraft and as it got nearer, it was so bright it lit up the banks and surrounding fields. The light tapered to the rear about 12 ft away and when it got overhead, it hovered, flashing on and off". Added Mr. Sharman "It was weird and frightening - after about 15 minutes, the light suddenly accelerated and disappeared".

Said another of the anglers, Mr. Walt Depledge, 21, of Shirland Lane, Sheffield "I have never seen anything like it before. It really put the wind up me".

26th October 1964 (UK) – UFO sighted

At 7pm, schoolboys – John Stuart McDougall and James Russell of Ringwood Road, Totton, in Hampshire – noticed an unusual *'bright light'* moving across the sky outside their house, and called Mrs McDougall. By the time she had arrived, there was no sign of it. As she was about to return into the house, another *'light'* appeared in the sky. Instead of continuing on its journey, *"it stopped and jerked backwards and forwards"*.

Knowing that James Russell – a school friend of the family, living a short distance away in Calmore Road – was interested in UFOs, they went off to tell him about the incident. However, by the time they arrived, the second object had faded away from view. Suddenly, a pair of *'lights'* – apparently in formation – appeared in the sky in the same direction, and at approximately the same height as the previous ones. After discussing what had been observed, the two boys – James and John – set off to walk back to John's house, when they saw a single *'light'* heading across the sky, followed by the solitary appearance of an aircraft – its lighting pattern totally unlike what they had seen before. This was followed by another pair of *'lights'*, a few minutes later, and then a single one.

Some days after, details were given to the local newspaper, the *Echo*, and a woman rang the McDougall's house, saying that her husband had seen *"an object, with 'flaps', hovering in the sky"* at about the same time as the sightings had taken place. (**Source: Isle of Wight UFO Society/***Southern Evening Echo*, 5.11.1964)

27th October 1964 (UK) – Two bright *'stars'* seen

Mr A.J. Macaulay of Morton Brading, Isle of Wight, was outside his house at 7.55pm, when:

> *"I saw what appeared to be two unusually bright 'stars', close together in flight. They were heading in a SSE direction, about 'three hands widths' above the horizon. I thought it was unusual, as I know that part of the sky well and am familiar with the stars. One of the 'stars' started to move at a speed slightly faster than an artificial satellite, but then stopped again due south, at a higher elevation. I took my eyes off them for a short time and when I looked back, at 8pm, there was no sign of either of them."*

(Source: Kath Smith, *UFOLOG*)

Liverpool UFOs

Miss Josephine Stirling – a nursing sister at a Liverpool factory – said that she saw two mysterious shapes; one brilliant, the other less intense but 'twinkling', from her home in Croxteth Road, at 5am.

(Source: *Liverpool Echo*, October 27th – 'Riddle of the Night Sky')

Police searched an area near Biggin Hill Aerodrome, Kent, after a report of a parachutist was seen falling to the ground. Nothing was found.

30th October 1964 (USA) – Beechcraft Bonanza pilot sights *'saucer'*

A silent saucer-shaped object was seen heading across the clear daylight sky, in a south-east to north-west direction, 15 miles west of Fort Jones, California, at a height of 11,500 feet, by a civilian pilot and his wife – out of view, seconds later. Explanation: Balloon. (**Source Project Blue Book**)

31st October 1964 (UK) – Inverted *'cone'* seen by police officer

David F. Smith – a Police Constable with the Hampshire Constabulary, who was familiar with aircraft recognition having served with the ATC – was having trouble sleeping, at 2am, and decided to go for a walk along Green Lane – a high point, overlooking the Millbrook Estate. Southampton.

"It was fairly cloudy, with about three quarters of the sky covered. I looked for the Plough constellation, when I saw a rather bright pulsating pale green 'star' in the sky, towards the south-west. I looked closer, and was stunned to see a huge inverted 'cone' underneath, tilted slightly to the right. I watched it for about 20 minutes, during which time the 'cone' slowly faded leaving the bright object. It, too, grew smaller as it moved away, before being obscured by clouds."

(Source: *UFOLOG*)

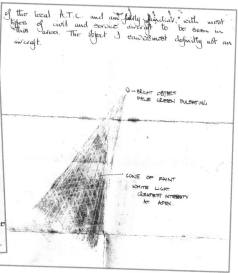

31st October 1964 (USA) – Photos of UFO from Project Blue Book

At South Charleston, Ohio, following a report of a UFO sighted, four photographs were taken. We have included one, but believe this was a hoax – although, of course, we may be wrong!

1st November 1964 (USA) – Parachute object seen

As dusk fell over Kirkwood, Missouri, a grey colored object – described as resembling a parachute, with the top made of metal, with ridges running from the top to the bottom – was seen stationary in the sky, at 25 degrees elevation. A vapour trail was seen, five minutes later, in another part of the sky. The object was seen to leave at an instantaneous speed. Explanation: A weather balloon, launched from Lambert St. Louis Airport. (**Source: Project Blue Book**)

2nd November 1964 (USA) – UFO photographed over Redwood City, California

At 6.20pm an object was seen in the sky at 30 degrees elevation, heading at an estimated speed of 90mph, by a motorist moving westwards along Bayshore Freeway. Blue Book had a look at the photo and suggested it was a film flaw, duplicating flaw or chip in the emulsion.

The object was described by the witness – an ex-Air Force employee, and well versed in astronomy – as rotating, the colour fluctuating from white to orange. *"At some stage it went to a string of lights and then back to one object."*

The camera used was a 35mm Leica. Several other people also saw the UFO.

Lieutenant Wolfram,

In reply to your letter on the 5th, here are some details. The sighting was made on Monday, November 1 at 18:20 to 18:40 hours on 6:20 PST on observation time. I was on Bayshore Freeway and the object was toward dayline. I first noticed it at the Whipple Street turnoff in Redwood City. The object appeared to be left and slightly north of me and appeared to be west of the coast range of hills. The object appeared to be composed of several lights connected together and rotating in a counter-clockwise direction. The object kept constant pace of about 30-40 miles per hour - it was slightly faster than the traffic on Bayshore but slower than any aircraft I have seen. The lights did not blink but were a steady white light which slowly went to ale orange back to white - to orange to white etc. Also, at times the single lights appeared to merge to form a one continuous round light similar to the round flourescent tubes found in a circle sometimes used in lighting a kitchen. Something like this ⟶ ◯ it might be described as a ring of light. Then it would switch back to individual lights again like this ⠿⠿⠿ the rotation was about way on the seconds and was constant. I stopped the car and got out twice and it appeared not different. The path of the object was swinging parallel to the coast, possibly a little toward the ocean. I saw it until I turned off at Bayshore for I had to go to work

arch #1

The duration of this sighting was about 15 minutes or a little less.

The camera used was a Leica M-3. The lens was a summicron 40 millimeter focal length f/2 summicron lens. Shutter speeds were varied between 1/30 second and 1/125 th second, all exposures were at f/2. & the film was Agfachrome CT-18. The film is being processed now and I will send you the transparencies when I recieve them back from the laboratory.

As to the credence of this report, I have the following qualifications. I have been an amateur astronomer since 1957, I have made my own reflector reflector telescopes. I was in the ground observer corps for several years and I am also a professional photographer. I have also observed weather balloons, mirages, planets, aircraft at night, helicopters at night, meteors, aurora Borealis and other assorted sky phenomena but this was not like any of those things I have seen previously. I would appreciate it if you would send me back the solution of this puzzle if you solve it. You will get the color slides as soon as they are returned to me.

Sincerely yours,

~~Redwood City~~
California

Major Walls,

In answer to your call, here is a description as I remember it.

Going back to work at 6:20, I turned onto Bayshore Freeway from the Whipple Street weapons at Redwood City and proceeded north. A bright light in the West caught my eye and I looked over. I saw a bright object going roughly parallel to my line of travel although later, I headed more to the ocean. Anyway, the object was about 20-30 degrees above the horizon and seemed to stay at a steady altitude in speed, it was a little faster than the traffic on Bayshore. The color of the light(s) they went from white to orange to white etc. The lights were rotating counterclockwise. Also, the object appeared to change from several smaller lights to merge into a "ring of light" then go back to single lights then merge again and so on. Duration of observation was 15 minutes for I had to turn off Bayshore at Brisbane avenue to go to work. I stopped the car twice and got out just to be sure I was actually seeing something.

Color slides were taken. Only one (1) is good enough to get data from. Here is information on that picture. Film was Agfachrome CT-18. Exposure 1/125 re for and at f 2.8. The camera is a Leica M-3. The lens is a 90 millimeter focal length f/2 Summicron (SUMMICRON)

arch #2
⟶

As to my background, I am a professional photographer, I was in the ground observer corps and I am an astronomer. Thus I have experience in observing sky phenomena such as weather balloons, meteors, aircraft at night, bright planets, aurora borealis, helicopters at night, heat inversions and so on. Also, the object had no noise.

The color slide is being sent in a separate package to make sure it will not be damaged in the mails.

Sincerely yours,

3rd November 1964 (USA)

Echo
8/65.

32 Shakespeare Road,
Eastleigh.
Hants
9 - 11 - 64.

Dear Sir,
I was interested to read your letter in tonights "Echo" on U.F.O. following the report last week by two youths from Totton.
On Tuesday nov 3rd 1964 about seven PM I was surveying the night sky (a hobby of mine) and noticed an unusually bright star to the West, lower than Capella and a little above Jupiter and of a brightness almost that of the latter.
Quickly going indoors to grab a hat and coat I was astonished to find on return that the "star" was moving quite rapidly, from then on I watched with fascination the object travel silently and stately across

the night sky. From where I watched at Eastleigh its course appeared to be in the direction of Portsmouth which would tie in to some extent the report from watcher at Totton, the exception of course being that my "spotting" was definately on Tuesday evening and that I only saw one object.
I should be very glad to learn the reason or purpose of the object if it is at all possible.

With best wishes
Your sincerely
L. Drayton.

Olmsted Falls, Ohio . . . November 6, 1964 . . . 6:06 P.M. . . . Schady Road . . . It was clear and completely dark when the 4 observers' attention was drawn to a brilliant object in the sky to their S. The object was "right next to the moon," when first seen, and their estimate of elevation was 40–45 degrees.

The object which was the apparent size of a quarter blinked completely on and off, was as bright as automobile headlights, silvery-white in color, and had a poor outline. (Blurred)

The object travelled N toward them and the nearby Turnpike, then turned westward, moving alongside the S side of the Turnpike. Its speed was described as faster than any aircraft seen by them before. (Cleveland Hopkins Intl. Airport is 2 miles SE of them.) The object was in view for 2 minutes. No sound or trail, level flight.

Observers: Mr. and Mrs. Alfred Haag, Luanne Haag 16, and Jack Dover 15-1/2.

4th November 1964 (USA)

At 8.05am, a doctor's wife was driving eastwards through Bath Township, Ohio. She noticed a shiny object in the eastern sky, which appeared to be stationary.

3rd/4th November 1964 (UK) – Spinning UFO

At 6.45pm a woman resident of Schofield Avenue, Cranbury Road, Eastleigh, in Hampshire, reported having sighted a bright object heading across the sky, which at one point stopped and spun around, before heading away towards the south-east.

Mystery Light Panics Couple

At 8:15 p. m. on 3 November 1964, Rudolph Huizen, 30, caretaker, and Duane Myers, 24, a nurseryman, were alerted by a barking dog at the Butano Girl Scout Camp near Pescadero, Californa. Both men went outside to investigate and immediately saw a very bright light "about the size of a half dollar" which was moving erratically in the northeast sky.

Huizen said it was " high in the sky" and "just for kicks" he flashed an SOS at it with his flashlight. The light began moving toward the men. It made no sound, just became larger and larger.

Huizen told deputies of the incident the next morning and said that after the first SOS the object came down and settled over the trees about a half a mile away and moved back and forth. Huizen flashed his light at it again and it "lit up the sky like a full moon. It was as big as a football.

At this point the two men ran into the house and brought their wives out to watch. The four watched for a while longer then signalled the SOS again. The object immediately responded and moved toward them. All four fled into the house and watched from the doorway as the object backed away and grew dim. "Then it toook off," Huizen reported, "no jet or any plane could go that fast."

Huizen called the Butano Forest Ranger Raymond Cavaliero, who called the sheriff's office. Deputies who went out to the Camp reported the object was gone.

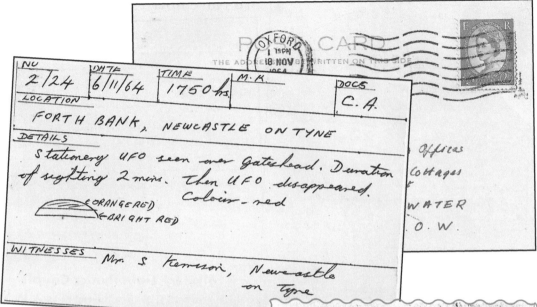

NU 2/24   DATE 6/11/64   TIME 1750 hrs   M.K.   DOCS C.A.

LOCATION

FORTH BANK, NEWCASTLE ON TYNE

DETAILS

Stationery UFO seen over Gateshead. Duration of sighting 2 mins. Then UFO disappeared. Colour - red

(ORANGE RED)
(BRIGHT RED)

WITNESSES   Mr S Kennison, Newcastle on Tyne

6th November 1963 (UK) (USA) – UFO sighted

A boy from Oklahoma City sighted what he took to be a meteor, which landed in a nearby river. He collected a sample, weighing 23lbs, and sent it to a local UFO Society, who posted it to Blue Book for analysis and evaluation. Blue Book concluded, following spectrographic and chemical analysis, that it did not have space residue. Unfortunately, the sample was destroyed during the process.

Meteorite Recovered

Bruce Baskerville, left, 5312 S. Monte Pl., and Rick Barnes, center, 3020 SW 53rd Pl., listen as Dale Johnson, staff member at Kirkpatrick planetarium, points out a piece of what is believed to be meteorite the boys found in southwest Oklahoma City Saturday. Young Barnes saw the meteorite fall about midnight Friday. The piece of material weighs 23 pounds.

23-Pound Meteorite Found In City Field

Two teen-age boys Saturday found what is believed to be a 23-pound meteorite

Baskerville, 5312 S. Monte Pl., found the meteorite Saturday morning in an open...

He said he went out to his car about this time and saw a "shooting star" flash down...

FTD (TDEW)
Wright-Patterson AFB, Ohio 45433
18 January 1965

Hayden C Hewes
Associate Director
IIOUFO
3005 West Eubanks
Oklahoma City, Oklahoma

Dear Hayden,

This is in reply to your letter of 26 December 1964. We received the Ray Stanford motion picture. It was forwarded to Chicago, Illinois for duplication by Kodak and returned to us. The original film was sent to you, airmail, registered, special delivery on the 11th of January under Register Number 664380. We do hope that it arrived in time for your lecture on the 12th. The images on the Ray Stanford film depicts clouds, a contrail and the planet Venus. In an independent evaluation of the movie the object was determined to be the planet Venus. Doctor J Allen Hynek has also evaluated the movie and he has determined the image to be the planet Venus. We appreciate your forwarding this film for our evaluation.

Regarding the fragments which you sent us on 9 November 1964. This fragment was forwarded and remained in the Post Office for approximately six weeks. There was an amount of postage due and we did not receive this object in our shop until the 23rd of December. We submitted the fragment to ASD for analysis and the Bowser-Morner Testing Laboratories, Incorporation conducted the spectrographic Semi-Quantative Analysis. The object was given preliminary tests and determined to have no space residue. The rock appears to be common to that portion of Oklahoma. A copy of the lab report is attached. Perhaps these events will clarify the statements in our letter of 11 December 1964 to you. No contact has been made with Doctor King or Doctor Hynek on this particular object. I would like to point out that meteor observations of this nature would be reported by many more observors and that should the object be a meteorite, the absence of sound would indicate that the impact point would be in excess of 300 miles from the point of observation.

The Fact Sheet is in the process of being printed. A courtesy copy will be forwarded to you upon completion. We are enclosing the statistics which will be included as attachments to the basic information.

8th November 1964 (UK) – UFO over Manchester

At 6.50pm, a strange *'star-like'* object was seen passing through the sky over Old Trafford, Manchester, by local resident – Christopher Ridgeway. After 10 minutes, it was lost from view. (**Source:** *UFOLOG*)

8th November 1964 (USA) – 'V'-shaped lights seen over Florida

Explanation: Insufficient data for evaluation. (**Source: Project Blue Book**)

Boca Raton, Fla.
33432

U.S.Air Force
Washington,D.C.

Dear Sir,

I hope you will be kind enough to forward this letter to the
authorities that deal with U.F.O. s.Thank you.
To begin with I am not a wide-eyed fanatic.I am an amature astronomer
and have not had,to the best of my knowledge,any hallucinations.I have
seen many astronomical phenomenas,from bolides to comets to satilites.
I am well informed from sorces such as Sky and Telescope and Reveiw of
Popular Astronomy.The point of all this is that I do not wish to be informed I've seen a meteor,a wheather balloon,or Venus.I am not trying
to tell you what it was that I saw,merely "discribing what I've seen."
Since this and one or two other sightings of which I am not certain of,
and thus will not mention,-I have read some books on the subject,but
found nothing concrete.I personaly believe that you are not taking a
very good stand.I remember in a statement use released several months
ago you said that there was no indication that these crafts,if they are
crafts, can do anything our plans can't do.I am wondering that if these
things are crafts and if you have been telling the truth about no unexplained radar contacts what do you call a craft or object that can
fly past America and not triger of the DEW equipment.

At any rate I will now tell you what happened.It has been a long
time since this night I am about to tell about,but I felt I wouldn't
bother to write to you.I did,however ,make a careful record.There was
one witness,whose name I will with hold.I'd better explain now that
I am only fourteen years old and if that demirts the letter,I am sorry.
I am still a competent amature astronomer.

The date and year was Nov.8,1964. The time:3:30 P.M. E.S.T.
My friend,who I will call "Paul", and I were over at his house useing
his telescope,a 2.4 in. refracter of Japanese make,taking turns at the
eyepiece.I looked up and started looking at the constellations,prehaps
trying to pick out the major stars in Ursa Major,a difficult feat I might
add with all those streetlights.Suddenly,and I mean very suddenly,a
moving object caught the corner of my eye.Turning my head towards the
northeast an open V-formation of tiny lights,too many to make out singly.
I saw

At the same time I gasped and "Paul " jerked his head up and followed my eyes.Now you must reliese this was all happening at once.The seeing out of the comer of my eye,the gasp and "Paul" seeing the thing too took no more than one second.The object or objects were in,as I've said,a V-formation,pointed part of the formation pointing in the direction of travel.The thing glowed with a blue-white light.Now we come to the most amazing things of the object.Its noise,or lack of it,and its motion.

The object crossed from one horizon to the other horizon in less than three seconds,if not faster(more like two seconds,but it is difficult to estimate such short amounts of time) and it was not jerkey in motion,more like a graceful glide.There was absolutly no sound whats so ever.

"Paul"also saw it for the greater part of its flight.His report checked out my own impression.

I do not try to explain it.I merely state that I saw something which is as I described and "Paul" saw the same.And I do state that this report is correct and wish it to go down on the record as such,

Sincerely,

P.S. I am sorry for the corrections I had to make in this letter. I am not good at typing.

9th November 1964 (UK) – Two UFOs seen

At 6.30pm a yellow object, with a green tail, some three feet in length, accompanied by a second smaller object, was seen moving across a clear night sky by Mr Olaf Davey and his wife – Doris, from Colomb Road, Goreleston, Great Yarmouth. The couple was in Olton Road, near Goreleston, at the time.

> *"It was heading inland from the coast and going westwards. Ten seconds later the first one vanished, leaving the smaller object to continue on its course. It was a clear night, with a light easterly wind."*

9th November 1964 (New Zealand) – UFO sighted

12th November 1964 (UK) – Lights seen

Mr Steel (80) – a resident of Great William Street, Aston Cantlow, near Stratford-upon-Avon – was outside his back door, close to the canal, in Great William Street, which faces north-east. He happened to look up into the sky at 9.45pm and see:

> *"...a row of lights, which at first I took to be a reflection of the street lights, or the tip of a TV aerial,*

Farmer Observes Sphere

At 8 p. m. on 9 November 1964 Trevor Foss of Kailoa Station, Gisborne, New Zealand, responded to his son John's call to watch a light in the northern sky. When Foss looked, he saw a ball of light brighter than any star traveling south toward him.

The Foss homestead is in the hills 1,000 feet above sea level. Using his night binoculars Foss, his son and another were able to view the object. It took 5 minutes to go from its position when first seen in the north to the southern horizon.

Foss, in a letter to Harold Fulton who was inquiring on behalf of APRO, said that two minutes prior to "first sighting the space ship", they had seen a bright ball disappearing in the east over Gisborne. The Foss farm is 22 air miles south of Gisborne. A quarter moon was in the west behind the observers.

The "space ship," as Foss referred to it, did not pass directly overhead, but rather "slightly away"—presenting a side view. The object presented a spherical appearance, the leading edge was outlined by a single dark line and it and the dark portion immediately behind were glowing hot with the major heat on the leading edge. The rotating light beams were a brilliant white and were projected downwards and toward the rear. The binoculars afforded a view which disclosed 6 jet-like objects at the rear, the lining or inside of which was golden-colored. The jets gave off a brilliant blue flame. Mr. Foss was unable to clearly discern what linked the tail of the disc with the rear jets but was able to get a clear view of the jets.

Foss, his son John (15) and a worker saw the object and Foss telephoned neighbors who also saw it but not as clearly as they were not equipped with binoculars.

but they were far too close together and in a gap between the houses. A few minutes later, another set of 'lights' appeared in the sky, heading northwards. Suddenly, they halted in the sky.

After watching them hanging there silently, for some time, I went inside."

13th November 1964 (UK) – Spinning UFO

At 8.45pm, Mrs Olive Hepell of Newcastle-on-Tyne was travelling west along Coast Road, when she saw:

"*...a bright white 'light' in the sky, shaped like a spinning top, about 200 yards away from near the Wills Cigarette factory on that road. I can't give you height, but saw it for five minutes.*"

(Source: *UFOLOG*)

NO.	DATE	TIME	MAP REF	DOCS
2/25	13/11/64	2045		C/A

LOCATION Nr. Wills Cigarette Factory, New Coast Rd, Newcastle on Tyne.

DETAILS Observer was travelling WEST along COAST RD in a car when she saw a bright white light shaped like a spinning top. It *was* spinning. Elev. 45°. 200yds ahead of car. Height not known. Seen for 5 mins. Also seen earlier in evening at 1915 hrs pro

WITNESSES Mrs O. Hepell, Newcastle on Tyne, 12

13th November 1964 (USA) – Orange UFO

At 6pm a woman from Shutesbury, Massachusetts, sighted an object she described as:

"*...like an orange harvest moon, several miles away, heading in a north-east to north-west direction – gone out of view in a minute.*"

14th November 1964 (USA) – Three *'lights'* seen

Dr. G.R. Wagner, MD, and two girls, saw three dim red *'lights'* flying through 60 degrees arc over Menomonee Falls, Wisconsin, heading in a north to south direction at 9.40pm. During flight they changed their positions.

(Source: Berliner/ Project Blue Book)

FLYING SAUCERS OVER ARGENTINA: On the night of November 14th, a mysterious object was observed by astronomers at the San Miguel Observatory, near Buenos Aires, Argentina. The red-colored UFO crossed the sky at about 4½ times the speed of a man-made earth satellite, according to a spokesman for the Observatory. A half hour later, the same object crossed the sky again, going in the opposite direction. It did not resemble any known type of satellite either in speed or orbital height.
      A few nights earlier, two men in a truck traveling along a highway near Parana in the northern province of Entre Rios, reported to police that a fast-moving brightly-lit object swooped down on their truck several times.
      These incidents are just two in a continuing Argentine flap, consisting of frequent near-landings, occasional landings, and scattered reports of little men. Unfortunately, our clipping services do not send us more than a small percentage of these reports.

15th November 1964 (USA) – Dome-shaped UFO

16th November 1964 (UK) (USA) – UFO sighted

At 4pm Anita Booth, from Whalley Range, Manchester was one of several people who sighted a strange silver object in the sky above Barlow Moor Road, Chorlton-cum-Hardy. *"It was roughly three times higher than a plane, and was hovering and rising. It was visible for 10-15 minutes till disappearing from view."* A spokesman for the Meteorological Office suggested they had seen the reflection of the setting sun on a satellite.

(Source: DIGAP/*Manchester Evening News & Chronicle* – 'Mystery light in the sky')

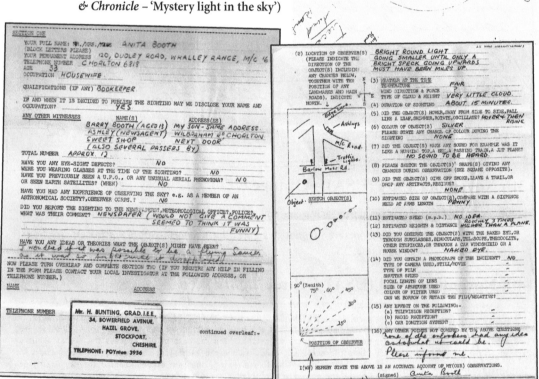

16th/17th/18th/19th November (USA) – Jet fighters launched to intercept UFOs

On 16th/17th/18th and 19th November, UFOs were tracked on radar by US Navy ships on patrol in the Caribbean. It is said that they emitted encrypted IFF Mode 1 transponder signals. The last occasion occurred while USS Gyatt was on patrol near Puerto Rico, at 18degrees 10.N, 66degrees 12' W. A jet fighter was launched, but failed to intercept the object. (**Source: Tony Rullan**)

UNCLASSIFIED

DETAILED EVENTS OF THE EVENING OF 19 NOVEMBER 1964

On the evening of 19 November 1964 while conducting project operations on board the USS GYATT in Latitude 20° 41.5 North 68° 34' West, the following sequence of events were noted by crew members of the USS GYATT (DD 712) and Norfolk Test and Evaluation Detachment personnel.

The radar used was the SPS-49 Radar, operating in the 850 - 942 mc range, manufactured by the Raytheon Co., Wayland, Massachusetts. The type video shown is Moving Target Resolver (MTR). The pictures were taken with the Universal Shipboard Radarscope Recorder, manufactured by the Heavy Military Electronics Department, General Electric Co., Syracuse, New York. The range of the video shown is 225 miles from GYATT with the range rings about forty-five miles apart.

The Naval aircraft involved was "SALT SPRAY 26", an F-8C aircraft of Utility Squadron EIGHT, based at Roosevelt Roads, Puerto Rico. This aircraft was flying at an altitude of thirty thousand feet from the commencement of the scheduled exercise at 2020Q until approximately 2101Q at which time "SALT SPRAY 26" reported a stranger closing very fast. At time 2102Q, "SALT SPRAY 26" by our record increased his altitude to 40,000 feet in an attempt to identify the object. While our records do not show it, due to poor communications, it is believed that "SALT SPRAY 26" climbed to 50,000 feet at some time later. At 2130Q "SALT SPRAY 26" reported still having some object on his port side but our photographs do not show it. "SALT SPRAY 26" was steered for Roosevelt Roads at 2134Q.

In the accompanying photographs, "SALT SPRAY 26" is identified by the letter "A" and what is believed to be the other object is identified by the letter "B". This identification was arrived at by commencing with the merged plot (No. 0751) and tracking backward in time.

At approximately 2110Q, the SPS-49 was jammed for a short period as shown in pictures 0758 to 0760. The source of the jamming is unknown.

The approximate range and bearing from GYATT to "SALT SPRAY 26" for applicable pictures is listed in the accompanying sheet.

Classification Cancelled
(or changed to _____)
Auth _____ TR ?
By _____
Date _____
AF-2305-1 para 2-17a
2 Jun 68

DOWNGRADED AT 3 YEAR INTERVALS;
DECLASSIFIED AFTER 12 YEARS.
DOD DIR 5200.10

UNCLASSIFIED

Enclosure (1) to COM-
NORTEVDET ltr ser
of December 1964
UNCLASSIFIED

JOINT MESSAGEFORM - CONTINUATION SHEET   SECURITY CLASSIFICATION   **UNCLASSIFIED**

FROM: , FTD, W P AFB, OHIO

SECRET/TDEW(UFO)_____ *01909* .

INFO FOR SAFOI, AFNIN FOR L/COL O'HARA, AFNINC FOR MAJ SMITH,

CINCONAD FOR L/COL SMITH, DIAST FOR COL WYNN. COMPREHENSIVE

ANALYSIS OF SCOPE PHOTOS INDICATES THAT BOGEY TRACKED BY USS GYATT

ON NIGHT OF 19 NOV 64 WAS CRUISING AT SUB-SONIC SPEEDS BETWEEN

20 HR 46 MIN 56 SEC AND 21 HR 07 MIN 32 SEC. BETWEEN 21 HR

07 MIN 32 SEC AND 21 HR 10 MIN 57 SEC BOGEY ACCELERATED SPEED,

HOWEVER, SCOPE PHOTOS INDICATE THAT HE DID NOT EXCEED 1515 KNOTS.

THE AVERAGE SPEED DURING PERIOD OF ACCELERATION IS 1200 KNOTS.

SPEED DURING PERIOD OF ACCELERATION IS SUBJECT TO ERROR DUE TO

SMALL SCALE AND CRITICAL INTERPRETATION OF THE SECOND HAND ON

CLOCK. UNABLE TO EXPLAIN ESTIMATED SPEED OF 3800 KNOTS REPORTED

IN UFO MESSAGE DCOI 34799 DTG 25/2204Z NOV FROM THE 72 BOMB WING.

(GROUP 3).

COORDINATION: TDEW _Fred P. Van Dame_ date 11 Dec '64
                    FRED P Van Dame

               TDEED _Bryant_ date 11 Dec 64
                    Bryant

DOWNGRADED AT 3 YEAR INTERVALS;
DECLASSIFIED AFTER 12 YEARS.
DOD DIR 5200.10

T64-79125

SYMBOL TDEW (UFO)   PAGE NR 2   NR OF PAGES 2   SECURITY CLASSIFICATION **UNCLASSIFIED**   INITIALS HQ

DD FORM MAY 55 173-1

☆ U. S. GOVERNMENT PRINTING OFFICE: 1955—352236

Examination of the declassified files archived with Project Blue Book gives a date of UFO activity between the 16th and 24th November 1964.

The objects were also seen visually from the air, by a pilot, as black or dark grey, 'delta-shaped', and about the size of a Jet fighter. Pursuit was given; pilot climbs to 52,000feet. The next night another intercept took place, but the pilot was 'hopelessly outclassed'. Explanation: Aircraft. (**Source: Project Blue Book**)

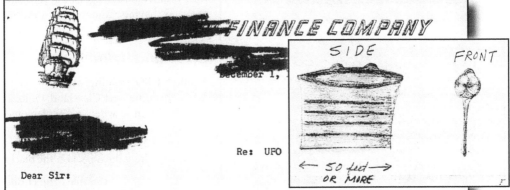

FINANCE COMPANY

December 1,

Re: UFO

SIDE   FRONT

← 50 feet →
OR MORE

Dear Sir:

The following is a complete summary of my experience which I will describe in detail:

On November 26, 1964 (Thanksgiving Day) at approximately 3:15 PM my wife and I saw an object in the sky which in the beginning appeared to be motionless. We were traveling north on Oahu Avenue and it appeared to be about a quarter of a mile ahead and above of us.

The reason why it seemed strange to me was because I have never before seen anything like it. I studied Air Science at the University and and also spent six years in the Air Force Reserve, with the limited knowledge I acquired throug these avenues, the object in the sky seemed to defy all laws of aerodynamics.

To get a better view I proceeded along the road to a point which was almost directly under the object. I turned the car motor off. It was hovering overhea between 500 to 600 up. It first appeared to be motionless pointing east to west (I couldn't front or back) then it slowly turned southward now moving at a sloww rate of speed. It then turned southwest and now seemed to be gaining altitude. It was getting closer to the mountain, at this time it swung around gaining more altitude traveling northwestward. It kept traveling in this direction till it slowly disappeared into the overcast. This was when I realized the tremendous size of it. During all this time there was not a sound that could be heard. It was absolutely noiseless. The color was dark either black of a very dark shade green.

On this day the islands here were receiving winds that were going from XXXXXXXXX XXXX southeast to northwest. At one point as I mentioned the object headed southward which only means it must have had some power to manuver. Not like a kite or a baloon. My wife and I had a full minute and a half to look at it.

Enclosed is a rough sketch of what we saw.

17th November 1964 (USA) – Diamond-shaped UFO seen

At Bridgewater, Massachusetts, two spinning lights were seen in the sky approaching each other, at incredible speed, 80 feet in the air and only 170 yards away from a number of schoolchildren. The sighting took place just after 9pm and the objects made a noise like a helicopter.

At 9.30pm a diamond-shaped object, covered with multicoloured lights, 20 yards away, was reported having come from the south-west direction.

Cleveland, Ohio

Another UFO sighting occurred on the same date – this time over Cleveland, Ohio, involving schoolchildren – when a circular object, with two appendages sticking out of it, was seen between 12.30pm and 12.40pm lunchtime. One of the boys drew the object on the blackboard.

(Source Project Blue Book)

25th November 1964 (USA) – Landed UFO, with occupants

What lay behind a claim of twelve humanoids seen over New Berlin, New York, following the landing of two *'discs'* on a hill, and that they appeared to be engaged in a repair operation for hours?

1st December 1964 (UK) – Cylindrical UFO

A UFO was seen in the sky by Handforth Primary schoolgirls – Marion Muir and Christine Bell – while returning home from a Brownie meeting at 8pm. Marion's mother:

> *"My daughter (9) came running home from Brownies, petrified, to tell me she had seen a strange cylindrical object in the sky. At the one end was a bright white pinpoint of light. Her face was ashen. When I asked her if she had seen a shooting star, she told me it couldn't have been one, as it was far too big and the wrong shape. When she went back to school, the headmaster – Mr Ringham – asked her to write the sighting out for the class."*

According to the Isle of Wight Society, a similarly described object was seen by people living in Chorlton-cum-Hardy, the same evening.

(Source: *Wilmslow County Express*, 3.12.1964 – 'Handforth children see flying object')

This matter was brought to the attention of Kath Smith, of the Isle of Wight UFO Society.

Wilmslow County Express 3/12/64
"Handforth children see flying object.

What was the unidentified flying object seen over Handforth and Manchester recently? Any local scientists who would venture an answer to this question would find their views welcomed by the "Advertiser" and by the children of Handforth Hall Primary School. Two pupils at the school both nine years old. Marion Muir of 9 Delamere Road Handforth and Christine Beth of Warburton Road, saw a bright white object in the sky when returning from their Brownie meeting at 8-0 p.m last Monday.

On the same night a Manchester paper reported that people in Chorlton-cum-Hardy had seen an object with same description as that given by Marion & Christine.

Marion's mother. Mrs Marion Muir told an "Advertiser" reporter last week:
"My daughter came running home from Brownies petrified. to tell me that she had seen a strange object flying in the sky. She said it was a bright white light, cylindrical in shape and at the end was a pinpoint of even brighter light. She added "Her face was ashen when she came in. She had really had a fright. When I asked her whether it was a shooting star she said it could not possibly have been one as it was too big and the wrong shape. She is a very sensible little girl and science is her pet subject, so she would be very interested to know what it was.

When she told her teachers at school they were most interested in it and the headmaster. Mr Ringham. asked her to write about it for the class so all the children are keen to find out what it could have been.

"My daughter came running home from Brownies petrified. to tell me that she had seen a strange object flying in the sky. She said it was a bright white light, cylindrical in shape and at the end was a pinpoint of even brighter light. She added "Her face was ashen when she came in. She had really had a fright. When I asked her whether it was a shooting star she said it could not possibly have been one as it was too big and the wrong shape. She is a very sensible little girl and science is her pet subject, so she would be very interested to know what it was.

When she told her teachers at school they were most interested in it and the headmaster. Mr Ringham. asked her to write about it for the class so all the children are keen to find out what it could have been.

4th December 1964 (USA) – Tracked on Radar

At 4.50am, over Baker, Oregon, a glowing, round, object – the size of a basketball in the sky – was seen by at least four observers. They included Harold H. Eves, Trainee Sergeant Radar Operations Crew Chief, city policeman Donald H. Stinett, Vernon W. Meador, of 821st Radar Squadron. Observations were made with binoculars and a surveyor's scope, con-firmed by radar returns observed on an AN/FPS-35 Search Radar. The duration of the sighting was two hours and involved 3-4 objects. (**Source:** Dan Wilson, *McDonald list*)

6th December 1964 (USA) – UFO sighted over Ohio

14th December 1964 (USA) – UFO display

A silver spinning object was seen over Needham High School, Massachusetts, at 4.20pm.

During the same date over Falls Church, Virginia, a sharply outlined object, fading into a dull red glow and appearing to be in two sections, was seen just above trees in the south-west direction of the sky, at 1.55am,

> *"...like the top of a mushroom, but without the stem".*

Explanation: Consistent with moon evaluation.

(Source: Project Blue Book)

RENDEVOUS OVER BEREA

Berea, Ohio . . . December 6, 1964 . . . 8:20 P.M. EST . . . A roaring, interference-ridden, TV set, a UFO conscious young man trespassing the property of an irate landowner, and startling happenings in the sky; these are the ingredients of this story.

David Meckel, 16, rushed out into his backyard. He spotted a blue-white object "over" the tall evergreen at the end of their back yard, to the West.

His calls brought his mother outdoors in time to see the object as it moved toward and over them in arcing flight. The object moved at "moderate" speed, turning in a smooth curve to the ESE. The boy ran S down Bevans St., then ran E on the first street crossing Bevans. When he was about 7 or 8 houses down that street, and with the large blue object in the clear, two white, dime-like objects were seen rising upwards from the East on an intercept course. When the two smaller objects were closing on the larger object, it suddenly stopped; there was a merger, and the two objects disappeared. After a few seconds (5-8), the remaining large object continued eastward, rising gradually and disappeared.

"It was as if they were sucked up by a vacuum cleaner," said David. No sound was heard from the three objects, no trail, no change in color or brightness. In estimating size, the original blue-white object was possibly 2 times Jupiter in length, and about as wide. (Jupiter at 30 degrees elevation) It was large enough to see a definite (fat cigar) outline. The smaller white objects were about 1/4 as large.

After scanning the sky for a few minutes, the boy returned to tell his mother what he had seen.

It was just a few minutes later when they saw a large red light approaching from the S. It was headed NE at low altitude. When it reached a position directly east of them, it stopped in mid-flight. Looking at it through the trees, the object was at elevation of about 15 degrees. It started blinking on and off at about one-second intervals.

Soon, David was inside the house for his 7x50 binoculars and a sweater. When he returned, the object was still stationary. He crossed Bevans, and ran full tilt down the alley until he had crossed the next street E. In his excitement and determination to get a better look at the red light, he was "carried" onto the lawn of one of the houses bordering the alleyway. Suddenly he was in the grasp of the irate landowner, who proceeded to shake him and accuse him of trespassing. Not only that, but that David was a "Peeping Tom." David fought off attempts by the "baron" to take his binoculars from him, and after some hot words, retreated. He had tried to explain about the red light to the man, but he was already "seeing red."

He looked, found the object, but before he could get that better look, it climbed steeply upward and disappeared. David and his mother agreed that it appeared to be larger than a traffic light at relatively close range.

No sound or trail, no details seen. Overall time of sightings: 15-20 minutes. Four objects seen.

David: The altitude of the (first) bluish-white object guessed to be medium or high altitude. (plane wise) Speed: much slower than planes usually seen. The two white objects that rose up from the east (?) might have been rising from low altitude or, arcing in from horizon at high altitude. (foreground of trees)

No color change or brightness change according to David. Mrs. Meckel said the first object was sun-like in color, but changed to a somewhat orangish color as it passed over. Weather: clear at the time of sightings. An hour later it was overcast. TV: no further trouble that night. This area is full of large trees. Cleveland Hopkins International Airport just a few miles away.

Page 5

27. In the following sketch, imagine that you are at the point shown. Place an "A" on the curved line to show how high the object was above the horizon (skyline) when you *first* saw it. Place a "B" on the same curved line to show how high the object was above the horizon (skyline) when you *last* saw it. Place an "A" on the compass when you *first* saw it. Place a "B" on the compass where you *last* saw the object.

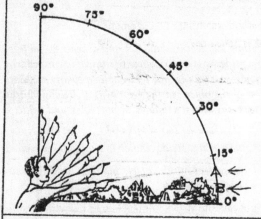

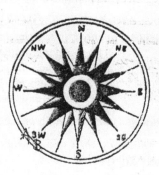

28. Draw a picture that will show the motion that the object or objects made. Place an "A" at the beginning of the path, a "B" at the end of the path, and show any changes in direction during the course.

29. IF there was MORE THAN ONE object, then how many were there? _____ 2 _____

Draw a picture of how they were arranged, and put an arrow to show the direction that they were traveling.

AT THIS POINT A SINGLE BRIGHT OBJECT ABOVE TREE TOPS

AT THIS POINT BLACKED OUT EXCEPT FOR A VERY DEEP DULL RED GLOW

AT THIS POINT - WHAT LOOKED LIKE TWO SEPARATE OBJECTS AS PICTURED - AND VERY BRIGHT

AT THIS POINT BOTH OBJECTS SEEMED TO MERGE AS SHOWN - STILL BRIGHTLY LIT - FINALLY SINKING BELOW TOPS OF TREES - AND AFTER SEVERAL MINUTES BLACKING OUT.

21st December 1964 (USA) – UFO lands and then takes-off

Mr Horace Burns – a gunsmith, who runs a small business on North Main Street, Harrisonburg, Virginia – was driving his station wagon on Route 250, towards Waynesboro in the Shenandoah Valley, at about 5pm.

A huge metallic object came down out of the sky from the north, and passed over the road 200 feet ahead of him. His car engine stopped with an abrupt jerk, while the UFO landed lightly *'like a bubble'* in a small meadow, some 100 yards away.

Mr Burns pushed his car to the side of the road and stood watching in amazement.

> *"The UFO resembled an inverted spinning top, some 125 feet in diameter and at least 80-90 feet high. In addition, I noticed that its circular sloping sides rose in six concentric convolutions, which decreased in diameter to the dome on top. Darkness was falling, but I was able to clearly see that the object was metallic. All around the perimeter of the object, at the base, was a glowing bluish coloured band, about 12-18 inches wide. I didn't see any doors, windows, or portholes, and neither any seams or joints; I couldn't see any landing gear either.*
>
> *The 'machine' had gently settled its base on the ground; its underside seemed to be slightly curved.*
>
> *Suddenly, with a whoosh, it rose straight up to about several hundred feet, and then headed away towards the north-east."*

Mr Burns got back into the car, which started straightaway, and drove home. He told his wife what he had witnessed but was reluctant to tell anyone else, until he heard an announcement on a local radio station about a UFO investigation club at the Eastern Mennonite College, in Harrisburg. Relieved, he contacted them and later received a visit by one of the group.

60,000 counts per minute found on Geiger counter

On the 30th December, Professor Ernest Gehman of the Eastern Mennonite College went to the location with a Geiger counter and quickly identified the spot where the incident had taken place. The Geiger counter recorded over 60,000 counts per minute. At this time he was joined by a Mr Harry Cook – a research engineer from Duponts – and a Mr Funk, also an engineer. They ascertained that the radioactivity was the alpha type and not the more dangerous gamma waves. A six page report was later sent to NICAP.

Airmen from Wright Patterson Air Force Base also visit location

On the 12th January 1965, two Air Force sergeants from Wright Patterson Air Force Base, together with Professor Gehman and Mr Funk, visited the area for themselves. Despite much rain and snow having fallen, the Geiger counter used by the airmen still recorded radioactivity.

Of interest was the observation that one of those airmen was a Sgt. Moody.

The Air Force report concluded, at the end of their investigations, that there had been no sighting of a UFO by Mr Burns, no landing and no radioactivity! (**Source:** *FSR*, May-June 1965, Volume 11, No. 3, **Opposition Flap, 1965, Charles Bowen and Gordon Creighton**)

29th December 1964 (USA) – UFOs tracked on radar

At Patuxent Naval Air Station, Maryland, USN control tower operator – Bernard Sujka – and two other operatives, tracked two large targets 10 miles apart, at 8.30pm, heading directly toward the radar station at about 7,000mph, swerving off at 15 miles range, then approaching again to 10 miles – then one target returned to eight miles range and made a high speed 160 degree turn. The incident was later explained away as being defective equipment. (**Sources:** *Daily Telegraph*, London/*Evening Standard*, 6.1.1965/NICAP)

OFFICIAL FILE COPY

TDEW

Analysis of Radar Targets, Patuxent Naval Air Station, Md   12 Jan 65

Hq USAF SAFOI-PB
Wash D C 20330

1. Based on results of a Navy investigation and analysis of the information supplied to Project Blue Book by the Navy, it has been determined that the target reported by the Patuxent Naval Air Station as an unidentified flying object on 29 Dec 1964 was not a valid target. Shape and illumination of the target, indicates that the target was created by some other electronic device within the station or was caused by intermittent abnormality within the circuitry of the radar set itself.

2. A check with an independent radar complex at Patuxent and with adjacent radar sector centers on the east coast revealed no unidentified targets.

FOR THE COMMANDER

HECTOR QUINTANILLA, Jr
Major, USAF
Chief, Aerial Phenomena Branch

UNCLASSIFIED

Enclosure (1)

AC
3700
Ser: 032

TRANSCRIPT FROM ARTCC TAPE RECORDING

PXT UFO RPT
12-19-64
Tape 5-29
Channel 26

2054 GMT

PXT   Washington Radar Patuxent Sector high altitude this is
Patuxent (unintel) fifty one line.

DCA   Washington, what sector do you want Patuxent.

PXT   Ah Patuxent sector ah somebody in high altitude. I got
a couple targets down here. Must be doing two thousand
knots. I just wanta see if they had 'em.

2055 GMT

DCA   Ah where abouts (pause) what area·

PXT   Ah they're forty ah I keep losing them and picking them
up forty miles southeast of Patuxent over to ah victor
one area and they're northwest bound and then they go
in for awhile and come back out and they're well over a
thousand knots -- they're giving me monstrous big targets
and on the forty mile scale here they jump about ten
miles a sweep.

DCA   Ah ah up around ah all the way up towards Salisbury way.

PXT   Yeah, well it'll be just a little bit south of Salisbury.

DCA   South of Salisbury

PXT   Ah southeast of Salisbury, I guess. Ah correction south-
west (pause) I don't know what they are. I don't paint
them on my ah long range radar.

DCA   I'm picking up a little bit of interference all the way
down from about ah twenty miles to the south of Salisbury up victor one to about ah thirty-five miles to the
northeast of Salisbury. I'm picking up interference
down there.

DOWNGRADED AT 3-YEAR INTERVALS

DECLASSIFIED AFTER 12 YEARS

DOD DIR. 5200.10

UNCLASSIFIED

Enclosure (1)

UNCLASSIFIED

Enclosure (1)

AO
3700
Ser: 032

PXT Yeah, I'm picking up that interference too and I'm
     picking it up every time they come inbound.

DCA Is that right.

2056 GMT

PXT Yeah, and these I (pause) I never saw a target move
     like them before. I never saw one give such a big radar
     return. They give a radar return on this radar scope
     about the size of a pencil eraser.

DCA Ah, I'm not (pause) I'm not picking that up at all.
     All I'm getting (pause) ah (pause) that interference
     there. I'll keep ----

PXT I'm only picking it up on the on the short range. I'm
     not picking it up on the long range radar.

DCA Is that right.

PXT Yeah.

DCA Well, I'm not picking anything up right now on it.

PXT Okay.

DCA Thank you.

Enclosure (1)

2

UNCLASSIFIED

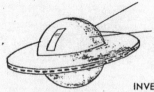

FSIC BULLETIN

PREPARED BY THE FLYING SAUCER
INVESTIGATING COMMITTEE OF AKRON, OHIO

P.O. DRAWER G   -   AKRON, OHIO 44305

VOL. 2   NO. 1

FOR
OCTOBER,
NOVEMBER,
DECEMBER, 1964
and
JANUARY,
FEBRUARY, 1965

GIGANTIC UFO LANDS NEAR STAUNTON, VIRGINIA

VIRGINIA HIT BY "SAUCERS"

Unidentified flying objects were everywhere — or so it seemed, during last December and January. Especially was this true in Augusta County in western Virginia. (38th parallel)

Many Virginians from various walks of life reported sightings of mysterious objects in the sky, on the ground, and even little men scurrying over the Virginia countryside.

Professor Ernest Gehman, of Eastern Mennonite College, at Harrisonburg, Va., entered the picture at that time. (Harrisonburg is 20-30 miles north). Prof. Gehman launched himself into the investigation, and found himself unexpectedly involved in a succession of fast moving discoveries.

The report is thorough, complete, and clearly written. But a greater value attaches; that of his first-hand contact with the Air Force investigations team. His keen observations and insights touch many familiar "bases" in the continuing controversy over UFOs.

Dr. Gehman's report follows, complete and unabridged.

GIGANTIC UFO LANDS NEAR STAUNTON, VIRGINIA
(Report on Sighting, Radiation, and Air Force Investigation)

Possibly the most remarkable sighting of an unidentified flying object ever reported to have taken place in the Shenandoah Valley occurred at 5 p.m. on Monday, Dec. 21, 1964. Mr. Horace Burns, living at Grottoes, Va., and conducting a small gunshop business on North Main Street in Harrisonburg, was driving his 58 Mercury station wagon a few miles east of Staunton on Route 250 toward Waynesboro, when he saw a huge metallic object coming out of the sky north of the highway. As it crossed Route 250 about 200 feet ahead of him, his motor stopped dead, "conked out," as he tells it, and his car seemed to come to an unnaturally quick stop.

The UFO landed lightly "like a bubble" in a small meadow at a spot about 100 yards from the highway. Mr. Burns guided his car to the side of the road, got out and stood beside it, and stared in amazement at the awesome spectacle. What he saw resembled in shape an upside-down toy top, but the size of it was astounding. "It was 125 feet in diameter, at least, and 80 to 90 feet high." he declares. And besides being generally cone-shaped, its circular, sloping sides rose in about 6 large, concentric convolutions that decreased in diameter to a dome at the top.

Although in the gathering twilight Craftsman Burns could not be sure of the exact nature of the material of which it was made, it appeared to be metallic, possibly of aluminum. He noted that all around the perimeter at the base of the monstrous machine there was a bluish glow in a band about a foot, possibly 18 inches, wide. He could see no windows, doors, portholes, or even seams anywhere on the object. Nor did there seem to be any sort of landing gear; the vehicle had gently settled flat on its bottom on the ground, although he noted that its underside was slightly curved.

The visitor from outer space rested on the meadow for from 60 to 90 seconds and then with a "whoosh," the sound no doubt caused by the air rushing under it, it suddenly rose straight up for several hundred feet and immediately took off in a northeasterly direction at a speed much greater than when it crossed the highway from the north the first time, which Mr. Burns estimates to have been about 15 miles per hour.

After it was gone, Burns got into his car again and was surprised to find, when he pressed the starter button, that there was nothing wrong with the engine and that it started off at once. As he drove away he was evidently very much excited and engrossed in his thoughts about the apparition (as who wouldn't be?), for he cannot recall seeing any other vehicles coming or going on Route 250 for possibly a mile. But no doubt other cars on that busy highway must have been halted by the UFO's tremendous magnetic field, and other drivers must have witnessed the sight; we are still hoping that any such will make the fact known.

Horace Burns went home and told Mrs. Burns the story of what he had seen, but declared he would not tell anyone else. "They'd think I'm crazy," he said. But six days later, when Mr. Jim Shipp of WSVA announced on the 6 p.m. newscast about the existence of the UFO Investigators as an extra-curricular club at Eastern Mennonite College, Mrs. Burns convinced her husband that he should report his experience. He told it on Monday to Mr. Shipp, who informed me, the undersigned sponsor of the UFO Investigators, and I taped the story on Tuesday as Mr. Burns told it in his gunshop. I had never known or heard of Horace Burns before that Monday afternoon. On Wednesday I made a preliminary testing of the area with a Geiger counter which revealed radioactivity of over 60,000 counts per minute. This was 9 days after the UFO had briefly rested there!

As an interesting and unplanned corroboration of Horace Burns' story, let me mention the fact that I found the exact landing area of the UFO by myself with the Geiger counter. Mr. Burns had intended to accompany me to the spot, but when the hour arrived for us to go to the place four miles east of Staunton (which is 28 miles south of Harrisonburg) he could not leave his gunshop until a certain dealer in West Virginia had come to pick up a lot of guns which Burns had repaired for the dealer's customers and which they had to have the next day to shoot out the old year and to shoot in the new!

(Continued on Page 2)

Diagram of the landing and departure of a gigantic UFO 4 miles east of Staunton, Virginia, at 5:00 p.m. on December 21, 1964.

Route 250 East

Band of light

Meadow drain

UFO 125 feet in dia, 80 ft. high.

At 1000 hours, 11 Jan 1965, The Aerial Phenomena Section of the Foreign
Technology Division received a letter (attached) from a civilian regarding an
alleged landing of an unidentified flying object in Harrisonburg, Virginia on
21 Dec 64. The letter indicated that the witness's car had stalled and that
radioactivity was present in the landing area. This radiation had been verified by one ████████ of Eastern Mennonite College. Upon receipt of this
letter a telephone call was made to ████████ to verify the alleged incident
and to determine if a check had been made on radiation. ████████ stated that
he had checked the area on 30 December with a geiger counter and that this check
showed radioactive returns.

In view of the report of radioactivity and car stalling it was decided that
an investigative team be sent from Wright-Patterson Air Force Base to conduct an
official investigation of the reported incident. At 1600, 11 Jan 65 TSgt David
N Moody and SSgt Harold T Jones departed W-P AFB for Harrisonburg, Virginia
(Orders Attached).

An investigation was conducted on 12 Jan 65 and the following information
was obtained. At 0900 a telephone call was made to ████████ home and
Sgt Moody was informed that he was in class at Eastern Mennonite College. Sub-
sequent contact was made and an appointment for an interview with the witness,
Mr ████████, and ████████ was arranged for 1330, 12 Jan. At 1330 Sgt Moody
and Sgt Jones arrived at ████████ gunshop at ████████s in
Harrisonburg, Virginia. Shortly thereafter ████████an and a student from Eastern
Mennonite College arrived. This party then departed for the area of the sighting.
The alleged landing site was on U S Route #250 between Waynesboro and Staunton,
near Fishersville, Virginia. During the drive of approximately forty-five minutes
the witness reported the essential details of his observation. Upon arrival
at the landing site pictures were taken of the area and the reported path and
description of the object were given by ████████. (Copies Attached)

DESCRIPTION OF OBJECT

The object was reported as tremendous in size, about eighty to ninety feet
high and 125 feet in diameter. The shape corresponded to a large beehive.
(Drawing Attached). No color was reported, the object being described only as
dark. When asked if colors of the cars and other objects could be identified,
Mr Burns stated that they could. He stated that the light condition at the time
of the sighting was such that colors of the cars and other objects could be identified. No features such as doors, windows, means of propulsion or other characteristics were noted with the exception of a narrow band of light surrounding the
object about six feet from the ground. This band of light was about 12 inches
in diameter which would have been above a man standing on the ground adjacent
to the object. No rays were noted and the light was described as florescent.
Mr ████s did not think the light could have been cuased by a heat source. It
was not similar to a welders torch or other flame. This light did not change
in intensity. It was not an extremely bright light and the edges were sharply
defined.

MOTION OF OBJECT

The object was first observed through the windshield in the upper left hand
corner. Object approached from the North at an altitude higher than a transmission

PAGE 6   THE A. P. R. O. BULLETIN   MAY-JUNE, 1965

Huge UFO At Staunton, Va.

Mr. Horace Burns, of Grottoes, Virginia, claims to have seen an 80-foot-high UFO four miles east of Staunton, Virginia at 5 p.m. on 21 December 1964. Drawings of the object show a general cone shape 125 feet in diameter with a band of bluish-white light on the bottom.

Burns claimed the metallic-appearing object came out of the sky north of the Highway, crossed Route 250 about 200 feet ahead of him and then his engine stopped. He said his car seemed to come to an "unnaturally" quick stop.

He also said the object landed lightly, "like a bubble" about 100 yards off the Highway. It had no visible portholes, wings or seams. See diagram. The object rested on the meadow for from 60-90 seconds, then with a sound of rushing air, it rose straight up for several hundred feet and then proceeded into the northeast. Burns claimed there was no traffic during this time, nor was there any for at least a mile ahead along the route which he drove his car after he started it up again.

Six days later Mr. Burns informed Ernest G. Gehman, a Professor of German at Eastern Mennonite College at Harrisonburg. On the following Tuesday Professor Gehman taped the story at Mr. Burns' gunshop. On Wednesday the Professor tested the area where the UFO had purportedly landed and his counter registered 60,000 counts per minute. This was 9 days after the UFO had rested on the spot.

On January 12 Sgt. David Moody and S/Sgt. H. Jones of Wright-Patterson AFB arrived to investigate the landing. They questioned Burns and Gehman.

Gehman, who was on the scene during the AF investigation, noted that Moody also got an indication of radioactivity. This was three weeks after the incident. Moody also indicated the Burns sighting was a "good" one by several remarks. However, in their 3-page report which they forwarded to Gehman, they inferred their doubts concerning the authenticity of Burns' claims.

To our knowledge no sighting of a UFO in that area which would tend to corroborate Burns' claims has come to light. It has been suggested that the lack of traffic on route 250 is most unusual at any time of day and especially at 5 p.m.

An examination of a state of Virginia road map shows Staunton intersected by two major highways and several smaller roads. Route 11 runs roughly SSW to NNE. Highway 250 where the huge UFO was alleged to have landed, runs WNW and ESE. This major U.S. Highway runs to Charlottesville and then to Richmond, ESE of Staunton. It does not

BAND OF LIGHT

80-90 FT.

LARRY E.

Shown above is the "beehive" shaped object reportedly observed near Staunton, Virginia, U.S.A. on 21 December, 1964.

seem likely that an 80-90 foot high UFO could land in daylight on a major thoroughfare and be seen by only one individual. Charlottesville, home of the University of Virginia is only 35 miles away to the ESE. Its population is in excess of 30,000. The population of Staunton is 20,000. Waynesboro, between Staunton and Charlottesville, has 13,000 residents.

This evidence seems to conflict with Burns' story—but on the other hand, we have the testimony of a respected University Professor concerning excessive radiation.

A short time ago, some strange holes and high radiation count were found in the woods near Glassboro, New Jersey. A tale of a glowing red object which had purportedly landed in the woods was told to the son of a known UFO enthusiast and NICAP member, by an unidentified youth. Police investigated and located a boy who was identified as the one who originally told of the alleged landing. He was taken into custody, admitted perpetrating a hoax by digging the holes and scattering certain chemicals to raise the radiation count. He was tried, found guilty, fined, warned about future shenanigans and released. His fine was also suspended.

We relate the latter case without pertinent details or names (the case is old and does not appear to be a true UFO report) because it is important in that radiation at an alleged UFO landing site can be simulated. However, such fake cases can be detected with a little investigation.

. Gilroy, Calif.

A number of County Park employees including Tom Goold and his son observed an object "larger" than an aircraft and of a bluish translucent color. Goold reported the incident and said he spotted the object over the Park's main office at 4 p.m. when it "circled past" in an east-west direction. It then seemed to halt in flight and made a right turn and proceeded into the south above the clouds. Goold said his son observed a similar phenomena about 2 p.m. the same day (28 December 1964) while riding bikes on Day Road and it appeared to be flying over Mt. Madonna. Goold said it didn't appear to be a weather balloon which ordinarily floats in one direction. . . .

Don Ramkin & Andrea Halford of Paranormal Research Kent

Don Ramkin is now the joint head of the above organisation, along with its founder Andrea Halford. Don has over 40 years experience in the field of paranormal and UFO research. He works with Andrea, who is trained in the field of psychic research under a popular well-known medium. She possesses considerable knowledge in the fields of 'mediumship, and demonology.

Don is well-known to the authors of this book, having spent many years visiting Rendlesham Forest, Suffolk – site of the famous incident, involving claims of a UFO seen during the end of December 1980. In addition he has, on a number of occasions, witnessed apports of stones and mysterious photographs during those excursions.

Andrea Halford

Don:

> *"Paranormal Research Kent has a team of three, but there are eight of us in total, who go out to locations on a very neutral level to both debunk activity as well as trying to find genuine evidence of activity, whether that be of an intelligent haunting or residual energies trapped in the fabric of the location."*

Electronic Voice Phenomena

The group have access to a wide range of equipment at their disposal. This includes original devices, as well as modern equipment, used to capture some amazing audio and EVPs (Electronic Voice Phenomena) and the use of infra-red cameras and video.

'Mediumship is the practice of certain people known as mediums – to purportedly mediate communication between spirits of the dead and living human beings.

Don:

> "We take great care to review each photo/video clip, to rule out the possibility of misidentification or contamination from a human or outside source. There has been much media interest in the paranormal over the years. Some documentaries sensationalise and attract ridicule with their thinly veiled scepticism; others offer an unbiased approach presenting evidence of inexplicable behaviour. With all due respect it is not a subject one should treat lightly, as there are negative forces out there which can appear to be hostile."

Authors: We agree with Don. Over the years we have come into contact with people who have been plagued by outbreaks of paranormal activity. Their stories are quite emotive and unbelievable to those that have never had the misfortune to endure actions orchestrated by an invisible force, whose origin is still shrouded in mystery and open to individual interpretation based on cultural belief.

Whilst there has been criticism directed at some individuals, over the years, who profess to carry out investigations into reported paranormal activity and then publish wild unsubstantiated exaggerated accounts of what took place in order to raise their profile, (never mind the ego), one can only thank Don and Andrea for their genuine commitment in trying to unravel the source that lies behind a phenomena which may be as real to the occupants in that plain of existence as we are to ours.

20th July 2014 – Babies Castle: apports of stones and a ring

Andrea:

"The photos below show apports, which appeared in a room at Babies Castle, Hawkhurst. [Formerly 'Hawkhurst Castle, until Banardos took it over] These all materialised into the middle of the 10ft x 10ft room, following response to questions asked by us. They appeared from different directions and were hot when handled. When this happened the K2 meter recorded red and a spirit box said 'ring'. Subsequently, we received a 'ring'; the spirit box also said 'American', so we asked for an American coin and received a 10 cents coin. Many photos of apports and strange lights around me, whilst on investigation, were picked up. It was an active night there. We used white noise and K2 continually measured red in this area. When words were spoken, items relating to those questions appeared – which is strange, as we have no control over what words are said using 'white noise'. The word knife was said; we responded with 'please, no knives', and received a paper knife."

'Hawkhurst is derived from Old English heafoc hyrst, meaning a wooded hill frequented by hawks. Unfortunately the building has now fallen into disrepair, although as of November 2014 there is work in progress on the site.

5th August 2014 – Dering Woods, Pluckley: apports of stones

Andrea:

"*The photo below was taken In Dering Woods, Pluckley (Screaming Woods) in an area known for witches' covens. It was a clear night. None of these stones could be found anywhere else in the woods. They arrived with a K2 meter going off. They were warm to touch and came over an hour's vigil, and were all roughly the same size, texture and colour.*"

The Old Coachhouse Inn, Littlebourne, Canterbury

Don:

"*We have been to this location (no longer in use and seemingly abandoned some time ago) a number of times between 2013 and the present, because psychically we have picked up on one or two entities – one being an angry spirit, who likes to try to throw his weight around even in the spirit realm; the other a child, who is apparently searching for her mum. She is friendly and likes to make her presence felt. We've actually heard her giggle. However, our main reason for returning is that we have had apports occurring – some objects being deliberately thrown at team members.*

Apports are physical objects believed materialised by spirits. They can include anything from stones, coins, books, jewellery – often warm or hot to the touch, which is measured with a laser thermometer to give an accurate temperature reading. The polar opposite of an apport is an asport – this being when something is taken or disappears, only to be found in a completely different area or place within that building."

Two eggcups

"We set-up base around a table in the bar lounge area where we sit around, throwing out questions whilst monitoring basic pieces of equipment installed around the area. We had concluded our base tests and visually noted what was on the bar and still hanging up on beams and shelving etc , but then spotted two eggcups on the bar, as well as dirty glasses, old bottles, and a disgusting looking jar of what I presumed was olives or whatever, but has now gone brown, resembling something out of a horror film."

Struck in the back

"Andrea was on the opposite side of the table with other members sat left and right of me. Andrea began to ask questions.

I now had my back to the darkness of the open lounge area, and we'd only been there less than 30minutes, when suddenly, and with what I can only describe as with intent, something hit me in the middle of my back and genuinely hurt. I jumped up and put my torch on. Straightaway, I noticed an eggcup on the floor behind my chair and made everyone aware of this. I bent down to pick it up, when Andrea shouted that she had just been hit in the chest by something. Switching on her torch, she noticed an eggcup by her feet. The eggcup that struck us both was very warm. One of the team immediately jumped up and went over to the bar and confirmed that the two eggcups had gone! Bizarre happenings like this just prove what spirits can actually do if they're strong enough.

Looking at earlier photos taken during our base tests and observations made, revealed the eggcups were definitely on the bar and were the very same ones that had just been thrown at us."

Pebbles and small stones thrown – even a coin!

"At other times we have had pebbles or small stones thrown – as if to get our attention, rather than anything aggressive – but on one occasion (and we didn't know this) Andrea had asked telepathically for a coin, BUT with a specific date on it (just for the purpose of authenticity as to how clever spirit can be or not). Within a minute or so of her doing this, something hit the table and bounced off, hitting the foot of another team member. This turned out to be not just a silver coin, but a coin with the exact date which Andrea had asked for. There have been other occasions when we have managed to explain rationally things that we have heard within the location, following investigation. Examples would be several knocks or bangs, which were caused by draughts or the wind getting in.

On a recent visit we invited two members from another team to join us, being aware of a very strong energy that seemed to linger around the area where the open fire used to be. One of our team, who always seems to be the focal point for any spirit who wants to be heard, or just "overshadow", went and stood in this area, inviting this energy to come close and 'overshadow' under Andrea's experienced guidance. It wasn't long before the spirit did indeed come very close, but seemed frustrated and angry. It began to shout out aggressively to one of the male team members, referring to him by name – so angrily that the man felt he was in a struggle to get the entity to back off. With Andrea's assistance, the situation was resolved."

Howling heard

"For me, the odd thing is that for almost a full minute whilst this was going on, I cannot say whether it was in the building or outside to the left, as I was sat at the back of the lounge area with only one of our guests for company, I clearly heard what sounded like howling and then it stopped.

Was this the spirit's pet dog, or maybe a couple of dogs, or was it something else? I've absolutely no idea but can only hope that what I heard had been captured on my recorder, so others can hear what I heard – taking into consideration there's a motorway outside the building on one side, but not one you hear much traffic on in the early hours, and nothing but overgrown woodland and bushes on the other. We will definitely be returning to this location a number of times again, because it's my sole belief that the more times you go somewhere that genuinely does have paranormal activity of the intelligent type, the more used to you they become and will start to be more forthcoming with their contact and trying to do things."

*Overshadowing is a form of Communication with the spirit world through a medium, an individual believed to possess the special ability to communicate with spirits existing in another dimension, and is referred to as spirit channelling. It is used to describe a situation where the spirit dominates the communication. When spirit links with a medium, the spirit communicator exerts various degrees of control, or overshadows the consciousness of the medium to a greater or lesser degree.

Overshadowing occurs to some degree in all channeling. The medium may retain some level of consciousness within the communication or may be completely overtaken (overshadowed) with the spirit controlling all speech and action, devoid of any translation by the medium. This does not denote any form of possession, as mediums typically control the level of overshadowing which they will allow. In some instances, the voice and mannerisms of the medium will change and reflect those of the spirit instead. This trance state is considered the deepest form of overshadowing. (Source: Wikipedia)

Transfiguration – only those with the appropriate experience can invite or allow spirit to enter and use their voice box to speak, where often the subject's face will physically look different to take on the appearance of the spirit/person they're allowing in.

The Old Church at a secret location

"Another team of researchers advised it was worth our while going there and seeing if anything could be picked up to tie-in with what they had obtained during a previous visit there. Five of us made our way there to conduct an investigation into the church, located in the middle of the countryside, surrounded by nothing but open fields and no sign of anyone or anything as far as the eye can see, although it has a cemetery that surrounds it and is to all intents and purpose a functioning church – yet apparently, this isn't the case."

Setting up the equipment

"We arrived and set-up our Electronic Voice Phenomena recorders. Mine was placed on the alter, along with a touch sensitive gadget that lights up and sounds an alarm, should it be touched or vibrated in any way. We then began by letting any spirits know that we were not there in any way to harm them, or to do harm to the building, but enter in love and light, to protect the team. It is important to bear in mind that not all old buildings will show paranormal phenomena in existence around those locations, or being so arrogant to expect paranormal activity wherever we conduct our enquiries, as experience in this field has shown us that while whole nights have been spent in supposedly haunted locations, absolutely nothing was noted.

Nothing happened initially, despite various team members asking questions out aloud – but then we all turned around having heard footsteps at the back of the church, yet there was nobody there. At one point we heard what sounded like groaning or moaning, right near the door, and thought it was children messing around – then we remembered we were in the middle of nowhere and that nobody knew we were there. Andréa and I went outside and checked . . . there was nobody there."

Communication of spoken words obtained

"At the conclusion of our visit, we summed it up. We had heard a few definite audible noises and seen a couple of shadows. On separate occasions we all saw a high up part of the church interior illuminate for a second, and a strange orange 'light' at a window. I switched on my Ovilus III, which takes readings from the environment by several sensors, including one for electromagnetic readings, and then uses a mathematical formula to convert these readings to a number that responds to a certain word, stored in its word database of more than 2,000 words. The result through its built-in speaker and text display identified the following words: reverend, bible, buried, and one or two words relevant to where we were. In addition, Andrea obtained one or two good photos of 'inexplicable lights', so we will definitely be returning to this location."

29th June 2014 – St. Augustine Hospital, Chartham

Don:

"This location is one that we have researched into several times as a single team event and with other teams. This location provides plenty of scope, as there are three houses and the huge main hospital at your disposal. It has been the scene of recurring paranormal activity over time and is a regular venue for us and other researchers. Over a number of visits we have made contact with an orderly from way back, who once worked there, and a couple of unpleasant entities who seriously try to make their presence felt by way of throwing objects at you, or by trying to 'overshadow' team members."

Bullying spirit

"The hospital has a number of spirit visitations, but a stronger entity appears to try to hold them back – almost in a bullying manner – as if it doesn't want them to tell their story."

Paranormal investigations can be dangerous!

"On our last visit, whilst conducting a vigil, we actually had one of our female team members 'overshadowed' by one of the more negative spirits to the point that she literally went from being perfectly fine to passing out and would have hit the concrete floor hard had one of our team not caught her as she fell. She now became a dead weight which, even with two of us holding her up, was a strain until we sat her down; her eyes had rolled back and she was well and truly out of it, until Andrea used a technique to force the negativity away and brought her back. Whilst Andrea was using her experience to bring her back, another female team member started feeling strange and said she felt like her energy was being sucked out, so I had to stand behind her and extend my own protection around her, before deciding that with the negativity in the atmosphere it would be best to take her outside. Thankfully this kind of experience doesn't happen to our team members often, and is a very rare occurrence, but illustrates what can happen when you allow your protection to drop – understanding the nature of investigations carried out at locations that have a history which may be good or bad dependant on what has occurred there.

We picked up some very good signals using the Ovillus III in various parts of the hospital – odd, considering there is absolutely no electricity anywhere in the location (our mobiles are switched off), accompanied by some good yes/no responses on the K2 meters."

Ghostly horse's hooves heard

"I also have an absolutely crystal clear audio recording of a horse's hooves clip-clopping, followed by it snorting, which I've played to various people without telling them what it is or sounds like, and immediately they say it sounds like a horse. The hospital was once used as a military field hospital, so this would actually tie-in with my audio. Whilst it is tedious having to painstakingly run through hours of recordings, we do obtain some very good evidence of spirit activity – anything ranging from a mere noise, like a door slamming, footsteps, to an entire sentence aimed at us, or to a two-way conversation between unseen entities."

Amputated arm on photo!

"There is also a very disquieting photo taken of myself with my right arm seemingly amputated, bearing in mind this was once a military field hospital and in modern times, too, where removal of limbs, following surgery, would have presumably taken place. This location has yielded apports, 'shadow people', the feeling of being touched, poked, pushed, as well as a sense of being observed, along with a feeling that the room seems charged with an electromagnetic force. Sadly, this location is being demolished to make way for housing or offices, but for us it has been a real pleasure to do several investigations here."

(Authors: Heaven help the new occupants – no doubt the manifestations will continue!)

Andrea:

"During a vigil at an old asylum, we had everything running – cameras, barrier beams, laser lights, 'white noise'. The atmosphere was heavy this night. We had already had some really big stuff thrown at us, and we have some great EVPs from the night. I was talking via 'white noise' and some mediumship to a caretaker. I told him that the place may need cleaning, to which he replied on EVP,

'I've cleaned it already'. Through 'white noise' we asked for cards. I said, 'we don't have any; maybe next time we come to visit we will bring some'. We were leaving and had started to clear our K2s off a table, when we discovered a playing card. We have photos throughout the night and its not there, and it only appeared after it was mentioned."

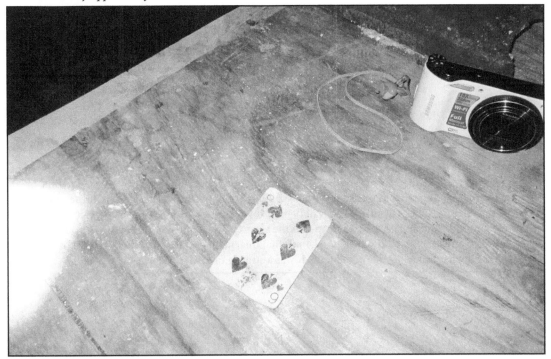

Margaret Westwood of the Birmingham UFO Group

Some years ago, before her untimely death, we had the pleasure of visiting Margaret and her husband, Geoffrey – both of whom were retired police officers, then living in the Harborne area of Birmingham. In the 1970s, the couple was head of a Birmingham-based UFO group, which catalogued reported UFO activity before passing it onto BUFORA. Sadly those sighting reports were mislaid and have never been found (much to Margaret's frustration), despite lengthy letters written to BUFORA in the late 1990s.

Margaret was an intelligent lady, whose enthusiasm for the UFO subject still shone as brightly as it ever did – despite the passing of years. She was an inspiration to us and we were sad to hear of her death.

On one occasion, following a report of UFO activity over the local golf course in 1974, Margaret recovered a sample of metal, which was analysed – following its fall to earth – with interesting results.

A few years before her death, Margaret called and asked us to visit her at her home, as she was puzzled about the inexplicable fall of a mirror positioned above the wooden fireplace in the bedroom.

As the reader can see, the mirror was fixed where the picture is now shown on the wall. Following a large thud heard, Margaret went to investigate and found the unbroken mirror on the floor, after it had collided with the right-hand side shelf of the dresser to the right of the picture – missing all of the ornaments as it did so.

Further inspection revealed the three metal rings, which had secured the mirror to the wall, had all snapped cleanly more-or-less in the same position, which defies comprehension. There is an indentation on the wooden surround of the mirror, consistent with it striking the dresser. In addition to this, the length of chain securing the mirror to the wall struck the wall behind it with another force, to mark it (as can be seen). It seems incredible that during its apparent leap into the air over the ornaments, on what was a narrow shelf, it did not disturb anything as it did so. One presumes that this incident was a total fluke, rather than anything else. Make of it what you will, but undoubtedly it was a strange one.

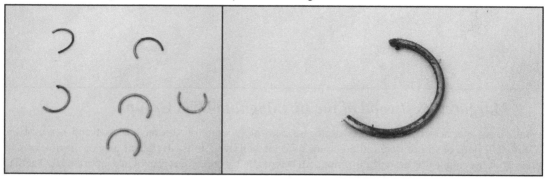

This is a photo of one of Margaret and Geoff's dogs. Margaret would have been pleased to see the article and her dog in print. RIP.

Rendlesham Forest – short update by Brenda Butler

Brenda Butler, from Leiston, whose dedication and enthusiasm for the UFO subject has earned her worldwide respect, has been photographing some amazing inexplicable photos, going back many years, during many walks through Rendlesham Forest, in Suffolk. Whether these anomalies – which include apports of stones and even a plastic elephant on one occasion – are connected to the UFO sightings of December 1980, is a matter which can only be speculation.

Brenda is pictured here with the sited UFO in Rendlesham Forest (constructed by the Forestry Commission), along with her close friend, Bernie, at the location known as where Colonel Halt had his sighting in December 1980 (following an erroneous attempt to label it by the Forestry Commission as where Jim Penniston had his sighting!). It was rumoured that this model would be opened by one of the servicemen involved in the UFO incident in September 2014, but this never came to fruition. It is now a focal point for anyone visiting the location, replete with information relating to the incident.

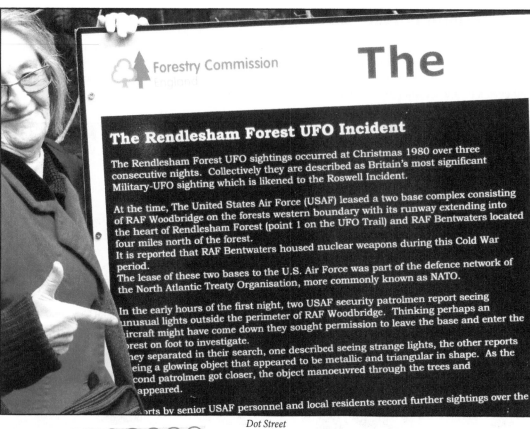

Forestry Commission England

The

The Rendlesham Forest UFO Incident

The Rendlesham Forest UFO sightings occurred at Christmas 1980 over three consecutive nights. Collectively they are described as Britain's most significant Military-UFO sighting which is likened to the Roswell Incident.

At the time, The United States Air Force (USAF) leased a two base complex consisting of RAF Woodbridge on the forests western boundary with its runway extending into the heart of Rendlesham Forest (point 1 on the UFO Trail) and RAF Bentwaters located four miles north of the forest.
It is reported that RAF Bentwaters housed nuclear weapons during this Cold War period.
The lease of these two bases to the U.S. Air Force was part of the defence network of the North Atlantic Treaty Organisation, more commonly known as NATO.

In the early hours of the first night, two USAF security patrolmen report seeing unusual lights outside the perimeter of RAF Woodbridge. Thinking perhaps an aircraft might have come down they sought permission to leave the base and enter the forest on foot to investigate.
They separated in their search, one described seeing strange lights, the other reports seeing a glowing object that appeared to be metallic and triangular in shape. As the second patrolmen got closer, the object manoeuvred through the trees and appeared.

...rts by senior USAF personnel and local residents record further sightings over the

Dot Street

Invitation to the London launch of 'You Can't Tell The People'

Brenda: *"On the 16th November 2000, Chris Pennington and I were invited to London to attend the launch of a book written by Georgina Bruni, to be held at the MOD building. We drove to London by car and then endured a horrendous journey on a bus before arriving at the MOD, where we were greeted by four beefeaters on the door. We were searched and then taken down under several floors, where we arrived at our destination. If we wanted to use the toilet, we had to be escorted by one of the beefeaters to the cubicle. Once Georgina knew we were there, she came over and introduced us to several*

Mr Chris Pennington
is cordially invited to attend the launch of

YOU CAN'T TELL THE PEOPLE
by Georgina Bruni

This event is combined with a benefit for
The British Limbless Ex-servicemen's Association
BLESMA

Tuesday 14 November 2000

King Henry VIII Wine Cellar
Ministry of Defence Main Building
(South Entrance)
Whitehall, London

19.00 hrs
Cocktails & Canapés served throughout the evening
Dress: Smart

Donations appreciated
(please see enclosed form)

RSVP
Telephone 020 7584 3939
Georgina Bruni, PO Box 697, Chelsea, London SW3 2BL

IMPORTANT
For security reasons guests are asked not to bring any bags other than handbags.
Please switch off mobile phones before entering the building. No photograph or film
equipment is allowed on the premises.

PRESS: Please contact Tony McEvoy with your requests Tel: 07710 754903
e-mail tony@apollo-fundraising.com

THE DEFINITIVE ACCOUNT OF THE
RENDLESHAM FOREST
UFO MYSTERY

**YOU CAN'T
TELL THE
PEOPLE**

GEORGINA BRUNI
WITH FOREWORD BY NICK POPE

Georgina Bruni at the Lapis Conference

senior 'top brass' and other guests whom we found a little overwhelming. Dot Street was already there. She had stayed the night in Georgina's flat. Once we had eaten, there was a draw. Georgina then gave a talk, followed by several other people. An auction of Bentwater's memorabilia was then held. It included photographs of the base, a map of the area, and Colonel Halt's famous memo – all for charity."

Brenda & Chris taken by Georgina at Coach & Horses, Melton, March 1999 *Brenda & Chris at Georgina's book signing 23.11.2000*

Charles Halt lecture – 11th July 2015

Brenda has assisted us, many times, in the preparation of the *Haunted Skies* series of books. She is a personal friend and is currently involved with a number of projects, including the forthcoming conference to be held at Woodbridge Community Hall, Suffolk, on the 11th July 2015, when Colonel Charles Halt will talk about his role.

David Bryant and his assessment of the UFO phenomenon

John Hanson and Dawn Holloway have invited me to make a regular editorial contribution to their excellent *Haunted Skies* encyclopaedia: it goes without saying that I am both delighted and flattered, but also a little perplexed! As some of you may know, I am a retired teacher/lecturer and now earn a living selling meteorites and space-flown memorabilia, as well as giving talks throughout the UK on astronomy-related topics: I have been part of the BBC's '*Stargazing Live*' since it began. Despite having my first experience (of several) of the UFO phenomenon at the age of 6, when John first suggested I become a regular contributor, I wondered what I could possibly bring to the party. I reviewed my career, involvement in 'UFOlogy' and contacts with John & Dawn.

1. I have a science background, with degree-level qualifications in Astronomy, Biochemistry and Cosmology: I have also completed a three-year teaching qualification.

2. I was (albeit briefly!) a pilot in the Royal Navy

3. As a professional meteoricist, I know the importance of scientific rigour, evidence and careful research.

4. I have met over thirty Astronauts socially, including eight of the twelve Moonwalkers, and spent time discussing, among other things, the UFO phenomenon.

5. I have acquired over the years a healthy cynicism about the way 'truth' is interpreted and manipulated within government and the media: I personally believe this is nowhere better exemplified than in the treatment of UFOs, their witnesses and chroniclers of the phenomenon such as John and Dawn.

6. I first visited Rendlesham Forest in 1983 and have thus seen the putative landing sites both before and after the hurricane and clearances. I met John and Dawn there at the 30th Anniversary Conference and we immediately became friends and have remained so ever since.

The media and the UFO phenomenon

"No UFOs have ever landed, no-one's been abducted – it's all bollocks!"

– Brian Cox on the *Rob Brydon Show*, BBC

When I give a talk about UFOs or merely mention them in conversation, I can virtually be certain of a sceptical – if not downright hostile – audience, chiefly based upon the way the subject is treated on TV and by the Press.

There has been a wave of primetime documentaries over the past couple of years: with a single exception these have been hosted or introduced by comedians or lightweight presenters such as Julia Bradbury, Ben Shephard, Andrew Maxwell and Mark Williams. Almost without fail the subject is treated in a dismissive and comedic fashion and the content generally focuses on the more bizarre and barely credible accounts of obvious attention seekers. ('I've had a ten year romance with a blond humanoid from Venus' or 'I can speak seven extraterrestrial languages fluently and communicate by means of this coat hanger on my head')

When public figures are persuaded to share their enthusiasm for the topic in a documentary, they tend to be treated badly, with post-production commentary that makes light of their beliefs or even holds them up for ridicule (e.g. Shaun Ryder and Danny Dyer).

I have often felt that as a society, we are becoming increasingly trusting of experts:

- We queued up at our local surgery for an untested (and, in the case of Swine Flu, it transpired, ineffective) vaccine that, we were assured, would protect us from a threat that in any event failed to materialise.

- We monitor our family's carbon footprint and worry that our high-wattage vacuum cleaner is going to contribute to the melting of the polar caps. We accept any level of extra taxation and loss of choice/personal freedom in the interest of slowing down climate change or some other imagined future apocalyptic event.

- We accept without demur any new research that proves that basic foods such as eggs, cheese, butter are bad for us, that items we are encouraged to purchase by high-power advertising (fast food, sweets, sugary 'energy' drinks) are responsible for the so-called obesity and diabetes epidemics, only to be thrown into confusion when a couple of years later we are told they are, in fact, good for us! Remember Edwina Curry?

- We concede that driving a car above 70mph is an anti-social criminal offence, despite the vastly improved brakes, suspension, and safety features of modern vehicles.

- One expert tells us fossil micro-organisms have definitely been discovered in a meteorite from Mars. A year later, another – working for the same organisation – says the observed structures are inorganic.

Why do we accept all these restraints and changes to our way of life? Because an expert said so!

When I was following a degree course in astronomy (not that long in the past!) the idea that planets might be found orbiting distant stars was considered ridiculous. The expert opinion was that our detection systems would never be up to the task, and that our Solar System might, in any case, be, if not unique, then at least a very rare occurrence. Now, of course, hundreds of such new worlds have been catalogued: it surely cannot be long until the experts begin to look for – and perhaps discover – evidence of carbon-based life forms on the more Earth-like of these planets.

This piece is headed by a quote from a current icon of science broadcasting: Dr Brian Cox. Like all of us, he is, of course, entitled to his private opinion. But does his background in particle physics give him a mandate to make statements like that above? He has been similarly casually offensive about those who question the Apollo Moon landings: again, is he an expert in Exobiology? Astronautics? Has he researched the UFO phenomenon with anything approaching rigour? Has he spoken to some of the thousands of credible witnesses such as Astronauts, military personnel, police officers, and air traffic controllers, who have had personal experiences? Why is his opinion more valid that that of Stanton Friedman, the American ufolgist and nuclear physicist? Could it be that his bigoted approach fits some BBC profile? It really does seem that any dissenter who puts his head above the parapet soon disappears from our screens (For example, David Bellamy and Nigel Calder)

To round this off, I'd just like to suggest that we all begin to think very carefully about whom we trust and what we decide to believe. There is no sell-by date on the truth and we should be wary of up and coming experts in any field who will espouse – and promote – any new idea, as part of their attempt to achieve recognition. If this includes following the established line of ridicule for contentious areas like the UFO phenomenon, that seems to be a price easily paid.

Fundamentally: if you know you have seen something in the sky that defies any easy rational explanation; don't be fobbed off by a self-proclaimed expert: and do remember, lighthouses in the real world don't fly around the fields of East Suffolk, whatever someone tries to tell you!

Brenda Butler recently issued this new account of her continuing investigations into the Rendlesham Forest UFO mystery. Co-authored by Philip Kinsella and published by Capall Bann in 2013.

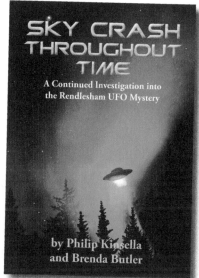

Birthday wishes to Amber....

Proud parents Sonya and Alex, April 2015

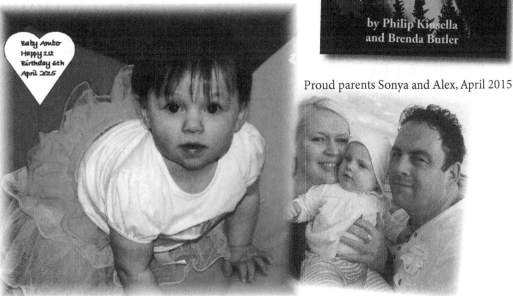

INDEX

C

D

E

F

G

H

T

V

CREDITS

DISCLAIMER

These books have cost us a great deal of money to produce, but we strongly believe that this information forms part of our social history and rightful heritage. It should therefore be preserved, despite the ridicule still aimed at the subject by the media. *All previous titles – pictured above – are currently available.*

If anyone is willing to assist us with the preparation of any illustrations, it would be much appreciated. We can be contacted by letter at **31, Red Lion St, Alvechurch, Worcestershire B48 7LG**, by telephone **0121 445 0340**, or email: **johndawn1@sky.com** • Website: **www.hauntedskies.co.uk**

For those that may wish to consider publishing their own books or magazines, our typesetter, Bob Tibbitts, is available to offer his design, layout and typesetting services – producing a final press-ready pdf file which can then be used for professional printing. He can be contacted on email: **isetcdart@tiscali.co.uk**

Volume 1 of *Haunted Skies* 1940-1959 *(Foreword by Timothy Good)*

We present sightings from the Second Word War. They include many reports from allied pilots, who describe seeing unidentified flying objects, while on bombing missions over Germany. Some pilots we interviewed told of being ordered to intercept a UFO; one pilot was even ordered to open fire! In addition to these are reports of early close encounters, involving allegations of abduction experiences.

Another report tells of strange 'beings' seen outside an RAF Base. We also outline a spectacular sighting, in 1957, that took place in Bedfordshire, which appears identical to that seen over Oregon by employees of the Ames Research Laboratory, San Francisco. There are also numerous reports of 'saucer', 'diamond' and 'cigar-shaped' objects seen during these years.

Volume 2 of *Haunted Skies* 1960-1965 *(Foreword by Jenny Randles)*

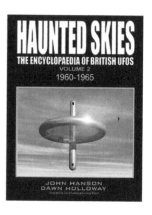

We re-investigated what may well be one of the earliest events, involving mysterious crop circles discovered in June 1960, at Poplar Farm, Evenlode. A 'V'-shaped UFO over Gloucestershire, and an example of a early 'Flying Triangle' over Tyneside in early September 1960. This type of object attracted much media interest in the early 1980s, following attempts by the Belgium Air Force to intercept what became labelled as 'Triangular' UFOs. This book contains many reports of saucer-shaped objects, and their occasional effect on motor vehicles. We also, wherever possible, include numerous personal letters and interviews with some of the researchers. We should not forget the early magazines, such as UFOLOG, produced by members of the (now defunct) Isle of Wight UFO Society.

Volume 3 of *Haunted Skies* 1966-1967 *(Foreword by Nick Redfern)*

This was two years before manned landings took place on the Moon. In October 1967, there was a veritable 'wave' of UFO sightings which took place in the UK, involving cross-shaped objects, reported from Northumberland to the South Coast, with additional reports from Ireland and the Channel islands. (The police in the USA also reported sightings of 'Flying Crosses'). The sightings took place at various times, mostly during the evening or early morning hours, and involved an object which was manoeuvrable, silent – and at times – apparently flying at a low altitude. Attempts were made by the police and various authorities to explain away the sightings as Venus, based on the fact that the planet was bright in the sky during this period, which is clearly, in the majority of sightings, not the answer.

Volume 4 of *Haunted Skies* 1968-1971 *(Foreword by Philip Mantle)*

This book begins with a personal reference to Budd Hopkins, by USA researcher – Peter Robbins.

We outline a close encounter from Crediton, in Devon, which was brought to the attention of the police. Further police sightings of UFOs have been tracked down from Derbyshire, and a police chase through Kent. Multiple UFO sightings occur over the Staffordshire area, which are brought to the attention of the MOD. UFO researchers – Tony Pace and Roger Stanway – travel to London to discuss the incidents with the MOD. Close encounters at Warminster are also covered. A domed object at Bristol and further UFO landings are covered. They include a chilling account from a schoolteacher, living near Stratford-upon-Avon, and a 'flying triangle' seen over Birmingham.

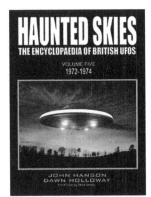

Volume 5 of *Haunted Skies* 1972-1975 *(Foreword by Matt Lyons, Chairman of BUFORA)*

Further examples of UFO activity at Warminster, involving classic 'sky watches' from such locations as Cradle Hill, was the focus of worldwide attention during this period. In addition to this are reports of mysterious footsteps heard. A visit from the 'Men in Black', and other amazing stories, form just a tiny part of some amazing material collected by us, over the years, during personal interviews with the people concerned. UFO fleets are seen over Reading, and a landed saucer-shaped object is seen at Lancashire.

A UFO, containing aliens, is seen at close range over Worcestershire. A local councillor also described seeing what he believes was an alien spaceship, with occupants. There is also an investigation into the famous Berwyn Mountain incident, when it was alleged, by some, that a 'craft' had landed.

Volume 6 of *Haunted Skies* 1976-1977 Jubilee edition *(Foreword by Kevin Goodman)*

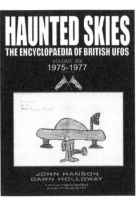

Strange globes of light, seen moving in formations of three (often referred to as triangular in overall shape). Warminster, Wiltshire – reports of mysterious black shadows, flying globes of light and a triangular-shaped UFO seen over Cleeve Hill, near Cheltenham by police officers. There is also an investigation into a number of reported landings of alien craft around the Dyfed area, in February 1977. We present some original illustrations, drawn by children at the local school (which will be reproduced in colour, in a later edition of Haunted Skies). A triangular UFO is seen over Stoke-on-Trent. Comprehensive details were also obtained, regarding Winchester woman, Joyce Bowles – who was to report many encounters with UFOs and their alien occupants.

Volume 7 of *Haunted Skies* 1978-1979 *(Foreword by David Bryant)*

The famous debate into UFOs, held at the United Nations, is covered. A UFO landing at Rowley Regis, West Midlands – involving housewife Jean Hingley – labelled by the Press as the 'Mince Pie Martian' case. Many original sketches and additional information supporting her claims are offered. Another classic UFO sighting is re-investigated, following interviews held with Elsie Oakensen – a housewife from the Daventry area – who sighted a dumb-bell shaped UFO while on the way home from work. Thanks to Dan Goring, editor of EarthLink we were able to include a large number of previously unpublished sighting reports from Essex and London. We also include a close encounter from Didsbury, Manchester involving Lynda Jones, who is known personally to us.

Volume 8 of *Haunted Skies* 1980 *(Foreword by Philip Mantle)*

This book covers the period of just one year and is now, for the first time in the *Haunted Skies* series of books, published in colour. Unfortunately, due to the increase in pagination and the use of colour, the price has been raised, but still represents extremely good value. The first part of the book covers the period from January to November 1980. This includes numerous reports of UFO sightings and encounters. In addition to this, we outline our investigation into the Zigmund Adamski death, and the UFO sighting involving Todmorden Police Constable Alan Godfrey. In the second part, which covers December 1980, we present a comprehensive overview of the events that took place in Rendlesham Forest, thanks to the assistance of retired Colonel Charles Halt and long-standing UFO researcher, Brenda Butler.

Volume 9 of *Haunted Skies* 1981-1986 *(Foreword by Nick Redfern)*
Over 450 pages, many in colour

The authors point out that the majority of the information contained within the *Haunted Skies* series of books will not be found in declassified UFO files, catalogued in the Public Records Office, Kew, London.

This book contains:

UFO sightings over RAF Woodbridge, Suffolk – the scene of much interest during the previous month; a landed UFO at South Yorkshire; UFOs seen over Kent – harrowing close encounters between UFOs and motorists are outlined. These include a report from three women, driving home along the A5 in rural Shropshire (UK), which can be contrasted with a similar allegation made by three women from Kentucky, USA. A close encounter over the M50 Motorway, Gloucestershire; a couple from Hampshire tell of their roadside encounter – which left the husband with some strange marks on his body; a man out fishing, in Aldershot – who was approached by aliens; mysterious apports of stones that occurred, over a number of years, at Birmingham, West Midlands, involving the police – who staked out the locality in a bid to catch the offender. In addition to this, falls of coins and stones in other parts of the world are also outlined.

Although primarily covering British UFO sightings – wherever space permits (always in short supply) – we now include other forgotten worldwide cases of interest, brought to the attention of the reader. One such incident tells of a triangular UFO, seen over Arizona; another of a UFO sighted by a Russian astronaut.

A bizarre story involving David Daniels, who approached a number of prominent worldwide UFO researchers during the early 1980s – he alleged he was from the Pleiades and claimed to be able to metamorphosise from a human body to a reptilian. While it is difficult to believe rationally that this could be true, the authors tell of visits made to influential people, such as the head of the MOD, and The Lord Hill-Norton. Fact is stranger than fiction!

Volume 10 of *Haunted Skies* 1987-1988 *(Foreword by Nick Pope)*
632 pages, many in colour

Includes a focus on UFO cases reported from USA, Australia and New Zealand, 1940-1962.

Volume 10 of *Haunted Skies* catalogues the results of over 20 years research into reported UFO activity by the authors. The majority of those sightings and personal experiences will not be found in any declassified MOD files. Despite promises by their department to release specific individual files from 1971 (which we brought to their notice), the situation remains unchanged.

This volume covers the period of 1987-1988; which documents not only British UFO activity but also UFO activity from New Zealand, Australia and the United States, and forms an ongoing process by the authors to document such matters. In addition, a number of historical UFO cases between the periods 1940 and 1962 is also presented.

The book contains over 600 pages – many in colour – including numerous original illustrations relating to increased UFO activity over the Essex area. In addition to this, the authors outline a mysterious incident in 1987, involving claims of a UFO crash-landing in Nottinghamshire, and a spectacular sighting of goblin-like creatures that invaded a farm in Kentucky. A number of thought-provoking images, captured on camera, are shown from locations such as Cumbria, Rendlesham Forest and the Sedona area of the United States.

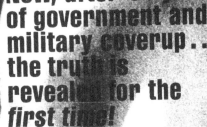

Now, after 30 years of government and military coverup... the truth is revealed for the first time!

We dare you not to believe after you've seen...

UFO'S ARE REAL

Brandon Chase presents A Group 1 Film UFO'S ARE REAL
Director of Photography HANANIA BAER Associate Producer GREG McCARTY Assistant Director DANA MacDUFF Graphics ED VARELA
Assistant Editor BRAD GOLDBERG Edited by LAWRENCE ROSS Music NEIMAN-TILLAR Technical Consultant STANTON FRIEDMAN
Written by EDWARD HUNT and STANTON FRIEDMAN Producer MARIANNE CHASE Director EDWARD HUNT
Color by DE LUXE   In Stereophonic Sound
Copyright© MCMLXXIX The Group 1 International Distribution Organization, Ltd.

G GENERAL AUDIENCES
All Ages Admitted

Lightning Source UK Ltd.
Milton Keynes UK
UKOW07f0731081115

262201UK00018B/12/P